1743 TO 1794	Antoine La[voisier]
1749 TO 1823	Edward Jen[ner]
1753 TO 1814	Count Rum[ford]
1766 TO 1844	John Dalto[n]
1769 TO 1832	Georges Cuvier: geology
1773 TO 1829	Thomas Young: wave theory of light
1791 TO 1867	Michael Faraday: electricity
1791 TO 1871	Charles Babbage: computing
1796 TO 1832	Sadi Carnot: thermodynamics
1797 TO 1875	Charles Lyell: geology
1800 TO 1882	Friedrich Wöhler: biochemistry
1804 TO 1881	Mathias Schleiden: cell theory
1809 TO 1882	Charles Darwin: evolutionary theory
1810 TO 1882	Theodore Schwann: cell theory
1813 TO 1878	Claude Bernard: biology, chemistry
1818 TO 1865	Ignaz Semmelweis: medicine
1821 TO 1894	Hermann von Helmholtz: biophysics
1822 TO 1884	Gregor Mendel: genetics
1822 TO 1895	Louis Pasteur: chemistry, medicine
1827 TO 1912	Joseph Lister: medicine
1831 TO 1879	James Maxwell: electromagnetism
1834 TO 1907	Dmitri Mendeleev: chemistry
1838 TO 1923	Edward Morley: physics, light
1852 TO 1931	Alfred Michelson: physics, light
1858 TO 1947	Max Planck: quantum physics
1866 TO 1945	Thomas Hunt Morgan: genetics
1867 TO 1934	Marie Curie: radioactivity
1878 TO 1968	Lise Meitner: nuclear physics
1879 TO 1955	Albert Einstein: relativity physics
1880 TO 1930	Alfred Wegener: continental drift
1885 TO 1962	Niels Bohr: quantum physics
1887 TO 1961	Erwin Schrödinger: quantum physics
1889 TO 1953	Carl Hubble: astronomy, cosmology
1901 TO 1976	Werner Heisenberg: quantum physics
1901 TO 1994	Linus Pauling: chemistry
1906 TO 1969	Harry Hess: plate tectonics
1908 TO 1993	J. Tuzo Wilson: plate tectonics
1911 TO 1988	Luis Alvarez: physics, mass extinctions
1912 TO 1954	Alan Turing: computing
1916 TO 2001	Claude Shannon: information theory
1916 TO 2004	Francis Crick: molecular biology
1924 TO –	Benoît Mandelbrot: chaos theory
1928 TO –	James Watson: molecular biology
1929 TO –	Murray Gell-Mann: particle physics
1942 TO –	Stephen Hawking: cosmology

PHILOSOPHY OF SCIENCE

Text with Readings

David Boersema

PEARSON

Prentice Hall

New York San Francisco Boston
London Toronto Sydney Tokyo Singapore Madrid
Mexico City Munich Paris Cape Town Hong Kong Montreal

To Doug

Editor-in-Chief: Dickson Musslewhite
Senior Editor: David Repetto
Supplements Editor: Brian Belardi
Marketing Manager: Lindsey Prudhomme
Production Manager: Eric Jorgensen
Project Coordination, Text Design, and Electronic Page Makeup:
    Pre-Press PMG
Cover Designer/Manager: Wendy Ann Fredericks
Cover Photo: Timothy McCarthy/Art Resource, NY
Visual Researcher: Rona Tuccillo
Senior Manufacturing Buyer: Roy L. Pickering, Jr.

For permission to use copyrighted material, grateful
acknowledgment is made to the copyright holders on
pp. 565–568, which are hereby made part of this copyright page.

Library of Congress Cataloging-in-Publication Data

Boersema, David.
    Philosophy of science / David Boersema.—1st ed.
        p. cm.
    Includes bibliographical references.
    ISBN-13: 978-0-321-43711-2
    ISBN-10: 0-321-43711-X
 1.   Science—Philosophy. I. Title.
    Q175.B665 2008
    501—dc22   2008004556

Please visit us at www.pearsonhighered.com

ISBN-13: 978-0-321-43711-2
ISBN-10:   0-321-43711-X

CONTENTS

PREFACE

This book is an introduction to the philosophy of science, with the emphasis on "introduction." My experience in teaching the philosophy of science over the past 25 years is that for most students such a course is more often than not their first, and frequently their only, philosophy course. This is true even if the course is listed as an upper-division undergraduate course (which it is at most colleges and universities). So, for many students it is both an introduction to the philosophy of science and to philosophy generally. Many students enroll in a philosophy of science course to fulfill a humanities requirement as part of their "general education" curriculum. As a result, students very often need careful and patient guidance through the complex and difficult philosophical material and argumentation in this subject. Likewise, although students who are science majors are often the students in this course, it is not unusual for them to be relatively unfamiliar with sciences outside their major. This is also true for the philosophy majors who enroll in the philosophy of science. So, not only is the content—both scientific and philosophical—of this course unfamiliar, but, as a first philosophy course, so too are the philosophical methods of analysis and critique.

At the same time, many texts that are available are compilations of articles culled from professional philosophy journals. These articles are written by professionals for professionals. Consequently, not having sufficient background in the subject, students are generally perplexed and frustrated when reading these essays and trying to comprehend them. All of us who have taught the philosophy of science know that we frequently need to spend a fair amount of class time not only explaining what is being said in the assigned articles, but also providing background context for them to even be approachable. This is not to chastise the editors of such anthologies. There are many excellent and valuable such works available. But the pedagogical reality is that they are pitched at such a level that many students, simply because they do not have the relevant background or training, must be "walked through" the readings before they are in the position to critique and evaluate them (i.e., before they are ready to "do" the philosophy of science).

As anyone who teaches the philosophy of science knows, this course is commonly the only course in which students will get a serious look at conceptual issues connected to the sciences. But this needs to be done in a way that is accessible to students and will motivate them to engage seriously with the material. This is why I have structured this book and written it this way. My goal is that the fascinating topic of the philosophy of science will be accessible, so I have written this book in a straightforward tone—speaking directly to the reader. Needless to say, I hope this is done without any "dumbing down" of the content. The specific topics covered in this book are quite standard for undergraduate courses in the philosophy of science: explanation, reductionism, confirmation, the structure of scientific change, and so on. These topics, however, are often unexpected and foreign to students who enroll in this course, as they—and quite often, their non-philosophy faculty—think of the philosophy of science as being equivalent to medical or environmental ethics. Besides the standard topics being covered in this book, there are also the usual suspects: Popper, Kuhn, Hempel, and so on. The structure, however, is to introduce these topics and characters not simply as a series of interesting issues, but in the context of three overarching philosophical foci: metaphysical concerns, epistemological concerns, and axiological concerns. By using these three philosophical bases, I hope to provide scaffolding for how these various topics cohere and for how they can be fruitfully addressed. It will, of course, be you, the users of this text, who will determine whether or not I have succeeded.

I would like to thank the reviewers of this book who provided feedback on the manuscript throughout its development:

Brett Coppenger, Western Michigan University; Paul Gregory, Washington & Lee University; Mary Gwin, Oklahoma State University; Christine James, Valdosta State University; John L. King, University of North Carolina at Greensboro; William Payne, Bellevue Community College; Naomi Zack, University of Oregon.

Their input was invaluable in giving shape to the book you now hold in your hands.

DAVID BOERSEMA

Major Shifts in Scientific Understanding

-600 to -400	Early Greek natural philosophy
-350 to -200	Aristotelian natural philosophy, including physical theories (e.g., mechanics), biological theories (e.g., teleology, potentiality), four elements of nature (earth, water, air, fire). Some aspects of Aristotelian natural philosophy lasted until the 1700s.
-200 to 200	Hellenistic natural philosophy
200 to 500	Roman science, with encyclopedic tradition, emphasis on technology and applied science
500 to 1200	Early medieval natural philosophy and Arab/Islamic natural philosophy
1200 to 1400	Late medieval natural philosophy ("medieval renaissance")
1400 to 1600	Renaissance natural philosophy
1600s	Early modern science ("the scientific revolution"), including movement toward mechanical, materialistic view of the world, Newtonian theory, emergence of modern instruments (e.g., microscope, telescope), emergence of scientific societies
1700s	"The Enlightenment," including final shift from alchemy to chemistry, beginnings of social science (e.g., Adam Smith and economics), emergence of geology from mineralogy and metallurgy, emergence of non-Euclidean geometry, probability theory, calculus, emergence of studies in electricity, first "new" planet (Uranus) discovered since classical times, emergence of new systematic biological taxonomy, emergence of modern studies in physiology, embryology
1800s	Nineteenth Century science, including evolutionary theory, cell theory, germ theory of disease, atomic theory, thermodynamics, organic chemistry, the periodic table of elements, concepts of chemical bonding and valence, theories of light and spectroscopy, electromagnetism and field theory
1900s	Recent science, including relativity theory, atomic structure, quantum theory, plate tectonics, genetics and molecular biology, ecology, cloning, emergence of neuroscience, emergence of modern biochemistry, cosmology and expanding universe, information theory and computing, chaos theory

CHAPTER ONE

What Is the Philosophy of Science?

IN THIS CHAPTER, WE WILL

- ◼ Identify the basic content and methods of philosophical analysis
- ◼ Identify the main topics of philosophical concern: metaphysics, epistemology, and axiology
- ◼ Identify the main topics of the philosophy of science, providing a preview of the upcoming chapters

What is the philosophy of science?

The simple answer is: *the philosophy of science is the analysis and evaluation of basic concepts and practices within science* (such as the nature of explanation) *and about science* (such as the role of science in society). The complicated, and better, answer is what this whole book is about. This book is a much fuller, although still introductory, examination of basic elements of science, their nature, their interrelationships, and their significance. Many people find the notion of the "philosophy of science" strange. What could be more different than philosophy and science, after all? Isn't philosophy just a matter of giving one's opinion on abstract although sometimes interesting issues? And isn't science a matter of discovering cold, hard facts, also sometimes interesting, about the world? Isn't philosophy about things like my (or your) view of the meaning of life or about impractical topics such as is reincarnation real? And isn't philosophy just subjective, without any "right" answers? Putting it in a more sophisticated way, isn't there simply no "philosophical method" for answering philosophical questions? Furthermore, other than having some interesting and perhaps fun bull sessions, what good is philosophy? (Every student who has ever majored in philosophy has been asked countless times: "Philosophy major? What can you do with that?")

On the other hand, isn't science about real things like chemistry and physics and medicine? Isn't science objective, with clear questions, such as "What is the speed of light?" and a clear "scientific method" to answer those questions? Doesn't science have definite right and wrong answers that are not just somebody's opinion? Furthermore, isn't it obvious that science is good, because we have airplanes and computers and advanced medicines? (Of course, we also have some unpleasant results from science, such as weapons of mass destruction, but it is still obvious that studying science is good.)

One of the goals of this book is to say that this characterization of philosophy is mistaken and the view of philosophy and science as such opposites is also mistaken. But there is still the question of what is the philosophy of science? Although that phrase "philosophy of science" might seem strange at first, in fact for most of our history, at least since the ancient Greeks, the types of people that we think of now as scientists were called "natural philosophers." That is, they were philosophers about nature. It was not until the 1800s that the term "scientist" was coined and gradually the term "natural philosopher" was abandoned.

But even if in the past being a philosopher and being a scientist (or "doing" philosophy and doing science) were not seen as dramatically opposite of each other, there is *still* the question of what philosophy of science is. Of course, scholars from various academic disciplines examine science. There is the history of science, the sociology of science, the psychology of science, and so on. So, there is yet much to say about the *philosophy* of science. Before specifically addressing that topic, however, we need to focus on the first word of the phrase, "philosophy of science," namely, philosophy.

What is philosophy?

There are three words in that phrase "philosophy of science." The first one—philosophy—means different things to different people. Even among philosophers themselves there is no single definition or notion that is universally accepted. A typical way that introductory philosophy textbooks begin to explain what is philosophy is by explaining the origin and meaning of the word "philosophy." It comes from two Greek terms, *philo,* which means "to love" and *sophia,* which means "wisdom." So, "philosophy" is "the love of wisdom" and a philosopher is a lover of wisdom. This is not very enlightening until we understand that the Greeks distinguished wisdom from simple knowledge. We can know lots of specific facts about the world, be great at Trivial Pursuit, but that is not the same as having wisdom. Wisdom is a matter of understanding how facts are interrelated, knowing underlying causes and connections, even knowing consequences or implications of those facts.

A term that often is associated with early Greek philosophers is *first principles.* The notion of a principle is meant to capture various things. First, principles are general, perhaps even universal, whereas facts are particular and specific. Being general, principles point to an interconnectedness between and among specific facts. Like laws, principles serve as a unifying notion. So, if there is an economic principle, for example, that higher interest rates reduce inflation, then what is being explained is not just some particular case of economic interaction, but general economic trends. Likewise, a moral principle, such as "murder is wrong," applies not to just some specific case of murder, but any case. The point is that principles are broader than facts and they "do" something; they display a unity among facts. First principles are the most basic, fundamental, and unifying underlying principles. Identifying first principles was the goal of philosophy, the attainment of wisdom.

Thales and first principles

Thales of Miletus, who lived around 600 B.C.E., is usually labeled as the first Western natural philosopher. He is famously credited with claiming that water is the source of all things. This seemingly simple and wrong (!) statement is just the sort of thing philosophers say that leads people to see philosophy as pointless, groundless speculation. Why, then, is he seen as being so important in the history of philosophy and the history of science? It is not because he correctly identified some fact about the world. Instead, he asked a question that went beyond particular facts. Behind the statement that "water is the source of all things" is the question of whether there is a single, basic underlying reality to what we know as being real. His answer is that there is, and the single basic underlying reality is something natural, namely, water (not something supernatural or unknowable or impossible for us to experience). Water is the source of *all* things, not just some things. In addition, water is the *source* of all things; it is something common to everything, something unifying. Now, we do not think that Thales was right and neither did his contemporaries, but that is not the point, and it is not why he is seen as important. He sought a first principle of natural philosophy (what, if anything, is the source of everything?), a fundamental, unifying, explanatory principle.

The goal of identifying first principles was—and is—held in different contexts. In the context of human behavior and interaction, we speak of moral principles. Again, the claim that "murder is wrong" is supposed to be applied generally, not just to particular people or situations. Or, if we claim that human rights should be respected, we do not mean just in Oregon, but anywhere and by everyone. So, looking for first principles of behavior is one context. This is the field of moral philosophy. Another context is accounting for what we discover about the natural world, and this was the field of natural philosophy. Here the question was "What are the first principles of nature?" Today, for science, we ask much the same question, but we say it differently. We ask questions like "What is everything made of?" or "What is the fundamental nature of matter?" or "What are the fundamental forces in nature?" The goal of looking for the most basic and unifying underlying reality is still there. The majesty of Isaac Newton's physical theories is that with three simple laws of motion and a law of universal gravitation (just four basic principles) he could offer a powerful account of the physical world. These simple laws could unify such apparently different and disparate phenomena as the orbits of the planets and the timing of the tides on Earth and why his famous apple fell.

This discussion of first principles is all to say that, originally at least, philosophy was a search for first principles, including—for natural philosophers—first principles of the natural world. Philosophy is still a quest for fundamental understanding. Although philosophers today rarely talk of seeking first principles, they do still have the goal of identifying basic concepts and showing how they relate to others. For example, today philosophers wrestle with questions such as, "What is consciousness?" or, among philosophers of science, "What is scientific explanation?" Philosophical questions such as these are informed by facts, but they are not just questions about facts. To answer the question about, say, the nature of consciousness, philosophers certainly need to take into consideration the facts that have been discovered by neuroscientists and by cognitive psychologists, not to mention by everyday experience. But those facts by themselves do not answer the question. Unless we can show that the mind is nothing but the brain, the facts coming from neuroscience will not be sufficient to account for consciousness. (At least, this is one philosophical perspective.) In addition, although the various sciences provide explanations for natural phenomena, no natural science or social science addresses the basic conceptual question of just what it means to give an explanation. That is a philosophical question.

Philosophical questions

We have all heard the expression that we should treat our family like company and company like family. This means that, because we tend to be on more polite terms and proper behavior with company, but more sincere, comfortable terms with family, that we ought to be a little nicer to our family and be a little less formal with our company. In a similar vein, one characterization of philosophy is that it makes the common uncommon and the uncommon common. That means that philosophers look at everyday, common notions and experiences and treat them as though they are uncommon; they need to be investigated and thought about more explicitly. So, most of us do not usually question that we have minds, but philosophers ask whether we do and just what it means to say that we do (or don't!). Likewise, philosophers tend to treat the uncommon as common. That is, they look for features or functions that show the things we take as strange or unfamiliar are in fact familiar, after all. It is just this attitude of treating the common as uncommon and the uncommon as common that motivates philosophical questions and points to why philosophical questions are often different than other sorts of questions. Here is an example: Consider the license plate of the next car you see. Suppose the plate number is: XYZ 123. Now, various kinds of questions could occur to you. (Yes, one might be: Why would I think about license plates? However, let's ignore that one.) One might be a simple arithmetical question: Given three letters and three numbers, how many different license plates are possible? (Although you might not care about this, state governments do, because they have to decide what to do once they come to plate ZZZ 999.) Another question might be fiscal: How much does it cost to make a license plate? Another might be historical: When did we start having license plates? Another might be sociological: Why do we require license plates for some vehicles, but not for others? A philosophical question is: What is a license? What does it mean to license something? These sorts of questions are basic, broad conceptual questions. They are like the stereotypical philosophical questions, "What is truth?" (or "goodness" or "beauty" or "reality," etc.). Philosophical questions often seem very abstract because they are, but this is not because they are not important. The value of asking such questions can often be that they make us think about common (and uncommon) phenomena in new ways that shed light on the topic at hand and often on other topics, too. And even if there is no recognized, single "right" answer to a philosophical question, it does not follow that asking and addressing that question is not valuable. For one thing, although we might not come up with a "right" answer, we could very well identify wrong answers. Just as we might not know the "right" answer to the question, "How many stars are there in the Milky Way galaxy?" we do know that "twelve" is a wrong answer. This question about stars is not a philosophical one, but the same point holds for questions about "What is a license?" or "What is truth?" and so on. We can identify wrong answers, even if we cannot or have not identified a "right" answer. One final point: taking the common as uncommon and vice versa is not, of course, unique to philosophy. When we ask "Why is the sky blue?" we are doing the same thing, but this is a scientific question, not a philosophical one, because the answer will finally be in terms of empirical facts about the world and scientific theories that account for those facts.

Philosophers tend to have two broad approaches to asking philosophical questions and answering them. First, philosophy is *analytical*. That is, it analyzes concepts. Socrates is famous for having persistently asked questions like, "What is knowledge?" or "What is piety?" or "What is friendship?" This remains a primary focus for philosophy today, to begin with the question, "What is X?"

A typical approach to answering a "What is X?" question is to look for necessary and sufficient conditions for something to be X. If you wanted to know what a flageolet is, one way to find out is to know what kinds of features something would have to have in order to be a flageolet. You might come to know that it is a musical instrument. But just knowing that does not tell you if a flageolet is different than a fipple flute, and if it is, how it is different. Simply being a musical instrument is not sufficient for something to be a flageolet, even though it might be necessary. Or, another example—a very common one—is to say what a bachelor is. To be a bachelor, something has to be male, so being male is a necessary condition for being a bachelor, but it is not a sufficient condition, because many males are not bachelors. Besides being male, another necessary condition is that the thing must be unmarried. If we wanted to distinguish bachelors from divorcés or widowers, we would need to say that the thing is not just unmarried, but never has been married. But, again, simply being unmarried (or never been married) is not by itself a sufficient condition for being a bachelor, because there are women who are not married, but they are not bachelors. In addition, we would need to stipulate other necessary conditions, like being a human (unless we want to include my tom cat Karloff as a bachelor), or being of a certain age (unless we want to say that a one-day-old human male baby is a bachelor).

Although this approach of looking to identify necessary and sufficient conditions in order to appropriately characterize something is philosophically common and fruitful, it does not always work. Some terms and concepts are vague and do not have necessary and sufficient conditions that easily answer a "What is X?" question. The point here, however, is that much of the job of philosophy, and what it is to "do" philosophy, is to analyze concepts. The underlying goal is to get clear, accurate, and fruitful understanding of just what we are talking about.

But analyzing concepts is not all that philosophy is about. Philosophy is also *synthetic,* that is, it is concerned with synthesizing and bringing together concepts and information. We're not just interested in conceptual clarity, but also in the presuppositions and implications and significance of issues. In the words of the philosopher Wilfred Sellars, we want to know how things, in the broadest sense of the term, hang together, in the broadest sense of the term. This is what most people think of when they think of philosophy, asking life's "big questions" in order to get the "big picture." We want the clear understanding that comes from philosophical analysis, but we also want to know what it means, how that clear understanding applies to anything.

These two concerns—philosophical analysis and synthesis—dovetail together. Here is an example, adapted from a case by James Rachels. In considering whether there is any important moral difference between actually killing someone or just letting them die, he suggested something like the following: Imagine a situation in which I am second in line for a large inheritance. The only person standing between that pot of money and me is my young nephew, Terry. I want that money and I am willing to eliminate Terry in order to get it. However, no one knows of my evil scheme and, in fact, everyone thinks that Uncle Dave likes Terry. So, one night Terry's parents go out for dinner and I volunteer to baby sit him. I tell them I will give him a nice bubble bath before putting him to bed. What I am planning, of course, is to get him in the tub and drown him. Later, I get the tub filled with water and Terry is happily taking his bath. I come in, knock him on the head and he does drown. I have killed him and we rightly think that I have done something that is morally wrong. But now, change the scenario slightly. This time, just as I am about to commit my heinous deed, Terry slips in the tub and drowns on his own, without me doing anything. I am again accused of having done something morally wrong by just standing by and watching him, but suppose I claim in my defense that I did not kill him, I just let him die. *Legally,* we might say there is a difference, but, Rachels says, there does not seem to be much of a difference *morally.* Now, and here comes the synthetic aspect of this case, if we think that this case demonstrates that there is no important moral distinction between killing and letting die (and, yes, that is an *if*), then we should apply this view to other cases and not just this one. So, if we know that other people are starving and we can help them, but we do not, then we cannot claim that we are being ok morally because we are not killing them, we are just letting them die. For our purposes here, it does not matter whether or not we are convinced by this case. The point is that one of the approaches of philosophy is to synthesize concepts, to show their presuppositions and implications, to engage in this intellectual enterprise to show how things are interrelated and why they matter.

Philosophical topics: metaphysics, epistemology, axiology

As with any academic discipline, there are many areas of study within philosophy. Besides the philosophy of science, the focus of this book, there are philosophy of law, philosophy of language, philosophy of education, logic, ethics, and many, many others. In very broad strokes, there are three major fields within philosophy: metaphysics, epistemology, and axiology. Metaphysics is the study of reality, the nature of reality. Epistemology is the study of knowledge, the nature of knowledge. Axiology is the study of value and values, the nature of value(s). As will be shown later in this book, the philosophy of science examines metaphysical, epistemological, and axiological issues within and about science. But before getting to those issues, a fuller introduction to these three fields would be helpful.

Metaphysics

Metaphysics, again, is the study of reality. The term comes from two Greek words, *meta*, which means "after" (or sometimes "before") and *phusis*, which means "physics," or at least what is physical. *Phusis* was, for the Greeks, the study of the physical world, so the term was broader than our contemporary term *physics*; it would have included other investigations of the physical world than just what we associate with physics today. Metaphysics is the study of reality more broadly even than phusis. It is not just the investigation of physical things, but asks even more fundamental questions about what *kinds* of things constitute reality. For example, there are concrete, specific things that we all acknowledge as being real, such as a white piece of paper. But what about abstract things, such as Harvard University? Harvard is not just a collection of concrete physical buildings or people. Are abstractions real, and, if so, in what sense, and what does it mean for something even to be an abstraction? A related question, but not exactly the same, about what kinds of things constitute reality is the question of universal objects versus particular objects. We know what particular objects are (though, as you might expect, philosophers even ask about just what it means to be a particular individual thing; it turns out that it is not so obvious, after all). But what about universal objects, such as the color white, which is not the same thing as the collection of all particular white objects?

Notice, with these examples I have used the words "things" and "objects." Another metaphysical question is about what else might be real besides or instead of things or objects. For example, we commonly speak of events, such as the battle of Waterloo. What are the nature and the status of events? That is a metaphysical question. Likewise, we speak of interactions and processes. Are these real? If so, are these "really" just things or objects, but we mistakenly talk about them as being something different? Again, this is a metaphysical question, and not one that particular sciences wrestle with. Consider also two common objects, say, a pencil and a standard piece of paper. Besides taking these two objects as real, we speak of the *properties* or traits of these objects. For instance, the piece of paper is white, it is rectangular, it is flat, it is smooth, no doubt, it has some flavor to it (taste it and see). Are these properties real as well as the object itself being real? In addition, the paper is larger than the pencil (at least, I am going to assume it is, not having seen your pencils or pieces of paper). The paper really is larger than the pencil; that is a fact of the world. Now, "is larger than" is not an object, like a pencil, and it is not a property of either object, like being rectangular. Rather, it is a relation between two objects, the paper and the pencil. (Sometimes relations are spoken of as *relational properties*, but that is not important here.) Are relations real? As just noted, we certainly say that the paper *really* is larger than the pencil. Asking about the nature and status of relations is a metaphysical question.

In addition to the types of broad metaphysical questions such as the nature and kinds of things that constitute reality, there are metaphysical questions about specific topics. Example of this are: "What is time?" or "What is possibility?" or "What is cause?" We frequently take these topics as ordinary and real; that is, that one event causes another. Metaphysicians take these common notions and treat them as uncommon, as needing further examination.

Now, as convoluted as this will sound, everything I have been saying about metaphysics above is the metaphysics of metaphysics! That is, it has been a brief discussion of the kinds of topics that metaphysics investigates. There are also epistemological issues about metaphysics, namely, what is metaphysical knowledge and how do we know? Is there some method of inquiry that will inform us about metaphysical issues or guarantee that our metaphysical *beliefs* constitute metaphysical *knowledge*? It seems that if the answer to metaphysical questions is a matter of bumping into the world and acquiring empirical facts, then wouldn't metaphysics just be something for the sciences to deal with? After all, they are pretty good at uncovering empirical facts. If metaphysical knowledge is not a matter of empirical facts, then how can/should we approach metaphysical questions—intuition? This is an epistemological issue about metaphysics.

In addition, there are axiological issues about metaphysics. Probably a basic axiological question about metaphysics, one you might well be asking yourself right now, is: What is the value of studying metaphysics? Who cares? Well, it turns out that metaphysical issues are quite important outside of the curiosity of philosophers. Here is an example: One metaphysical topic is the nature of *personhood*. That is, what is a person? Persons are not just human beings, as the notion of human is a biological one; if X has the appropriate genetic structure, X is human. But that is not the same as being a person. Persons are things in social contexts, with rights and responsibilities, and so on. An obvious, very practical, question connected to personhood is: Is a human fetus a person? We all agree that a human fetus is a human (again, that is a biological matter), but not everyone agrees—because it is not obvious—that a human fetus is a person. Here is another practical case, one that is perhaps less emotionally charged: A man named Andrija Artukovic was arrested in 1984 in the United States and accused of crimes committed in Europe 40 years earlier during World War II. The assumptions that underlie the attempt to punish him were that he was in fact the same person as the one who committed the crimes, that he (the same person) was responsible, and that, being responsible, he was legitimately punishable. Should the man named "Andrija Artukovic," almost 90 years old at the time of his trial, be punished for crimes committed by the man, referred to as "the butcher of the Balkans," for actions committed 40 years earlier? A necessary condition for such a punishment being appropriate is that this old man is the same person as the younger killer, and what constitutes being the same person is the very issue of personal identity. So, there are important value issues connected to metaphysics.

Epistemology

The second major field of philosophy noted above is epistemology, the study of knowledge. Epistemology addresses questions about the nature of knowledge, the source(s) of knowledge, the justification for claims to knowledge, forms of knowledge, even whether we have any knowledge at all. All of us claim to know lots of things: I know when I have a toothache, I know that 2 plus 2 equals 4, I know that the sun is larger than the earth, I know how to drive a car, and so on. These examples illustrate different kinds of knowledge. Sometimes by "knowledge" we mean *knowledge by acquaintance,* or knowledge of something with which we are immediately connected to (or acquainted with), such as having a toothache. There is also *propositional knowledge,* or knowledge that something is the case (i.e., knowledge that some proposition is true), such as knowing that the sun is larger than the earth. In addition, there is *practical knowledge,* which in this case means knowing how, such as knowing how to drive a car. One issue within epistemology is the examination of how these various kinds of knowledge are related to each other. For example, is all propositional knowledge based finally on knowledge by acquaintance?

Besides knowing things, I believe lots of things. However, I am not sure that I know them. I believe Socrates spoke Greek, I believe that humans will some day walk on Mars, and I believe that there is no largest prime number. I believe I can successfully fix the motor on my ceiling fan. Clearly, there are many things we believe, but it does not follow that we know those things. We make a distinction between belief and knowledge. This distinction points to a long-standing issue in epistemology: What is knowledge?

A traditional answer to the question, "What is knowledge?," at least for propositional knowledge, is that knowledge is Justified True Belief. Philosophers usually state this in this way: *S knows that p* (meaning some person S knows that some proposition p is the case) involves three necessary conditions. Those conditions are: (1) S believes that p, (2) p is true, and (3) S is justified in believing p. The first condition, the *belief condition,* simply says that for us to know something, we have to at least believe it. It would be strange to claim that I know that Seattle is in Washington, but I don't believe it. So, believing that p is a necessary condition for knowing that p. But it is not sufficient, because we can believe things without knowing them. A second condition for knowledge is the *truth condition.* This states that p, the proposition we know, is true. This means that we cannot know something that is false. Now, we can know that something is false. For instance, I know that it is false that my cat is a dog. I can know that a proposition is false, but I cannot know a false proposition. Another way of saying this is that, although there can be false beliefs, there cannot be false knowledge. Again, I cannot know that 2 plus 2 equals 3 or that the sun is smaller than the earth, no matter how strongly I believe it. In those cases, I am just wrong.

The third traditional condition for knowledge is the *justification condition.* The first two conditions by themselves, having a true belief, are not enough for knowledge. I must also have justification for the belief. We all have true beliefs but that is not the same as having knowledge. Every student who has been faced with multiple-choice exams has had the experience of making a lucky guess at an answer and getting it right. In such as case, they had a true belief ("I think the answer is (d) none of the above"), but it certainly was not a case of knowing. (Admit it; you have done this too many times to remember!) So knowledge cannot just be true belief, otherwise any lucky guess that turned out correct would be a case of knowledge.

This traditional notion of knowledge as justified true belief has been examined and criticized by philosophers for a long time. Our present concern is not with that, but there are some more things to say about each of these three conditions. First, with respect to belief, it is not the same as just having an opinion. We can have—and, sadly, too many people do—opinions about anything without having any sort of evidence or warrant for those opinions. This is not the same as having a belief. A belief involves the acceptance of some fact or process, with a readiness to act on that acceptance. If I really believe something, rather than just saying that I do, then I take it as given that certain facts are the case and my future behavior is affected as a result.

As for truth, there are a number of philosophical views about just what truth is. A common sense view is called by philosophers the *correspondence* conception of truth. This view of truth states that what makes a particular proposition or belief true is that it corresponds to facts in the world. If my belief that the sun is larger than the earth is true, it is because in fact the sun is larger than the earth. It is that simple; if my belief corresponds to the facts, it is true (indeed, that is what makes it true), and if it does not correspond, it is not true. Another philosophical view of truth is called the *coherence* conception of truth. This view of truth states that what makes a particular proposition or belief true is that it coheres with other accepted propositions or beliefs. That is, no proposition or belief exists in isolation and when we say some belief is true (or false, for that matter) what we mean is that it is consistent with other beliefs. Many, probably most, of those other beliefs are ones concerning facts about the world, so truth is not just some coherent fairy tale, according to the supporters of this view. A third view of truth is called the *pragmatist* conception of truth. This view of truth states that what makes a particular proposition or belief true is how it affects us in the future, that is, what consequences follow from taking it as true. The point here is that "true" is not just a descriptive property of propositions or beliefs, but, rather, that "true" is also a prescriptive notion, directing our future beliefs and actions. As one pragmatist, William James, said *truth happens to an idea, it is made true by events, and its verity is itself an event or process.* Now, the point for us with respect to philosophy of science is not to resolve the nature of truth, but to see that one epistemological concern is the nature of truth, especially as it relates to the nature of knowledge.

Let me say one more word about truth here. It is quite common to have someone say that truth is relative or that something is "true for me." There are several things to say about this. First, there is a difference between *relativity* and *subjectivism.* When people say something is "true for me," that statement really is a claim that truth is subjective and that there are no objective standards for assessing whether some belief is true or not. To say that truth is relative is not the same thing. We can speak of beliefs being judged true or false relative to certain standards (e.g., legal standards of evidence or proof versus scientific standards of evidence or mathematical standards of proof), but that is not the same as saying that it is subjective. So, one point is that the notion of truth as relative is not the same as the notion of truth as subjective. Beyond that, when someone says that something is "true for me," that really comes down to just saying that "I believe it" (and perhaps believe it so strongly that I will act in certain ways on that belief). But there must be some reason why something is "true for me" as opposed to being "false for me." In saying it is "true for me," the "for me" part doesn't really add anything. It just says that I believe it. That does not get us anywhere toward distinguishing true beliefs and false beliefs nor to what makes some beliefs true and others false. This points to the third condition of knowledge discussed above, namely, the justification condition.

When asked what kinds of support or evidence or warrant justify propositions or beliefs, philosophers traditionally spoke of *empiricist* justification or *rationalist* justification. An empiricist view of justification is the view that the source of all knowledge, and, so, the final justification of all knowledge, comes down to immediate sensory experience. Quite simply, we bump into the world. If we claim to know something and that claim cannot be shown finally to be based in sensory experience, then, under an empiricist view, that claim is not a case of knowledge. Clearly, matters get more complex than this, for example, we often, especially within science, have to base claims on probabilities and statistical analyses, but the point remains the same: for some belief to be knowledge, it ultimately must be based on sensory experience, however complex that experience is.

A rationalist view of justification rejects the view that the source, and justification, of all knowledge is sensory experience. The rationalist view says this empiricist view is false, because there are things we know that are not based on sensory experience, such as mathematical or logical knowledge. Although, as children, we might come to learn that 2 plus 2 equals 4, numbers and addition and equality are not things in the world that we bump into. We can demonstrate our knowledge of, in this case, simple arithmetic by showing two apples and two more apples give us four apples, but, say the rationalists, that is just a demonstration of knowledge, not the knowledge itself. (In addition, we know that $\sqrt[3]{5} < 29$, but not because we have ever bumped into $\sqrt[3]{5}$ apples in the world.) So, according to the rationalist view, not all knowledge is based on sensory experience and, in fact, there are "truths of reason" (which is why this view is called rationalism) that we know and are not a matter of sensory experience of things in the world. Besides the example of mathematical knowledge, rationalists claim that other basic concepts that we use, basic categories such as causality or unity or possibility, are not known by sensory experience (that is, we see objects in the world, but we do not "see" cause or unity).

This dispute between an empiricist view and a rationalist view of justification of beliefs generated more philosophical writing than you would ever want to know about! Today philosophers tend to address the issue of the justification of beliefs not so much in terms of empiricism and rationalism as in terms of *externalism* and *internalism*. Simply put, externalism is the view that what justifies a person's beliefs must be something external to the person, whereas internalism is the view that something internal to the believer can (at least in part) be relevant to justifying that person's beliefs. Again, as with the various topics covered in this chapter, the point here is not to fully engage in the philosophical debates, but to illustrate the kinds of issues dealt with in these areas of philosophy.

Besides the issues of belief and truth and justification, there are numerous other epistemological topics. For example, there is the broad question of whether we are ever justified in claiming to actually know something or if we might always be mistaken about our beliefs. This is the issue of *skepticism,* and it has to do with the kinds and level of justification that is required for a belief to be justified to such an extent or in such a way as to really be knowledge. There are also more specific epistemological topics, such as the nature of perception and other modes of belief (e.g., intuition, revelation). As will be seen later in this book, there are important epistemological issues connected to the philosophy of science, like the nature of evidence and confirmation.

Axiology

The third broad area of philosophical concern is axiology, the study of value(s). This is the area that probably most people think of when they think of philosophy, especially in the sense of moral value(s). When people think of the meaning of life or questions about how we should live or what's really important in life, they are asking axiological questions. Now, axiology, as the study of value(s), does encompass ethics and morality, but it is broader than that. There are other kinds of values than ethical values. For instance, there are artistic values. The field of study that focuses on artistic value(s) is often called *aesthetics,* although today the term "philosophy of art" is used more and more. In any case, aesthetics involves the examination of value(s) where the value(s) might have nothing at all to do with ethics and morality. When we say that some book or movie or song or statue is a good one, we do not mean that it was morally good (well, at least most of us do not mean that). A song might be good because it has a beat that makes it easy to dance to, not because it carries some approved moral message. So, there are artistic values that fall under the umbrella of axiology, but have nothing to do with morality.

Nevertheless, ethics and morality are the axiological topics that most of us think about and philosophers mostly examine. First, a point of terminology: *morality* is a matter of actions and judgments pertaining to particular actions and kinds of actions, whereas *ethics* (sometimes called *moral philosophy*) is the study of moral values, including analyzing, justifying, prioritizing, integrating them, and so on. So, "murder is wrong" is a moral statement, whereas "whatever promotes the greatest good for the greatest number" or "the good is defined in terms of what promotes the greatest good" is an ethical statement. The distinction is analogous to saying that biology is the study of life forms; it is not the life forms themselves.

There are, of course, many subtopics within ethics. There is the issue of the origin of moral values; do they come from biology, society, intuition, God, and so on? There is also the issue of the justification of moral values. What justifies the claim that murder is wrong? Does it come down to being wrong (assuming that it is, indeed, wrong) because it violates people's rights or

because it violates God's commandments or because it creates
social unrest or some other reason? This is similar to the externalism versus internalism debate mentioned above with respect
to epistemology. This—what justifies moral values—is what most
moral philosophy is about.

Origin versus justification of value(s)

Although the origin and the justification of value(s) are related issues,
they are not the same thing. Consider this example: Suppose we are
talking and I make some outrageous sexist or racist remark. You are as-
tonished and you ask me, "Why do you believe that?" I answer, "Well,
that's what my father told me." Now, I have given you the origin of my
belief/value, namely, it came from my family upbringing. But, clearly, I
have not given a justification for that belief/value. You would be quite
right in thinking that not only am I reprehensible, but so is my father.
The point is that answering a "why" question simply by providing the
origin sometimes does not really answer the question. The "why" did
not refer to "how did I come to have this belief/value?" but to "what
would justify having this belief/value?" These are not at all necessarily
the same thing.

One other subfield of axiology is social/political philosophy.
This is obviously related to ethics and morality, but, again, they
are not the same. Social/political philosophy deals with topics
such as the nature of the state, legitimate regulation of people's
behavior, the relation of the individual and the group or community, the nature of civil laws, and so on. There is certainly an overlap of ethics and morality with social and political philosophy, but
the notion of *person* is not the same as the notion of *citizen*, and
the study of values relevant to being a person are not necessarily
those relevant to being a citizen. I could be a good citizen of a
community by paying my taxes on time, recycling regularly, not
annoying my neighbors, and so on—that is, be a model citizen—
even though I might be a scoundrel in my personal life. No, there
is not a sharp, mutually exclusive division between the public and
the private, but the point should be clear: persons and citizens are

not identical notions, and social/political philosophy focuses on the latter.

Philosophy of science

This brief summary of philosophy gives us a grounding—finally!—to say something directly about philosophy of science. The three broad areas of concern for philosophers—metaphysics, epistemology, and axiology—are all relevant when philosophers turn their attention to particular human endeavors, such as law or education or religion or language, and so on. Take religion (and, in Chapter Thirteen, we will look more closely at the relationships between science and religion). There are metaphysical issues connected to religion, such as the nature of supernatural beings (e.g., God or gods, angels) as well as of other "things" like a human soul. There are epistemological issues connected to religion, such as "ways of religious knowledge" (e.g., revelation, scriptural authority, faith, signs in nature). There are axiological issues connected to religion, such as the role of religion in public education or why bad things happen to good people.

Likewise, when philosophers turn to philosophically examining science, metaphysical, epistemological, and axiological issues arise. Indeed, the very ways that we characterize science, or distinguish science from non-science, are along the lines of metaphysics, epistemology, and axiology. For example, when asking what science is, we might focus on what science investigates (as opposed to what, say, art investigates). We might say that there are kinds of questions that science does and can properly ask, which are different kinds of questions than those that artists ask. So, what makes something science is *what* it investigates. Or, we might claim that what makes something science is not what it investigates, but *how* it is investigated. That is, what distinguishes science from non-science is not the content of its investigations, but the method(s) used. Both astronomers and poets might talk about the same thing, the moon, but how they approach their topic is what makes their disciplines different. Finally, recognizing that it is scientists who do the investigating, people who live in cultural and historical contexts, we might focus on *why* certain things are investigated, as well as why they are investigated using certain kinds of methods. Science is a social institution, influencing and influenced by the larger contexts in which it is housed. *These three approaches to looking at the nature of science (the what, the how, the why) correspond to the three broad categories of philosophical concern: metaphysics (the what), epistemology (the how), and axiology (the why).*

I mentioned at the beginning of this chapter that people usually think of philosophy and science as being not only quite different from each other, but pretty much in opposition to each other. I hope that, given what you've read so far, that notion of philosophy *versus* science is already fading. They are not in opposition to each other; at least they certainly do not need to be. Of course, that does not mean that they are not different; they are. They ask different questions, they answer those questions in different ways, and they have different goals. Or, to be more careful about it, they do not have the same questions or go about answering them in the same ways or have the same goals. They overlap, often in important and dramatic ways. One of the ways is in terms of the implications of scientific information or theories or practices. For example, some people have claimed that indeterminacy and uncertainty at the subatomic level that quantum physicists speak of implies that humans have free will. After all, if even the motions of subatomic particles are not determined, how could human behavior be? Needless to say, others have questioned that implication. Or, more familiar to all of us, theories of biological evolution make implications about the nature and origin of the human species. As we all know, these implications have excited and agitated lots of folks. These kinds of issues (implications of science, critique of particular claims or theories or even practices, even influences of culture and society as a whole on science) are ones that philosophy of science deals with. But even more so, philosophy of science is concerned with the analysis and evaluation of scientific methodologies and fundamental concepts connected to science. Typical topics here are things like the nature of explanation, the nature of laws, the nature of evidence, the relation between models and data, how science changes and progresses, the role of values in scientific practice and evaluation, and so on. These are the types of topics that this book will investigate.

One final comment before we actually dig in and start doing some philosophy of science. Philosophers of science sometimes are seen by scientists as treading where they do not belong, or at least as acting like they can talk about things (namely, science) that they do not really know about. They are philosophers, after all, not scientists! How can they meaningfully talk about the nature of science? Well, there are several things to say about this. First, most philosophers of science in fact do have training in science and can speak knowledgeably about it. You will see this with the reading selections in the upcoming chapters. No, they are not scientific specialists, but they are not ignorant, either. Second, they are not *doing* science; they are doing philosophy. That is, they are asking *philosophical* questions, not scientific ones. They happen to be philosophical questions about things connected to science, just as historians of science ask historical questions about science and sociologists of science ask sociological questions about science. Of course, philosophers of science defer to scientists about the science part of philosophy of science! Third, when this concern is raised ("Who do philosophers think they are spouting off about science?"), it is sometimes raised as if philosophers of science are up to no good, that they are trying to tell scientists how to do science or what science is really all about. This is a remnant of that philosophy versus science view that is unfortunate. Imagine if politicians said that nobody other than politicians had any legitimate business investigating the nature of politics, because only politicians have the expertise and political knowledge and skills involved in politics? We rightly would not buy that line. Philosophers and scientists have much to learn from one another; philosophy of science is just one bridge between them that (I hope, at least!) allows them to find common ground. With that all being said, let's start doing philosophy of science.

What is science?

Just as the typical philosophical question is "What is X?" it would naturally occur to begin with the question of what science is. Consider the following story about a purported science, umbrellaology:

UMBRELLAOLOGY

John Somerville

"Dear Sir: I am taking the liberty of calling upon you to be a judge in a dispute between me and an acquaintance who is no longer a friend. The question at issue is this: Is my creation, umbrellaology, a science? Allow me to explain this situation. For the past eighteen years, assisted by a few faithful disciples, I have been collecting materials on a subject hitherto almost wholly neglected by scientists, the umbrella. The results of my investigation to date are embodied in the nine volumes which I am sending to you under separate cover. Pending their receipt, let me describe to you briefly the nature of their contents and the method I pursued in compiling them. I began on the Island of Manhattan. Proceeding block by block, house by house, family by family, and individual by individual, I ascertained (1) the number of umbrellas possessed, (2) their size, (3) their weight, (4) their color. Having covered Manhattan after many years, I eventually extended the survey to the other boroughs of the City of New York, and at length completed the entire city. Thus I was ready to carry forward the work of the rest of the state and indeed the rest of the United States and the whole world.

"It was at this point that I approached my erstwhile friend. I am a modest man, but I felt I had the right to be recognized as the creator of a new science. He, on the other hand, claimed that umbrellaology was not a science at all. First, he said, it was silly to investigate umbrellas. Now this argument is false because science scorns not to deal with any object, however humble, even to the 'hind leg of a flea.' Then why not umbrellas? Next he said that umbrellaology could not be recognized as a science because it was of no use or benefit to mankind. But is not the truth the most precious thing in life? And are not my nine volumes filled with the truth about my subject? Every word is true. Every sentence contains a hard, cold fact. When he asked me what was the object of umbrellaology I was proud to say, "To seek and discover the truth is object enough for me." I am a pure scientist; I have no ulterior motives. Hence it follows that I am satisfied with truth alone. Next, he said my truths were dated and that any one of my findings might cease to be true tomorrow. But this, I pointed out, is not an argument against umbrellaology, but rather an argument for keeping it up to date, which is exactly what I propose. Let us have surveys monthly, weekly or even daily to keep our knowledge abreast of the changing facts. His next contention was that umbrellaology had entertained no hypotheses and had developed no theories or laws. This is a great error. In the course of my investigations, I employed numerous hypotheses. Before entering each new block and each new section of the city, I entertained an hypothesis as regards the number and characteristics of the umbrellas that would be found there, which hypotheses were either verified or nullified by my subsequent observations, in accordance with proper scientific procedure, as explained in authoritative texts. (In fact, it is interesting to note that I can substantiate and document every one of my replies to these objections by numerous quotations from standard works, leading journals, public speeches of eminent scientists and the like.) As for theories and laws, my work presents an abundance of them. I will here mention only a few by way of illustration. There is the Law of Color Variation Relative to Ownership by Sex. (Umbrellas owned by women tend to a great variety of color, whereas those owned by men are almost all black.) To this law I have given exact statistical formulation. (See Vol. 6, Appendix I, Table 3, p. 582.) There are the curiously interrelated laws of Individual Ownership of Plurality of Umbrellas, and Plurality for Owners of Individual Umbrellas. The interrelationship assumes the form, in the first law, of almost direct ratio to annual income, and in the second, of almost inverse ratio to annual income. (For an exact statement of the modifying circumstances, see Vol. 8, p. 350.) There is also the Law of Tendency towards Acquisition of Umbrellas in Rainy Weather. To this law I have given experimental verification in chapter 3 of Volume 3. In the same way I have performed numerous other experiments in connection with my generalization.

"Thus I feel that my creation is in all respects a genuine science, and I appeal to you for substantiation of my opinion."

Is umbrellaology a science? Or, put a different way: Is umbrellaology scientific? I am not going to answer this question here because I hope that you (either on your own or in class discussion) will try to answer it. What is important is what reasons you give for why you take umbrellaology to be science/scientific or not. The reasons you give (either pro or con) point to what you take as necessary or sufficient conditions for something to be science/scientific.

As you debate the scientific status of umbrellaology, consider also these following two characterizations of science, the first one taken from a geology textbook and the second from an economics textbook:

> First the scientists observes, then he formulates a problem concerning his observations. He thinks out a possible explanation, or hypothesis, which he then tests with experiments. The experiments then prove or disprove his hypothesis, and if it is proved, he can state a law.

> First, all facts would be observed and recorded, *without selection* or *a priori* guess as to their relative importance. Secondly, the observed and recorded facts would be analyzed, compared, and classified, without *hypothesis* or *postulates*, other than those necessarily involved in the logic of thought. Third, from this analysis of the facts, generalizations would be inductively drawn as to the relations, classificatory or causal, between them. Fourth, further research would be deductive as well as inductive, employing inferences from previously established generalizations.

In upcoming chapters, there will be plenty to say about these characterizations of science, but for now, think about how they compare with the umbrellaology case. My hope is that, having considered the scientific status of umbrellaology here at the beginning of this book, you will return to this case by the end of the book, after you have been immersed in philosophy of science issues, to see whether and in what ways your views about umbrellaology—and science, broadly—change.

The point of bringing up the umbrellaology case is to address the question of what science is. I will proceed with the assumption that we do not have a single, fully accepted definition (with necessary and sufficient conditions) of "science." Indeed, here are various definitions that are in the dictionary:

- the state of fact or knowing
- knowledge or cognizance of something specified or implied
- knowledge acquired by study

- trained skill
- the kind of knowledge or intellectual activity of which the various "sciences" are examples
- a branch of knowledge that is concerned either with a connected body of demonstrated truths or with observed facts systematically classified and more or less colligated by being brought under general laws and that includes trustworthy methods for the discovery of new truth within its own domain

Obviously, these various definitions characterize science in vastly different ways. Some features do stand out, though. Science is seen as a form of knowledge (a product) and also as a skill or ability (a process). One difficulty with them all, even with the last one, is that they apply to disciplines that we do not normally take as science, such as philosophy.

A more useful approach to examining the philosophical issues connected to science than beginning with a single definition of science is to consider features that are basic to all those fields that are taken as science. They might not be distinctive of science (that is, these features can be found in non-sciences), but they certainly are part of anything that is science. Those features are the following:

- *Gathering information:* direct observation, instrument-aided observation, measurement, case studies, field studies, experiments
- *Organizing gathered information:* classifications, measurement scales, models, theories, paradigms
- *Alternative modes of organization:* refinement, reduction, replacement
- *Accounting for phenomena:* explanation, prediction, control
- *Data enhancement/extrapolation:* evidence, confirmation, falsification, hypothesis testing

Whatever science is, however we meaningfully distinguish science and non-science, even if we cannot come up with a single, clear definition, anything that is science will involve these various features (at least most of them). Whatever counts as science is certainly going to require the gathering of information, frequently via experimentation. In addition, it will involve organizing and making sense of that information. No science is without models and theories. Furthermore, as any science proceeds, new information leads to refinement or reduction or replacement of the models and theories that have come before. As we will see later, that is exactly one claim about what makes any investigation scientific, namely, that new information leads to restructuring our understanding of old information. Likewise, explaining, not merely describing, phenomena is basic to anything that is science. Again, these features might not provide a set of necessary and sufficient conditions for what science is or be a collection of distinguishing features of science (meaning they distinguish all science from all non-science), but they do provide a good starting point for philosophical analysis of science. And that is what the rest of the book is about.

Because this is a book on the *philosophy* of science, the basic approach it will take is to examine metaphysical, epistemological, and axiological aspects of science. This will happen in two ways: First, the overall structure of the topics covered here reflects these three concerns. The first section of the book—Chapters Two through Seven—are what I am calling the metaphysical elements of science. By this I mean the topics covered in those chapters are what I have labeled the "components" of science, that is, basic aspects of any science. These topics include observation and measurement, experimentation and realism, models and theories, explanation, confirmation and hypothesis testing, reductionism, and the unity of science. Each of them is also certainly a matter of epistemology (for example, observation is an epistemological topic since it has to do with what and how we know), but for the purposes of this book, I am treating them as basic components of what science is.

I call these topics basic elements of science, and hence the metaphysical components of science, because they are the conceptual *what* of science, that is, the content of all sciences, not content that is specific to a particular science. So, although issues about the nature of adaptation are part of the philosophy of *biology*, issues of the nature of explanation are part of the philosophy of science generally speaking, because all sciences attempt to provide explanations of phenomena. In these chapters then, we are investigating and examining "What is X?" and "X" includes these topics of observation, explanation, reductionism, and so on.

The second section of the book—covering Chapters Eight through Ten—is meant to be the epistemological focus on science. That is, in these chapters, the primary focus is on models of *how* science changes (or progresses). Six models of the nature of scientific change, two in each chapter, will be examined. Of course, metaphysical and epistemological issues often overlap and topics in the "metaphysics" chapters, such as the nature of experimentation, could easily be seen as epistemological. However, the intent here is to emphasize epistemological aspects of science in terms of how scientific knowledge has changed, and that is the focus of the second section of the book.

The third section—Chapters Eleven through Fourteen—form the axiological approach to a philosophical look at science. The topics covered are science and technology, science and values, science and religion, and science and society. The emphasis is on value issues related to science, both within science (such as the desirability of quantifiable data) and about science (such as political ramifications and concerns). Finally, the book ends with a chapter that is devoted to a single case study, the current ongoing debates about the history of mass extinctions of life on the earth. We will see metaphysical, epistemological, and axiological issues—as we come to understand them vis-à-vis the topics covered in the earlier chapters—revealed and displayed in this contemporary case of scientific practice and controversy.

Above I mentioned that this book takes the approach of looking at science via metaphysical, epistemological, and axiological lenses in two ways. The first was the overall structure of the book, which I just remarked on. The second way that this approach is taken is that for many of the particular topics, for example, science and religion, I will identify the metaphysical, epistemological, and axiological issues that pertain to those particular topics. For example, with the issue of science and religion, there is the metaphysical concern of the content (the *what*) of what science and religion assert. Here a focus will be on the issue of intelligent design/evolutionary theory. An epistemological concern is on method (the *how*), in the sense of how religion and science investigate the world and in what ways the methods of science and religion are similar or dissimilar. Finally, there are axiological value concerns (the *why*), for example, how questions of human origin (as they are understood via religion or science) matter to human dignity.

So, the approach in this book to philosophical concerns relating to science will have a three-pronged conceptual approach (metaphysics, epistemology, axiology), both in terms of the overall structure of topics and in terms of issues within particular topics.

I have one final word about the upcoming chapters. At the end of each chapter, there is a case study drawn from the history of science. The intent of these case studies is to test the philosophical and conceptual claims and issues in that chapter to some particular episode in the history of actual scientific practice. As stated earlier in this chapter, philosophy is not science; it is also not history. Philosophy, although concerned with actual scientific practices, both past and present, is not merely a descriptive account or summary of those practices. There is also the analytical and evaluative focus of philosophy. Nevertheless, it is valuable to see how the philosophical claims and models proposed by philosophers of science stack up to actual scientific practice. So, in each chapter there will be a historical case study as well as samples of contemporary scientific practice. These are intended both to shed light on the philosophical claims and to serve as conceptual sounding boards and tests for those claims. As you go through this book, it will be obvious that many of the topics in one chapter overlap with topics in another. Likewise, the case studies from the different chapters can be considered from the perspective of issues that are raised and discussed in other chapters. For example, in Chapter Two the case study is on Gregor Mendel and the focus is on issues about observation and measurement. However, one could also look at that same case study from the perspective of issues raised in Chapter Three (experimentation) or Chapter Five (explanation), and so on. My hope is that you will indeed go back over the various case studies from the perspective of later chapters, as they present additional philosophical topics. The history of science is filled with fascinating episodes and events and these particular case studies were chosen because they are so fruitful with philosophical applications.

Chapter Summary

The philosophy of science is the analysis and evaluation of basic concepts and practices within science and about science. Philosophy, as a process, involves two approaches. The first is the analysis of concepts, often a matter of looking for necessary and sufficient conditions for the nature of a concept. For example, it is a necessary condition of being a bachelor that something be male, but being male is not sufficient for something being a bachelor; other necessary conditions must also be satisfied. The second approach in philosophy is the synthesis of concepts and understanding; that is, investigating implications and presuppositions of concepts and showing interconnection among concepts. For example, if there is no important moral difference between killing and letting die, then people could be morally responsible for not only doing something bad but also for failing to do something good. The main areas of philosophical concern are metaphysics (the study of reality), epistemology (the study of knowledge), and axiology (the study of values). The philosophical study of science reflects these three areas in terms of looking at science as content (what science investigates), science as method (how science investigates), and science as social institution (why science investigates). Although there is no single definition of science, there are common features of the sciences that serve as a means of focusing philosophical examination of science: gathering information, organizing gathered information, alternative modes of organization, accounting for phenomena, and data enhancement and extrapolation.

CASE STUDY
Albert Einstein

Identify the metaphysical, epistemological, and axiological aspects of the following passage from a lecture given by Albert Einstein (1879–1955) in 1933. How does it relate to the characterization of science that is given in the textbook quotes on page 24?

A LECTURE ON THE THEORY OF RELATIVITY
Albert Einstein

Let us now cast an eye over the development of the theoretical system, paying special attention to the relations between the content of the theory and the totality of empirical fact. We are concerned with the eternal antithesis between the two inseparable components of our knowledge, the empirical and the rational, in our department.

We reverence ancient Greece as the cradle of western science. Here for the first time the world witnessed the miracle of a logical system which preceded from step to step with such precision that every single one of its propositions was absolutely indubitable—I refer to Euclid's geometry. The admirable triumph of reasoning gave the human intellect the necessary confidence in itself for its subsequent achievements. If Euclid failed to kindle your youthful enthusiasm, then you were not born to be a scientific thinker.

But before mankind could be ripe for a science which takes in the whole of reality, a second fundamental truth was needed, which only became common property among philosophers with the advent of Kepler and Galileo. Pure logical thinking cannot yield us any knowledge of the empirical world; all knowledge starts from experience and ends in it. Propositions arrived at by purely logical means are completely empty as regards reality. Because Galileo saw this, and particularly because he drummed it into the scientific world, he is the father of modern physics—indeed, of modern science altogether.

If then, experience is the alpha and the omega of all our knowledge of reality, what is the function of pure reason in science?

A complete system of theoretical physics is made up of concepts, fundamental laws which are supposed to be valid for those concepts and conclusions to be reached by logical deduction. It is these conclusions which must correspond to our separate experiences; in any theoretical treatise their logical deduction occupies almost the whole book.

This is exactly what happens in Euclid's geometry, except that there the fundamental laws are called axioms and there is no question of the conclusions having to correspond to any sort of experience. If, however, one regards Euclidean geometry as the science of the possible mutual relations of practically rigid bodies in space, that is to say, treats it as a physical science, without abstracting from its original empirical content, the logical homogeneity of geometry and theoretical physics becomes complete.

We have thus assigned to pure reason and experience their places in a theoretical system of physics. The structure of the system is the work of reason; the empirical contents and their mutual relations must find their representation in the conclusions of the theory. In the possibility of such a representation lie the sole value and justification of the whole system, and especially of the concepts and fundamental principles which underlie it. Apart from that, these latter are free inventions of the human intellect, which cannot be justified either by the nature of that intellect or in any other fashion *a priori*.

These fundamental concepts and postulates, which cannot be further reduced logically, form the essential part of a theory, which reason cannot touch. It is the grand object of all theory to make these irreducible elements as simply and as few in number as possible, without having to renounce the adequate representation of any empirical content whatever.

The view I have just outlined of the purely fictitious character of the fundamentals of scientific theory was by no means the prevailing one in the eighteenth and nineteenth centuries. But it is steadily gaining ground from the fact that the distance in thought between the fundamental concepts and laws on the one side and, on the other, the conclusions which have to be brought into relation with our experience grows larger and larger, the simpler the logical structure becomes—that is to say, the smaller the number of logically independent conceptual elements which are found necessary to support the structure.

Newton, the first creator of a comprehensive, workable system of theoretical physics, still believed that the basic concepts and laws of his system could be derived from experience. This is no doubt the meaning of his saying, *hypotheses non fingo* [I make no hypotheses].

Actually the concepts of time and space appeared at that time to present no difficulties. The concepts of mass, inertia, and force, and the laws connecting them, seemed to be drawn directly from experience. Once this basis is accepted, the expression for the force of gravitation appears derivable from experience, and it was reasonable to expect the same in regard to other forces.

We can indeed see from Newton's formulation of it that the concept of absolute space, which comprised that of absolute rest, made him feel uncomfortable; he realized that there seemed to be nothing in experience corresponding to this last concept. He was also not quite comfortable about the introduction of forces operating at a distance. But the tremendous practical success of his doctrines may well have prevented him and the physicists of the eighteenth and nineteenth centuries from recognizing the fictitious character of the foundations of his system.

The natural philosophers of those days were, on the contrary, most of them possessed with the idea that the fundamental concepts and postulates of physics were not in the logical sense free inventions of the human mind but could be deduced from experience by "abstraction"—that is to say, by logical means. A clear recognition of the erroneousness of this notion really only came with the general theory of relativity, which showed that one could take account of a wider range of empirical facts, and that, too, in a more satisfactory and complete manner, on a foundation quite different from the Newtonian. But quite apart from the question of the superiority of one or the other, the fictitious character of fundamental principles is perfectly evident from the fact that we can point to two essentially different principles, both of which correspond with experience to a large extent; this proves at the same time that every attempt at a logical deduction of the basic concepts and postulates of mechanics from elementary experiences is doomed to failure.

If, then, it is true that the axiomatic basis of theoretical physics cannot be extracted from experience but must be freely invented, can we ever hope to find the right way? Nay, more, has this right way any existence outside our illusions? Can we hope to be guided safely by experience at all when there exist theory (such as classical mechanics) which to a large extent do justice to experience, without getting to the root of the matter? I answer without hesitation that there is, in my opinion, a right way, and that we are capable of finding it. Our experience hitherto justifies us in believing that nature is the realization of the simplest conceivable mathematical ideas. I am convinced that we can discover by means of purely mathematical constructions the concepts and the laws connecting them with each other, which furnish the key to the understanding of natural phenomena. Experience may suggest the appropriate mathematical concepts, but they most certainly cannot be deduced from it. Experience remains, of course, the sole criterion of the physical utility of a mathematical construction. But the creative principle resides in mathematics. In a certain sense, therefore, I hold it true that pure thought can grasp reality, as the ancients dreamed.

Further Reading

Boyd, Richard et al. *The Philosophy of Science*. Boston: MIT, 1991.

Brody, Baruch and Richard Grandy. *Readings in the Philosophy of Science, 2nd ed.* Englewood Cliffs, NJ: Prentice Hall, 1989.

Chalmers, Alan. *What Is This Thing Called Science?*, 3rd ed. Indianapolis, IN: Hackett, 1999.

Curd, Martin and J.A. Cover. *Philosophy of Science*. New York, NY: Norton, 1998.

Giere, Ronald. *Understanding Scientific Reasoning*, 4th ed. Fort Worth, TX: Harcourt Brace, 1997.

Godfrey-Smith, Peter. *Theory and Reality*. Chicago, IL: University of Chicago, 2003.

Hung, Edwin. *The Nature of Science*. Belmont, CA: Wadsworth, 1997.

Klee, Robert. *Introduction to the Philosophy of Science*. Oxford: Oxford University Press, 1997.

Kosso, Peter. *Reading the Book of Nature*. Cambridge: Cambridge University Press, 1992.

Kourany, Janet. *Scientific Knowledge*, 2nd ed. Belmont, CA: Wadsworth, 1998.

Ladyman, James. *Understanding Philosophy of Science*. New York, NY: Routledge, 2001.

Losee, John. *A Historical Introduction to the Philosophy of Science*, 4th ed. Oxford: Oxford University Press, 2001.

Machamer, Peter and Michael Silberstein. *The Blackwell Guide to the Philosophy of Science*. Oxford: Blackwell, 2002.

McErlean, Jennifer. *Philosophies of Science*. Belmont, CA: Wadsworth, 2000.

Okasha, Samir. *Philosophy of Science*. Oxford: Oxford University Press, 2002.

Pine, Ronald. *Science and the Human Prospect*. Belmont, CA: Wadsworth, 1989.

Rosenberg, Alexander. *The Philosophy of Science: A Contemporary Introduction*. New York, NY: Routledge, 2000.

Salmon, Marilee et al. *Introduction to the Philosophy of Science*. Englewood Cliffs, NJ: Prentice-Hall, 1992.

Schick, Jr., Theodore. *Readings in the Philosophy of Science*. Mountain View, CA: Mayfield, 2000.

Zucker, Arthur. *Introduction to the Philosophy of Science*. Englewood Cliffs, NJ: Prentice-Hall, 1996.

CHAPTER TWO

Observation and Measurement

IN THIS CHAPTER, WE WILL

- Identify some metaphysical, epistemological, and axiological aspects of observation and measurement
- Examine the thesis that observation is theory-laden
- Consider the relation between observation and objectivity
- Examine the conceptual underpinnings of measurement as a basic aspect of scientific investigation

In Chapter One, we noted various elements of science, including the gathering of information; organizing and making sense of that information via the construction of models and theories; testing, altering, and even jettisoning those models and theories in light of further investigations, and so on. This chapter focuses on two particular issues that relate especially to gathering and making sense of information: observation and measurement. Specifically, this chapter will look at some philosophical concerns as they relate to the topics of observation and measurement. Some of these philosophical concerns are metaphysical in focus (about the *what* of observation and measurement). For example, there is the issue of just what kinds of things we can and do observe and measure. Sometimes we observe and measure objects, such as the number of hatchlings in a given brood of animals; sometimes traits or properties of those objects, such as the mass or spin of a subatomic particle; sometimes relations between or among objects, such as rates of valence between given molecules. Sometimes the *what* that we observe or measure is what is *not* there, such as the absence of some particular organism or characteristic.

Epistemological issues concerning observation and measurement are not always easy to separate from metaphysical issues. For example, if we ask about the very nature of observation, we are most likely interested in knowing the mechanisms and processes of observation, such as what particular olfactory cells detect specific odors and react to what specific chemical stimuli. This is not only a question of the *what* of observation, but also the *how*, that is, epistemological matters. Likewise, we might want to consider observation or measurement as opposed to other forms of knowing the world, such as intuition or logical inference. Yet another issue related to how we observe and measure (the epistemological focus) is how observation and measurement yields reliable, or for that matter, unreliable, information. Indeed, there is the question of just what information is and how observation and measurement are related to information. It is one thing to know the mechanisms of tactile stimulation, but it is another to know how tactile stimulation gives us information about the world (for example, information such as just what it is that I feel when I am tactilely stimulated right now).

The issue of reliability of observation and measurement folds over into axiological (value-focused) concerns. For example, why is precision of measurement or accuracy of measurement significant in scientific investigation? Or why is replicability or quantifiability of measurement significant in scientific investigation? Assuming that objectivity matters to us in science, how is objectivity related to observation and measurement?

Of course, to the extent that the answers to these questions are a matter of describing things and events in the world, such as identifying and describing just what olfactory cells react to what chemical stimuli, these issues are not philosophical. For much of the philosophical literature on observation and measurement, a major point of attention has been on the role of observation and measurement in science (are they indeed the "starting point" of scientific investigation?) and their relation to the claim and value of objectivity in science (do they provide unbiased means by which we test hypotheses and theories?). In the rest of the chapter, then, we will focus primarily on these philosophical concerns relating to the role of observation and measurement and questions about their status as the most fundamental elements in scientific practice.

Observation

What could be more basic to investigating the world than simply to observe it? From our earliest experiences of science projects in elementary school we are trained to watch how ants carry bits of food or count and describe the number and color of bird's eggs in a nest. Bumping into the world—that is, observing phenomena—seems basic not only to describing and explaining the world but also to distinguishing science from mere speculation. Of course, observation is much more complex than it might appear at first blush. For one thing, it is not just a matter of what we can *see*, although vision is usually what comes to mind when we think of observation. There are other senses by which we perceive and observe phenomena, such as smell and sound. Sometimes our different senses give us different or even (apparently) conflicting information about the world, as when we visually perceive a stick partially immersed in water as being bent but we can tactilely feel it as straight.

Beyond the multiplicity of information that is given by our various senses, we rarely (if ever) observe phenomena as disconnected bits of information. We perceive patterns and structures. We do not see a baseball as a patch of color(s) and some particular shape, but we see a baseball, a unified phenomenon. Or, we see someone walking, not a series of disconnected colors and shapes in motion.[1] Indeed, over the years psychologists have noted many factors that affect observation. The state of the observer affects what is observed. This can include the observer's expectations, previous experience, and even desires and interests (or what the observer hopes to observe). For example, in cognitive experiments observers frequently claim to "see" a black ace of hearts when playing cards are flashed on a screen. In addition, repeated performances of a particular task affect what an observer observes (this is often referred to as the *adaptation of the percipient*). Other noncognitive factors affect observation, such as limitations of the sensory apparatus. For instance, humans can directly perceive certain parts of the electromagnetic spectrum (visible light), but not other parts (ultraviolet radiation). Nonhuman observers (e.g., microscopes) also have limitations to what they can "observe." The sorts of factors that affect observation that philosophers focus on are commonly termed the *theory-laden* aspects of observation. Theory-ladenness refers to how expectations, previous experience, training, and so on influence the categories by which we observe objects, events, processes, rates, and so on. The argument that observation is theory-laden is often associated with the writings of Norman R. Hanson. In the following selection, he states his classic view:

PATTERNS OF DISCOVERY

Norman R. Hanson

Consider two microbiologists. They look at a prepared slide; when asked what they see, they may give different answers. One sees in the cell before him a cluster of foreign matter: it is an artifact, a coagulum resulting from inadequate staining techniques. This clot has no more to do with the cell, *in vivo*, than the scars left on it by the archeologist's spade have to do with the original shape of some Grecian urn. The other biologist identifies the clot as a cell organ, a "Golgi body." As for techniques, he argues: "The standard way of detecting a cell organ is by fixing and staining. Why single out this one technique as producing artifacts, while others disclose genuine organs?"

The controversy continues. It involves the whole theory of microscopical technique; nor is it obviously an experimental issue. Yet it affects what scientists say they see. Perhaps there is a sense in which two such observers do not see the same thing, do not begin from the same data, though their eyesight is normal and they are visually aware of the same object . . .

Some philosophers have a formula ready for such situations: "Of course they see the same thing. They make the same observation since they begin from the same visual data. But they interpret what they see differently. They construe the evidence in different ways." The task is then to show how these data are molded by different theories or interpretations or intellectual constructions . . .

These biological examples are too complex. Let us consider Johannes Kepler: imagine him on a hill watching the dawn. With him is Tycho Brahe. Kepler regarded the sun as fixed: it was the earth that moved. But Tycho followed Ptolemy and Aristotle in this much at least: the earth was fixed and all other celestial bodies moved around it. *Do Kepler and Tycho see the same thing in the east at dawn?*

We might think this an experimental or observational question, unlike the question, "Are there Golgi bodies?" Not so in the sixteenth and seventeenth centuries. Thus Galileo said to the Ptolemaist ". . . neither Aristotle nor you can prove that the earth is *de facto* the center of the universe . . . ." "Do Kepler and Tycho see the same thing in the east at dawn?" is perhaps not a *de facto* question either, but rather the beginning of an examination of the concepts of seeing and observation.

The resultant discussion might run:

"Yes, they do."

"No, they don't."

"Yes, they do!"

"No, they don't!"

That this is possible suggests that there may be reasons for both contentions. Let us now consider some points in support of the affirmative answer.

The physical processes involved when Kepler and Tycho watch the dawn are worth noting. Identical photons are emitted from the sun; these traverse solar space, and our atmosphere. The two astronomers have normal vision; hence these photons pass through the cornea, aqueous humor, iris, lens, and vitreous body of their eyes in the same way. Finally, their retinas are affected. Similar electro-chemical changes occur in their selenium cells. The same configuration is etched on Kepler's retina as on Tycho's. So they see the same thing . . .

[But] seeing the sun is not seeing retinal pictures of the sun. The retinal images which Kepler and Tycho have are four in number, inverted and quite tiny. Astronomers cannot be referring to these when they say they see the sun. If they are hypnotized, drugged, drunk or distracted they may not see the sun, even though their retinas register its image in exactly the same way as usual.

Seeing is an experience. A retinal reaction is only a physical state—a photochemical excitation. Physiologists have not always appreciated the differences between experiences and physical states. People, not their eyes, see. Cameras, and eyeballs, are blind. Attempts to locate within the organs of sight (or within the neurological reticulum behind the eyes) some nameable called "seeing" may be dismissed. That Kepler and Tycho do, or do not, see the same thing cannot be supported by reference to the physical states of their retinas, optic nerves or visual cortices: there is more to seeing than meets the eyeball.

Naturally, Tycho and Kepler see the same physical object. They are both visually aware of the sun. If they are put into a dark room and asked to report when they see something—anything at all—they may both report the same object at the same time. Suppose that the only object to be seen is a certain lead cylinder. Both men see the same thing: namely this object—whatever it is. It is just here, however, that the difficulty arises, for while Tycho sees a mere pipe, Kepler will see a telescope, the instrument about which Galileo has written to him.

Unless both are visually aware of the same object there can be nothing of philosophical interest in the question of whether or not they see the same thing. Unless they both see the sun in the prior sense our question cannot even strike a spark.

Nonetheless, both Tycho and Kepler have a common visual experience of some sort. This experience perhaps constitutes their seeing the same thing. Indeed, this may be a seeing logically more basic than anything expressed in the pronouncement "I see the sun" (where each means something different by "sun"). If what they meant by the word "sun" were the only clue, then Tycho and Kepler could not be seeing the same thing, even though they were gazing at the same object.

If, however, we ask, not "Do they see the same thing?" but rather "What is it that they both see?", an unambiguous answer may be forthcoming. Tycho and Kepler are both aware of a brilliant yellow-white disc in a blue expanse over a green one. Such a "sense-datum" picture is single and uninverted. To be unaware of it is not to have it. Either it dominates one's visual attention completely or it does not exist . . . In this sense Tycho and Kepler see the same things at dawn. The sun appeared to them in the same way. The same view, or scene, is presented to them both.

Normal retinas and cameras are impressed similarly by Fig. 1. Our visual sense-data will be the same too. If asked to draw what we see, most of us will set out a configuration like Fig. 1.

Do we all see the same thing? Some will see a perspex cube viewed from below. Others will see it from above. Still others will see it as a kind of polygonally cut gem. Some people see only crisscrossed lines in a plane. It may be seen as a block of ice, an aquarium, a wire frame for a kite—or any of a number of other things.

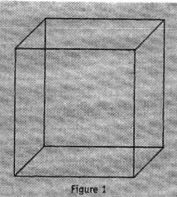

Figure 1

Here the "formula" re-enters: "These are different *interpretations* of what all observers see in common. Retinal reactions to Fig. 1 are virtually identical; so too are our visual sense-data, since our drawings of what we see will have the same content. There is no place in the seeing for these differences, so they must lie in the interpretations put on what we see."

So, the standard (common sense) view is that we observe the same things, but we might interpret what we observe differently. This view, for Hanson, is mistaken. He claims (below) that there are not two events taking place, one being an observation and the second being an interpretation. Rather, observation, *as an experience,* inherently involves some categorization. Seeing is always "seeing as." My experience of a particular set of retinal images is of, say, a baseball. I see the object as a baseball. My observational experience is not of a set of images that I then interpret to be a baseball. That is, for Hanson, we never merely see and then interpret; rather, the observational experience is of a "categorized" object. Continuing his discussion of Figure 1, Hanson rejects the two-step view of observation as (1) sensation followed by (2) interpretation:

PATTERNS OF DISCOVERY *(continued)*
Norman R. Hanson

This [view of same observation but different interpretations] sounds as if I do two things, not one, when I see boxes and bicycles. Do I put different interpretations on Fig. 1 when I see it now as a box from below, and now as a cube from above? I am aware of no such thing. I mean no such thing when I report that the box's perspective has snapped back into the page. If I do not mean this, then the concept of seeing which is natural in this connection does not designate two diaphanous components, one optical, the other interpretative. Fig. 1 is simply seen now as a box from below, now as a cube from above; one does not first soak up an optical pattern and then clamp an interpretation on it. Kepler and Tycho just see the sun. That is all. That is the way the concept of seeing works in this connection . . .

Ordinary accounts of the experiences appropriate to Fig. 1 do not require visual grist going into an intellectual mill: theories and interpretations are "there" in the seeing from the outset. How can interpretations "be there" in the seeing? How is it possible to see an object according to an interpretation? "The question represents it as a queer fact; as if something were being forced into a form it did not really fit. But no squeezing, no forcing took place here." . . .

A trained physicist could see one thing in Fig. 2: an X-ray tube viewed from the cathode. Would Sir Lawrence Bragg and an Eskimo baby see the same thing when looking at an X-ray tube? Yes, and no. Yes—they are visually aware of the same object. No—the ways in which they are visually aware are profoundly different. Seeing is not only the having of a visual experience; it is also the way in which the visual experience is had . . .

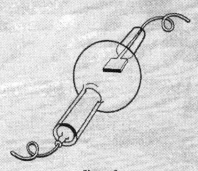

Figure 2

The visitor must learn some physics before he can see what the physicist sees. Only then will the context throw into relief those features of the objects before him which the physicist sees as indicating resistance.

This obtains to all seeing. Attention is rarely directed to the space between the leaves of a tree, save when a Keats brings it to our notice. (Consider also what was involved in Crusoe's seeing a vacant space in the sand as a footprint.) Our attention most naturally rests on objects and events which dominate the visual field. What a blooming, buzzing, undifferentiated confusion visual life would be if we all arose tomorrow without attentions capable of dwelling only on what had heretofore been overlooked.

The infant and the layman can see: they are not blind. But they cannot see what the physicist sees; they are blind to what he sees. We may not hear that the oboe is out of tune, though this will be painfully obvious to the trained musician. (Who, incidentally, will not hear the tones and *interpret* them as being out of tune, but will simply hear the oboe to be out of tune. We simply see what time it is; the surgeon simply sees a wound to be septic; the physicist sees the X-ray tube's anode overheating.) The elements of the visitor's visual field, though identical with those of the physicist, are not organized for him as for the physicist; the same lines, colors, shapes are apprehended by both, but not in the same way. There are indefinitely many ways in which a constellation of lines, shapes, patches, may be seen . . .

There is a sense, then, in which seeing is a "theory-laden" undertaking. Observation of x is shaped by prior knowledge of x. Another influence on observations rests in the language or notation used to express what we know, and without which there would be little we could recognize as knowledge.

Observation, then, for Hanson, is theory-laden. As an experience that provides information, there is never a "pure" observation, absent some conceptualization or other. Many philosophers have claimed that a consequence of this is that objectivity both *in* observation and *from* observation is suspect. That is to say, observations themselves are not objective (no objectivity *in* observation), if the informational experience of observation is theory-laden. In addition, observations cannot serve as an objective starting point of science or as an objective test of scientific claims (no objectivity *from* observation). This does *not* mean, however, that we can observe or perceive whatever we want or fail to observe what is "right in front of us." That is, claiming that observation is theory-laden does not mean that the world does not put constraints or demands of what is observed or observable. We still experience something external to us, for example, Hanson's x-ray tube. So, advocating the theory-ladenness of observation is the not the same thing as advocating the philosophical view of idealism, that only mental experiences are real. Rather, it is to say that because observation is inherently shaped (at least in part) by mental categories—which themselves are shaped by various factors such as expectation, the nature and status of the observer, and so on—then observation is not thoroughly objective and not a basis for scientific objectivity. It is also to question the notion that observation is the starting point of scientific practice, because the point is that observation is not neutral or theory-free.

Not all philosophers agree with this conclusion. One who does not is Israel Scheffler, who argues below that although observations might well be conceptualization-based (or, theory-laden) and, so, they indeed shape how we classify and understand the content of what we observe, nevertheless, the content of what we observe and the information we receive are not determined by those conceptualizations. Scheffler agrees with Hanson on a number of points: observation does not occur in isolation from some conceptualization; observation is alterable by conceptual change; observation is not ineffable (that is, observation is not incapable of being expressed in words); observational descriptions are not certain (that is, we could be mistaken about what we observe). In spite of agreeing on these points, however, Scheffler argues that objectivity, both in and from observation, is not necessarily negated even if observations are theory-laden. Using an analogy to a filing system, Scheffler argues that such a system might categorize and influence how we file, say, letters of correspondence, but it does not determine what those items are that we file.

SCIENCE AND SUBJECTIVITY
Israel Scheffler

I turn . . . to the problem of objectivity in observation. In its broadest terms, the fundamental issue may be stated as follows: Observation needs to be construed as independent of conceptualization if conceptualization is not to be simply arbitrary; yet, it cannot plausibly be thought to be independent of conceptualization. On the contrary, it is shot through with interpretation, expectation, and wish. Were it not so, indeed, we should be powerless to take hold of anything in experience: equally receptive to everything in awareness and uniformly undiscriminating, we could not properly be said to observe anything at all; at best we should confront a flat and undifferentiated given incapable of providing any control over our thought. So, on the one hand, observation must be independent, and, on the other hand, it cannot be. To suppose it is independent commits us to an implausibly pure observational given, and makes a mystery of observational control over thought. To suppose, on the other hand, that it is not independent commits us rather to the view that apparent observational control is always circular and hence incapable of restricting the arbitrariness of conception; it further commits us to the impossibility of common observation across the barrier of conceptual differences. In any event, the standard notion of observation as providing objective control over conception needs to be abandoned.

Up to this point, Scheffler has simply stated what he sees as the problem of objectivity and observation, namely, how can we make sense of objectivity either in or from observation if observation is theory-laden? His answer is this:

SCIENCE AND SUBJECTIVITY *(continued)*
Israel Scheffler

The first step we need to take is to break down the notion of conceptualization, for its unanalyzed use blurs a broad distinction critical for our topic. This distinction may be put in somewhat different ways, but the variations are irrelevant to the main issues at hand. We may express it, for example, as a distinction between concepts on the one hand and propositions on the other, between general terms or predicates on the one hand and statements on the other, between a vocabulary on the one hand and a body of assertions on the other, between categories or classes on the one hand and expectations or hypotheses as to category membership on the other.

A general term or concept applies to each of a number of things which may be said to belong to the class or category determined by it. To adopt a given term is, in effect, to commit oneself to recognizing anything satisfying this term; it is to adopt a certain scheme for he acknowledgement of instances . . . A vocabulary of terms or concepts thus may be said to represent a means of delimiting and sorting what are taken to be things; it is a device of reference. Concepts or terms are not, however, in themselves capable of conveying propositions, beliefs, or assertions nor, hence, of making claims to evidential warrant or truth. The latter functions are dependent upon an available conceptual apparatus, to be sure, but they do not simply reduce to this apparatus; they represent rather a specialized accomplishment that may result from its proper use, going beyond mere reference, to the level of *statement* . . .

Putting the matter in terms of categories and simplifying, we may express the point as follows: Conceptualization relates both to the idea of categories for the sorting of items and to the idea of expectation, belief, or hypothesis as to how items will actually fit available categories; it links up with the notion of *category* and, also, with the quite different notion of *hypothesis*. The very same category system is, surely, compatible with alternative, and indeed conflicting hypotheses: that is, having adopted a given category system, our hypotheses as to the actual distribution of items within the several categories are not prejudged. Conversely, the same set of hypotheses may be formed compatibly with different category systems: the categories specifically referred to in these hypotheses may belong, as a common possession, to the different systems in question. Simply to set up an alphabetical filing system for correspondence is not yet to determine how tomorrow's correspondence will need to be filed. Conversely, to guess that the next letter will need to be filed under "E" or "L" is a prediction that may be made whether or not we a place for "X" in our system.

A filing system may be said to determine in advance how correspondence is to be sorted. It does not determine in advance how any particular letter will be sorted. The second step in dealing with our problem is to separate these two notions of determination. A category system, within a limited context, may be described as imposing order in general and in advance on whatever experience in that context may bring. It commits us to ways of delimiting items to be recognized, as well as to modes of classifying them. Lacking such order altogether, we may, indeed, aptly be described as facing an undifferentiated chaos, since we lack the very recognition of things—that is to say, we do not individuate and separate items as objects of reference. Yet having a category system, we do not thereby prejudge the manner in which we shall need to apply it in the future. Without a vocabulary and grammar, we can describe nothing; having a vocabulary and grammar, our descriptions are not thereby determined.

Categorization does not, in other words, decide the forms of distribution which items will in fact display, nor does it, in itself, determine the categorical assignments of any particular item or class of items yet to be encountered. Such special anticipations may, however, be expressed by suitable hypotheses. Categorization provides the pigeonholes; hypothesis makes assignments to them. It is crucial to see that alternative assignments stipulated by different hypotheses are yet possible with the same categorization, for this provides at least the beginnings of an answer to our main problem. It means that we can understand a hypothesis which conflicts with our favored hypothesis of the moment, in terms of the very category system to which the latter appeals. In order for us to grasp such a conflicting hypothesis we do not need to decategorize and unstructure our thought, for such a conflicting hypothesis represents simply a different assignment under the selfsame category system. It follows that stripping away a given hypothesis is not tantamount to destroying our conceptual apparatus, so that we are left to cope only with a homogenized and ineffable given. On the contrary, it is compatible with retention of our category system, by reference to which conflicting assignments may be formulated and understood, and by means of which new data may continue to be processed, independently of our initial hypotheses.

To say that a categorization is independent of—in the sense that it does not prejudge—the particular hypotheses expressible through it means that observation may be conceived as thoroughly molded by such categorization and yet equally independent of these hypotheses. We simply have a false dichotomy in the notion that observation must be either a pure confrontation with an undifferentiated given, or else so conceptually contaminated that it must render circular any observational test of a hypothesis. Observation may be considered as shot through with categorization, while yet supporting a particular assignment which conflicts with our most cherished current hypothesis. It may be crucially independent of such hypothesis while retaining its full categoricity, for categorization is itself, as we have seen, independent of any particular assignment of items to categories. We have here a fundamental source of control over the arbitrariness of belief . . .

You will no doubt remind me that the psychological considerations earlier cited provide strong empirical support not only for the importance of categorical schemata in observation, but also for the enormous influence of expectations and beliefs, that is, of particular *hypotheses*, upon observational mode and even upon content. Categorization itself may not completely determine any special assignment of items, but acceptance of a hypothesis in advance does, in fact, limit our perception of alternative assignments, expressible though they are under the category system in question. Accepting a hypothesis tends to restrict our view to certain of our categories, that is, to those which accord with the hypothesis itself. Expecting the next item to belong to a particular category, we tend generally to see it so. To be sure, the possibility that this item falls outside the category in question is expressible in terms of our category system, and is ascertainable, if realized, by observation which is molded by this system. Nevertheless, the possibility in question is less likely to be seriously entertained in observation, the firmer our commitment to a hypothesis which denies it. So much seems indeed to be the lesson of psychology and everyday life.

The fact seems to me undeniable: Observational support for an assignment contrary to an accepted hypothesis needs to persist longer and fight harder for a hearing than observational data which accord with expectations. Yet such contrary indications can and do make themselves felt. Our expectations strongly structure what we see, but do not wholly eliminate unexpected sights. To suppose that they do would be, absurdly, to deny the common phenomena of surprise, shock, and astonishment, as well as the reorientations of belief consequent upon them.

What is the upshot? There is here no evidence for a general capacity to learn from contrary observations, no proof of a pre-established harmony between what we believe and what we see. In the disharmony between them, indeed, lies the source of observational control over belief. Our categorizations and expectations guide by orienting us selectively toward the future; they set us, in particular, to perceive in certain ways and not in others. Yet they do not blind us to the unforeseen. They allow us to recognize what fails to match anticipation, affording us the opportunity to improve our orientation in response to disharmony. The genius of science is to capitalize upon such disharmony for the sake of a systematic learning from experience.

Measurement

"How long is the coast of Britain?" Benoit Mandelbrot asked this question and the "answer" to it reveals the complexity of the concept of measurement, which—like observation—is taken by many people to be straightforward in itself and a basic element in scientific practice. However, like observation, a closer look at the notion of measurement shows that it is conceptually layered and complex. Mandelbrot's answer to the question, "How long is the coast of Britain?" is that there is no single correct answer. This is not because we are not careful enough in our measurements, but because there is no single "thing" that is the coast of Britain. Nor is it because the coast keeps changing as coastal waters wash some of it away or tides cover some of it up. Even if we could freeze time and physical events so that nothing changed, the length of the coast of Britain would depend on some chosen scale of measurement as well as just what physical parts of the world we included as being part of Britain. For Mandelbrot, as we try to get more and more precise about just what object we want to measure, it becomes less and less clear just what the object is (much like magnifying a picture to get a closer and closer look at some detail; the overall picture gets more and more blurry) and the number we get as the answer gets larger and larger.

Nevertheless, measurement is basic to scientific practice and scientists are astonishingly precise and accurate in their measurements. As we know, environmental scientists can measure the toxicity of a sample down to a few parts per billion; physicists can measure the speed of light down to feet per fraction of a second; chemists can measure the mass of an electron down to millionths of a gram. But as the question becomes more "scientific," the background knowledge and level of abstraction becomes greater and greater. For example, if we want to measure the mass of a gallon of water, it is pretty easy to do: put it on a scale. Of course, such a measurement is not very interesting from a scientific perspective. But, if we want to measure the mass of the earth or the mass of an electron (which is more scientifically interesting), the task of measuring gets far more complicated and complex. How can we measure the mass of the earth? We cannot plop it onto a gigantic scale. Here is a description of one way:

MATHEMATICS AND THE PHYSICAL WORLD
Morris Kline

One of the rather simple yet spectacular deductions that can be made on the basis of the law of gravitation is to calculate the mass of the earth. To do this we shall first make an auxiliary calculation. Suppose that an object of mass m is suspended at C on a string AC [Figure 3]. Of course gravity pulls straight down on this mass. Nearby a one-ton mass of lead is placed and it pulls the mass m to B. The position of the lead is adjusted until it is on the same level and one yard from B. Hence the mass m remains suspended at B and the string now has position AB.

Let us analyze the forces acting on the mass m at B. The force of gravity continues to pull it straight down and the lead pulls it to the left. The combined action of these two forces is some force that acts in an oblique direction somewhere between straight down and horizontally to the left. This resultant force must in fact lie along the line AB because the tension in the string just opposed the resultant and keeps the mass m motionless at B. It is helpful to make a separate diagram of the forces acting on the mass m. Thus the line PQ [Figure 4] represents the force of gravity and the line PR represents the attractive force of the lead. It is known from experience that forces combine like velocities; that is, the combined effect of the forces PQ and PR is the diagonal of the rectangle determined by PQ and PR. This resultant force PS, as noted above, must have the same slope as the line AB. Hence angle SPQ = angle A. But

$$(1) \quad \tan SPQ = QS/PQ = PR/PQ.$$

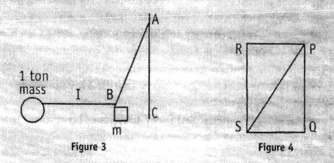

Figure 3　　　　　　　　　　　　　**Figure 4**

Since angle A can be measured we also know angle SPQ. It turns out to be a very small angle, $0.000,000,45°$. From tables one can find that tan $SPQ = 8 \times 10^{-9}$, that is, 8 divided by one billion. Hence we know the ratio of the force PR to the force PQ.

Let us now use the law of gravitation to calculate the same ratio of the two forces PQ and PR. The force of gravitation PQ acting straight down on the mass m is given by

$$(2)\ PQ = GmM/(4000 \times 1760)^2$$

where M is the mass of the earth, and the number in the parentheses is the distance from the mass m to the center of the earth in yards [and G is the gravitational constant]. The force of attraction PR of the one-ton mass of lead on the mass m one yard away is given by

$$(3)\ PR = Gm \times 1/1^2.$$

The ratio of PR to PQ is then obtained by dividing equation (3) by equation (2). The result is

$$PR/PQ = (4000 \times 1760)^2/M.$$

But we have already found the ratio of PR to PQ to be 8×10^{-9}. Hence

$$8 \times 10^{-9} = (4000 \times 1760)^2/M.$$

Then

$$M = (4000 \times 1760)^2/8 \times 10^{-9} = 6.5 \times 10^{21}.$$

The quantity 6.5×10^{21} is tons of mass, since our unit of mass has been tons. Thus we have the remarkable result, the mass of the earth.

Notice what is involved in this ingenious measurement of the mass of the earth. In large part the entire process is a matter of algebraic, geometrical, and trigonometric calculations, not weighing something like we would weigh a gallon of water. The calculations themselves rely on presumptions about forces, such as gravity. Had this been a case of measuring the mass of an electron, the types and level of presumed background theory would have been even greater. (For example, the force of gravity would be far less significant than electromagnetic forces.) The point, again, is not that scientists cannot make precise and accurate measurements. It is that doing so involves background theory and categorizations, etc. This, then, leads to the question of the nature and role of measurement in the larger context of understanding science generally.

In spite of the remarkable precision and accuracy and replicability of scientific measurement, there are some fundamental philosophical questions about the nature of the concept of measurement. Physicist Roger Jones claims that, "Science's claim to objectivity rests ultimately on its ability to make exact and reproducible measurements." Yet underlying the most basic of measurements reveals a very complex set of operations and conceptual decisions. To illustrate this, he details the variety of factors that are involved in something as simple as measuring the length of, say, a table. To measure any length at all, much less to measure it with extreme accuracy and precision, involves several steps. The first step is stipulating a standard unit of measurement. We could measure the distance from the earth to distant stars in terms of inches or the length of a table in terms of light-years, but these would make our measurements outrageously complex. The second step is defining the "object" to be measured. "Object" is in quotes here because often what we want to measure is not a physical object, but a process or a rate of change. For some sciences, for example, particle physics, this might mean abandoning the notion of the object to be measured as being solid matter with well-defined boundaries. The third step is determining a measuring device. For simple everyday measurements, say measuring the length of a table, we would use a simple device such as a yardstick or for measuring the mass of a baseball we would use a simple balance scale. However, if we want to measure the distance to a distant galaxy, yardsticks won't do; if we want to measure the mass of the earth, a balance scale won't do. So, just what will function well as a measuring device often is not a minor matter. Indeed, the technology needed for a well-functioning and practical measuring device can be a significant challenge.

Besides having a standard unit of measure, determining the object to be measured, and having a useful measuring device, another step in the process of measurement is comparing the object with the measuring device. Although this might seem obvious and straightforward, for many scientific measurements such a comparison is quite difficult. Jones argues in the following selection that even for something as simple as measuring the length of a table, such a comparison involves complexity. Minimally, two decisions must be made; first, the coincidence, or relative proximity, of two points must be set (one point being the "edge" of the "object" being measured and the other point being the "edge" of the measuring device), and, second, the relative position of three points must be set (two points on the measuring device and one point being the "edge" of the "object"). With respect to the first decision, deciding whether two points are coincident boils down to making judgments about the distance (in the case of length) between two points. Two points are said to be coincident when the distance between them is negligible in comparison with any meaningful distance involved in the measurement. In other words, two points are coincident when the distance between them is less than any distance that matters for the purposes of the measurement. (If you are baking a cake and need a cup of sugar, the level of precision for having a cup does not come down to counting out specific grains of sugar; you have a cup when the amount of sugar is close enough to a cup for your tastes!) With respect to the second decision involved in comparing the object being measured with the measuring device, determining the relative position of three points requires the ability to identify and label the points, which in turn requires the ability to locate positions in space (again, using the example of length), and that ability requires the prior notion of length.

Using language from our previous discussion about observation, the conclusion of Jones' argument is that measurement is theory-laden is many and varied ways. Something as simple as measuring the length of a table involves many decisions and choices. To the extent that scientific measurement is even more complex, such as measuring the mass or velocity or charge of an electron or measuring the age of a fossil, the measurement is that much more theory-laden. This is not to say that we cannot or do not make very careful, precise, and accurate measurements. We do. But, for Jones, we can do this only in the context of judgments and decisions and choices, all of which are non-objective, that is, not "given" or determined by the world. Here is Jones' argument:

PHYSICS AS METAPHOR

Roger Jones

In this [reading] we shall explore in some detail the process of measuring the length of a table in order to expose the fundamental and irreducible subjective nature of measurement itself. The reason for all this fuss is that science's claim to objectivity rests ultimately on its ability to make exact and reproducible measurements . . .

It is an amazing fact about physics that none of its concepts are ever really defined. What we are given instead of a definition is a prescription for measurement. To build a rocket and send it to the moon, you need only measure space, not define it. The measurement of space is the only specification of it needed for scientific purposes, and this is called an operational definition . . .

I wish to measure the length of a table. I choose to adopt the definition of length used in physics, for, as we have seen, it is an operational definition, telling me *how* to measure length. I take as my standard unit of length the meter (equal to 39.37 inches) . . . First, I must locate and identify two unique points that will form the limit of the measurement. My table is rectangular, and so the two ends of the longer dimension are the points in question, and the distance between these points is defined as the length of the table. Now, if I am measuring for a tablecloth, I can afford to be pretty sloppy about all of this. A tablecloth has enough overhang that 10 or 20 centimeters either way will not matter much. If, instead, I want a glass plate made to fit neatly on the tabletop, I should be much more careful. An error of a couple of millimeters is as much as I can tolerate for a good fit. But to understand the definition of length, I should first ask for the most precise possible measurement of the length of the table. This is really asking for trouble.

The problem is that in trying to make an ultimate measurement of the table, we need to think in terms of a microscopic, or even atomic, determination of the limiting points. We now lose the everyday concept of a table as a solid object with well-defined boundaries. Instead, we must use the modern picture of matter as molecules in motion, and we must try to imagine how to define the edges of the table in terms of the rapidly speeding molecules that make it up. To make matters worse, the atom of modern physics is, strictly speaking, not even visible in principle. The atom is not the hard little ball of popular illustrations and high school science texts. It is something of a mathematical abstraction whose description in terms of the spacetime of our everyday world requires some compromise. Today's physicists use such terms as electron clouds and probability densities in describing atoms. These terms have fairly precise mathematical definitions. But their use to represent atoms visually as fuzzy-looking balls, dumbbells, and ellipsoids is usually misleading . . .

It might be argued that such a level of accuracy is meaningless anyway since a length of measurement at the atomic level cannot be performed in practice. But we are discussing the principle of the definition of length. Furthermore, even if we do give up the atomic level for the definition, down to what level does the table have a meaningful length? We see that length is not well defined, even in principle, but has a built-in unspecifiable uncertainty . . .

Before I can perform the . . . step of counting the number of meters that fit along the edge of the table, I must compare the defined interval (the length of the table between its two ends) with the meter stick. This will allow me to decide which points on the meter stick determine the starting and stopping points for the count. To locate these two points, two kinds of decisions have to be made: the first about the coincidence or relative proximity of the two points, and the second about the relative position of three points.

We begin by lining up one end of the meter stick with the left end of the table. (This involves a decision about the coincidence of two points.) We assume that the meter stick or tape measure is longer than the table, so that all I need do is decide between which two marks of the meter stick the right end of the table lies. (This involves a decision about the relative position of three points.)

In practice, deciding whether two points are coincident boils down to making judgments about the distance between two points. Point A on the table and Point B on the meter stick cannot literally be coincident, for two objects cannot occupy the same space at the same time. I should call the points coincident when the distance between them appears to be negligible in comparison with any meaningful distances involved in the measurement, for example, in comparison with the smallest unit of distance on the meter stick. This presents some difficulties. First, the judgment of sufficient closeness or negligible distance, however obvious it may seem, is still a matter of human judgment and thus subjective. Nor can we avoid this problem by making an "objective" measurement of the distance between the points in question with some more precise measuring device. For then we are simply starting the length-measuring process over again at Step 1 and will sooner or later have to return to the problem of judging the coincidence of two points at some magnified level. Second, judging closeness means estimating or measuring distance. But we are in the process of giving an objective definition of length by means of its measurement. (Recall that this operational definition of length is the only definition of length we have in physics.) We find that we must be able to estimate length in order to measure or define it. A prior understanding of length is needed for the definition. Such a circular definition is no definition at all.

I must emphasize, at the risk of repeating myself, that although this logical problem seems to have no bearing on the practical application of the concept of length (for example, we can measure space well enough to send people to the moon and back), it is of paramount importance in debunking the notion that an objective definition of a measurable length guarantees the independent existence of objects.

The other kind of decision we make in comparing the ruler and table is about the relative order of three points. We must decide between which two marks on the meter stick the right end of the table lies. We have three points, A, B, and C, and we wish to establish that B, the end point of the table, lies between A and C, two particular marks on the meter stick . . .

To observe the order of three points, we must be able to identify and label the points. Indeed, we have assumed this in calling B the right end point of the table and A and C the two particular marks on the meter stick that flank B . . . A mathematical point has no properties whatsoever. Only one property can distinguish one point from another—its position in space. But, of course, to specify a position in space, we must assume the measurement of length. We are stuck again. There is no purely objective description of anything that does not depend on a prior perception of length.

Now, as with observation, the claim of conceptual complexity with the nature of measurement does not negate the amazing precision and accuracy of scientific measurement. It is a fact that we are able to make exceedingly fine measurements. The philosophical issues include: what is the nature of measurement and how is it related to the nature of science as a whole? If measurement is theory-laden, what does this say about its role(s) in scientific practice; for example, is it a basis for objectivity; is it a "starting point" of scientific inquiry; does the reliability of measurement vary depending upon the presumptions that must be made (such as the measurement scale, the stability of the "object" being measured, etc.)? To see the complexity involved, consider the following, rather common, example of a research project:

UNHEALTHY CHANGE: DIVERSITY IN A BACTERIAL COLONY CAN PROLONG INFECTIONS

C. Brownlee

Researchers have long known that diversification strengthens large groups, from the stocks in a winning portfolio to the wildflowers in a field. New findings suggest that the same idea applies to bacterial communities and may explain why some infections are notoriously difficult to treat.

Many species of bacteria that form lump-shaped colonies can also live as biofilms, large clusters of organisms encased in a self-produced slime. Biofilms frequently capitalize on vulnerable sites in people, such as eyes irritated by contact lenses or open wounds, to cause chronic infections that are tough to eradicate.

While studying biofilms in the lungs of cystic fibrosis patients, Pradeep Singh and his colleagues at the University of Iowa in Iowa City noticed a strange phenomenon. When they used a small number of identical *Pseudomonas aeruginosa* bacteria to start a biofilm culture, the microbes quickly diversified into several types that looked and behaved differently.

Individuals isolated from the new biofilms had different nutritional needs, swimming styles, and defensive-chemical programs. Previous studies had noted that *P. aeruginosa* creates several different colony types.

Singh's team speculated that diversity within biofilms could give the bacteria an advantage in maintaining chronic infections. To test their hypothesis, the researchers exposed different groups of the bacteria to the disinfectant hydrogen peroxide. While biofilm communities composed of multiple *P. aeruginosa* types weathered the chemical onslaught, colonies containing only one bacterial type quickly perished.

The researchers traced the source of the species' diversity to a gene called *recA*. Biofilms composed of mutant bacteria missing the *recA* gene showed far less diversity and died rapidly, much as individual colonies did, when exposed to hydrogen peroxide.

Singh and his colleagues say that these results which [were] published in the Nov. 23 [2004] *Proceedings of the National Academy of Sciences,* parallel previous findings about diversity in other biological communities. When plant or animal groups are composed of several subpopulations, differences between individual members of a community can help the entire population survive environmental changes. Ecologists frequently refer to this idea as the "insurance hypothesis."

Although scientists are just beginning to consider bacterial groups as communities defined by cooperative interactions among individuals, Singh's team suggest that the insurance hypothesis may apply to the bacteria in biofilms.

"Basically, everyone knew that there was diversity [within *P. aeruginosa* bacteria] and that diversity is a good thing because it might help survival. But nobody did the experiment to show that a diverse population survives better and a less diverse population doesn't," says Bill Costerton, a microbiologist at Montana State University in Bozeman and an author of a commentary accompanying Singh's report. Other researchers "did the experiments in their heads and assumed the results," Costerton says.

Singh suggests that once researchers are convinced that a biofilm's survival hinges on diversity, they may develop new ideas for fighting chronic infections. "It may be that we should start thinking of chronic infections from the ecological perspective," he says. "One would have to account for the capabilities of a diverse group instead of a large number of identical clones."

What is being measured in this case is the behavior of collections of bacteria. "Behavior," though, is not a straightforward property of something like mass or shape. (Of course, even mass and shape are not really that straightforward, either, as they both vary relative to an object's velocity; as any physicist will say: rest mass is not the same thing as relativistic mass.) So, some decisions must be made about what constitutes *behavior* of the bacteria (rather than, say, the mere effect of gravity), just as among a person's movements some will be behavior (actions) rather than mere motions (effects of one's physicality). In addition, some decision must be made about what exactly constitutes "identical *Pseudomonas aeruginosa* bacteria." Decisions must be made about what constitutes "different nutritional needs, swimming styles, and defensive-chemical programs." Decisions must be made about what constitutes relevant criteria for "diversity" since some features remain constant across the each bacterium and some features do not. Even the notion of the *recA* gene is itself housed within a prior theoretical, though thoroughly established, context of genetics. Notice that these types of conceptual decisions are in place not only for issues about measurement but also for issues about observation. And, once again, the point here is not that this was a flawed study or that the observations and measurements were not reliable, but, rather, that in everyday scientific practice the very important features of observation and measurement are themselves very complex and, as they are more and more informative to scientists, they rely on previous background assumptions, categories, and theories.

Chapter Summary

Observation and measurement are basic to whatever counts as science; they are necessary conditions for anything to be considered scientific. Often these two elements of science are taken as fundamental to science, not only in the sense of being necessary but also in the sense of being the starting point for scientific practice. Many people see them as being independent of the "later" elements of science, such as models and theories. Some philosophers of science have questioned this belief of observation and measurement as being either independent of, or prior to, models and theories. Norman Hanson, for example, has argued that observation, as an informative experience, is theory-laden, that is, inherently shaped by background knowledge, expectations, categories, and so on. Being theory-laden, Hanson questions the notion that there can be objectivity in observation or from observation. Israel Sheffler, although acknowledging the background influences on observation, rejects the conclusion that because of the categorizational nature of observation that objectivity is lost. Though observation might be theory-laden, he claims, the content of what we observe and the information we receive are not determined by those conceptualizations. Along the lines of Hanson, physicist Roger Jones argues that measurement is extremely conceptually complex, imbued throughout with conceptual decisions. Consequently, measurement, no matter how precise and accurate, does not provide an objective foundation to science.

CASE STUDY
Gregor Mendel

Read the following account of Gregor Mendel's (1822–1884) famous experiments in plant genetics. Consider the conceptual issues connected to observation and measurement. For example, what exactly did Mendel observe? How, if at all, did prior theory, categorization, expectation, and so on influence what was observed? What "objects" did he measure (keeping in mind that the "objects" might be events, processes, rates, characteristics, etc.). What measuring device(s) did he use?

PLANT-HYBRIDIZATION
Gregor Mendel

Experience of artificial fertilization, such as is effected with ornamental plants in order to obtain new variations in color, has led to the experiments which will here be discussed. The striking regularity with which the same hybrid forms always reappeared whenever fertilization took place between the same species induced further experiments to be undertaken, the object of which was to follow up the developments of the hybrids in their progeny . . .

Division and Arrangement of the Experiments

If two plants which differ constantly in one or several characters be crossed, numerous experiments have demonstrated that the common characters are transmitted unchanged to the hybrids and their progeny; but each pair of differentiating characters, on the other hand, unite in the hybrid to form a new character, which in the progeny of the hybrid is usually variable. The object of the experiment was to observe these variations in the case of each pair of differentiating characters, and to deduce the law according to which they appear in the successive generations . . .

The characters which were selected for experiment relate:

1. To the *difference in the form of the ripe seeds*. These are either round or roundish; the depressions, if any, occur on the surface, being always only shallow; or they are irregularly angular and deeply wrinkled (*P. quadratum*).
2. To the *difference in the color of the seed albumen* (endosperm). The albumen of the ripe seeds is either pale yellow, bright yellow and orange colored, or it possesses a more or less green tint. The difference of color is easily seen in the seeds as their coats are transparent.
3. To the *difference in the color of the seed coat*. This is either white, with which character white flowers are constantly correlated, or it is grey, grey-brown, leather-brown, with or without violet spotting, in which case the color of the standards is violet, that of the wings purple, and the stem in the axils of the leaves is of a reddish tint. The grey seed-coats become dark brown in boiling water.
4. To the *difference in the form of the ripe pods*. These are either simply inflated, not contracted in places; or they are deeply constricted between the seeds and more or less wrinkled (*P. saccharatum*).
5. To the *difference in the color of the unripe pods*. They are either light to dark green, or vividly yellow, in which coloring the stalks, leaf-veins, and calyx participate.
6. To the *difference in the position of the flowers*. They are either axial, that is, distributed along the main stem; or they are terminal, that is, bunched at the top of the stem and arranged almost in a false umbel; in this case the upper part of the stem is more or less widened in section (*P. umbellatum*).

7. To the *difference in the length of the stem*. The length of the stem is very various in some forms; it is, however, a constant character for each, in so far that healthy plants, grown in the same soil, are only subject to unimportant variations in this character.

The Forms of the Hybrids

Experiments which in previous years were made with ornamental plants have already afforded evidence that the hybrids, as a rule, are not exactly intermediate between the parental species . . . That is . . . the case with the Pea-hybrids. In the case of each of the seven crosses the hybrid-character resembles that of one of the parental forms so closely that the other either escapes observation completely or cannot be detected with certainty. This circumstance is of great importance in the determination and classification of the forms under which the offspring of the hybrids appear. Henceforth in this paper those characters which are transmitted entire, or almost unchanged in the hybridization, and therefore in themselves constitute the characters of the hybrid, are termed the *dominant*, and those which become latent in the process *recessive*. The expression "recessive" has been chosen because the characters thereby designated withdraw or entirely disappear in the hybrids, but nevertheless reappear unchanged in their progeny, as will be demonstrated later on.

It was furthermore shown by the whole of the experiments that it is perfectly immaterial whether the dominant character belong to the seed-bearer or to the pollen-parent; the form of the hybrid remains identical in both cases . . .

Of the differentiating characters which were used in the experiments the following are dominant:

1. The round or roundish form of the seed with or without shallow depressions.
2. The yellow color of the seed albumen.
3. The grey, grey-brown, or leather-brown color of the seed-coat, in association with violet-red blossoms and reddish spots in the leaf axils.
4. The simply inflated form of the pod.
5. The green coloring of the unripe pod in association with the same color in the stems, the leaf-veins and the calyx.

6. The distribution of the flowers along the stem.
7. The greater length of stem . . . .

The First Generation [Bred] from the Hybrids

In this generation there reappear, together with the dominant characters, also the recessive ones with their peculiarities fully developed, and this occurs in the definitely expressed average proportion of three to one, so that among four plants of this generation three display the dominant character and one the recessive. This relates without exception to all the characters which were investigated in the experiments . . . . *Transitional forms were not observed in any experiment* . . .

If now the results of the whole of the experiments be brought together, there is found, as between the number of forms with the dominant and recessive characters, an average ratio of 2.98 to 1, or 3 to 1.

The dominant character can here have a *double signification*.—viz., that of a parental character, or a hybrid character. In which of the two significations it appears in each separate case can only be determined by the following generation. As a parental character it must pass over unchanged to the whole of the offspring; as a hybrid-character, on the other hand, it must maintain the same behavior as in the first generation.

The Second Generation [Bred] from the Hybrids

Those forms which in the first generation exhibit the recessive character do not further vary in the second generation as regards this character; they remain constant in their offspring.

It is otherwise with those which possess the dominant character in the first generation (bred from the hybrids). Of these *two*-thirds yield offspring which display the dominant and recessive characters in the proportion of 3 to 1, and thereby show exactly the same ratio as the hybrid forms, while only *one*-third remains with the dominant character constant.

In each of these experiments a certain number of plants came constant with the dominant character. For the determination of the proportion in which the separation of the forms with the constantly persistent character results, the two first experiments are of especial importance, since in these a larger number of plants can be compared. The ratios 1.93 to 1 and 2.13 to 1 gave together almost exactly the average ratio of 2 to 1. The sixth experiment gave a quite concordant result; in the others the ratio varies more or less, as was only to be expected in view of the smaller number of 100 trial plants. Experiment 5, which shows the greatest departure, was repeated, and then, in lieu of the ratio of 60 and 40, that of 65 and 35 resulted. *The average ratio of 2 to 1 appears, therefore, as fixed with certainty.* It is therefore demonstrated that, of those forms which possess the dominant character in the first generation, two-thirds have the hybrid-character, while one-third remains constant with the dominant character.

The ratio of 3 to 1, in accordance with which the distribution of the dominant and recessive characters results in the first generation, resolves itself therefore in all experiments into the ratio of 2:1:1 if the dominant character be differentiated according to its significance as a hybrid-character or as a parental one. Since the members of the first generation spring directly from the seed of the hybrids, *it is now clear that the hybrids form seeds having one or the other of the two differentiating characters, and of these one-half develop again the hybrid form, while the other half yield plants which remain constant and receive the dominant or the recessive characters in equal numbers.*

The Subsequent Generations [Bred] from the Hybrids

The proportions in which the descendants of the hybrids develop and split up in the first and second generations presumably hold good for all subsequent progeny. Experiments 1 and 2 have already been carried through six generations, 3 and 7 through five, and 4, 5, and 6 through four, these experiments being continued from the third generation with a small number of plants, and no departure from the rule has been perceptible. The offspring of the hybrids separated in each generation in the ratio of 2:1:1 into hybrids and constant forms.

If *A* be taken as denoting one of the two constant characters, for instance the dominant, *a*, the recessive, and *Aa* the hybrid form in which both are conjoined, the expression

$$A + 2Aa + a$$

shows the terms in the series for the progeny of the hybrids of two differentiating characters . . .

The Offspring of Hybrids in which Several Differentiating Characters Are Associated

In addition, further experiments were made with a smaller number of experimental plants in which the remaining characters by twos and threes were united as hybrids; all yielded approximately the same results. There is therefore no doubt that for the whole of the characters involved in the experiments the principle applies that *the offspring of the hybrids in which several essentially different characters are combined exhibit the terms of a series of combinations, in which the developmental series for each pair of differentiating characters are united.* It is demonstrated at the same time that *the relation of each pair of different characters in hybrid union is independent of the other differences in the two original parental stocks . . . .*

Note

[1] It is true, of course, that various areas of the brain process different aspects of sensation independently, so one could, in fact, experience shape without color or motion without shape, but that is separate from the point being made here.

Further Reading

Berka, Karel. *Measurement: Its Concepts, Theories and Problems.* Boston: Reidel, 1982.

Bishop, Owen. *Yardsticks of the Universe.* New York: Peter Bedrick Books, 1982.

Brown, Harold. *Observation and Objectivity.* Oxford: Oxford University Press, 1987.

Cartwright, Nancy. *Nature's Capacities and Their Measurement.* New York: Clarendon Press, 1989.

Chang, Hasok. *Inventing Temperature: Measurement and Scientific Progress.* Oxford: Oxford University Press, 2004.

Ellis, Brian. *Basic Concepts of Measurement.* Cambridge: Cambridge University Press, 1968.

Grundy, Richard (ed.). *Theories and Observation in Science.* Englewood Cliffs: Prentice-Hall, 1973.

Kline, Morris. *Mathematics and the Physical World.* New York: Dover Books, 1959.

Kosso, Peter. *Reading the Book of Nature.* Cambridge: Cambridge University Press, 1992.

Kyburg, Jr., Henry E. *Theory and Measurement.* Cambridge: Cambridge University Press, 1984.

Nagel, Ernst, et al. *Observation and Theory in Science.* Baltimore: Johns Hopkins Press, 1971.

Radder, Hans. *The World Observed/The World Conceived.* Pittsburgh: University of Pittsburgh Press, 2006.

CHAPTER THREE

Experimentation and Realism

IN THIS CHAPTER, WE WILL

- Consider notions of experimental design and criteria for experimental evaluation
- Identify some metaphysical, epistemological, and axiological aspects of experimentation
- Consider various conceptions of scientific realism and constructivism
- Examine arguments for an against both realism and constructivism

Some old-timers (probably your professor) fondly remember the line from Bobby "Boris" Pickett: "As I was working in my lab late one night, my eyes beheld an eerie sight; my monster from his slab began to rise, when suddenly to my surprise . . . he did the Mash; he did the Monster Mash!" Although we might not normally associate scientists as creating Frankenstein monsters (in spite of Hollywood's too-often portrayal of scientists), there is probably no more common image of scientists than that of them engaging in experimentation in their laboratories. Indeed, if anything is seen as the most basic means by which scientists come to understand the world, it is rigorous and detailed experimentation. Just as I hope the previous chapter demonstrated that something so basic as observation and measurement are, in fact, conceptually quite complex, in this chapter we will explore some philosophical aspects of another basic component of science, experimentation. There are many points relating to experimentation that could be considered, but this chapter will focus on one in particular, the issue that philosophers of science often call *scientific realism*. We will spend much of this chapter exploring this issue, but for the moment take it to mean this: In what ways and to what extent do we take the goal of science and the results of scientific investigation (both experimental and theoretical) to be that of providing a true picture of how the world really is (independent of our investigations)? We will get at that question, and examine various answers, by first looking at features and concerns relating explicitly to that basic component of science, experimentation.

Experiments and experimentation

There are many types of experiments and many kinds of experimental designs. This stands to reason, because not only are there many different things and kinds of things that are the subjects of experimentation, but there are many different aims that we have when we engage in experimentation. For example, in the December 2, 2006 issue of *Science News,* there are articles discussing experimentation relating to genes, butterflies, red dwarf stars, wine, ancient human technology, the earth's climate, viruses, mussels, sharks, bird blood samples, and others. Some of these experiments were intended simply to find out information that was previously unknown, while others were designed to test rival claims and hypotheses, and still others to lead to the production of new products. Throughout this chapter, as we consider metaphysical, epistemological, and axiological matters relating to experimentation, we will see that these matters often overlap. For instance, what counts as a certain type of experiment (a *what* issue) is intimately connected to the aim(s) of that experiment (a *why* issue). One overriding point that I hope comes through in the following discussion, though, is that—just as with observation and measurement, and just as with other features of science to be discussed in upcoming chapters—experimentation, that is, the very concept of experimentation, is not a simple matter, but is conceptually quite complex. And, remember, one of the goals of a philosophical look at science is to help us take a longer and harder look at those aspects of science that we assume are pretty straightforward. That being said, let's look more closely at experiments and experimentation.

The first point, already mentioned above, is that there are many types of experiments. There are *methodological* experiments, in which the goal is to develop/improve some particular technique or inquiry. Pilot studies are commonly this type of experiment. For instance, we might wish to find out if delivering an antidote for some infection is better accomplished via an oral pill versus an injection directly into the bloodstream. Another type of experiment is a *heuristic* one, in which we hope to provide leads for further or even new lines of inquiry. A fairly standard version of a heuristic type of experiment is a trial and error type. Perhaps the most common, or at least commonly thought of, type of experiment is a *fact-finding* experiment, that is, one intended to determine some particular/well-defined phenomenon, such as measuring the speed of light even more precisely than we already have. Later in this chapter, we'll have a reading that discusses Millikan's oil drop experiment; it is a fact-finding type.

Another type of experiment is a *creative* experiment, wherein we (attempt to) create some new phenomenon. For instance, we have all heard of large particle accelerators with which physicists smash atoms together in an attempt (among other things) to create a new, perhaps theoretically predicted, particle. There are also what are sometimes called *boundary* experiments, that is, fact-finding experiments designed to fix the range of application of laws. For example, cognitive psychologists often test to discover perceptual thresholds. Closely related to boundary and fact-finding experiments are ones that are sometimes called *nomological* experiments. These are aimed at testing laws or general hypotheses, with the aim of confirming or disconfirming them. A famous example of this type is experiments to determine whether or not light is affected by a gravitational field. (This case will be discussed in Chapter Eight.) There are *simulation* experiments (more and more done only via computers), which are designed to learn from models how the real world operates. A very common example of this type of experiment is a wind tunnel experiment that auto companies use to test potential gas mileage of their automobiles. Perhaps, as students, the type of experiment you are most familiar with is *illustrative* experiments, namely, experiments that are designed to train you about science and experimentation. The aim here is not really to discover new facts or really to test known hypotheses, and so on, but to train the experimenter in how to experiment. Finally, there are *thought* experiments, in which the experiment is performed only conceptually. (You probably already know that Einstein was famous for arguing along the lines of thought experiments.)

Now, the point of this little taxonomy of experiments is that even at the beginning of a consideration of experiments and experimentation, we can see that things are not so simple as to merely talk about experiments. There are quite a few types of experiments, not to mention how they are carried out (for example, in laboratories, in the field, via computer simulations, just conceptually).

One straightforward axiological element of experiments and experimentation is the notion of criteria of experimental evaluation; that is, identifying features of a good experiment. There are a number of features that we insist upon in order to make the evaluation that a particular experimental design is good. Here are some:

- Replicability—we expect that the "same" experiment can be repeated by the same experimenter or by other experimenters in order to test the reliability of the initial experiment;
- Accuracy—we expect that a good experiment yields accurate and clearly measurable results;
- Precision—we expect that meaningful results will be clearly understandable and analyzable and that they lead to some fairly definitive interpretation; (By the way, accuracy and precision are not the same thing. Think of someone shooting arrows at a particular target. The shooter could be accurate by getting lots of bull's eyes, that is, hitting the center of the target, but the shooter could also be precise by getting lots of shots grouped together in the same area even if that area isn't the bull's eye.)
- Generalizability—we want the results of our experiment to go beyond the specifics of that particular experiment; we want to be able to apply the results and conclusions of a given experiment to other cases;
- Simplicity—all things being equal, we want simpler experiments to more complicated ones, both in terms of

the design of the experiment and in terms of the analysis of it;
- Focus/clarity (of purpose)—we want clearly defined experiments in the sense of clearly defined hypotheses being tested and in terms of what would count as meaningful results and answers;
- Absence of systematic error—we want experiments designed and executed in such as way as to eliminate (or at least minimize) built-in error, such as not accounting for multiple variables or lack of clear criteria for a control group;
- Utility—much like generalizability, we want the experiment to provide us with useful information;
- Consistency—we want the design of the experiment to be consistent with (that is, not contradict) already accepted procedures or information or theories.

Now, there are several points to make about this list of experimental desiderata (things to be desired). First, it is not exhaustive. There are many features that we desire for a good experiment; these nine are ones I take to be fairly obvious. Second, they are open to debate and interpretation. For example, I claim that we desire consistency with already accepted procedures or information or theories. Obviously, there are times when an experiment is inconsistent with these things. That, in and of itself, certainly does not mean that the experiment is not a good one. But in such a case, we would need to explain why the inconsistency is important and fruitful. Third, these experimental desiderata are values that we hold about experiments and experimentation. They are not "out there" in the data and information or objects of the world; we, as scientists, decide that replicability is important for scientific reliability. Features such as replicability, consistency, accuracy, etc. are what, in Chapter Twelve, we will call *epistemic values,* and we will discuss them much more fully at that point.

Just as there are values about the desirable features of experiments, there are factors that affect the worthwhile nature of experiments, both in terms of the experimental process and the experimental product, or results. For example, with respect to the experimental process, here are some relevant factors (at least for some experiments):

- History—this refers to events that occur between measurements that are outside the scope of the given test or experiment (one example of this is sometimes called *mortality*, which refers to the loss of experimental subjects between measurements);
- Maturation—this refers to events or processes within the experimental subjects that could produce a nondesigned change as a function of time (for example, simple fatigue on the part of the experimental subjects, when fatigue or stamina are not factored into the experimental design);
- Instability—this refers to unreliability of measures or, perhaps, fluctuations in sampling, again not factored into the experimental design;
- Reflexivity—this refers to the effect of test-taking on future test trials (for example, when the experimental subjects infer—rightly or wrongly—what results the experimenters are expecting or desiring);
- Instrumentation—this refers to changes in calibration of instruments, observers, and so on, again not factored into the experimental design;
- Selection—this refers to bias resulting from differential recruitment for comparison groups

Without going into such detail, there are also factors that could affect the reliability of the experimental results include. For instance, results could be less reliable because of the reflexivity concern mentioned above (this is sometimes referred to as "interaction effects of testing"). In addition, the test setting might be atypical or at least not reflective of conditions beyond the test (sometimes referred to as "reactive effects of experimental arrangements"). For example, there has long been a complaint about EPA gas mileage estimates that are made in test settings that don't really duplicate conditions "on the road" of everyday drivers. The result is that EPA mileage estimates are almost always higher than what drivers actually observe when they drive their vehicles. There are other sorts of concerns about the reliability of experimental results, such as how representative is the test sample for the population beyond the sample or how relevant are the features that are being measured versus features in the experiment that are not being measured, and so on. But you get the point—there are numerous factors that affect the worth and value of experiments. These factors are among the epistemological concerns of experiments and experimentation, though, because they are also value issues, they are among the axiological concerns, as well. So, if we want to get a better understanding of this basic component of science, that is, experiment and experimentation, we could and should identify these underlying philosophical, conceptual complexities.

Interpretation and theory

Besides noting some basic philosophical issues relating to experiment and experimentation, I want here to mention one other philosophical matter before turning to the relation between experimentation and scientific realism. That other matter is the notion of the theory-ladenness of experimentation. Recall from Chapter Two, the claim was made concerning the theory-ladenness of observation and measurement. That claim, of ineliminable underlying background assumptions, applies also to experimentation, at least according to many philosophers of science. One of those philosophers (actually, a nineteenth-century physicist) was Pierre Duhem (who will be discussed again briefly in Chapter Eight). As an experimental physicist himself, Duhem argued the following:

THE AIM AND STRUCTURE OF PHYSICAL THEORY
Pierre Duhem

An experiment in physics is the precise observation of phenomena accompanied by an *interpretation* of these phenomena; this interpretation substitutes for the concrete data really gathered by observation abstract and symbolic representations which correspond to them by virtue of the theories admitted by the observer . . .

The point, I hope, is clear. Not only must the *results* of any experiment be interpreted, and, for Duhem, that means theory-laden, but also any experimental *design* must also rely on many background assumptions, so that prior theory enters into experimentation even before the setting up of an experiment, indeed, for an experiment to even be possible. Because we want to get to the issue of realism, I will not go further into this issue of theory-ladenness of experimentation. Besides, having discussed that in our previous chapter, you know the sorts of conceptual concerns related to this topic.

As a "test case" for the philosophical concerns that have been raised so far in this chapter, consider this story below of a recent experiment involving gene regulation and cancer. Try to identify the type(s) of experiments that are discussed as well as the features and factors that would point to the reliability of the experiment(s) involved. In addition, try to identify the observational and interpretational elements are, as well as what prior theory is assumed. Following that, we'll turn to the topic of scientific realism.

GENE REGULATES PROGESTERONE EFFECT ON BREAST CELLS

Nathan Seppa

Since its discovery in 1994, the BRCA1 gene has given up its secrets grudgingly. Early on, scientists recognized that it kept cancer at bay. Women carrying a mutation in the gene face an extremely high risk of breast and ovarian cancer. Researchers have struggled to understand how the protein encoded by a normal BRCA1 gene works.

A study in mice now suggests one possibility. The BRCA1 protein moderates the hormone progesterone's effect in breast cells. The protein appears to calm those cells when progesterone urges them to divide and grow.

Earlier research had shown that BRCA1 protein orchestrates the repair of damaged DNA. But since that process occurs continuously in every cell throughout the body, the finding failed to explain how a mutated BRCA1 would predispose a woman specifically to cancers of the breasts and ovaries.

In the new study, the researchers genetically engineered mice so that they didn't make BRCA1 protein. Breast tissue is these animals grew abnormally, creating many branching mammary ducts of a type usually seen only in pregnant mice, says Eva Y.-H.P. Lee, a molecular biologist at the University of California, Irvine.

Compared with normal breast cells, the breast cells in the genetically altered mice were also three times as likely to have progesterone receptors—proteins on the cell surface that serve as docks for the hormone. When progesterone binds to the receptor, it sends a signal that's transferred to the cell nucleus. Progesterone typically instructs a cell to proliferate.

Normally, after a progesterone receptor transmits a growth signal, the cell destroys the receptor, Lee says. However, animals lacking BRCA1 failed to complete this routine cleanup process, she and her colleagues report in the Dec. 1 [2006] *Science*. In some cases, other progesterone molecules bind to the already used receptor, generating more proliferation signals.

All the mice in a group bereft of BRCA1 protein developed tumors within 5 to 9 months, the researchers found. But when similar mice received the anti-progesterone drug mifepristone, they showed no cancer during the 12 months of observation.

The study "places the progesterone receptor right in the middle of the physiology" of BRCA1-related breast cancers, says physician Steven Narod of the University of Toronto.

"This provides compelling evidence that abnormal branching [in mammary glands] is due to aberrant progesterone signaling," says oncologist Nicholas Turner of the Breakthrough Breast Cancer Research Centre in London.

However, Narod notes that mice aren't a perfect model for the human disease because healthy women with BRCA1 mutations don't exhibit the abnormal duct branching seen in the animals in this study.

Antiprogesterone drugs might control abnormal signaling, thereby preventing or treating cancers in some women with the BRCA1 mutation, says oncologist Eliot M. Rosen of Georgetown University in Washington, D.C. At present, "the most effective protection [against breast cancer for women with a BRCA1 mutation] is drastic surgery to remove the ovaries and both breasts," he says. An antiprogesterone "might be a non-surgical approach," he adds.

Narod cautions that determining the preventive effects of an antiprogesterone drug would require a massive clinical trial of healthy women. A test of an antiprogesterone as a treatment for breast cancer might come first, he says.

Realism

You certainly have heard of Copernicus and the claim that he revolutionized astronomy by arguing that the earth was "merely" a planet that orbits the sun, not the center of the universe with the sun, planets and stars orbiting it. Almost just as surely as you have heard of Copernicus, you have *not* heard of Nicole Oresme, who argued in the mid-1300s—200 years before Copernicus—for a solar system (i.e., sun-centered) with the earth as one planet. (If you haven't heard of Oresme, this is a shame. He is one of many important medieval thinkers who clearly belie the claim that the sciences made little progress during the Middle Ages. Get a good history of science book and read about him!) In his book entitled, *On the Book of the Heavens and the World of Aristotle,* Oresme argued that our experiences and observations are consistent with a stationary earth (in which the heavens move) or a moving earth (in which the heavens appear to move because the earth itself moves). In either case, to us on earth, it would appear that the heavens move. Reminiscent of claims made by Einstein almost 600 years later, Oresme argued for a relativity of motion and that there is no obvious "privileged" perspective. As he put it: "If *a* is at rest and *b* is moved, it will appear to him [someone at *a*] that *b* is moved. On the other hand, if *a* is moved and *b* is at rest, it will appear to him as before that *a* is at rest and that *b* is moved." He proceeded to claim, with respect to the universe, that "one cannot demonstrate by any experience whatever that the heavens are moved with daily movement, because, regardless of whether it has been posited that the heavens and not the earth are so moved or that the earth and not the heavens is moved, if an observer is in the heavens, and he sees the earth clearly, it (the earth) would seem to be moved . . . Yet, nevertheless, everyone holds, and I believe, that they (the heavens), and not the earth, are so moved, for 'God created the orb of the earth, which will not be moved' (Psalms 92:1), notwithstanding the arguments to the contrary. This is because they are 'persuasions' which do not make the conclusions evident. But having considered everything which has been said, one could by this believe that the earth and not the heavens is so moved, and there is no evidence to the contrary. Nevertheless, this seems prima facie as much, or more, against natural reason as are all or several articles of faith."

So, the gist of Oresme's claims here is that there is no evidence that favors either the view that the earth moves or the view that the earth is stationary and the heavens move. Some historians of science have interpreted his remarks as suggesting that in such a case where natural reason cannot solve a problem that revelation or appeal to scripture should be the deciding factor in favoring one hypothesis over another. So, although Oresme said the earth might indeed really be a planet orbiting the sun, this was just a hypothesis that is consistent with empirical data, but it doesn't mean that is how the universe *really* is. Other historians of science have suggested that Oresme really did think a moving earth is how the universe really is but did not want to come right out and say so, fearing that he would get in trouble with the Church if he did.

What this case points to, besides the fact that Copernicus wasn't as revolutionary as we are usually told, is the issue that philosophers of science refer to as *scientific realism*. In a nutshell, scientific realism is the view that there is a real world out there, independent of our theories and beliefs about it. Science, at least good science, discovers what that world is really like. This nutshell view, though, is too simplistic, even just for characterizing what scientific realism is. For one thing, the claim is not simply that there is a real, independent world out there, but that there is one world and, so, ultimately one correct description of that world. We will talk more about this issue of one correct description later in Chapter Seven (on the unity of science). For now, though, as it turns out, different philosophers mean different things by the term scientific realism. Jarrett Leplin has identified at least ten different notions of scientific realism:

1. The best current scientific theories are at least approximately true.
2. The central terms of the best current scientific theories are genuinely referential.
3. The approximate truth of a scientific theory is sufficient explanation of its predictive success.
4. The approximate truth of a scientific theory is the only possible explanation of its predictive success.
5. A scientific theory might be approximately true even if referentially unsuccessful.
6. The history of at least the mature sciences shows progressive approximation to a true account of the physical world.
7. The theoretical claims of scientific theories are to be read literally, and so read, are definitely true or false.
8. Scientific theories make genuine, existential claims.
9. The predictive success of a theory is evidence for the referential success of its central terms.
10. Science aims at a literally true account of the physical world, and its success is to be reckoned by its progress toward achieving this goal.

Notice that these various notions of scientific realism focus on different philosophical matters. For example, the emphasis on science as getting true, or approximately true, or closer-to-the-whole-truth accounts, is one (epistemological) focus. Notions that emphasize referential success or making genuine, existential claims, are another (metaphysical) focus. Nevertheless, there is a pretty common sense, clear position that, as I mentioned earlier, the world is the way it is independent of how we think of it (a metaphysical, or ontological, claim). Furthermore, good science gives us a correct picture of the world by giving us true (or true-like) representations of the world (an epistemological claim). In addition, the history of science shows us that we are getting better at describing the world the way it really is; that is, our current models and theories are closer-to-the-whole-truth than previous models and theories were. The things and events and processes that our models and theories talk about and refer to (for example, electrons and genes and electromagnetic fields) are really "out there" in the world and to the extent that our models and theories are good, they correctly identify and describe and make use of these things and events and processes. One way that philosophers like to speak of this last point is that our best models and theories "cut nature at its joints," meaning that we correctly describe the natural classes of things as they really are.

Who could disagree with this common sense view and why? Well, as you can probably imagine, quite a few people can and do, especially many philosophers of science. They disagree with different aspects of the various characterizations of realism noted above and they disagree for various reasons. Let's begin with laying out different labels that have been used for critics of scientific realism (some of these labels are used by the critics themselves, others by realists when they talk about those critics). The first label is *antirealism*. We will see one prominent realist, Ian Hacking, who uses this label for critics. I will be upfront and say that I think this label is not very useful and probably unfair. It certainly gives the connotation that advocates of this view are somehow opposed to the notion of a real world and this is simply not a correct picture of these critics. Another label that is sometimes used, though less often now than it used to be, is *idealism*. The root of this word is not "ideal," but "idea." Idealism is the metaphysical view that what is really real, or most real, are ideas in some mind, not physical substances in themselves. To the extent that things "out there" in the world are real, it is because they are thought of, or conceived. Closely related to idealism is another label, *phenomenalism*. Phenomenalism is the view that we perceive only the appearances of things (i.e., phenomena) as they arise in our experiences, so the only meaningful reality to talk about is the reality of phenomena. *Instrumentalism* is a different label for a different version of critics of realism. Instrumentalism implies that scientific models and theories are instruments, tools, for allowing us to make sense of phenomena that we encounter. As tools, the concern is how well they work, not on whether or not they are true. Another label that is often used, especially by the critics of realism themselves, is *constructivism*. The emphasis here is that we construct conceptions of the world, that there are multiple correct ways of describing the world, that we do not just discover what kinds of things there are in the world, but (at least in part) we construct them, that we do not "cut nature at its joints," but we determine what joints there are to be cut. Even another label for critics of realism is *constructive empiricism.* This view is that the goal of science is to provide empirically adequate accounts of the phenomena that we encounter. It is successful prediction and explanation of phenomena that matters, not truth. For constructive empiricists, the most renown being the philosopher of science, Bas van Fraassen, claiming that a theory is true does not carry any explanatory force; what matters for science is the ability to describe, predict, and control phenomena, to be able to provide coherent and complete accounts of the phenomena we encounter. Some have suggested that the label *nonrealism* be used as a sort of umbrella term for all of these various views. However, for some this still has the connotation that critics of realism deny reality (which they do not) or that their view is simply a reaction and rejection of realism, without offering any full-fledged positive view (which they claim they do). Besides, not all critics of realism agree with each other (e.g., constructive empiricists are not idealists). So, the term "nonrealism" has not stuck and the most neutral phrase to use is just "critics of realism."

Realists counter these critics by claiming that truth does in fact have explanatory force. It is precisely because good science describes the world the way it really is that science "works." What explains the success of, say, relativity physics or molecular genetics or geological plate tectonics is that they match the way the world is.

The following selection, by Ian Hacking, gives an argument for realism. In this selection, Hacking makes a distinction between realism about entities (those things we take to be real, or, as he says, that we actually use in science) and realism about theories (those accounts we give for phenomena). He argues in favor of realism about entities and is not concerned so much about realism about theories. Before getting to those two types of realism, though, he first describes an experiment in physics that he claims convinced him of realism about entities. As you read this selection, keep in mind the various features and factors about experiments and experimentation we discussed earlier in this chapter.

This selection is a very nice transition from experimentation to scientific realism and demonstrates a close connection between these two issues. So, here is Hacking:

REPRESENTING AND INTERVENING
Ian Hacking

Scientific realism says that the entities, states and processes described by correct theories really do exist. Protons, photons, fields of force, and black holes are as real as toe-nails, turbines, eddies in a stream, and volcanoes. The weak interactions of small particle physics are as real as falling in love. Theories about the structure of molecules that carry genetic codes are either true or false, and a genuinely correct theory would be a true one.

Even when our sciences have not yet got things right, the realist holds that we often get close to the truth. We aim at discovering the inner constitution of things and at knowing what inhabits the most distant reaches of the universe. Nor need we be too modest. We have already found out a good deal.

Anti-realism says the opposite: there are no such things as electrons. Certainly there are phenomena of electricity and of inheritance but we construct theories about tiny states, processes and entities only in order to predict and produce events that interest us. The electrons are fictions. Theories about them are tools for thinking. Theories are adequate or useful or warranted or applicable, but no matter how much we admire the speculative and technological triumphs of natural science, we should not regard even its most telling theories as true. Some anti-realists hold back because they believe theories are intellectual tools which cannot be understood as literal statements of how the world is. Others say that theories must be taken literally—there is no other way to understand them. But, such anti-realists contend, however much we may use the theories we do not have compelling reasons to believe they are right. Likewise, anti-realists of either stripe will not include theoretical entities among the kinds of things that really exist in the world: turbines, yes, but photons no.

We have indeed mastered many events in nature, says the anti-realist. Genetic engineering is becoming as commonplace as manufacturing steel, but do not be deluded. Do not suppose that long chains of molecules are really there to be spliced. Biologists may think more clearly about an amino acid if they build a molecular model out of wire and colored balls. The model may suggest new microtechnology, but it is not a literal picture of how things really are. I could make a model of the economy out of pulleys and levers and ball bearings and weights. Every decrease in weight M (the "money supply") produces a decrease in angle I (the "rate of inflation") and an increase in the number N of ball bearings in this pan (the number of unemployed workers). We get the right inputs and outputs, but no one suggests that this is what the economy is.

If you can spray them, then they are real

For my part I never thought twice about scientific realism until a friend told me about an ongoing experiment to detect the existence of fractional electric charges. They are called quarks. Now it is not the quarks that made me a realist, but rather electrons. Allow me to tell the story. It ought not to be a simple story, but a realistic one, one that connects with day to day scientific research. Let us start with an old experiment on electrons.

The fundamental unit of electric charge was long thought to be the electron. In 1908 J.A. Millikan devised a beautiful experiment to measure this quantity. A tiny negatively charged oil droplet is suspended between electrically charged plates. First it is allowed to fall with the electric field switched off. Then the field is applied to hasten the rate of fall. The two observed terminal velocities of the droplet are combined with the coefficient of viscosity of the air and the densities of the air and oil. These, together with the known value of gravity, and of the electric field, enable one to compute the charge on the drop. In repeated experiments the charges on these drops are small integral multiples of a definite quantity. This is taken to be the minimum charge, that is, the charge on the electrons. Like all experiments, this one makes assumptions that are roughly correct: that the drops are spherical, for instance. Millikan at first ignored the fact that the drops are not large compared to the mean free path of air molecules so they get bumped about a bit. But the idea of the experiment is definitive.

The electron was long held to be the unit of charge. We use e as the name of that charge. Small particle physics, however, increasingly suggests an entity, called a quark, that has a charge of 1/3e. Nothing in theory suggests that quarks have independent existence; if they do come into being, theory implies, then they react immediately and are gobbled up at once. This has not deterred an ingenious experiment started by LaRue, Fairbank and Hebard at Stanford. They are hunting for "free" quarks using Millikan's basic idea.

Since quarks may be rare or short-lived, it helps to have a big ball rather than a tiny dorp, for then there is a better chance of having a quark stuck to it. The drop used, although weighing less than 10^{-4} grams, is 10^7 times bigger than Millikan's drops. If it were made of oil it would fall like a stone, almost. Instead it is made of a substance called niobium, which is cooled below its superconducting transition temperature of 9°K. Once an electric charge is set going round this very cold ball, it stays going, forever. Hence the drop can be kept aloft in a magnetic field, and indeed driven back and forth by varying the field. One can also use a magnetometer to tell exactly where the drop is and how fast it is moving.

The initial charge placed on the ball is gradually changed, and, applying our present technology in a Millikan-like way, one determines whether the passage from positive to negative charge occurs at zero or at +/– 1/3e. If the latter, there must surely be one loose quark on the ball. In their most recent preprint [in the early 1980s], Fairbank and his associates report four fractional charges consistent with +1/3e, four with –1/3e, and 13 with zero.

Now how does one alter the charge on the niobium ball? "Well, at that stage," said my friend, "we spray it with positrons to increase the charge or with electrons to decrease the charge." From that day forth I've been a scientific realist. *So far as I'm concerned, if you can spray them then they are real.*

Hacking's point is quite obvious: if you can spray electrons, then electrons are real! We will see whether or not a critic of realism (in our case, the person is Arthur Fine) agrees that realism is the best—or only—conclusion to draw as an explanation for being able to spray electrons. But, again, consider the conceptual features of experiments and experimentation and ask yourself, at this point, how those features support (or do not) a commitment to realism. Meanwhile, here is Hacking again, arguing that realism about entities is what is crucial and that such realism is not only assumed by scientists, but explains their practices and successes.

REPRESENTING AND INTERVENING *(continued)*
Ian Hacking

Experimental work provides the strongest evidence for scientific realism. This is not because we test hypotheses about entities. It is because entities that in principle cannot be "observed" are regularly manipulated to produce new phenomena and to investigate other aspects of nature. They are tools, instruments not for thinking but for doing. The philosopher's favorite theoretical entity is the electron. I shall illustrate how electrons have become experimental entities, or experimenter's entities. In the early stages of our discovery of an entity, we may test the hypothesis that it exists. Even that is not routine. When J.J. Thomson realized in 1897 that what he called "corpuscles" were boiling off hot cathodes, almost the first thing he did was to measure the mass of these negatively charged particles. He made a crude estimate of e, the charge, and measured e/m. He got m about right, too. Millikan followed up some ideas already under discussion at Thomson's Cavendish Laboratory, and by 1908 had determined the charge of the electron, that is, the probably minimum unit of electric charge. Hence from the very beginning people were less testing the existence of electrons than interacting with them. The more we come to understand some of the causal powers of electrons, the more we can build devices that achieve well-understood effects in other parts of nature. By the time that we can use the electron to manipulate other parts of nature in a systematic way, the electron has ceased to be something hypothetical, something inferred. It has ceased to be theoretical and has become experimental.

Experimenters and Entities

The vast majority of experimental physicists are realists about some theoretical entities, namely the ones they *use*. I claim that they cannot help being so. Many are also, no doubt, realists about theories too, but that is less central to their concerns.

Experimenters are often realists about the entities that they *investigate*, but they do not have to be so. Millikan probably had few qualms about the reality of electrons when he set out to measure their charge. But he could have been skeptical about what he would find until he found it. He could even have remained skeptical. Perhaps there is a least unit of electric charge, but there is no particle or object with exactly that unit of charge. Experimenting on an entity does not commit you to believing that it exists. Only *manipulating* an entity, in order to experiment on something else, need do that . . .

There is an important experimental contrast between realism about entities and realism about theories. Suppose we say that the latter is belief that science aims at true theories. Few experimenters will deny that. Only philosophers doubt it. Aiming at the truth is, however, something about the indefinite future. Aiming a beam of electrons is using present electrons. Aiming a finely tuned laser at a particular atom in order to knock off a certain electron to produce an ion is aiming at present electrons. There is in contrast no present set of theories that one has to believe in. If realism about theories is a doctrine about the aims of science, it is a doctrine laden with certain kinds of values. If realism about entities is a matter of aiming electrons next week, or aiming at other electrons the week after, it is a doctrine much more neutral between values. The way in which experimenters are scientific realists about entities is entirely different from ways in which they might be realists about theories . . .

Making

Even if experimenters are realists about entities, it does not follow that they are right. Perhaps it is a matter of psychology: maybe the very skills that make for a great experimenter go with a certain cast of mind that objectifies whatever it thinks about. Yet this won't do. The experimenter cheerfully regards neutral bosons as merely hypothetical entities, while electrons are real. What is the difference?

There are an enormous number of ways in which to make instruments that rely on the causal properties of electrons in order to produce desired effects of unsurpassed precision. I shall illustrate this. The argument—it could be called the experimental argument for realism—is not that we infer the reality of electrons from our success. We do not make the instruments and then infer the reality of the electrons, as when we test an hypothesis, and then believe it because it passed the test. That gets the time-order wrong. By now we design apparatus relying on a modest number of home truths about electrons, in order to produce some other phenomenon that we wish to investigate.

This may sound as if we believe in electrons because we predict how our apparatus will behave. That too is misleading. We have a number of general ideas about how to prepare polarized electrons, say. We spend a lot of time building prototypes that don't work. We get rid of innumerable bugs. Often we have to give up and try another approach. Debugging is not a matter of theoretically explaining or predicting what is going wrong. It is partly a matter of getting rid of "noise" in the apparatus. Although it also has a precise meaning, "noise" often means all the events that are not understood by any theory. The instrument must be able to isolate, physically, the properties of the entities that we wish to use, and damp down all the other effects that might get in the way. *We are completely convinced of the reality of electrons when we regularly set out to build—and often enough succeed in building—new kinds of device that use various well-understood causal properties of electrons to interfere in other more hypothetical parts of nature.*

Now, as noted earlier, critics of realism come in a variety of versions (phenomenalists, constructivists, constructive empiricists, etc...). The philosopher included on the following page is Arthur Fine. As you will see when he declares, "Realism is dead," he definitely disagrees with Hacking that realism, even realism about entities, provides an explanation for the success of science. In fact, he portrays realism's "explanation" as mainly stomping one's foot and saying, "Really!" In the selection, Fine claims that critics of realism can accept the results of science, including positing the existence of electrons, without being committed to the view that therefore there really are electrons or that theories about electrons are therefore true (and, hence, that truth has any explanatory force). In fact, Fine claims that part of the reason to reject realism as an explanation for the success of science is that some very basic, successful, scientific theories, most notably quantum physics, challenge realist assumptions. In the reading below, after asserting that realism is dead, Fine discusses what he calls "the small handful" argument. By that he means that for any given scientific concern at any one time there is only a small handful of viable accounts. Fine claims that critics of realism actually have better accounts for the phenomenon of small handfuls than does realism.

THE NATURAL ONTOLOGICAL ATTITUDE
Arthur Fine

Realism is dead. Its death was announced by the neopositivists who realized that they could accept all the results of science, including all the members of the scientific zoo [i.e., the multitude of subatomic particles], and still declare that the questions raised by the existence claims of realism were mere pseudoquestions. Its death was hastened by the debates over the interpretation of quantum theory, where Bohr's nonrealist philosophy was seen to win out over Einstein's passionate realism. Its death was certified, finally, as the last two generations of physical scientists turned their backs on realism and have managed, nevertheless, to do science successfully without it. To be sure, some recent philosophical literature . . . has appeared to pump up the ghostly shell and to give it new life. But I think these efforts will eventually be seen and understood as the first stage in the process of mourning, the stage of denial . . . I think we shall pass through this first stage and into that of acceptance, for realism is well and truly dead, and we have work to get on with, in identifying a suitable successor. To aid that work I want to do three things in this essay. First, I want to show that the arguments in favor of realism are not sound, and that they provide no rational support for belief in realism. Then, I want to recount the essential role of nonrealist attitudes for the development of science in this [i.e., the 20th] century, and thereby (I hope) to loosen the grip of the idea that only realism provides a progressive philosophy of science. Finally, I want to sketch out what seems to me a viable nonrealist position, one that is slowly gathering support and that seems a decent philosophy for postrealist times.

Arguments for Realism

Recent philosophical argument in support of realism tries to move from the success of the scientific enterprise to the necessity for a realist account of its practice. As I see it, the arguments here fall on two distinct levels. On the ground level, as it were, one attends to particular successes; such as novel, confirmed predictions, striking unifications of disparate-seeming phenomena (or fields), successful piggybacking from one theoretical model to another, and the like. Then, we are challenged to account for such success, and told that the best and, it is slyly suggested, perhaps, the *only* way of doing so is on a realist basis. I do not find the details of these ground-level arguments at all convincing. Larry Laudan has provided a forceful and detailed analysis which shows that not even with a lot of hand waving (to shield gaps in the argument) and charity (to excuse them) can realism itself be used to explain the very successes to which it invites our attention. But there is a second level of realist argument, the methodological level, that derives from Popper's attack on instrumentalism as inadequate to account for the details of his own, falsificationist methodology . . . These [methodological] arguments focus on the methods embedded in scientific practice, methods teased out in ways that seem to me accurate and perceptive about ongoing science. We are then challenged to account for why these methods lead to scientific success and told that the best, and (again) perhaps, the only truly adequate way of explaining the matter is on the basis of realism . . .

A typical realist argument on the methodological level deals with what I shall call the problem of the "small handful." It goes like this. At any time, in a given scientific area, only a small handful of alternative theories (or hypotheses) are in the field. Only such a small handful are seriously considered as competitors, or as possible successors to some theory requiring revision. Moreover, in general, this handful displays a sort of family resemblance in that none of these live options will be too far from the previously accepted theories in the field, each preserving the well-confirmed features of the earlier theories and deviating only in those aspects less confirmed. Why? Why does this narrowing down of our choices to such a small handful of cousins of our previously accepted theories work to produce good successor theories?

The realist answers this as follows. Suppose that the already existing theories are themselves approximately true descriptions of the domain under consideration. Then surely it is reasonable to restrict one's search for successor theories to those whose ontologies and laws resemble what we already have, especially where what we already have is well confirmed. And if these earlier theories were approximately true, then so will be such conservative successors. Hence, such successors will be good predictive instruments; that is, they will be successful in their own right . . .

The problem of the small handful raises three challenges: why small, why narrowly related, and why does it work. The realist has no answer for the first of these, begs the question as to the truth of explanatory hypotheses on the second, and has no resources for addressing the third. For comparison, it may be useful to see how well his archenemy, the instrumentalist, fares on the same turf. The instrumentalist, I think, has a substantial basis for addressing the questions of smallness and narrowness, for he can point out that it is extremely difficult to come up with alternative theories that satisfy the many empirical constraints posed by the instrumental success of theories already in the field. Often it is hard enough to come up with even one such alternative. Moreover, the common apprenticeship of scientists working in the same area certainly has the effect of narrowing down the range of options by channeling thought into the commonly accepted categories. If we add to this the instrumentally justified rule, "If it has worked well in the past, try it again," then we get a rather good account, I think, of why there is usually only a small and narrow handful. As to why this strategy works to produce instrumentally successful science, we have already noted that for the most part it does not. Most of what this strategy produces are failures. It is a quirk of scientific memory that this fact gets obscured, much as do the memories of bad times during a holiday vacation when we recount all our "wonderful" vacation adventures to a friend. Those instrumentalists who incline to a general account of knowledge as a social construction can go further at this juncture, and lean on the sociology of science to explain how the scientific community "creates" its knowledge. I am content just to back off here and note that over the problem of the small handful, the instrumentalist scores at least two out of three, whereas the realist, left to his own devices, has struck out.

Following this rejection of realism, Fine argues below that there is a more acceptable account of scientific practice and scientific success, one that he believes has explanatory force. He calls this view the *natural ontological attitude* (or NOA). By NOA he means the view that scientific claims and truths are not that different from what he calls "homely truths," that is, everyday, common sense notions of what things there are (an ontology) and how we come to know them and call claims about them true or false (an epistemology) and what we want science to do for us (an axiology). Fine talks about accepting these homely truths as "the core position," because he claims that both realists and their critics can and do accept them (contrary, for Fine, to what Hacking says). What really distinguishes realists from their critics, he says, is what they add to the core position. It is here that Fine claims that realists only add foot stomping, whereas critics of realism add other accounts (such as constructing empirically adequate models) that are precisely the accounts that realists say are empty or false. At this point Fine offers his NOA, which he says in not really realist or antirealist, although many philosophers of science have interpreted this view as far more aligned with the critics of realism than with realism. See for yourself:

THE NATURAL ONTOLOGICAL ATTITUDE *(continued)*
Arthur Fine

. . . What is it to accept the evidence of one's senses and, *in the same way*, to accept confirmed scientific theories? It is to take them into one's life as true with all that implies concerning adjusting one's behavior, practical and theoretical, to accommodate these truths. Now, of course, there are truths, and truths. Some are more central to us and our lives, some less so. I might be mistaken about anything, but were I mistaken about where I am right now, that might affect me more than would my perhaps mistaken belief in charmed quarks. Thus, it is compatible with the homely line of argument that some of the scientific beliefs that I hold are less central than some, for example, perceptual beliefs. Of course, were I deeply in the charmed-quarks business, giving up that belief might be more difficult than giving up some at the perceptual level. (Thus we get the phenomenon of "seeing what you believe," as is well known to all thoughtful people.) When the homely line asks us, then, to accept the scientific results "in the same way" in which we accept the evidence of our senses, I take it that we are to accept them both as true. I take it that we are being asked not to distinguish between two kinds of truth or modes of existence or the like, but only among truths themselves, in terms of centrality, degrees of belief, or such . . .

Let me use the term "antirealist" to refer to any of the many different specific enemies of realism: the idealist, the instrumentalist, the phenomenalist, the empiricist (constructive or not), the conventionalist, the constructivist, the pragmatist, and so forth. Then, it seems to me that both the realist and the antirealist must toe what I have been calling "the homely line." That is, they must both accept the certified results of science as on a par with more homely and familiarly supported claims. That is not to say that one party (or the other) cannot distinguish more from less well-confirmed claims at home or in science; nor that one cannot single out some particular mode of inference (such as inference to the best explanation) and worry over its reliability, both at home and away. It is just that one must maintain parity. Let us say, then, that both realist and antirealist accept the results of scientific investigations as "true," on a par with more homely truths. (I realize that some antirealists would rather use a different word, but no matter.) And call this acceptance of scientific truths the "core position." What distinguishes realists from antirealists, then, is what they add onto this core position.

The antirealist may add onto the core position a particular analysis of the concept of truth, as in the pragmatic and instrumentalist and conventionalist conceptions of truth. Or the antirealist may add on a special analysis of concepts, as in idealism, constructivism, phenomenalism, and in some varieties of empiricism. These addenda will then issue in a special meaning, say, for existence statements. Or the antirealist may add on certain methodological strictures, pointing a wary finger at some particular aspects of science (e.g., explanations or laws). Typically, the antirealist will make several additions to the core.

What then of the realist, what does he add to his core acceptance of the results of science as really true? My colleague, Charles Chastain, suggested what I think is the most graphic way of stating the answer—namely, that what the realist adds on is a desk-thumping, foot-stamping shout of "Really!" So, when the realist and antirealist agree, say, that there really are electrons and that they really carry a unit negative charge and really do have a small mass (of about 9.1×10^{-28} grams), what the realist wants to add is the emphasis that all this is really so. "There really are electrons, really!" This typical realist emphasis serves both a negative and a positive function. Negatively, it is meant to deny the additions that the antirealist would make to that core acceptance which both parties share. The realist wants to deny, for example, the phenomenalistic reduction of concepts or the pragmatic conception of truth. The realist thinks that these addenda take away from the substantiality of the accepted claims to truth or existence. "No," he says, "they *really* exist, and not in just your diminished antirealist sense." Positively, the realist wants to explain the robust sense in which *he* takes these claims to truth or existence, namely, as claims about reality—what is really, really the case. The full-blown version of this involves the conception of truth as correspondence with the world, and the surrogate use of approximate truth as near-correspondence . . .

It seems to me that when we contrast the realist and the antirealist in terms of what they each want to add to the core position, a third alternative emerges—and an attractive one at that. It is the core position itself, *and all by itself.* If I am correct in thinking that, at heart, the grip of realism only extends to the homely connection of everyday truths with scientific truths, and that good sense dictates our acceptance of the one on the same basis as our acceptance of the other, then the homely line makes the core position, all by itself, a compelling one, one that we ought to take to heart. Let us try to do so, and to see whether it constitutes a philosophy, and an attitude toward science, that we can live by.

The core position is neither realist nor antirealist; it mediates between the two. It would be nice to have a name for that position, but it would be a shame to appropriate another "ism" on its behalf, for then it would appear to be just one of the many contenders for ontological allegiance. I think it is not just one of that crowd but rather, as the homely line behind it suggests, it is for commonsense epistemology—the natural ontological attitude. Thus, let me introduce the acronym *NOA* (pronounced as in "Noah"), for *natural ontological attitude*, and, henceforth, refer to the core position under that designation.

To begin showing how NOA makes for an adequate philosophical stance toward science, let us see what it has to say about ontology. When NOA counsels us to accept the results of science as true, I take it that we are to treat truth in the usual referential way, so that a sentence (or statement) is true just in case the entities referred to stand in the referred-to relations. Thus, NOA sanctions ordinary referential semantics and commits us, via truth, to the existence of the individuals, properties, relations, processes, and so forth referred to by the scientific statements that we accept as true. Our belief in their existence will be just as strong (or weak) as our belief in the truth of the bit of science involved, and degrees of belief here, presumably, will be tutored by ordinary relations of confirmation and evidential support, subject to the usual scientific canons. In taking this referential stance, NOA is not committed to the progressivism that seems inherent in realism. For the realist, as an article of faith, sees scientific success, over the long run, as bringing us closer to the truth. His whole explanatory enterprise, using approximate truth, forces his hand in this way. But a "noaer" (pronounced "knower") is not so committed. As a scientist, say, within the context of the tradition in which he works, the noaer, of course, will believe in the existence of those entities to which his theories refer. But should the tradition change, say in the manner of the conceptual revolutions that Kuhn dubs "paradigm shifts," then nothing in NOA dictates that the change be assimilated as being progressive, that is, as a change where we learn more accurately about *the same things*. NOA is perfectly consistent with the Kuhnian alternative, which construes such changes as wholesale changes of reference. Unlike the realist, adherents to NOA are free to examine the facts in cases of paradigm shift, and to see whether or not a convincing case for stability of reference across paradigms can be made without superimposing on these facts a realist-progressivist superstructure. I have argued elsewhere that if one makes oneself free, as NOA enables one to do, then the facts of the matter will not usually settle the case; and that this is a good reason for thinking that cases of so-called "incommensurability" are, in fact, genuine cases where the question of stability of reference is indeterminate. NOA, I think, is the right philosophical position for such conclusions. It sanctions reference and existence claims, but it does not force the history of science into prefit molds . . .

Because of its parsimony, I think the minimalist stance represented by NOA marks a revolutionary approach to understanding science. It is, I would suggest, as profound in its own way as was the revolution in our conception of morality, when we came to see that founding morality on God and His Order was *also* neither legitimate nor necessary. Just as the typical theological moralist of the eighteenth century would feel bereft to read, say, the pages of [the present-day philosophical journal] *Ethics*, so I think the realist must feel similarly when NOA removes that "correspondence to the external world" for which he so longs. I too have regret for that lost paradise, and too often slip into the realist fantasy. I use my understanding of twentieth-century physics to help me firm up my convictions about NOA, and I recall some words of Mach, which I offer as a comfort and as a closing. With reference to realism, Mach writes

It has arisen in the process of immeasurable time without the intentional assistance of man. It is a process of nature, and preserved by nature. Everything that philosophy has accomplished . . . is, as compared with it, but an insignificant and ephemeral product of art. The fact is, every thinker, every philosopher, the moment he is forced to abandon his one-sided intellectual occupation . . ., immediately returns [to realism].

Nor is it the purpose of these "introductory remarks" to discredit the standpoint [of realism]. The task which we have set ourselves is simply to show why and for what purpose we hold that standpoint during most of our lives, and why and for what purpose we are . . . obliged to abandon it.

These lines are taken from Mach's *The Analysis of Sensations* (Sec. 14). I recommend that book as effective realism-therapy, a therapy that works best (as Mach suggests) when accompanied by historicophysical investigations . . . For a better philosophy, however, I recommend NOA.

Chapter Summary

Experimentation is a fundamental component of science. Just as there are numerous types of experiments, there are numerous philosophical and conceptual features of experiments and experimentation, including criteria of evaluation of experimental design (the process) and experimental results (the product). Physicist Pierre Duhem, argued that experiments always involve observation and interpretation; because of the latter, they are necessarily theory-laden. In addition, though, Duhem claimed that the very design of any experiment is theory-laden. A major philosophical concern connected to experimentation is scientific realism. The debate about scientific realism among philosophers of science is in what ways and to what extent scientific practice and scientific success must be explained by claiming that science provides a true (or approximately true) account of phenomena. There are many versions of scientific realism and many versions of criticism of scientific realism. One realist, Ian Hacking, argues that experimentation provides the strongest argument for scientific realism because scientists (must) take the entities they use as real. This view is sometimes called entity realism, as opposed to theory realism. Arthur Fine is a critic of scientific realism. He argues that scientific realism does not really have any explanatory force to account for the phenomena that science encounters and works with. Instead, he argues for what he calls the natural ontological attitude, which, he says, is not committed to the progressivism (i.e., science makes progress by and because of getting closer and closer to a single, correct account of the world) that seems inherent in realism. The natural ontological attitude is a working approach to scientific practice, in which it is assumed that scientists are accounting for actual entities in the world, but there is not necessarily a single way the world is, so there is not necessarily a single, correct account; describing things as "real" adds nothing to scientific accounts. Scientific realists, then, claim that there is a way the world is and that ultimately there is a correct scientific account of the way the world is. Science succeeds by "getting it right," that is, by describing the features of the world, which are independent of our theories and descriptions; "getting it right" is epistemological in the sense of science having a correct theory about those metaphysical features that constitute the world. Critics of realism challenge realism on both the epistemological issues (that there is one correct account of the world) and the metaphysical issues (that there is one way the world is).

CASE STUDY

Evangelista Torricelli (Air Pressure)

In the mid-1600s Evangelista Torricelli (1608–1647) performed a series of experiments related to the question of whether a vacuum could exist in nature. His experiments led him to the conclusion that there existed such a thing as the weight of air, or what we would now call air pressure. Consider what type of experiment this is, what its aim is and to what extent it satisfies the various features of a good experiment. Does this case provide greater support for a realist view over a nonrealist one?

THE PRESSURE OF THE AIR
Evangelista Torricelli

I have already called attention to the fact that there are in progress certain philosophical experiments, I do not know just what, relating to vacuum, designed not simply to make a vacuum but to make an instrument which will show the changes in the atmosphere, as it is now heavier and more gross and now lighter and more subtle. Many have said that a vacuum does not exist, others that it does exist in spite of the repugnance of nature and with difficulty; I know of no one who has said it exists without difficulty and without a resistance from nature. I argued thus: If there can be found a manifest cause from which the resistance can be derived which is felt if we try to make a vacuum, it seems to me foolish to try to attribute to vacuum those operations which follow evidently from some other cause; and so by making some very easy calculations, I found that the cause assigned by me (that is, the weight of the atmosphere) ought by itself alone to offer a greater resistance than it does when we try to produce a vacuum. I say this because a certain philosopher, seeing that he cannot escape the admission that the weight of the atmosphere causes the resistance which is felt in making a vacuum, does not say that he admits the operation of the heavy air, but persists in asserting that nature also concurs in resisting the vacuum. We live submerged at the bottom of a sea of elemental air, which by experiment undoubtedly has weight, and so much weight that the densest air in the neighborhood of the surface of the earth weighs about one four-hundredth part of the weight of water. Certain authors have observed after twilight that the vaporous and visible air rises above us to a height of fifty or fifty-four miles, but I do not think it is so much, because I can show that the vacuum ought to offer a much greater resistance that it does, unless we use the argument that the weight which Galileo assigned applies to the lowest atmosphere, where men and animals live, but that on the peaks of high mountains the air begins to be more pure and to weigh much less than the four-hundredth part of the weight of water. We have made many vessels of glass like those shown as *A* and *B* (Figure 1.) and with tubes two cubits long. These were filled with quicksilver, the open end was closed with the finger, and they were then inverted in a vessel where there was quicksilver *C*; then we saw that an empty space was formed and that nothing happened in the vessel where this space was formed; the tube between *A* and *D* remained always full to the height of a cubit and a quarter and an inch over. To show that the vessel was entirely empty, we filled the bowl with pure water up to *D* and then, raising the tube little by little, we saw that, when the opening of the tube reached the water, the quicksilver fell out of the tube and the water rushed with great violence up to the mark *E*. It is often said in explanation of the fact that the vessel *AE* stands empty and the quicksilver, although heavy, is sustained in the tube *AC*, that, as has been believed

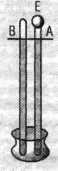

Figure 1

hitherto, the force which prevents the quicksilver from falling down, as it would naturally do, is internal to the vessel AE, arising either from the vacuum or from some exceedingly rarefied substance; but I assert that it is external and that the force comes from without. On the surface of the liquid which is in the bowl there rests the weight of a height of fifty miles of air; then what wonder is it if into the vessel CE, in which the quicksilver has no inclination and no repugnance, not even the slightest, to being there, it should enter and should rise in a column high enough to make equilibrium with the weight of the external air which forces it up? Water also in a similar tube, though a much longer one, will rise to about 18 cubits, that is, as much more than quicksilver does as quicksilver is heavier than water, so as to be in equilibrium with the same cause which acts on the one and the other. This argument is strengthened by an experiment made at the same time with the vessel A and the tube B in which the quicksilver always stood at the same horizontal line AB. This makes it almost certain that the action does not come from within; because the vessel AE, where there was more rarefied substance, should have had a greater force, attracting much more activity because of the greater rarefaction than that of the much smaller space B. I have endeavored to explain by this principle all sorts of repugnances which are felt in the various effects attributed to vacuum, and I have not yet found any with which I cannot deal successfully.

Further Reading

Cartwright, Nancy. *How the Laws of Physics Lie.* Oxford: Clarendon Press, 1983.

Cartwright, Nancy. *Nature's Capacities and Their Measurements.* Oxford: Oxford University Press, 1989.

Churchland, Paul and Clifford Hooker (eds.). *Images of Science: Essays on Realism and Empiricism.* Chicago: University of Chicago Press, 1985.

Fine, Arthur. *The Shaky Game: Einstein, Realism, and the Quantum Theory, 2nd edition.* Chicago: University of Chicago Press, 1996.

Franklin, Allan. *The Neglect of Experiment.* Cambridge: Cambridge University Press, 1986.

Galison, Peter. *How Experiments End.* Chicago: University of Chicago Press, 1987.

Hacking, Ian. *Representing and Intervening.* Cambridge: Cambridge University Press, 1983.

Kitcher, Philip. *The Advancement of Science.* Oxford: Oxford University Press, 1993.

Latour, Bruno and Stephan Woolgar. *Laboratory Life.* Princeton: Princeton University Press, 1986.

Leplin, Jarrett (ed.). *Scientific Realism.* Berkeley: University of California Press, 1984.

Sorensen, Roy A. *Thought Experiments.* Oxford: Oxford University Press, 1992.

van Fraassen, Bas. *The Scientific Image.* Oxford: Clarendon Press, 1980.

CHAPTER FOUR

Theories and Models

IN THIS CHAPTER, WE WILL

- Identify some metaphysical, epistemological, and axiological aspects of scientific theories and models
- Examine claims about the nature and value of scientific theory
- Consider the relationship between theory and models as well as the nature of models

In 2002 the school board in Cobb County, Georgia (a suburb of Atlanta), adopted a policy to require, for science textbooks used in its school district, that stickers be added to those books saying, "Evolution is a theory, not a fact." The unstated, but clearly intended implication, is that evolution is *merely* a theory. In Chapter Thirteen we will look much more closely at the issue of evolutionary theory and the broader issue of the relationship between science and religion. Here, however, the focus will be on philosophical issues related to the nature of scientific theories and models. What is it about theories and models that make it seem reasonable to some people to treat them as tentative or unreliable or even simple guesswork?

Theories

What is a scientific theory? In a moment we will look at various definitions of them, but, first, we should note that the word "theory" is usually contrasted with a number of different terms. As we just noted above, "theory" is sometimes contrasted with "fact." Even without a distinct definition of either term, we know that when this contrast is being made, the point is that facts are definite, proven knowledge or information, whereas theories are not (they are merely theories). Although it is not necessarily implied here that theories are somewhat negative, they certainly are not treated with the positive connotation of (proven) facts; it is reasonable to challenge theories, but not so (or less so) for facts. On a more positive spin, however, "theory" is also contrasted with "guess." That is, simply guessing about some phenomenon is not at all the same thing as having a theory about it. Surely, however tentative a theory might be, it is not simply guesswork.

We distinguish "theory" from other terms, too. For example, we contrast "theory" with "assumption." Although a theory might serve among assumptions we have about some phenomenon, clearly a theory is not simply an assumption. Likewise, "theory" is more inclusive and encompassing than "hypothesis." A hypothesis—at least, a good, testable one—is fairly precise and particular. A theory, on the other hand, is broader than that; we do not have theories about one particular phenomenon. On the other end of the spectrum, "theory" is narrower than, say, "world view." The point, of course, is not that the word "theory" is vague or means whatever anyone wants it to mean, but that we use that word in various contexts and usually to contrast it with some other notion.

The variability of the term "theory" can be seen with the different senses of it that are found among the different sciences. Consider these various definitions of the word "theory":

- (1) A speculative plan; (2) a formulation of underlying principles of certain observed phenomena, which has been verified to some degree; (3) the principles of an art or science rather than its practices (from Webster's Dictionary).
- A supposition or an assumption based on certain evidence or observations but lacking scientific proof (from a medical dictionary).
- A system of assumptions, accepted principles and rules of procedure devised to analyze, predict, or otherwise explain the nature or behavior of a specific set of phenomena (from an occupational therapy textbook).
- A statement that organizes a set of concepts in a meaningful way by explaining the relationship between them (from a sociology textbook).

- An explanation of the general principles of certain phenomena with considerable evidence or facts to support it (from a chemistry textbook).
- A scientific statement based on experiments that verify a hypothesis; the usual last step in scientific procedure (from a zoology textbook).

These various definitions cover quite a range of conceptions of what a theory is. A speculative plan is a far cry from a statement that organizes a set of concepts in a meaningful way by explaining the relationship between them. Although each of these definitions differs from the others, there are some common features that emerge: theories (at least scientific theories) relate to observation and evidence; theories are principled, in the sense that they are generalized statements or conceptions rather than specific particular claims and hypotheses; theories have the function of explaining, predicting, verifying, and so on. These different features certainly apply to the "big" scientific theories that scientists employ and refer to. For example, evolutionary theory is said to encompass lots of specific phenomena and information and provide a basis for predicting future observations, as well as give a principled explanation for the observed phenomena. In addition, as a theory, it is not simply dreamed up by someone to account for phenomena, but is closely aligned with evidence and facts. Likewise, the Newtonian theory of motion and gravitation was much more than simple guesswork and far broader than a simple hypothesis or assumption. It allowed many instances of phenomena and many types of phenomena to be accounted for with the same underlying physical principles.

Although there might not be a single definition of "theory" that is accepted by all (or even nearly all) scientists, there are normative features of theories that are widely accepted. That is to say, there are widely accepted criteria for what counts as a good scientific theory. For example, a theory should be *extensive*, or correlate a large amount of phenomena. Plate tectonics gave an account of not only of why mountain ranges are where they are but also why earthquakes occur where they do. In a word, the theory extends to a vast array of phenomena.

A second criterion of a good scientific theory is that it is *fecund*, or fruitful. In other words, a good theory should stimulate and generate new questions and new research; it not only accounts for information we are already aware of but also it is forward looking in the sense of nudging us toward further information. Plate tectonics led to new questions about the geochemical structure of continental shelves versus the geochemical structure of the seafloor.

A third criterion of a good scientific theory is that it is *predictive and explanatory*. Theories do not simply describe phenomena that we encounter, but give a basis for making predictions and provide a basis for explaining those phenomena that we encounter. As we will see in Chapter Five, there are a number of conceptions of what it means to provide an explanation (and prediction), but the point here is that whatever model of explanation we embrace, theories provide explanations and, indeed, a basis for particular explanations. For example, plate tectonics gives an explanation for why mountain ranges are where they are (and tend to be along the edges of continents); it is because mountain ranges emerge where plates collide, resulting in the uplift of parts of the earth's surface. This also provides for prediction, say, of where earthquake zones are likely to be.

Another criterion for a good scientific theory is *simplicity*. That is to say, everything being equal, a simpler theory is better than a more complex theory. Phenomena, of course, can be quite complex and so can a good account of those phenomena. Simplicity in and of itself, then, is not the crucial point here. Rather, if two different theories can account for the same phenomena, the simpler theory is preferable to the more complicated theory. One of the reasons that Newton's theory of motion and gravitation was seen as so impressive is that with just a few basic laws, he could account for many phenomena. Along with simplicity, another criterion of a good scientific theory is *plasticity*, or the modifiability of a theory to accommodate new information. Evolutionary theory, for instance, as propounded by Charles Darwin was committed to gradualism, that is, the changes in species as a result of many, small, gradual modifications in the features of organisms. Later information suggested that some species changes might be much more accelerated and not so gradual, after all. Darwinian evolutionary theory could easily accommodate this new information without abandoning its fundamental core.

Yet another criterion of a good scientific theory is that it is *coherent*. This means that the theory is internally consistent—it does not contradict itself—and also that it is externally consistent—it coheres with other established facts, laws, and theories. As with simplicity, this criterion is not crucial, since some good theories do in fact run counter to what is taken at the time to be established knowledge. Evolutionary theory, for example, was thought at the start of the 20th century to be in conflict with the prevailing views from physics about the age of the earth. (The prevailing view turned out to be mistaken!)

Finally, many scientists take a criterion of a good scientific theory to be that the theory is *quantitative*. In other words, the content of the theory should be essentially expressible in quantitative, mathematical formulae. Though it is not obvious that all scientific theories are essentially expressible in this way, it is usually assumed that the more quantitative a theory is, the better it is.

Now, the point of all of this is that there are widely accepted features of scientific theories that certainly point to them as far more important than simple guesswork and far broader in scope than hypotheses and far more integrative and comprehensive than facts. In addition, as you have probably already determined, there are metaphysical elements of theories (what they are; how they differ from hypotheses, and so on), epistemological elements (how they function; what they do; how they are knowledge-producing), and axiological elements (why they matter in science; what constitutes good theory).

In the following reading, Norman Campbell fleshes out the nature of scientific theory. He argues that theories are closely related to, though distinct from, scientific laws. Theories, he says, explain laws—and, so, this indicates that theories are also closely related to, though distinct from, explanations. (We will look much more closely at various notions of scientific explanation in the next chapter.) Campbell argues that how theories explain laws is by showing that the laws are deducible from the (broader and more inclusive) theories. In large part the explanatory power of theories is a result of "translating" the information from the laws into more familiar contexts, by taking what we already know and showing that the data from the laws in question are instances of or analogs of this already-known general knowledge. In addition, and this is crucial for the value and power of a theory, a theory provides predictability. It is the vehicle by which we can formulate testable hypotheses about what we do not yet know and, hence, provide an extension of our present base of knowledge. Without predictability, we have only descriptions and explanations, but not full-fledged theory. Finally, the power of theories is that they display a commitment to the reality of the objects and phenomena talked about in the theories (and in the laws explained by the theories). As he says, if a theory about gases is true and the behavior of gases is explained by treating them as collections of molecules, then the theory explains because it correctly describes actual behavior of actual things (molecules). Here, then, is Campbell:

WHAT IS SCIENCE?
Norman Campbell

What is a Theory?

How then does science explain laws? It explains them by means of "theories," which are not laws, although closely related to laws. We will proceed at once to learn what a theory is, and how it explains laws . . . A great many laws are known, concerning the physical properties of all gases; air, coal-gas, hydrogen and other gases, differ in their chemical properties, but resemble each other in obeying these laws. Two of these laws state how the pressure, exerted by a given quantity of gas on its containing vessel, varies with the volume of the vessel, and with the temperature of the gas. Boyle's Law states that the pressure is inversely proportional to the volume, so that if the volume is halved the pressure is doubled; Gay-Lussac's states that, at a constant volume, the pressure increases proportionally to the temperature (if a certain scale of temperature is adopted, slightly different from that in common use). Other laws state the relation between the pressure of the gas and its power of conducting heat and so on. All these laws are "explained" by a doctrine known as the Dynamical Theory of Gases, which was proposed early in the [19th] century and is accepted universally today. According to this theory, a gas consists of an immense number of very small particles, called molecules, flying about in all directions, colliding with each other and with the wall of the containing vessel; the speed of the flight of these molecules increases with the temperature; their impacts on the walls of the vessel tend to force the walls outwards and represent the pressure on them; and by their motion, heat is conveyed from one part of the gas to another in the manner called *conduction*.

When it is said that this theory explains the laws of gases, two things are meant. The first is that if we assume the theory to be true we can prove that the laws that are to be explained are true. The molecules are supposed to be similar to rigid particles, such as marbles or grains of sand; we know from the general laws of dynamics (the science which studies how bodies move under forces) what will be the effect on the motions of the particles of their collisions with each other and with the walls; and we know from the same laws how great will be the pressure exerted on the walls of the vessel by the impacts of a given number of particles of given mass moving with given speed. We can show that particles such as are imagined by the theory, moving with the speed attributed to them, would exert the pressure that the gas actually exerts, and that this pressure would vary with the volume of the vessel and with the temperature in the manner described in Boyle's and Gay-Lussac's Laws. In other words, from the theory we can deduce the laws.

This is certainly one thing that we mean when we say that the theory explains the laws; if the laws could not be deduced from the theory, the theory would not explain the laws and the theory would not be true. But this cannot be all that we mean. For if it were, clearly any other theory from which the laws could be deduced, would be equally an explanation and would be equally true. But there is an indefinite number of "theories" from which the laws could be deduced; it is a mere logical exercise to find one set of propositions from which another set will follow; and anyone could invent in a few hours twenty such theories. For instance, that the two propositions (1) that the pressure of a gas increases as the temperature increases (2) that it increases as the volume decreases, can be deduced from the single proposition that the pressure increases with the increase of temperature and decrease of volume. But of course the single proposition does not explain the two others; it merely states them in other words. But that is just what logical deduction consists of; to deduce a conclusion from premises is simply to state the premises in different words, though the words are sometimes so different as to give quite a different impression. If all that we required of a theory was that laws could be deduced from it, there would be no difference between a theory which merely expressed the laws in different words without adding anything significant and a theory which, like the example we are considering, does undoubtedly add something significant.

It is clear that when we say the theory explains the laws we mean something additional to this mere logical deduction; the deduction is necessary to the truth of the theory, but it is not sufficient. What else do we require? I think the best answer we can give is that, in order that a theory may explain, we require it—to explain! We require that it shall add to our ideas, and that the ideas which it adds to shall be acceptable. The reader will probably feel that this is true of the explanation of the properties of gases offered by the dynamical theory. Even if he did not know (and probably does not know apart from what I have just told him) that the laws can be deduced from the theory, he would feel that the mere introduction of moving particles and the suggestion that the properties of a gas can be represented as due to their motion would afford some explanation of those properties. They would afford some explanation, even if the laws could not be deduced correctly; they would then offer an explanation, although the explanation would not be true.

And this is, I believe, the reason why he would feel thus. Only those who have practiced experimental physics, know anything by actual experience about the laws of gases; they are not things which force themselves on our attention in common life, and even those who are most familiar with them never think of them out of working hours. On the other hand, the behavior of moving solid bodies is familiar to every one; every one knows roughly what will happen when such bodies collide with each other or with a solid wall, though they may not know the exact dynamical laws involved in such reactions. In our common life we are continually encountering moving bodies, and noticing their reactions;

indeed, if the reader thinks about it, he will realize that whenever we do anything which affects the external world, or whenever we are passively affected by it, a moving body is somehow involved in the transaction. Movement is just the most familiar thing in the world; it is through motion that everything and anything happens. And so by tracing a relation between the unfamiliar changes which gases undergo when their temperature or volume is altered, and the extremely familiar changes which accompany the notions and mutual reactions of solid bodies, we are rendering the former more intelligible; we are explaining them . . . .

Difference between Theories and Laws

It was stated before that it has been usually held that the explanation of laws consists in showing that they are particular examples of more general laws. If this view were applied to the example under discussion, it might be urged that the dynamical theory explains the properties of gases because it shows that they are particular examples of the laws of dynamics; the properties of gases are explained because they are shown to be the consequences of the subjection of the molecules, of which the gases consist, to the general laws of all moving bodies. Here, it might be said, is the clearest possible instance of explanation by generalization, a simple extension of the process involved in the discovery of laws.

But, against this view, it must be pointed out that the most important feature of the theory is not that it states that molecules are subject to dynamic laws, but that which states that there are such things as molecules, and that gases are made up of them. It is that feature of the theory which makes it a real explanation. Now this part of the theory is not a particular instance of any more general law; indeed it is not a law or anything that could be an instance of a law . . .

We conclude therefore—and the conclusion is vital to the view of science presented here—that a theory is not a law, and consequently, that the explanation afforded by a theory cannot simply be the explanation by generalization which consists in the exhibition of one law as a particular instance of another. It does not follow that theories have nothing to do with laws, and that it is immaterial for the theory that the laws of dynamics are true, and of very great generality. We shall see presently that this feature is of great importance. But it does not involve that the theory is itself a law.

The Value of Theories

After this protest against a dangerous misunderstanding, let us return and develop further our view of theories. So far the truth of a theory has been based on two grounds; first, that the laws to be explained can be deduced from it; second, that it really explains in the sense that has been indicated. But actually there is in addition, a third test of the truth of a theory, which is of great importance; a true theory will not only explain adequately the laws that it was introduced to explain; it will also predict and explain in advance laws which were unknown before. All the chief theories in science (or at least in physics) have satisfied this test; they have all led directly to the discovery of new laws which were unsuspected before the theory was proposed.

It is easy to see how a theory may predict new laws. The theory, if it is worthy of consideration at all, will be such that the old laws can be deduced from it. It may easily be found on examination that not only these laws, but others also can be deduced from it; so far as the theory is concerned, these others differ in no way from the known laws, and if the theory is to be true, these laws that are consequences of it must be true. As a matter of fact, it is seldom that a theory, *exactly* in its original form, predicts any laws except those that it was proposed to explain; but a very small and extremely natural development of it may make it predict new laws. Thus, to take our example, in order to explain the laws (Boyle's and Gay-Lussac's) to which the theory was originally applied, it is unnecessary to make any assumption about the size of the molecules; those laws can be deduced from the theory whatever that size (so long as it is below a certain limit) and the assumption was at first made for simplicity that the molecules were mathematical points without any size at all. But obviously it was more natural to assume that the molecules, though extremely small, have some size and once that assumption is made, laws are predicted which had not been discovered at the time and would never have been suspected apart from the theory. Thus, it is easy to see that, if the molecules have a definite size, the behavior of a gas, when the number of molecules contained in a given vessel is so great that the space actually occupied by the molecules is nearly the whole space in the vessel, will be very different from its behavior when there are so few molecules that practically all that space is unoccupied. This expectation, a direct result of the theory, is definitely confirmed by experiments which show a change in the laws of a gas when it is highly compressed, and all its molecules forced into a small volume.

This test of predicting new and true laws is always applied to any theory when it is proposed. The first thing we do when anyone proposes a theory to explain laws, is to try to deduce from the theory, or from some slight but very natural development of it, new laws, which were not taken into consideration in the formulation of the theory. If we can find such laws and prove by experiment that they are true, then we feel much more confidence in the theory; if they are not true, we know that the theory is not true; but we may still believe that a relatively slight modification will restore its value. It is in this way that most new laws are actually suggested . . . almost all advances in the formulation of new laws follow on the invention of theories to explain the old laws . . .

The Analogies of Theories

. . . The explanation offered by a theory (that is to say, the part of the theory which does not depend simply on the deduction from it of the laws to be explained) is always based on analogy, and the system with which an analogy is traced is always one of which the laws are known; it is always one of those systems which form part of that external world of which the subject-matter of science consists. The theory always explains laws by showing that if we imagine that the system to which those laws apply consists in some way of other systems to which some other known laws apply, then the laws can be deduced from the theory. Thus our theory of gases explains the laws of gases on the analogy of a system subject to dynamical laws. The theory of evolution explains the laws involved in the assertion that there are such-and-such living beings by supposing that these living beings are the descendents of others whose characters have been modified by reaction to their surroundings in a manner which is described by laws applicable to living beings at the present day. Again the immense theory involved in the whole science of geology explains the structure of the earth as it exists today by supposing that this structure is the result of the age-long operation of influences, the action of which is described by laws observable in modern conditions. In each case the "explaining" system is supposed to operate according to known laws, but it is not a system of which those laws can be asserted as laws, because it is, by the very supposition underlying the theory, one which could never be observed—either because it is too small or too remote in the past or for some similar reason—and therefore does not form part of the proper subject-matter of science . . .

Are Theories Real?

And here we come to our last question. I have been at pains to distinguish theories from laws, and to insist that theories are not laws. But if that contention is true, are not theories deprived of much of their value? Laws, it may be said, are statements about real things, about real substances (such as iron), about real objects (such as the earth or the planets or existing living beings). Laws are valuable because they tell us the properties of these real objects. But if theories are not laws, and if the statements they make are about things than cannot ever be the subject of laws, do they tell us about anything real? Are the molecules (by means of which we explain the properties of gases) or the countless generations of unknown animals and plants (by means of which we explain the connections between known animals and plants) or the forces on the planets (by means of which we explain their orbit)—are these molecules and animals and forces mere products of our fantasy, or are they just as real as the gases and the animals the laws of which they are led to explain? Are theories merely explanatory, are they like the fairy tales by means of which our ancestors explained to themselves the world about them, are they like the tales we often tell to our children with the same object of explanation, or are they truly solid fact about the real things of the world? . . .

I should reply to the questioner by asking him what he means by "real" and why he is so sure that a piece of iron, or a dog, is a real object. And the answer that I should suggest to him is that he calls these things real because they are necessary to make the world intelligible to him; and that it is because they are necessary to make the world intelligible to him that he resents so strongly (as he will if he is a plain man) the suggestions that some philosophers have made that these things are not real. It is true that these suggestions are often not interpreted rightly, and that what the philosophers propose is not so absurd as appears at first sight; but the fact remains that these ideals are of supreme importance to him in making the world intelligible, and that he dislikes the notion that they are in any sense less valuable than other ideas which, for him at least, do not make the world so intelligible. The invariable associations which are implied by the use of the ideas "iron" and "dog" are extremely important in all his practical life; it is extremely important for him that a certain hardness and strength and density and so on are invariably associated in the manner which we assert when we say that there is iron, and that a certain form and sound and behavior are invariably associated in the way that we assert when we say that there are dogs. When the plain man says iron and dogs are real objects he means (I suggest) to assert that there are such invariable associations, that they are extremely important, and that they are rendered intelligible only by the assertion that there is iron and there are dogs.

If we accept this view it is clear that we must answer in the affirmative the question from which we started. Theories are also designed to make the world intelligible to us, and they play quite as important a part as do laws in rendering it intelligible. And if anything is real that renders the world intelligible, then surely the ideas of theories—molecules and extinct animals and all the rest of it—have just as much claim to reality as the ideas of laws.

One well-known critic of Campbell's view about theories is Nancy Cartwright. We saw in the previous chapter different views related to the topic of realism. Part of Cartwright's criticisms has to do with the realism of Campbell's view on theories. But even more, she disagrees with the underlying view regarding laws and their relation to theory. In her book, *How the Laws of Physics Lie* (from which the reading on pages 112–114 is taken), she proposes what she calls a "simulacrum" view. A simulacrum is something that has the form or appearance of something else but without possessing the substance or proper qualities of that something else. (So, a scarecrow or a robot could be a simulacrum of a human.) She claims that to explain a phenomenon is to construct a model that fits the phenomenon into a theory. The fundamental laws of a theory, she says, are true of the objects *in the model*. Fundamental laws do not govern objects in reality, but in models. Models, then, have a significant role in science, including—for the present concerns—in the nature and role of theories. So, Cartwright's selection not only speaks to theories, but also serves as an introduction to looking more closely at scientific models, which we will do in the second half of this chapter.

In her reading, Cartwright states that a theory's laws do not literally match up to reality. This is because laws do not and cannot include all of the particularities of the instances that are said to be governed by those laws. For example, the law of universal gravitation is often expressed as: $F = Gm_1 \times m_2/r^2$, where F is the gravitational force (or mutual attraction) of two bodies of mass (m_1 and m_2), G is the gravitational constant (approximately 6.673×10^{-11}), and r is the distance between the centers of the two bodies of mass (m_1 and m_2). Because real bodies are extended over a certain amount of space, their mass is spread out. This is why we weigh very slightly less on a mountaintop that we do at sea level. Or, another example is the velocity of light, which varies depending upon the medium through which it travels. There are always, then, particularities that attend to every instance governed by a law. Philosophers and scientists refer to this as *ceteris paribus*, which means "other things being equal." When a *ceteris paribus* clause is invoked, that is meant to imply the absence of unusual or interfering or otherwise irrelevant conditions. A very simple example of this is that a match will ignite when it is struck, but it is assumed (that is, *ceteris paribus*) there is oxygen present or the match is not immersed in water, etc. There are always *ceteris paribus* clauses pertinent to laws, says Cartwright.

Another feature of models and laws is that they often involve idealizations. For example, they might assume frictionless planes or objects in a vacuum or objects that are not extended in space even though they have mass. Such idealizations are, of course, for that reason removed from actual experience, but they also allow underlying salient features of the phenomena (and of the model) to be highlighted and analyzed. But, again, the point here of her reading is not so much about realism or the nature of explanation—though those are important and relevant—but about models and their relation to theories. Here, then, is Cartwright:

HOW THE LAWS OF PHYSICS LIE
Nancy Cartwright

To explain a phenomenon is to find a model that fits into the basic framework of the theory and that thus allows us to derive analogues for the messy and complicated phenomenological laws which are true of it. The models serve a variety of purposes, and individual models are to be judged according to how well they serve the purpose at hand. In each case we aim to "see" the phenomenon through the mathematical framework of the theory, but for different problems there are different emphases. We may wish to calculate a particular quantity with great accuracy, or to establish its precise functional relationship to another. We may wish instead to replicate a broader range of behavior, but with less accuracy. One important thing we sometimes want to do is to lay out the causally relevant factors as realistically as possible, in both sense of "realistic." But this may well preclude treating other factors realistically. We should not be misled into thinking that the most realistic model will serve all purposes best.

In order to stress this "anti-realistic" aspect of models, I call my view of explanation a "simulacrum" account. The second definition of "simulacrum" in the *Oxford English Dictionary* says that a simulacrum is "something having merely the form or appearance of a certain thing, without possessing its substance or proper qualities." This is just what I have been urging that models in physics are like. Is a helium-neon laser really a van der Pol oscillator? Well, it is really a mix of helium and neon atoms, in about the ratio of nine to one, enclosed in a cavity with smooth walls and reflecting mirrors at both ends, and hooked up to a device to pump the neon atoms into their excited state. It is not literally a triode oscillator in a d.c. circuit. If we treat it with van der Pol's equation for a triode oscillator, we will be able to replicate a good deal of its behavior above threshold, and that is our aim. The success of the model depends on how much and how precisely it can replicate what goes on.

A model is a work of fiction. Some properties ascribed to objects in the model will be genuine properties of the objects modeled, but others will be merely properties of convenience. The term "properties of convenience" was suggested by H.P. Grice, and it is apt. Some of the properties and relations in a model will be real properties, in the sense that other objects in other situations might genuinely have them. But they are introduced into this model as a convenience, to bring the objects modeled into the range of the mathematical theory.

Not all properties of convenience will be real ones. There are the obvious idealizations of physics—infinite potentials, zero time correlations, perfectly rigid rods, and frictionless planes. But it would be a mistake to think entirely in terms of idealizations—of properties which we conceive as limiting cases, to which we can approach closer and closer in reality. For some properties are not even approached in reality. They are pure fictions.

I would want to argue that the probability distributions of classical statistical mechanics are an example. This is a very serious claim, and I only sketch my view here as an illustration. The distributions are essential to the theory—they are what the equations of the theory govern—and the theory itself is extremely powerful, for example in the detailed treatment of fluid flow. Moreover, in some simple special cases the idea of the probability distribution can be operationalized; and the tests support the distributions ascribed by the theory.

Nevertheless, I do not think these distributions are real. Statistical mechanics works in a massive number of highly differentiated and highly complex situations. In the vast majority of these it is incredible to think that there is a true probability distribution for that situation; and proofs that, for certain purposes, one distribution is as good as another, do not go any way to making it plausible that there is one at all. It is better, I think, to see these distributions as fictions, fictions that have a powerful organizing role in any case and that will not mislead us too much even should we take them to be real in the simple cases.

. . . [On] the simulacrum account, models are essential to theory. Without them there is just abstract mathematical structure, formulae with holes in them, bearing no relation to reality. Schroedinger's equation, even coupled with principles which tell what Hamiltonians to use for square-well potentials, two-body Coulomb interactions, and the like, does not constitute a theory of anything. To have a theory of the ruby laser, or of bonding in a benzene molecule, one must have models for those phenomena which tie them to descriptions in the mathematical theory. In short, on the simulacrum account the model is the theory of the phenomenon . . .

I want to focus on the details of what actually happens in concrete situations, whether these situations involve theoretical entities or not, and how these differ from what would happen if even the best of our fundamental laws played out their consequences rigorously. In fact, the simulacrum account makes the stronger claim: it usually does not make sense to talk of the fundamental laws of nature playing out their consequences in reality. For the kind of antecedent situations that fall under the fundamental laws are generally the fictional situations of a model, prepared for the needs of the theory, and not the blousy situations of reality. I do not mean that there could never be situations to which the fundamental laws apply. That is only precluded if the theory employs properties or arrangements which are pure fictions, as I think classical statistical mechanics does. One may occur by accident, or, more likely, we may be able to construct one in a very carefully controlled experiment, but nature is generally not obliging enough to supply them freely.

Let me repeat a point I have made often before. If we are going to argue from the success of theory to the truth of theoretical laws, we have better have a large number and a wide variety of cases. A handful of careful experiments will not do; what lead to conviction is the widespread application of theory, the application to lasers, and to transistors, and to tens of thousands of other real devices. Realists need these examples, application after application, to make their case. But these examples do not have the right structure to support the realist thesis. For the laws do not literally apply to them.

Models

As with theories, scientific models are a means by which scientists explore and account for phenomena. Also, as with theories, there are a variety of characterizations of models. For example, Webster's Dictionary gives the following definitions of "model": (1) a small representation of a planned or existing object; (2) a person or a thing regarded as a standard of excellence to be imitated; (3) a style or design; (4) a structural isomorphism to theories or objects. Although these four different characterizations are quite distinct, and although the last one seems on the surface to be the most directly connected to scientific models, all four actually point to salient features of scientific models. The first definition emphasizes that models are representations of something. That is, we construct and use models in science usually for two purposes, *exploratory* and *explanatory*. Sometimes we construct and use models in order to have a basis for generating focused questions and avenues for future research. This exploratory purpose or function is often referred to as the heuristic function of models. In addition to this function, models are also constructed and used to evaluate or give a basis for explaining phenomena. In either case, exploratory or explanatory, we construct and use models to represent some set of phenomena. How we represent those phenomena is different depending upon the type of model we use. Some models are mathematical, whereas some are physical. Usually the representation is some sort of *isomorphism* ("same shape") between features of the phenomena and features of the model, which is the emphasis of the fourth definition above. So, for instance, those little plastic models of cars represent real cars by resembling real cars at a smaller scale, at least resembling them in ways that matter to us. So, the color of the plastic might not be so important to us in order to represent the real car, the placement of the wheels do matter. (It would be a pretty bad model of a real VW Beetle if the little plastic model had only three wheels and they were placed on top of the car.) So, displaying a one-to-one resemblance between the model and the real object, at least of those features that matter to us, is fundamental to the representative nature of a model.

The second definition from Webster's pointed to the normative nature of models. That is to say, models reflect focused, purposive concerns that we have. In some respects, they are idealized. In other words, if we wanted a model of a VW Beetle, we would want that model to reflect the features of an "idealized" real Beetle, not one that has been smashed up or altered to look like a freakish mini-Batmobile. We often speak of a "model student" meaning one who does all of her assignments on time, is self-motivated, attends class all the time, etc. This is also pointing to the normative nature of models. Again, with respect to scientific models, what are meant here are the "idealized" and valued features of the phenomena and model at issue. Webster's third definition was that a model is a style or design. This, too, speaks to the purposive nature of models. They do not just happen; they are designed and constructed with particular purposes and object-phenomena in mind. As with theories, there are features of models that are desirable: simplicity, testability, consistency, fecundity, (perhaps) quantifiability, and so on.

So, models have metaphysical elements (they are structural representations of something beyond themselves), epistemological elements (they have a function of leading us from what we know to what we do not know, either by providing exploratory avenues or by providing explanations), and axiological elements (they are designed for particular purposes and function only against a background of what are taken as relevant features being investigated).

Above we saw that Nancy Cartwright claims that models are a crucial component for explanation in science and for relating theories and laws to phenomena. Her simulacrum account points to the significance of models in scientific practice—both in terms of exploration and explanation—but she does not analyze the nature of models in great detail. For example, there might be certain reasons for *suggesting* some particular model (or some hypothesis on the basis of some particular model) and quite different reasons for *accepting* some particular model (or some hypothesis on the basis of some particular model). This is analogous to the issues of theory *construction* and theory *evaluation*. In the following reading, however, Margaret Morrison and Mary S. Morgan do just this; that is, they analyze the nature and function of scientific models. Not dissimilar to Cartwright, they argue that models are not merely applications of theories, but are autonomous instruments of scientific investigation. Of particular importance about models is that they *represent* aspects of the world (and also of theories). There are many issues that could be addressed about the representative nature of models: what exactly gets represented; what features of the model do the representing; how do those features of the model represent features of the world (or of theories); is representation "just" a matter of resemblance; if not, what else or different is involved in representing? For example, in the early 20th century there was what was called the plum pudding model of the atom. This model was suggested by the British physicist J. J. Thomson prior to the discovery of the nucleus of the atom. Thomson suggested that the structure of the atom was much like a bowl of plum pudding, in which the plums represented electrons, randomly scattered throughout the atom (the bowl of pudding). Obviously, plums do not resemble electrons in many ways or in normally relevant ways, that is, ways that relate to why we normally care about either electrons or plums. They are not structurally like electrons and they do not really behave like electrons. Nonetheless, for the purposes of suggesting a structure of the atom, they were offered as representations of electrons. The reading by Morrison and Morgan raise some issues about representation and models in the context of other features of models. As you read the selection, consider how their views cohere or do not cohere with what Cartwright said about models:

MODELS AS MEDIATING INSTRUMENTS
Margaret Morrison and Mary S. Morgan

Models are one of the critical instruments of modern science. We know that models function in a variety of different ways within the sciences to help us learn not only about theories but also about the world. So far, however, there seems to be no systematic account of *how* they operate in both of these domains . . . One of the points we want to stress is that when one looks at examples of the different ways that models function, we see that they occupy an autonomous role in scientific work. [Here] we want to outline . . . an account of models as *autonomous agents*, and to show how they function as *instruments* of investigation. We believe there is a significant connection between the autonomy of models and their ability to function as instruments. It is precisely because models are partially independent of both theories and the world that they have this autonomous component and so can be used as instruments of exploration in both domains.

In order to make good our claim, we need to raise and answer a number of questions about models. We outline the important questions here before going on to provide detailed answers. These questions cover four basic elements in our account of models, namely how they are constructed, how they function, what they represent and how we learn from them.

Construction

What gives models their autonomy? Part of the answer lies in their construction. It is common to think that models can be derived entirely from theory or from data. However, if we look closely at the way models are constructed we can begin to see the sources of their independence. It is because they are neither one thing nor the other, neither just theory nor data, but typically involve some of both (and often additional "outside" elements), that they can mediate between theory and the world. In addressing these issues we need to isolate the nature of this partial independence and determine why it is more useful than full independence or full dependence.

Functioning

What does it mean for a model to function autonomously? Here we explore the various tasks for which models can be used. We claim that what it means for a model to function autonomously is to function like a tool or instrument. Instruments come in a variety of forms and fulfill many different functions. By its nature, an instrument or tool is independent of the thing it operates on, but it connects with it in some way. Although a hammer is separate from both the nail and the wall, it is designed to fulfill the task of connecting the nail to the wall. So too with models. They function as tools or instruments and are independent of, but mediate between things; and like tools, can often be used for many different tasks.

Representing

Why can we learn about the world and about theories from using models as instruments? To answer this we need to know what a model consists of. More specifically, we must distinguish between instruments which can be used in a purely instrumental way to effect something and instruments which can also be used as investigative devices for learning something. We do not learn much from the hammer. But other sorts of tools (perhaps just more sophisticated ones) can help us learn things. The thermometer is an instrument of investigation; it is physically independent of a saucepan of jam, but it can be placed into the boiling jam to tell us its temperature. Scientific models work like these kinds of investigative instruments—but how? The critical difference between a simple tool, and a tool of investigation is that the latter involves some form of representation: models typically represent either some aspect of the world, or some aspect of our theories about the world, or both at once. Hence the model's representative power allows it to function not just instrumentally, but to teach us something about the thing it represents.

Learning

Although we have isolated representation as the mechanism that enables us to learn from models we still need to know *how* this learning takes place and we need to know what else is involved in a model functioning as a mediating instrument. Part of the answer comes from seeing how models are used in scientific practice. We do not learn much from looking at a model—we learn more from building the model and from manipulating it. Just as one needs to use or observe the use of a hammer in order to really understand its function, similarly, models have to be used before they will give up their secrets. In this sense, they have the quality of a technology—the power of the model only becomes apparent in the context of its use. Models function not just as a means of intervention, but also as a means of representation. It is when we manipulate the model that these combined features enable us to learn how and why our interventions work . . .

2.1 Construction

Independence in Construction

When we look for accounts of how to construct models in scientific texts we find very little on offer. There appear to be no general rules for model construction in the way that we can find detailed guidance on principles of experimental design or on methods of measurement. Some might argue that it is because modeling is a tacit skill, and has to be learnt not taught. Model building surely does involve a large amount of craft skill, but then so does designing experiments and any other part of scientific practice. This omission in scientific texts may also point to the creative element involved in model building, it is, some argue, not only a craft but also an art, and thus not susceptible to rules. We find a similar lack of advice available in philosophy of science texts. We are given definitions of models, but remarkably few accounts of how they are constructed . . . [There is] an explicit account of model construction by Marcel Boumans who argues that models are built by a process of choosing and integrating a set of items which are considered relevant for a particular task. In order to build a mathematical model of the business cycle, the economists that he studied typically began by bringing together some bits of theories, some bits of empirical evidence, a mathematical formalism and a metaphor which guided the way the model was conceived and put together. These disparate elements were integrated into a formal (mathematically expressed) system taken to provide the key relationships between a number of variables. The integration required not only the translation of the disparate elements into something of the same form (bits of mathematics), but also that they be fitted together in such a way that they could provide a solution equation which represents the path of the business cycle.

. . . A similar situation arises in Mauricio Suárez's discussion of the London brothers' model of superconductivity. They were able to construct an equation for the superconducting current that accounted for an effect that could not be accommodated in the existing theory. Most importantly, the London equation was not derived from electromagnetic theory, nor was it arrived at by simply adjusting parameters in the theory governing superconductors. Instead, the new equation emerged as a result of a completely new conceptualization of superconductivity that was supplied by the model. So, not only was the model constructed without the aid of theory, but it became the impetus for a new theoretical understanding of the phenomena.

The lesson we want to draw from these accounts is that models, by virtue of their construction, embody an element of independence from both theory and data (or phenomena); it is because they are made up from a *mixture* of elements, including those from outside the original domain of investigation, that they maintain this partially independent status.

. . . [T]heory does not provide us with an algorithm from which the model is constructed and by which all modeling decisions are determined. As a matter of practice, modeling always involves certain simplifications and approximations which have to be decided independently of the theoretical requirements or of data conditions . . . .

2.2 Function

Because model construction proceeds in part independently of theory and data, models can have a life of their own and occupy a unique place in the production of scientific knowledge. Part of what it means to situate models in this way involves giving an account of what they do—how it is that they can function autonomously and what advantages that autonomy provides in investigating both theories and the world. One of our principle claims is that the autonomy of models allows us to characterize them as instruments. And, just as there are many different kinds of instruments, models can function as instruments in a variety of ways.

Models in Theory Construction and Exploration
One of the most obvious uses of models is to aid in theory construction. Just as we use tools as instruments to build things, we use models as instruments to build theories . . . [In addition, models] are often used as instruments for exploring or experimenting on a theory that is already in place. There are several ways in which this can occur; for instance, we can use a model to correct a theory. Sir George Francis FitzGerald, a nineteenth-century British physicist, built mechanical models of the aether out of pulleys and rubber bands and used these models to correct Maxwell's electromagnetic theory. The models were thought to represent particular mechanical processes that must occur in the aether in order for a field theoretic account of electrodynamics to be possible. When processes in the model were not found in the theory, the latter was used as the basis of correction for the former . . .

In other cases, models are used to explore the implications of theories in concrete situations. This is one way to understand the role of the twentieth-century conception of "rational economic man." This idealized and highly simplified characterization of real economic behavior has been widely used in economists' microeconomic theories as a tool to explore the theoretical implications of the most single-minded economizing behavior. More recently this "model man" has been used as a device for benchmarking the results from experimental economics. This led to an explosion of theories accounting for the divergence between the observed behavior of real people in experimental situations and that predicted from the theory of such a model man in the same situation . . . .

2.3 Representation

The first question we need to ask is how an instrument can represent. We can think of a thermometer representing in a way that includes not simply the measurement of temperature but the representation of the rise and fall in temperature through the rise and fall of the mercury in the column. Although the thermometer is not a model, the model as an instrument can also incorporate a representational capacity. Again, this arises because of the model's relation to theory or through its relation to the world or to both.

Representing the World, Representing Theory

Above we saw the importance of maintaining a partial independence of the model from both theory and the world; but, just as partial independence is required to achieve a level of autonomy so too a *relation* to at least one domain is necessary for the model to have any representative function whatsoever. In some cases the model may, in the first instance, bear its closest or strongest relation to theory. For example, Morrison's case of the model of a pendulum functions specifically as a model of a theory—Newtonian mechanics—that describes a certain kind of motion. In other words, the pendulum model is an instance of harmonic motion. Recall that we need the model because Newton's force laws alone do not give us an adequate description of how a physical pendulum (an object in the world) behaves. The pendulum model represents certain kinds of motion that are both described by the theory and produced by the real pendulum. To that extent, it is also a model of the physical object. Fisher's mechanical balance model (discussed by Morgan) provided a representation of the theory of the monetary system. This model enabled him to explore theoretical aspects of the dynamic adjustment processes in the monetary economy and the phenomena of the business cycle in a way that the existing theoretical representation (the equation of exchange) did not allow.

Alternatively, the model-world representation may be the more prominent one. The early statistical business barometers, constructed to represent (in graphic form) the path of real-world economic activity through time, were used to help determine the empirical relationships between various elements in the economy and to forecast the turning points in that particular economy's cycle. In contrasting cases, such model-world representations may be used to explore theory by extending its basic structure or developing a new theoretical framework. Such was the case with the nineteenth-century mechanical aether models of Kelvin and FitzGerald discussed above. Recall that their function was to represent dynamical relations that occurred in the aether, and based on the workings of the model FitzGerald was able to make corrections to Maxwell's field equations. In the previous section we saw how manipulating these models had the status of experiment. This was possible only because the model itself was taken as a *representation* of aether . . .

As we can see from the examples above, the idea of representation used here is not the traditional one common in the philosophy of science; in other words, we have not used the notion of "representing" to apply only to cases where there exists a kind of mirroring of a phenomenon, system or theory by a model. Instead, a representation is seen as a kind of rendering—a partial representation that either abstracts from, or translates into another form, the real nature of the system or theory, or one that is capable of embodying only a portion of a system . . . .

2.4 Learning

Learning from Construction

Modeling allows for the possibility of learning at two points in the process. The first is in constructing the model. As we have pointed out, there are no rules for model building and so the very activity of construction creates an opportunity to learn: what will fit together and how? Perhaps this is why modeling is considered in many circles an art or craft; it does not necessarily involve the most sophisticated mathematics or require extensive knowledge of every aspect of the system. It does seem to require acquired skills in choosing the parts and fitting them together, but it is wise to acknowledge that some people are good model builders, just as some people are good experimentalists.

Models as Technologies for Investigation

The second stage where learning takes place is in using the model. Models can fulfill many functions as we have seen; but they generally perform these functions not by being built, but by being used. Models are not passive instruments, they must be put to work, used, or manipulated. So, we focus here on a second, more public, aspect of learning from models, and one which might be considered more generic. Because there are many more people who use models than who construct them we need some sense of how "learning from using" takes place.

Models may be physical objects, mathematical structures, diagrams, computer programs or whatever, but they all act as a form of instrument for investigating the world, our theories, or even other models. They combine three particular characteristics which enable us to talk of models as a technology, the features of which have been outlined in previous sections of this essay. To briefly recap: first, model construction involves a partial independence from theories and the world but also a partial dependence on them both. Secondly, models can function autonomously in a variety of ways to explore theories and the world. Thirdly, models represent either aspects of our theories, or aspects of the world, or more typically aspects of both at once. When we use or manipulate a model, its power as a technology becomes apparent: we make use of these characteristics of partial independence, functional autonomy and representation to learn something from the manipulation . . . .

We showed earlier (in section 2.2) how models function as a technology that allows us to explore, build and apply theories, to structure and make measurements, and to make things work in the world. It is in the process of using these technologies to interrogate the world or our theory that learning takes place. Again, the pendulum case is a classic example. The model represents, in its details, both the theory and a real world pendulum (yet is partially independent of both), and it functions as an autonomous instrument which allows us to make the correct calculations for measurements to find out a particular piece of information about the world.

The general way of characterizing and understanding this second way of "learning from using" a model is that models are manipulated to teach us things about themselves. When we build a model, we create a mind of representative structure. But, when we manipulate the model, or calculate things within the model, we learn, in the first instance, about the model world—the situation depicted by the model . . . .

Conclusion

We have argued . . . that scientific models have certain features which enable us to treat them as a technology. They provide us with a tool for investigation, giving the user the potential to learn about the world or about theories or both. Because of their characteristics of autonomy and representational power, and their ability to effect a relation between scientific theories and the world, they can act as powerful agents in the learning process. That is to say, models are both a means to and a source of knowledge. This accounts for their broad applicability, and the extensive use of models in modern science.

Our account shows the range of functions and variety of ways in which models can be brought to bear in problem-solving situations. Indeed, our goal is to stress the significance of this point especially in light of the rather limited ways that models have, up to now, been characterized in the philosophical literature. They have been portrayed narrowly as a means for applying theory, and their construction was most often described either in terms of "theory simplification" or derivation from an existing theoretical structure. These earlier views gave not only a limited, but in many cases an inaccurate, account of the role of models in scientific investigation. Our view of models as mediating instruments . . . go some way toward correcting the problem and filling a lacuna in the existing literature.

A virtue of our account is that it shows how and why models function as a separate tool amongst the arsenal of available scientific methods. The implication of our investigations is that models should no longer be treated as subordinate to theory and data in the production of knowledge. Models join with measuring instruments, experiments, theories and data as one of the essential ingredients in the practice of science. No longer should they be seen just as "preliminary theories" in physics, nor as a sign of the impossibility of making economics a "proper" science.

Chapter Summary

Theories and models are both significant elements of science. They are used to account for phenomena that scientists investigate, both in terms of exploring phenomena and in terms of explaining phenomena. Theories are broader and more inclusive than models, though many of the criteria for assessing theories are also relevant for assessing models: simplicity, fecundity, consistency, predictive and explanatory power, and so on. Norman Campbell argues that theories are the vehicle for explaining laws of nature. Theories explain by both showing laws are deducible from them and by making the features of laws instances of broader, already-understood features of the world that the theory has accounted for. In addition, theories have predictive power and also generate and reflect a commitment to the reality of the phenomena explained. Nancy Cartwright disagrees. She claims that to explain a phenomenon is to construct a model that fits the phenomenon into a theory. The fundamental laws of a theory, she says, are true of the objects *in the model.* Fundamental laws do not govern objects in reality, but in models. Models have a significant role in science, including—for the present concerns—in the nature and role of theories. Models, then, not theories, serve the primary explanatory, as well as exploratory, function in science. Far from a commitment to realism and the reality of phenomena, models, she says, are fictions. Margaret Morrison and Mary S. Morgan extend Cartwright's analysis and detail various functions and features of models, including their construction, functions, representational power, and possibility of learning. Models, they claim, function as autonomous agents (that is, separable from theories and other aspects of science) and as instruments of investigation. Like Cartwright, they see models as the primary vehicle for both scientific exploration and explanation.

CASE STUDY

Rene Descartes

In the 1600s, Rene Descartes (1596–1650) was renowned as a philosopher, scientist, and mathematician. In his work, Principles of Philosophy, *he postulated an account of the physical world that was thoroughly materialistic. The structure and the features of the world were ultimately to be accounted for in terms of material bodies in motion. With respect to his account of the motions of the planets and heavenly bodies, he claimed that space was not empty, but was filled with a subtle material and that planets were carried along by vortices of this subtle material. As a result, historians of science often speak of Descartes' account as the* vortex theory *or* vortex model. *Though Isaac Newton wrote several decades after Descartes, his theory—namely that gravity, as a force, accounted for the orbits of the planets—was discarded by Descartes as violating a strong commitment to materialism. This is because gravity was seen as* action at a distance. *That is, Descartes rejected the notion that one body could be causally affected by another body that was not contiguous with it. Action at a distance, and any view of gravity that went along with that notion, was labeled by Descartes (and many others) as an "occult quality," incapable of truly accounting for any phenomenon and, indeed, an ad hoc claim that substituted for any genuine materialistic account. Of course, history favored Newton in the long run, but Descartes' account was taken as a serious challenge by many at the time. Below are selections from Descartes to account for the motions of bodies (particularly planets). Consider what features of theories and models are exhibited here, as well as the features of good theories and models discussed earlier in this chapter and how they relate to this account.*

PRINCIPLES OF PHILOSOPHY

René Descartes

Part Two: On the Principles of Material Objects

27. That movement and rest are merely diverse modes of the body in which they are found. We are not concerned here with the action which is understood to be in whatever initiates or stops the motion of a body, but only with the body's transference and absence of transference, or rest. It is obvious that this transference cannot exist apart from the body which is moved, and that it is only a case of the body being differently inclined when it is being transported that when it is not transported, or is at rest. Thus, movement and rest are merely two diverse modes of that body.

28. That movement, properly understood, concerns only the bodies contiguous to the body which is moving. I have also added that the transference is effected *from the vicinity of those bodies contiguous to it into the vicinity of others*, and not from one place to another; because, as has been explained above, "place" can be understood in several ways, depending on our conception. However, when we take movement to be the

transference of a body from the vicinity of those contiguous to it, we cannot attribute to that moving body more than one movement at any given time; because at any given time, only a certain number of bodies can be contiguous to it . . .

37. The first law of nature: that each thing, as far as in its power, always remains in the same state; and that consequently, when it is once moved, it always continues to move . . .

39. The second law of nature: that all movement is, of itself, along straight lines; and consequently, bodies which are moving in a circle always tend to move away from the center of the circle which they are describing . . .

40. The third law: that a body, upon coming into contact with a stronger one, loses none of its motion; but that, upon coming in contact with a weaker one, it loses as much as it transfers to that weaker body . . .

Part Three: Of the Visible Universe

25. That the heavens carry with them all the bodies which they contain. But it seems to me that many who seek to attribute to the heavens the property of fluidity are mistaken in imagining it to be an entirely empty space, which not only offers no resistance to the motion of other bodies, but also lacks the force [to move them and] carry them along with it. For in addition to the fact that such a void cannot exist in nature, there is a factor which all fluids have in common: the reason that they do not offer so much resistance to the motions of other bodies is [not that they contain less matter, but] that they also have motion [of their particles] in themselves. And since this motion can be easily determined in any direction, if it has been determined in some single direction, then a fluid will necessarily, by the force of this motion, carry with it all the bodies which it contains and which are not prevented from following it by some external cause, even though these bodies may be entirely at rest, and hard and solid; as manifestly follows from what has been said above [about the nature of fluid bodies] . . .

26. That the Earth is at rest in its heaven which nevertheless carries it along . . . . [S]ince we see that the Earth is not supported by columns or suspended in air by means of cables but is surrounded on all sides by a very fluid heaven, let us assume that it is at rest and has no innate tendency to motion, since we see no such propensity in it. However, we must not at the

same time assume that this prevents it from being carried along by [the current of] that heaven or from following the motion of the heaven without however moving itself: in the same way as a vessel, which is neither driven by the wind or by oars, nor restrained by anchors, remains at rest in the middle of the ocean; although it may perhaps be imperceptibly carried along by [the ebb and flow of] this great mass of water.

27. That the same is to be believed of all the Planets. And just as the other planets resemble the Earth in being opaque and reflecting the rays of the Sun, we have reason to believe that they also resemble it in remaining at rest, each in its own part of the heaven, and that the variation we observe in their position results solely from the motion of the matter of the heaven which contains them . . .

30. That all the planets are carried around the Sun by the heaven. Now that we have, by this reasoning, removed any possible doubts about the motion of the Earth, let us assume that the matter of the heaven, in which the Planets are situated, unceasingly revolves, like a vortex having the Sun as its center, and that those of its parts which are close to the Sun move more quickly than those further away; and that all the Planets (among which we [shall from now on] include the Earth) always remain suspended among the same parts of this heavenly matter. For by that alone, and without any other devices, all their phenomena are very easily understood. Thus, if some straws [or other light bodies] are floating in the eddy of a river, where the water doubles back on itself and forms a vortex as it swirls; we can see that it carries them along with them and makes them move in circles with it. Further, we can often see that some of these straws rotate about their own centers, and that those which are closer to the center of the vortex which contains them complete their circle more rapidly than those which are further away from it. Finally, we see that, although these whirlpools always attempt a circular motion, they practically never describe perfect circles, but sometimes become too great in width or in length, [so that all the parts of the circumference which they describe are not equidistant from the center]. Thus we can easily imagine that all the same things happen to the Planets; and this is all we need to explain all their remaining phenomena . . .

33. How the Earth is also moved around its own center and the Moon around the Earth. In addition, in the great vortex which forms a heaven

[having the Sun at its center], there are other smaller ones which we can compare to those I have often seen in eddies of rivers where they [all follow the current of the larger vortex which carries them, and] move in the direction in which it moves. One of these vortices has Jupiter at its center, and moves with it the four satellites which revolve around Jupiter, at speeds so proportional that the most distant of the four completes its revolution in about sixteen days, the next one in seven, the third in eighty-five hours and that closest to the center in forty-two hours; and thus, they revolve several times around Jupiter while it describes a large circle around the Sun. Similarly, the vortex which has the Earth at its center carries the Moon around the Earth in the space of a month, while the Earth turns on its own axis in the space of twenty-four hours; and in the time it takes the Earth and the Moon to describe the circle which is common to them [and which forms the year], the Earth revolves on its axis [approximately] three hundred and sixty-five times and the Moon revolves [approximately] twelve times around the Earth.

34. That the movements of the heavens are not perfectly circular. Finally, we must not think that all the centers of the Planets are always situated exactly on the same plane, or that the circles they describe are absolutely perfect; let us instead judge that, as we see occurring in all other natural things, they are only approximately so, and also that they are continuously changed by the passing of the ages . . .

119. How a fixed star is transformed into a Planet or a Comet. Now we must consider how such a hard and opaque sphere composed of an accumulation of many spots must move when it begins to be carried along [in this way] by one of its neighboring vortices. Specifically, it rotates with the matter of this vortex in such a way that it will be driven [by that matter] toward the center of this rotation, as long as it has less agitation than [the parts of] that matter [which surround it]. But the particles of [the matter which forms] a vortex are not all equal, either in speed or in size. Rather, their movement is slower, in proportion to their distance from the circumference, until a certain point; below which they are both smaller and move more rapidly in proportion to their closeness to the center, as was said earlier. Therefore, if this globe is so solid that, before descending to the point at which the parts of the vortex move the most slowly, it acquires a degree of agitation equal to that of those parts among which it is located; it descends

no further, and will proceed into other vortices, and become a Comet. On the other hand, if it is not sufficiently solid to acquire so much agitation, and therefore descends below that point [at which the parts of the vortex move the most slowly], it will remain a certain distance from the star which occupies the center of this vortex; and will become a Planet revolving around it.

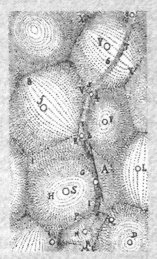

Figure 1 Drawing of Descartes' vortex theory

Part Four: Of the Earth

23. <u>How all parts of the Earth are driven downward by this heavenly matter, and thus become heavy.</u> Next, it must be noted that the force which the individual parts of the heavenly matter have to recede from [the center of] the Earth cannot produce its effect unless, while those parts are ascending, they press down and drive below themselves some terrestrial parts into whose places they rise. For, seeing that all the spaces which are around the Earth are occupied either by particles of terrestrial bodies or by the heavenly matter; and seeing that all the globules of this heavenly matter have an equal propensity to move away from the Earth: individually they have no force to drive other similar globules from their place. However, since such a propensity is not as great in the particles of terrestrial bodies; whenever the heavenly globules have some of these terrestrial particles above them, the former must bring this force of theirs to bear upon the latter in every way. Thus, the weight of each terrestrial

body is not, strictly speaking, produced by all the heavenly matter flowing around it, but rather only by that portion of the heavenly matter which immediately ascends into the place of the descending body, and which, therefore, is exactly equal to it in size . . .

27. That weight drives bodies down toward the center of the Earth. Finally, it must be noted that, although the particles of heavenly matter are agitated at the same time by many diverse movements, yet all of their actions harmonize and, as it were, counterbalance one another in such a way that, due solely to their encounter with the bulk of the earth which resists their movements, they strive to move away equally in all directions from its vicinity, as if from its center; unless by chance some exterior cause introduces diversity into this matter. Now, several such causes can be imagined; but I have not yet been able to ascertain whether their effect is sufficiently great to be perceived by the senses.

Further Reading

Ben-Ari, Moti. *Just a Theory: Exploring the Nature of Science.* New York: Prometheus Books, 2005.

Cartwright, Nancy. *How the Laws of Physics Lie.* Oxford: Oxford University Press, 1983.

Colodny, Robert G. (ed.). *The Nature and Function of Scientific Theories.* Pittsburgh: University of Pittsburgh Press, 1970.

da Costa, Newton C.A. and Steven French. *Science and Partial Truth.* Oxford: Oxford University Press, 2005.

Earman, John. *Testing Scientific Theories.* Minneapolis: University of Minnesota Press, 1983.

Giere, Ronald N. *Science Without Laws.* Chicago: University of Chicago Press, 1999.

Hesse, Mary. *Models and Analogies in Science.* Notre Dame: University of Notre Dame Press, 1966.

Hoover, Kenneth R. *The Elements of Social Scientific Thinking, 3rd ed.* New York: St. Martin's Press, 1984.

Morgan, Mary S. and Margaret Morrison (eds.). *Models as Mediators.* Cambridge: Cambridge University Press, 1999.

Savage, C. Wade (ed.). *Scientific Theories.* Minneapolis: University of Minnesota Press, 1990.

Suppe, Frederick. *The Structure of Scientific Theories.* Urbana: University of Illinois Press, 1977.

Wartofsky, Max W. and Robert S. Cohen (eds.). *Models, Representation and the Scientific Understanding (Boston Studies in the Philosophy of Science, vol. 48).* Dordrecht: D. Reidel, 1979.

CHAPTER FIVE

Scientific Explanation

IN THIS CHAPTER, WE WILL

▓ Identify some metaphysical, epistemological, and axiological aspects of scientific explanation

▓ Examine several models of scientific explanation: the Covering-Law model, the Causal model, the Pragmatic model, the Unification model, and the Information model

The following item appeared in the science newsmagazine, *Science News*, in 1995:

ICY THEORY EXPLAINS STRANGE SLIDING STONES—DEATH VALLEY NATIONAL PARK PHENOMENA CAUSED BY WINDS PUSHING STONES ON ICE, AND POSSIBLY MUD

Richard Monastersky

For decades, geologists have struggled to interpret strange trails etched into the surface of Racetrack Playa, a dry lake bed neighboring Death Valley. At the end of each track sits a stone, the obvious perpetrator. But no one has actually witnessed the rough boulders—measuring up to one-half meter across and weighing around 300 kilograms—sliding across the flat ground.

According to textbooks, strong winds push the rocks after infrequent rains cover the lake surface with a thin film of mud. But geologists from Hampshire College and the University of Massachusetts, both in Amherst, now challenge the established idea. Their measurements of friction on the playa surface suggest that winds can budge the boulders only with the help of ice.

"The concept you have when you stand out there is that the wind should be able to blow these things around with ease. In fact, the coefficient of friction for the biggest rock was about 0.8. It's a 700-pound rock; that means it would take a 600-pound force to move the thing. The wind can't possibly blow strong enough to do it," says Hampshire's John B. Reid, Jr.

Reid and his coworkers wet the playa and measured how much force it took to move large and small blocks of dolomite. Since dolomite is rough, it doesn't move readily, even across slick mud, they report in the September *Geology*.

Individually, the stone do not provide enough surface area for the wind to push on, say the researchers. But when the lake surface freezes after a rain, wind passing over a large sheet of ice could generate enough force to drag several rocks embedded in the same ice, they suggest.

This theory, first proposed in 1955, was later rejected. But Reid's group found support for the idea while doing precise surveys of the track-ways. Separate trails display exactly the same turns—which would be possible only if ice connected individual rocks.

Geologist John S. Shelton of La Jolla, Calif., however, suggests that some of the rocks move without ice. Shelton, who studies the problem on and off for 25 years, believes that winds can push rocks when a thin layer of mud covers frozen ground, which Reid's group did not simulate.

The title of this news article was, "Icy Theory Explains Strange Sliding Stones." It is clear that these researchers were offering an *explanation* for this particular phenomenon and not merely a *description* of it. They were not simply saying here is what happened, but were suggesting how or why it happened. This is exactly what we want and expect from science, namely, that it explain things and events and processes; it does not just describe them. One of the features of the umbrellaology case from the introductory chapter that spoke against its status as science was the absence of explanation. It described how many umbrellas were to be found in certain areas and who was most likely to use just black ones. But no explanation was given for those phenomena; in fact, there was not even an attempt at giving an explanation.

Now, the philosophical question here is: what is an explanation? What does it mean to say that these researchers in the sliding stones case have explained this phenomenon? There are many sorts of explanations that can be given for some phenomenon. For example, suppose we come into a room and find the notorious gangster, Smith, lying dead on the floor. Smith has obviously been shot. We say, "What happened here?" We want to know how/why Smith died. His partner in crime, Jones, answers, "Because Smith double-crossed Brown." The captain of the local police answers, "Because Smith was shot." The medical examiner answers, "Well, not everyone who is shot dies. The reason Smith died was because the bullet punctured his lungs and, basically, he suffocated." With respect to different purposes, each of these answers provides an explanation. Jones gave a behavioral or psychological explanation (if Smith had not double-crossed Brown, Smith would not have been killed), whereas the police captain and the medical examiner gave more physiological explanations (piercing bullets or punctured lungs result in death of humans). A biochemist would no doubt give an even more detailed account of what happens when the lungs are punctured and why that kills. Perhaps a television evangelist would give a different sort of explanation altogether: Smith lived a life of sin and died because of that. You get the point: there are lots of types of explanations and they are geared toward lots of types of cognitive goals. So, what we really want to get at here is: what is a *scientific* explanation (or: what does it mean to scientifically explain some phenomenon)?

As with any topic in the philosophy of science generally, there are metaphysical issues with respect to explanation, epistemological issues, and axiological issues. Among the metaphysical issues are: what kinds of things are explained (or explainable); what kinds of things can "do the explaining." We take it that particular events (like Smith's death) or general processes or states of affairs (like the fact that it rains or certain kinds of molecules bond together) are the kinds of things that can be explained. It is pretty easy and common sense to say what kinds of things get explained. It is harder to say what kinds of things "do the explaining." In fact, this entire chapter is devoted in large part to that issue.

Among the epistemological issues relating to explanation are: how does something get explained; how do we know if/when something has been explained. Again, throughout this chapter these issues will emerge as we look at various models of explanation. Sometimes the metaphysical and epistemological issues are difficult to separate. For instance, if we ask whether there are degrees of explanation (that is, that *A* explains *E* better than *B* explains *E*), this contains metaphysical and epistemological elements, since we would need to know not only what an explanation is as well as whether explanations can come in degrees, but also standards or criteria for evaluating rival purported explanations. That last notion, of evaluating explanations, points to axiological issues relating to explanation. There are other value issues: what is the goal (or goals) of explanation; how do they function both "inside" of science and also "outside" of science (i.e., as we evaluate science vs. non-science). These sorts of issues, too, will emerge as we cover a number of models of explanation, which is what we will turn to now.

Models of explanation
Covering law model

Although philosophers and scientists have thought about the nature of explanation for quite a long time, the first fully worked out model of scientific explanation is usually attributed to Carl Hempel and Paul Oppenheim. Around the middle of the 20th century, they gave us an apparently straightforward way of knowing what a scientific explanation is, their Covering-Law model. If there was some event to be explained (the *explanandum*), say, that my car would not start this morning or that the jar broke when it fell, this was explained by providing the appropriate explanatory conditions (the *explanans*). Some of those conditions would consist of particular facts relevant to the case at hand (e.g., that the jar was made of glass, not rubber). But those particular relevant facts were not enough. What was also needed was some sort of covering-law (or laws) that connected those particular facts with the event to be explained. So, we might need to cite laws dealing with fragility or friction coefficients or even gravity (because the jar would probably not have broken if I had been orbiting the earth on the space shuttle, but would have gently floated around). Explanations, then, for Hempel and Oppenheim, had the structure of a logical argument; indeed they were arguments. This Covering Law model came in various versions. One version was called the Deductive-Nomological (or D-N) model. Here are a couple of examples of this D-N model:

All sodium salts impart a yellow color to a Bunsen flame.
<u>This crystal is a sodium salt.</u>
Therefore, this crystal imparts a yellow color to a Bunsen flame.

Metals conduct electricity.
<u>This rod is copper (a metal).</u>
So, this rod conducts electricity.

In both these examples, the final sentence is the *explanandum*, that is, the thing to be explained, and the first two sentences are the *explanans*, that is, what does the explaining. We want to know why this crystal imparts a yellow color to a Bunsen flame and the answer (the explanation) is that it is a sodium salt and sodium salt does that. Or, we want to know why this rod conducts electricity (maybe we got zapped when we touched it!). The answer is because it is metal and metals conduct electricity.

An important point here is that the explanans contains two types of claims, or evidence. The first sentence in each example is a general sentence. It expresses a law, or at least a law-like claim (*all* sodium salts do such-and-such). The second sentence in each example expresses a particular claim; it speaks to particular facts that relate to the explanandum. Both types of claims, or evidence, are needed for a scientific explanation. We want to know why some event took place (e.g., why this flame turned yellow when we stuck this stuff in it). To explain why, we need to know some particular conditions (e.g., it was *this* stuff we stuck in the flame). Much of the time, that is all we normally consider when we explain things. For example, why did my car not start this morning? Because the spark plugs were wet. But, for a full scientific explanation, that is not enough. We also need evidence like the sort that the first sentences provide, namely, laws or general claims that connect the particular conditions in the explanans with the particular explanandum.

Those general claims are Covering Laws; they provide the context that covers cases like these, that shows the connection between the second and third sentences in the examples. This is why the model is called a Covering Law model; some covering law (or laws) is necessary for there to be a genuine explanation. Otherwise, there is no accounting for how the second sentence (the particular conditions) is relevant to the third sentence (the event or thing to be explained). However, the particular conditions are also necessary for the explanation, because they provide the specific connection between the covering law and the event or thing to be explained. So the structure of a scientific explanation is this:

Explanans: Covering Law(s)
               <u>Particular relevant conditions</u>
Explanadum: Events or thing to be explained

Besides the Deductive-Nomological version, Hempel and Oppenheim recognized that many of our explanations involve probabilistic covering laws, and these were portrayed as exhibiting an Inductive-Statistical (or I-S) argument structure. Here is an example:

Most cases of streptococcus infection clear up quickly with the administration of penicillin.
<u>Schmoe was given penicillin.</u>
Therefore, it is likely that Schmoe will recover quickly from his streptococcus infection.

The structure of this explanation is the same as in the cases above, except that the covering law in the first sentence is not universal, but probabilistic. The explanandum will not necessarily follow from the explanans, but likely will.

Here is what Hempel and Oppenheim themselves had to say about the Covering Law model:

STUDIES IN THE LOGIC OF EXPLANATION
Carl Hempel and Paul Oppenheim

To explain the phenomena in the world of our experience, to answer the question "why?" rather than only the question "what?" is one of the foremost objectives of empirical science. While there is rather general agreement on this point there exists considerable difference of opinion as to the function and the essential characteristics of scientific explanation. The present essay is an attempt to shed some light on these issues by means of an elementary survey of the basic pattern of scientific explanation and a subsequent more rigorous analysis of the concept of law and the logical structure of explanatory arguments . . .

Part I. Elementary Survey of Scientific Explanation

2. Some Illustrations

A mercury thermometer is rapidly immersed in hot water; there occurs a temporary drop of the mercury column, which is then followed by a swift rise. How is this phenomenon to be explained? The increase in temperature affects at first only the glass tube of the thermometer; it expands and thus provides a larger space for the mercury inside, whose surface therefore drops. As soon as by heat conduction the rise in temperature reaches the mercury, however, the latter expands, and as its coefficient of expansion is considerably larger than that of glass, a rise of the mercury level results. This account consists of statements of two kinds. Those of the first kind indicate certain conditions which are realized prior to, or at the same time as, the phenomenon to be explained; we shall refer to them briefly as antecedent conditions. In our illustration, the antecedent conditions include, among others, the fact that the thermometer consists of a glass tube which is partly filled with mercury, and that it is immersed into hot water. The statements of the second kind express certain general laws; in our case, these include the laws of the thermic expansion of mercury and of glass, and a statement about the small thermic conductivity of glass. The two sets of statements, if adequately and completely formulated, explain the phenomenon under consideration: they entail the consequence that the mercury will first drop, then rise. Thus, the event under discussion is explained by subsuming it under general laws, that is, by showing that it occurred in accordance with those laws, in virtue of the realization of certain specified antecedent conditions.

Consider another illustration. To an observer in a rowboat, that part of an oar which is under water appears to be bent upwards. The phenomenon is explained by means of general laws—mainly the law of refraction and the law that water is an optically denser medium than air—and by reference to certain antecedent conditions—especially the facts that part of the oar is in the water, part in the air, and that the oar is practically a straight piece of wood. Thus, here again, the question "Why does the phenomenon occur?" is construed as meaning "according to what general laws, and by virtue of what antecedent conditions does the phenomenon occur?"

So far, we have considered only the explanation of particular events occurring at a certain time and place. But the question "why?" may be raised also in regard to general laws. Thus, in our last illustration, the question might be asked: Why does the propagation of light conform to the law of refraction? Classical physics answers in terms of the undulatory theory of light, that is, by stating that the propagation of light is a wave phenomenon of a certain general type, and that all wave phenomena of that type satisfy the law of refraction. Thus, the explanation of a general regularity consists in subsuming it under another, more comprehensive regularity, under a more general law. Similarly, the validity of Galileo's law for the free fall of bodies near the earth's surface can be explained by deducing it from a more comprehensive set of laws, namely Newton's laws of motion and his law of gravitation, together with some statements about particular facts, namely, about the mass and the radius of the earth.

3. The Basic Pattern of Scientific Explanation

From the preceding sample cases let us now abstract some general characteristics of scientific explanation. We divide an explanation into two major constituents, the *explanandum* and the *explanans*. By the explanandum, we understand the sentence describing the phenomenon to be explained (not that phenomenon itself); by the explanans, the class of those sentences which are adduced to account for the phenomenon. As was noted before, the explanans falls into two subclasses; one of these contains certain sentences $C_1, C_2, \ldots, C_k$ which state specific antecedent conditions; the other is a set of sentences $L_1, L_2, \ldots, L_r$ which represent general laws.

If a proposed explanation is to be sound, its constituents have to satisfy certain conditions of adequacy, which may be divided into logical and empirical conditions. For the following discussion, it will be sufficient to formulate these requirements in a slightly vague manner . . .

I. Logical Conditions of Adequacy

(R1) The explanandum must be a logical consequence of the explanans; in other words, the explanandum must be logically deducible from the information contained in the explanans; for otherwise, the explanans would not constitute adequate grounds for the explanandum.

(R2) The explanans must contain general laws, and these must actually be required for the derivation of the explanandum. We shall not make it a necessary condition for a sound explanation, however, that the explanans must contain at least one statement which is not a law; for, to mention just one reason, we would surely want to consider as an explanation the derivation of the general regularities governing the motion of double stars from the laws of celestial mechanics, even though all the statements in the explanans are general laws.

(R3) The explanans must have empirical content; that is, it must be capable, at least in principle, of test by experiment or observation. This condition is implicit in (R1); for since the explanandum is assumed to describe some empirical phenomenon, it follows from (R1) that the explanans entails at least one consequence of empirical character, and this fact confers upon it testability and empirical content . . .

II. Empirical Condition of Adequacy

(R4) The sentences constituting the explanans must be true. That in a sound explanation, the statements constituting the explanans have to satisfy some condition of factual correctness is obvious. But it might seem more appropriate to stipulate that the explanans has to be highly confirmed by all the relevant evidence available rather than that it should be true. This stipulation, however, leads to awkward consequences. Suppose that a certain phenomenon was explained at an earlier stage of science, by means of an explanans which was well supported by the evidence then at hand, but which has been highly disconfirmed by more recent findings. In such a case, we would have to say that originally the explanatory account was a correct explanation, but that it ceased to be one later, when unfavorable evidence was discovered. This does not appear to accord with sound common usage, which directs us to say that on the basis of the limited initial evidence, the truth of the explanans, and thus the soundness of the explanation, had been quite probable, but that the ampler evidence now available makes it highly probable that the explanans is not true, and hence that the account in question is not—and never has been—a correct explanation. . .

Some of the characteristics of an explanation which have been indicated so far may be summarized in the following schema:

Explanans

$C_1, C_2, \ldots, C_k$ Statements of antecedent conditions

Logical deduction $\dfrac{L_1, L_2, \ldots, L_r \text{ General Laws}}{}$

E Description of the empirical

Explanandum   phenomenon to be explained

Let us note here that the same formal analysis, including the four necessary conditions, applies to scientific prediction as well as to explanation. The difference between the two is of a pragmatic character. If E is given, that is, if we know that the phenomenon described by E has occurred, and a suitable set of statements $C_1, C_2, \ldots, C_k, L_1, L_2, \ldots, L_r$ is provided afterwards, we speak of an explanation of the phenomenon in question. If the latter statements are given and E is derived prior to the occurrence of the phenomenon it describes, we speak of a prediction. It may be said, therefore, that an explanation of a particular event is not fully adequate unless its explanans, if taken account of in time, could have served as the basis for predicting the event in question. Consequently, whatever will be said in this article concerning the logical characteristics of explanation or prediction will be applicable to either, even if only one of them should be mentioned.

Many explanations which are customarily offered, especially in prescientific discourse, lack this predictive potential force, however. Thus, we may be told that a car turned over on the road "because" one of its tires blew out while the car was traveling at a high speed. Clearly, on the basis of just this information, the accident could not have been predicted, for the explanans provides no explicit general laws by means of which the prediction might have been effected, nor does it state adequately the antecedent conditions which would be needed for the prediction. The same point may be illustrated by reference to W.S. Jevons's view that every explanation consists in pointing out a resemblance between facts, and that in some cases this process may require no reference to laws at all and "may involve nothing more than a single identity, as when we explain the appearance of shooting stars by showing that they are identical with portions of a comet." But clearly, this identity does not provide an explanation of the phenomenon of shooting stars unless we presuppose the laws governing the development of heat and light as the effect of friction. The observation of similarities has explanatory value only if it involves at least tacit reference to general laws.

In some cases, incomplete explanatory arguments of the kind here illustrated suppress parts of the explanans simply as "obvious"; in other cases, they seem to involve the assumption that while the missing parts are not obvious, the incomplete explanans could at least, with appropriate effort, be so supplemented as to make a strict derivation of the explanandum possible. This assumption may be justifiable in some cases, as when we say that a lump of sugar disappeared "because" it was put into hot tea, but it surely is not satisfied in many other cases. Thus, when certain peculiarities in the work of an artist are explained as outgrowths of a specific type of neurosis, this observation may contain significant clues, but in general it does not afford a sufficient basis for a potential prediction of those peculiarities. In cases of this kind, an incomplete explanation may at best be considered as indicating some positive correlation between the antecedent conditions adduced and the type of phenomenon to be explained, and as pointing out a direction in which further research might be carried on in order to complete the explanatory account.

In addition, Hempel and Oppenheim seem to claim that there must be one final correct scientific explanation; there cannot be multiple correct scientific explanations. Remember, they claim that on the basis of evidence at a given point in time, we offer an explanation, but then later, with newer, fuller evidence we how say that our earlier "explanation" was wrong. This certainly suggests that they hold the view that there is one, single correct scientific explanation of any given explanandum. This relates back to the discussion of scientific realism in Chapter Three.[1]

Very soon after its enunciation by Hempel and Oppenheim, the Covering Law model of explanation was criticized on a number of grounds. Some criticisms focused on the internal inadequacy of the model, that is, on whether it made sense on its own grounds. People came up with cases that fit the structure of the

Covering Law model, but which no one took as legitimate cases of scientific explanation. Here are some examples:

> All samples of table salt that have had a dissolving spell cast upon them dissolve in water.
> <u>This sample of table salt has had a dissolving spell cast upon it.</u>
> Therefore, this sample of table salt dissolved in water.

> Every male who regularly takes birth control pills avoids pregnancy.
> <u>Schmoe (a male) has taken birth control pills regularly for the past year.</u>
> So, Schmoe has avoided pregnancy for the past year.

Here is one aimed against the I-S version of the Covering Law model:

> Most colds clear up within a week after the administration of large doses of vitamin C.
> <u>Schmoe took large doses of vitamin C.</u>
> Therefore, Schmoe's cold cleared up within a week.

(In case you don't know, the reason this last example is seen as a counter-example to the Covering Law model is because most colds clear up within a week regardless of whether or not someone takes large doses of vitamin C.)

Among the criticisms of the Covering Law model, the philosopher Sylvain Bromberger proposed his well-known flagpole counter-example. (We will come back to this particular counter-example later in this chapter.) Here a vertical flagpole of a certain height stands on a flat level piece of ground. The sun is at a certain elevation resulting in the flagpole casting a shadow of a certain length. Given these particular facts, along with a law of rectilinear propagation of light, the length of the shadow can be deduced, in line with the Covering Law model. In addition, given the length of the shadow and the position of the sun and the same law about light, the height of the flagpole can be deduced. Yet no one, said Bromberger, would seriously suggest that the flagpole's height is explained by the length of its shadow (even if it could be predicted by the length of its shadow).

Besides criticisms that focused on the internal inadequacy of this model, other criticisms focused on its overall inadequacy. For example, a number of philosophers, including Michael Scriven and Sam Gorovitz, suggested that this model omitted the importance of causation in accounting for explanation. After all, even at a common sense level we say X happened *because* (by the cause of) Y. The upshot of numerous concerns about the Covering Law model was that by the beginning of the 1970s, other models of explanation were proposed. In this chapter, we will look at four of these models: the Causal model, the Unification model, the Pragmatic model, and the Information model.

Causal model

Though early nods toward a causal model came from Gorovitz and Scriven, among others, the Causal model of explanation is most often today associated with the work of Wesley Salmon. We will begin with his own remarks and then say some things about them:

SCIENTIFIC EXPLANATION AND THE CAUSAL STRUCTURE OF THE WORLD

Wesley Salmon

Much of the contemporary literature on scientific explanation arises directly or indirectly in response to the classic 1948 Hempel-Oppenheim paper, "Studies in the Logic of Explanation." In it the authors attempt to provide a precise explication of what has come to be known as the deductive-nomological or D-N model of scientific explanation. They did not invent this mode of scientific explanation, nor were they the first philosophers to attempt to characterize it. As mentioned previously, its roots go back at least to Aristotle, and it is strongly suggested in such works as Arnaud's *The Art of Thinking* ("Port-Royal Logic") and Laplace's *Philosophical Essay on Probabilities*. In none of the anticipations by these or other authors, however, do we find the precision and detail of the Hempel-Oppenheim account. One might almost say that 1948 marks the division between the prehistory and the history of the philosophical study of scientific explanation . . . According to [this view], particular facts are explained by subsuming them under general laws, while general regularities are explained by subsumption under still broader laws. If a particular fact is successfully subsumed under a lawful generalization, it is, on this view, completely explained . . . .

Most proponents of this subsumption theory maintain that some events can be explained statistically by subsumption under statistical laws in much the same way that other events—such as the fact that the penny just inserted behind the fuse conducts electricity—are explained by appeal to universal laws. Thus we can explain the fact that a particular window was broken by pointing out that it was struck by a flying baseball, even though not all, but only most, windows so struck will shatter.

Although I disagreed from the beginning with the proponents of the *standard* subsumption view about the nature of the relation of subsumption of particular facts under universal or statistical generalizations, I did for some time accept the notion that *suitable* subsumption under generalizations is sufficient to explain particular facts. In *Statistical Explanation and Statistical Relevance* (Salmon et al., 1971), I tried to give a detailed account of what seemed to me the appropriate way to subsume facts under general laws for the purposes of explanation. This effort led to the elaboration of the statistical-relevance (S-R) model of scientific explanation. As the name suggests, statistical relevance relations play a key role in this model of scientific explanation.

Let's pause Salmon for a moment, to make sure this last part is clear. We saw above that people criticized Hempel and Oppenheim with examples like men taking birth control pills and Schmoe taking large doses of vitamin C. The problem, of course, is that the fact of men taking birth control pills or Schmoe taking large doses of vitamin C are just irrelevant to explaining why men do not get pregnant or why Schmoe recovered. To really explain these phenomena, we want and need *relevant* evidence and information. This is what Salmon was addressing in the 1970s with his S-R model, namely, identifying an explanans that was relevant to the explanandum. (There were fancy ways of saying this, such as "demarcating the maximal class of maximal specificity," but that is what he and others were up to.) Now, back to Salmon:

SCIENTIFIC EXPLANATION AND THE CAUSAL STRUCTURE OF THE WORLD *(continued)*
Wesley Salmon

Subsequent reflection has convinced me that subsumption of the foregoing sort is only part—not all—of what is involved in the explanation of particular facts. It now seems to me that explanation in a two-tiered affair. At the most basic level, it is necessary, for purposes of explanation, to subsume the event-to-be-explained under an appropriate set of statistical relevance relations, much as was required under the S-R model. At the second level, it seems to me, the statistical relevance relations that are invoked at the first level must be explained in terms of *causal* relations. The explanation, on this view, is incomplete until the causal components of the second level have been provided. This constitutes a sharp divergence from the approach of Hempel, who explicitly rejects the demand for causal laws . . .

Causal Connections and Common Causes

Let us begin by reconsidering one of our simple examples. Two students, Adams and Baker, submit essentially identical term papers in a particular course. There is, of course, the logical possibility that the two papers were produced entirely independently, and that the resemblance between them is a matter of pure chance. Given the overwhelming improbability of this sort of coincidence, no one takes this suggestion seriously. Three reasonable explanatory hypotheses are available: (1) Baker copied from Adams, (2) Adams copied from Baker, or (3) both copied from a common source . . . There is either a causal process running from Adams's production of the paper to Baker's, (2) a causal process running from Baker's production of the paper to Adams's, or (3) a common cause—for example, a paper in a fraternity file to which both Adams and Baker had access. [Salmon wrote this prior to the internet, the plagiarism source of choice today.] In the case of the third alternative, there are two distinct causal processes running from the paper in the file to each of the two papers submitted by Adams and Baker, respectively . . .

According to the viewpoint I am attempting to develop, statistical relevance relations require causal explanations. In order to explain these relations, let us introduce the concept of *causal relevance*. We shall need two kinds of causal relevance—direct and indirect. Let us say that we have *direct causal relevance* of one event to another if there is a causal process connecting them, and if that causal process is responsible for the transmission of causal influence from one to the other. Let us say that we have *indirect causal relevance* if the two events are results of a common cause as characterized in terms either of an interactive fork or a conjunctive fork . . . a common cause—of either the conjunctive or the interactive variety—requires causal processes connecting the common cause to each of the separate effects. We can now say, quite generally, that statistical relevance relations are to be explained in terms of causal relevance relations.

In the example of the two plagiarists, let us assume that careful investigation reveals that neither copied directly from the other. In that case, we hypothesize the existence of a common cause, and this hypothesis is amenable to direct observational confirmation. Moreover, the causal processes connecting the common cause to the effects are themselves observable; indeed, they were observed by the plagiarists. In many other circumstances, however, we postulate the existence of causal processes and/or common causes when they are not directly observable . . .

The Mechanical Philosophy

I have tried to say something constructive about some of the mechanisms that function in certain domains of our world; in other worlds, or in other domains of this world, mechanisms of radically different sort might operate. I have focused upon causal mechanisms; however, mechanisms of a noncausal sort might be found. I have tried to describe certain kinds of causal mechanisms that happen to exist in our world; perhaps causality can take different forms. I make no claim for universal applicability of my characterization of scientific explanation in all domains of our world, let alone for universality across all possible worlds. Thus I agree with Achinstein (1983, chap. 4) in rejecting the universalist viewpoint regarding scientific explanation. But I do maintain that scientific explanation is designed to provide understanding, and such understanding results from *knowing how things work*. In this sense, the theory of scientific explanation that I have been attempting to develop is an expression of a *mechanical philosophy* . . .

Explanation and Understanding

If we correctly identified those factors that are statistically relevant to the event-to-be-explained, we have completed the bottom tier of our explanatory structure. A completed S-R basis—one that incorporates all statistically relevant factors—is, of course, something we rarely possess; it is an idealization. Nevertheless . . . it is philosophically important to have an adequate account of the ideal statistical basis.

The next step is to provide causal accounts of the statistical relevance relations involved in the S-R basis. There is no presumption that the causal relations can be "read off" in any automatic or routine fashion. We must formulate causal hypotheses and apply standard scientific procedures to test them. According to the causal/mechanical approach I have been advocating, there are fundamental sorts of causal mechanisms that figure crucially in providing scientific explanations of statistical relevance relations. Given a statistical relevance relation between events of type A and events of type B, there may be a direct causal connection. Causal connections are causal processes. In the case of a direct causal connection, there must be a causal process connecting any given event A_i with the corresponding event B_j; the causal influence may be transmitted from A_i to B_j or it may go in the opposite direction . . . Causal processes transmit energy, information, structure, and causal influence; they also transmit propensities to enter into various kinds of interactions under appropriate circumstances. A moving billiard ball carries a propensity to interact with another billiard ball in specifiable ways if their paths intersect, a golf ball carries a propensity to be deflected in specifiable ways if it encounters a tree branch, and an energetic photon carries a propensity to interact with an electron in a Compton scattering event. Some of these propensities may be deterministic; other seems clearly to be probabilistic.

If the statistical relevance relation between A and B that we are trying to explain does not arise out of a direct causal relation, we search for an indirect causal relation that obtains an account of a common cause. Causal forks of the conjunctive and interactive varieties . . . constitute the mechanisms. If an interactive fork is invoked, there must be an intersection C of processes that lead from C to A and B, respectively. C must, of course, be a causal interaction, and the processes must be causal processes . . .

Causal processes and causal interactions are governed by basic laws of nature. Photons, for instance, travel in null geodesic paths unless they are scattered or absorbed upon encountering material particles. Freely falling material particles follow paths that are nonnull geodesics. Linear and angular momentum are conserved when particles interact with one another. Energy is conserved in isolated physical systems. *The causal/mechanical version of the ontic conception of scientific explanation is as much a covering-law conception as any version of the epistemic conception.*

What Salmon means at the end of this reading by the epistemic conception and the ontic conception of explanation is this: the epistemic conception treats explanations as arguments, like the Hempel and Oppenheim model, such that we make an inference to the explanandum based on the explanans, whereas in Salmon's ontic conception, explanation is treated as referring to and even exhibiting causal connections in the world. So, again, for Salmon, explanation involves having a set of factors that are statistically relevant to the explanandum, along with pertinent probability values of how strong the connection is between the explanans and the explanandum, as well as causal accounts of the relevance relations. As he put it in an article called, "Why Ask 'Why'?": "Subsumption of a particular occurrence under statistical regularities—which, we recall, does not imply anything about the construction of deductive or inductive arguments—is a necessary part of any adequate explanation of its occurrence, but it is not the whole story. The causal explanation of the regularity is also needed."[2] Salmon even claims that without this causal requirement the patterns we perceive in nature would be miracles and our subsequent explanations would be groundless.

This causal model makes lots of intuitive sense. As we noted earlier, this view certainly seems to square with many of our intuitions that an explanation is of the form: event E occurred *because* (i.e., by the cause) of X. Nonetheless, other philosophers have raised concerns about it. Much of the focus of these critics as well as of Salmon, himself, has been on fleshing out a robust notion of causation, an issue that has not yet been settled.

Another concern is over the notion of statistical relevance. Whether, and to what degree, one thing is relevant to another is often claimed to be dependent upon some goal or concern external to those things themselves. For example, whether (or to what degree) the color of my favorite lamp is relevant to the color scheme in my living room depends on lots of things other than the lamp and the room (my tastes, for instance). Now, that example is not about providing an explanation for some event, but the point should be clear. To give an example relating to explanation, let's return to the flagpole case that was mentioned earlier in the discussion about Hempel and Oppenheim. If you remember, Sylvain Bromberger claimed that we could derive the height of a flagpole from the length of its shadow and theories about the propagation of light. Bromberger said, and lots of folks agreed, that we would not say that the height of the flagpole is explained by the length of its shadow. And, given Salmon's causal model that we just looked at, we certainly would not say that the length of the shadow causes the height of the flagpole (and, so, for Salmon, we certainly would not want to say that the shadow's length explains the flagpole's height). But, there is another model of scientific explanation that does say it could make sense to do exactly that! Part of what this model will attempt to show is that what counts as being statistically relevant (remember, that is the point we are talking about right now) is not just "given out there in the world." It is determined, at least in part, by our interests and concerns. Let's turn to that alternative model.

Pragmatic model

Why would anyone seriously suggest that (1) we could explain the height of a flagpole by the length of its shadow, and (2) we could even claim that the length of the shadow causes, or at least is part of the cause, of the height of the flagpole? This sounds peculiar! But consider this little scenario: Remember my nephew, Terry, from the introductory chapter, the one I wanted to drown so I could get an inheritance? Well, suppose that Terry got wind of my dastardly designs and decided to bury his pot of gold somewhere. He decided to bury it in a secret spot, but he did not want to leave any sort of map or message anywhere, in case I might find some written record. So, he found a secret spot on the ground, made some calculations, and then built a flagpole so that the very tip of the flagpole's shadow touched that secret spot at exactly high noon on summer solstice. In other words, what mattered to him was that the shadow end right at the exact spot where the treasure was buried. Given that spot, he then built a flagpole to be exactly the right height such that its shadow would end up exactly on the ground where it would reveal the treasure (to him, anyway). So, given his goal of hiding and later being able to find his treasure, he built the flagpole a specific height because he wanted its shadow to end up at exactly that spot. In other words, we could explain the height of the flagpole on the basis of the length of its shadow. Indeed, we could claim that the length of the shadow is part of the causal basis for the height of the flagpole, at least to the extent that we take design and goal and purpose as part of the cause, not just hammering and welding, etc. This is part of the pragmatic model of explanation, namely, that purpose or goal or context, is an inherent part of any explanation.

This model is most often associated with Bas van Fraassen. In laying out a pragmatic model, he sees explanation as a relation of three parts: theory, fact, and context. Explanations, he says, are answers to why-questions and why-questions consist of three elements: a topic of concern, a contrast class, and a relevance relation. An example, provided by van Fraassen, to illustrate these features is the question, "Why is this conductor warped?" The topic of concern is the presupposition that, in fact, there is a warped conductor. The contrast class, or set of alternatives, in this case, is conductors. (We want to know why *this*, not *that*, conductor is warped.) The relevance relation is the feature that provides a context for the possibility of explanation. It is the pragmatic aspects of what we want explained. So, what question is being asked, and, hence, what set of answers would be possible, depends on all three of these features. To give another (now well-worn) example: Willie Sutton, a notorious bank robber, when asked, "Why do you rob banks?" replied, "That's where the money is." The topic here is robbing banks (or Sutton robbing banks); the contrast class is, for the questioner, occupations (bank robber vs. philosophy professor) and, for Sutton, places to rob (banks vs. boutiques). The relevance relation is, in this case, motivation.

Underlying van Fraassen's model of explanation is a view about questions. There can be a single statement that is in the form of a question, but that form might actually reveal several questions. For example, if I ask:

Have you read the latest Harry Potter book?

I might really be asking any one of these questions:

Have *you* read the latest Harry Potter book? (You, not someone else)

Have you *read* the latest Harry Potter book? (Read, not listened to an audio book)

Have you read the *latest* Harry Potter book? (The latest one, not an earlier one)

Have you read the latest *Harry Potter* book? (Harry Potter, not James Bond)

What counts as an appropriate answer will depend on just which of these questions was really being asked. And, of course, some questions require direct answers (such as a "yes" or "no" answer), whereas others do not (say, ones that offer a choice, such as "What's your favorite flavor of ice cream?"). Back to explanation; here is van Fraassen in his own words:

THE SCIENTIFIC IMAGE
Bas van Fraassen

A Model for Explanation

I shall now propose a new theory of explanation. An explanation is not the same as a proposition, or an argument, or list of propositions; it is an *answer*. (Analogously, a son is not the same as a man, even if all sons are men, and every man is a son.) An explanation is an answer to a why-question. So, a theory of explanation must be a theory of why-questions . . .

A Theory of Why-questions

There are several respects in which why-questions introduce genuinely new elements into the theory of questions. Let us focus first on the determination of exactly what question is asked, that is, the contextual specification of factors needed to understand a why-interrogative. After that is done (a tale which ends with the delineation of the set of direct answers) and as an independent enterprise, we must turn to the evaluation of those answers as good or better. This evaluation proceeds with reference to the part of science accepted as "background theory" in that context.

As example, consider the question "Why is this conductor warped?" The questioner implies that the conductor is warped, and is asking for a reason. Let us call the proposition that the conductor is warped the *topic* of the question (following Henry Leonard's terminology, "topic of concern"). Next, this question has a *contrast-class*, as we saw, that is, a set of alternatives. I shall take this contrast-class, call it X, to be a class of propositions which includes the topic. For this particular interrogative, the contrast could be that it is *this* conductor rather than *that* one, or that the conductor has warped rather than retained its shape. If the question is "Why does this material burn yellow?" the contrast-class could be the set of propositions: this material burned (with a flame of) color x.

Finally, there is the respect-in-which a reason is requested, which determines what shall count as a possible explanatory factor, the relation of *explanatory relevance*. In the first example, the request might be *for events "leading up to" the warping*. That allows as relevant an account of human error, of switches being closed or moisture condensing in those switches, even spells cast by witches (since the evaluation of what is a good answer comes later). On the other hand, the events leading up to the warping might well be known, in which case the request is likely to be for the standing conditions that made it possible for those events to lead to this warping: the presence of a magnetic field of a certain strength, say. Finally, it might already be known, or considered immaterial, exactly how the warping is produced, and the question (possibly based on a misunderstanding) may be about exactly what function this warping fulfills in the operation of the power station. Compare "Why does the blood circulate through the body?" answered (1) "because the heart pumps the blood through the arteries" and (2) "to bring oxygen to every part of the body tissue."

In a given context, several questions agreeing in topic but differing in contrast-class, or conversely, may conceivably differ further in what counts as explanatorily relevant. Hence we cannot properly ask what is relevant to this topic, or what is relevant to this contrast-class. Instead we must say of a given proposition that it is or is not relevant (in this context) to the topic with respect to that contrast-class. For example, in the same context one might be curious about the circumstances that led Adam to eat the apple rather than the pear (Eve offered him an apple) and also about the motives that led him to eat it rather than refuse it. What is "kept constant" or "taken as given" (that he ate the fruit; that what he did, he did to the apple) which is to say, the contrast-class, is not to be dissociated entirely from the respect-in-which we want a reason.

Summing up then, the why-question Q expressed by an interrogative in a given context will be determined by three factors:

The *topic* P_k
The *contrast-class* $X = \{P_1, \ldots, P_k \ldots\}$
The *relevance relation* R

and, in a preliminary way, we may identify the abstract why-question with the triple consisting of these three:

$$Q = <P_k, X, R>$$

A proposition A is called *relevant to* Q exactly if A bears relation R to the couple $<P_k, X>$.

We must now define what are the direct answers to this question. As a beginning let us inspect the form of words that will express such an answer:

(*) P_k *in contrast to* (the rest of) X *because* A

This sentence must express a proposition. What proposition it expresses, however, depends on the same context that selected Q as the proposition expressed by the corresponding interrogative ("Why P_k?"). So some of the same contextual factors, and specifically R, may appear in the determination of the proposition expressed by (*).

What is claimed in answer (*)? First of all, that P_k is true. Secondly, (*) claims that the other members of the contrast-class are not true. So much is surely conveyed already by the question—it does not make sense to ask why Peter rather than Paul has paresis if they both have it. Thirdly, (*) says that A is true. And finally, there is that word "because": (*) claims that A is a *reason*.

This fourth point we have awaited with bated breath. Is this not where the inextricably modal or counterfactual element comes in? But not at all; in my opinion, the word "because" here signifies only that A is relevant, in this context, to this question. Hence the claim is merely that A bears relation R to $<P_k, X>$. For example, suppose you ask why I got up at seven o'clock this morning, and I say "because I was woken up by the clatter the milkman made." In that case I have interpreted your question as asking for a sort of reason that at least includes events-leading-up-to my getting out of bed, and my word "because" indicates that the milkman's clatter was that sort of reason, that is, one of the events in which Salmon would call the causal process. Contrast this with the case in which I construe your request as being specifically for a motive. In that case I would have answered "No reason, really. I could easily have stayed in bed, for I don't particularly want to do anything today. But the milkman's clatter had woken me up, and I just go up from force of habit I suppose." In this case, I do not say "because" for the milkman's clatter does not belong to the relevant range of events, as I understand your question . . .

Conclusion

Let us take stock. Traditionally, theories are said to bear two sorts of relation to observable phenomena: *description* and *explanation*. Description can be more or less accurate, more or less informative; as a minimum, the facts must "be allowed by" the theory (fit some of its models), as a maximum the theory actually implies the facts in question. But in addition to a (more or less informative) description, the theory may provide an explanation. This is something "over and above" description; for example, Boyle's law describes the relationship between pressure, temperature, and volume of a contained gas, but does not explain it—kinetic theory explains it. The conclusion was drawn, correctly I think, that even if two theories are strictly empirically equivalent they may differ in that one can be used to answer a given request for explanation while the other cannot.

Many attempts were made to account for such "explanatory power" purely in terms of those features and resources of a theory that make it informative (that is, that allow it to give better descriptions). On Hempel's view, Boyle's law does explain these empirical facts about gases, but minimally. The kinetic theory is perhaps better *qua* explanation simply because it gives so much more information about the behavior of gases, relates the three quantities in question to other observable quantities, has a beautiful simplicity, unifies our over-all picture of the world, and so on. The use of more sophisticated statistical relationships by Wesley Salmon and James Greeno (as well as by I.J. Good, whose theory of such concepts as weight of evidence, corroboration, explanatory power, and so on deserves more attention from philosophers), are all efforts along this line. If they had succeeded, an empiricist could rest easy with the subject of explanation.

But these attempts ran into seemingly insuperable difficulties. The conviction grew that explanatory power is something quite irreducible, a special feature differing in kind from empirical adequacy and strength. An inspection of examples defeats any attempt to identify the ability to explain with any complex of those more familiar and down-to-earth virtues that are used to elevate the theory *qua* description. Simultaneously it was argued that what science is really after is understanding, that this consists in being in a position to explain, hence what science is really after goes well beyond empirical adequacy and strength. Finally, since the theory's ability to explain provides a clear reason for accepting it, it was argued that explanatory power is evidence for the *truth* of the theory, special evidence that goes beyond any evidence we may have for the theory's empirical adequacy . . .

Once you decide that explanation is something irreducible and special, the door is opened to elaboration by means of further concepts pertaining thereto, all equally irreducible and special. The premises of an explanation have to include lawlike statements; a statement is lawlike exactly if it implies some non-trivial counterfactual conditional statement; but it can do so only by asserting relationships of necessity in nature. Not all classes correspond to genuine properties; properties and propensities figure in explanation. Not everyone has joined this return to essentialism or neo-Aristotelian realism, but some eminent realists have publicly explored or advocated it.

Even more moderate elaborations of the concept of explanation make mysterious distinctions. Not every explanation is a scientific explanation. Well then, that irreducible explanation-relationship comes in several distinct types, one of them being scientific. A scientific explanation has a special form, and adduces only special sorts of information to explain—information about causal connections and causal processes. Of course, a causal relationship is just what "because" must denote; and since the *summum bonum* of science is explanation, science must be attempting even to describe something beyond the observable phenomena, namely causal relationships and processes.

These last two paragraphs describe the flights of fancy that become appropriate if explanation is a relationship *sui generis* between theory and fact. But there is no direct evidence for them at all, because if you ask a scientist to explain something to you, the information he gives you is not different in kind (and does not sound or look different) from the information he gives you when you ask for a description. Similarly in "ordinary" explanations: the information I adduce to explain the rise in oil prices, is information I would have given you to a battery of requests for description of oil supplies, oil producers, and oil consumption. To call an explanation scientific, is to say nothing about its form or the sort of information adduced, but only that the explanation draws on science to get this information (at least to some extent) and, more importantly, that the criteria of evaluation of how good an explanation it is, are being applied using a scientific theory (in the manner I have tried to describe).

The discussion of explanation went wrong at the very beginning when explanation was conceived of as a relationship like description: a relation between theory and fact. Really it is a three-term relation, between theory, fact, and context. No wonder that no single relation between theory and fact ever managed to fit more than a few examples! Being an explanation is essentially relative, for an explanation is an *answer*. (In just that sense, being a daughter is something relative: every woman is a daughter and every daughter is a woman, yet being a daughter is not the same thing as being a woman.) Since an explanation is an answer, it is evaluated *vis-à-vis* a question, which is a request for information. But exactly what is requested, by means of a question "Why is it the case that P?", differs from context to context. In addition, the background theory plus data relative to which the question is evaluated, as arising or not arising, depends on the context. And even what part of that background information is to be used to evaluate how good the answer is, *qua* answer to that question, is a contextually determined factor. So to say that a given theory can be used to explain a certain fact, is always elliptical for: there is a proposition which is a telling answer, relative to this theory, to the request for information about certain facts (those counted as relevant for *this* question) that bear on a comparison between this fact which is the case, and certain (contextually specified) alternatives which are not the case.

So scientific explanation is not (pure) science but an application of science. It is a use of science to satisfy certain of our desires; and these desires are quite specific in a specific context, but they are always desires for descriptive information. (Recall: every daughter is a woman.) The exact content of the desire, and the evaluation of how well it is satisfied, varies from context to context. It is not a single desire, the same in all cases, for a very special sort of thing, but rather, in each case, a different desire for something of a quite familiar sort.

Hence there can be no question at all of explanatory power as such (just as it would be silly to speak of the "control power" of a theory, although of course we rely on theories to gain control over nature and circumstances). Nor can there be any question of explanatory success as providing evidence for the truth of a theory that goes beyond any evidence we have for its providing an adequate description of the phenomena. For in each case, a success of explanation is a success of adequate and informative description. And while it is true that we seek for explanation, the value of this search for science is that the search for explanation is *ipso facto* a search for empirically adequate, empirically strong theories.

As you know by now, no philosopher proposes any view or model without others criticizing it. You, yourself, have probably already come up with some concerns or questions about what van Fraassen says about explanation. For example, we might all agree that context is important in providing an explanation for some phenomenon. And we might all agree that we need to be precise about the question we are asking (Have you *read* the latest Harry Potter book? versus Have you read the *latest* Harry Potter book?). But we still want to know: in virtue of what is some phenomenon explained and, in addition, is there some structure or pattern to what counts as an explanation, any explanation? Just how do the components of theory, fact, and context (van Fraassen's three elements of an explanatory relation) explain some phenomenon? Could those same three components fail to explain that phenomenon? Also, when we looked at Hempel and Oppenheim, they seemed to be committed to saying that there was one, single correct explanation for a given phenomenon. Is van Fraassen denying this? Of course, different interests and different contexts might give us satisfying answers. For instance, when we asked how/why Smith died, we got different answers and, in given contexts, any and all of the proposed explanations were satisfactory. But does that mean that any satisfactory explanation is the correct explanation? Although van Fraassen wants to say that there is no single correct explanation *per se*, there are different correct explanations depending upon context, many others are uncomfortable with that view. That seems to suggest that in two competing, and perhaps contradictory, theories could each have a correct explanation of some phenomenon. So, Ptolemaic astronomy might give one correct explanation for why Mars appears to move backward in the sky (relative to Earth) during part of the year and Copernican astronomy might give a different correct explanation for that. But those two theories contradict each other, so how could they both give a correct explanation for the same phenomenon?

Unification model

Another model of explanation is the Unification model, associated with Michael Friedman and Philip Kitcher, although there is not complete agreement between them. This model emphasizes the goal of explanation as understanding, along with the sense that understanding the world is enhanced to the extent that we recognize and establish interconnections among phenomena. We think that evolutionary theory provides (correct) explanations because it makes sense of lots of phenomena, including lots of different kinds of phenomena. When we explain, then, we show how a given phenomenon is related to other phenomena, how things hang together.

Friedman identifies three features that we would want for any model of explanation: (1) that it be sufficiently general, (2) that it be objective (i.e., not depend upon idiosyncrasies and changing tastes), and (3) that it be connective to our understanding. As he puts it:

EXPLANATION AND SCIENTIFIC UNDERSTANDING
Michael Friedman

Why does water turn to steam when heated? Why do the planets obey Kepler's laws? Why is light refracted by a prism? These are typical of the questions science tries to answer. Consider, for example, the answer to the first question: Water is made of tiny molecules in a state of constant motion. Between these molecules are intermolecular forces, which, at normal temperatures, are sufficient to hold them together. If the water is heated, however, the energy, and consequently the motion, of the molecules increases. If the water is heated sufficiently the molecules acquire enough energy to overcome the intermolecular forces—they fly apart and escape into the atmosphere. Thus, the water gives off steam. This account answers our question. Our little story seems to give us understanding of the process by which water turns to steam. The phenomenon is now more intelligible or comprehensible. How does this work? What is it about our little story, and scientific explanations generally, that gives us understanding of the world—what is it for a phenomenon to be scientifically understandable?

Two aspects of our example are of special interest. First, what is explained is a general regularity or pattern of behavior—a law, if you like—that is, that water turns to steam when heated. Although most of the philosophical literature on explanation deals with the explanation of particular events, the type of explanation illustrated by the above account seems much more typical of the physical sciences. Explanations of particular events are comparatively rare—found only perhaps in geology and astronomy. Second, our little story explains one phenomenon, the changing of water into steam, by relating it to another phenomenon, the behavior of the molecules of which water is composed. This relation is commonly described as *reduction:* the explained phenomenon is said to be reduced to the explaining phenomenon; for example, the behavior of water is reduced to the behavior of molecules. Thus, the central problem for the theory of scientific explanation comes down to this: what is the relation between phenomena in virtue of which one phenomenon can constitute an explanation of another, and what is it about this relation that gives understanding of the explained phenomenon?

. . . . Consider a typical scientific theory—for example, the kinetic theory of gases. This theory explains phenomena involving the behavior of gases, such as the fact that gases approximately obey the Boyle-Charles law, by reference to the behavior of the molecules of which gases are composed. For example, we can deduce that any collection of molecules of the sort that gases are, which obeys the laws of mechanics will also approximately obey the Boyle-Charles law. How does this make us understand the behavior of gases? I submit that if this were all the kinetic theory did we would have added nothing to our understanding. We would have simply replaced one brute fact with another. But this is not all the kinetic theory does—it also permits us to derive other phenomena involving the behavior of gases, such as the fact that they obey Graham's law of diffusion and (within certain limits) that they have the specific-heat capacities that they do have, from the same laws of mechanics. The kinetic theory effects a significant *unification* in what we have to accept. Where we once had three independent brute facts—that gases approximately obey the Boyle-Charles law, that they obey Graham's law, and that they have the specific-heat capacities they do have—we now have only one—that molecules obey the laws of mechanics. Furthermore, the kinetic theory also allows us to integrate the behavior of gases with other phenomena, such as the motions of the planets and of falling bodies near the earth. This is because the laws of mechanics also permit us to derive both the fact that planets obey Kepler's laws and the fact that falling bodies obey Galileo's laws. From the fact that *all* bodies obey the laws of mechanics it follows that the planets behave as they do, falling bodies behave as they do, and gases behave as they do. Once again, we have reduced a multiplicity of unexplained, independent phenomena to one. I claim that this is the crucial property of scientific theories we are looking for; this is the essence of scientific explanation—science increases our understanding of the world by reducing the total number of independent phenomena that we have to accept as ultimate or given. A world with fewer independent phenomena is, other things being equal, more comprehensible than one with more . . .

On the view of explanation I am proposing, the kind of understanding provided by science is global rather than local. Scientific explanations do not confer intelligibility on individual phenomena by showing them to be somehow natural, necessary, familiar, or inevitable. However, our overall understanding of the world is increased; our total picture of nature is simplified via a reduction in the number of independent phenomena that we have to accept as ultimate. . . We don't simply replace one phenomenon with another. We replace one phenomenon with a *more comprehensive* phenomenon, and thereby effect a reduction in the total number of accepted phenomena. We thus genuinely increase our understanding of the world.

Philip Kitcher, although also proposing that explanation is a matter of unification, rejects Friedman's emphasis on phenomenon reduction. Although, indeed, we want an account of explanation to advance our understanding of the world, we must see explanation as a form of activity, not as an argument. This activity, Kitcher claims, involves an ordered pair consisting of a proposition and an act type. For Kitcher, the history of science indicates that scientific practitioners draw from a set of possible explanatory arguments (what he calls an *explanatory store*) and adopt the one that provides the greatest epistemic coherence, where coherence involves various epistemic values we associate with scientific understanding, such as predictive power, promise of future understanding, consistency with accepted laws, simplicity of theory, and so on. For instance, the history of science shows that theory acceptance is based not just on simplicity and predictive power, but also on explanatory promise. That is, we have reason to believe that the theory hasn't necessarily already explained important or lots of phenomena but that it is successful enough for us to believe that it will likely provide explanations. It was just this kind of promise that led scientists to embrace, and continue to embrace, Newton's mechanics. There is not space in this chapter to fully flesh out Kitcher's version of a unificationist model, but you can find more on it in his book, *Scientific Explanation* (co-edited with Wesley Salmon and mentioned at the end of this chapter in "Further Reading").

Information model

A fourth model to mention here is the Information model of explanation, associated primarily with Joseph Hanna and James

Greeno, as well as in some writings of Samuel Gorovitz. Like the Pragmatic model, this model emphasizes the insight that explanations are contextual and presuppose some identified contrast class of possible explanations. A difference is that for the Information model, the measure of explanatory power of a given answer is the level of information that is transmitted relative to background expectations. As Hanna puts it: "Information . . . has an obvious connection with the explanatory power of scientific theories. After all, to produce a satisfactory explanation of some phenomenon is, at the same time, to acquire information concerning the empirical variables that are 'causally implicated' in the phenomenon. Moreover, in their informal use, both of the terms 'information' and 'explanation' have the connotation of change-in-expectation."[3] Though not using the language of information, Gorovitz expresses essentially the same view with what he calls an attention to differentiating factors: ". . . he who seeks the cause of an event undertakes an inquiry that can be described as the attempt to identify the factor that makes the difference between the actual course of events and one or more particular courses of events or situations that might otherwise have occurred. The cause is, then, the factor that differentiates the actual situation from some particular standard of comparison for causal inquiry."[4] So, explanations are relative to some standard of comparison (for Gorovitz) or some generic experiment (for Hanna) or contrast class (for van Fraassen). Contrary to the Pragmatic model, though, the Information model emphasizes the explicit and measurable information that is transmitted, that is, the probability of an event relative to expected prior probabilities. As Karl Popper (we will talk quite a bit about him in Chapter Eight) pointed out, the information provided by a statement is inversely proportional to its prior expected probability. For example, the statement that tomorrow it will either rain or not rain at a specific place and time has a probability of being true of 100%, but an informative value of zero. We learn nothing from that claim. van Fraassen might put it as: we need to specify more precisely the contrast class. Relative to this class, what will count as providing the most information (or, what will end up as the differentiating factor) is what constitutes the explanation. The philosopher Peter Railton has developed the Information model of explanation more recently, but I will let Hanna's account represent this view in this chapter. Here he is:

EXPLANATION, PREDICTION, DESCRIPTION, AND INFORMATION
Joseph F. Hanna

The distinction between explanation and prediction has been much discussed in recent literature, but the equally important distinction between explanation and description has received very little attention. It is evident that explanations differ from descriptions, that an explanatory account of some phenomenon differs from a descriptive account of it, but it is difficult to separate the logical from the pragmatic aspects of these distinct scientific methods. The principle objective of this paper is to clarify this recognized distinction. As a by-product, the present analysis also provides a fresh approach to the controversy surrounding the relation between explanation and prediction.

The concept of transmitted information is the basis for distinguishing between the predictive or explanatory power of a theory on the one hand, and its descriptive power on the other hand. In brief, predictive or explanatory power is identified with information transmitted by empirical factors which can be determined prior to the data, while descriptive power is identified with total transmitted information, including information transmitted by the data. Thus, the difference between the descriptive power and the predictive or explanatory power of a theory can be attributed to information transmitted by the data itself . . .

The concept of information provides an intuitive measure of predictive power with several desirable formal properties. Any observation, e.g., the outcome of a specific experiment, may be viewed as containing a fixed amount of information, the quantity depending on the observer's background of knowledge and belief. For instance, in glancing out the window to see if snow has fallen during the night, I obtain an amount of information which generally depends on the actual state of affairs as well as upon my beliefs regarding the a-priori likelihood of various meteorological events. If it is a June morning and the ground is covered with snow, the observation will be quite informative, because surprising; if it is a January morning with snow on the ground, the observation will convey less information. Thus, the information content of an observation depends on the unexpectedness of its outcome; I am informed by an observation just to the extent that its outcome is surprising when considered in the context of my other beliefs.

Following the classic work of Shannon, we adopt the logarithm of the likelihood as a numerical measure of information. Specifically, let e be an experiment with initial conditions s and outcome r, and let $P_0(r|s)$ be the a-priori probability of response r given stimulus s, then the *a-priori information content of e given response r is* $I_0 = \log_k 1/P_0(r|s)$, where k is the unit of information.

The a-priori probability of a specific experiment is determined in large part by vaguely articulated theoretical considerations. A particular outcome may appear improbable, and thus informative, simply on the basis of introspection or intuition, or possibly in view of previous experimental results. Often, there will be no good reason to consider one outcome any more likely than another; in such cases the *principle of insufficient reason* suggests that all outcomes be assigned equal a-priori probability.

The effect of an articulated theory (e.g., a stochastic model) is to alter the a-priori probabilities of the possible outcomes of an experiment. The revised probabilities determined by a formal theory will be referred to as a-posteriori probabilities. In altering the a-priori likelihood of a given observation, a formal theory also alters its uncertainty or surprise value and thereby alters its information content. Specifically, if the a-posteriori probability of an observed outcome *exceeds* its a-priori probability, then the formal theory has accounted for some of the a-priori information in the observation. On the other hand, if the a-posteriori probability of the observed outcome is *less* than its a-priori probability, then the formal theory is misinformative. Or using somewhat different terminology, we may say that if it increases the likelihood, a formal theory *transmits* information concerning the observation, while if it decreases the likelihood, it transmits misinformation . . .

To summarize the above discussion: predictions in the experimental sciences characteristically refer to generic rather than to specific experiments. In effect, predictions are open-ended—always subject, in principle, to disconfirmation—irrespective of whether they are deterministic or stochastic in form. Predictions of uniform (as well as of stochastic) "stimulus-response" associations involve projections over an indefinite range of specific experiments. Thus, on the one hand, no prediction is ever finally safe from disconfirmation, while, on the other hand, it is in principle always open to the theorist to reject any apparent disconfirmation of a prediction due to failure to meet boundary conditions.

A similar account holds for explanation in the experimental sciences. Explanations provide answers to "why questions," but the scope of such questions extends over generic experiments (i.e., to event types or events under a description); it is never limited just to specific experiments (i.e., to concrete events). Though one might account for the outcome of Jones' experiment in laboratory X by means of a deductive or statistical explanation, the scope of the proffered explanation would never be limited to that specific experiment. In particular, failure of the explanation to account for the outcome of Smith's replication of Jones' experiment would raise doubts, at the very least, about the adequacy of the "original" explanation.

Thus, by analogy with the condition of predictive consistency*, to explain why response r is invariably associated (under appropriate boundary conditions) with stimulus s, one produces a model instance M_a such that $P_a(r|s) = 1$. More generally, to explain why stimulus s and response r are associated with frequency p (again, under appropriate boundary conditions) one produces a model instance M_a such that $P_a(r|s) = p$. This account makes it clear that the adequacy of any particular explanation in the experimental sciences is again an open-ended question: explanations of general uniform regularities, and even more so explanations of stochastic regularities, are unbounded in scope. However, the coefficient of predictive (or explanatory) power enable one to assess the adequacy of such explanations, as well as can be done, on the basis of limited and incomplete data.

Descriptive Power of Models

Although formal models are frequently used in the social sciences to generate predictions and provide explanations of empirical phenomena, they undoubtedly function more extensively as descriptions. The purpose of this section is to clarify this distinction between the predictive or explanatory role of models, on the one hand, and their descriptive role, on the other hand.

Broadly speaking, to describe a phenomenon is to classify it or to place it appropriately in a hierarchy of concepts. For example, to describe an imprint in the sand as a human footprint or a set of data points as a straight line, is to place these phenomena in appropriate classes: the class of human footprints and the class of straight lines, respectively. Notice, however, that this aspect of description is not sufficient to distinguish it from explanation and prediction; for as Hempel and others have argued, to explain (or predict) a phenomenon is to bring it under appropriate covering laws, a procedure which at least implicitly involves classification. For example, in explaining a storm on the basis of atmospheric pressure, humidity, temperature, etc., a meteorologist *classifies* the situation as being in a specific way storm producing. Thus, the distinction between explanation and description involves more than simply the presence or absence of classification.

From the present point of view, the nature of the substantiating evidence provides the basis for distinguishing between an explanatory (or predictive) and a descriptive account of some phenomenon: specifically, the distinction lies in the *source* of the evidence, whether from environmental factors or from the data, that is included in the account. The decision to classify or describe a particular imprint as a human footprint, for example, rests on a consideration of its physical properties: its size and shape, the texture of the sand, etc. In short, the description rests on information that could only be obtained in investigating the imprint. By contrast, explanations and predictions characteristically involve evidence (information) which is temporally prior and logically independent of the explanandum event. Thus, one *describes* the imprint as a human footprint on the basis of its physical properties, and from this description it follows (logically) that the imprint was made by some human (of an appropriate size and shape) moving (in an appropriate manner) on the beach. One *explains* the imprint, on the other hand, as due to some human (of an appropriate size and shape) having moved (in an appropriate manner) on the beach, from which it follows (logically) that the imprint is a human footprint. The distinction depends, then, on the source of the evidence (information) contained in the account.

[*What Hanna means by the *Condition of Predictive Consistency* is this: If one predicts on the basis of evidence s that event r will occur with probability *p*, then one is committed to project *r* with probability *p* under any circumstances in which the evidence statement s is true. In particular, the prediction that s and r are uniformly associated commits one to project r on every occasion in which s is realized.]

Chapter Summary

Science attempts not simply to describe phenomena, but to explain it. Explanations involve the phenomenon to be explained (or the explanandum) as well as what is appealed to as a way of "doing the explaining" (or the explanans). There are various models of what explanation is in science: the Covering Law model, the Causal model, the Pragmatic model, the Unificationist model, and the Information model. The Covering Law model portrays explanation as a form of argument, in which the explanandum is the conclusion. The premises of the argument form (the explanans) include both particular, relevant conditions and also covering-laws (i.e., general statements or laws that relate the particular conditions to the explanandum). Most philosophers of science have rejected the Covering Law model because not only are there counter-examples to it but also because it omits elements of explanation, such as causation, that most scientists and philosophers see as necessary for genuine explanation. The Causal model identifies the cause(s) of some phenomenon as the explanation of it and insists on the importance of causally relevant phenomena, though critics have questioned the clarity of both the notion of causation and relevance. The Pragmatic model stresses the view that relevance is central to explanation but that it is also a matter of context, of what pragmatic concerns are in play for a given explanation. The Unification model emphasizes the goal of explanation as understanding, along with the sense that understanding the world is enhanced to the extent that we recognize and establish interconnections among phenomena; we explain some phenomenon by placing it in a broader context of knowledge (i.e., by unifying it with other knowledge). The Information model draws on various elements of each of the preceding models but focuses on explanation as a measure of information or surprise.

CASE STUDY

Count Rumford (Heat)

Benjamin Thomson, Count Rumford (1753–1814) explained the nature of heat; it is a form of motion. Given Rumford's explanation of the nature of heat below, in what ways does it fit, or not, with the various models of explanation covered in this chapter? Which of the models best captures how the nature of heat is explained here?

THE NATURE OF HEAT AS MOTION
Count Rumford

It frequently happens that in the ordinary affairs and occupations of life opportunities present themselves of contemplating some of the most curious operations of nature; and very interesting philosophical experiments might often be made, almost without trouble of expense, by means of machinery contrived for the mere mechanical purposes of the arts and manufactures.

I have frequently had occasion to make this observation, and am persuaded that a habit of keeping the eyes open to everything that is going on in the ordinary course of the business of life has oftener led, as it were by accident, or in the playful excursions of the imagination, put into action by contemplating the most common appearances, to useful doubts, and sensible schemes for investigation and improvement, than all the more intense meditations of philosophers, in the hours expressly set apart for study.

It was by accident that I was led to make the experiments of which I am about to give an account; and, though they are not perhaps of sufficient importance to merit so formal an introduction, I cannot help flattering myself that they will be thought curious in several respects, and worthy of the honor of being made known to the Royal Society.

Being engaged, lately, in superintending the boring of cannon, in the workshops of the military arsenal at Munich, I was struck with the very considerable degree of heat which a brass gun acquires, in a short time, in being bored; and with the still more intense heat (much greater than that of boiling water, as I found by experiment) of the metallic chips separated from it by the borer.

The more I meditated on these phenomena the more they appeared to me to be curious and interesting. A thorough investigation of them seemed even to bid fair to give a further insight into the hidden nature of heat; and to enable us to form some reasonable conjectures respecting the existence, or non-existence, of an igneous fluid: a subject on which the opinions of philosophers have, in all ages, been much divided.

In order that the Society may have clear and distinct ideas of the speculations and reasonings to which these appearances gave rise in my mind, and also of the specific objects of philosophical investigation they suggested to me, I must beg leave to state them at some length and in such manner as I shall think best suited to answer this purpose.

From whence comes the heat actually produced in the mechanical operation above mentioned?

Is it furnished by the metallic chips which are separated by the borer from the solid mass of metal?

If this were the case, then, according to the modern doctrines of latent heat, and of caloric, the capacity for heat of the parts of the metal, so reduced to chips, ought not only to be changed, but the change undergone by them should be sufficiently great to account for all the heat produced.

But no such change had taken place; for I found, upon taking equal quantities, by weight, of these chips, and of thin slips of the same block of metal separated by means of a fine saw, and putting them, at the same temperature (that of boiling water) into equal quantities of cold water (that is to say, at the temperature of $59^{1/2\circ}$F), the portion of water into which the chips were put was not, to all appearance, heated either less or more than the other portion, in which the slips of metal were put.

This experiment being repeated several times, the results were always so nearly the same that I could not determine whether any, or what change, had been produced in the metal, in regard to its capacity for heat, by being reduced to chips by the borer.

From hence it is evident that the heat produced could not possibly have been furnished at the expense of the latent heat of the metallic chips. But, not being willing to rest satisfied with these trials, however conclusive they appeared to me to be, I had recourse to the following still more decisive experiment. [Rumford devised an apparatus in which a 130 lb. cylinder of brass was bored with a dull drill in an insulated tank of water.]

The result of this beautiful experiment was very striking, and the pleasure it afforded me amply repaid me for all the trouble I had in contriving and arranging the complicated machinery used in making it.

The cylinder, revolving at the rate of about thirty-two times in a minute, had been in motion but a short time when I perceived, by putting my hand into the water and touching the outside of the cylinder, that heat was generated; and it was not long before the water which surrounded the cylinder began to be sensibly warm.

At the end of one hour I found, by plunging a thermometer into the water in the box (the quantity of which fluid amounted to 18.77 pounds avoirdupois, or $2^{1/4}$ wine gallons) that its temperature had been raised no less than 47 degrees; being now 107° of Fahrenheit's scale.

When thirty minutes more had elapsed, or one hour and thirty minutes after the machinery had been put into motion, the heat of the water in the box was 142°.

At the end of two hours, reckoning from the beginning of the experiment, the temperature of the water in the box was found to be raised to 178°.

At two hours twenty minutes it was 200°; and at two hours thirty minutes it *actually boiled*.

By mediating on the results of all these experiments we are naturally brought to that great question which has so often been the subject of speculation among philosophers; namely: What is heat? Is there any such thing as an *igneous fluid*? Is there anything that can with propriety be called *caloric*?

We have seen that a very considerable quantity of heat may be excited in the friction of two metallic surfaces and given off in a constant stream or flux, *in all directions*, without interruption or intermission, and without any signs of diminution or exhaustion.

From whence came the heat which was continually given off in this manner, in the foregoing experiments? Was it furnished by the small particles of metal, detached from the larger solid masses, on their being rubbed together? This, as we have already seen, could not possibly have been the case.

Was it furnished by the air? This could not have been the case; for, in three of the experiments, the machinery being kept immersed in water, the access of the air of the atmosphere was completely prevented.

Was it furnished by the water which surrounded the machinery? That this could not have been the case is evident; first, because this water was continually *receiving heat* from the machinery and could not, at the same time, be *giving to*, and *receiving heat from*, the same body; and secondly, because there was no chemical decomposition of any part of this water. Had any such decomposition taken place (which indeed could not reasonably have been expected), one of its component elastic fluids (most probably inflammable air) must, at the same time, have been set at liberty, and in making its escape into the atmosphere would have been detected; but though I frequently examined the water to see if any air bubbles rose up through it, and had even made preparations for catching them, in order to examine them, if any should appear, I could perceive none, nor was there any sign of decomposition of any kind whatever, or other chemical process, going on in the water.

Is it possible that the heat could have been supplied by means of the iron bar to the end of which the blunt steel borer was fixed? Or by the small neck of gun metal by which the hollow cylinder was united to the cannon? These suppositions appear more improbable even than either of those before mentioned; for heat was continually going off, or *out of the machinery*, by both these passages, during the whole time the experiment lasted.

And, in reasoning on this subject, we must not forget to consider that most remarkable circumstance, that the source of the heat generated by friction, in these experiments, appeared evidently to be *inexhaustible*.

It is hardly necessary to add that anything which any *insulated* body, or system of bodies, can continue to furnish *without limitation* cannot possibly be a *material substance:* and it appears to me to be extremely difficult, if not quite impossible, to form any distinct idea of anything, capable of being excited and communicated, in the manner the heat was excited and communicated in these experiments, except it be MOTION.

Notes

[1] There is a lot more to Hempel and Oppenheim's model of explanation than this reading gives. They had quite a bit to say about the nature of scientific laws. They also discussed teleological, or goal-directed, explanations.

Some of the issues raised in their comments above are ones that we won't get into in this chapter. For example, as you saw, they drew a very strong connection between explanation and prediction. This has been called the Structural Identity Thesis, meaning that the structure of an explanation and the structure of a prediction are identical; the only difference is that explanations are after the fact (of the explanandum) and predictions are before the fact.

[2] This quote is from Salmon's essay, "Why Ask 'Why'?" *Proceedings and Addresses of the American Philosophical Association* 51 (1978), page 704.

[3] This quote is from Hanna's essay, "On Transmitted Information as a Measure of Explanatory Power." *Philosophy of Science* 45 (1978), page 531.

[4] This quote is from Gorovitz's essay, "Aspects of the Pragmatics of Explanation." *Nous* 3 (1969), page 62.

Further Reading

Achinstein, Peter. *The Nature of Explanation.* New York: Oxford University Press, 1983.

Garfinkel, Alan. *Forms of Explanation.* New Haven: Yale University Press, 1981.

Hempel, Carl. *Aspects of Scientific Explanation and Other Essays in the Philosophy of Science.* New York: The Free Press, 1965.

Kitcher, Philip and Wesley Salmon (eds.). *Scientific Explanation.* Minneapolis: University of Minnesota Press, 1989.

McLaughlin, Peter and Michael Ruse. *What Functions Explain.* Cambridge: Cambridge University Press, 2000.

Pitt, Joseph (ed.). *Theories of Explanation.* Oxford: Oxford University Press, 1980.

Rescher, Nicholas. *Scientific Explanation.* New York: Free Press, 1970.

Ruben, David-Hillel (ed.). *Explanation.* Oxford: Oxford University Press, 1993.

Salmon, Wesley. *Causality and Explanation.* Oxford: Oxford University Press, 1997.

Salmon, Wesley. *Scientific Explanation and the Causal Structure of the World.* Princeton: Princeton University Press, 1984.

Salmon, Wesley, Richard C. Jeffrey, and James G. Greeno. *Statistical Explanation and Statistical Relevance.* Pittsburgh: University of Pittsburgh Press, 1971.

Salmon, Wesley. *Four Decades of Scientific Explanation.* Minneapolis: University of Minnesota Press, 1990.

van Fraassen, Bas. *The Scientific Image.* Oxford: Oxford University Press, 1980.

Wallace, William A. *Classical and Contemporary Science (Causality and Scientific Explanation).* New York: University Press of America, 1981.

Wilson, Fred. *Explanation, Causation and Deduction.* Dordrecht: Reidel, 1985.

CHAPTER SIX

Evidence and Confirmation

IN THIS CHAPTER, WE WILL

- Identify some metaphysical, epistemological, and axiological aspects of evidence and confirmation
- Consider early 20th-century notions of the logic of confirmation
- Examine the contemporary view called Bayesianism
- Examine criticisms of Bayesianism and investigate Achinstein's view of evidence as good reasons to believe

In 1859, the year that Darwin published *The Origin of Species,* Alfred Wilks Drayson published a book of his own, *The Earth We Inhabit.* In his book, Drayson argued that the earth was expanding; he calculated the rate of expansion to be such that the circumference of the earth grew around one centimeter per kilometer per year. He claimed as evidence of the truth of his view that among the effects of this expansion would be the case that telegraph wires eventually would stretch and begin to snap. This raises a question: Would telegraph wires that stretched and snapped in the future be evidence of the truth of Drayson's claims? (Well, it raises lots of questions, but this is the one we care about in this chapter!)

Or, consider this (true) story: Stanford philosopher John Perry tells of a time he once followed a trail of sugar on a supermarket floor, pushing his cart down the aisle on one side of a tall counter and back the aisle on the other, seeking the shopper with the torn sack to tell him he was making a mess. With each trip around the counter, the trail became thicker, but Perry seemed unable to catch up with the offending shopper. Finally it dawned on him that he was the person he was trying to catch.

Was the trail of sugar evidence for John Perry as to who was the offending shopper?

What can we say about these two stories? In Drayson's telegraph wire case, the failure of snapping telegraph wires seems to speak to whether or not some particular hypothesis has been supported. The hypothesis in this case is might be any one of the following (or, for that matter, any number of other hypotheses):

h: The earth is expanding;

h*: The earth is expanding at the rate of 1cm/km/year;

h**: An expanding earth will cause wires of particular tension to snap.

Whatever the particular hypothesis involved, the snapping or failure of snapping of telegraph wires would be seen as being relevant evidence, relevant to supporting or failing to support the truth of some particular hypothesis. That is, the phenomenon of snapping wires (or the phenomenon of the failure of wires to snap) would be taken as evidence for some hypothesis and in the context of justifying some hypothesis.

In Perry's sugar case, the phenomenon of the sugar trail was not taken as evidence for any specific hypothesis beyond "Some local shopper has a torn bag of sugar." It was not taken as evidence that one hypothesis, say:

h: Smith's bag of sugar is torn

was more likely than a second hypothesis, say:

h*: Jones' bag of sugar is torn.

Rather, Perry saw the phenomenon of the trail of sugar as evidence that someone's bag of sugar was torn and this motivated him to seek the offending shopper. Perry was taking a phenomenon as evidence more in a context of discovery. That is, he did not have some particular hypothesis in mind for which this phenomenon was said to justify or help justify. (We might say that the trail of sugar was evidence *of* a torn sugar bag, but not necessarily evidence *for* any particular hypothesis.)

Now, the point of raising these two cases is that scientists consider the notion of evidence in various contexts and for various concerns. Sometimes some phenomenon is taken as evidence in the context of trying to test the truth of some particular hypothesis. Sometimes some phenomenon is taken as evidence that some particular hypothesis, rather than a different hypothesis, is true (or, at least, better supported). Sometimes some phenomenon is taken as evidence that some line of inquiry is more fruitful than another. In a nutshell, scientists treat phenomena as evidence for a variety of reasons and in a variety of concerns. We will see in the latter part of this chapter that this point is stressed by the philosopher of science, Peter Achinstein.

The logic of confirmation

There are, of course, many questions about the notion of evidence (and confirmation) that arise, both for scientists and philosophers. Probably the most basic is simply: what is evidence? What does it mean for some phenomenon, usually some observation, to be evidence? The first thing to notice is that evidence is a relation: some phenomenon is evidence for some hypothesis (or perhaps of some other phenomenon). If something is evidence, it is *evidence that* some hypothesis is the case (or perhaps that some event occurred). This, unfortunately, does not tell us much. Just what makes some phenomenon evidence that some hypothesis is the case? Right now, as I write these words, there is a jar of peanuts sitting on my desk. That is a phenomenon. Is it evidence that some hypothesis is the case? Is it evidence that some particular hypothesis is more probable than some other hypothesis? Can it be evidence for an unlikely hypothesis? For multiple hypotheses? For conflicting hypotheses?

Evidence is obviously an epistemological notion, but it also has axiological aspects. For example, we assume that for some phenomenon to be evidence that some hypothesis is the case that phenomenon must be relevant to the hypothesis. (Can this jar of peanuts on my desk be evidence that the theory of plate tectonics is true—or false, for that matter?) Relevance, though, is a matter of interest and values. At least most philosophers of science would take certain features of some phenomenon to be relevant to a particular hypothesis because certain issues are taken as salient and important rather than other issues. There is also the interest-based (or value-based) issue of what types of evidence matter for a particular concern as well as how much evidence matters. This is certainly the case in the context of law, where secondhand evidence (such as hearsay) is less significant than, say, physical evidence; also, the legal standard of clear and convincing evidence is different than the legal standard of preponderance of evidence. In the context of science, there is also the issue of what types of evidence matter and how much evidence. A single case of experimental results that support a particular hypothesis is rarely taken very seriously if a given experiment can be repeated. However, in some situations, say in cosmology where scientists are much more constrained in setting up repeatable experiments, a single confirming instance might carry more weight. The point is that there are interest- and value-based decisions to be made about evidence.

In terms of the history of philosophers of science being concerned with the issue of evidence, the first half of the 20th century involved what was called the logic of confirmation. A major concern for these philosophers was how to justify our beliefs, including our scientific beliefs. Empirical, scientific beliefs are rarely, if ever, deductively warranted. Many scientific claims, especially generalizations and laws, rest on inductive support, but philosophers have long questioned the reliability of inductive reasoning. Nevertheless, scientists certainly seem to proceed on inductive logic and certainly seem to produce very reliable claims about the world. In particular, philosophers of science began to ask about the "logic of confirmation," that is, what structure and form underlay the relation between hypotheses and phenomena that served as evidence. Carl Hempel (whose work on the nature of explanation we looked at in the previous chapter), for one, proposed that confirmation (or the nature of evidence) be understood as a logical relation between sentences (hypotheses on the one hand and sentences stating some observation on the other). The question became whether or not these sentences entailed the other; that is, did the truth of some particular hypothesis entail certain observational sentences, or did certain observational sentences entail the truth of some particular hypothesis?

We do not need to go into detail about this approach to understanding confirmation and evidence, but Hempel himself acknowledged various problems that arose. Two, in particular, were seen as notorious. The first problem is sometimes referred to as *armchair confirmation*. The problem is this: If we have a hypothesis, say, that "all ravens are black," then common sense seems to tell us that every time we encounter an instance of a black raven, that encounter is evidence for the truth of the hypothesis that all ravens are black. That makes sense. Likewise, if we have a statement that "all non-black things are non-ravens," then every time we encounter an instance of some non-black thing that is a non-raven (e.g., a blue book), that encounter is evidence for the truth of the statement that all non-black things are non-ravens. However, the statement "all ravens are black" turns out to be logically equivalent to the statement that "all non-black things are non-ravens." As a result, it seems that when we encounter a blue book, that encounter is evidence for the truth of the hypothesis that all ravens are black! As we sit in our armchairs and look around the room to see blue books, white pieces of paper, mauve tissue boxes, chartreuse lamps, that crusty, some weird color of "stuff" under the sofa cushion—all those non-black, non-raven things—help to confirm (or provide evidence for) the hypothesis that all ravens are black. At best this is counter-intuitive and it certainly is not in keeping with scientific practice.

The second problem is a formal proof that *anything confirms anything* (or: any phenomenon provides evidence for any hypothesis). This proof rests on two seemingly reasonable conditions. First, there is the *Consequence Condition:* If e confirms (or is evidence for) hypothesis h, and if h^* is a consequence of h, then e confirms (or is evidence for) h^*. For example, let h be Newton's theory of gravity. Let h^* be the hypothesis that there is gravity on the moon equal to value k. Then if e confirms (is evidence for) h, e also confirms (is evidence for) h^*. Second, there is the *Converse-Consequence Condition:* If e confirms (or is evidence for) hypothesis h^* and h^* is a consequence of hypothesis h, then e confirms (or is evidence for) h. For example, let h^* be Kepler's Laws. Let h be Newton's theory of gravity. Then if e confirms (or is evidence for) Kepler's Law, it also confirms (or is evidence for) Newton's theory. The proposed proof that anything confirms anything (or: anything provides evidence for any hypothesis) is as follows:

Let h^* be Newton's theory of gravity.
Let h^{**} be the hypothesis that the moon is made of cheese.
Let h be the conjunction of h^* & h^{**}.
Let e be evidence for h^*.

Then: e confirms (or is evidence for) h^* (Given). h^* is a consequence of h (By logical deduction). So, e confirms (or is evidence for) h (By the Converse-Consequence Condition). h^{**} is a consequence of h (By logical deduction). So, e confirms (or is evidence for) h^{**} (By the Consequence Condition). The absurd conclusion is that *any* evidence for Newton's theory of gravity confirms (or is evidence for) the hypothesis that the moon is made of cheese. Indeed, more generally, this shows that *any* evidence for *any* hypothesis confirms (or is evidence for) *any other* hypothesis, no matter how absurd or irrelevant! This result is, of course, outlandish, though the proof is valid. We could avoid the apparent problem here by rejecting either or both the Consequence Condition or Converse-Consequence Condition, however, both seem to be reasonable rules of inference. In any case, we certainly have arrived at an unacceptable result, so there is clearly a problem here. And, indeed, philosophers of science wrestled with some other way of understanding what it is to confirm, or provide evidence for, a hypothesis.

Bayesianism

One such conceptual move was to emphasize the notion of comparative confirmation, that is, whether and how some phenomenon supports one hypothesis over another hypothesis, along with the notion of degrees of confirmation, that is, how well some phenomenon supports some hypothesis. The sense of "how well" was spelled out in terms of assessing the probability of a hypothesis being supported by the evidence provided by the phenomenon. The basic claim here is this: We can determine and assign probabilities for some hypothesis being true; if we can also show that the probability of that hypothesis being true is increased because of encountering some phenomenon (that is, the phenomenon makes the hypothesis more likely to be true), then not only can we measure this, but we have a criterion for what counts as evidence, namely, phenomena that increase the probability of a hypothesis being true.

Now, what I just said was a little bit quick and dirty, but it gets explained admirably well below in a selection by the philosopher of science, Peter Godfrey-Smith. Before turning directly to what he says, there is a point of terminology to clear up. There is a difference between "probability" and "likelihood," even though in everyday contexts we often use them interchangeably. The philosopher of biology, Elliot Sober, gives a nice example to illustrate the difference. To begin with, Sober says, there is a difference between the odds of a hypothesis being true *given some phenomenon* and a phenomenon happening *given some hypothesis*. Suppose, he says, that you and I are sitting in a cabin one night and we hear a rumbling noise in the attic. We wonder what could have produced that noise. I suggest the hypothesis that there are gremlins in the attic and they are bowling. You reject this suggestion. Now, the probability of my hypothesis is pretty low; that is, the odds of there being gremlins in the attic given a rumbling noise are pretty low. But, the likelihood of the hypothesis is actually relatively high; that is, *if* there are gremlins in the attic, it could be fairly likely that they are causing the rumbling noise by bowling. The gremlin hypothesis is not very plausible; its probability is quite low, but its likelihood is reasonably high. A slightly more technical way of stating this is that the probability of a hypothesis being true on the basis of some phenomenon is not necessarily the same as the likelihood of some phenomenon being the case on the basis of some hypothesis. We'll see below how Godfrey-Smith notes this distinction in explaining a current perspective on evidence. In the reading below, Godfrey-Smith explains, and also critiques, the most prevalent view today regarding evidence and confirmation, a view that is called *Bayesianism*, named for a theorem articulated by Thomas Bayes:

BAYESIANISM AND MODERN THEORIES OF EVIDENCE

Peter Godfrey-Smith

Through much of the twentieth century, the unsolved problem of confirmation hung over philosophy of science. What is it for an observation to provide evidence for, or confirm, a scientific theory? . . . The logical empiricists wanted to start from simple, obvious ideas—like the idea that seeing many black ravens confirms the hypothesis that all ravens are black—and build from there to an "inductive logic" that would help us understand testing in science. They failed, and we left the topic in a state of uncertainty and frustration.

. . . . The situation has now changed. Once again a large number of philosophers have real hope in a theory of confirmation and evidence. The new view is called *Bayesianism*. The core ideas of this approach developed slowly through the twentieth century, but eventually these ideas started to look like they might actually solve the problem . . .

Although Bayesianism is the most popular approach to solving these problems today, I am not in the Bayesian camp. Some parts of Bayesianism are undeniably powerful, but I would cautiously put my money on some different ideas . . .

Understanding Evidence with Probability

At this point I will shift my terminology. The term "confirmation" was used by the logical empiricists, but more recent discussions tend to focus on the concept of *evidence*. From now on I will follow this usage.

Bayesianism tries to understand evidence using probability theory. This idea is not new. It has often seemed natural to express some claims about evidence in terms of probability. Rudolf Carnap spent decades trying to solve the problem in this way. And outside philosophy this idea is familiar; we say that seeing someone's car outside a party makes it very *likely* that he is at the party. The mathematical fields of statistics and data analysis use probability theory to describe the kinds of conclusions that can be drawn from surveys and samples. And in law courts, we have become familiar with the description of forensic evidence, like DNA evidence, in terms of probability.

Consequently, many philosophers have tried to understand evidence using probability. Here is an idea that lies behind many of these attempts: when there is an uncertainty about a hypothesis, observational evidence can sometimes *raise or lower the probability* of the hypothesis.

Bayesianism is one version of this idea. For Bayesians, there is a formula that is like a magic bullet for the evidence problem: *Bayes's theorem*. Thomas Bayes, an English clergyman, proved his theorem in the eighteenth century. As a theorem—as a piece of mathematics—his ideas is very simple. But the Bayesians believe that Thomas Bayes struck gold.

Here is the magic formula in its simplest form:

$$P(h|e) = P(e|h)P(h)/P(e).$$

Here it is in a form that is more useful for showing how it works in philosophy of science:

$$(2) \quad P(h|e) = \frac{P(e|h)P(h)}{P(e|h)P(h) + P(e|not\text{-}h)P(not\text{-}h)}.$$

Here is how to read formulas of this kind: $P(X)$ is the probability of X. $P(X|Y)$ is the probability of X conditional upon Y, or the probability of X *given* Y.

How does this formula help us to understand confirmation of theories? Read "h" as a hypothesis and "e" as a piece of evidence. Then think of $P(h)$ as the probability of h measured without regard for evidence e. $P(h|e)$ is the probability of h given e, or the probability of the hypothesis *in the light of e*. Bayes's theorem tells us how to compute this latter number. As a consequence, we can measure what *difference* evidence e makes to the probability of h. So we can say that evidence e *confirms* h if $P(h|e) > P(h)$. That is, e confirms h if it *makes h more probable* than it would otherwise be.

Picture someone changing her beliefs as evidence comes in. She starts out with $P(h)$ as her assessment of the probability of h. If she observes e, what should her new view be about the probability of h? It seems that her new view of the probability of h should be given by $P(h|e)$, which Bayes's theorem tells us how to compute. So Bayes's theorem tells us how to *update* probabilities in the light of evidence. (More on this updating later.)

There are two central ideas in Bayesiansism: the idea that e *confirms* h if e raises the probability of h, and the idea that probabilities should be *updated* in a way dictated by Bayes's theorem.

Bayes's theorem expresses $P(h|e)$ as a function of two different kinds of probability. Probabilities of hypotheses of the form $P(h)$ are called *prior* probabilities. Looking at formula 2, we see $P(h)$ and $P(not\text{-}h)$; these are the prior probability of h and the prior probability of the negation of h. These two numbers must add up to one. Probabilities of the form

$P(e|h)$ are often called "likelihoods," or the likelihood of evidence on theory. In formula 2, we see two different likelihoods, $P(e|h)$ and $P(e|not\text{-}h)$. (These need not add up to any particular value.) Finally, $P(h|e)$ is the "posterior probability" of h.

Suppose that all these probabilities make sense and can be known; let's see what Bayes's theorem can do. Imagine you are unsure about whether someone is at a party. The hypothesis that he is at the party is h. Then you see his car outside. This is evidence e. Suppose that before seeing the car, you think the probability of his going to the party is 0.5. And the probability of his car's being outside if he *is* at the party is 0.8, because he usually drives to such events, while the probability of his car's being outside if he is *not* at the party is only 0.1. Then we can work out the probability that he is at the party *given* that his car is outside. Plugging the numbers into Bayes's theorem, we get $P(h|e) = (.5)(.8)/[(.5)(.8) + (.5)(.1)]$, which is almost 0.9. So seeing the car raises the probability of h from 0.5 to about 0.9; seeing the car strongly confirms the hypothesis that the person is at the party.

This all seems to be working well. We can do a lot with Bayes's theorem, *if* it makes sense to talk about probabilities in these ways. It is common to think that it is not too hard to interpret probabilities in the form $P(e|h)$, the likelihoods. Scientific theories are supposed to tell us *what we are likely to see*. Some Bayesians underestimate the problems that can arise with this idea, but there is no need to pursue that yet. The probabilities that are more controversial are the prior probabilities of hypotheses, like $P(h)$. What could this number possibly be measuring? And the posterior probability of h can only be computed if we have its prior probability. So although it would be good to use Bayes's theorem to discuss evidence, many interpretations of probability will not allow this because they cannot make sense of prior probabilities of theories. If we want to use Bayes's theorem, we need an interpretation of probability that will allow us to talk about prior probabilities. And that is what Bayesians have developed. This interpretation of probability is called the *subjectivist* interpretation.

The Subjectivist Interpretation of Probability
Most attempts to analyze probability have taken probabilities to measure some real and "objective" feature of events. A probability value is seen as

measuring the *chance* of an event happening, where this chance is somehow a feature of the event itself and its location in the world. That is
how we usually speak about the probabilities of horses winning races, for
example. But according to the subjectivist interpretation, probabilities
are *degrees of belief*. A probability measures a person's degree of confidence in the truth of some proposition. So if someone says that the probability of the horse "Tom B" will win its race tomorrow is 0.4, he is saying
something about his *degree of confidence* that the horse will win.

. . . Subjectivism sees probabilities as degrees of belief in propositions or hypotheses about the world. To find out what someone's degree
of belief in a proposition is, we do not ask him or look inside his mind.
Instead, we see his degrees of belief as revealed in his *gambling behavior,*
both actual and possible. Your degrees of belief are revealed in which
bets you would accept and which you would reject. Real people may be
averse to gambling, even when they think the odds are good, or they may
be prone to it even when the odds are bad. Here and in other places,
Bayesianism seems to be treating not *actual* people but *idealized* people.
But let us not worry too much about that. To read off a person's degree of
belief from his gambling behavior, we look for the odds on a given bet
such that the person would be *equally willing to take either side* of the
bet. If we know a person's subjectively fair odds for a bet, we can read
off his degree of belief in the proposition that the bet is about.

For example, suppose you think that 3:1 is fair for a bet on the truth
of *h*. That is, a person who bets that *h* is true wins \$1 if she is right and
loses \$3 is she is wrong. More generally, let us say that to bet on *h* at
odds of *X*:1 is to be willing to risk losing \$*X* if *h* is false, in return for a
gain of \$1 if *h* is true. So a large *X* corresponds to a lot of confidence in
h. And if your subjectively fair odds for a bet on h are *X:1*, then your degree of belief in h is $X/(X + 1)$.

So far we have just considered one proposition, *h*. But your degrees
of belief for *h* will be related to your degrees of belief for other propositions as well. You will have a degree of belief for *h & j* as well, and for *not-h*,
and so on. To find your subjective probability for *h & j*, we find your subjectively fair odds for a bet on *h & j*. So a person's belief system at a particular time can be described as a network of subjective probabilities.
These subjective probabilities work in concert with the person's preferences ("utilities") to generate his or her behavior. From the Bayesian

point of view, all of life is a series of gambles, in which our behavior manifests our bets about what the world is like.

Bayesians claim to give a theory of when a person's total network of degrees of belief is "coherent," or rational. They argue that a coherent set of degrees of belief has to follow the standard rules of the mathematics of probability.

. . . Let us now connect these ideas to the problem of evidence. The ideas about belief and probability discussed in this section so far apply to a person's beliefs *at a specific time*. But we can use these ideas to give a theory of the rational *updating* of beliefs as evidence comes in. Bayes's theorem tells us about the relations between $P(h)$ and $P(h|e)$. Both those assignments of probability are made *before e* is observed. Then suppose *e* is actually observed. According to Bayesianism, the rational agent will update her degrees of belief so that her *new* overall confidence in *h* is derived from her *old* value of $P(h|e)$. So the key relationship in this updating process is

$$(3) \quad P_{new}(h) = P_{old}(h|e).$$

The probability $P_{new}(h)$ then becomes the agent's new *prior* probability for *h*, for use in assessing how to react to the *next* piece of evidence. So "today's posteriors are tomorrow's priors." . . .

Assessing Bayesianism

Bayesianism is an impressive set of ideas. There is a big literature on these topics, and I will not try to predict whether Bayesianism will work in the end. But many of the debates have to do with the role of prior probabilities, so they are worth further discussion.

In standard presentations of Bayesianism, a person is imagined to start out with an initial set of prior probabilities for various hypotheses, which are updated as evidence comes in. The initial set of prior probabilities is a sort of *free choice*; no initial set of prior probabilities is better than another so long as the axioms of probability are followed. This feature of Bayesianism is sometimes seen as a strength and sometimes as a weakness.

It can seem to be a weakness because Bayesianism cannot criticize very strange initial assignments of probability. And, one might think, where you end up after updating your probabilities must depend on where you start.

But this is only true in a sense. Bayesians would argue that although prior probabilities are freely chosen and might be weird initially, the starting point gets "washed out" by incoming evidence, so long as updating is done rationally. The starting point matters less and less as more evidence is taken into account.

This idea is usually expressed as a kind of *convergence*. Consider two people with very different prior probabilities for h, but the same likelihoods for all possible pieces of evidence (e_1, e_2, e_3, . . .). And suppose the two people see all the same actual evidence. Then these two people's probability for h will get closer and closer. It can be proved that for *any* amount of initial disagreement about h, there will be *some* amount of evidence that will get the two people to any specified degree of closeness in their final probabilities for h. That is, if having final probabilities within (say) 0.001 of each other counts as being in close agreement, then no matter how far apart people start, there is some amount of evidence that will get them within 0.001 of each other by the end. So initial disagreement is eventually washed out by the weight of evidence.

This convergence could, however, take a very long time. These "in the limit" proofs may not help much. As Henry Kyburg likes to put it, we must also accept that for *any* amount of evidence, and any measure of agreement, there is *some* initial set of priors such that this evidence will *not* get the two people to agree by the end. So some Bayesians have tried to work out a way of "constraining" the initial assignments of probability that Bayesianism allows.

I think there is a more basic problem with the arguments about convergence or the "washing out" of prior probabilities. The convergence proofs assume that when two people start with very different priors, they nonetheless agree about all the *likelihoods* (probabilities of the form $P(e_1|h)$, etc.). That is needed for disagreements about the priors to "wash out." But why should we expect this agreement about likelihoods? Why should two people who disagree massively on many things have the same likelihoods for all possible evidence? Why don't their disagreements affect their views on the *relevance* of possible observations? This agreement *might* be present, but there is no general reason why it should be . . . This argument suggests that convergence results do not help much with problems about theory choice in science.

Evidence as good reasons to believe

In his book, *The Book of Evidence,* philosopher of science Peter Achinstein remarked that a dean at his university, who was also a scientist, complained to him that, "you have never made a contribution of interest to scientists." Harsh! Achinstein took his remarks to mean not just him (Peter Achinstein), but philosophers of science generally. (Nice move!) This motivated Achinstein to (re)consider what philosophers of science had to say, and had been saying, about evidence. We'll see shortly what Achinstein concluded.

As mentioned at the beginning of this chapter, there are a variety of concerns that scientists have that are related to the notion of evidence. Sometimes (often) evidence matters in terms of providing justification for accepting or rejecting some particular hypothesis. Other times evidence matters in terms of deciding between competing hypotheses. Still others times evidence matters less in terms of justifying hypotheses and more in terms of generating avenues of research (that might well later lead to formulating particular hypotheses). So, some phenomenon (such as a trail of sugar on a supermarket floor) might be evidence of some other phenomenon (such as some shopper's bag of sugar is torn and spilling). The latter could be formulated as a particular hypothesis to be tested, but not necessarily. Indeed, it is often the case that scientists encounter some phenomenon and this leads to a "I wonder if . . ." moment. For example, in 1820, when Hans Oersted accidently and surprisingly noticed that an electrical current affected a magnetic needle, he was not testing the hypothesis that it would. But he took the (surprising) phenomenon of the moving needle as evidence that there might be some connection between electricity and magnetism. Only later did he formulate a hypothesis for testing and then claim that there was evidence for this hypothesis. (Some philosophers will argue that he really was testing an implicit hypothesis here.) My point, however, is simply that scientists take the notion of evidence sometimes in the context of testing and justifying hypotheses, but sometimes in other contexts.

Besides various contexts and concerns that scientists have for evidence, there are also various kinds of evidence. By this I do not mean that some kinds of evidence are physical and others are something else. Rather, I mean that sometimes what counts as evidence is the presence of some phenomenon and other times what counts as evidence is the absence of some phenomenon. That is, when something does *not* happen, that can be evidence for some hypothesis or evidence of some other phenomenon. For instance, in the case study at the end of this chapter, Michelson and Morley were testing to see if they could detect and measure a change in the behavior of light in a particular experiment. What they got was "negative" evidence, that is, the absence of any relevant change. This was taken by various physicists as evidence for competing hypotheses. Likewise, in the plate tectonics case study (on pages 348–365), the absence of a land bridge between Africa and South America was taken as evidence for competing hypotheses.

Now, in terms of considering actual scientific practice, it is often the case that some phenomenon is treated by different scientists as evidence for competing hypotheses. That is to say, that scientists who advocate different hypotheses—often competing hypotheses that are incompatible with each other—point to the same empirical phenomenon as support evidence for their own particular hypothesis. From their perspective, concerns about evidence are focused on issues such as: was this phenomenon predicted by our background theory, is this phenomenon consistent with the hypothesis in question, is the phenomenon a one-time event or can it be repeated, was the experimental design that produced or detected this phenomenon reliable, is this phenomenon explainable by only this given hypothesis or by others as well, and so on. Given these types of concerns by scientists, it is small wonder that they are puzzled by the emphasis of philosophers of science to discuss evidence in terms of subjective degrees of confidence and gambling odds. At the very least, it is not obvious how the latter (gambling odds) helps to answer questions about how and why some phenomenon serves as evidence, much less how and why it serves as good evidence for some hypothesis (or even good evidence of some other phenomenon to be investigated). At best, they say, all this Bayesian talk provides a means of *measuring* evidence (or our confidence in something as being evidence), but not in *explaining* the nature of evidence. Because of this, Achinstein has argued that philosophers, in their quest to understand the nature of evidence, need to shift their focus from subjective degrees of confidence to the issue of having good reasons to believe (1) that some phenomenon actually is evidence for something and (2) that it is evidence that matters to scientists in their various concerns regarding evidence (e.g., concerns that are sometimes justificatory and sometimes exploratory).

In the reading below, Achinstein provides a brief summary and critique of other notions of evidence, especially subjectivist ones. He rejects these on two grounds; they are largely mistaken and they are largely irrelevant to working scientists. To support this claim he identifies two assumptions that he sees underlying the standard philosophical views about evidence, what he calls the "weakness assumption" (that philosophers provide a pretty weak understanding of evidence) and the "a priori assumption" (that philosophers do not take evidence to be an empirical matter). First, we will see what he says about these and then, later, turn to his alternative, objective conception of evidence. So, here is Achinstein:

THE BOOK OF EVIDENCE
Peter Achinstein

. . . [Philosophers] of science have developed theories or definitions of evidence that are designed to do at least two things for scientists: first, to clarify what it means to say that some fact is evidence that a hypothesis is true; second, and relatedly, to help scientists determine whether (and to what extent) putative evidence supports a hypothesis. These goals are championed by a range of philosophers who have developed theories of evidence . . . .

By and large, however, philosophical theories of evidence are ignored by scientists. You don't find scientists with disagreements of the sort in question turning to philosophers for help. Why not? Is this just a matter of people in very different fields ignoring one another's work? That may be part of the answer, but I don't think that is the main problem or the most interesting one. I think the problem is deeper, and stems from two very basic, but questionable, assumptions philosophers usually make about evidence.

The first assumption is that evidence is a very weak notion. You don't need very much to have evidence that something is the case. The second is that the evidential relation is a priori and not empirical. It is a logical, or semantic, or mathematical relation that can be established by "calculation." The philosophers who make both assumptions are concerned with an objective, not subjective, notion of evidence. On their view, whether some fact e is evidence that hypothesis h is true, and how that evidence is, does not depend on what anyone believes about e, h, or their relationship. Not all philosophers who talk about evidence recognize, or are interested in, objective evidence. Subjective Bayesians, for example, reject such a notion. But a range of philosophers accept the idea . . . [Here] I will defend the claim that although there are occasions on which scientists employ a subjective concept of evidence, the important concept for them is objective . . .

The Weakness Assumption

I will illustrate this assumption [that the concept of evidence is weak] by reference to three standard theories of evidence. The first theory is a Bayesian one: for a fact e to be evidence that a hypothesis h is true, it is both necessary and sufficient that e increase h's probability over its prior probability. So, for example, since my buying one ticket in a million-ticket lottery increases the probability that I will win, this fact is evidence that I will win. To be sure, it is not a lot of evidence; it is certainly not decisive; but it is *some*. According to *The New York Times*, there is 1 elevator accident per 6 million rides. Using this as a basis for a probability judgment, since my riding this elevator today raises the probability that I will be involved in an elevator accident today, it is evidence that I will. Not a lot, but some, perhaps a tiny bit of evidence. Such a notion of evidence . . . is too weak to be taken seriously. To be sure, the bigger the probabilistic boost e gives to h, the stronger the evidence. But the fact remains that for e to be evidence that h, on this view, all that is required is that e raise h's probability.

A second standard theory of objective evidence is hypothetico-deductive (h-d). For e to be evidence that h it suffices for e to be derivable deductively from h. So, for example, since the fact that light travels in straight lines is derivable from the classical wave theory of light, it is evidence that light is a classical wave motion. This is a very weak notion of evidence, because it allows the same fact to be evidence for a range of conflicting theories. (The same is true of the previous Bayesian account.) For example, since the rectilinear propagation of light is also derivable from the classical particle theory, it is evidence that light is composed of classical particles.

A third approach to objective evidence is a "satisfaction" theory of the sort proposed by Hempel. The basic idea is that an observation report is confirming evidence for a hypothesis if the hypothesis is satisfied by the class of individuals mentioned in that report. To use Hempel's famous example, on observation report that a particular raven observed is black is evidence that all ravens are black. So is the fact that a particular nonblack thing observed is a nonraven. Glymour devises a more complex bootstrap approach that takes Hempel's idea of satisfaction as basic.

Let me say why I believe such notions of evidence are too weak for scientists to take an interest in. Why do scientists want objective evidence for their hypotheses? What does evidence give them? My answer . . . is that in the case of the two most important types of objective evidence (which I call potential and veridical evidence) it gives them a good reason to believe their hypotheses. Not necessarily a conclusive one, or the best possible one, but a good one nonetheless. If the results of a biopsy constitute evidence that the patient's tumor is malignant then there is good reason to believe the patient has cancer. By contrast, if you visit your doctor complaining of a stomach ache persisting for the last few days I don't believe the doctor would or should count this fact by itself as evidence that you have cancer, even if the probability that you do is raised slightly by this symptom. By itself it is not a good reason to believe this hypothesis. Similarly, although the fact that I am entering an elevator increases my chances of being in an elevator accident, it is not evidence that this will be so, even a little bit of evidence, since by itself it fails to provide any reason to believe this hypothesis.

. . . [E]vidence is related to probability, but . . . it is a "threshold" concept with respect to probability. In order for e to be evidence that h there must be a certain threshold of probability that e gives to h, not just any amount greater than zero. What is the threshold? Returning to the idea that evidence provides a good reason to believe, a basic principle . . . is that if e is a good reason to believe h, then it cannot also be a good reason to believe *not-h* or some proposition incompatible with *h*. (It might of course be the case that e is an equally good reason to believe *h* as to believe *not-h*. But that does not make it a good reason to believe both or either.) So, for example, the fact that I am tossing this fair coin is not a good reason to believe that it will land heads, because it is an equally good reason to believe it will land tails; that is, it is not a good reason to believe either hypothesis . . .

Does this mean that it is impossible to have evidence for conflicting theories? Yes and no. Yes, it is impossible for the same fact to be evidence for conflicting theories. The fact that I am about to toss this fair coin is not evidence that it will land heads and evidence that it will land tails. It is not evidence—not even a little bit of evidence—that either "theory" is true . . .

Some philosophers who are objective Bayesians about evidence suggest that there is a concept of evidence according to which *e* is evidence that *h* if and only if *h*'s probability on *e* is sufficiently high, say greater than $\frac{1}{2}$. This notion is much stronger than the weak increase-in-probability account. And it has the advantage of ruling out the unwanted lottery, elevator, and stomach ache cases. However, even if probability of greater than $\frac{1}{2}$ is a necessary condition, it is not sufficient. High probability by itself is too weak for evidence, since *h*'s probability may be high with or without *e*. It may have nothing to do with *e*. Let *e* be the fact that Michael Jordan eats Wheaties. (He used to promote Wheaties on TV.) Let *h* be the hypothesis that Michael Jordan will not become pregnant. Now *h*'s probability with or without *e* is close to 1. Yet surely the fact that Michael Jordan eats Wheaties is not evidence, or a good reason to believe, that he will avoid pregnancy. For *e* to be evidence that *h*, for *e* to be a good reason to believe *h*, not only must *h*'s probability on *e* be sufficiently high, but there must be some other connection between *e* and *h*, or the probability of such a connection: *e* must have "something to do" with [i.e., be relevant to] *h* . . .

On all of these [above] views of evidence it is too easy to get evidence. To be sure, each of these theories could be strengthened. For example, instead of demanding just any increase in probability, that view could be altered to require a very significant increase. In addition to high probability, that view could impose some further condition(s). The h-d and satisfaction views, respectively, could require the hypothesis to entail, or to be satisfied by, not just some single instance but a range of them. [But] "significant" increases in probability do not suffice for evidence. Nor will "many instances" entailed or satisfied by the hypothesis. This is due to the fact that what you get in such cases does not necessarily give you a good reason to believe a hypothesis. High probability is necessary, but we need to consider a lot more than this for the putative evidence to provide a good reason, or indeed any reason, to believe a hypothesis.

This, then, is the first reason scientists do not and should not take such philosophical accounts of evidence seriously: they are too weak to be taken seriously. They do not give scientists what they want, or enough of what they want, when they want evidence.

The A Priori Assumption

The second assumption made by many philosophers who try to provide objective accounts of evidence is that the evidential relation is a priori: whether e, if true, is evidence that h, and how strong that evidence is, is a matter to be determined completely by a priori calculation, not by empirical investigation.

. . . [R]ecent scientists offered an empirical reason for rejecting the claim that the burned animal bones in the same layer as stone tools and sediment that looks like wood ash is evidence that the first culinary campfires were built by Peking Man in caves in China between 200,000 and 500,000 years ago. The empirical reason was the new discovery that although the sediment looks like wood ash, it is in fact not this but fine minerals and clay deposited by water.

I am not claiming that all evidential statements are empirical. There are cases . . . where enough information is packed into the e-statement to make the claim that e is evidence for h a priori. But these cases are the exception, not the rule. Nor am I denying that it is possible to transform an empirical evidential claim into an a priori one by incorporating a sufficient amount of additional information of a sort that might be used in defending the empirical evidential claim. But even if this is possible, that will not suffice to alter the empirical character of the original evidential claim, or demonstrate that the original claim is incomplete until this transformation occurs. An empirical claim, whether evidential or not, is not necessarily incomplete or lacking in truth-value if its defense is not provided; nor does the original claim lose its empirical character if it is replaced by an a priori claim. Furthermore, an empirical evidential claim may be true, and very useful, even if a scientist who makes the claim does not have a sufficient defense of it that could transform the claim into an a priori one.

If evidential claims, or many of them, are empirical, not a priori, then it is scientists, not philosophers, who are in the best position to judge whether e, if true, is evidence that h, and how strong that evidence is. If evidential claims are, by and large, empirical, that is and ought to be an important reason why scientists do not consult philosophical theories of evidence when they try to settle disagreements over evidential claims. Philosophical theories would make such disagreements settleable on a priori grounds. Accordingly, scientists may find philosophical theories of evidence wanting because they give a very mistaken idea of how evidential disputes are usually settled.

Having criticized other accounts of evidence, Achinstein claims that there are different concepts of evidence that scientists use. He identifies four such concepts: (1) subjective evidence, (2) epistemic-situation evidence, (3) veridical evidence, and (4) potential evidence. Subjective evidence is the concept that something can count as evidence for some particular audience at some particular point in time. For example, having no better account for why some planets appeared sometimes to move backward in their orbits, Ptolemaic epicycles provided an explanation, and this retrograde motion was evidence to support the epicycle view. It is subjective, however, with the emphasis that something is evidence *for someone in particular* with the emphasis on someone *believing* some hypothesis on the basis of some phenomenon. Epistemic-situation evidence, although somewhat similar to subjective evidence, emphasizes that *anyone* in a particular epistemic situation is *justified* in believing h on the basis of e. This concept, says Achinstein, is objective in the sense that there is an objectively describable epistemic situation such that there is a justifiable basis for *h* on the basis of *e*. It is not important whether or not anyone in fact actually believes anything about *h* or *e* or their relation to each other or even whether or not anyone is actually in the relevant epistemic situation. The point is that in a given epistemic situation, there is justification for *h* on the basis of *e*.

These two concepts of evidence, subjective and epistemic-situation, allow for the possibility that some phenomenon could be evidence for a false hypothesis. Again, the retrograde motion of some planets was taken as evidence for the Ptolemaic epicycle account of planetary motion and the structure of the universe. This account, we now say, is false (and was false then, too); but, under these two notions of evidence, there was evidence that supported that account. Achinstein's concept of veridical evidence, however, disallows evidence for false hypotheses. ("Veridical" means truthful, genuine.) Under this concept, retrograde motion was never evidence for the Ptolemaic view, even though they believed it at the time and even though they had some justification for believing it at the time. The concept of veridical evidence rules out that any phenomenon can actually be evidence for any false hypothesis. Evidence is objective and nonrelativized. Under this concept, *e* is a good reason to believe *h*, regardless of whether or not anyone does believe *h* or is even aware of *e*. Potential evidence is a weaker version of veridical evidence because it is objective, but does not require that *h* be true. For example, Achinstein says, suppose someone has spots on his skin that are typically associated with the measles virus, but it turns out that the person does not in fact have measles. Those spots are not veridical evidence (because the hypothesis that the person has measles is false), but are potential evidence, because they provide a good objective reason to believe the measles hypothesis.

Now, what is important about this discussion, for Achinstein, is that he claims that scientists use all four concepts of evidence, so any philosophical account of evidence needs to acknowledge and deal with all of them. Continuing from his book, he makes his case on the following page for this view:

THE BOOK OF EVIDENCE *(continued)*
Peter Achinstein

What Type of Evidence is Most Important for Scientists?

Scientists seek veridical evidence, not just potential or ES-[epistemic-situation] evidence. They want their hypotheses to be true. And they want to provide a good reason for believing them in a sense of "good reason" that requires truth. They are not satisfied with providing only a justification of belief for those in certain epistemic situations, even their own, since the belief might turn out to be false. Nor are they satisfied with providing a good reason for belief in the weaker [potential] sense . . .

If veridical and not simply E-S or potential evidence is what scientists desire, is it attainable? One might think that this is too high to aim, since veridical evidence requires the truth of the hypothesis, and not simply probability. Let us be clear regarding what is and what is not required to obtain veridical evidence. It is not required that one obtain conclusive evidence; it is not required that the evidence prove the hypothesis (that the probability of the hypothesis on the evidence be 1). Nor is it even required that one knows that one has obtained veridical evidence. To show that veridical evidence is not attainable one would need to show either that truth, or that good reasons for belief, or both, are not attainable. Even if one is a philosophical sceptic who denies that knowledge of the truth of any hypothesis is possible, that would not commit one to the view that veridical evidence is unattainable, but only to the view that it is impossible to know that one has it. Scepticism does not preclude veridical evidence. Scientists, who tend to reject skepticism, certainly believe that they have obtained veridical evidence for many of their hypotheses. These scientists believe that such evidence is both desirable and attainable.

Are All Four Concepts Employed? When?

My answer to the first question is yes, at least in this sense. Statements of the following types, each of which corresponds to one of the concepts distinguished, make good sense:

1. Anyone who knows or justifiably believes such and such would be justified in believing that *e* is evidence that *h*. For such a person, *e* should count as evidence that *h*.

2. *e* is *X*'s evidence that *h*; *e* is what *X* proposes as, takes to be, evidence that *h*.
3. Potentially, *e* is evidence that *h*; *e* is the sort of fact that is usually evidence that a hypothesis such as *h* is true.
4. *h* is true, since *e* is genuine evidence that it is . . .

Under what conditions is each concept employed? That is, why are four concepts needed? At the simplest level, there are occasions when all one wants to know are the reasons some person has or had for believing something, whether or not these are good reasons, whether or not the person was justified in believing a hypothesis for those reasons. This is so in historical contexts when an investigator simply wants to learn what some scientist of the past proposed as evidence. Such a concept is also employed by scientists concerned with a hypothesis *h* who what to know what evidence some other scientist has proposed for *h*. In such situations one may ask for the scientist's evidence without implying or presupposing that it is ES-, potential, or veridical evidence. When one speaks of evidence in these cases no evaluation of that evidence is being made.

The other three concepts involve evaluations of different types. With ES-evidence one's concern is with justification of belief for someone in a certain epistemic situation . . . Whether *e* is (was) ES-evidence for a particular scientist can be a difficult historical question to answer, since one needs to know what epistemic situation the scientist was actually in with respect to the hypothesis, as well as whether one in that epistemic situation is justified in believing the hypothesis. For this reason, scientists themselves, in contrast to historians, do not have very much interest in this question . . .

The usual interest of scientists is not historical, nor is it restricted to particular or types of epistemic situation, not even their own. To be sure, when a scientist claims that *e* is evidence that *h*, he believes and hopes that, given his knowledge, he is justified in believing *h* on the basis of *e*. But he believes and hopes for something much more. That is why for scientists potential and (particularly) veridical evidence are crucial.

A scientist wants to know whether some experimental results reported in *e* provide a good reason for believing a hypothesis *h*—not a good reason for him, but a good reason period, independent of epistemic situations. And he wants to know whether *e* is a good reason in the strong sense. His goal is to obtain veridical evidence, since he seeks true hypotheses. He is not satisfied with potential evidence that he knows or believes is not veridical. And whether it is veridical evidence has nothing to do with what he or anyone else knows or believes. It is not veridical evidence for one type of epistemic situation but not another.

What role remains for potential evidence? The main one is to serve as a vehicle for obtaining veridical evidence and for demonstrating that some experimental result is not veridical evidence. A necessary condition for e's being veridical evidence is that it is potential evidence. A necessary condition for e's being a good reason in the strong sense is that it is a good reason in the weak sense. Accordingly, in searching for veridical evidence one must search for something that is at least potential evidence. One can refute someone's claim that e is veridical evidence by showing that it is not even potential evidence . . .

The Empirical Character of Evidence Statements

My final question is this: Are evidence statements of the form

(a) e is evidence that h, as these are understood in terms of the four concepts of evidence, empirical statements?

My initial answer is very simple: All evidence statements of all four types are empirical. Their truth is not establishable by a priori calculation. The reason can be stated briefly. Potential, veridical, and ES-evidence all require e to be true. Whether e is true . . . is an empirical question, not settleable a priori. Subjective evidence does not require e to be true. But it does require that the person or community whose evidence it is hold certain beliefs about e and h (including the belief that e is evidence that h, and the belief that h is true or probable). Whether such beliefs are in fact held is an empirical matter, not an a priori one.

Given Achinstein's insistence on truth, you might conclude that he takes the concept of veridical evidence as the central and most important of the four concepts. He certainly does take it to be the strongest concept. Nevertheless, he argues that it, along with the subjective and ES concepts, can be characterized in terms of potential evidence. Indeed, since we just do not *know* whether or not our hypotheses are true (after all, we might have lots of good reasons to believe they are true, but we might be wrong), actual scientific practice proceeds on the basis of potential evidence. In addition, Achinstein states that there is an obvious relationship between evidence and explanation, as evidence should help provide us with some explanatory account for a hypothesis. As he puts it: if, given e (and other background information, b), the probability is high that there is an explanatory connection between h and e, then, given e and b, e is a good reason to believe h. With this notion of the high probability of an explanatory connection, he then characterizes veridical evidence in this way:

> e is veridical evidence that h, given b, if and only if: e is potential evidence that h, given b; h is true; and there is an explanatory connection between e's being true and h's being true.

ES-evidence becomes:

> e is ES-evidence that h (with respect to an epistemic situation ES) if and only if: e is true and anyone in ES is justified in believing that e is (probably) veridical evidence that h.

And subjective evidence becomes:

> e is X's subjective evidence that h at time t if and only if: at t, X believes that e is (probably) veridical evidence that h, and X's reason for believing h true (or probable) is that e is true.

Potential evidence, then, captures the reality of scientific practice, says Achinstein, because it both emphasizes the desire to provide a true account of phenomena while at the same time acknowledging that we cannot take it for granted that our hypotheses and theories are true. We want not just confidence, but confidence in what is actually the case.

We saw in Chapter Three that many philosophers of science question the view (and sometimes, assumption) of realism. Yet, this seems to be part of Achinstein's notion of evidence. That is, potential (and veridical) evidence is understood only in the sense of an objective truth, whether or not we know it. Some philosophers, then, have been hesitant to adopt a concept of evidence that requires or presupposes truth, along with the notion that there cannot be "real" (potential or veridical) evidence for false hypotheses. Likewise, there have been questions about the nature of explanation with respect to the importance of Achinstein's requirement of explanatory connection. In addition, there has been a question about relevance as part and parcel for evidence to be understood and fruitfully characterized. How is it determined whether or not some phenomenon is relevant and evidentiary for a hypothesis? These are questions that remain and point to the need for further exploration and elaboration of the notion of evidence.

Chapter Summary

The notion of evidence is fundamental to science. In terms of generating questions and even hypotheses, we speak of phenomena (observations, events in the world) as evidence of some other phenomenon. For example, a scab on one's arm is evidence that the person was wounded or injured. We also, and even moreso, speak of phenomena as evidence for some hypothesis being true or probable (or, evidence that some hypothesis). A basic philosophical question, then, is what exactly is evidence? What makes some phenomenon an evidentiary phenomenon? There are also questions of how much and what types of evidence matter, as well as how and in what ways some phenomenon is relevant to some hypothesis. Early 20th-century discussions about evidence were framed in terms of the logic of confirmation (how phenomena confirmed or helped confirm hypotheses or theories and how to formalize that relationship). Several problems and paradoxes arose from these discussions, which led philosophers of science to reframe the issue of confirmation to that of evidence and to propose different conceptions of evidence. One proposal, which has been endorsed by many philosophers, is that of Bayesianism, which embraces a common sense notion that for some phenomenon to be evidence for a hypothesis it must be that it enhances the probability that the hypothesis is the case (that is, that the hypothesis is more likely to be true given that phenomenon than without that phenomenon). One concern about this approach to understanding evidence is that it often interprets probability in subjective terms of degrees of confidence or gambling odds. Another conception of evidence, said to be objective, is Peter Achinstein's view that evidence is good reason to believe; if some phenomenon is evidence that some hypothesis is the case, then that phenomenon provides good reason to believe the hypothesis, where "good reason" gets fleshed out in terms of a high probability of an explanatory connection between the evidence and the hypothesis.

CASE STUDY

A.A. Michelson & E.W. Morley

An important experiment in the history of physics was made by the team of Albert A. Michelson (1852–1931) and Edward W. Morley (1838–1923). Underlying this experiment was the belief that light was a wave and, as such, light required some medium through which it travels. This medium was referred to as aether. It was believed that the universe was filled with this extremely rarified medium. But, however rarified the aether was, the view was that as the earth moved in its orbit around the sun, it would meet some sort of resistance because of the aether. In addition, as a wave, light would (and, indeed, does) display what are called interference patterns. That is, given certain experimental conditions, the waves of light interfere with each other and produce interference patterns. As a result, the assumption was that with a very delicate and precise experiment, physicists should be able to detect a change in the interference patterns of light as the earth moved in its orbit through the presumed aether, because sometimes the earth would be moving "upstream" in the aether, sometimes "downstream" and sometimes "cross-stream." By manipulating the experimental apparatus so that it sometimes did all of these (that is, move upstream, downstream, cross-stream), there should be a detectable change in the interference patterns. What resulted from the Michelson-Morley experiments was that no detectable change in the interference patterns was found. With respect to different physicists, this result was taken as evidence in a variety of ways. That is, some physicists took these result as evidence that there was no aether, others that the measuring apparatus itself was affected by the movement through the aether, and so on. Given the description by Michelson and Morley of their experiment, consider what features of evidence are relevant to what they were trying to do, how and why this phenomenon—in this case, the absence of a change—functioned for them and for others as evidence, what it was taken as evidence of and for. Also, does this case fit with Achinstein's account of evidence; with a Bayesian account? In what ways does it lend credence to either account and in what ways does it not? (The "emission theory" that they speak of is the view that light is a particle, being emitted from some source, and the "undulatory theory" is the view that light is a wave.)

THE RELATIVE MOTION OF THE EARTH AND THE LUMINIFEROUS ETHER

A.A. Michelson & E.W. Morley

The discovery of the aberration of light was soon followed by an explanation according to the emission theory. The effect was attributed to a simple composition of the velocity of light with the velocity of the earth in its orbit. The difficulties in this apparently sufficient explanation were overlooked until after an explanation on the undulatory theory of light was proposed. This new explanation was at first almost as simple as the former. But it failed to account for the fact proved by experiment that the aberration was unchanged when observations were made with a telescope filled with water. For if the tangent of the angle of aberration is the ratio of the velocity of the earth to the velocity of light, then, since the latter velocity in water is three-fourths its velocity in a vacuum, the aberration observed with a water telescope should be four-thirds of its true value.

On the undulatory theory, according to Fresnel, first, the aether is supposed to be at rest, except in the interior of transparent media, in which, secondly, it is supposed to move with a velocity less than the velocity of the medium in the ratio $n^2 - 1/n^2$, where n is the index of refraction. These two hypotheses give a complete and satisfactory explanation of aberration. The second hypothesis, notwithstanding its seeming improbability, must be considered as fully proved, first, by the celebrated experiment of Fizeau, and secondly, by the ample confirmation of our own work. The experimental trial of the first hypothesis forms the subject of the present paper.

If the earth were a transparent body, it might perhaps be conceded, in view of the experiments just cited, that the intermolecular aether was at rest in space, notwithstanding the motion of the earth in its orbit; but we have no right to extend the conclusion from these experiments to opaque bodies. But there can hardly be any question that the aether can and does pass through metals. Lorenz cites the illustration of a metallic barometer tube. When the tube is inclined, the aether in the space above the mercury is certainly forced out, for it is incompressible. But again we have no right to assume that it makes its escape with perfect freedom, and if there be any resistance, however slight, we certainly could not assume an opaque body such as the whole earth to offer free passage through its entire mass . . .

In April, 1881, a method was proposed and carried out for testing the question experimentally.

In deducing the formula for the quantity to be measured, the effect of the motion of the earth through the aether on the path of the ray at right angles to this motion was overlooked. The discussion of this oversight and of the entire experiment forms the subject of a very searching analysis by H.A. Lorenz, who finds that this effect can by no means be disregarded. In consequence, the quantity to be measured had in fact but half the value supposed, and as it was already barely beyond the limits of errors of experiment, the conclusion drawn from the result of the experiment might well be questioned; since, however, the main portion of the theory remains unquestioned, it was decided to repeat the experiment with such modifications as would insure a theoretical result much too large to be masked by experimental errors. The theory of the method may be briefly stated as follows:

Let sa (Fig. 1) be a ray of light which is partly reflected in ab, and partly transmitted in ac, being returned by the mirrors b and c, along ba and ca. ba is partly transmitted along ad, and ca is partly reflected along ad. If then the paths ab and ac are equal, the two rays interfere along ad. Suppose now, the aether being at rest, that the whole apparatus moves in the direction sc, with the velocity of the earth in its orbit, the directions and distances traversed by the rays will be altered thus:— The ray sa is reflected along ab (Fig. 2); the angle bab_1, being equal to the aberration $= a$ is returned along ba_1, $(aba_1 = 2\alpha)$, and goes to the focus of the telescope, whose direction is unaltered. The transmitted ray goes along ac, is returned along ca_1, and is reflected at a_1, making ca_1e, equal $90 - a$, and therefore still coinciding with the first ray. It may be remarked that the rays ba_1 and ca_1 do not now meet exactly in the same point a_1, though the difference is of the second order; this does not affect the validity of the reasoning. Let it now be required to find the difference in the two paths aba_1, and aca_1.

Let $V =$ velocity of light.
$v =$ velocity of the earth in its orbit.

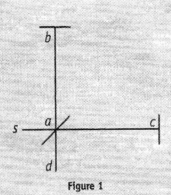

Figure 1

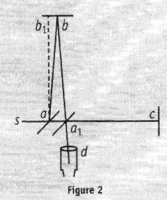

Figure 2

D = distance of ab or ac (Fig. 1).
T = time light occupies to pass from a to c.
T_1 = time light occupies to return from c to a_1 (Fig. 2).

Then

$$T = D/V - \nu \qquad T_1 = D/V + \nu$$

The whole time of going and coming is

$$T + T_1 = 2D \, V/V^2 - \nu^2,$$

and the whole distance traveled in this time is

$$2D \, V^2/V^2 - \nu^2 = 2D(1 + \nu^2/V^2),$$

neglecting terms of the fourth order. The length of the other path is evidently $2D \sqrt{(1 + \nu^2/V^2)}$, or to the same degree of accuracy,

$2D \, (1 + \nu^2/2V^2)$. The difference is therefore $D \, \nu^2/V^2$. If now the whole apparatus be turned through 90°, the difference will be in the opposite direction, hence the displacement of the interference-fringes should be $2D\nu^2/V^2$. Considering only the velocity of the earth in its orbit, this would be $2D \times 10^{-8}$. If, as was the case in the first experiment, $D = 2 \times 10^6$ waves of yellow light, the displacement to be expected would be 0.04 of the distance between the interference-fringes . . . .

In what precedes, only the orbital motion of the earth is considered. If this is combined with the motion of the solar system, concerning which but little is known with certainty, the result would have to be modified; and it is just possible that the resultant velocity at the time of the observations was small, though the chances are much against it. The experiment will therefore be repeated at intervals of three months, and thus all uncertainty will be avoided.

It appears from all that precedes reasonably certain that if there be any relative motion between the earth and the luminiferous aether, it must be small . . . .

Further Reading

Achinstein, Peter. *The Book of Evidence.* Oxford: Oxford University Press, 2001.

Achinstein, Peter (ed.). *The Concept of Evidence.* Oxford: Oxford University Press, 1983.

Earman, John. *Bayes or Bust? A Critical Examination of Bayesian Confirmation Theory.* Cambridge: The MIT Press, 1992.

Glymour, Clark. *Theory and Evidence.* Princeton: Princeton University Press, 1980.

Goodman, Nelson. *Fact, Fiction, and Forecast, 4th ed.* Cambridge: Harvard University Press, 1983.

Hesse, Mary. *The Structure of Scientific Inference.* Berkeley: University of California Press, 1974.

Horwich, Paul. *Probability and Evidence.* Cambridge: Cambridge University Press, 1982.

Howson, Colin and Peter Urbach. *Scientific Reasoning: The Bayesian Approach, 2nd ed.* Chicago: Open Court, 1993.

Jeffrey, Richard. *The Logic of Decision.* New York: McGraw-Hill, 1965.

Salmon, Wesley. *The Foundations of Scientific Inference.* Pittsburgh: University of Pittsburgh Press, 1967.

Skyrms, Brian. *Choice and Chance, 3rd ed.* Belmont: Wadsworth, 2000.

Stove, David C. *The Rationality of Induction.* Oxford: Oxford University Press, 1986.

CHAPTER SEVEN

Reductionism and Unity of Science

IN THIS CHAPTER, WE WILL

- Identify some metaphysical, epistemological, and axiological aspects of reductionism and the unity of science
- Examine the case in favor of reductionism and a resulting unity of science
- Consider the case against reductionism as either necessary or sufficient for unity of science

You know, of course, that water is H_2O; that is, a molecule composed of two hydrogen atoms joined to one oxygen atom. After reading the Case Study in Chapter Five in this book, you now know (if you did not already) that heat is the motion of molecules. You might also know that light is one form of electromagnetic radiation (something we learned from physicists, especially Michael Faraday and James Clerk Maxwell). In addition, you might have heard of what physicists call the Theory of Everything, in which all of the fundamental forces of nature are unified into one theory that accounts for them. (They do not yet have that Theory of Everything—or, TOE, as they like to say—but they are working on it!) So, what is the point of mentioning these things? It is that a very basic and very common aspect of scientific investigation is to construct an account of the phenomena of the world in such a way as to yield the most complete and accurate and coherent account possible. If there is a way the world is then ideally there is (or will be) a single, correct scientific account of the world. Now, there is a lot (including a lot of controversy) built into that simple statement, which is the subject of this chapter. In particular, this chapter will look at the notions that (1) there is, or ought to be, a unity of science and (2) such a unity is the result of acknowledging that more complex phenomena can be reduced to less complex phenomena. This statement, too, has a lot built into it, which we will investigate. So, let's get started.

Ontological, epistemological, and axiological unity of science

We will begin with a statement by E.O. Wilson, a renowned entomologist. In this statement, he notes how, as a student, he became captivated by science and what he called "the Ionian Enchantment." What he speaks of is both the power of science to explain natural phenomena and also of the unifying nature of this power. As he says, he came to embrace the unity of science, a unity that he ultimately refers to as *consilience*, and a unity that, for him, ultimately encompasses all human knowledge, not just the natural sciences. Here is what he says:

CONSILIENCE
E.O. Wilson

I had experienced the Ionian Enchantment. That recently coined expression I borrow from the physicist and historian Gerald Holton. It means a belief in the unity of the sciences—a conviction, far deeper than a mere working proposition, that the world is orderly and can be explained by a small number of natural laws. Its roots go back to Thales of Miletus, in Ionia, in the sixth century B.C. The legendary philosopher was considered by Aristotle two centuries later to be the founder of the physical sciences. He is of course remembered more concretely for his belief that all matter consists ultimately of water. Although the notion is often cited as an example of how far astray early Greek speculation could wander, its real significance is the metaphysics it expressed about the material basis of the world and the unity of nature.

The Enchantment, growing steadily more sophisticated, has dominated scientific thought ever since. In modern physics its focus has been the unification of all the forces of nature—electroweak, strong, and gravitation—the hoped-for consolidation of theory so tight as to turn the science into a "perfect" system of thought, which by sheer weight of evidence and logic is made resistant to revision. But the spell of the Enchantment extends to other fields of science as well, and in the minds of a few it reaches beyond into the social sciences, and still further . . . to touch the humanities. The idea of the unity of science is not idle. It has been tested in acid baths of experiment and logic and enjoyed repeated vindication. It has suffered no decisive defeats. At least not yet, even though at its center, by the very nature of the scientific method, it must be thought always vulnerable . . .

There is only one way to unite the great branches of learning and end the culture wars [that is, the division between the sciences and the humanities, with respect to content, methods, and aims]. It is to view the boundary between the scientific and literary cultures not as a territorial line but as a broad and mostly unexplored terrain awaiting cooperative entry from both sides. The misunderstandings arise from ignorance of the terrain, not from a fundamental difference in mentality. The two cultures share the following challenge. We know that virtually all of human behavior is transmitted by culture. We also know that biology has an important effect on the origin of culture and its transmission. The question remaining is how biology and culture interact, and in particular how they interact across all societies to create the commonalities of human nature. What, in the final analysis, joins the deep, mostly genetic history of the species as a whole to the more recent cultural histories of its far-flung societies? That, in my opinion, is the nub of the relationship between the two cultures. It can be stated as a problem to be solved, the central problem of the social sciences and the humanities, and simultaneously one of the great remaining problems of the natural sciences.

. . . From diverse vantage points in biology, psychology, and anthropology, [researchers] have conceived a process called *gene-culture coevolution*. In essence, the conception observes, first, that to genetic evolution the human lineage has added the parallel track of cultural evolution, and, second, that the two forms of evolution are linked . . . Gene-culture coevolution is a special extension of the more general process of evolution by natural selection.

Notice that, for Wilson, the consilience between the sciences and the humanities really amounts to the problems and concerns of the humanities ultimately being framed and addressed within the sciences, so, although both genes and cultures have an impact on human evolution, both are finally to be accounted for in scientific terms. Whether or not we agree with his view, the more important point for us right now is that Wilson's statement displays two notions. The first notion is that there is a unity of phenomena. That is, there is a world "out there" to be explained and that world is what it is, independent of our beliefs or theories about it. There are electrons and genes and earthquakes and all sorts of phenomena in the world and they exist independent of our beliefs and theories. That is what *discovery* is all about; we find out things about the world that we never knew. In addition, there is just one world "out there," which is incredibly complex and varied, but, still, it is just one world. We might think about it in a variety of ways and those ways might change over time (and, indeed, they have), but nevertheless, the world is what it is and the phenomena are what they are. So, there is a unity of phenomena, or, if you prefer, a unity of the world. As philosophers put it, there is *ontological unity*.

Furthermore, Wilson's statement makes clear that he sees a unity of science in terms of that ontological unity being explained ultimately by a grand scientific theory. As he says, gene-culture coevolution is a special extension of the more general process of evolution by natural selection. The notion that different and varied phenomena can be explained by a single scientific theory is, of course, one of the goals of scientific theorizing and is taken as one mark of a good scientific theory. The point here is that one sense of unity of science is that unity comes about because different phenomena are unified under a single account. There is unity of explanation. As philosophers put it, there is *epistemological unity*.

Having gotten this far into this book, you know what comes next! That's right, *axiological unity*. In other words, another sense of unity of science is the notion that the aims and goals (and other values) of scientific investigations are also unified. This last sense of unity, axiological unity, is sometimes not discussed very much. The reason is because many scientists and philosophers (and just ordinary folks, for that matter) take it for granted that the aims and goals of all of the sciences are an understanding of how the world works, perhaps with some other aspects as well in terms of aiding that understanding. For example, accurate predictions are a goal of the various sciences, but mainly as a measure of how good our theories and models are, which then finally tell us if we really do have a good understanding of phenomena. We will actually discuss these issues in greater detail in Chapters Twelve and Fourteen, although we will certainly touch on them later in this chapter.

So, to begin with, as we consider the notion of the unity of science, we see right away that the term "unity of science" can mean ontological unity, epistemological unity, or axiological unity, depending upon whether we are talking about the unity of scientific content or method(s) or aims and values.

Reductionism

A notion that is related to the unity of science is that of reductionism. That is to say, one way that science can be unified is by showing that all the various sciences are really aspects of one single science and the "higher level" sciences (say, biology or psychology) can be shown to actually be reduced to more a "basic level" science (say, physics). Philosophers and scientists sometimes speak of one theory being reduced to another or of some phenomenon being explained in terms of another phenomenon or even of one kind of thing "just being" an example of another kind of thing. For example, at the beginning of this chapter, we noted that water *just is* H_2O. In other words, one kind of thing—an everyday fluid with certain features—*really is* another kind of thing: chemical molecules with certain features (quite unlike the features we usually associate with the everyday fluid). Historically, water was taken as a basic element, not something that could be broken down into simpler parts, for centuries. It was not until the 1700s that it was discovered, via experimentation, that water was composed of ("just is") a particular configuration of two gases. As we now say, water just is H_2O. This is *ontological reduction;* one kind of phenomenon is shown to be really an instance of another, more basic, kind of phenomenon. What makes this ontological, of course, is that we take it to be true that water just is H_2O independent of whether or not we discovered that fact; it is something true about the world. Yes, we have come to believe this because of experimentation and scientific theory, but it was not experimentation that created the fact that water is H_2O, rather experimentation allowed us to discover that water is H_2O. Again, the emphasis of ontological reduction is that particular kinds of phenomena are said to actually be instances of other kinds of phenomena. This is true not just of water, but, as we noted at the beginning of the chapter, of light as electromagnetic radiation and many other features of the world.

Additionally, this ontological reduction is not just a one-step process. Not only do we say that water is really composed of hydrogen and oxygen molecules, but we also say that hydrogen and oxygen are themselves really just particular configurations of even smaller entities, electrons and protons (and neutrons). Physicists speak of leptons and quarks as making up these protons and neutrons. The point is that what some physical object "really" is—say, my cat Karloff—is a bunch of subatomic particles configured in certain ways. As we said, this is the notion of ontological reduction: complex phenomena (whether objects or events or processes) are constituted by smaller and simpler phenomena, such that what is "really" real are the smaller, simpler constituents.

Another sense of reduction is *epistemological* reduction. There are many concepts, models, theories, and so on that scientists use to explore and explain phenomena. The various sorts of concepts, models, theories, and so on that scientists use to explore and explain phenomena can themselves be reduced to the concepts, models, theories, and so on of the more basic sciences. Almost always the story goes like this: If we had good enough theories of individual behavior, say, from economics or psychology, we could—at least in principle—give a complete account of collective behavior. So, a "complete" psychology could explain everything that sociology now explains. As such, sociology would be perhaps convenient, but superfluous and not necessary. Anything it could explain, psychology could explain. But the story continues; if we had a complete understanding of biology, we would not need a science of psychology. After all, psychology deals with certain features of biological organisms. So, a complete biology would be able to explain everything that psychology explains and more (e.g., there are aspects of biology that psychology does not and cannot explain). Of course, we will not stop there: a complete biochemistry could—again, at least in principle—explain all of biology and a complete chemistry could explain all of biochemistry and, finally (at least for most reductionists), a complete physics could explain all of chemistry. Everything that is physical must be subject to the laws of physics, so a complete physics would, in the long run, give a full account of all physical nature and that includes everything all the other sciences deal with.

As the famous physicist, Ernest Rutherford, once remarked, "All science is either physics or stamp collecting." This, at least, is the core of epistemological reduction. What are reduced in epistemological reduction are the concepts, models, theories, and so on of the "less basic" sciences.

We will soon look at two readings that flesh out the nature and details of what such an epistemological reduction would be, but first let me give you a fairly simple example. In the early 1600s, the astronomer Johannes Kepler formulated three laws of the motion of the planets in our solar system. These laws were (1) planetary orbits are ellipses (not circles), with the sun as one of the foci; (2) in any two equal periods of time, equal areas are swept out by a line from the sun to a given planet; and (3) the squares of the periodic times are proportional to the cubes of the mean distances from the sun to a given planet. Now, several decades later, Isaac Newton formulated his famous laws of motion, which were: (1) every body continues in its state of rest, or of uniform motion in a right line, unless it is compelled to change that state by forces compressed on it; (2) the change of motion is proportional to the motive force impressed, and is made in the direction of the right line in which that force is impressed; and (3) to every action there is always opposed an equal reaction, or the mutual actions of two bodies upon each other are always equal and directed to contrary parts. What Newton showed (he gave the mathematical calculations) was that Kepler's three laws of planetary motion were one instance of his (Newton's) broader laws of motion (along with the law of gravitation). In other words, Kepler's model (or, theory) could be fully explained and even derived from Newton's model (or, theory), but not vice versa. Newton's theory is said, then, to reduce Kepler's theory. Here we are not talking directly about ontological reduction (we are not saying that the planets are reduced to simpler things), but about epistemological reduction; in this case, a reduction of one model or set of laws to another model or set of laws.

This sense of *theoretical* or *explanatory* reduction—that is, reducing one theory to another or showing that one theory explains everything that another theory does (plus more)—is the most common version of epistemological reduction. Another important epistemological aspect of scientific inquiry is, of course, exploration, meaning the techniques and practices that scientists use to explore the world in the hopes of eventually explaining the world. Reduction as it applies to this epistemological notion of exploration is referred to as *methodological* reduction.

Now, with respect to epistemological reduction, we noted above that the usual claim is that *in principle* there is a hierarchy of sciences that reflect the nature of the subject matter of those sciences, with physics almost always identified as the most basic science, followed by chemistry on up to the social sciences. Not all scientists or philosophers accept the "reductionist program" and even some who do accept it to some degree do not necessarily accept the view that reductionism is either necessary or sufficient for unity of science, as we will see in the selection by the philosopher Jerry Fodor that begins on page 226. Some philosophers—and scientists, for that matter—accept the notion of reduction in principle, but not necessarily in practice. For example, some biologists and philosophers of biology agree that biological organisms are, of course, physical entities (and, so, perhaps ontological reduction might make sense), but they deny that epistemological reduction of biology to physics is likely or plausible or even desirable. In addition, though it is unstated, there is the underlying issue of the purpose or aim of reductionism. What do we *hope* to achieve in the attempt to reduce biology to physics. Those in support of a reductionist program claim that what we hope to achieve is a better understanding of phenomena and with this better understanding comes better applications of this knowledge. For example, the more we know about biochemical and physiological features of organisms, the better we can develop therapeutic medicines. Critics disagree and we will look at this issue directly and more completely in Chapters Twelve and Fourteen.

Arguments for and against unity of science from reduction

The above discussion centered around two notions: unity of science and reduction(ism). Among both scientists and philosophers there are varying views about these two notions, including how they relate to one another. Some people claim that there is no unity of science, that the various sciences have different content, methods, and goals. Those differences, for some, are not just differences, but incompatible differences. For example, many biologists (and social scientists) think of explanation in terms of functional explanation, that is, some phenomena are goal-directed (such as, the function of the heart is to circulate blood). Physics does not speak of functional explanation. So, not everyone thinks that there can be a single, unified science, even if there is a single, unified world of phenomena. (Some philosophers and scientists would even deny that there is a single, unified world of phenomena.) On the other hand, among those scientists and philosophers who do embrace the notion of a unity of science, some do not claim that such a unity is a matter of reducing "higher level" sciences to more "basic" sciences. For example, we will see that Jerry Fodor argues that there is a confusion between the view of reductionism as being true and the view of the generality of physics. The first view claims that all other sciences can be reduced to physics; the second view claims that all other sciences cannot contradict physics (since physical laws, if true, apply to all physical things). So, although the notions of unity of science and reductionism are clearly related, not everyone agrees on the nature of that relationship. The two readings that make up the rest of this chapter, indeed, offer two different views on this issue. The first reading is by Paul Oppenheim and Hilary Putnam. They argue for a reductionist version of unity of science. The second reading is by Jerry Fodor, who argues against a reductionist version of unity of science.

Oppenheim and Putnam address various issues in the following selection. They suggest that reductionism should be thought of as a working hypothesis for scientists. Clearly, the higher level sciences at present have not been reduced to physics. However, there have been a number of reductionistic successes in the past (such as Kepler's laws being reduced to Newton's laws). So, reductionism seems a plausible working hypothesis, they say. In addition, it has the practical benefit of providing a good synopsis of scientific activity and relations among the various sciences. Indeed—although they do not say this explicitly—non-reductionist views of science would seem to suggest a non-unified world of phenomena. So, given some past success and given no good (or, at least, no better) alternative working hypothesis, reductionism seems to be the most reasonable approach to take for scientific inquiry.

In the following selection, Oppenheim and Putnam begin with laying out various conceptions of unity of science. One conception is *unity of language*. What they mean by this is that the terms and concepts of one science can be replaced by the terms and concepts of another (more basic) science, and still have everything in the first science accounted for. So, we could reduce the concept of light to the concept of electromagnetic radiation (and understand that whenever we use the term "light" we are actually just referring to electromagnetic radiation). A second conception is *unity of laws*. Here it is not just the terms and concepts of one science being reduced to another science, but the laws of the first science can be translated, as it were, into laws of the more basic science (but not vice versa). So, again, Kepler's laws could be formulated as just an example of Newton's laws. A third conception of unity of science, and one that Oppenheim and Putnam only mention but do not explore here, is the notion of unity of science as "connected" laws. What they mean is that the various laws of a higher level science can be not only formulated in terms of the laws of a more basic science, but that the more basic science shows a connection among the laws of the higher level science, perhaps by showing that two separate laws of the higher level science can be formulated as just instances of a single law in the more basic science. (But, again, the selection below does not discuss this.)

There are two other notions of unity of science that Oppenheim and Putnam mention. First, they speak of a *unity of method*, by which they mean that different sciences can be unified by having the same standards of explanation, evidence, and so on. To the extent that they do not have the same such standards, they are not unified. The second notion, a sort of unity of language, is that unity of science comes from defining all scientific terms in *sensationalistic predicates*. That really just means defining them all in terms of observable qualities or features of physical things. Neither of these two notions are ones that Oppenheim and Putnam assume. So, here they are:

UNITY OF SCIENCE AS A WORKING HYPOTHESIS
Paul Oppenheim and Hilary Putnam

Introduction

1.1 The expression "Unity of Science" is often encountered, but its precise content is difficult to specify in a satisfactory manner. It is the *aim of this paper* to formulate a precise concept of Unity of Science; and to examine to what extent that unity can be attained.

A concern with Unity of Science hardly needs justification. We are guided especially by the conviction that Science of Science, i.e., the meta-scientific study of major aspects of science, is the natural means for counterbalancing specialization by promoting the integration of scientific knowledge. The desirability of this goal is widely recognized; for example, many universities have programs with this end in view; but it is often pursued by means different from the one just mentioned, and the conception of the Unity of Science might be especially suited as an organizing principle for an enterprise of this kind.

1.2 As a preliminary, we will distinguish, in order of increasing strength, three broad concepts of Unity of Science.

First, Unity of Science in the weakest sense is attained to the extent to which all the terms of science are reduced to the terms of some one discipline (e.g., physics, or psychology). This concept of *Unity of Language* may be replaced by a number of sub-concepts depending on the manner in which one specifies the notion of "reduction" involved. Certain authors, for example, construe reduction as the *definition* of the terms of science by means of those in the selected basic discipline (reduction by means of biconditionals); and some of these require the definitions in question to be analytic, or "true in virtue of the meanings of the terms involved" (epistemological reduction); others impose no such restriction upon the biconditionals effecting reduction. The notion of reduction we shall employ is a wider one, and is designed to include reduction by means of biconditionals as a special case.

Second, Unity of Science in a stronger sense (because it implies Unity of Language, whereas the reverse is not the case) is represented by *Unity of Laws*. It is attained to the extent to which the laws of science become reduced to the laws of some one discipline. If the ideal of such an all-comprehensive explanatory system were realized, one could call it *Unitary Science*. The exact meaning of "Unity of Laws" depends, again, on the concept of "reduction" employed.

Third, Unity of Science in the strongest sense is realized if the laws of science are not only reduced to the laws of some one discipline, but the laws of that discipline are in some intuitive sense "unified" or "connected."

It is difficult to see how this last requirement can be made precise; and it will not be imposed here . . .

1.3 In the present paper, the term "Unity of Science" will be used in two senses, to refer, first, to an ideal *state* of science, and, second, to a pervasive *trend* within science, seeking the attainment of that ideal.

In the first sense, "Unity of Science" means the state of unitary science. It involves the two constituents mentioned above: unity of vocabulary, or "Unity of Language"; and unity of explanatory principles, or "Unity of Laws." That Unity of Science, in this sense, can be fully realized constitutes an over-arching, meta-scientific hypothesis which enables one to see a unity in scientific activities that might otherwise appear disconnected or unrelated, and which encourages the construction of a unified body of knowledge.

In the second sense, "Unity of Science" exists as a trend within scientific inquiry, whether or not unitary science is ever attained, and notwithstanding the simultaneous existence (and, of course, legitimacy) of other, even *incompatible*, trends.

1.4 The expression "Unity of Science" is employed in various other senses, of which two will be briefly mentioned in order to distinguish them from the sense with which we are concerned. In the first place, what is sometimes referred to is something that we may call the *Unity of Method* in science. This might be represented by the thesis that all the empirical sciences employ the same standards of explanation, of significance, of evidence, etc.

In the second place, a radical reductionist thesis (of an alleged "logical," not an empirical kind) is sometimes referred to as the thesis of the Unity of Science. Sometimes the "reduction" asserted is the definability of all the terms of science in terms of *sensationalistic predicates;* sometimes the notion of "reduction" is wider and predicates referring to *observable qualities of physical things* are taken as basic. These theses are epistemological ones, and ones which today appear doubtful. The epistemological uses of the terms "reduction," "physicalism," "Unity of Science," etc., should be carefully distinguished from the use of these terms in the present paper.

Let's stop at this point because the next section of their paper has some terminology that should be mentioned. In the next section, Oppenheim and Putnam speak of observational and theoretical vocabularies. By "observational predicates" they mean the terms we use to speak of the properties or features of things that we can directly observe; by "theoretical predicates" they mean the terms we use to speak of the properties or features of things that we cannot directly observe. They also speak of "universe of discourse." That just means the sort of things that are talked about by a given theory or science. For example, physicists talk about quarks while economists talk about business cycles; they have different universes of discourse.

In the section below, the authors focus on two questions: first, *how* can unity of science be attained and, second, *can* unity of science be attained. Their answer to the first question is that unity of science can (best, perhaps only) be attained by what they call *micro-reduction.* Micro-reduction is the notion that there is a "part-whole" relation used by a given science, namely, we conceive of the whole of something as composed of the parts that make it up and can be understood in terms of what is true about those parts. Their answer to the second question (*can* unity of science be attained?) is that it is the most plausible working hypothesis.

One very important point that Oppenheim and Putnam claim is that (micro-) reductions have a cumulative character. That is, while it seems preposterous to suggest that economics could be directly reduced to physics—after all, how could we possibly explain business cycles in terms of electromagnetic forces or gravitation?—it is not preposterous to suggest that laws (or objects and interactions) of chemistry could be reduced to laws of physics and, in addition, laws of biology could be reduced to laws of chemistry, and, in addition, laws of psychology could be reduced to laws of biology, and so on. Here, then, again are Oppenheim and Putnam:

UNITY OF SCIENCE AS A WORKING HYPOTHESIS *(continued)*

Paul Oppenheim and Hilary Putnam

Unity of Science and Micro-reduction

2.1 In this paper we shall employ a concept of reduction introduced by Kemeny and Oppenheim in their paper on the subject ["Systematic Power"

Philosophy of Science 22 (1955): 27–33], to which the reader is referred for a more detailed exposition. The principle requirements may be summarized as follows: given two theories T_1 and T_2, T_2 is said to be reduced to T_1 if and only if:

1. The vocabulary of T_2 contains terms not in the vocabulary of T_1.
2. Any observational data explainable by T_2 are explainable by T_1.
3. T_1 is at least as well systematized as T_2. (T1 is normally more complicated than T_2; but this is allowable, because the reducing theory normally explains more than the reduced theory. However, the "ratio," so to speak, of simplicity to explanatory power should be at least as great in the case of the reducing theory as in the case of the reduced theory.)

Kemeny and Oppenheim also define the reduction of a branch B_2 by another branch B_1 (e.g., the reduction of chemistry to physics). Their procedure is as follows: take the accepted theories of B_2 at a given time t as T_2. Then B_2 *is reduced to B_1 at time t* if and only if there is some theory T_1 in B_1 at t such that T_1 reduces T_2. Analogously, if *some* of the theories of B_2 are reduced by some T_1 belonging to branch B_1 at t, we shall speak of a partial reduction of B_2 to B_1 at t. This approach presupposes (1) the familiar assumption that some division of the total vocabulary of both branches into theoretical and observational terms is given, and (2) that the two branches have the same observational vocabulary.

2.2 The essential feature of a *micro*-reduction is that the branch B_1 deals with the parts of the objects dealt with by B_2. We must suppose that corresponding to each branch we have a specific universe of discourse U_{B1}; and that we have a part-whole relation Pt. Under the following conditions we shall say that the reduction of B_2 to B_1 is a *micro-reduction*: B_2 is reduced to B_1; and the objects in the universe of discourse of B_2 are wholes which possess a decomposition into proper parts all of which belong to the universe of discourse of B_1. For example, let us suppose B_2 is a branch of science which has multicellular living beings as its universe of discourse. Let B_1 be a branch with cells as its universe of discourse. Then the things in the universe of discourse of B_2 can be decomposed into proper parts belonging to the universe of discourse of B_1. If, in addition, it is the case that B_1 reduces B_2 at the time t, we shall say that B_1 *micro-reduces B_2 at time t.*

We shall also say that a branch B_1 is a *potential micro-reducer* of a branch B_2 if the objects in the universe of discourse of B_2 are wholes which possess a decomposition into proper parts all of which belong to the universe of discourse of B_1. The definition is the same as the definition of "micro-reduces" except for the omission of the clause "B_2 is reduced to B_1."

Any micro-reduction constitutes a step in the direction of *Unity of Language* in science. For, if B_1 reduces to B_2, it explains everything that B_2 does (and normally, more besides). Then, even if we cannot define in B_1 analogues for some of the theoretical terms of B_2, we can *use B_1 in place of B_2*. Thus any reduction, in the sense explained, permits "reduction" of the total vocabulary of science by making it possible to dispense with some terms. Not every reduction moves in the direction of Unity of Science; for instance reductions *within* a branch lead to a simplification of the vocabulary of science, but they do not necessarily lead in the direction of Unity of Science as we have characterized it (although they may at times fit into that trend). However, *micro*-reductions, and even partial micro-reductions, insofar as they permit us to replace some of the terms of one branch of science by terms of another, *do* move in this direction.

Likewise, the micro-reduction of B_2 to B_1 moves in the direction of *Unity of Laws;* for it reduces the total number of scientific laws by making it possible, in principle, to dispense with the laws of B_2 and explain the relevant observations by using B_1.

The relations "micro-reduces" and "potential micro-reducer" have very simple properties: (1) they are transitive (this follows from the transitivity of the relations "reduces" and "Pt"); (2) they are irreflexive (no branch can micro-reduce itself); (3) they are asymmetric (if B_1 micro-reduces B_2, B_2 never micro-reduces B_1). The two latter properties are not purely formal; however, they require for their derivation only the (certainly true) empirical assumption that there does not exist in infinite descending chain of proper parts, i.e., a series of things $x_1, x_2, x_3, \ldots$ such that x_2 is a proper part of x_1, x_3 is a proper part of x_2, etc.

The just-mentioned *formal* property of the relation "micro-reduces"—its transitivity—is of great importance for the program of Unity of Science. It means that micro-reductions have a *cumulative* character. That is, if a branch B_3 is micro-reduced to B_2, and B_2 is in turn micro-reduced to B_1, then B_3 is automatically micro-reduced to B_1. This simple fact is sometimes overlooked in objections to the theoretical possibility of attaining unitary science by means of micro-reduction. Thus it has been contended that one manifestly cannot explain human behavior by reference to the laws of atomic physics. It would indeed be fantastic to suppose that the simplest regularity in the field of psychology could be explained directly—i.e., "skipping" intervening branches of science—by employing subatomic theories. But one may believe in the attainability of unitary science without thereby committing oneself to this absurdity. It is not absurd to suppose that psychological laws may eventually be explained in terms of the behavior of individual neurons in the brain; that the behavior of individual cells—including neurons—may eventually be explained in terms of their biochemical constitution; and that the behavior of molecules—including the macromolecules that make up living cells—may eventually be explained in terms of atomic physics. If this is achieved, then psychological laws will have in *principle*, been reduced to laws of atomic physics, although it would nevertheless be hopelessly impractical to try to derive the behavior of a single human being directly from his constitution in terms of elementary particles.

2.3 *Unitary* science certainly does not exist today. But will it ever be attained? It is useful to divide this question into two subquestions: (1) If unitary science can be attained at all, *how* can it be attained? (2) *Can* it be attained at all?

First of all, there are variously abstracted possible ways in which unitary science might be attained. However, it seems very doubtful, to say the least, that a branch B_2 could be reduced to a branch B_1, if the things in the universe of discourse of B_2 are not themselves in the universe of discourse of B_1 and also do not possess a decomposition into parts in the universe of discourse of B_1. ("They don't speak about the same things.")

It does not follow that B_1 must be a potential *micro*-reducer of B_2, i.e., that all reductions are micro-reductions.

There are many cases in which the reducing theory and the reduced theory belong to the same branch, or to branches with the same universe of discourse. When we come, however, to branches with different universes—say, physics and psychology—it seems clear that the possibility of reduction depends on the existence of a structural connection between the universes *via* the "Pt" relation. Thus one cannot plausibly suppose—for the present at least—that the behavior of inorganic matter is explainable by reference to psychological laws; for inorganic materials do not consist of living parts. One supposes that psychology may be reducible to physics, but not that physics may be reducible to psychology!

Thus, the only method of attaining unitary science that appears to be seriously available at present is micro-reduction.

To turn now to our second question, *can* unitary science be attained? We certainly do not wish to maintain that it has been *established* that this is the case. But it does not follow, as some philosophers seem to think, that a tentative acceptance of the hypothesis that unitary science can be attained is therefore a mere "act of faith." We believe that this hypothesis is *credible*; . . . [and] think the assumption that unitary science can be attained through cumulative micro-reduction recommends itself *as a working hypothesis*. That is, we believe that it is in accord with the standards of reasonable scientific judgment to tentatively accept this hypothesis and to work on the assumption that further progress can be made in this direction, without claiming that its truth has been established, or denying that success may finally elude us . . .

4.6 Let us mention in passing certain *pragmatic* and *methodological* points of view which speak in favor of our working hypothesis:

1. It is of *practical* value, because it provides a good synopsis of scientific activity and of the relations among the several scientific disciplines.
2. It is, as has often been remarked, *fruitful* in the sense of stimulating many different kinds of scientific research. By way of contrast, belief in the *irreducibility* of various phenomena has yet to yield a single accepted scientific theory.
3. It corresponds *methodologically* to what might be called the "Democritean tendency" in science; that is, the pervasive methodological tendency to try, insofar as is possible, to explain apparently dissimilar phenomena in terms of qualitatively identical parts and their spatio-temporal relations.

Past Successes

5.1 . . . Many writers believe that there are some laws common to all forms of animal association, including that of humans. Of greater potential relevance to such laws are experiments dealing with "pecking order" among domestic fowl. In particular, experiments showing that the social structure can be influenced by the amount of male hormone in individual birds suggests possible parallels farther up the evolutionary scale.

With respect to the problem of human social organization, as will be seen presently, two things are striking: (1) the most developed body of theory is undoubtedly in the field of *economics*, and this is at present entirely micro-reductionistic in character; (2) the main approaches to *social* theory are *all* likewise of this character. (The technical term "micro-reduction" is not, of course, employed by writers in these fields. However, many writers have discussed "the Principle of Methodological Individualism;" and this is nothing more than the special form our working hypothesis takes in application to human social groups.)

In economics, if very weak assumptions are satisfied, it is possible to represent the way in which an individual orders his choices by means of an individual preference function. In terms of these functions, the economist attempts to explain group phenomena, such as the market, to account for collective consumer behavior, to solve the problems of welfare economies, etc. As theories for which a micro-reductionistic derivation is accepted in economics we could cite all the standard macro-theories; e.g., the theories of the business cycle, theories of currency fluctuation (Gresham's law to the effect that bad money drives out good is a familiar example), the principle of marginal utility, the law of demand, laws connecting change in interest rate with changes in inventory, plans, equipment, etc. The relevant point is while the economist is no longer dependent on the oversimplified assumption of "economic man," the explanation of economic phenomena is still in terms of the preferences, choices, and actions available to *individuals* . . .

Concluding Remarks

The possibility that all science may one day be reduced to microphysics (in the sense in which chemistry seems today to be reduced to it), and the presence of a unifying trend toward micro-reduction running through much of scientific activity, have often been noticed both by specialists in the various sciences and by meta-scientists. But these opinions have, in general, been expressed in a more or less vague manner and without very deep-going justification. It has been our aim, first, to provide precise definitions for the crucial concepts involved, and, second, to reply to the frequently made accusation that belief in the attainability of unitary science is "a mere act of faith." We hope to have shown that, on the contrary, a tentative acceptance of this belief, an acceptance of it as a working hypothesis, is *justified,* and that the hypothesis is *credible,* partly on methodological grounds (e.g., the simplicity of the hypothesis, as opposed to the bifurcation that rival suppositions create in the conceptual system of science), and partly because there is really a large mass of direct and indirect evidence in its favor.

We noted earlier that some scientists and philosophers accept the view that science is, or at least can be, unified, but they do not thereby embrace reductionism as the means of unification. One philosopher who rejects reductionism, but not necessarily unity of science, is Jerry Fodor. In the following selection Fodor claims that those who support reductionism rightly embrace the generality of physics, because physical laws apply to all physical objects and those objects include biological organisms. However, even if we accept the generality of physics, it does not necessarily follow that all sciences are reducible to physics. Fodor uses the term "special sciences" to talk of these other sciences and argues that they do not have the same content, methods, or aims of physics and, hence, are not reducible to physics. The behavior of higher-level things (such as human economic exchanges) are not causally determined or physically captured by the behavior of lower-level ones. We might be concerned from a scientific standpoint if these higher-level behaviors (or also laws) contradicted physics, to the extent that we are dealing with physical objects, but that is not the same thing as adopting reductionism.

In this selection, Fodor claims that those who favor the reductionist thesis take it as an empirical one. That is, they claim that it is true and supported by past successes. However, he says, it does not have the empirical support that it is claimed to have, but is instead (*pace* Oppenheim and Putnam) a working hypothesis; one which he argues is mistaken. Indeed, he says, reductionism actually plays a regulative role for its adherents, such that they dismiss non-reductionist views and practices.

Some of what Fodor says in the following selection needs to be clarified here. He speaks of "bridge laws" and "nomologically necessary contingent event identities" and "token physicalism." Here's what he means by these. Bridge laws are laws that define the items in the higher-level science in terms of items in the lower-level science. That is, these laws serve as a bridge between the two sciences by showing how the items from the one can be defined (and, hence, reduced) to the items of the other. By "nomologically necessary contingent event identities" Fodor means that bridge laws are (1) laws (the root of the term "nomological") and (2) necessary (as laws they do not just happen to describe phenomena, but they capture how phenomena must be). Now, the "contingent event identities" refer to events described in one science (the higher-level one) that the law is saying are really (identical with) events described in another science (the lower-level one). So, as he says, a reduction of psychology to neurology would entail that any event which consists of an instantiation (or instance) of a psychological property is identical with some event which consists of the instantiation of some neurological property. (Again, in this example, whatever we can say about psychology can be defined in terms of neurology.) "Token physicalism" needs some unpacking, too. Tokens are particular instances of types. For example, my cat Karloff is a token (a particular instance) of a type (cats). Or, this series of numerals: "2 2 2" is made up of three tokens (the three particular instances) or a single type (the number two). Physicalism is, of course, the view that whatever is real is physical. So, "token physicalism" means that for any particular thing x (including behaviors or processes, as well as objects), there is some particular physical thing y such that x really just is y. For example, this particular belief I have that Karloff is wonderful really just is a particular neuronal state of my brain. So, given all of this, here is Fodor:

SPECIAL SCIENCES

Jerry Fodor

A typical thesis of positivistic philosophy of science is that all true theories in the special sciences should reduce to physical theories in the long run. This is intended to be an empirical thesis, and part of the evidence which supports it is provided by such scientific successes as the molecular theory of heat and the physical explanation of the chemical bond. But the philosophical popularity of the reductivist program cannot be explained by reference to these achievements alone. The development of science has witnessed the proliferation of specialized disciplines at least as often as it has witnessed their reduction to physics, so the widespread enthusiasm for reduction can hardly be a mere induction over its past successes.

I think that many philosophers who accept reductivism do so primarily because they wish to endorse the generality of physics vis-à-vis the special sciences: roughly, the view that all events which fall under the laws of any science are physical events and hence fall under the laws of physics. For such philosophers, saying that physics is basic science and saying that theories in the special sciences must reduce to physical theories have seemed to be two ways of saying the same thing, so that the latter doctrine has come to be a standard construal of the former.

In what follows, I shall argue that this is a considerable confusion. What has traditionally been called "the unity of science" is a much stronger, and much less plausible, thesis than the generality of physics. If this is true it is important. Though reductionism is an empirical doctrine, it is intended to play a regulative role in scientific practice. Reducibility to physics is taken to be a *constraint* upon the acceptability of theories in the special sciences, with the curious consequence that the more the special sciences succeed, the more they ought to disappear. Methodological problems about psychology, in particular, arise in just this way: the assumption that the subject-matter of physics is taken to imply that psychological theories must reduce to physical theories, and it is this latter principle that makes the trouble. I want to avoid the trouble by challenging the inference.

I

Reductivism is the view that all the special sciences reduce to physics. The sense of "reduce to" is, however, proprietary. It can be characterized as follows.
Let

$$(1) \ S_1 x \rightarrow S_2 x$$

be a law of the special science S. ((1) is intended to be read as something like "all S_1 situations bring about S_2 situations." I assume that a science is individuated largely by reference to its typical predicates, hence that if S is a special science S_1 and S_2 are not predicates of basic physics. I also assume that the "all" which quantifies laws of the special sciences needs to be taken with a grain of salt; such laws are typically *not* exceptionless. This is a point to which I shall return at length.) A necessary and sufficient condition of the reduction of (1) to a law of physics is that the formulas (2) and (3) [below] be laws, and a necessary and sufficient condition of the reduction of S to physics is that all its laws be so reducible.

$$(2a)\ S_1 x \leftrightarrow P_1 x$$

$$(2b)\ S_2 x \leftrightarrow P_2 x$$

$$(3)\ P_1 x \rightarrow P_2 x$$

P_1 and P_2 are supposed to be predicates of physics, and (3) is supposed to be a physical law. Formulas like (2) are often called "bridge" laws. Their characteristic feature is that they contain predicates of both the reduced and the reducing science. Bridge laws like (2) are thus contrasted with "proper" laws like (1) and (3). The upshot of the remarks so far is that the reduction of a science requires that any formula which appears as the antecedent or consequent of one of its proper laws must appear as the reduced formula in some bridge law of other . . .

In what follows I shall assume a reading of reductivism which entails token physicalism. Bridge laws thus state nomologically necessary contingent event identities and a reduction of psychology to neurology would entail that any event which consists of the instantiation of a psychological property is identical with some event which consists of the instantiation of some neurological property.

Where we have got to is this: reductivism entails the generality of physics in at least the sense that any event which falls within the universe of discourse of a special science will also fall within the universe of discourse of physics. Moreover, any prediction which follows from the laws of a special science and a statement of initial conditions will also follow from a theory which consists of physics and the bridge laws, together with the statement of initial conditions. Finally, since "reduces to" is supposed to be an asymmetric relation, it will also turn out that physics is *the* basic science; that is, if reductivism is true, physics is the only science that is general in the sense just specified. I now want to argue that reductivism is too strong a constraint upon the unity of science, but that the relatively weaker doctrine will preserve the desired consequences of reductivism: token physicalism, the generality of physics, and its basic position among the sciences.

Fodor, then, accepts token physicalism, the generality of physics, and even that physics is the most basic science. These, he takes it, are the "desired consequences" of reductionism. However, he goes on to reject reductionism as unnecessary for unity of science as characterized by token physicalism and the generality of physics. He argues that the kinds, or natural kinds, that different sciences deal with are not all reducible to physical kinds that physics deals with. For example, one such kind in economics is monetary exchange. But the laws of economics that describe the behaviors of monetary exchange cannot, he says, be defined (reduced, characterized by) the natural kinds that belong to physics. For one thing, monetary exchange is not about specific physical objects (such as dollar bills) being exchanged. Dollars are abstract entities, even if dollar bills (the physical tokens) are concrete physical objects. But laws about monetary exchange are about dollars, not dollar bills.

Beyond this objection to reductionism, Fodor says that the generalizations that typify the laws of the special sciences are not like the generalizations that typify the laws of physics. The interestingness of the generalizations of the special sciences—and, so, why we find them informative and valuable—are not explainable in terms of what is true of the physicality of the objects involved in those generalizations. (The physical mass and spatio-temporal features of dollar bills are quite irrelevant to their monetary exchange value.) Noting that we have different sciences, with their corresponding taxonomies and universes of discourse, to address different subject matters and different purposes, Fodor states that the informativeness that comes from special sciences is simply not to be captured by attempting to reduce those sciences to physical things or features. Again, here is Fodor:

SPECIAL SCIENCES *(continued)*

Jerry Fodor

II

Every science implies a taxonomy of the events in its universe of discourse. In particular, every science employs a descriptive vocabulary of theoretical and observation predicates such that events fall under the laws of the science by virtue of satisfying those predicates. Patently, not every true description of an event is a description in such a vocabulary. For example, there are a large number of events which consist of things having been transported to a distance of less than three miles from the Eiffel Tower. I take it, however, that there is no science which contains "is transported to a distance of less than three miles from the Eiffel Tower" as part of its descriptive vocabulary. Equivalently, I take it that there is no natural law which applies to events in virtue of their being instantiations of the property *is transported to a distance of less than three miles from the Eiffel Tower* (though I suppose it is conceivable that there is some law that applies to events in virtue of their being instantiations of some distinct but coextensive property). By way of abbreviating these facts, I shall say that the property *is transported . . .* does not determine a *natural kind,* and that predicates which express that property are not natural kind predicates.

. . . [W]e can now characterize the respect in which reductivism is too strong a construal of the doctrine of the unity of science. If reductivism is true, then *every* natural kind is, or is coextensive with, a physical natural kind. (Every natural kind *is* a physical natural kind if bridge laws express proper identities, and every natural kind is coextensive with a physical natural kind if bridge laws express event identities.) This follows immediately from the reductivist premise that every predicate which appears as the antecedent or consequent of a law of the special sciences must appear as one of the reduced predicates in some bridge, together with the assumption that the natural kind predicates are the ones whose terms are the bound variables in proper laws. If, in short, some physical law is related to each law of a special science in the way that (3) [above] is related to (1), then every natural kind predicate of a special science is related to a natural kind predicate of physics in the way that (2) relates S_1 and S_2 to P_1 and P_2.

I now want to suggest some reasons for believing that this consequence of reductivism is intolerable . . . The reason it is unlikely that every natural kind corresponds to a physical natural kind is just that (a) interesting generalizations (e.g., counterfactual supporting generalizations) can often be made about events whose physical descriptions have nothing in common, (b) it is often the case that *whether* the physical descriptions of the events subsumed by these generalizations have anything in common is, in an obvious sense, entirely irrelevant to the truth of the generalizations, or to their interestingness, or to their degree of confirmation or, indeed, to any of their epistemologically important properties, and (c) the special sciences are very much in the business of making generalizations of this kind.

I take it that these remarks are obvious to the point of self-certification; they leap to the eye as soon as one makes the (apparently radical) move of taking the special sciences at all seriously. Suppose, for example, that Gresham's "law" really is true. (If one doesn't like Gresham's law, then any generalization of any conceivable future economics will probably do as well.) Gresham's law says something about what will happen in monetary exchanges under certain conditions. I am willing to believe that physics is general *in the sense that it implies any event which consists of monetary exchange* (hence any event which falls under Gresham's law) *has a true description in the vocabulary of physics and in virtue of which it falls under the laws of physics*. But banal considerations suggest that a description which covers all such events must be wildly disjunctive. Some monetary exchanges involve strings of wampum. Some involve dollar bills. And some involve signing one's name to a check. What are the chances that a disjunction of physical predicates which covers all these events (i.e., a disjunctive predicate which can form the right hand side of a bridge law of the form "x is a monetary exchange $\leftrightarrow$ . . .") expresses a physical natural kind? In particular, what are the chances that such a predicate forms that antecedent or consequent of some proper law of physics? The point is that monetary exchanges have interesting things in common; Gresham's law, if true, says what one of these interesting things is. But what is interesting about monetary exchanges is surely not their commonalities under *physical* description. A natural kind like a monetary exchange *could* turn out to be coextensive with a physical natural kind; but if it did, that would be an accident on a cosmic scale.

In fact, the situation for reductivism is still worse than the discussion thus far suggests. For, reductivism claims not only that all natural kinds are coextensive with physical natural kinds, but that the coextensions are nomologically necessary: bridge laws are *laws*. So, if Gresham's law is true, it follows that there is a (bridge) law of nature such that "x is a monetary exchange $\leftrightarrow x$ is P," where P is a term for a physical natural kind. But, surely, there is no such law. If there were, then P would have to cover not only all the systems of monetary exchange that there *are*, but also all the systems of monetary exchange that there *could be*; a law must succeed with the counterfactuals. What physical predicate is a candidate for P in "x is a nomologically possible monetary exchange if P_x"?

To summarize: an immortal econophysicist might, when the whole show is over, find a predicate in physics that was, in brute fact, coextensive with "x is a monetary exchange." If physics is general—if the ontological biases of reductivism are true—then there must *be* such a predicate. But (a) to paraphrase a remark Donald Davidson made in a slightly different context, nothing but brute enumeration could convince us of this brute extensivity, and (b) there would seem to be no chance at all that the physical predicate employed in stating the coextensivity is a natural kind term, and (c) there is still less chance that the coextension would be lawful (i.e., that it would hold not only for the nomologically possible world that turned out to be real, but for any nomologically possible world at all).

I take it that the preceding discussion strongly suggests that economics is not reducible to physics in the proprietary sense of reduction involved in claims for the unity of science. There is, I suspect, nothing special about economics in this respect; the reasons why economics is unlikely to reduce to physics are paralleled by those which suggest that psychology is unlikely to reduce to neurology.

. . . [W]e could, if we liked, *require* the taxonomies of the special sciences to correspond to the taxonomy of physics by insisting upon distinctions between the natural kinds postulated by the former wherever they turn out to correspond to distinct natural kinds in the latter. This would *make* the laws of the special sciences exceptionless if the laws of basic science are. But it would also lose us precisely the generalizations which we want the special sciences to express. (If economics were to posit as many *kinds* of monetary systems as there are kinds of physical realizations of monetary systems, then the generalizations of economics *would* be exceptionless, but, presumably, only vacuously so, since there would be no generalizations left to state. Gresham's law, for example, would have to be formulated as a vast, open disjunction about what happens in monetary system, or monetary system, under conditions which would themselves defy uniform characterization. We would not be able to say what happens in monetary systems *tout court* since, by hypothesis, "is a monetary system" corresponds to no natural kind predicate of physics.)

In fact, what we do is precisely the reverse. We allow the generalizations of the special sciences to *have* exceptions, thus preserving the natural kinds to which the generalizations apply. But since we know that the *physical* descriptions of the natural kinds may be quite heterogeneous, and since we know that the physical mechanisms which connect the satisfaction of the antecedents of such generalizations to the satisfaction of their consequents may be equally diverse, we expect both that there will be exceptions to the generalizations and that these exceptions will be "explained away" at the level of the reducing science. This is one of the respects in which physics really is assumed to be bedrock science; exceptions to *its* generalizations (if there are any) had better be random, because there is nowhere "further down" to go in explaining the mechanism whereby the exceptions occur.

This brings us to why there are special sciences at all. Reductivism as we remarked at the outset, flies in the face of the facts about the scientific institution: the existence of a vast and interleaved conglomerate of special scientific disciplines which often appear to proceed with only the most token acknowledgement of the constraint that their theories must turn out to be physics "in the long run." I mean that the acceptance of this constraint, *in practice*, often plays little or no role in the validation of theories. Why is this so? Presumably, the reductivist answer must be *entirely* epistemological. If only physical particles weren't so small (if only brains were on the *out*side, where one can get a look at them), *then* we would do physics instead of paleontology (neurology instead of psychology; psychology instead of economics; and so on down). There is an epistemological reply; namely, that even if brains were out where they can be looked *at*, as things now stand, we wouldn't know what to look *for*: for we lack the appropriate theoretical apparatus for psychological taxonomy of neurological events . . .

Physics develops the taxonomy of its subject matter which best suits its purposes: the formulation of exceptionless laws which are basic in several senses discussed above. But this is not the only taxonomy which may be required if the purposes of science in general are to be served: e.g., if we are to state such true, counterfactual supporting generalizations as there are to state. So, there are special sciences, with their specialized taxonomies, in the business of stating some of these generalizations. If science is to be unified, then all such taxonomies must apply *to the same things*. If physics is to be basic science, then each of these things had better be a physical thing. But it is not further required that the taxonomies which the special sciences employ must themselves reduce to the taxonomy of physics. It is not required, and it is probably not true.

Chapter Summary

Many scientists and philosophers desire a unity of science. This desire springs from the belief that the world is a certain way, so ideally there is a single, coherent, correct account of the world. Unity of science can mean ontological unity, the notion that there is a unity of things, epistemological unity, the notion that there is unity of explanation and theory, or axiological unity, the notion that there is unity of aims and purposes (and perhaps of standards and criteria for evaluating methods of inquiry). Frequently, the embracing of unity of science is related to the view of reductionism, that is, the view that the content, methods, and goals of the "higher-level" sciences (such as the social sciences) can be fully accounted for (or, reduced to) the content, methods, and goals of the more basic sciences. Because physics deals with all physical objects, events, processes, and forces, it is almost always seen as the most basic science such that ideally all other sciences can be, in principle, accounted for in terms of physics. Just as unity of science can mean ontological, epistemological, and axiological unity, so, too, reductionism can mean ontological reduction (higher-level things "really are" just instances of lower-level things), epistemological reduction (higher-level accounts can be formulated as lower-level accounts), and axiological reduction (aims and standards of higher-level sciences can be formulated and explained in terms of lower-level sciences). E.O. Wilson speaks of this reductionistic unity of science as the Ionian Enchantment and claims it has always been the driving goal and force of scientific inquiry. Paul Oppenheim and Hilary Putnam argue that this view is the most plausible working hypothesis for science. Jerry Fodor, on the other hand, argues that unity of science is not dependent upon reductionism and that, in fact, reductionism is mistaken.

CASE STUDY
Claude Bernard

Claude Bernard (1813–1878) was important in the history of medicine and physiology as an experimenter who made discoveries regarding the role of the pancreas in digestion and effects of toxins in the body, among others. He was also instrumental in challenging the contemporary view of vitalism, the notion that there was a special feature of living organisms that accounted for life. Bernard urged an alternative thoroughgoing materialist account. In the following selection, consider what types of reductionism Bernard seems to be committed to, as well as whether or not he provides sufficient evidence and reasons for any commitment to a reductionist view.

INTRODUCTION TO THE STUDY OF EXPERIMENTAL MEDICINE
Claude Bernard

The Physiological Phenomena of Higher Organisms Occur in Organic Interior Environments Perfected by and Endowed with Constant Physico-Chemical Properties

It is very important, in order to understand completely the application of experimentation to living beings, to be perfectly clear about the ideas which we are developing at this point. When we examine a higher living organism, that is to say, a complex being, and when we observe it carrying out its different functions in the general cosmic environment common to all phenomena of nature, the organism seems independent of that environment up to a certain point. But this appearance results from our illusions concerning the simplicity of the phenomena of life. The external phenomena which we perceive in that living being are fundamentally very complex, and they represent the result of a host of intimate properties of organic elements who manifestations are linked to the physico-chemical conditions of the internal environments in which these elements are immersed. In our explanations, we do away with this internal environment and only see the external environment which is before our eyes. But the real explanation of the phenomena of life rests on the study and knowledge of the most tenuous and subtle particles which form the organic elements of the body. This idea, set down in biology long ago by the great physiologists, appears more and more valid as the study of the organization of living beings makes greater progress. We must learn in addition that these *intimate particles* of the organization only manifest their vital activity by a necessary physicochemical relation with *intimate environments* which we should equally study and know. Otherwise, if we limit ourselves to the examination of the total phenomena visible from the outside, we might falsely believe that there is a unique force in living beings which violates the physico-chemical laws of the general cosmic environment, in the same way an ignorant person could believe that there is a special force which violates the laws of gravity in a machine which mounts into the air or runs along the ground. Now a living organism is nothing but an amazing machine endowed with the most marvelous properties and activated by the aid of the most complex and delicate mechanisms. There are no opposing forces struggling with one another; nature only knows order and disorder, harmony and discord.

In experimentation on organic bodies, we only need to take into account a single environment, the external cosmic environment; while in higher living beings, there are at least two environments to consider: the *external environment* or extra-organic, and the internal environment or intra-organic. Each year in my course on physiology in the Faculty of Sciences, I develop these new ideas on organic environments, ideas which I consider the basis of general physiology; they also necessarily form the basis of general pathology, and these same concepts will guide us in the application of experimentation to living beings. As I have said elsewhere, the complexity due to the existence of an organic internal environment is the only reason for the great difficulties which we encounter in the experimental determination of the phenomena of life and in the application of the means capable of modifying these phenomena.

With the aid of the thermometer, the barometer, and all the instruments which record and measure the properties of the external environment, the physicist and the chemist who experiment on inert bodies, having only to consider the external environment, can always set up identical conditions. For the physiologist, these instruments no longer suffice, and besides, it is in the internal environment which he must employ them. In effect it is the internal environment of living beings which is always in immediate relation with the normal or pathological vital manifestations of the organic elements. The higher one travels up the scale of living beings, the more the organization becomes more complicated, and the more the organic elements become more delicate and require a more perfect internal environment. All the circulating fluids, the blood serum and the intra-organic fluids, in reality constitute this internal environment.

In all living beings, the internal environment, which is a true *product of the organism*, preserves the necessary relations of exchange and equilibrium with the external cosmic environment; but, as the organism becomes more perfect, the organic environment becomes more specialized and in some manner isolates itself more and more from the ambient environment. In plants and cold-blooded animals, as we have said before, this isolation is less complete than in hot-blooded animals; in hot-blooded animals, the blood maintains an almost fixed and constant temperature and composition. But these different conditions do not create differences in nature among different living beings; they only represent improvements in the environmental mechanisms of isolation and protection. The vital manifestations of animals only vary because the physico-chemical conditions of their internal environments vary; thus a mammal whose blood has been cooled, either by natural hibernation, or by certain lesions of the nervous system, completely resembles, in the properties of its tissues, a true cold-blooded animal.

In sum, one can, according to what has been said, construct an idea of the enormous complexity of the phenomena of life and the almost insurmountable difficulties in exactly determining them which confront the physiologist when he is forced to carry out experimentation in these interior or organic environments. Nevertheless, these obstacles will not frighten us if we are convinced that we are traveling along the right path. In effect, there is an absolute determinism in all vital phenomena; hence there exists a biological science, and consequently, all the studies to which we devote ourselves will not be in vain. General physiology is the fundamental biological science towards which all the other biological sciences converge. Its main concern is to determine the elementary conditions of the phenomena of life. Pathology and therapeutics also rest on this common foundation. It is through the normal activity of the organic elements that life maintains a state of health; it is the abnormal manifestation of these same elements which characterizes disease, and in the end through the intermediary of the organic environment modified by the means of certain toxic or medicinal substances, therapeutics can act on the organic elements. To arrive at a resolution of these various problems, it is necessary to break down the organism successively, as one takes apart a machine in order to understand it and to study all the workings; this means, that before experimenting on the elements, it is first necessary to experiment on the apparatus and the organs. We must have recourse to a successive analytical study of the phenomena of life by using the same experimental method which the physicist and the chemist use to analyze the phenomena of inorganic bodies. The difficulties which result from the complexity of the phenomena of living bodies, arise solely in the application of the experimentation, because in the end the goal and the principles of the method always remain exactly the same.

Further Reading

Agazzi, Evandro (ed.). *The Problem of Reductionism in Science.* Dordrecht: Kluwer, 1991.

Batterman, Robert W. *The Devil in the Details: Asymptotic Reasoning in Explanation, Reduction, and Emergence.* Oxford: Oxford University Press, 2001.

Causey, Robert L. *Unity of Science.* Dordrecht: D. Reidel, 1977.

de Jong, Huib Looren, et al. *Rethinking Reductionism.* Oxford: Blackwell, 2006.

Dupré, John. *The Disorder of Things: Metaphysical Foundations of the Disunity of Science.* Cambridge: Harvard University Press, 1993.

Giere, Ronald. *Scientific Perspectivism.* Chicago: University of Chicago Press, 2006.

Kellert, Stephen, et al. *Scientific Pluralism.* Minneapolis: University of Minnesota Press, 2006.

Sarkar, Sahotra. *Genetics and Reductionism.* Cambridge: Cambridge University Press, 1998.

Silberstein, Michael. "Reduction, Emergence, and Explanation." In *The Blackwell Guide to the Philosophy of Science.* Edited by Peter Machamer and Michael Silberstein. Oxford: Blackwell, 2002. Pages 80–107.

Suppes, Patrick. "The Unity of Science—Plurality of Nature." In *PSA 1978, Volume 2.* Edited by P.D. Asquith and Ian Hacking. East Lansing: Philosophy of Science Association, 1981. Pages 3–16.

CHAPTER EIGHT

Inductivism and Falsificationism

IN THIS CHAPTER, WE WILL

- Examine the inductivist model of scientific change
- Examine the falsificationist model of scientific change

Most people would agree that we know more about the natural world today than we did 1,000 years ago or 100 years ago (perhaps even one year ago). For example, in the year 1900 we knew nothing about how geologic tectonic plates shaped the history of the earth; we knew nothing of Einsteinian relativistic physics; we knew nothing about an expanding cosmos; we knew nothing about molecular genetics. The list can go on and on. There unquestionably has been change in our scientific view of the world with respect to the content of our scientific theories and models and what we take as established facts. In addition, there has been scientific change in terms of methods used to investigate the world (for example, double-blind studies in medicine) and in criteria and standards for evaluating scientific claims (for example, probability tests and reliability standards). Not only would most people agree that there has been change in our scientific understanding of the world (in terms of content, methods, and evaluative criteria), but most people would agree that this change has been one of progress, that is, that our scientific understanding is not simply different than it used to be but is better than it used to be. To put it simply, for most people, the sciences have made progress toward the goal of understanding (i.e., fully describing and explaining) the world. Though we will see over this and the next two chapters that there is some question over the issue of progress, there is no question that the sciences have changed over time. This and the next two chapters will look at various models that try to spell out just what has been—and is—the nature of scientific change, and, to that extent, the nature of science. This chapter in particular will cover two of these models: inductivism and falsificationism.

Inductivism

A common conception of how science proceeds (often called, "the scientific method") is that scientists begin by observing certain phenomena in the world. Often they notice some pattern to the phenomena and then investigate what could account for that pattern. That investigation would include formulating some hypothesis about the phenomena and then taking further observations to see if that pattern holds. These further observations should be structured and focused via careful measurements and carefully designed experiments. If some empirical generalizations can be culled from the investigation, perhaps a broader hypothesis can be formulated and likewise tested. Eventually, some theory might be proposed to encompass and explain the observations and experimental results. That theory, in turn, will be tested against future observations of other phenomena. This process, or model of scientific procedure, is often referred to as *inductivism*. This label is meant to capture the conception of science as beginning with particular observational data and then, through testing, leading to broader, more general facts, finally culminating in a full-fledged theory. The reason it is called "inductivist" is because a long-standing notion of reasonable and reliable inference is that we generalize from some specific, particular cases or facts to some broader statement that subsumes those specific cases or facts. Inductive inference is usually distinguished from deductive inference where the latter is said to involve reasoning from general statements to some specific conclusion. A typical example of deductive reasoning is the following: Because all humans are mortal (a general claim), and Socrates is a human, then Socrates is moral (a specific claim). Now, inductivism as a model of how science proceeds is more than simply saying that scientists make inductive inferences. It is the view that the basic mode and method of scientific practice and change is inductive in nature; good science operates on the basis of inductive reasoning, which is the structure of reliable scientific practice.

As an illustration that this is a popular notion of scientific procedure, look again at the quotes from textbooks back on page 24.

As a statement of how science proceeds, the movement from specific data to generalized conclusions is quite straightforward. As was mentioned at the beginning of this chapter, one of the most obvious features of science is that science, and our scientific understanding of the world, has changed over time. This is true not only of the content of scientific models and theories (the *what*, or the metaphysical aspects), but also of the particular procedures and techniques we use to investigate the world (the *how*, or epistemological aspects), and even some purposes and goals we attach to this content and these procedures (the *why*, or axiological aspects). Inductivism, then, is a model not only of scientific procedure but also of scientific change over time. In a nutshell, change in our scientific understanding of the world is a result of cumulative observations and tests of those observations over time where the tests are a matter of applying inductive patterns of reasoning to the data. A classic attempt to systematize and explicate these patterns as they relate to science was made in the 1800s and we will now turn to that.

Mill's Methods

The 19th-century British philosopher, John Stuart Mill, claimed that there are a number of common patterns of inductive argumentation, particularly for establishing causal relations. These patterns, which have come to be dubbed "Mill's Methods," reflect some basic forms of inference that are associated with scientific reasoning. Irving Copi elaborates on these patterns in the following examples:

> The Democratic Party is clearly a 'war' party. Democratic presidents have gotten us into many major wars: Wilson in World War I, Roosevelt in World War II, Truman in Korea, Kennedy in Vietnam, Clinton in Kosovo.

The line of reasoning here is that the presence of one fact (having a Democratic president) is correlated with the presence of another fact (going to war). This has been called the *Method of Agreement*. The pattern is said to reveal a causal connection based on instances or features that "agree," that is, where the same effect follows from the same cause over the course of various cases. Here is a scientific example of this Method of Agreement:

> Edward Jenner kept neatly detailed records of his work on cowpox and smallpox. After years of individual studies of people who had been inoculated with cowpox, he concluded that such an inoculation rendered them immune to smallpox. He performed his crucial experiment in 1796. He took cowpox matter from the hands of Sarah Nelmes, a dairymaid, and with it he vaccinated the arm of James Phipps. Two months later, Jenner inoculated Phipps with smallpox on both arms and several months later repeated the inoculation. The result was none of the symptoms of smallpox, but instead only a trivial sore at the point of inoculation, typical of immunity.

In this case, the presence of one fact (immunity to smallpox) was causally associated with the presence of another fact (vaccination by inoculation of cowpox).

Of course, the presence of correlated facts or events does not in itself entail that they are causally connected. Each year I get older and each year the universe expands, but no matter how many times those two events occur in tandem, we do not conclude that my getting older causes the universe to expand. As Mill noted, there are other inference patterns that we commonly use in scientific and causal reasoning. One such pattern is called the *Method of Difference*. It is important to know not merely how many times two events are present together, but also to know if and when they are not present together. A simple example of this is the following:

> People in several parts of the country have lower rates of tooth decay. An investigation showed that the only thing different about these parts of the country was that their water supply contains fluorine.

So, what is important is not just that where one fact is present so is another fact, but where one fact is not present that second fact is also missing. In the context of the larger study, it's the difference in input that seems particularly relevant to the difference in output. Another example from biology demonstrates this pattern:

> In 1861 Pasteur at last carried general conviction against spontaneous generation. He boiled meat broth in a flask with a very long thin neck until no bacteria were left. This was shown by the fact that he could

now keep broth in the flask for an indefinite period without change setting in, the narrow neck admitting nothing. Then he broke off the neck and in a few hours the liquid showed micro-organisms, and the meat was in full decay. That the air carried such organisms he proved by twice filtering it through sterile filters and showing that with the first filter, but not the second, he could set up putrefaction.

The relevant difference, and hence the inferred relevant causal factor, was whether or not unfiltered air was admitted into the flasks.

The third of Mill's Methods is a combination of the previous two and is called the *Method of Agreement and Difference*. Here is a simple example of this method:

In a study of the heart rate of athletes and how it corresponds to various factors, the only significant correlation found was that those who do aerobic exercise—and only those who do—have lower heart rates.

In this example, there is the agreement ("those who do") between the presence of aerobic exercise and the presence of lower heart rates. There is also the difference ("only those who do"), that is, where aerobic exercise is absent, lower heart rates is also absent. An example from the history of science of this method of agreement and difference is:

Eijkman fed a group of chickens exclusively on white rice. They all developed polyneuritis and died. He fed another group of fowl unpolished rice. Not a single one of them contracted the disease. Then he gathered up the polishings from rice and fed them to other polyneuritic chickens, and in a short time the birds recovered. He had accurately traced the cause of polyneuritis to a faulty diet. For the first time in history, he had produced a food deficiency disease experimentally, and had actually cured it.

A fourth method of causal inference is the *Method of Residues*. Related to the previous three, especially to the method of difference, this method identifies a causal agent by screening out other known factors and then isolating what is left over (the "residue"). For a homespun example:

About a month ago I bought two aralia plants for my apartment and both looked healthy. But now one of them seems to be dying.

The only thing I can figure out is that it needs to be moved out of the direct sunlight, since I water both of them the same and I've checked both of them for bugs and they're both potted in the same kind of soil.

Among the various possible correlations (or causal factors), it cannot be the water, it cannot be bugs infesting one of the plants but not the other, it cannot be the soil they are in (since in all of these cases the input is the same, but the output is not—one plant is healthy and the other is not). The factor that is left over, the residue among the identified possible causes, is the level of direct sunlight. Though very similar to the method of difference, this method of inference already identifies a specific list of possible causes and by a process of elimination specifies one as the residual relevant difference. For an example from science, consider the following case:

> It was not merely the amount of water in circulation which was influenced by temperature . . . It was the total amount of hemoglobin. The mystery was: "Whence came this outpouring of hemoglobin?" It was not credible that the bone-marrow could have provided the body with new corpuscles at the rate required. Moreover, there was no evidence of increase in immature corpuscles in circulation . . .

> The question was then forced upon us: Has the body any considerable but hidden store of hemoglobin which can be drawn upon in case of emergency? . . . In searching for a locality which might fulfill such as condition one naturally seeks in the first instance for some place where the red corpuscles are outside the circulatory system—some backwater outside the arteries, capillaries, and veins. There is only one such place of any considerable size in the body— that place is the spleen.

The obvious causal agent for the higher-than-expected levels of hemoglobin is the spleen, other reasonable sources having been ruled out.

Finally, the fifth of Mill's Methods is the *Method of Concomitant Variation*. This is an academic-sounding name for the common pattern of reasoning in which we correlate two facts because they vary in accordance with one another. A very basic example of this is:

> When Caroline was a kid, she made a wonderful discovery. As she moved the volume control dial on her dad's stereo up and down, she found that the music got louder and softer.

What Caroline discovered was that as one factor varied (in this case, the movement of the volume dial), another varied (the volume of the music). In this case, the varying together (the concomitant variation) was positive, but concomitant variations can also be negative (inverse variations), when increasing one factor (the cause) results in a concomitant decreasing of another factor (the effect). A scientific example of this method is:

> Even as Banting was slaying dogs to save men, Evans was achieving a startling discovery in this field with another mysterious gland, *hypophysis cerebri,* commonly called the *pituitary.* This is a bit of an organ safely housed in a small pocket of bone attached to the base of the brain. Both Galen and Vesalius knew of this gland and thought it supplied the body with spit (in Latin, *sputum*). It is one of the most inaccessible glands in the living body. For many years, there appeared to be some connection between body growth and the functioning of this gland. In 1783 John Hunter had bargained with an undertaker for the body of an Irish giant of eight feet, four inches—Charles O'Brien, who had died at the age of twenty-two. The physician finally bought the body for twenty-five hundred dollars, and found a pituitary almost as large as a hen's egg. That of a normal adult man weighs hardly more than half a gram. A century later, *acromegaly,* an enlargement of the hands, feet, nose, lips, and jaw, was declared to be due to a tumor of the pituitary. The pituitary glands of dwarfs, some of them only eighteen inches high, showed relatively small development or partial atrophy.

The line of inference is fairly clear: larger pituitary gland, larger body; smaller pituitary gland, smaller body.

Now, the point of Mill's Methods—indeed, the point of discussing them here—is that they illustrate basic modes of inductive reasoning within science, in these cases, focused on identifying the causes of phenomena. However, as noted earlier, inductivism as a model of scientific change is more than simply invoking inductive patterns of inference. It is a statement of how science, certainly good science, does and should operate.

Criticisms of inductivism

Although inductivism has been said to be a common conception of scientific change, there have been many criticisms of it as a sufficient or adequate model. Indeed, some features that have been associated with inductivism have been questioned in earlier chapters. For example, inductivism is usually attributed with the view that unbiased observation is the starting point of scientific inquiry, a view we considered—and questioned—in Chapter Two. We will be looking at other models of scientific change in this and the next two chapters, all of which challenge inductivism on a number of points. Here, however, we will focus on one particular criticism, namely, the reliability of inductive inference itself and its actual role in testing scientific hypotheses and theories. This criticism is raised by Sir Karl Popper, a very influential philosopher of science and who is the main proponent of an alternative model of scientific change, usually called *falsificationism* (which we will examine in the second half of this chapter). In the following selection, Popper argues that induction is not a legitimate method for either the discovery of scientific information or the justification of scientific information. One problem with induction, Popper says, is that the principle of induction itself cannot be justified. For Popper, there simply is not sufficient warrant for any universal statements, such as a scientific law or theory, based on singular statements or particular data. No matter how many particular cases support some general conclusion that general conclusion does not necessarily follow from those cases. Indeed, the very principle of induction itself can only be "justified" by appealing to the principle of induction, which is to say, for Popper, that it cannot be justified. In addition, Popper thinks that induction is not how sciences genuinely proceed in the testing of its hypotheses and theories. Now, this is not to say that scientists do not make inductive inferences, but it is to say, for Popper, that inductive methods do not capture genuine scientific methodologies. As a model of how science changes, inductivism is inadequate and misleading. Here's what Popper says:

THE LOGIC OF SCIENTIFIC DISCOVERY
Karl Popper

A scientist, whether theorist or experimenter, puts forward statements, or systems of statements, and tests them step by step. In the field of the empirical sciences, more particularly, he constructs hypotheses, or systems of theories, and test them against experience by observation and experiment.

I suggest that it is the task of the logic of scientific discovery, or the logic of knowledge, to give a logical analysis of this procedure; that is, to analyze the method of the empirical sciences.

But what are these "methods of the empirical sciences?" And what do we call "empirical science?"

According to a widely accepted view—to be opposed in this [selection]—the empirical sciences can be characterized by the fact that they use "*inductive methods*," as they are called. According to this view, the logic of scientific discovery would be identical with inductive logic, i.e., with the logical analysis of these inductive methods.

It is usual to call an inference "inductive" if it passes from *singular statements* (sometimes also called "particular" statements), such as accounts of the results of observations or experiments, to *universal statements*, such as hypotheses or theories.

Now it is far from obvious, from a logical point of view, that we are justified in inferring universal statements from singular ones, no matter how numerous; for any conclusion drawn in this way may always turn out to be false: no matter how many instances of white swans we may have observed, this does not justify the conclusion that *all* swans are white.

The question whether inductive inferences are justified, or under what conditions, is known as *the problem of induction*.

The problem of induction may also be formulated as the question of how to establish the truth of universal statements which are based on experience, such as the hypotheses and theoretical systems of the empirical sciences. For many people believe that the truth of these universal statements is "*known by experience*;" yet it is clear that an account of an experience— of an observation or the result of an experiment—can in the first place be only a singular statement and not a universal one. Accordingly, people who say of a universal statement that we know its truth from experience usually mean that the truth of this universal statement can somehow be reduced to the truth of singular ones, and that these singular ones are known by experience to be true; which amounts to saying that the universal statement is based on inductive inference. Thus to ask whether there are natural laws known to be true appears to be only another way of asking whether inductive inferences are logically justified.

Yet if we want to find a way of justifying inductive inferences, we must first of all try to establish a *principle of induction*. A principle of induction would be a statement with the help of which we could put inductive inferences into a logically acceptable form. In the eyes of the upholders of inductive logic, a principle of induction is of extreme importance for scientific method: ". . . this principle," says [Hans] Reichenbach, "determines the truth of scientific theories. To eliminate it from science would mean nothing less than to deprive science of the power to decide the truth or falsity of its theories. Without it, clearly, science would no longer have the right to distinguish its theories from the fanciful and arbitrary creations of the poet's mind." . . .

Some who believe in inductive logic are anxious to point out, with Reichenbach, that "the principle of induction is unreservedly accepted by the whole of science and that no man can seriously doubt this principle in everyday life either." Yet even supposing this were the case—for after all, "the whole of science" might err—I should still contend that a principle of induction is superfluous, and that it must lead to logical inconsistencies.

That inconsistencies may easily arise in connection with the principle of induction should have been clear from the work of [David] Hume; also, that they can be avoided, if at all, only with difficulty. For the principle of induction must be a universal statement in its turn. Thus if we try to regard its truth as known from experience, then the very same problems which occasioned its introduction will arise all over again. To justify it, we should have to employ inductive inferences; and to justify these we should have to assume an inductive principle of a higher order; and so on. Thus the attempt to base the principle of induction on experience breaks down, since it must lead to an infinite regress . . .

My own view is that the various difficulties of inductive logic here sketched are insurmountable. So also, I fear, are those inherent in the doctrine, so widely current today, that inductive inference, although not "strictly valid," *can attain some degree of "reliability" or of "probability."* According to this doctrine, inductive inferences are "probable inferences." "We have described," says Reichenbach, "the principle of induction as the means whereby science decides upon truth. To be more exact, we should say that it serves to decide upon probability. For it is not given to science to reach either truth or falsity . . . but scientific statements can only attain continuous degree of probability whose unattainable upper and lower limits are truth and falsity."

At this stage I can disregard the fact that the believers in inductive logic entertain an idea of probability that I shall later reject as highly unsuitable for their own purposes. I can do so because the difficulties mentioned are not even touched by an appeal to probability. For if a certain degree of probability is to be assigned to statements based on inductive inference, then this will have to be justified by invoking a new principle of induction, appropriately modified. And this new principle in its turn will have to be justified, and so on. Nothing is gained, moreover, if the principle of induction, in its turn, is taken not as "true" but only as "probable." In short, like every other form of inductive logic, the logic of probable inference, or "probability logic," leads either to an infinite regress, or to the doctrine of *apriorism*.

The theory to be developed in the following pages stands directly opposed to all attempts to operate with the ideas of inductive logic. It might be described as the theory of *the deductive method of testing*, or as the view that a hypothesis can only be empirically *tested*—and only *after* it has been advanced . . .

According to the view that will be put forward here, the method of critically testing theories, and selecting them according to the results of tests, always proceeds on the following lines. From a new idea, put up tentatively, and not yet justified in any way—an anticipation, a hypothesis, a theoretical system, or what you will—conclusions are drawn by means of logical deduction. These conclusions are then compared with one another and with other relevant statements, so as to find what logical relations (such as equivalence, derivability, compatibility, or incompatibility) exist between them.

We may if we like distinguish four different lines along which the testing of a theory could be carried out. First there is the logical comparison of the conclusions among themselves, by which the internal consistency of the system could be tested. Secondly, there is the investigation of the logical form of the theory, with the object of determining whether it has the character of an empirical or scientific theory, or whether it is, for example, tautological. Thirdly, there is the comparison with other theories, chiefly with the aim of determining whether the theory would constitute a scientific advance should it survive our various tests. And finally, there is the testing of the theory by way of empirical applications of the conclusions which can be derived from it.

The purpose of this last kind of test is to find out how far the new consequences of the theory—whatever may be new in what it asserts—stand up to the demands of practice, whether raised by purely scientific experiments, or by practical technological applications. Here too the procedure of testing turns out to be deductive. With the help of other statements, previously accepted, certain singular statements—which we may call "predictions"—are deduced from the theory; especially predictions that are easily testable or applicable. From among these statements, those are selected which are not derivable from the current theory, and more especially those which the current theory contradicts. Next we seek a decision as regards these (and other) derived statements by comparing them with the results of practical applications and experiments. If this decision is positive, that is, if the singular conclusions turn out to be acceptable, or *verified*, then the theory has, for the time being, passed its test: we have found no reason to discard it. But if the decision is negative, or in other words, if the conclusions have been *falsified*, then their falsification also falsifies the theory from which they were logically deduced.

It should be noticed that a positive decision can only temporarily support the theory, for subsequent negative decisions may always overthrow it. So long as a theory withstands detailed and severe tests and is not superseded by another theory in the course of scientific progress, we may say that it has "proved its mettle" or that it is *"corroborated."*

Nothing resembling inductive logic appears in the procedure here outlined. I never assume that we can argue from truth of singular statements to the truth of theories. I never assume that by force of "verified" conclusions, theories can be established as "true," or even as merely "probable."

Having seen Popper's criticisms of inductivism as a model of scientific change, we can now turn to an examination of a model that he proposes as an alternative, falsificationism.

Falsificationism

In his rejection above of inductivism, Popper gestures toward his own view of a model of scientific change. The primary emphasis of scientific method is to propose some hypothesis (or model or theory) and then subject it to empirical testing. Scientific practice, at least good scientific practice, is a matter of making conjectures and then subjecting those conjectures to robust tests, or, in other words, attempting to refute those conjectures. This process of conjecture and refutation is even the name of one of Popper's books (in fact, the source of the next reading). If a conjecture passes those robust tests, that is, survives our attempts at refutation, it is a pretty good indication that the conjecture is warranted. It is this process and goal of *testing* hypotheses that is paramount for Popper, not merely accumulating supporting evidence. After all, says Popper, we could come up with evidence to support pretty much any hypothesis we could imagine. Popper's concerns are about what is sometimes called the *demarcation problem*, that is, on what criteria we demarcate science from non-science. It cannot simply be on the basis of what gets investigated, since as we noted in Chapter One, poets and philosophers can talk about planets and stem cells and supply/demand equilibriums. Rather, for Popper, what sets science apart from non-science (or pseudo-science) is the requirement of testability, or falsifiability. What he means by falsifiability is that for a given hypothesis, it is possible that there is some observation or fact that would be inconsistent with that hypothesis and which we would accept as having shown the hypothesis in question to be false. Of course, if we have a good hypothesis, it might pass all the tests we put to it, so it might in fact not get falsified. But as long as it is falsifiable, that is, it *could* be falsified, that is what is important.

As the reading beginning on page 253 shows, Popper claims that any hypothesis that explains every relevant observation (that is, that is consistent with every relevant case) in fact does not really explain anything, because (apparently) no observation serves as a test for the hypothesis. This means that such a hypothesis provides no information to us about the world, since any prediction based on it would turn out to be supportable. What we want, then, for Popper, is hypotheses (conjectures) that are falsifiable. Furthermore, we want hypotheses that will actually give us information about the world, or, as he puts it, we don't just want any old conjecture, we want *bold* conjectures, that is, conjectures that are risky given our background knowledge and expectations. For example, I could conjecture that tomorrow in my hometown it will either rain or not rain. Well, clearly it will do one or the other, so my conjecture is certain to turn out true. It is far from being a bold conjecture; it is quite a safe (timid?) conjecture. However, it is also totally uninformative. I have no idea on the basis of that conjecture whether or not to carry an umbrella. Or, to take a more scientific example, consider the following three conjectures:

1. Material bodies attract one another.
2. Material bodies attract one another, stronger when closer together, weaker when further apart.
3. $F = GmM/r2$ [Newton's formula for the force of gravitation]

Now, conjecture three is less likely to be true than conjecture two and it, in turn, is less likely to be true than conjecture one. Conjecture one is a timid conjecture, whereas conjecture three is a bold one, because there are observations that could refute, or at least be inconsistent with, conjecture three that would not refute or be inconsistent with conjecture one. So, although three is riskier, it is also more informative; if it passes our tests (i.e., turns out to be consistent with our future observations), we will have gained more information about the world than we would from conjecture one.

Besides this notion of conjecture and refutation as the appropriate model of scientific discovery, justification, and change, and besides the proposal that bold conjectures are better than timid ones, a feature of Popper's model is that we can never know if a given hypothesis is true. We can know if it is false, because it can fail our tests. But even if it passes all the tests we throw at it, perhaps there is another test (some future observation) that could occur in the future that might falsify the hypothesis. Two points emerge from this. The first is that whenever an observation that could have refuted the hypothesis fails to do so (i.e., when the hypothesis passes the test), what we have, for Popper, is not confirming evidence, but corroborating evidence. That is, the observation that supports the hypothesis does not actually confirm it, but is does not disconfirm it. The term "corroboration" is often used in law to identify evidence that supports in the sense of not contradicting. For example, if a crime is committed on Main Street at 10:00 pm and some witness testifies that she saw me somewhere else at a time that would make it highly unlikely that I was on Main Street at 10:00 pm, that testimony would corroborate my claim that I did not commit the crime. It does not prove it, but it functions as supporting evidence. Likewise, for Popper, when a conjecture is tested by some observation and that observation turns out not to refute the hypothesis, it is said to be corroborating evidence. (Again, for Popper, we can disconfirm a hypothesis, but we cannot confirm one.)

The second point that emerges from the features of Popper's model is that we can never prove a hypothesis is true (though we can prove that it is false). As just mentioned above, there might always be some future test that the hypothesis fails. So, rather than saying that we have a true hypothesis, or more broadly, rather than saying that science gives us a true picture of the world, the best that we can say is that we get closer and closer to the truth, whatever that is. The term he uses is that our theories have a certain level of *verisimilitude*. That is to say, we might be getting closer and closer to "the truth," though we would never know it. Or, given two hypotheses, H_1 and H_2, if H_1 passes more tests than does H_2, we can say that H_1 has greater verisimilitude than does H_2.

With these notions of conjecture/refutation, falsifiability, informativeness, corroboration, and verisimilitude in hand, we can now let Popper summarize his model:

CONJECTURES AND REFUTATIONS: THE GROWTH OF SCIENTIFIC KNOWLEDGE

Karl Popper

[I will] give you a report on my own work in the philosophy of science, since the autumn of 1919 when I first began to grapple with the problem, *"When should a theory be ranked as scientific?"* or *"Is there a criterion for the scientific character or status of a theory?"*

The problem which troubled me at the time was neither, "When is a theory true?" nor, "When is a theory acceptable?" My problem was different. *I wished to distinguish between science and pseudo-science;* knowing very well that science often errs, and that pseudo-science may happen to stumble on the truth.

I knew, of course, the most widely accepted answer to my problem: that science is distinguished from pseudo-science—or from "metaphysics"—by its *empirical method,* which is essentially *inductive,* proceeding from observation or experiment. But this did not satisfy me. On the contrary, I often formulated my problem as one of distinguishing between a genuinely empirical method and a non-empirical or even a pseudo-empirical method—that is to say, a method which, although it appeals to observation and experiment, nevertheless does not come up to scientific standards. The latter method may be exemplified by astrology, with its stupendous mass of empirical evidence based on observation—on horoscopes and on biographies.

But as it was not the example of astrology which led me to my problem I should perhaps briefly describe the atmosphere in which my problems arose and the examples by which it was stimulated. After the collapse of the Austrian Empire there had been a revolution in Austria: the air was full of revolutionary slogans and ideas, and new and often wild theories. Among the theories which interested me Einstein's theory of relativity was no doubt by far the most important. Three others were Marx's theory of history, Freud's psycho-analysis, and Alfred Adler's so called "individual psychology."

There was a lot of popular nonsense talked about these theories, and especially about relativity (as still happens even today), but I was fortunate in those who introduced me to the study of the theory. We all—the small circle of students to which I belonged—were thrilled with the result of Eddington's eclipse observations which in 1919 brought the first important confirmation of Einstein's theory of gravitation. It was a great experience for us, and one which had a lasting influence on my intellectual development.

The three other theories I have mentioned were also widely discussed among students at that time. I myself happened to come into personal contact with Alfred Adler, and even to cooperate with him in his social work among the children and young people in the working-class districts of Vienna where he had established social guidance clinics.

It was during the summer of 1919 that I began to feel more and more dissatisfied with these three theories—the Marxist theory of history, psycho-analysis, and individual psychology; and I began to feel dubious about their claims to scientific status. My problem perhaps first took the simple form, "What is wrong with Marxism, psycho-analysis, and individual psychology? Why are they so different from physical theories, from Newton's theory, and especially from the theory of relativity?"

To make the contrast clear I should explain that few of us at the time would have said that we believed in the *truth* of Einstein's theory of gravitation. This shows that it was not my doubting the *truth* of those other three theories which bothered me, but something else. Yet neither was it that I merely felt mathematical physics to be more *exact* than the sociological or psychological type of theory. Thus what worried me was neither the problem of truth, at that stage at least, nor the problem of exactness or measurability. It was rather that I felt that these other three theories, though posing as sciences, had in fact more in common with primitive myths than with science; that they resembled astrology rather than astronomy.

I found that those of my friends who were admirers of Marx, Freud, and Adler, were impressed by a number of points common to those theories, and especially by their apparent *explanatory power*. These theories appeared to be able to explain practically everything that happened within the fields to which they referred. The study of any of them seemed to have the effect of an intellectual conversion or revelation, opening your eyes to a new truth hidden from those not yet initiated. Once your eyes were thus opened you saw confirming instances everywhere: the world was full of *verifications* of the theory. Whatever happened always confirmed it. Thus its truth appeared manifest; and unbelievers were clearly people who refused to see it, either because it was against their class interest, or because of their repressions which were still "un-analyzed" and crying aloud for treatment.

The most characteristic element in this situation seemed to me the incessant stream of confirmations, of observations which "verified" the theories in question; and this point was constantly emphasized by their adherents. A Marxist could not open a newspaper without finding on every page confirming evidence for his interpretation of history; not only in the news, but also in its presentation—which revealed the class bias of the paper—and especially of course in what the paper did *not* say. The Freudian analysts emphasized that their theories were constantly verified by their "clinical observations." As for Adler, I was much impressed by a personal experience. Once, in 1919, I reported to him a case which to me did not seem particularly Adlerian, but which he found no difficulty in analyzing in terms of his theory of inferiority feelings, although he had not even seen the child. Slightly shocked, I asked him how he could be so sure. "Because of my thousandfold experience," he replied; whereupon I could not help saying: "And with this new case, I suppose your experience has become thousand-and-one-fold."

What I had in mind was that his previous observations may not have been much sounder than this new one; that each in its turn had been interpreted in the light of "previous experience," and at the same time counted as additional confirmation. What, I asked myself, did it confirm? No more than that a case could be interpreted in the light of the theory. But this meant very little, I reflected, since every conceivable case could be interpreted in the light of Adler's theory, or equally of Freud's. I may illustrate this by two very different examples of human behavior; that of a man who pushes a child into the water with the intention of drowning it; and that of a man who sacrifices his life in an attempt to save the child. Each of these two cases can be explained with equal ease in Freudian and in Adlerian terms. According to Freud the first man suffered from repression (say, of some component of his Oedipal complex), while the second man had achieved sublimation. According to Adler the first man suffered from feelings of inferiority (producing perhaps the need to prove to himself that he dared to commit some crime), and so did the second man (whose need was to prove to himself that he dared to rescue the child). I could not think of any human behavior which could not be interpreted in terms of either theory. It was precisely this fact—that they always fitted, that they were always confirmed—which in the eyes of their admirers constituted the strongest argument in favor of these theories. It began to dawn on me that this apparent strength was in fact their weakness.

With Einstein's theory the situation was strikingly different. Take one typical instance—Einstein's prediction, just then confirmed by the findings of Eddington's expedition. Einstein's gravitational theory had led to the result that light must be attracted by heavy bodies (such as the sun), precisely as material bodies were attracted. As a consequence it could be calculated that light from a distant fixed star whose apparent position was close to the sun would reach the earth from such a direction that the star would seem to be slightly shifted away from the sun; or, in other words, the stars close to the sun would look as if they had moved a little away from the sun, and from one another. This is a thing which cannot normally be observed since such stars are rendered invisible in daytime by the sun's overwhelming brightness; but during an eclipse it is possible to take photographs of them. If the same constellation is photographed at night one can measure the distances on the two photographs, and check the predicted effect.

Now the impressive thing about this case is the *risk* involved in a prediction of this kind. If observation shows that the predicted effect is definitely absent, then the theory is simply refuted. The theory is *incompatible with certain possible results of observation*—in fact with results which everybody before Einstein would have expected. This is quite different from the situation I have previously described, when it turned out that the theories in question were compatible with the most divergent human behavior, so that it was practically impossible to describe any human behavior that might not be claimed to be a verification of these theories.

These considerations led me in the winter of 1919–20 to conclusions which I may now reformulate as follows:

1. It is easy to obtain confirmations, or verifications, for nearly every theory—if we look for confirmations.
2. Confirmations should count only if they are the result of *risky predictions*; that is to say, if, unenlightened by the theory in question, we should have expected an event which was incompatible with the theory—an event which would have refuted the theory.
3. Every "good" scientific theory is a prohibition: it forbids certain things to happen. The more a theory forbids, the better it is.
4. A theory which is not refutable by any conceivable event is nonscientific. Irrefutability is not a virtue of a theory (as people often think) but a vice.
5. Every genuine *test* of a theory is an attempt to falsify it, or to refute it. Testability is falsifiability; but there are degrees of testability: some theories are more testable, more exposed to refutation, than others; they take, as it were, greater risks.
6. Confirming evidence should not count *except when it is the result of a genuine test of the theory;* and this means that it can be presented as a serious but unsuccessful attempt to falsify the theory. (I now speak in such cases of "corroborating evidence.")
7. Some genuinely testable theories, when found to be false, are still upheld by their admirers—for example by introducing *ad hoc* some auxiliary assumption, or by reinterpreting the theory *ad hoc* in such a way that it escapes refutation. Such a procedure is always possible, but it rescues the theory from refutation only at the price of destroying, or at least lowering, its scientific status. (I later described such a rescuing operation as a "conventionalist twist" or a "conventionalist stratagem.")

One can sum up all this by saying that the criterion of the scientific status of a theory is its falsifiability, or refutability, or testability.

Criticisms of falsificationism

Popper's model of scientific change seems both reasonable and quite descriptive of scientific practice. Indeed, quite a few scientists over the years have made explicit reference to Popper as having captured their conception of how science operates and what distinguishes science from non-science (or pseudo-science). Nevertheless, there have been a number of criticisms leveled against falsificationism as an adequate or sufficient model of scientific change. The next two chapters will flesh out other alternative models and present criticisms in that context. Here I will discuss just two criticisms, neither of which relies on any other conception of scientific change.

The first criticism is that, contrary to Popper's model, we never test a single hypothesis in isolation, and, so, a disconfirming observation does not necessarily disconfirm the hypothesis in question. Rather, so goes this criticism, whenever we test a given hypothesis, we are also, in effect, testing a whole array of background assumptions, or auxiliary hypotheses. Here is an example to illustrate this: A prevailing view among ancient Greek astronomers was that the earth was at the center of the universe and the stars as well as the planets, including the sun and our moon, orbited around the earth in circular orbits. However, observations taken over a long period of time showed that some planets didn't actually appear to follow these nice circular orbits. Mars, for instance, displayed what was called retrograde motion. That is, in its movements across the sky, at times Mars appeared to slow down and even move backwards (relative to background stars) in its orbit before then later moving forward again. There were several efforts to explain this apparent retrograde motion. The most widely accepted attempt was to suggest that the planets not only orbited the earth in circular paths or cycles, but they also moved along smaller cycles (epicycles) in the process of moving along the main cycles. Another attempt, made by Aristarchus (310–230 BCE) was to suggest that, in fact, Mars did not really orbit around the earth, but that both of them orbited the sun. However, the earth orbited the sun faster than Mars did and so, at some points in their respective orbits, Mars appeared to slow down relative to the earth's movements and even move backwards. In addition to the earth moving in an orbit around the sun, it also rotated on its axis, accounting for the apparent movement of the heavenly bodies around it. (That is, because the earth spins on its axis, it looks as if the stars and sun and planets move around it, but they do not really.)

Now, there were plenty of common sense observations that ran counter to this "moving earth" view. For example, if the earth was orbiting around the sun and spinning on its axis, why don't we feel hurricane force winds all the time? When we throw things into the air, why don't they fall slightly behind where we threw them, because the earth would have rotated slightly during that time? We certainly do not feel the earth moving! But, more importantly, in terms of examining Popper's model, an observational test was formulated to see if the "moving earth" hypothesis made sense. This test is often referred to as the *stellar parallax test*. The test is this: If the earth orbits the sun, then in a six-month interval, the earth will be on opposite sides of the sun in its orbit around the sun (points 1 and 2 in Figure 1.). From the perspective of position 1, the close star appears to lie in front of (or very near) star B. Six months later, when the earth is at position 2 in its orbit of the sun, the same close star now appears to be in front of (or very near) star A. The angle Θ represents the parallax, or degree of apparent change, and, since we are talking about the apparent change in the star's movement relative to background stars, this is called the stellar parallax.

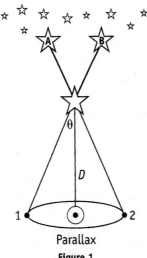

Parallax

Figure 1

Now, the point here is that the hypothesis that the earth moves in an orbit around the sun—a bold conjecture, given prevailing views—leads to a prediction of a certain observation, namely, that astronomers would be able to detect a stellar parallax. However, when they looked, after six months, no parallax was detected. Naturally, they rejected the hypothesis that the earth moves in an orbit around the sun. That hypothesis seemed quite clearly to have been falsified.

What we now know, of course, is that the hypothesis was in fact true, but there were other assumptions, or auxiliary hypotheses, that were mistaken. For example, there was an assumption about the distances to the stars. It turns out that there is a parallax, but the angle is so small that the ancient Greek astronomers could not detect it. There was also an assumption that the stars did not move, certainly not in ways that we now understand them to. So—and here is the point of the criticism—it is never the case that any single hypothesis is tested in isolation. As a result, negative results might not in fact falsify the hypothesis in question.

Such a criticism was raised by the French physicist, Pierre Duhem (although not directly raised against Popper, as Duhem preceded Popper), who claimed that there can never be a "crucial experiment," because we can never test any single hypothesis in isolation, but only a whole group of hypotheses and, so, disconfirming experimental results only indicate that at least one of the hypotheses in the group is mistaken, but do not indicate which one(s).

A second criticism that has been raised against Popper's falsificationist model of scientific change is that it is not clear when a modification to a hypothesis or theory is ad hoc. Remember, his objection was that when a hypothesis or theory is found to be false (or, at least appears to be), it is sometimes still upheld by its admirers by introducing ad hoc hypotheses to rescue it from the (apparent) falsifying evidence. To this extent, Popper says, the hypothesis or theory is diminished in its status as science. However, so goes the criticism, this is exactly what often is done, especially for a hypothesis or theory that has displayed great explanatory power previously. Furthermore, it is not clear from what Popper says just what constitutes an ad hoc modification. Let me give first a homespun example and then a more serious one. The homespun example is that as I was in my first physics lab and we were doing experiments to try to measure the force of gravity, I was (and, sad to say, still remain) a complete bungler. The results I got gave a force of gravity that was about ten times the real value. My physics professor certainly did not think that I had falsified centuries of previous detected values. He said, "Boersema, you really are pathetic in this lab, aren't you? Make sure your equipment is working properly." (He really did say this!) Now, would it have been an ad hoc modification to suggest that my equipment might have malfunctioned? Well, probably in this case, but, in fact, for real scientists who get surprising results that run counter to what was predicted, checking their equipment is a very reasonable thing to do, especially as the work is more and more dependent on sophisticated, sensitive equipment. The point, though, is that it does not at all seem to be ad hoc to "save the hypothesis" by looking for a variety of reasons or causes as to why a hypothesis seemed to be falsified.

The more serious example is that, in the 1800s as astronomers noted the erratic, or at least surprising, orbit of Uranus, one proposal to account for this was that a further, yet undetected and even unsuspected, planet existed, whose gravitational attraction could affect the orbit of Uranus. This turned out to be the case (it was Neptune), but the question here is: was that an ad hoc, and hence non-scientific, move to rescue the current Newtonian theory? So, the broader issue of the rationality of modifications, including what seem to be ad hoc, is a more complex matter than it appears that Popper takes it to be. This type of concern will arise in the course of the next two chapters as we look at other models of scientific change.

Chapter Summary

Inductivism is a model of how science changes. It claims that science begins with specific observations or data and, through experimentation and further observation, identifies patterns in the data, leading ultimately to generalized conclusions (laws or theories). John Stuart Mill attempted to elucidate various common inductive patterns of establishing causal connections, dubbed "Mill's Methods." These methods of determining cause among phenomena include the Methods of Agreement, Difference, Agreement and Difference, Residues, and Concomitant Variation. Karl Popper (among others) criticized inductivism as an inadequate model for scientific change. Popper argued that the principle of induction cannot be justified as a model for discovery or justification of scientific theories. In fact, he claimed, the principle of induction itself cannot be justified as a means of establishing general scientific claims. In addition, the search for confirming instances of some hypothesis or theory is a poor test of the scientific worth of that hypothesis or theory. Rather, what distinguishes science from non-science (or pseudo-science) is the proffering of bold, risky conjectures followed by the attempt to genuinely test those conjectures against further observation. The attempt to test, or falsify, a hypothesis is the real test of its scientific status. Finally, no hypothesis can be truly verified, but only corroborated and we can never claim that a hypothesis is true, but only speak of its verisimilitude.

CASE STUDY

Lazaro Spallanzani

The following is a selection from the biological researches of Lazaro Spallanzani (1729–1799). This selection is an account of his experiments on the nature of digestion. Consider in what ways this case supports or fails to support the inductivist model of scientific change or the falsificationist model. For example, are any of Mill's Methods displayed here? Is a general conclusion drawn from specific premises? Does Spallanzani propose any bold conjectures? Does he offer any ad hoc explanations for his results? In what senses, if any, is he attempting to falsify any hypothesis?

ON DIGESTION

Lazaro Spallanzani

I must now turn to man, to conclude my investigations upon digestion in different animals with membranous stomachs. It is true that the studies designed for this purpose on numerous animals of this class—especially birds of prey, cats and dogs, whose stomachs are very like ours—lead us to conclude that their digestive functions are the same as our own: this, however, is proof by analogy and is, therefore, only a probability; besides, after having reached certain positive conclusions with regard to animals, I had at least to try and do the same with regard to man. Glancing over the works of doctors, both ancient and modern, I find the commonest object of their study is human digestion, but, if I may be allowed to say so, they have sought to guess the way in which digestion works rather than to discover it. Direct experiments on man are altogether lacking and all that has been done is limited to more or less doubtful conjectures and hypotheses. If, therefore, I had to have recourse to my own experiments when dealing with animal digestion, how much more necessary was it to do so with regard to human digestion.

Thinking over the most important experiments which it would be possible to make on man, it seemed to me that they could be brought under two principle groups, i.e., those in which human gastric juice is obtained in order to repeat the experiments made with the same juice in animals, and those in which tubes containing various animal and vegetable substances are swallowed, in order to study the changes which they will have undergone when they emerge from the body.

I intended to make these experiments on myself, but I admit that those involving the use of tubes seemed to me rather dangerous, for I knew that bodies held up in the stomach without being digested had led to dire consequences and, after a considerable time, had been vomited up. I remembered, too, cases where similar bodies had been held up in the intestines. However, the various contradictory facts which are current encouraged me to try these experiments. I knew that very hard stones, like those of cherries, morellas, medlars, and plums were swallowed with impunity by children and country people and that they passed through the anus very easily without causing the slightest discomfort. In the midst of this struggle, the previous events which I have recorded induced me to overcome my reluctance . . .

It was a question of swallowing a little linen bag, containing 52 grains of masticated bread. I began this experiment one morning on rising and while fasting, and the circumstances which I am about to relate to all my experiments of this kind. I retained the bag for 23 hours, without experiencing any ill effects; on emerging it contained no bread, the thread with which the two sides of the bag had been sewn was neither broken nor damaged; the same applied to the thread at the mouth of the bag. The linen was not torn in any way, so that, evidently, it had not undergone any alteration either in the stomach or intestine. The success of this experiment encouraged me to try others; I repeated it with two similar bags, containing an equal amount of masticated bread, but with this difference, one of the bags was made of two thicknesses of linen, the other of three. You may guess, from what I have said elsewhere, that I wanted to find out whether the thickness of the bag would make digestion more difficult. I observed as follows: the two small bags emerged from my body after twenty-seven hours; the bread in the bag made of two thicknesses had been entirely digested, but there was a little left in the one made of three thicknesses . . .

Having discovered that I could digest meat which had been cooked and masticated, I wanted to find out whether I could digest the same meat unmasticated; I swallowed, therefore, 80 grains of gristly meat from a chicken's breast in a small bag: I ejected it only after 37 hours. It had lost 56 grains and what was left, far from being gelatinous or tender, was dry and the inmost fleshy fibers seemed less dry than those outside. Otherwise, digestion appeared to have taken place equally, as the piece of meat kept the shape into which I had cut it.

CASE STUDY

Plate Tectonics

On pages 348–365, read the account of the emergence of plate tectonics, a revolutionary geological theory that arose in the mid-20th century. What aspects of this case fit or do not fit the inductivist or falsificationist models of scientific change?

Further Reading

Ackermann, Robert. *The Philosophy of Karl Popper*. Amherst: University of Massachusetts Press, 1976.

Chalmers, A.F., *What Is This Thing Called Science?* St. Lucia: University of Queensland Press, 1976.

Copi, Irving. *Introduction to Logic*. New York: Macmillan, 1953.

Mill, J.S. *A System of Logic*. London:, 1843.

O'Hear, Anthony (ed.). *Karl Popper: Philosophy and Problems*. Cambridge: Cambridge University Press, 1995.

Popper, Karl. *Conjectures and Refutations: The Growth of Scientific Knowledge*. London: Routledge & Kegan Paul, 1963.

Popper, Karl. *The Logic of Scientific Discovery*, Karl Popper; London: Hutchinson, 1959.

Popper, Karl. *The Myth of the Framework*. London: Routledge, 1994.

Popper, Karl. *Objective Knowledge*. Oxford: Clarendon Press, 1972.

Popper, Karl. *Realism and the Aim of Science*. London: Hutchinson, 1983.

Schillp, P.A. (ed.). *The Philosophy of Karl Popper*. LaSalle: Open Court, 1974.

CHAPTER NINE

Paradigms and Research Programs

IN THIS CHAPTER, WE WILL

- Examine the Paradigm model of scientific change, particularly associated with Thomas Kuhn
- Examine the Research Programs model of scientific change, particularly associated with Imre Lakatos

The terms *paradigm* and *paradigm shift* have become mainstream. For example, in October 2005, Malcolm D. Knight, General Manager of the Bank for International Settlements, spoke at an international conference in India on commerce and banking. He began his speech with these remarks:

> It is a great pleasure to be here today to deliver the inaugural
> address at the fourth Annual Conference of the Federation of
> Indian Chambers of Commerce and Industry (FCCI). The last time
> I participated in the FCCI Conference was in September 2003. The
> theme then was "Indian banking—global benchmarks." Today it is
> "Global banking—paradigm shift." This subtle change of emphasis
> in themes—from Indian banking to global banking—clearly reflects
> today's reality: the increasing globalization of the Indian economy.

Now, what does this have to do with the philosophy of science? Indian banking, not much; the notion of paradigm shift, a lot! Although the word "paradigm" has been around for centuries, it became a household word—among academicians, anyway—beginning in the 1960s and it was solely because of the work of one philosopher/historian of science, Thomas Kuhn. Kuhn used the term in his enormously influential book, *The Structure of Scientific Revolutions (SST)*, which was published in 1962. He used this term, which can be traced back to a Greek word for *pattern*, to argue that scientific change is largely the result of scientific revolutions, themselves a matter of major changes in how a scientific community understands the world. Since Kuhn published *SST*, it has become commonplace to speak of a Newtonian paradigm or Darwinian paradigm or Freudian paradigm. In addition, it has become commonplace to speak of major scientific revolutions as *paradigm shifts*. This terminology became so widespread in the academic community that, as the banker quote above exemplifies, the terms *paradigm* and *paradigm shift* spread and are now used commonly outside of academics. (Google them and see for yourself!)

Paradigms (and historicism)

In *SST*, Kuhn challenged the prevailing philosophical views of the nature of science, especially scientific change and progress, and did so in such a compelling manner that, ever since, philosophers of science spoke of pre-Kuhnian and post-Kuhnian views. At the time, the prevailing theories of the nature of science were that science could clearly be demarcated from non-science either on an inductivist model or on a falsificationist model. As we saw in the previous chapter, the inductivist view argued that science (at least, good science) proceeded from an unbiased observational foundation, followed precisely defined procedures ("the scientific method"), and, as a result, made cumulative progress in modeling an independent, objectively-known world. Good science, it was said, was a value-free, inductively based, cumulatively progressing means of gaining knowledge. Although Popper offered some strong rebuttals and criticisms of inductivism, his alternate falsificationist model also argued that science (at least, good science) was primarily rational and changed as a result of clearly defined, logically structured criteria. Kuhn, armed with his understanding of the history of science, challenged these models of the nature of science.

Change and progress in science, he claimed, are not the result of a cumulative collection of facts that result from value-free observations and theories inductively inferred from those observations nor of bold conjectures with clearly articulated falsifiability criteria and standards. Rather, change and progress in science is a matter of the replacement of paradigms. Paradigms are defined sociologically from the perspective of scientific communities. A scientific community, for Kuhn, is defined in terms of actual communication linkages, such as sharing professional organizations, professional journals, attending conferences, citing specific published works, and so on. A scientific community shares a particular paradigm in the sense that those members of the community point to the same, or similar, scientific exemplars (or achievements) and the same, or similar, disciplinary matrices (or values, instrumentation, etc.). To the extent that science can be demarcated from non-science, it is because science is guided by a predominant paradigm at any given time. A Newtonian paradigm, for example, rests on a commitment to absolute space and time, whereas an Einsteinian paradigm does not. While a scientific community operates within the confines of a paradigm, which gives structure to that community's work, non-science (and also a science in its infancy) will not be governed or guided by a paradigm; instead, many schools will coexist, arguing from the fundamentals on up, with no accepted methodology. Kuhn called paradigm-governed science "normal science," in which the scientific community engages primarily in solving particular puzzles, such as gathering more detailed data or increasing the precision of agreement between observation and theoretical predictions or determining more accurately the values of certain constants (such as the speed of light). Within normal science, the underlying paradigm is assumed, not tested. Scientists, not having to continually argue for the fundamentals, can specialize and focus on specific problems and details, thus accounting for progress. Here is his account of typical activities of normal science:

THE STRUCTURE OF SCIENTIFIC REVOLUTIONS
Thomas Kuhn

The Route to Normal Science

In this essay, "normal science" means research firmly based upon one or more past scientific achievements, achievements that some particular scientific community acknowledges for a time as supplying the foundation for its further practice. Today such achievements are recounted, though seldom in their original form, by science textbooks, elementary and advanced. These textbooks expound the body of accepted theory, illustrate many or all of its successful applications, and compare these applications with exemplary observations and experiments. Before such books became popular early in the nineteenth century (and even until more recently in the newly matured sciences), many of the famous classics of science fulfilled a similar function. Aristotle's *Physica*, Ptolemy's *Almagest*, Newton's *Principia* and *Opticks*, Franklin's *Electricity*, Lavoisier's *Chemistry*, and Lyell's *Geology*—these and many other works served for a time implicitly to define the legitimate problems and methods of a research field for succeeding generations of practitioners. They were able to do so because they shared two essential characteristics. Their achievement was sufficiently unprecedented to attract an enduring group of adherents away from competing modes of scientific activity. Simultaneously, it was sufficiently open-ended to leave all sorts of problems for the redefined group of practitioners to resolve.

Achievements that share these two characteristics I shall henceforth refer to as "paradigms," a term that relates closely to "normal science." By choosing it, I mean to suggest that some accepted examples of actual scientific practice—examples which include law, theory, application, and instrumentation together—provide models from which spring particular coherent traditions of scientific research. These are the traditions which the historian describes under such rubrics as "Ptolemaic astronomy" (or "Copernican"), "Aristotelian dynamics" (or "Newtonian"), "corpuscular optics" (or "wave optics"), and so on. The study of paradigms, including many that are far more specialized than those named illustratively above, is what mainly prepares the student for membership in the particular scientific community with which he will later practice . . .

Why is the concrete scientific achievement, as a locus of professional commitment, prior to the various concepts, laws, theories, and points of view that may be abstracted from it? In what sense is the shared paradigm a fundamental unit for the student of scientific development, a unit that cannot be fully reduced to logically atomic components which might function in its stead? When we encounter them [below], answers to these questions and to others like them will prove basic to an understanding both of normal science and of the associated concept of paradigms. That more abstract discussion will depend, however, upon a previous exposure to examples of normal science or of paradigms in operation. In particular, both these related concepts will be clarified by noting that there can be a sort of scientific research without paradigms, or at least without any so unequivocal and so binding as the ones named above. Acquisition of a paradigm and of the more esoteric type of research it permits is a sign of maturity in the development of any given scientific field.

. . . In the absence of a paradigm or some candidate for paradigm, all of the facts that could possibly pertain to the development of a given science are likely to seem equally relevant. As a result, early fact-gathering is a far more nearly random activity than the one that subsequent scientific development makes familiar. Furthermore, in the absence of a reason for seeking some particular form of more recondite information, early fact-gathering is usually restricted to the wealth of data that lie ready to hand. The resulting pool of facts contains those accessible to casual observation and experiment together with some of the more esoteric data retrievable from established crafts like medicine, calendar making, and metallurgy. Because the crafts are one readily accessible source of facts that could not have been casually discovered, technology has often played a vital role in the emergence of new sciences.

. . . No natural history can be interpreted in the absence of at least some implicit body of intertwined theoretical and methodological belief that permits selection, evaluation, and criticism. If that body of belief is not already implicit in the collection of facts—in which case more than "mere facts" are at hand—it must be externally supplied, perhaps by a current metaphysics, by another science, or by personal and historical accident. No wonder, then, that in the early stages of the development of any science different men confronting the same range of phenomena, describe and interpret them in different ways. What is surprising, and perhaps also unique in its degree to the fields we call science, is that such initial divergences should ever largely disappear.

The Nature of Normal Science

. . . Paradigms gain their status because they are more successful than their competitors in solving a few problems that the group of practitioners has come to recognize as acute. To be more successful is not, however, to be either completely successful with a single problem or notably successful with any large number. The success of a paradigm—whether Aristotle's analysis of motion, Ptolemy's computation of planetary position, Lavoisier's application of a balance, or Maxwell's mathematization of the electromagnetic field—is at the start largely a promise of success discoverable in selected and still incomplete examples. Normal science consists in the actualization of that promise, an actualization achieved by extending the knowledge of those facts that the paradigm displays as particularly revealing, by increasing the extent of the match between those facts and the paradigm's predictions, and by further articulation of the paradigm itself.

Few people who are not actually practitioners of a mature science realize how much mop-up work of this sort a paradigm leaves to be done or quite how fascinating such work can prove in the execution. And these points need to be understood. Mopping-up operations are what engage most scientists throughout their careers. They constitute what I am here calling normal science. Closely examined, whether historically or in the contemporary laboratory, that enterprise seems an attempt to force nature into the preformed and relatively inflexible box that the paradigm supplies. No part of the aim of normal science is to call forth new sorts of phenomena; indeed those that will not fit the box are often not seen at all. Nor do scientists normally aim to invent new theories, and they are often intolerant of those invented by others. Instead, normal-scientific research is directed to the articulation of those phenomena and theories that the paradigm already supplies.

. . . There are, I think, only three normal foci for factual scientific investigation, and they are neither always nor permanently distinct. First is that class of facts that the paradigm has shown to be particularly revealing of the nature of things. By employing them in solving problems, the paradigm has made them worth determining both with more precision and in a larger variety of situations. At one time or another, these significant factual determinations have included: in astronomy—stellar position and magnitude, the periods of eclipsing binaries and of planets; in physics—the specific gravities and compressibilities of materials, wave lengths and spectral intensities, electrical conductivities and contact potentials; and in chemistry—composition and combining weights, boiling points and acidity of solutions, structural formulas and optical activities . . .

A second usual but smaller class of factual determinations is directed to those facts that, though often without much intrinsic interest, can be compared directly with predictions from the paradigm theory . . . The existence of the paradigm sets the problem to be solved; often the paradigm theory is implicated directly in the design of apparatus able to solve the problem. Without the *Principia*, for example, measurements made with the Atwood machine [to demonstrate Newton's second law] would have meant nothing at all.

A third class of experiments and observations exhausts, I think, the fact-gathering activities of normal science. It consists of empirical work undertaken to articulate the paradigm theory, resolving some of its residual ambiguities and permitting the solution of problems to which it had previously only drawn attention. This class proves to be the most important of all, and its description demands its subdivision. In the more mathematical sciences, some of the experiments aimed at articulation are directed to the determination of physical constants . . . Efforts to articulate a paradigm are not, however, restricted to the determination of universal constants. They may, for example, also aim at quantitative laws: Boyle's Law relating gas pressure to volume, Coulomb's Law of electrical attraction, and Joule's formula relating heat generated to electrical resistance and current are all in this category . . . Finally, there is a third sort of experiment which aims to articulate a paradigm. More than the others this one can resemble exploration, and it is particularly prevalent in those periods and sciences that deal more with the qualitative than with the quantitative aspects of nature's regularity . . .

These three classes of problems—determination of significant fact, matching of facts with theory, and articulation of theory—exhaust, I think, the literature of normal science, both empirical and theoretical. They do not, of course, quite exhaust the literature of science. There are also extraordinary problems, and it may well be their resolution that makes the scientific enterprise as a whole so particularly worthwhile. But extraordinary problems are not to be had for the asking. They emerge only on special occasions prepared in advance of normal research. Inevitably, therefore, the overwhelming majority of the problems undertaken by even the very best scientists usually fall into one of the three categories outlined above. Work under the paradigm can be conducted in no other way, and to desert the paradigm is to cease practicing the science it defines. We shall shortly discover that such desertions do occur. They are the pivots about which scientific revolutions turn.

So, we can see from what Kuhn says above why he has called normal science "dogmatic." What he means is that scientists work within a given paradigm and accept that paradigm, usually because that was what they learned explicitly or implicitly as students when they began to study their particular field. The basic tenets of the paradigm are not challenged or questioned or, for that matter, really even thought about; they are the given background. Because the basic tenets of the paradigm are just assumed, to that extent science is dogmatic, but Kuhn does not at all mean that as a criticism. Indeed, it is because of that dogmatic attitude that the scientific community can proceed to carry out its normal science functions.

Inevitably, however, unexpected phenomena—*anomalies*—occur. Often these anomalies can be resolved within the paradigm. For Kuhn, the presence of an anomaly does not result in the falsification of a given hypothesis (contra Popper). Certainly, the history of science, including what is agreed to be good science, abundantly demonstrates that the presence of anomalies did not result in the abandonment of a given hypothesis or even, often, in the perceived falsification of that hypothesis. Nevertheless, sometimes these anomalies build in number or strike at the heart of the paradigm. If a large number or particularly significant anomalies arise, this can produce a crisis for the paradigm. Especially important for Kuhn is that these anomalies might arise for non-scientific (i.e., political, social, philosophical) reasons. When a crisis produces "profound professional insecurity," and rival paradigms are seriously considered, the community has shifted from normal science to extraordinary science. An example of this is the shift from a Ptolemaic, geocentric view to a Copernican, heliocentric view. Scientific revolutions, such as the Copernican revolution, are the abandonment of one paradigm for another, and this occurs when the new paradigm resolves the old paradigm's anomalies and appears to hold promise to solve even more "normal" puzzles. New normal science then emerges within the new paradigm. We can summarize Kuhn's picture of scientific change in the following diagram:

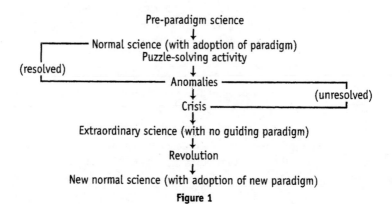

Figure 1

Kuhn's views were striking for a number of reasons. First, he emphasized the revolutionary aspect of science, not the "normal," cumulative aspect. Science changes and progresses, he claimed, not because it steadily accumulates and assimilates more and more information, but because it makes sudden leaps. Second, these revolutions can be seen to have structure; there are enunciable stages to scientific revolutions. Third, scientific change is, to a large extent, non-rational. The observations made within normal science, said Kuhn, are theory-laden; what is accepted as legitimate observation is influenced by background theories and assumptions. In addition, as noted above, what is seen as legitimate and as anomalous might be motivated and justified along non-scientific grounds. Finally, the abandonment of one paradigm for another is often gestalt-like or analogous to a conversion experience, with the consequence, according to Kuhn, that different paradigms are "incommensurable," such that scientists understand the world differently across rival paradigms. We will go over in more detail just what Kuhn means by the notion of *incommensurability*, but first here he is again, with his explanation of scientific revolution and paradigm shift:

THE STRUCTURE OF SCIENTIFIC REVOLUTIONS (continued)
Thomas Kuhn

The Nature and Necessity of Scientific Revolutions

What are scientific revolutions, and what is their function in scientific development? Much of the answer to these questions has been anticipated in earlier sections. In particular, the preceding discussion has indicated that scientific revolutions are here taken to be those non-cumulative developmental episodes in which an older paradigm is replaced in whole or in part by an incompatible new one. There is more to be said, however, and an essential part of it can be introduced by asking one further question. Why should a change of paradigm be called a revolution? In the face of the vast and essential differences between political and scientific development, what parallelism can justify the metaphor that finds revolutions in both?

One aspect of the parallelism must be already apparent. Political revolutions are inaugurated by a growing sense, often restricted to a segment of the political community, that existing institutions have ceased adequately to meet the problems posed by an environment that they have in part created. In much the same way, scientific revolutions are inaugurated by a growing sense, again often restricted to a narrow subdivision of the scientific community, that an existing paradigm has ceased to function adequately in the exploration of an aspect of nature to which that paradigm itself had previously led the way. In both political and scientific development the sense of malfunction that can lead to crisis is prerequisite to revolution . . .

This genetic aspect of the parallel between political and scientific development should no longer be open to doubt. The parallel has, however, a second and more profound aspect upon which the significance of the first depends. Political revolutions aim to change political institutions in ways that those institutions themselves prohibit. Their success therefore necessitates the partial relinquishment of one set of institutions in favor of another, and in the interim, society is not fully governed by institutions at all. Initially it is crisis alone that attenuates the role of political institutions as we have already seen it attenuate the role of paradigms. In increasing numbers individuals become increasingly estranged from political life and behave more and more eccentrically within it. Then, as the crisis deepens, many of these individuals commit themselves to some concrete proposal for the reconstruction of society in a new institutional framework. At that point the society is divided into competing camps or parties, one seeking to defend the old institutional constellation, the others seeking to institute some new one. And once that polarization has occurred, *political recourse fails*. Because they differ about the institutional matrix within which political change is to be achieved and evaluated, because they acknowledge no supra-institutional framework for the adjudication of revolutionary difference, the parties to a revolutionary conflict must finally resort to the techniques of mass persuasion, often including force. Though revolutions have had a vital role in the evolution of political institutions, that role depends upon their being partially extrapolitical or extrainstitutional events.

. . . the historical study of paradigm change reveals very similar characteristics in the evolution of the sciences. Like the choice between competing political institutions, that between competing paradigms proves to be a choice between incompatible modes of community life. Because it has that character, the choice is not and cannot be determined merely by the evaluative procedures characteristic of normal science, for these depend in part upon a particular paradigm, and that paradigm is at issue. When paradigms enter, as they must, into a debate about paradigm choice, their role is necessarily circular. Each group uses its own paradigm to argue in that paradigm's defense.

The resulting circularity does not, of course, make the arguments wrong or even ineffectual. The man who premises a paradigm when arguing in its defense can nonetheless provide a clear exhibit of what scientific practice will be like for those who adopt the new view of nature. That exhibit can be immensely persuasive, often compellingly so. Yet, whatever its force, the status of the circular argument is only that of persuasion. It cannot be made logically or even probabilistically compelling for those who refuse to step into the circle. The premises and values shared by the two parties to a debate over paradigms are not sufficiently extensive for that. As in political revolutions, so in paradigm choice—there is no standard higher than the assent of the relevant community. To discover how scientific revolutions are effected, we shall therefore have to examine not only the impact of nature and of logic, but also the techniques of persuasive argumentation effective within the quite special groups that constitute the community of scientists.

Revolutions as Changes of World View

Examining the record of past research from the vantage of contemporary historiography, the historian of science may be tempted to exclaim that when paradigms change, the world itself changes with them. Led by a new paradigm, scientists adopt new instruments and look in new places. Even more important, during revolutions scientists see new and different things when looking with familiar instruments in places they have looked before. It is rather as if the professional community had been suddenly transported to another planet where familiar objects are seen in a different light and are joined by unfamiliar ones as well. Of course, nothing of quite that sort does occur: there is no geographical transplantation; outside the laboratory everyday affairs usually continue as before. Nevertheless, paradigm changes do cause scientists to see the world of their research-engagement differently. In so far as their only recourse to that world is through what they see and do, we may want to say that after a revolution scientists are responding to a different world.

It is as elementary prototypes for these transformations of the scientist's world that the familiar demonstrations of a switch in a visual gestalt prove so suggestive. What were ducks in the scientist's world before the revolution are rabbits afterwards. The man who first saw the exterior of the box from above later sees its interior from below. Transformations like these, though usually more gradual and almost always irreversible, are common concomitants of scientific training. Looking at a contour map, the student sees lines of a paper, the cartographer a picture of a terrain. Looking at a bubble-chamber photograph, the student sees confused and broken lines, the physicist a record of familiar subnuclear events. Only after a number of such transformations of vision does the student become an inhabitant of the scientist's world, seeing what the scientist sees and responding as the scientist does. The world that the student then enters is not, however, fixed once and for all by the nature of the environment, on the one hand, and of science, on the other. Rather, it is determined jointly by the environment and the particular normal-scientific tradition that the student has been trained to pursue. Therefore, at times of revolution, when the normal-scientific tradition changes, the scientist's perception of his environment must be re-educated—in some familiar situations he must learn to see a new gestalt. After he has done so the world of his research will seem, here and there, incommensurable with the one he had inhabited before. That is another reason why schools guided by different paradigms are always slightly at cross-purposes . . .

Do we, however, really need to describe what separates Galileo from Aristotle, or Lavoisier from Priestley, as a transformation of vision? Did these men really *see* different things when *looking at* the same sorts of objects? Is there any legitimate sense in which we can say that they pursued their research in different worlds? Those questions can no longer be postponed, for there is obviously another and far more usual way to describe [such examples]. Many readers will surely want to say that what changes with a paradigm is only the scientist's interpretation of observations that themselves are fixed once and for all by the nature of the environment and of the perceptual apparatus. On this view, Priestley and Lavoisier both saw oxygen, but they interpreted their observations differently; Aristotle and Galileo both saw pendulums, but they differed in their interpretations of what they both had seen.

Let me say at once that this very usual view of what occurs when scientists change their minds about fundamental matters can be neither all wrong nor a mere mistake. Rather it is an essential part of a philosophical paradigm initiated by Descartes and developed at the same time as Newtonian dynamics. That paradigm has served both science and philosophy well. Its exploitation, like that of dynamics itself, has been fruitful of a fundamental understanding that perhaps could not have been achieved in another way. But as the example of Newtonian dynamics also indicates, even the most striking past success provides no guarantee that crisis can be indefinitely postponed. Today research in philosophy, psychology, linguistics, and even art history, all converge to suggest that the traditional paradigm is somewhat askew. That failure to fit is also made increasingly apparent by the historical study of science to which most of our attention is necessarily directed here.

None of these crisis-promoting subjects has yet produced a viable alternate to the traditional epistemological paradigm, but they do begin to suggest what some of that paradigm's characteristics will be. I am, for example, acutely aware of the difficulties created by saying that when Aristotle and Galileo looked at swinging stones, the first saw constrained fall, the second a pendulum. The same difficulties are presented in an even more fundamental form by the opening sentences of this section: though the world does not change with a change of paradigm, the scientist afterwards works in a different world. Nevertheless, I am convinced that we must learn to make sense of statements that at least resemble these. What occurs during a scientific revolution is not fully reducible to a reinterpretation of individual and stable data. In the first place, the data are not unequivocally stable. A pendulum is not a falling stone, nor is oxygen dephlogisticated air. Consequently, the data that scientists collect from these diverse objects are, as we shall shortly see, themselves different. More important, the process by which either the individual or the community makes the transition from constrained fall to the pendulum or from dephlogisticated air to oxygen is not one that resembles interpretation. How could it do so in the absence of fixed data for the scientist to interpret? Rather than being an interpreter, the scientist who embraces a new paradigm is like the man wearing inverted lenses. Confronting the same constellation of objects as before and knowing that he does so, he nevertheless finds them transformed through and through in many of their details.

None of these remarks is intended to indicate that scientists do not characteristically interpret observations and data. On the contrary, Galileo interpreted observations on the pendulum, Aristotle observations on falling stones, Musschenbroek observations on a charge-filled bottle, and Franklin observations on a condenser. But each of these interpretations presupposed a paradigm. They were parts of normal science, an enterprise that, as we have already seen, aims to refine, extend, and articulate a paradigm that is already in existence . . . Given a paradigm, interpretation of data is central to the enterprise that explores it.

But that interpretive enterprise—and this was the burden of the paragraph before last—can only articulate a paradigm, not correct it. Paradigms are not corrigible by normal science at all. Instead, as we have already seen, normal science ultimately leads only to the recognition of anomalies and to crises. And these are terminated, not by deliberation and interpretation, but by a relatively sudden and unstructured event like the gestalt switch. Scientists then often speak of the "scales falling from the eyes" or of the "lightning flash" that "inundates" a previously obscure puzzle, enabling its components to be seen in a new way that for the first time permits its solution. On other occasions the relevant illumination comes in sleep. No ordinary sense of the term "interpretation" fits these flashes of intuition through which a new paradigm is born. Though such intuitions depend upon the experience, both anomalous and congruent, gained with the old paradigm, they are not logically or piecemeal linked to particular items of that experience as an interpretation would be. Instead, they gather up large portions of that experience and transform them to the rather different bundle of experience that will thereafter be linked piecemeal to the new paradigm but not to the old.

. . . [But] neither scientists nor laymen learn to see the world piecemeal or item by item. Except when all the conceptual and manipulative categories are prepared in advance—e.g., for the discovery of an additional transuranic element or for catching sight of a new house—both scientists and laymen sort out whole areas together from the flux of experience. The child who transfers the word "mama" from all humans to all females and then to his mother is not just learning what "mama" means or who his mother is. Simultaneously he is learning some of the differences between males and females as well as something about the ways in which all but one female will behave toward him. His reactions, expectations, and beliefs—indeed, much of his perceived world—change accordingly. By the same token, the Copernicans who denied its traditional title "planet" to the sun were not only learning what "planet" meant or what the sun was. Instead, they were changing the meaning of "planet" so that it could continue to make useful distinctions in a world where all celestial bodies, not just the sun, were seen differently from the way they had been seen before. The same point could be made about any of our earlier examples. To see oxygen instead of dephlogisticated air, the condenser instead of the Leyden jar, or the pendulum instead of constrained fall, was only one part of an integrated shift in the scientist's vision of a great many related chemical, electrical, or dynamical phenomena. Paradigms determine large areas of experience at the same time . . .

To conclude this section, let us henceforth neglect retinal impressions and again restrict attention to the laboratory operations that provide the scientist with concrete though fragmentary indices to what he has already seen. One way in which much laboratory operations change with paradigms has already been observed repeatedly. After a scientific revolution many old measurements and manipulations become irrelevant and are replaced by others instead. One does not apply all the same tests to oxygen as to dephlogisticated air. But changes of this sort are never total. Whatever he may see then, the scientist after a revolution is still looking at the same world. Furthermore, though he may previously have employed them differently, much of his language and most of his laboratory instruments are still the same as they were before. As a result, postrevolutionary science invariably includes many of the same manipulations, performed with the same instruments and described in the same terms, as its prerevolutionary predecessor. If these enduring manipulations have been changed at all, the change must lie either in their relation to the paradigm or in their concrete results.

Now, just prior to the passage above, I noted that Kuhn said that different paradigms are incommensurable. What did Kuhn mean by that? Well, the term is taken from mathematics and it would help first to say what "commensurable" means. It means that two systems can be put into a one-to-one relationship with each other. For example, the integers (1, 2, 3, . . .) can be put into a one-to-one relation with their squares (1, 4, 9, . . .). In other words, for every integer, there is its square (and vice versa), such that we could draw two lines (one of the integers and one of their squares) and each point on one line would match up exactly with one point on the other line, like this:

1	2	3	4	5	6	7...
↓	↓	↓	↓	↓	↓	↓
1	4	9	16	25	36	49...

When it comes to natural science, it is not matching up numbers that is important, but matching up concepts and data. But, says Kuhn, different paradigms are not commensurable. Some basic terms such as "mass" and "planet" simply do not mean the same thing in different paradigms. This does not mean that there are no terms that mean the same thing across different paradigms; in fact a great many terms do not change their meaning or their function. But, for Kuhn, some do change their meanings and functions, so there is not a clean, conceptual one-to-one relationship of terms across paradigms. This point about incommensurability was one that led many philosophers of science to challenge Kuhn and he spent much of his life after *SST* was published in trying to clarify and elucidate this notion of incommensurability (see, especially, his essays compiled in *The Road Since Structure*). This issue of incommensurability was intimately bound up with his efforts, seen in the passage above, to say in what ways scientists across different paradigms respond to a *different world*.

Criticisms of Kuhn

Kuhn's model of scientific change was a conceptual earthquake. While many academicians hailed his "sociological turn," others were quick to criticize his views as portraying science as being irrational and ideological. Kuhn spent much of the next three decades responding to critics and clarifying his views, insisting that he was giving a historically based description of scientific practice, not necessarily a normative prescription. In addition, he insisted that science is not irrational and ideological, but proceeds on the basis of rigorous checks and balances. Good science and the evaluation of rival theories can be characterized around values such as accuracy, consistency, breadth, simplicity, and fecundity. Nevertheless, one criticism of Kuhn is that his view is too conventionalist; that is, he places far too much emphasis on the importance of extra-scientific matters in evaluating science. Too much of what he says, critics claim, make it sound as if the standards and criteria of good scientific work is simply a matter of politics or personal influence or religion or other non-rational factors. Kuhn seems to be rejecting or at least severely restricting the value and significance of objective standards of evaluation as well as simple facts about the world settling disputes.

In addition, critics have pointed out that the very notion of "paradigm" is much too vague to be fruitful. One critic early after the publication of *SST* claimed that Kuhn used the term "paradigm" in at least 22 different ways! Although he responded to this concern, many philosophers of science still see the notion as not very clear (and, hence, not very useful or explanatory).

Another criticism of Kuhn's view of scientific change is that he rejects (or, at least, seems to reject) the notion of cumulative progress in science. Surely, say critics, our understanding of the physical world after Einstein is not simply different than our understanding prior to Einstein, but it is better! We have a fuller picture of the world and it is a better picture than Newton's. Yet, if Kuhn is correct, they say, the notion of progress across paradigms is not possible. Because progress is possible—indeed, actual—Kuhn's model of scientific change must be mistaken.

Even another criticism of Kuhn is that he is mistaken with respect to mature sciences being guided by a single paradigm at any given point in time. Sciences are always in a state of competition of different paradigms (or, to use a term preferred by these critics, *research programs*) and not by a series of single dominant paradigms. This leads to our survey of the next model of scientific change—rational reconstructionism—associated most closely with the work of Imre Lakatos, to whom we will now turn.

Rational reconstructionism

Supporters of Kuhn's view often label it as "historicism," because of his emphasis on considering the actual history of scientific practice as the appropriate means of identifying and understanding standards and criteria of scientific change. Opponents, however— at least, some opponents—often label his view as "conventionalism," because it appears that his view embraces (or at least does not condemn) "mere convention" as the final standard and criterion for determining what constitutes good science. One such critic was Imre Lakatos, who remarked that in Kuhn's view there can be no logic, or clear standards of evaluation, but only a psychology of discovery with respect to scientific change and progress. Lakatos went so far as to say that in Kuhn's view scientific revolution is irrational and a matter of "mob psychology." Harsh words! But they have been shared by many who see, as we noted above, Kuhn's view of science as *too* sociological and historical and political. Nevertheless, Lakatos thought that Kuhn served as a corrective to naïve versions of inductivism and falsificationism. Drawing on what he saw as the correct insights of both Popper and Kuhn while also rejecting what he saw as points where they were mistaken, Lakatos offered an alternative account of scientific change.

Broadly speaking, Lakatos claimed that scientific change is the result of competing rival *research programs*. In the selections on the following pages, what is meant by "research programs" will be spelled out, but for now consider it as a set of methodological rules for pursuing scientific investigations of the world and for evaluating scientific activity. Like Kuhn's paradigms, research programs are more than simply a given theory about some phenomena; minimally, they involve a series of theories. More importantly, however, they are *heuristic,* meaning they are guides for discovery or, as mentioned a moment ago, they provide sets of methodological rules (sometimes explicitly, sometimes implicitly). Even more importantly, for Lakatos, this means that there are rational standards and criteria for appraising scientific change, something he was insistent upon, especially in light of his criticisms of Kuhn.

In the passage below, Lakatos speaks of *internal history* and *external history*. What he means by these terms is the following: internal history is historical matters internal to the scientific community, such as specific scientific problems, methods, goals, standards of evaluation; external history is historical matters external to the scientific community, such as philosophical, religious, social contexts with their own problems, methods, goals, and standards of evaluation. One of Lakatos's criticisms of Kuhn is that Kuhn allowed (even embraced) far too much external history in his account of scientific change. In this passage, Lakatos lays out basic features of four accounts of scientific change (what he calls "logics of discovery"): inductivism, conventionalism (i.e., Kuhn), methodological falsificationism (i.e., Popper), and his own methodology of scientific research programs.

THE METHODOLOGY OF SCIENTIFIC RESEARCH PROGRAMMES
Imre Lakatos

"Philosophy of science without history of science is empty; history of science without philosophy of science is blind." Taking its cue from this paraphrase of Kant's famous dictum, this paper intends to explain *how* the historiography of science should learn from the philosophy of science and not *vice versa*. It will be argued that (a) philosophy of science provides normative methodologies in terms of which the historian reconstructs "internal history" and thereby provides a rational explanation of the growth of objective knowledge; (b) two competing methodologies can be evaluated with the help of (normatively interpreted) history; (c) any rational reconstruction of history needs to be supplemented by an empirical (socio-psychological) "external history."

The vital demarcation between normative-internal and empirical-external is different for each methodology. Jointly, internal and external historiographical theories determine to a very large extent the choice of problems for the historian. But some of external history's most crucial problems can be formulated only in terms of one's methodology; thus internal history, so defined, is primary, and external history only secondary.

Indeed, in view of the autonomy of internal (but not of external) history, external history is irrelevant for the understanding of science.

Rival Methodologies of Science

There are several methodologies afloat in contemporary philosophy of science; but they are all very different from what used to be understood as "methodology" in the seventeenth or even eighteenth century. Then it was hoped that methodology would provide scientists with a mechanical book of rules for solving problems. This hope has now been given up: modern methodologies or "logics of discovery" consist merely of a set of (possibly not even tightly knit, let alone mechanical) rules for the *appraisal* of ready, articulated theories. Often these rules, or systems of appraisal, also serve as "theories of scientific rationality," "demarcation criteria" or "definitions of science." Outside the legislative domain of these normative rules there is, of course, an empirical psychology and sociology of discovery.

I shall now sketch four different "logics of discovery." Each will be characterized by rules governing the (scientific) *acceptance* and *rejection* of theories or research programs. These rules have a double function. Firstly, they function as *a code of scientific honesty* whose violation is intolerable; secondly, as hard cores of *(normative) historiographical research programs*. It is their second function on which I should like to concentrate.

(a) Inductivism

One of the most influential methodologies of science has been inductivism. According to inductivism only those propositions can be accepted into the body of science which either describe hard facts or are infallible inductive generalizations from them. When the inductivist *accepts* a scientific proposition, he accepts it as provenly true; he *rejects* it if it is not. His scientific rigor is strict: a proposition must be either proven from facts, or—deductively or inductively—derived from other propositions already proven.

Each methodology has its specific epistemological and logical problems. For example, inductivism has to establish with certainty the truth of "factual" ("basic") propositions and the validity of inductive inferences. Some philosophers get so preoccupied with their epistemological and logical problems that they never get to the point of becoming interested in actual history; if actual history does not fit their standards they may even have the temerity to propose that we start the whole business of science anew. Some others take some crude solution of these logical and epistemological problems for granted and devote themselves to a rational reconstruction of history without becoming aware of the logico-epistemological weakness (or, even, untenability) of their methodology.

Inductivist criticism is primarily skeptical: it consists in showing that a proposition is unproven, that is, pseudoscientific, rather than in showing that it is false. When the inductivist historian writes the *prehistory* of a scientific discipline, he may draw heavily upon such criticisms. And he often explains the early dark age—when people were engrossed by "unproven ideas"—with the help of some "external" explanation, like the socio-psychological theory of the retarding influence of the Catholic Church.

The inductivist historian recognizes only two sorts of *genuine scientific discoveries: hard factual propositions* and inductive *generalizations.* These and only these constitute the backbone of his *internal history.* When writing history, he looks out for them—finding them is quite a problem. Only when he finds them can he start the construction of his beautiful pyramids. Revolutions consist in unmasking (irrational) errors which then are exiled from the history of science into the history of pseudoscience, into the history of mere beliefs: genuine scientific progress starts with the latest scientific revolution in any given field.

Each internal historiography has its characteristic victorious paradigms. The main paradigms of inductivist historiography were Kepler's generalizations from Tycho Brahe's careful observations; Newton's discovery of his law of gravitation by, in turn, inductively generalizing Kepler's "phenomena" of planetary motion; and Ampère's discovery of his law of electrodynamics by inductively generalizing his observations of electric currents. Modern chemistry too is taken by some inductivists as having really started with Lavoisier's experiments and his "true explanations" of them.

But the inductivist historian cannot offer a *rational* "internal" explanation for *why* certain facts rather than others were selected in the first instance. For him this is a *non-rational, empirical, external* problem. Inductivism as an "internal" theory of rationality is compatible with many different supplementary empirical or external theories of problem-choice. It is, for instance, compatible with the vulgar-Marxist view that problem-choice is determined by social needs, indeed, some vulgar-Marxists identify major phases in the history of science with the major phases of economic development. But choice of facts need not be determined by social factors; it may be determined by extra-scientific intellectual influences. And inductivism is equally compatible with the "external" theory that the choice of problems is primarily determined by inborn, or by arbitrarily chosen (or traditional) theoretical (or "metaphysical") frameworks.

(b) Conventionalism

Conventionalism allows for the building of any system of pigeon holes which organizes facts into some coherent whole. The conventionalist decides to keep the center of such a pigeonhole system intact as long as possible: when difficulties arise through an invasion of anomalies, he only changes and complicates the peripheral arrangements. But the conventionalist does not regard any pigeonhole system as provenly true, but only as "true by convention" (or possibly even as neither true nor false). In *revolutionary* brands of conventionalism one does not have to adhere forever to a given pigeonhole system: one may abandon it if it becomes unbearably clumsy and if a simpler one is offered to replace it. This version of conventionalism is epistemologically, and especially logically, much simpler than inductivism: it is in no need of valid inductive inferences. Genuine *progress* of science is cumulative and takes place on the ground level of "proven" facts; the *changes* on the theoretical level are merely instrumental. Theoretical "progress" in only in convenience ("simplicity"), and not in truth-content. One may of course, introduce revolutionary conventionalism also at the level of "factual" propositions, in which case one would accept "factual" propositions by decision rather than by experimental "proofs." But then, if the conventionalist is to retain the idea that the growth of "factual" science has anything to do with objective, factual truth, he must devise some metaphysical principle which he then has to superimpose on his rules for the game of science. If he does not, he cannot escape skepticism or, at least, some radical form of instrumentalism . . .

For the conventionalist historian, major discoveries are primarily inventions of new and simpler pigeonhole systems. Therefore he constantly compares for simplicity: the complications of pigeonhole systems and their revolutionary replacement by simpler ones constitute the backbone of his internal history.

The paradigmatic case of a scientific revolution for the conventionalist has been the Copernican revolution. Efforts have been made to show that Lavoisier's and Einstein's revolutions too were replacements of clumsy theories by simple ones.

Conventionalist historiography cannot offer a *rational* explanation of why certain facts were selected in the first instance or of why certain particular pigeonhole systems were tried rather than others at a stage when their relative merits were yet unclear. Thus conventionalism, like inductivism, is compatible with various supplementary empirical "externalist" programs.

Finally, the conventionalist historian, like his inductivist colleague, frequently encounters the problem of "false consciousness." According to conventionalism for example, it is a "matter of fact" that great scientists arrive at their theories by flights of their imaginations. Why then do they often claim that they derive their theories from facts? The conventionalist's rational reconstruction often differs from the great scientists' own reconstruction—the conventionalist historian relegates these problems of false consciousness to the externalist.

(c) Methodological Falsificationism

Contemporary falsificationism arose as a logico-epistemological criticism of inductivism, and of Duhemian conventionalism. Inductivism was criticized on the grounds that its two basic assumptions, namely, that factual propositions can be "derived" from facts and that there can be valid inductive (content-increasing) inferences, are themselves unproven and even demonstrably false. Duhem was criticized on the grounds that comparison of intuitive simplicity can only be a matter for subjective taste and that it is so ambiguous that no hard-hitting criticism can be based on it. Popper proposed a new "falsificationist methodology." This methodology is another brand of revolutionary conventionalism: the main difference is that it allows factual, spatio-temporally singular "basic statements," rather than spatio-temporally universal theories, to be accepted by convention. In the code of honor of the falsificationist a theory is scientific only if it can be *made* to conflict with a basic statement. Popper also indicated a further condition that a theory must satisfy in order to qualify as scientific: it must predict facts which are *novel*, that is, unexpected in the light of previous knowledge. Thus, it is against Popper's code of scientific honor to propose unfalsifiable theories or "*ad hoc*" hypotheses (which imply no *novel* empirical predictions)—just as it is against the (classical) inductivist code of scientific honor to propose unproven ones.

The great attraction of Popperian methodology lies in its clarity and force. Popper's deductive model of scientific criticism contains empirically falsifiable spatio-temporally universal propostions, initial conditions and their consequences. The weapon of criticism is the *modus tollens:* neither inductive logic nor intuitive simplicity complicate the picture . . .

The Popperian historian looks for great, "bold," falsifiable theories and for great negative crucial experiments. These form the skeleton of his reconstruction. The Popperians' favorite paradigms of great falsifiable theories are Newton's and Maxwell's theories, the radiation formulas of Rayleigh, Jeans and Wien, and the Einsteinian revolution; their favorite paradigms for crucial experiments are the Michelson-Morley experiment, Eddington's eclipse experiment, and the experiments of Lummer and Pringsheim . . .

Popperian internal history, in turn, is readily supplemented by external theories of history. Thus Popper himself explained that (on the positive side) (1) the main *external* stimulus of scientific theories comes from unscientific "metaphysics," and even from myths (this was later beautifully illustrated, mainly by Koyré); and that (on the negative side) (2) facts do *not* constitute such external stimulus—factual discoveries belong completely to internal history, emerging as refutations of some scientific theory, so that facts are only noticed if they conflict with some previous expectation. Both these are cornerstones of Popper's *psychology* of discovery . . .

(d) Methodology of Scientific Research Programs

According to my methodology the great scientific achievements are research programs which can be evaluated in terms of progressive and degenerating problemshifts; and scientific revolutions consist of one research program superceding (overtaking in progress) another. This methodology offers a new rational reconstruction of science. It is best presented by contrasting it with falsificationism and conventionalism, from both of which it borrows essential elements.

From conventionalism, this methodology borrows the license rationally to accept by convention not only spatio-temporally singular "factual statements" but also spatio-temporally universal theories: indeed, this becomes the most important clue to the continuity of scientific growth. The basic unit of appraisal would not be an isolated theory or conjunction of theories but rather a *"research program,"* with a conventionally accepted (and thus by provisional decision "irrefutable") *"hard core"* and with a *"positive heuristic"* which defines problems, outlines the construction of a belt of auxiliary hypotheses, foresees anomalies and turns them victoriously into examples, all according to a preconceived plan. The scientist lists anomalies, but as long as his research program sustains its momentum, he may freely put them aside. *It is primarily the positive heuristic of his program, not the anomalies, which dictate the choice of his problems.* Only when the driving force of the positive heuristic weakens, may more attention be given to anomalies. The methodology of research programs can explain in this way *the high degree of autonomy of theoretical science;* the naïve falsificationist's disconnected chains of conjectures and refutations cannot . . .

The methodology of research programs presents a very different picture of the game of science from the picture of the methodological falsificationist. The best opening gambit is not a falsifiable (and therefore consistent) hypothesis, but a research program. Mere "falsification" (in Popper's sense) must not imply rejection . . . Mere "falsifications" (that is, anomalies) are to be recorded but need not be acted upon. Popper's great negative crucial experiments disappear; "crucial experiment" is an honorific title, which may, of course, be conferred on certain anomalies, but only *long after the event,* only when one program has been defeated by another one. According to Popper, a crucial experiment is described by an accepted basic statement which is inconsistent with a theory—according to the methodology of scientific research programs, no accepted basic statement *alone* entitles the scientist to reject a theory. Such a clash may present a problem (major or minor), but in no circumstance a "victory." Nature may shout *no,* but human ingenuity . . . may always be able to shout louder. With sufficient resourcefulness and some luck, any theory can be defended "progressively" for a long time, even if it is false. The Popperian pattern of "conjectures and refutations," that is the pattern of trial-by-hypothesis followed by error-shown-by-experiment, is to be abandoned: no experiment is crucial at the time—let alone before—it is performed (except, perhaps, psychologically).

. . . [However, contra conventionalism] I inject some hard Popperian elements into the appraisal of whether a program progresses or degenerates or of whether one is overtaking another. That is, I give criteria of progress and stagnation within a program and also rules for the "elimination" of whole research programs. A research program is said to be *progressing* as long as its theoretical growth anticipates its empirical growth, that is as long as it keeps predicting novel facts with some success ("*progressive problemshift*"); it is *stagnating* if its theoretical growth lags behind its empirical growth, that is, as long as it gives only *post hoc* explanations either of chance discoveries or of facts anticipated by, and discovered in, a rival program ("*degenerating problemshift*"). If a research program progressively explains more than a rival, it "supercedes" it, and the rival can be eliminated (or, if you wish, "shelved").

Let's take stock at this point of what Lakatos has been saying. Having identified three other models of scientific change—inductivism, conventionalism, and (naïve) falsificationism—he proposed his own methodology of scientific research programs. On the next page, in another passage, his own view will be spelled out more fully. For now, however, keep in mind that he intends to preserve the notion that scientific change is a rational process (hence his objections to Kuhn and conventionalism), even though it is historically sensitive (hence his objections to Popper and falsificationism), meaning that the history of science demonstrates that scientists were correct not to be driven by anomalies. Although research programs function in some ways like Kuhn's paradigms—in the sense of serving as background assumptions involving content, methodological prescriptions and proscriptions, as well as goals and values—nevertheless, they are different than paradigms in the sense that scientific change is a result of comparative problemshifts. In other words, Lakatos saw Kuhn's notion of normal science, in which the scientific community is all in agreement and guided by a dominant single paradigm, as mistaken, both descriptively and prescriptively. That is, Lakatos thought that scientists always work in the context of *competing* rival research programs, not simply under a single paradigm, and, in addition, he thought that science should *never become* guided by a single dominant paradigm because progress means progress relative to rivals. As he will say below, a research program is (and should be) rejected only if a rival research program has greater heuristic power. These points will (I hope) be clearer with his following remarks:

THE METHODOLOGY OF SCIENTIFIC RESEARCH PROGRAMMES *(continued)*

Imre Lakatos

If we look at the historical details of the most celebrated crucial experiments, we have to come to the conclusion that either they were accepted as crucial for no rational reason, or that their acceptance rested on rationality principles radically different from ones [discussed by falsificationists]. First of all, our falsificationist must deplore the fact that stubborn theoreticians frequently challenge experimental verdicts and have them reversed. In the falsificationist conception of scientific "law and order" we have described there is no place for such successful appeals. Further difficulties arise from the falsification of theories to which a *ceteris paribus* clause is appended. Their falsification as it occurs in actual history is *prima facie* irrational by the standards of our falsificationist. By his standards, scientists frequently seem to be irrationally slow: for instance, eighty-five years elapse between the acceptance of the perihelion of Mercury as an anomaly and its acceptance as a falsification of Newton's theory, in spite of the fact that the *ceteris paribus* clause was reasonably well corroborated. On the other hand, scientists frequently seem to be irrationally rash: for instance, Galileo and his disciples accepted Copernican heliocentric celestial mechanics in spite of the abundant evidence against the rotation of the Earth; or Bohr and his disciples accepted a theory of light emission in spite of the fact that it ran counter to Maxwell's well-corroborated theory.

Indeed, it is not difficult to see at least two crucial characteristics common to both dogmatic and our methodological falsificationism which are clearly dissonant with the actual history of science: that (1) *a test* is—or must be made—a two-cornered fight between theory and experiment so that in the final confrontation only these two face each other; and (2) the only interesting outcome of such confrontation is (conclusive) falsification: "[the only genuine] discoveries are refutations of scientific hypotheses." However, history of science suggests that (1') test are—at least—three-cornered fights between rival theories and experiment and (2') some of the most interesting experiments result, prima facie, in confirmation rather than falsification.

But if—as seems to be the case—the history of science does not bear out our theory of scientific rationality, we have two alternatives. One alternative is to abandon efforts to give a rational explanation of the success of science. Scientific method (or "logic of discovery"), conceived as the discipline of rational appraisal of scientific theories—and of criteria of progress—vanishes. We may, of course, still try to explain changes in "paradigms" in terms of social psychology. This is Polanyi's and Kuhn's way. The other alternative is to try at least to reduce the conventional element in falsificationism (we cannot possibly eliminate it) and replace the naive versions of methodological falsificationism—characterized by the theses (1) and (2) above—by a sophisticated version which would give a new rationale of falsification and thereby rescue methodology and the idea of scientific progress. This is Popper's way, and the one I intend to follow . . .

For the naïve falsificationist, a theory is falsified by a ("fortified") "observational" statement which conflicts with it (or which he decides to interpret as conflicting with it). For the sophisticated falsificationist a scientific theory T is falsified if and only if another theory T' has been proposed with the following characteristics: (1) T' has excess empirical content over T: that is, predicts novel facts, that is, facts improbable in the light of, or even forbidden by, T; (2) T' explains the previous success of T, that is, all the unrefuted content of T is included (within the limits of observational error) in the content of T'; and (3) some of the excess content of T' is corroborated . . .

Let us take a series of theories, $T_1, T_2, T_3, \ldots$ where each subsequent theory results from adding auxiliary clauses to (or from semantical representations of) the previous theory in order to accommodate some anomaly, each theory having at least as much content as the unrefuted content of its predecessor. Let us say that such a series of theories is theoretically progressive (or "constitutes a theoretically progressive problemshift") if each new theory has some excess empirical content over its predecessor, that is, if it predicts some novel, hitherto unexpected fact. Let us say that a theoretically progressive series of theories is also *empirically progressive* (or "constitutes an empirically progessive problemshift") if some of this excess empirical content is also corroborated, that is, if each new theory leads us to the actual discovery of some *new fact*. Finally, let us call a problemshift *progressive* if it is both theoretically and empirically progressive, and *degenerating* if it is not. We "*accept*" problemshifts as "scientific" only if they are at least theoretically progressive; if they are not, we "*reject*" them as "pseudoscientific." Progress is measured by the degree to which the series of theories leads us to the discovery of novel facts. We regard a theory in the series "falsified" when it is superceded by a theory with higher corroborated content.

Finally, here is a fuller account of his notions of positive and negative heuristics:

THE METHODOLOGY OF SCIENTIFIC RESEARCH PROGRAMMES (*continued*)

Imre Lakatos

I have discussed the problem of objective appraisal of scientific growth in terms of progressive and degenerating problemshifts in series of scientific theories. The most important such series in the growth of science are characterized by a certain *continuity* which connects their members. This continuity evolves from a genuine research program adumbrated at the start. The program consists of methodological rules: some tell us what paths of research to avoid (*negative heuristic*), and others what paths to pursue (*positive heuristic*).

Even science as a whole can be regarded as a huge research program with Popper's supreme heuristic rule: "devise conjectures which have more empirical content than their predecessors." . . . But what I have primarily in mind is not science as a whole, but rather *particular* research programs, such as the one known as "Cartesian metaphysics." Cartesian metaphysics, that is, the mechanistic theory of the universe—according to which the universe is a huge clockwork (and system of vortices) with push as the only cause of motion—functioned as a powerful heuristic principle. It discouraged work on scientific theories—like (the "essentialist" version of) Newton's theory of action at a distance—which were inconsistent with it (*negative heuristic*). On the other hand, it encouraged work on auxiliary hypotheses which might have saved it from apparent counterevidence—like Keplerian ellipses (*positive heuristic*).

(a) Negative Heuristic: The "Hard Core" of the Program

All scientific research programs may be characterized by their "hard core." The negative heuristic of the program forbids us to direct the *modus tollens* at this "hard core." Instead, we must use our ingenuity to articulate or even invent "auxiliary hypotheses," which form a *protective belt* around this core, and we must redirect the *modus tollens* to *these*. It is this protective belt of auxiliary hypotheses which has to bear the brunt of tests and get adjusted and re-adjusted, or even completely replaced, to defend the thus-hardened core. A research program is successful if all this leads to a progressive problemshift; unsuccessful if it leads to a degenerating problemshift.

The classical example of a successful research program is Newton's gravitational theory: possibly the most successful research program even. When it was first produced, it was submerged in an ocean of "anomalies" (or, if you wish, "counterexamples"), and opposed by the observational theories supporting these anomalies. But Newtonians turned, with brilliant tenacity and ingenuity, one counter-instance after another into corroborating instances, primarily by overthrowing the original observational theories in the light of which this "contrary evidence" was established. In the process they themselves produced new counter-examples which they again resolved. They "turned each new difficulty into a new victory of their program."

In Newton's program the negative heuristic bids us to divert the *modus tollens* from Newton's three laws of dynamics and his law of gravitation. This "core" is "irrefutable" by the methodological decision of its proponents: anomalies must lead to changes only in the "protective" belt of auxiliary, "observational" hypotheses and initial conditions . . .

(b) Positive Heuristic: The Construction of the "Protective Belt" and the Relative Autonomy of Theoretical Science

Research programs, besides their negative heuristic, are also characterized by their positive heuristic.

Even the most rapidly and consistently progressive research programs can digest their "counter-evidence" only piecemeal: anomalies are never completely exhausted. But it should not be thought that yet unexplained anomalies—"puzzles" as Kuhn might call them—are taken in random order, and the protective belt build up in an eclectic fashion, without any preconceived order. The order is usually decided in the theoretician's cabinet, independently of the *known* anomalies. Few theoretical scientists engaged in a research program pay undue attention to "refutations." They have a long-term research policy which anticipates these refutations. This research policy, or order of research, is set out—in more or less detail—in the *positive heuristic* of the research program. The negative heuristic specifies the "hard core" of the program which is "irrefutable" by the methodological decision of its proponents; the positive heuristic consists of a partially articulated set of suggestions or hints on how to change, develop the "refutable variants" of the research program, how to modify, sophisticate, the "refutable" protective belt.

The positive heuristic of the program saves the scientist from becoming confused by the ocean of anomalies. The positive heuristic sets out a program which lists a chain of ever more complicated *models* simulating reality: the scientist's attention is riveted on building his models following instructions which are laid down in the positive part of his program. He ignores the *actual* counterexamples, the available "data." Newton first worked out his program for a planetary system with a fixed point-like sun and one single point-like planet. It was in this model that he derived his inverse square law for Kepler's ellipse. But this model was forbidden by Newton's own third law of dynamics, therefore the model had to be replaced by one in which both sun and planet revolved around their common center of gravity. This change was not motivated by any observation (the data did not suggest an "anomaly" here) but by a theoretical difficulty in developing the program. Then he worked out the program for more planets as if there were only heliocentric by no interplanetary forces. Then he worked out the case where the sun and the planets were not mass-points but mass-*balls*. Again, for this change he did not *need* the observation of an anomaly: infinite density was forbidden by an (inarticulated) touchstone theory, therefore planet *had* to be extended. This change involved considerable mathematical difficulties, held up Newton's work—and delayed the publication of the *Principia* by more than a decade. Having solved this "puzzle," he started work on *spinning balls* and their wobbles. Then he admitted interplanetary forces and started work on *perturbations*. At this point he started to look more anxiously at the facts. Many of them were beautifully explained (qualitatively) by this model, many were not. It was then that he started to work on *bulging* planets, rather than round planets, etc.

Newton despised people who, like Hooke, stumbled on a first naïve model but did not have the tenacity and ability to develop it into a research program, and who thought that a first version, a mere aside, constituted a "discovery." He held up publication until his program had achieved a remarkable progressive problemshift.

Most, if not all, Newtonian "puzzles," leading to a series of new variants superceding each other, were foreseeable at the time of Newton's first naïve model and no doubt Newton and his colleagues *did* foresee them: Newton must have been fully aware of the blatant falsity of his first variants. Nothing shows the existence of a positive heuristic of a research program clearer than this fact: this is why one speaks of "models" in research programs. A "*model*" is a set of initial conditions (possibly together with some of the observational theories) which one knows is *bound* to be replaced during the further development of the program, and one even knows, more or less how. This shows once more how irrelevant "refutations" of any specific variant are in a research program: their existence is fully expected, the positive heuristic is there as the strategy both for predicting (producing) and digesting them. Indeed, if the positive heuristic is clearly spelt out, the difficulties of the program are mathematical rather than empirical.

One may formulate the "positive heuristic" of a research program as a "metaphysical" principle. For instance one may formulate Newton's program like this: "the planets are essentially gravitating spinning-tops of roughly spherical shape." This idea was never *rigidly* maintained: the planets are not *just* gravitational, they have also, for example, electromagnetic characteristics which may influence their motion. Positive heuristic is thus in general more flexible than negative heuristic. Moreover, it occasionally happens that when a research program gets into a degenerating phase, a little revolution or a *creative shift* in its positive heuristic may push it forward again. It is better therefore to separate the "hard core" from the more flexible metaphysical principles expressing the positive heuristic.

Our considerations show that the positive heuristic forges ahead with almost complete disregard of "refutations:" it may seem that it is the *"verifications"* rather than the refutations which provide the contact points with reality. Although one must point out that any "verification" of the $(n + 1)$th version of the program is a refutation of the nth version, we cannot deny that *some* defeats of the subsequent versions are always foreseen; it is the "verifications" which keep the program going, recalcitrant instances notwithstanding.

We may appraise research programs, even after their "elimination," for their *heuristic power*: how many new facts did they produce, how great was "their capacity to explain their refutations in the course of their growth?" . . .

Thus the methodology of scientific research programs accounts for the *relative autonomy of theoretical science*: a historical fact whose rationality cannot be explained by the earlier falsificationists. Which problems scientists working in a powerful research program rationally choose, is determined by the positive heuristic of the program. Only those scientists have to rivet their attention on anomalies who are either engaged in trial and error exercises or who work in a degenerating phase of a research program when the positive heuristic ran out of steam.

Criticisms of rational reconstructionism

In being sensitive to the history of science as well as to rational standards and criteria of scientific change, Lakatos claimed that a given research program could be progressive at one point in time, become degenerating later on, but then become progressive again even later. For example, as physicists investigated the nature of light, Newton argued strongly for the view that light is a particle (though he did not quite phrase it that way). During the 1800s, however, there was fairly overwhelming evidence that light is in fact a wave. But in the very early 1900s, as a result of the work of Einstein and others, the view of light as a particle (now called a "photon") was resurrected. This example is not exactly an example of a research program, but it is a close enough analogy. The point, for Lakatos, was that a research program's status as being progressive or degenerating can and does change, perhaps from progressive to degenerating and back again to progressive. Some critics, in particular another philosopher of science, Paul Feyerabend, quickly argued that this fact suggested that the rational thing to do would be not to abandon any research program, but simply to "wait longer" with the hope (and hard work to ensure) that a degenerating research program might once again become progressive. Pushed even further, this suggested that no research program should be abandoned, because—who knows?—it might become viable and progressive again in the future. Lakatos, of course, thought this criticism failed to be realistic with respect to actual scientific practice.

Other critics claimed that the details of research programs also were not clear or fruitful. For example, it is not obvious what is meant by excess empirical content between rivals if each explains different bits or types of phenomena; it is not obvious what is meant by a protective belt of auxiliary hypotheses that protects a hard core of the negative heuristic when those hypotheses are often not explicit. The point of asking for further clarification of research programs in general as well as of the details was not simply to have an accurate picture of the history of science, but to have a useful and instructive model of scientific change and critics of Lakatos claimed that lack of clarity diminished the usefulness and instructive power of his model. Another sort of criticism, less focused on details, came from Larry Laudan and others, who stated that Lakatos actually was not that different from Popper and Kuhn in fundamental assumptions about models of scientific change. We will get to that criticism directly in the next chapter.

Chapter Summary

Kuhn's "historicist" view is a model of scientific change. The emphasis is on getting an accurate account of how science changes via a study of how it has changed. What such a study reveals, according to Kuhn, is that scientific change is not a matter of cumulative, slow steady progress toward a single description of the world, nor a matter of proposing bold conjectures and attempting to then falsify them. Rather, science changes primarily because of episodic revolutions, which entail dramatic shifts in our understanding of phenomena. Scientists are guided by paradigms—"world views"—which explicitly or implicitly guide normal scientific inquiry by identifying content, methods, and goals for scientists. Scientists operate within a guiding paradigm and attempt to solve empirical or conceptual puzzles generated by the paradigm. As anomalies (unexpected phenomena) arise, they can sometimes become so significant that the paradigm fails to resolve them and the scientific community enters a crisis. Scientific revolutions occur when the guiding paradigm is overthrown in favor of a new paradigm, resulting in its turn in new normal science (i.e., new puzzles to be solved). Extra-scientific matters—for example, social, religious, philosophical—play a role in paradigm shifts, not just matters within typical scientific inquiry. Kuhn has been criticized by some philosophers of science as making scientific change too irrational. Among those critics is Imre Lakatos, who offered an alternative model of scientific change, his methodology of scientific research programs. In this model, there is never (or, there never should be) a single, dominant paradigm in science, but rival competing research programs. As long as a research program is progressive, it is rational for scientists to pursue it. Research programs consist of a negative heuristic, which "tells" scientists what matters not to question or pursue, and a positive heuristic, which tells them what matters and questions to pursue.

CASE STUDY
Phlogiston

Phlogiston theory emerged in the 1600s as a means of explaining chemical change, that is, changes in the nature and properties of bodies, especially when heated. The term "phlogiston" derives from the Greek word meaning "to inflame." Not until the very end of the 1700s and into the early 1800s was it abandoned, largely because of the work of the French chemist, Antoine Laurent Lavoisier (1743–1794). On the following pages are passages from four chemists, Georg Ernst Stahl (1660–1734), Carl Wilhelm

Scheele (1742–1786), Joseph Priestly (1733–1804), and Lavoisier, ex-hibiting a movement from the formulation of the phlogiston theory (Stahl) to its explanatory incorporation for experimental result (Scheele and Priestly) to its rejection (Lavoisier). How well do the models of Kuhn and Lakatos fit the history of phlogiston theory? Does the phlogiston view con-stitute a Kuhnian paradigm? What would count as the hard core of phlo-giston theory and what the protective belt? What, if anything, constituted a degenerative problem-shift?

A SOURCE BOOK IN CHEMISTRY, 1400–1900
Henry M. Leicester and Herbert S. Klickstein (editors)

Stahl

The same thing works very well with sulfur, when certainly two parts, or better, three parts of alkali salt and one of pulverized sulfur are succes-sively poured into and fused in a crucible. There is formed liver of sul-fur. This, in the space of a quarter of an hour more or less, by fire alone, without any addition, can be converted to such a salt as is obtained from oil of sulfur *per campanum* [H_2SO_4] and salt of tartar, that which is commonly called *vitriolated tartar*. There is no more trace of sulfur or al-kali salt, and in place of the red color of the liver, this salt is very bit-ter; in place of the easy solution, nay, the spontaneous deliquescence of the liver, by reason of its alkali salt, this salt is the most difficult of all salts except tartar of wine to be dissolved; in place of the impossi-bility of crystallizing the liver, this is very prone to form almost octa-hedral crystals; in place of the fusibility of the liver, this is devoid of all fusion.

If this new salt, from the acid of sulfur and alkaline salt formed as stated above when the phlogiston has been used up, is treated with charcoal, in the space of a quarter of an hour the original liver of sulfur reappears, and this can be so converted a hundred times . . .

I can indeed show by various other experiments how phlogiston from fatty substances and charcoal enters very promptly into metals them-selves and regenerates them from the burned calx into their own *fusible, malleable,* and *amalgamable* state.

Now the first thing to consider concerning the principle of sulfur is its properties, as follows:

1. Behavior toward fire
2. Display of colors
3. Subtle and intimate mixing with other metal substances
4. Behavior toward water and humidity
5. Its own great and wonderful subtlety
6. Its own form in the dry or fluid state
7. Where it can be found or occurs

According to these conditions and intentions, I now have demonstrable grounds to say, first,

Toward fire, this sulfur principle behaves in such a manner that it is not only suitable for the movement of fire but is also one and the same being, yes, even created and designed for it.

But also, according to a reasonable manner of speaking, it is the corporeal fire, the essential fire material, the true basis of fire movement in all inflammable compounds.

However, except in compounds, no fire at all occurs, but it dissipates and volatilizes in invisible particles, or at least, develops and forms a finely divided and invisible fire, namely, heat.

On the other hand, it is very important to note that this fire material, of an by itself and apart from other things, especially air and water, is not found united and active, either as a liquid or in an attenuated state. But if once by the movement of fire, with the addition of free air, it is attenuated and volatilized, then by this in all such conditions it is lost through unrecognizable subtlety and immeasurable attenuation, so that from this point on no science known to man, no human art, can collect it together or bring it into narrow limits, especially if this occurred rapidly and in quantity.

But how enormously attenuated and subtle material becomes through the movement of fire is shown by experience, which furnishes a field for thought and which also delights us.

From all these various conditions, therefore, I have believed that it should be given a name, as the first, unique, basic, inflammable principle. But since it cannot, until this hour, be found by itself, outside of all compounds and unions with other materials, and so there are no grounds or basis for giving a descriptive name based on properties, I have felt that it is most fitting to name it from its general action, which it customarily shows in all its compounds. And therefore I have chosen the Greek name phlogiston . . .

Scheele

Air must be Composed on Elastic Fluids of Two Kinds

First experiment. I dissolved one ounce of alkaline liver in sulfur in eight ounces of water; I poured four ounces of this solution into an empty bottle capable of holding twenty-four ounces of water and closed it most securely with a cork; I then inverted the bottle and placed the neck in a small vessel with water; in this position I allowed it to stand for fourteen days. During this time the solution had lost a part of its red color and had also deposited some sulfur: afterwards I took the bottle and held it in the same position in a larger vessel with water, so that the mouth was under and the bottom above the water-level, and withdrew the cork under the water; immediately water rose with violence into the bottle. I closed the bottle again, removed it from the water, and weighed the fluid which it contained. There were ten ounces. After subtracting from this the four ounces of solution of sulfur there remained six ounces, consequently it is apparent from this experiment that of twenty parts of air six parts have been lost in fourteen days . . .

Sixth experiment. I collected in a bladder the nitrous air which arises on the dissolution of the metals in acid of nitre, and after I had tied the bladder tightly I laid it in a flask and secured the mouth very carefully with a wet bladder. The nitrous air gradually lost its elasticity, the bladder collapsed, and became yellow as if corroded by *aqua fortis*. After fourteen days I made a hole in the bladder tied over the flask, having previously held it, inverted, under water; the water rose rapidly into the flask, and it remained only two thirds empty.

Seventh experiment. (a) I immersed the mouth of a flask in a vessel with oil of turpentine. The oil rose in the flask a few lines every day. After the lapse of fourteen days the fourth part of the flask was filled with it; I allowed it to stand for three weeks longer, but the oil did not rise higher. All those oils which dry in the air and become converted into resinous substances, possess this property. Oil of turpentine, however, and linseed oil rise up sooner if the flask is previously rinsed out with a concentrated corrosive ley. (b) I poured two ounces of colorless and transparent animal oil of Dippel into a bottle and closed it very tightly; after the expiry of two months the oil was thick and black. I then held the bottle, inverted, under water and drew out the cork; the bottle immediately became one fourth filled with water.

Eighth experiment. (a) I dissolved two ounces of vitriol of iron in thirty-two ounces of water, and precipitated this solution with a caustic ley. After the precipitate had settled, I poured away the clear fluid and put the dark green precipitate of iron so obtained, together with the remaining water, into the before mentioned-bottle [from the first experiment] and closed it tightly. After fourteen days (during which time I shook the bottle frequently) this green calx of iron had acquired the color of crocus of iron, and of forty parts of air twelve had been lost. (b) When iron filings are moistened with some water and preserved for a few weeks in a well-closed bottle, a portion of the air is likewise lost. (c) The solution of iron in vinegar has the same effect upon air. In this case the vinegar permits the dissolved iron to fall out in the form of a yellow crocus and becomes completely deprived of the metal. (d) The solution of copper prepared in closed vessels with spirit of salt likewise diminishes air. In none of the foregoing kinds of air can either a candle burn or the smallest spark appear.

It is seen from these experiments that phlogiston, this simple inflammable principle, is present in each of them. It is known that the air strongly attracts to itself the inflammable matter of substances and deprives them of it: not only may this be seen from the experiments cited, but it is at the same time evident that on the transference of the inflammable matter to the air a considerable part of the air is lost . . .

It may also be seen from the above experiments, that a given quantity of air can only unite with, and at the same time saturate, a certain quantity of the inflammable principle: . . . Thus much I see from the experiments mentioned, that the air consists of two fluids differing from each other, the one of which does not manifest in the least the property of attracting phlogiston while the other, which composes between the third and the fourth part of the whole mass of the air, is peculiarly disposed to such attraction. But where this latter kind of air has gone to after it has united with the inflammable matter, is a question which must be decided by further experiments, and not by conjecture.

Priestley

Of Dephlogisticated Air, and of the Constitution of the Atmosphere

There are, I believe, very few maxims of philosophy that have laid firmer hold upon the mind, than that air, meaning atmospherical air (free from various foreign matters, which were always supposed to be dissolved, and intermixed with it) is a *simple elementary substance*, indestructible, and unalterable, at least so much so as water is supposed to be. In the course of my inquiries, I was, however, soon satisfied that atmospherical air is not an unalterable thing; for that the phlogiston with which it becomes loaded from bodies burning in it, and animals breathing it, and various other chemical processes, so far alters and depraves it, as to render it altogether unfit for inflammation, respiration, and other purposes to which it is subservient; and I had discovered that agitation in water, the process of vegetation, and probably other natural processes, by taking out the superfluous phlogiston, restore it to its original purity. But, I own, I had no idea of the possibility of going any farther in this way, and thereby procuring air purer than the best common air. I might, indeed, have naturally imagined that such would be air that should contain less phlogiston than the air of the atmosphere; but I had no idea that such a composition was possible.

It will be seen in my last publication, that, from the experiments which I made on the marine acid air, I was led to conclude that common air consisted of some acid (and I naturally inclined to the acid that I was then operating upon) and phlogiston; because the union of this acid vapor and phlogiston made inflammable air; and inflammable air, by agitation in water, ceases to be inflammable, and becomes respirable. And though I could never make it quite so good as common air, I thought it very probably that vegetation, in more favorable circumstances than any in which I could apply it, or some other natural process, might render it more pure.

Upon this, which no person can say was an improbably supposition, was founded my conjecture, of volcanoes having given birth to the atmosphere of this planet, supplying it with a permanent air, first inflammable, then deprived of its inflammability by agitation in water, and farther purified by vegetation.

Several of the known phenomena of the *nitrous acid* might have led me to think that this was more proper for the constitution of the atmosphere than the marine acid: but my thoughts had got into a different train, and nothing but a series of observations, which I shall now distinctly relate, compelled me to adopt another hypothesis, and brought me, in a way which I had then no idea, to the solution of the great problem, which my reader will perceive I have had in view ever since my discovery that the atmospherical air is alterable, and therefore that it is not an elementary substance, but a *composition*, viz. what this composition is, or *what is the thing that we breathe*, and how it is to be made from its constituent principles.

At the time of my former publication, I was not possessed of a *burning lens* of any considerable force; and for want of one, I could not possibly make many of the experiments that I had projected, and which, in theory, appeared very promising. I had, indeed, a *mirror* of force sufficient for my purpose. But the nature of this instrument is such that it cannot be applied, with effect, except upon substances that are capable of being suspended, or resting on a very slender support. It cannot be directed at all upon any substance in the form of a *powder*, nor hardly upon any thing that requires to be put into a vessel of quicksilver; which appears to me to be the most accurate method of extracting air from a great variety of substances, as was explained in the Introduction of this volume. But having afterwards procured a lens of twelve inches diameter, and twenty inches focal distance, I proceeded with great alacrity to examine, by the help of it, what kind of air a great variety of substances, natural and factitious, would yield, putting them into [various vessels], which I filled with quicksilver, and kept inverted in a basin of the same. Mr. Warltire, a good chymist, and lecturer in natural philosophy, happening to be at that time in Calne, I explained my views to him, and was furnished by him with many substances, which I could not otherwise have procured.

With this apparatus, after a variety of other experiments, an account of which will be found in its proper place, on the 1st of August, 1774, I endeavored to extract air from *mercurius calcinatus per se;* and I presently found that, by means of this lens, air was expelled from it very readily. Having got about three or four times as much as the bulk of my materials, I admitted water to it, and I found that it was not imbibed by it. But what surprised me more than I can well express, was, that a candle burned in this air with a remarkably vigorous flame, very much like that enlarged flame with which a candle burns in nitrous air, exposed to iron or liver of sulfur; but as I had got nothing like this remarkable appearance from any kind of air besides this particular modification of nitrous air, and I knew no nitrous acid was used in the preparation of *mercurius calcinatus*, I was utterly at a loss how to account for it . . .

In this air [from a later experiment], as I had expected a candle burned with a vivid flame; but what I observed new at this time, and which surprised me no less than the fact that I had discovered before, was, that, whereas a few moments agitation in water will deprive the modified nitrous air of its property of admitting a candle to burn in it; yet, after more than ten times as much agitation as would be sufficient to produce this alteration in the nitrous air, no sensible change was produced in this. A candle still burned in it with a strong flame; and it did not, in the least, diminish common air, which I have observed that nitrous air, in this state, in some measure does.

But I was much more surprised, when, after two days, in which this air had continued in contact with water (by which it was diminished about 1/20th of its bulk) I agitated it violently in water about five minutes, and found that a candle still burned in it as well as in common air. The same degree of agitation would have made phlogisticated nitrous air fit for respiration indeed, but it would certainly have extinguished a candle.

These facts fully convinced me, that there must be a very material difference between the constitution of the air from *mercurius calcinatus*, and that of phlogisticated nitrous air, notwithstanding their resemblance in some particulars. But though I did not doubt that air from *mercurius calcinatus* was fit for respiration, after being agitated in water, as every kind of air without exception, on which I had tried the experiment, had been, I still did not suspect that it was respirable in the first instance; so far was I from having any idea of this air being, what it really was, much superior, in this respect, to the air of the atmosphere.

Lavoisier

Memoir on the Nature of the Principle which Combines with Metals During their Calcinations and which Increases their Weight

Are there different kinds of air? Is it sufficient that a body be in a durable state of expansability in order to be a species of air? Finally, are the different airs which occur in nature or which we may produce separate substances or merely modifications of the air of the atmosphere?

Such are the principle questions which encompass the plan which I have formed and whose successive development I propose to bring before the eyes of the Academy. But the time devoted to our public meetings does not permit me to treat any of these questions extensively, and I will confine myself today to a particular case and limit myself to showing that the principle which combines with metals during their calcinations, which increases their weight and constitutes them in the state of a calx, is nothing other than the most salubrious and purest portion of the air and such that, it appears in an eminently respirable state more capable than the air of the atmosphere of sustaining ignition and combustion.

The majority of metallic calces are not to be reduced, that is, returned to the metallic state, without the immediate contact of a carbonaceous material or any substance whatsoever containing what we call *phlogiston*. The charcoal which is used is completely destroyed in this operation if it be present in suitable proportion; whence it follows that the air which is evolved in metallic reductions with carbon is not a simple substance but in some manner is the result of the combination of the elastic fluid disengaged from the metal and that disengaged from the carbon. Therefore the fact that this fluid is obtained as fixed air gives us no right to conclude that it existed in this form in the metallic calx before its combination with the carbon.

These considerations showed me that in order to clear up the mystery of the reduction of metallic calces it would be necessary to experiment with those calces which are reducible without the addition of anything. The calx of iron offered me this property and actually, of all those calces, either natural or artificial, which we have exposed at the foci of the large burning glasses either of the Regent or of Mr. Trudaine, there have been none which have not been completely reduced without addition.

I tried, consequently, to reduce by means of a burning glass several species of the calx of iron under large glass bells inverted in mercury, and I succeeded in disengaging by this means a large quantity of elastic fluid. But at the same time this elastic fluid became mixed with the common air contained in the bell, and this circumstance threw much uncertainty on my results, so that none of the tests which I conducted upon this air were perfectly conclusive and it was impossible for me to be certain whether the phenomena I obtained arose from the common air, from that disengaged from the calx of iron, or from the combination of the two. The experiments having failed of fully filling my purpose, I omit their details here; they will, however, find their natural place in other memoirs . . .

Memoir on Combustion in General

As dangerous as is the desire to systematize in the physical sciences, it is, nevertheless, to be feared that in storing without order a great multiplicity of experiments we obscure the science rather than clarify it, render it difficult to access to those desirous of entering upon it, and, finally, obtain at the price of long and tiresome work only disorder and confusion. Facts, observations, experiments—these are the materials of a great edifice, but in assembling them we must combine them into classes, distinguish which belongs to which order and to which part of the whole each pertains.

Systems in physical science, considered from this point of view, are no more than appropriate instruments to aid the weakness of our organs: they are, properly speaking, approximate methods which put us on the path to the solution of the problem; these are the hypotheses which, successively modified, corrected, and changed in proportion as they are found false, should lead us infallibly one day, by a process of exclusion, to the knowledge of the true laws of nature.

Encouraged by these reflections, I venture to propose to the Academy today a new theory of combustion, or rather, to speak with the reserve which I customarily impose upon myself, a hypothesis by the aid of which we may explain in a very satisfactory manner all the phenomena of combustion and calcinations, and in part event he phenomena which accompany the respiration of animals. I have already laid out the initial foundations of this hypothesis. . . , but I acknowledge that, having little confidence in my own ability, I did not then dare to put forward an opinion which might appear peculiar and was directly contrary to the theory of Stahl and to those of many celebrated men who have followed him.

While some of the reasons which held me back perhaps remain today, facts which appear to me to be favorable to my ideas have increased in number since and have strengthened me in my opinion. These facts, without being perhaps too strong, have made me more confident, and I believe that the proof or at least the probability is sufficient so that even those who are not of my opinion will not be able to blame me for having written.

We observe in the combustion of bodies generally four recurring phenomena which would appear to be invariable laws of nature; while these phenomena are implied in other memoirs which I have presented, I must recall them here in a few words.

First phenomenon. In all combustion the matter of fire or light is evolved.

Second phenomenon. Materials may not burn except in a very few kinds of air, or rather, combustion may take place in only a single variety of air: that which Mr. Priestley has named *dephlogisticated air* and which I name here *pure air* [i.e., oxygen]. Not only do those bodies which we call *combustible* not burn either in vacuum or in any other species of air, but on the contrary, they are extinguished just as rapidly as if they had been plunged into water or any other liquid.

Third phenomenon. In all combustion, pure air in which the combustion takes place is destroyed or decomposed and the burning body increases in weight exactly in proportion to the quantity of air destroyed or decomposed.

Fourth phenomenon. In all combustion the body of which is burned changes into an acid by the addition of the substance which increases its weight. Thus, for example, if sulfur is burned under a bell, the product of the combustion is vitriolic acid; if phosphorus be burned, the product of the combustion is phosphoric acid; if a carbonaceous substance be burned, the product of the combustion is fixed air, formerly called the acid of chalk, etc . . .

These different phenomena of the calcinations of metals and of combustion are explained in a very nice manner by the hypothesis of Stahl, but it is necessary to suppose with Stahl that the material of fire, of phlogiston, is fixed in metals, in sulfur, and in all bodies which are regarded as combustible. Now if we demand of the partisans of the doctrine of Stahl that they prove the existence of the matter of fire in combustible bodies, they necessarily fall into a vicious circle and are obliged to reply that combustible bodies contain the matter of fire because they burn and that they burn because they contain the matter of fire. Now it is easy to see that in the last analysis this is explaining combustion by combustion.

The existence of the matter of fire, of phlogiston in metals, sulfur, etc., is then actually nothing but a hypothesis, a supposition which, once admitted, explains, it is true, some of the phenomena of calcinations and combustion; but if I am able to show that these phenomena may be explained in just as natural a manner by an opposing hypothesis, that is to say without supposing that the matter of fire or phlogiston exists in combustible materials, the system of Stahl will be found to be shaken to its foundation . . .

Pure air, according to this, that which Mr. Priestley calls *dephlogisticated air*, is an igneous combination in which the matter of fire or light enters as a dissolvent and in which another substance enters as a base. Now if in any dissolution whatsoever we present to the base a substance with which it has more affinity, it unites instantly and the dissolvent which it has left becomes free; it regains all its properties and escapes with the characteristics by which it is known, that is to say, with flame, heat, and light.

Reflections on Phlogiston, Serving to Develop the Theory of Combustion and Calcination

. . . My only object in this memoir has been to give the new development of the theory of combustion which I published in 1777 and to show that the phlogiston of Stahl is an imaginary thing whose existence has been gratuitously supposed in metals, sulfur, phosphorus, and all combustible bodies; that all the phenomena of combustion and calcinations may be explained in a far simpler and easier manner without phlogiston than with it. I do not expect that my ideas will be adopted all at once; human nature bends toward one viewpoint, and those who have envisaged nature from a certain point of view during a part of their career change only with difficulty to new ideas: it is for time, then, to confirm or destroy the opinions which I have presented. In the meantime I see with great satisfaction that the young people who are commencing to study the science without prejudice, the geometricians and the natural philosophers who bring fresh minds to bear on chemical truths, believe no longer in a phlogiston in the sense that Stahl presented it and regard all the doctrine as a scaffolding more encumbering than useful for continuing the edifice of chemical science.

CASE STUDY
Plate Tectonics

On pages 348–365, read the account of the emergence of plate tectonics, a revolutionary geological theory that arose in the mid-20th century. What aspects of this case fit or do not fit the historicist (Kuhnian) or rational reconstructionist (Lakatosian) models of scientific change? For example, was there a single guiding paradigm and later a paradigm shift or were there concurrent competing research programs? If there were research programs, what, exactly, were the elements of the hard core and the protective belt?

Further Reading

Barnes, Barry. *T.S. Kuhn and Social Science.* New York: Columbia University Press, 1982.

Gutting, Gary, ed. *Paradigms and Revolutions.* Notre Dame: University of Notre Dame Press, 1980.

Hacking, Ian (ed.). *Scientific Revolutions.* Oxford: Oxford University Press, 1981.

Hacking, Ian. *Representing and Intervening.* Cambridge: Cambridge University Press, 1983.

Hoyningen-Huene, Paul. *Reconstructing Scientific Revolutions* Chicago: University of Chicago Press, 1993.

Kuhn, Thomas. *The Copernican Revolution.* Cambridge: Harvard University Press, 1957.

Kuhn, Thomas. *The Structure of Scientific Revolutions* (with a second edition in 1970), Kuhn, Thomas. *The Essential Tension.* Chicago: University of Chicago Press, 1977. Kuhn, Thomas. *Black Body Theory and Quantum Discontinuity, 1894–1912.* Oxford: Oxford University Press, 1978.

Kuhn, Thomas. *The Road Since Structure.* Edited by James Conant and John Haugeland. Chicago: University of Chicago Press, 2000.

Lakatos, Imre. *The Methodology of Scientific Research Programmes. Philosophical Papers, Volume 1.* Cambridge: Cambridge University Press, 1978.

Lakatos, Imre and Alan Musgrave (eds.) *Criticism and the Growth of Knowledge.* Cambridge: Cambridge University Press, 1970.

Newton-Smith, W.H. *The Rationality of Science.* London: Routledge, 1981.

CHAPTER TEN

Problem-Solving Research Traditions and Technologism

IN THIS CHAPTER, WE WILL

- Examine the Research Traditions model of scientific change, particularly associated with Larry Laudan
- Examine the Technologist model of scientific change, particularly associated with Joseph Pitt

As noted in the previous chapter, one of the criticisms leveled against Kuhn's view is that it seems to at least diminish rationality as a factor both in scientific change and in assessing scientific change. That is, critics (including Lakatos) claimed that Kuhn described the history of scientific change as displaying a structure in which extra-scientific matters played a crucial role, such that actual scientific change was often the result of nonrational factors, for example, philosophical or religious or political pressures and commitments. In addition, the critics claimed, when philosophers of science (or anyone else, for that matter) assess scientific change—rather than simply describe it—Kuhn's model precludes, or at least downplays, rational criteria and standards for such an assessment. After all, if scientific revolutions go hand-in-hand with paradigm shifts such that there is incommensurability across paradigms, in what senses can we evaluate progress or the reasonableness of scientific activity across those paradigms? As also mentioned in the previous chapter, Kuhn thought that such an antirational, or at least nonrational, characterization of his model was incorrect.

What is important, however, is the underlying assumption that science is (primarily) a rational activity and hence that scientific change can best be understood as a rational activity and via rational criteria. Indeed, this is very much part of the view of the inductivist and falsifcationist models of scientific change. As we saw in Chapter Eight, inductivism argued for clear criteria to demonstrate the rational nature of science, namely, beginning with unbiased descriptive observations, scientists should describe patterns uncovered in and from those observations, formulate clear hypotheses, test them under rigorous conditions and, if possible, identify further empirical generalizations, leading ultimately to laws and theories that should account for the experienced phenomena. Likewise, although critical of inductivism, falsificationism offered very precise criteria and conditions for scientific practice and evaluation: conjectures and refutations, with the unambiguous *modus tollens* form of argumentation as the rational standard. Nevertheless, as we have seen over the previous two chapters, each of these models of scientific change has been subject to plausible and telling criticisms. In this current chapter, we will consider two more models of scientific change. The first is associated with Larry Laudan and is often referred to as the Research Traditions (or Problem-Solving) model; the second is associated with Joseph Pitt and, for lack of any better term, is labeled the Technologist model. As we will see over the course of looking at these two models, they have several points in common. First, they begin with the point of view that science is always a goal-based activity and, as a result, any good model of scientific change must both describe and assess such change in light of what goals are being sought by scientists.

Second, as this is very important for them, it is the identification and understanding of what counts as a problem to be solved (for Laudan) and how it actually gets solved (for Pitt) that defines scientific rationality. This really is basic and important for these two models, so let me explain this more fully. Laudan claims that the earlier models of scientific change began with assumptions concerning criteria and standards of rationality in and for science. For example, falsificationism took the *modus tollens pattern* of argumentation as the characterizing nature of good science. So, as we saw for Popper, good science should conform to the *modus tollens* pattern; we should formulate bold hypotheses that make clear predictions; we should then check to see if those predictions are borne out; if they are, the hypothesis has been corroborated and is ready to stand for further testing; if those predictions are not borne out, then the hypothesis has clearly been falsified and should be jettisoned. The point is that there is a clear and clean rational standard here—the deductively valid logical argument pattern, *modus tollens*. So, there is some given standard of scientific rationality in place (*modus tollens*) and we can then determine whether there has been scientific progress relative to that preexisting standard of scientific rationality.

Now, a crucial element of Laudan's Problem-Solving model is that this relationship between rationality and progress is in fact reversed! Rather than defining progress in terms of rationality, Laudan argues that we should define rationality in terms of progress. That is, Laudan argues that what really matters for scientists is solving particular problems, where those problems are always identified against a background of some goal(s). To the extent that the goals are met via the solving of the problems, progress is made, for Laudan, and there is no further standard for what counts as scientific rationality. This is a fairly major departure, at least Laudan claims it is, from the earlier models of scientific change. It is, for him, a matter of turning the relationship of rationality and progress on its head, by now defining rationality in terms of progress rather than progress in terms of rationality. (I will say more about how Pitt's model relates to this issue when we turn directly to him in the second part of this chapter.)

A third point to note about both Laudan's model and Pitt's model is that, given the goal-based starting point and given the insistence on defining rationality in terms of progress, both of them emphasize the "materiality" of scientific change. What I mean by "materiality" is that it is not timeless, abstract standards or criteria (such as *modus tollens*) that are basic for understanding or assessing scientific change, but rather material, historical conditions and goals that serve as the standards and criteria. These conditions and goals can change (and, historically, have changed), so that progress (and, hence, rationality) should not be viewed non-historically. Although this might sound similar to aspects of Kuhn's and Lakatos' models—and there certainly are some similarities—differences between them and these two new models will be shown later in this chapter as we flesh out Laudan's and Pitt's views.

Research traditions

In the following selection, Larry Laudan stresses the close relationship between rationality and progress in science. Science is, he insists, a rational endeavor and it does not merely change, but makes progress. However, scientific progress and rationality should not be understood or characterized by some set of atemporal, abstract criteria or standards. Rather, progress occurs when particular problems get solved. How it is determined that they get solved will depend on the standards and criteria of evaluation that scientists accept at any given point in time and by the goals that scientists are striving toward. For example, today the use of double-blind studies in the context of medical experiments is commonplace and seen as a rational standard. A double-blind study is one in which neither the researchers nor the subjects of the study know who among the subjects is receiving the experimental drug, say, or a control substance. The purpose, of course, of such an experimental design is to eliminate or at least diminish any bias in the experimental process. The concern is that if either the researchers or the subjects know if they are or are not receiving the experimental drug, they might give subtle (or not so subtle) cues that could skew the results of the experiment. So, double-blind experimental design is seen as a means of promoting valid, reliable experimental data and, so, is seen as a rational standard of scientific practice and evaluation. However, double-blind studies are relatively new to medical research given the centuries of human medical practice and experimentation. For example, a major accomplishment in the history of medicine is often referred to as the "germ theory of disease" (see the case study at the end of this chapter). Yet, double-blind studies were not used in the development of this theory. A major point, in Laudan's view, is that the standards and criteria that were used at the time of the development of the germ theory (basically the 1800s) were quite rational and the scientists at the time could understand and assess progress relative to the problems they were addressing. It would be mistaken, he says, to look back on those scientists from our current views about rationality and change and argue that they were not behaving rationally because their standards were different than ours (or would today be considered faulty standards).

Here is another example: For a long time the dominant view of health was what was called the *humor theory*. No, it is not about laughter being the best medicine or anything funny. It is the view that health is a balance of four humors, or bodily fluids. The four humors were blood, phlegm, yellow bile, and black bile. Each of them was associated with varying conditions of heat and moisture. For example, blood was associated with a positive level of heat (it is warm) and moisture (it is wet). Phlegm, on the other hand, is wet but cool. Good health was seen as a balance of these humors and disease, or at least ill health, was seen as an imbalance of these humors. For instance, fever in which a person is hot and sweating was seen as an overabundance of blood, because the person is too hot and too wet. The remedy for someone who is feverish is to reduce the proportion of blood in the body, because the feverish conditions must be caused by an abundance of blood. If you are too hot and too wet, then to restore the balance of humors, one would have to either increase the level of the other humors or decrease the level of the offending humor, in this case, blood. A typical treatment, then, would be blood-letting, that is, extracting blood from the body of a feverish person. Now, today we would see blood-letting as definitely not a good idea for treating a feverish condition. However, given the underlying theory about health, we can see that blood-letting was not an irrational treatment. Today we reject the treatment because we reject the underlying theory of health. For Laudan, it would be inappropriate to criticize these earlier physicians for their practice of blood-letting based on our current theories of health.

This does *not* mean that Laudan thinks that there are no bases for critiquing or criticizing any scientific views other than our own. As will be seen in the following selection, he is quite explicit about laying out just what conditions do count as scientific progress, and, hence, as grounds for assessing other views, or research traditions, as he will call them. In a nutshell, his claim is that we can identify problems for a given research tradition. Those problems will be either empirical (about phenomena in the world) or conceptual (about non-empirical matters such as fruitfulness or consistency or simplicity of our

theories). Although standards and criteria of rationality might
vary over time and different research traditions, what we can
identify objectively is the problem-solving effectiveness of any
given research tradition. The basic aim of science, for Laudan,
is to maximize problem-solving effectiveness and, given this
goal, we can identify progress in the sense of comparing the
problem-solving effectiveness of rival theories or research traditions, without appealing to some timeless, abstract standard
or criterion of rationality. So, we can judge the problem-solving
effectiveness of the humor theory relative to the germ theory.
How we can do that is the focus of Laudan's selection (though
he does not speak to this particular example of theories of
health). In this first selection, he begins by identifying what he
sees as things to be desired (desiderata) for a model of scientific change and lays out what he sees as the aim of science
and types of problems that face science, empirical and conceptual, as well as what he means by "progress with cumulative
retention."

A PROBLEM-SOLVING APPROACH TO SCIENTIFIC PROGRESS
Larry Laudan

Desiderata

Studies of the historical development of science have made it clear
that any normative model of scientific rationality which is to have
the resources to show that science has been largely a rational enterprise must come to terms with certain persistent features of scientific
change. To be specific, we may conclude from the existing historical
evidence that:

1. Theory transitions are generally non-cumulative, i.e. neither the logical nor empirical content (nor even the "confirmed consequences")
   of earlier theories is wholly preserved when those theories are supplanted by new ones.

2. Theories are generally not rejected simply because they have anomalies nor are they generally accepted simply because they are empirically confirmed.

3. Changes in, and debates about, scientific theories often turn on conceptual issues rather than on questions of empirical support.

4. The specific and "local" principles of scientific rationality which scientists utilize in evaluating theories are not permanently fixed, but have altered significantly through the course of science.

5. There is a broad spectrum of cognitive stances which scientists take towards theories, including accepting, rejecting, pursuing, entertaining, etc. Any theory of rationality which discusses only the first two will be incapable of addressing itself to the vast majority of situations confronting scientists.

6. There is a range of levels of generality of scientific theories ranging from laws at the one end to broad conceptual frameworks at the other. Principles of testing, comparison, and evaluation of theories seem to vary significantly from level to level.

7. Given the notorious difficulties with notions of "approximate truth"—at both the semantic and epistemic levels—it is implausible that characterizations of scientific progress which view evaluation towards greater truthlikeness as the central aim of science will allow one to represent science as a rational activity.

8. The co-existence of rival theories is the rule rather than the exception, so that theory evaluation is primarily a comparative affair.

The challenge to which this essay is addressed is whether there can be a normatively viable philosophy of science which finds a place for most or all of these features of science *wie es eigentlich gewesen ist* [as it actually was].

The Aim of Science

To ask if scientific knowledge shows cognitive progress is to ask whether science through time brings us closer to achieving our cognitive aims or goals. Depending upon our choice of cognitive aims, one and the same temporal sequence of theories may be progressive or non-progressive. Accordingly, the stipulative task of specifying the aims of science is more than an academic exercise. Throughout history, there has been a tendency to characterize the aims of science in terms of such transcendental properties as truth or apodictic certainty. So conceived, science emerges as non-progressive since we evidently have no way of ascertaining whether our theories are more truthlike or more nearly certain than they formerly were. We do not yet have a satisfactory semantic characterization of truthlikeness, let alone any epistemic account of when it would be legitimate to judge one theory to be more nearly true than another. Only by setting goals for science which are in principle achievable, and which are such that we can tell whether we are able to make a positive claim about the progressive character of science. There are many non-transcendent immanent goals in terms of which we might attempt to characterize science; we could view science as aiming at well-tested theories, theories which predict novel facts, theories which "save the phenomena," or theories which have practical applications. My own proposal, more general than these, is that the aim of science is to secure theories with a high problem-solving effectiveness. From this perspective, *science progresses just in case successive theories solve more problems than their predecessors.*

The merits of this proposal are two-fold: (1) it captures much that has been implicit all along in discussions of the growth of science; and (2) it assumes a goal which (unlike truth) is not intrinsically transcendent and hence closed to epistemic access. The object of this essay is to spell out this proposal in some detail and to examine some of the consequences that a problem-solving model of scientific progress has for our understanding of the scientific enterprise.

Kinds of Problem-Solving: A Taxonomy

Despite the prevalent talk about problem-solving among scientists and philosophers, there is little agreement about what counts as a problem, what kinds of problems there are, and what constitutes a solution to a problem. To begin with, I suggest that we separate *empirical* from *conceptual* problems.

At the empirical level, I distinguish between potential problems, solved problems, and anomalous problems. "Potential problems" constitute what we take to be the case about the world, but for which there is as yet no explanation. "Solved" or "actual" problems are that class of putatively germane claims about the world which have been solved by some viable theory or other. "Anomalous problems" are actual problems which rival theories solve but which are not solved by the theory in question. It is important to note that, according to this analysis, unsolved or potential problems need not be anomalies. A problem is only anomalous for some theory if that problem has been solved by a viable rival. Thus, a prima facie falsifying instance for a theory, T, may not be an anomalous problem (specifically, when no other theory has solved it); and an instance which does not falsify T may none the less be anomalous for T (if T does not solve it and one of T's rivals does).

In addition to empirical problems, theories may be confronted with *conceptual* problems. Such problems arise for a theory, T, in any of the following circumstances:

1. when T is internally inconsistent or the theoretical mechanisms it postulates are ambiguous;
2. when T makes assumptions about the world that run counter to other theories or to prevailing metaphysical assumptions, or when T makes claims about the world which cannot be warranted by prevailing epistemic and methodological doctrines;
3. when T violates principles of the research tradition of which it is a part (to be discussed below);
4. when T fails to utilize concepts from other, more general theories to which it should be logically subordinate.

Conceptual problems, like anomalous empirical problems, indicate liabilities in our theories (i.e. partial failures on their part to serve all the functions for which we have designed them) . . . .

The centrality of conceptual concerns here represents a significant departure from earlier empirical philosophers of science. Many types of conceptual difficulties that theories regularly confront have been given little or no role to play by these philosophers in their models of scientific change. Even those like Popper who have paid lip service to the heuristic role of metaphysics in science leave no scope for rational conflicts between a theory and prevailing views about scientific methodology. This is because they have assumed that the meta-scientific evaluative criteria which scientists use for assessing theories are immutable and uncontroversial.

Why do most models of science fail at this central juncture? In assessing prior developments, they quite properly attend carefully to what evidence a former scientist had and to his substantive beliefs about the world, but they also assume without argument that earlier scientists adhered to our views about the rules of theory evaluation. Extensive scholarship on this matter makes it vividly clear that the views of the scientific community about how to test theories and about what counts as evidence have changed dramatically through history. This should not be surprising, since we are as capable of learning more about how to do science as we are of learning more about how the world works. The fact that the evaluative strategies of scientists of earlier eras are different from our strategies makes it quixotic to suppose that we can assess the rationality of their science by ignoring completely *their* views about how theories should be evaluated . . . it is anachronistic to judge the rationality of the work of an Archimedes, a Newton, or an Einstein by asking whether it accords with the contemporary methodology of a Popper or a Lakatos. The views of former scientists about how theories should be evaluated must enter into judgments about how rational those scientists were in testing their theories in the ways that they did. The problem-solving model [argued for here] brings such factors into play through the inclusion of conceptual problems, one species of which arises when a theory conflicts with a prevailing epistemology. Models of science which did not include a scientist's theory of evidence in a rational account of his actions and beliefs are necessarily defective.

I have talked of problems, but what of solutions? In the simplest cases, a theory solves an *empirical* problem when it entails, along with appropriate initial and boundary conditions, a statement of the problem. A theory solves or eliminates a *conceptual* problem when it fails to exhibit a conceptual difficulty of its predecessor. It is important to note that on this account, *many different theories may solve the same* (empirical or conceptual) *problem*. The worth of a theory will depend *inter alia* on how many problems it solves. Unlike most models of explanation which insist that a theory does not really explain anything unless it is the best theory (or possesses a high degree of confirmation), the problem-solving approach allows a problem solution to be credited to a theory, independent of how well established the theory is, just so long as the theory stands in a certain formal relation to (a statement of) the problem . . .

Progress without Cumulative Retention

Virtually all models of scientific progress and rationality (with the exception of certain inductive logics which are otherwise flawed) have insisted on wholesale retention of content or success in every progressive-theory transition. According to some well-known models, earlier theories are required to be contained in, or limiting cases of, later theories; while in others, the empirical content or confirmed consequences of earlier theories are required to be sub-sets of the content or consequence classes of the new theories. Such models are appealing in that they make theory choice straightforward. If a new theory can do everything its predecessor could and more besides, then the new theory is clearly superior. Unfortunately, history teaches us that theories rarely if ever stand in this relation to one another, and recent conceptual analysis even suggests that theories could not possibly exhibit such relations under normal circumstances.

What is required, if we are to rescue the notion of scientific progress, is a breaking of the link between cumulative retention and progress, so as to allow for the possibility of progress even when there are explanatory losses as well as gains. Specifically, we must work out some machinery for setting off gains against losses. This is a much more complicated affair than simple cumulative retention and we are not close to having a fully developed account of it. But the outlines of such an account can be perceived. Cost-benefit analysis is a tool developed especially to handle such a situation. Within a problem-solving model, such analysis proceeds as follows: for every theory, assess the number and the weight of the empirical problems it is known to solve; similarly, assess the number and weight of its empirical anomalies; finally, assess the number and centrality of its conceptual difficulties or problems. Constructing appropriate scales, our principle of progress tells us to prefer the theory which comes closest to solving the largest number of important empirical problems while generating the smallest number of significant anomalies and conceptual problems . . .

To recap, every theory encounters both empirical and conceptual problems, and it is the resolution of these problems that is the focal point of scientific efforts, as well as the focal point of assessment and evaluation of rival theories. Echoing Lakatos, Laudan insists that theory appraisal is comparative; one theory is evaluated in terms of its problem-solving effectiveness vis-à-vis rival theories, so that rarely (if ever) is there a single, dominant Kuhnian-style paradigm. Specific principles of scientific rationality change over time, but problem-solving effectiveness can be identified across time and across theories. Scientific progress can be enunciated, then, but it is not (at least, not necessarily) cumulative. With these features in mind, Laudan suggests that the significant vehicle of theory evaluation, and the more meaningful vehicle for understanding scientific change, is not so much any particular theory or set of theories, but rather a *research tradition*. Reminiscent of Kuhn's paradigms, Laudan's research traditions include sets of beliefs about metaphysics (what sorts of entities and processes make up a given domain of inquiry), epistemology (what sorts of methods or practices are appropriate), and axiology (what aims and goals are appropriate and desirable). Like Kuhn's paradigms and Lakatos' research programs, research traditions do not necessarily explicitly "tell" scientists these things, but scientists are trained to understand and appreciate the kinds of questions to ask and not ask, the kinds of techniques to use and not use, the kinds of background assumptions to make and not make about what is already established knowledge, and so on. An additional conclusion of Laudan's view is that there is no sharp demarcation between science and non-science (which is not to say that there are no differences at all, but that there is no mutually exclusive conditions between them). Here is what Laudan says:

A PROBLEM-SOLVING APPROACH TO SCIENTIFIC PROGRESS (continued)

Larry Laudan

Theories and Research Traditions

Theories represent exemplifications of more fundamental views about the world, and the manner in which theories are modified and changed only makes sense when seen against the backdrop of those more fundamental commitments. I call the cluster of beliefs which constitute such fundamental views "research traditions." Generally, this consist of at least two components: (i) a set of beliefs about what sorts of entities and processes make up the domain of enquiry and (ii) a set of epistemic and methodological norms about how the domain is to be investigated, how theories are to be tested, how data are to be collected, and the like.

Research traditions are not directly testable, both because their ontologies are too general to yield specific predictions and because their methodological components, being rules or norms, are not straightforwardly testable assertions about matters of fact. Associated with any active research tradition is a family of theories. Some of these theories, for instance, those applying the research tradition to different parts of the domain, will be mutually consistent while other theories, for instance, those which are rival theories with the research tradition, will not. What all the theories have in common is that they share the ontology of the parent research tradition and can be tested and evaluated using its methodological norms.

Research traditions serve several specific functions. Among others: (a) they indicate what assumptions can be regarded as uncontroversial "background knowledge" to all the scientists working in that tradition; (b) they help to identify those portions of a theory that are in difficulty and should be modified or amended; (c) they establish rules for the collection of data and for the testing of theories; (d) they pose conceptual problems for any theory in the tradition which violates the ontological and epistemic claims of the parent tradition.

Adequacy and Promise

Compared to single theories, research traditions tend to be enduring entities. Where theories may be abandoned and replaced very frequently, research traditions are usually long-lived, since they can obviously survive the demise of any of their subordinate theories. Research traditions are the units which endure through theory change and which establish, along with solved empirical problems, much of what continuity there is in the history of science. But even research traditions can be overthrown. To understand how, we must bring the machinery of problem-solving assessment into the picture.

Corresponding to the idealized modalities of acceptance and pursuit are two features of theories, both related to problem-solving efficiency. Both of these features can be explained in terms of the problem-solving effectiveness of a theory, which is itself a function of the number and importance of the empirical problems a theory has solved and of the anomalies and conceptual problems which confront it. One theory is more adequate (i.e. more acceptable) than a rival just in case the former has exhibited a greater problem-solving effectiveness than the latter. One research tradition is more adequate than another just in case the ensemble of theories which characterize it at a given time are more adequate than the theories making up any rival research tradition.

If our goal was only that of deciding which theory or research tradition solved the largest number of problems, these tools would be sufficient. But there is a *prospective* as well as retrospective element in scientific evaluation. Our hope is to move to theories which can solve more problems, including potential empirical problems, than we are now able to deal with. We seek theories which promise fertility in extending the range of what we can now explain and predict. The fact that one theory (or research tradition) is now the most adequate is not irrelevant to, but neither is it sufficient grounds for, judgments about promise or fertility. New theories and research traditions are rarely likely to have managed to achieve a degree of problem-solving effectiveness as high as that of old, well-established theories. How are we to judge when such novel approaches are worth taking seriously? A natural suggestion involves assessing the progress or rate of progress of such theories and research traditions. That progress is defined as the difference between the problem-solving effectiveness of the research tradition in its latest form and its effectiveness at an earlier period. The rate of progress is a measure of how quickly a research tradition has made whatever progress it exhibits.

Obviously, one research tradition may be less adequate than a rival and yet more progressive. Acknowledging this fact, one might propose that highly progressive theories should be explored and pursued whereas only the most adequate theories should be accepted. Traditional philosophies of science (e.g. Carnap's, Popper's) and some more recent ones (e.g. Lakatos's) share the view that both adequacy and promise are to be assessed by the same measure. My approach acknowledges that we evaluate scientific ideas with different ends in view and that different measures are appropriate to those ends. How progressive a research tradition is and how rapidly it has progressed are different, if equally relevant, questions from asking how well supported the research tradition is.

Patterns of Scientific Change

According to Thomas Kuhn's influential view, science can be periodized into a series of epochs, the boundaries between which are called scientific revolutions. During periods of normal science, one paradigm reigns supreme. Raising fundamental conceptual concerns or identifying anomalies for the prevailing doctrine or actively developing alternative "paradigms" are, in Kuhn's view, disallowed by the scientific community, which has a very low tolerance for rival points of view. The problem-solving model gives rise to a very different picture of the scientific enterprise. It suggests that the co-existence of rival research traditions is the rule rather than the exception. It stresses the centrality of debates about conceptual foundations and argues that the neglect of conceptual issues (a neglect which Kuhn sees as central to the "normal" progress of science) is undesirable. That the actual development of science is closer to the picture of permanent co-existence of rivals and the omnipresence of conceptual debates than to the picture of normal science seems clear. It is difficult, for instance, to find any lengthy period in the history of any science in the last 300 years when the Kuhnian picture of "normal science" prevails. What seems to be far more common is for scientific disciplines to involve a variety of co-present research approaches (traditions). At any given time, one or other of these may have the competitive edge, but there is a continuous and persistent struggle taking place, with partisans of one view or another pointing to the empirical and conceptual weaknesses of rival points of view and to the problem-solving progressiveness of their own approach. Dialectical confrontations are essential to the growth and improvement of scientific knowledge; like nature, science is red in tooth and claw.

Criticisms of research traditions

Although many philosophers of science have endorsed Laudan's distinction between the reasonableness of different cognitive aims with respect to science—for example, it is one thing to pursue a line of research (exploratory aim) and another thing to accept that line (explanatory aim)—nevertheless, they have had some qualms about other aspects of Laudan's model. The concerns mostly arise with respect to two issues: (1) the vagueness of the notion of a scientific problem and (2) the historically contextual standards and criteria of assessment.

As for the vagueness of the notion of a scientific problem, even though Laudan spells out a difference between empirical and conceptual problems, and insists that both are important for the assessment of a scientific theory or research tradition, critics claim that what even counts as a problem at all is left unclear. For example, for some accounts of life on earth, the issue of design (how there is such order among complexity of organisms and within organisms) is a problem, whereas for other accounts it is not a problem—where "problem" means some phenomenon that needs explaining at all, not that it is difficult to explain. Beyond just what counts as a problem, critics have argued that Laudan's statements regarding the respective weighing of problems—his calculus of rationality, so to speak—is not clear at all. How can the relative "weights" of empirical and conceptual problems be determined? Is one conceptual problem equal to one empirical problem? Is there even a sharp distinction between what is an empirical vs. a conceptual problem (is design an empirical or conceptual problem)? Is it really as simple to compare rival theories or research traditions as counting up solved problems vs. anomalies and unsolved problems?

The second concern, regarding historically based standards of rationality, is one that has been raised at Kuhn and Lakatos, as well. Is it really the case, critics ask, that the germ theory of disease is not "really" (i.e., objectively) a better account of disease than the humor theory? Although Laudan might not embrace Kuhnian incommensurability, isn't he saddled with it, ask critics.

A third form of concern comes from the next (and last) model of scientific change to be explored here, namely, the Technologist model of scientific change. Joseph Pitt, though he shares some of the criticisms that Laudan has with earlier models, is critical of Laudan as well as focusing on theories and ideas as the driving force of scientific change. As we will see in the following selection, it is not theories (or paradigms or research programs or research traditions, etc.) that Pitt sees as accounting for actual scientific change, rather it is material, technological achievement. For all his emphasis on problem-solving, Laudan is still guilty, for Pitt, of seeing science as essentially an intellectual, cognitive enterprise, to be described and explained in virtue of ideas and theories. The history of science, he says, is described—wrongly, for Pitt—as the history of theories and ideas, and this includes Laudan. What does Pitt see as the more appropriate description? That is what we will now see.

Technologism

A recent issue (November 18, 2006) of the weekly magazine, *Science News,* contained multiple references or allusions to technology in the context of describing current scientific research: the Hubble telescope shedding light on cosmic expansion, computer analyses of Neandertal DNA, self-scrutinizing robots, sonogram analysis of chicken vocalizations, tests of stem cells and their connection to canine muscular dystrophy, data recorded by ocean buoys, and numerous other examples. It is inconceivable today to think of scientists functioning without a necessary reliance on technology. Of course, tools and machines have been a part of human history, and of scientific inquiry, since the beginnings of civilization. Much of what we usually call "the scientific revolution" of the 1600s is intimately connected with the invention of instruments such as the telescope, microscope, and air pump (allowing the creation of functional vacuums) that allowed the scientists of the time to investigate whole new fields of study that previously had been impractical, unthinkable, even impossible. There is simply no question that science has changed and continues to change as a direct result of changes and advancements in technology.

Although the next chapter in this book will focus on the issue of science and technology, here the concern is looking at another model of scientific change, a model associated with the work of the philosopher of science (and philosopher of technology), Joseph Pitt. Pitt does not call his model of scientific change *technologism,* but, for ease of having a label, I will. This model is included in this chapter because it represents a growing emphasis among many philosophers of science (and of technology) that other models of scientific change have simply ignored or downplayed the very fundamental role of technology in science. In addition, as mentioned at the start of this chapter, Pitt's model shares a number of features with Laudan's problem-solving research traditions model, namely, the importance and prominence of solving particular problems as the major focus of scientific inquiry, as well as a rejection of atemporal, abstract standards and criteria of scientific progress (and rationality).

Though Kuhn and Laudan, and to some extent, Lakatos, all talk about the significance of historical contexts in which scientists engage in their pursuits, Pitt claims that they don't take these contexts seriously enough. They especially ignore what he calls *the technological infrastructure of science*, by which he means the political, economic, and other social networks that underlie and make possible the material conditions for scientists to do their work. Scientists do not work in a vacuum. For example, today most scientific research is funded by government granting agencies or by private industries. Or, even at a more mundane level, scientific research is done by scientists who have to balance that research with other responsibilities, such as teaching and raising their kids. In addition, for Pitt, this underlying technological infrastructure is not merely equipment and machines, but social structures, as well. As he remarks, legal systems are just as much tools as hammers.

In the selection below, Pitt describes what he means by the technological infrastructure of science and argues that scientific change and progress—and, by implication, scientific rationality—is a consequence of this technological infrastructure and, in large part, of the specific technologies that arise and are used by scientists.

THINKING ABOUT TECHNOLOGY
Joseph Pitt

Theories of Scientific Change

There are numerous theories of scientific change in the literature. And they all have one thing in common. In accounting for the succession of scientific theories over time, they ignore the contribution of the support systems in which the activities of scientists are embedded. This support system is what . . . I [have] called *the technological infrastructure of science*. By the technological infrastructure of science, I mean: *the historically* defined set of mutually supporting sets of artifacts and structures without which the development and refinement of scientific knowledge is not possible. [For instance,] Galileo's development and use of the telescope took place in the context of his role as, first, a professor at Padua and an employee of the Doge of Venice, and then as Chief Mathematician and Philosopher for Cosimo d'Medici of Florence. First the university and then the d'Medici court provided support systems for Galileo to develop the instruments that he used to make the observations that forced significant changes in the theories of the heavens.

What I intend by the use of the phrase "technological infrastructure" is to recognize the social, political, economic, technical, and scientific contexts in which specific scientists are embedded and the contribution those contexts make to their work. Science does not develop and make what progress it does outside of society. By including the social structures that support science in this account, I am merely . . . [claiming] that social structures such as legal systems are as much tools as are hammers and automobiles. But I also intend the phrase "the technological infrastructure of science" to suggest more than merely a recognition of the social dimension of science. With this idea I want to emphasize the extent to which scientific development, which depends so much on new discoveries, is likewise, and for that very reason, dependent on the development of new forms of instrumentation, data processing, and analysis . . .

On the topic of technological change as a counter part concept to scientific change, my underlying thesis is this: following Derek Price, it seems clear that progress in science is a direct function of increasing sophistication not merely in instrumentation, but in the technological infrastructure that underlies and makes mature science possible.

Price claimed: "historically, the arrow of causality is largely from the technology to the science," but this is only part of the story. By emphasizing the causal priority of technology in scientific progress, Price was attempting to overcome a popular characterization of the relation between science and technology in which technology is placed in a second-class position as the offshoot of science or sometimes its "handmaiden." Price was on the right track, pointing out that despite the fact that historians and philosophers of science from Kuhn to Laudan have a tendency to talk about progress in science in terms of the history of ideas, a significant role is played by technology, a role largely ignored by these same philosophers and historians of science. The typical history-of-ideas story of science proceeds by relating that, for example, Newton's mechanics replaced Aristotle's, and the relativity theory replaced Newton's mechanics.

The story is usually told in Kuhnian fashion, without any mention of the means by which anomalies were discovered. It is merely announced that following a certain experiment, it was decided that so-and-so's theory was false, and it was replaced by another. Thus, a typical bad history would tell you that Michelson's and Morley's experiment was developed to test for aether drift, as predicted by Newton's theory. Once it was discovered that drift did not occur, Newton had to be abandoned. Enter Einstein, and all is saved. Very few historians reveal that Newton did not talk about aether drift; the notion evolved over a hundred years in the course of his successors' efforts to adjust his theory in light of their experience with it. Likewise, very few accounts tell you about the details of the Michelson-Morely experiment. The point here is that on the history of ideas account the history of progress in science is made to read like merely the replacement of one bad theory by another once the bad theory is somehow discovered to be faulty. All of this rests on the presumption that the models of the logic of confirmation produced by philosophers have some bearing on what scientists do, which isn't at all clear. What is ignored is the role in all of this of *the technological infrastructure* within which the falsification and/or confirmation of theories takes place, to the extent that theories are falsified and/or confirmed . . .

The Technological Infrastructure of Science

I now turn more explicitly to the role of the technological infrastructure of science in the growth of knowledge generally. I start by reviewing some features of the manner in which Galileo's development and use of the telescope helped create an initial technological infrastructure for astronomy, and then move to a sketchy reconsideration of that notion as it occurs in modern guise. In doing so, I hope to make plain what is meant by a technological infrastructure of science. Instead of attempting to argue one side or another of the old science/technology debate, I have recast some of the issues so as to demonstrate the epistemological importance of a technological infrastructure construed as interrelated sets of artifacts and structures. Furthermore, just as it makes no sense to talk broadly of technology, it makes no sense to speak of the history and development or importance of a single artifact, suggesting, as this does, that once invented, artifacts remains stable over time. My general thesis is direct: *the development of new information in a mature science is, by and large, a function of its technological infrastructure.* In short, scientific discovery today depends almost completely on the technological context without which modern science would be impossible. I will not raise the question of the merits of this situation until the end of my discussion, although I will provide a hint: in this age of increasingly theoretical science, the technology behind the science may be our only contact with reality, and even so, it is at best a tenuous one. But now let us turn to the relationship between new and improved artifacts of science . . .

Having enunciated what he means by the technological infrastructure of science and why he sees this as basic and crucial for understanding scientific change, Pitt goes on, in the selection on the next page, to provide a specific case to support his argument, the case of Galileo and the advent and further development of the telescope. Before directly laying out the Galileo case, Pitt discusses the related matter of discovery and invention, because both are intimately connected to scientific change and progress. He raises this issue of discovery and invention in the context of the realism/ constructivism debate (remember, Chapter Three), as this debate surrounds some of the controversy about Kuhn and others, and their models of scientific change. In particular, this issue is related to technology, for Pitt, because he claims that advances in technology don't simply give us new or additional information, but they provide us with new *kinds* of information, even new *ways* of discovering and inventing information. Indeed, technology often *forces* us to see the world differently, both in terms of new kinds of information and in terms of new ways we need to acquire information. To the extent, then, that we understand science as a set of practices (that is, as method) rather than merely as a set of statements about the world (that is, as content), changing technology is changing practice; scientific change is just (or, at least primarily) technological change. To put this in Kuhnian terms, for Pitt, the reason there are paradigm shifts is because there are technological changes and changes in the technological infrastructure. Pitt claims to demonstrate this via his discussion of Galileo, but claims that this is even truer for contemporary science, which relies even more on technology and associated infrastructures. So, here is Pitt again:

THINKING ABOUT TECHNOLOGY (continued)
Joseph Pitt

Returning then to the problem of articulating the technological infrastructure of science, we are going to need some definitions. Three, in particular, are relevant to our concerns.

Discovery: the cognitive apprehension of that which has not been so apprehended or apprehended in that manner before.
Technology: humanity at work.
The technology of discovery: humanity at work cognitively apprehending that which has not been so apprehended or apprehended in that manner before.

These definitions present us with a few problems when viewed from the perspective of the realist/constructivist debate. For example, do we, in cognitively apprehending electrons using an electron microscope for the first time, invent or discover electrons? The way to avoid getting stuck back in the very situation we are trying to avoid is to take our definitions seriously. The definition offered for discovery makes no ontological claims, only an epistemological one. One must "cognitively apprehend something new or in a new way." It doesn't follow that such an act entails that what is cognitively apprehended must exist. Thus this account of discovery, it is to be hoped, avoids the old problems of the realist and the constructivist, at least in the manner in which these were plagued by them.

Turning back to the definitions, I want to lay them out so as to help clarify some of the issues that are before us. But we seem to have both too much and too little in these definitions to be able to understand the role of the technological infrastructure of science. Attending to "cognitively apprehending people at work in a new way" is not going to help us explore the sense in which sets of artifacts generate new scientific discoveries. We need something else; we need to know the manner in which further scientific work depends on new developments in the artifacts, i.e., an account of the *invention* and modification of the relevant artifacts in these circumstances. That is considerably more complicated. It requires our account of "technological infrastructure," characterized as before:

> *A technological infrastructure:* an historically determined set of mutually supporting artifacts and structures that enable human activity and provide the means for its development.

The notion of *mutually supporting* sets of artifacts is difficult to nail down in the abstract. What is ultimately perhaps most important is not the notion that science works within a framework of interrelated sets of artifacts, but the realization, nay, the *discovery* that the technological infrastructure has itself grown and developed over time in conjunction with those features of the activity we call science. Thus I am not claiming that science, whenever and however it is or was practiced, has this kind of technological infrastructure. I will argue, however, that the development of a technological infrastructure is essential if science is going to *continue* to provide us with new discoveries about how the universe works. In short, after slow and modest beginnings, a *developed* science *requires* this kind of technological framework. The sorts of investigations and explanations it is called upon to produce require more than mere unaided human thinking alone can produce. I will return to consider the consequences of this claim later. For now, this is enough by way of speculation; let's start to build the case by looking again at Galileo and his telescope . . .

. . . I am not claiming that Galileo was the first to use an instrument to investigate the heavens and that he thereby forced astronomy onto its historical path. The use of instruments to assist us in our exploration of the heavens already had a long and rich history by Galileo's time. The astrolabe, for example, a device for determining the positions of the planets and the stars, was prominent in Arabic as well as in European astronomy. The quadrant was also a well-used device for determining positions in the heavens.

But unlike the astrolabe or the quadrant, the telescope produced fundamentally new kinds of information. The telescope did not, as did the astrolabe, merely assist in the refinement of measurements according to an established theory. It produced fundamentally new information about the structure and population of the heavens. This information conflicted with the then-established astronomical theories that determined what could and could not be the case astronomically. In this sense then, the telescope forced a transformation in cosmology. The instrument, in effect, required a major overhaul of theory. What was being demanded of theory then in turn forced a reworking and refinement of the instrument, demanding better and more accurate observations to confirm the new theory, which in turn pushed the matter even harder toward further theory revision. A basic new feature had been added to the activity of science: the *interplay* between instruments and theory. It was no longer the case that theories merely used instruments to confirm assumptions. Now we see instruments that are not necessarily coupled to any particular theory (remember that Galileo did not develop the telescope for astronomical purposes), yielding information that forces the scientists defending certain theories to rework their theories in order to accommodate the new data. But, as in any such successful reworking of a theory, the new theory will not only accommodate the new data, it will also suggest opportunities for new discoveries. This then forces revisions of or changes to or even the invention of new instruments, which in turn force the theories to be reworked, etc.

Thus, in Galileo's case, following the first use of the telescope to look at the moon with Cosimo d'Medici, the simple single instrument was to become a complex of instruments. Galileo originally intended his telescope to be handheld for maritime use. But for astronomical purposes it needed a base, then a fixed position from which the observations could be regularized. Tables of sightings could now be corrected, and the need for further refinements in the tables would force refinements in the telescope itself.

For example, a major problem in astronomy was determining the size of the planets. For this, Galileo's telescope, with its concave lens, was not the optimal instrument. In the 1630s it began to be replaced by what van Helden calls "the astronomical telescope," which had a convex ocular and produced greatly improved clarity in its images. It also had a broader field of vision, which permitted the introduction of a micrometer into the instrument itself, thereby improving the precision of measurements. This was the kind of instrument Huygens used to measure the diameters of the planets. Slowly, Galileo's simple device was becoming a set of things, each part of which could be separately refined, and which in so doing would ramify its effects on the others—perhaps not all the others all the time, but a kind of domino effect was evident. Furthermore, the availability of increasingly precise measurements of particular features of the observable universe also forced changes in the manner in that the relative distances of the planets were calculated. So now we have the instruments and their refinements forcing changes not only in cosmology but in the auxiliary methods that augment it. In this manner, the discovery of the size and structure of the solar system and then the universe was undertaken.

The story could be told without mentioning the instruments. For example, we could say:

Galileo showed there was more than one center around which planets revolved, forcing a revision of the geocentric theory of the universe. His methods were developed in such a way as to allow for the determination of the distances between planets and the relative sizes of the planets. Modern astronomy continues his program of empirical investigation of the universe.

That says what we have been saying, but the picture it provides of science is, to say the least, impoverished. The mechanism behind the changing ideas is lost, without which we truly have no explanation.

The need for a refined explanation is, I maintain, the proper motivation for including the technological infrastructure of science in our history of culture. For if we want an explanation for the development of science, we need to offer more than a recitation of the sequence of ideas produced by scientists. We need an account of how those ideas were developed and why they were abandoned and/or refined. We are thus dealing with an issue of historiography. An historically sensitive *explanation* of scientific progress and discovery requires appeal to some mechanism. It will not suffice merely to provide a list of dates of events for the selection of those events, for there is a need to justify the selection of those events. Traditionally one selected those events that can be shown to be in a direct line with current developments. I am urging that the events in question be selected for the importance in their own setting, whether or not they eventually lead to something that we deem important today.

That is why the traditional history-of-ideas approach, with its base in the present, is inadequate. I am proposing that *the mechanism* that makes the discoveries of science possible and scientific change mandatory *is the technological infrastructure* within which that science operates, and that to understand why a science worked the way it did and why it works the way it does, you need to understand its context, which happens to include in important ways its technological infrastructure. In short, you can no longer do philosophy of science, history of science, or even sociology of science without the philosophy and history of technology . . .

What we have to face is the fact that while there is no one necessary way to investigate nature, the mechanisms—read "technological infrastructure"—we develop to assist us set a complicated process in motion in which the imagination and creativity are sparked and fed by the interplay between idea and artifact. Artifacts stimulate us to seek uses for them—how to couple them with other artifacts; they also present us with the problem of interpreting the results. Given different sets of artifacts—by definition different simulations—we get different results. But we start small and go large in quick order. Compare Galileo's simple telescope with the complex that we need for a modern mountain-top observatory.

What are the consequences of accepting this characterization of the role of our technologies? It is not the case, as I am sure some determinist will be sure to suggest, that it means not only that society is run by technology, but that now science is too! No, that is not the proper conclusion to draw. It is not a question of which disembodied and reified nonentity, science or technology, controls anything. What a careful look at history will show is that *as instruments are made more complex by individuals with specific objectives in mind (objectives sometimes, but not always, generated by endorsing certain theories), a complex of interrelated activities develops through which, by choosing certain ways to augment the technological infrastructure, certain options are opened or shut for theoretical testing and exploration.* People still make the choices, and they may choose badly, taking us down a dead end. Or they may opt for a system that odes not have the backup to support it. This is what happened to the nineteenth-century astronomer, William Herschel. He built a forty-inch telescope that was certainly a technological marvel. Only there were severe problems. The mounting for it proved unstable. The mirror was made of metal and lost it reflective capacity. It fell into disuse.

My point is that if you want to explain the changing claims and face of science, you have to go beneath the ideas to the technological infrastructure and then you have to unravel the interactions between its parts and the mass of theories with which it is involved. It is that complex that makes it possible to apprehend new things or to apprehend things previously known, but in a new way. The discovery of structures in nature is a function of this complicated, mutually interacting set of artifacts, ideas, systems, and, of course, men and women . . .

Conclusion

I have looked at technological change as a counterpart concept to scientific change. I have argued that understanding scientific change requires putting the science in context, and one of the more important contexts—for there are many—in which to see science, especially mature science, is its technological infrastructure. The strong conclusion emerging from this discussion is that there can be no analysis of changes in a well-developed science without considering a massive support system of artifacts and social institutions. Thus the growth of science can be seen in similar terms as the growth of human culture, that is, made possible by the tools and mutually interactive support systems we have come to call technology. By shifting the burden of the production of knowledge from individuals to groups, we also take steps toward insuring that the infrastructures do not constrain the search for knowledge but, in fact, help create the dynamics that makes the relations between the sciences and our technologies so exciting. So what is the relation between science and technology? There isn't one; there are many, and that is the way it ought to be.

Criticisms of technologism

Who would deny that changes in technology have led to changes in science? No one. It is obvious that the advent of the telescope allowed astronomers to discover new information about the cosmos and that it forced new questions to be asked that would not have been thinkable before. If this is so, critics of Pitt ask, what's all the fuss? Couldn't Kuhn simply say that changes in technology are just a part of normal science or, if they really do generate significant anomalies and even crises, they are a part of revolutionary science? Likewise, couldn't Lakatos see technology and technological infrastructures as merely a part of research programs (and, for Laudan, a part of research traditions, with their problem-solving agendas)? Is Pitt's model just normal science in disguise?

The point of these questions, of course, is to say that one criticism of Pitt's model is that it really is not an alternative model of scientific change, but actually a "closer-to-the-ground" look at the details of scientific practices. Obviously, Pitt sees things differently and argues that his model is a fairly radical departure from previous models. It is a departure because the explanation for scientific change is based on material grounds, not on abstract ideas. When push comes to shove, it is practice (based on technology) that drives theory, not the reverse, which he accuses previous models of asserting.

A second criticism of Pitt's model is that it is subject to some of the same criticisms that were made of Kuhn, namely, that there seem to be no standards of progress beyond what the historical conventions allow or demand at the time. For example, although Galileo's telescope seemed to require a change in astronomical thinking (toward a heliocentric view), there were actually very good grounds at the time to reject his observations and the conclusions drawn from his observations. Those good reasons included the fact that theories of optics did not provide a thorough justification for accepting this new instrument to be so accurate and trustworthy as to overturn contrary observations and conclusions. That is, technology itself needs theoretical backing to warrant its use and reliability. Observations in themselves, whether aided or generated by technology, do not necessarily function as trumps; they require interpretation and theoretical support. Pitt's response to this concern is that he does not deny the importance of theory to help warrant the use and reliability of technology. As he noted, "The discovery of structures in nature is a function of this complicated, mutually interacting set of artifacts, ideas, systems, and, of course, men and women . . ." But, he says, this interacting set is ever-changing and there are no context-free standards or criteria.

Chapter Summary

Two models of scientific change that rely primarily on material problem-solving concerns are Laudan's Research Traditions model and Pitt's Technologist model. Laudan argues that previous models of scientific change, such as Popper, Kuhn, and Lakatos, presume some timeless, abstract standards or criteria of scientific rationality and then measure scientific progress against those standards or criteria. This is both descriptively and prescriptively backwards, for Laudan, who claims that actual change (and progress) in science is the result of solving actual problems. These problems can be either empirical or conceptual. What determines if scientific activity is rational is whether or not it solves these problems. Standards and criteria of rationality, then, can change (and have changed) over time; what is "objective" is whether or not actual problems have been solved. Research traditions, like paradigms or research programs, provide the background contexts for the identification and addressing of problems.

Pitt's technologist model of scientific change argues that scientific change is the result of technological advances and the background infrastructures that make technologies possible and functional. It is *how* problems are solved—via technologies—that defines scientific change and progress (and rationality). Technologies allow, even force, new kinds of information, new ways of comprehension, and new practices and it is these features of science that account for change and progress.

CASE STUDY

Germ Theory of Disease

Following the invention of the microscope in the 17th century, scientists discovered microorganisms. Over the next several centuries, this led to various concerns such as the issue of the genesis of life (often referred to as the question of spontaneous generation). By the 1800s this led to a new conception of disease, usually today called the germ *theory of disease. This is the view that contact with (some) microorganisms is the cause of disease. Two very significant figures in the emergence and acceptance of this view (though neither represented in this Case Study) were Louis Pasteur (1822–1895) and*

Robert Koch (1843–1910). However, the scientists included here—Edward Jenner (1749–1823), Ignaz Semmelweis (1818–1865), and Joseph Lister (1827–1912)—all made particular contributions to the germ theory. Consider what elements (if any) of Laudan's problem-solving research traditions view and Pitt's technology-focused view are in fact illustrated in these selections. For example, are there identifiable empirical and conceptual problems that are being addressed? If so, what are they? What technological instruments (if any) seem to play an important role in the formulation or resolution of problems?

SOURCE BOOK OF MEDICAL HISTORY
Logan Clendening (editor)

Edward Jenner

There is a disease to which the horse, from his state of domestication, is frequently subject. The farriers call it the grease. It is an inflammation and the swelling in the heel, from which issues matter possessing properties of a very peculiar kind, which seems capable of generating a disease in the human body (after it has undergone the modification which I shall presently speak of), which bears so strong a resemblance to the smallpox that I think it highly probable it may be the source of the disease.

. . . the disease makes it progress from the horse to the nipple of the cow, and from the cow to the human subject.

Morbid matter of various kinds, when absorbed into the system, may produce effect in some degree similar; but what renders the cow-pox virus so extremely singular is that the person who has been thus affected is forever secure from the infection of the smallpox; neither exposure to the variolous effluvia, nor the insertion of the matter into the skin, producing this distemper.

In support of so extraordinary a fact, I shall lay before my readers a great number of instances [only one given here].

Case 1. Joseph Merret, now as under gardener to the Earl of Berkeley, lived as a servant with a farmer near this place in the year 1770, and occasionally assisted in milking his master's cows. Several horses belonging to the farm began to have sore heels, which Merret frequently attended. The cows soon became affected with the cow-pox, and soon after several sores appeared on his hands. Swellings and stiffness in each axilla followed, and he was so much indisposed for several days as to be incapable of pursuing his ordinary employment. Previously to the appearance of the distemper among the cows there was no fresh cow brought into the farm, nor any servant employed who was affected with the cow-pox.

In April 1795, a general inoculation taking place here, Merret was inoculated with his family; so that a period of twenty-five years had elapsed from his having the cow-pox to this time. However, though the variolous matter was repeatedly inserted into his arms, I found it impracticable to infect him with it; an efflorescence only, taking on an erysipelatous look about the center, appearing on the skin near the punctured parts. During the whole time that his family had the smallpox, one of whom had it very full, he remained in the house with them, but received no injury from exposure to the contagion.

Ignaz Semmelweis

Supported by the experiences which I have collected in the course of fifteen years in three different institutions all of which were visited from time to time by puerperal fever to a serious extent, I maintain that puerperal fever, without the exception of a single case, is a resorption fever produced by the resorption of decomposed animal organic material. The first result of this resorption is a blood-dissolution; and exudations result from the blood-dissolution.

The decomposed animal organic material which produces child-bed fever is, in the overwhelming majority of cases, brought to the individual from without, and that is the infection from without; these are the cases which represent child-bed fever epidemics; these are the cases which can be prevented.

In rare cases the decomposed animal matter which when absorbed causes child-bed fever, is produced within the limits of the affected organism. These are the cases of self-infection, and these cases cannot all be prevented.

The source whence the decomposed animal organic material is derived from without is the cadaver of any age, of either sex, without regard to the antecedent disease, without regard to the fact whether the dead body is that of a puerperal or non-puerperal woman. Only the degree of putrefaction of the cadaver has to be taken into consideration . . .

At the Obstetric Clinic of the Faculty of Medicine at Pesth, it was physiologic human blood and normal lochia which were the etiological factor of a puerperal fever, inasmuch as they were left for a long time soaking the bed-linen and undergoing decomposition.

The carrier of the decomposed animal organic material is the examining finger, the operating hand, the bed-clothes, the atmospheric air, sponges, the hands of midwives and nurses which come into contact with the excrementa of sick lying-in-women or other patients, and then come again into contact with the genitals of women in labor or just confined; in a word the carrier of the decomposed animal organic material is everything which can be rendered unclean by such material and then come into contact with the genitals of the patient.

The site of infection by the decomposed animal organic material is the internal os uteri and upward from there. The inner surface of the uterus . . . is robbed of its mucosa and presents an area where absorption occurs with extreme readiness. The other parts of the mucosa are well clad with epithelium and do not absorb unless they are wounded. If it is injured any portion of the genitals becomes capable of absorption.

With regard to the time of infection, it seldom occurs during pregnancy because of the inaccessibility of the inner absorbing surface of the uterus by reason of the closure of the os internum. In cases in which the internal os uteri is open during pregnancy infection may occur then, but these cases are rare because there is seldom any need for passing the finger within the cervix uteri . . .

The time within which infection most frequently occurs is during the stage of dilatation. This is owing to frequent examinations made with the object of ascertaining the position of the fetus.

A proof of this is that before the introduction of chlorine disinfection nearly all the patients after labor, protracted in the dilatation period, died of puerperal fever.

Infection seldom takes place during the expulsion stage because the surface of the uterus cannot then be reached . . .

When we declare that child-bed fever is a resorption fever in which as the result of absorption a blood-poisoning occurs, and then exudation follows, we do not imply that puerperal fever is peculiar to the lying-in woman and restricted in its incidence to lying-in women. We have met with the disease in pregnant women and in new-born infants without regard to sex . . . we find it affecting anatomists, surgeons, and patients who have undergone surgical operations.

Puerperal fever is not a contagious disease. By contagious disease we understand the sort of disease which itself produces the contagion by which it is propagated, and this contagion again produces in another individual the same disease. Smallpox is a contagious disease because smallpox produces the contagion by which smallpox can be reproduced in another individual. Smallpox produces in another individual smallpox and no other disease . . .

Puerperal fever is not a contagious disease, but puerperal fever is conveyable from a sick to a sound puerperal by means of a decomposed animal organic material.

Joseph Lister

The frequency of disastrous consequences in compound fracture, contrasted with the complete immunity from danger to life or limb in simply fracture is one of the most striking as well as melancholy facts in surgical practice.

If we inquire how it is that an external wound communicating with the seat of fracture leads to such grave results, we cannot but conclude that it is by inducing, through access of the atmosphere, decomposition of the blood which is effused in greater or less amount around the fragments and among the interstices of the tissues, and losing by putrefaction its natural bland character, and assuming the properties of an acid irritant, occasions both local and general disturbance.

We know that blood kept exposed to the air at the temperature of the body, in a vessel of glass or other material chemically inert, soon decomposes; and there is no reason to suppose that the living tissues surrounding a mass of extravasted blood could preserve it from being affected in a similar manner by the atmosphere. On the contrary, it may be ascertained as a matter of observation, that, in a compound fracture, twenty-four hours after the accident the colored serum which oozes from the would is already distinctly tainted with the odor of decomposition, and during the next two or three days, before suppuration has set in, the smell of the effused fluids becomes more and more offensive . . .

Turning now to the question how the atmosphere produces decomposition of organic substances, we find that a flood of light has been thrown upon this most important subject by the philosophic researches of M. Pasteur, who has demonstrated by thoroughly convincing evidence that it is not to its oxygen or to any of its gaseous constituents that the air owes this property, but to minute particles suspended in it, which are the germs of various low forms of life, long since revealed by the microscope, and regarded as merely accidental concomitants of putrescence, but now shown by Pasteur to be its essential cause, resolving the complex organic compounds into substances of simpler chemical constitution, just as the yeast plant converts sugar into alcohol and carbonic acid . . .

Applying these principles to the treatment of compound fracture, bearing in mind that it is from the vitality of the atmospheric particles that all the mischief arises, it appears that all that is requisite is to dress the wound with some material capable of killing these septic germs, provided that any substance can be found reliable for this purpose, yet not too potent as a caustic . . .

My attention having for several years been much directed to the subject of suppuration, more especially in its relation to decomposition, I saw that such a powerful antiseptic was peculiarly adapted for experiments with a view to elucidating that subject, and while I was engaged in the investigation the applicability of carbolic acid for the treatment of compound fracture naturally occurred to me.

My first attempt of this kind was made in the Glasgow Royal Infirmary in March 1865, in a case of compound fracture of the leg. It proved unsuccessful, in consequence, as I now believe, of improper management; but subsequent trials have more than realized my most sanguine anticipations . . .

Case 2. Patrick F—, a healthy laborer, aged 32, had his right tibia broken on the afternoon of the 11th of September, 1865, by a horse kicking him with its full force over the anterior edge of the bone about its middle. He was at once taken to the infirmary, where Mr. Miller, the house surgeon in charge, found a wound measuring about an inch by a quarter of an inch, from which blood was welling profusely.

He put up the fracture in pasteboard splints, leaving the wound exposed between their anterior edges, and dressing it with a piece of lint dipped in carbolic acid, large enough to overlap the sound skin about a quarter of an inch in every direction. In the evening, he changed the lint for another piece, also dipped in carbolic acid, and covered this with oiled paper. I saw the patient the next day, and advised the daily application of a bit of lint soaked in carbolic acid over the oiled paper; and this was done for the next five days. On the second day there was an oozing of red fluid from beneath the dressing, but by the third day this had ceased entirely. On the fourth day, when, under ordinary circumstances, suppuration would have made its appearance, the skin had a nearly natural aspect, and there was no increase in swelling, while the uneasiness he had previously felt was almost entirely absent. His pulse was 64, and his appetite improving. On the seventh day, though his general condition was all that could be wished, he complained again of some uneasiness, and the skin about the still adherent crust of blood, carbolic acid, and lint was found to be visicated, apparently in consequence of the irritation of the carbolic acid. From the seventh day the crust was left untouched till the eleventh day, when I removed it, disclosing a concave surface destitute of granulation, and free from suppuration. Water dressing was now applied, and by the sixteenth day the entire sore, with the exception of one small spot where the bone was bare, presented a healthy granulating aspect, the formation of pus being limited to the surface of the granulations.

CASE STUDY

Plate Tectonics

On pages 348–365, read the account of the emergence of plate tectonics, a revolutionary geological theory that arose in the mid-20th century. What aspects of this case fit or do not fit the fallibalist (Laudanian) or technologist (Pittian) models of scientific change? For example, are there identifiable rival research traditions? What are the empirical and conceptual problems to be solved? Are there identifiable elements of a technological infrastructure? In what ways is the revolution a result of technological matters?

Further Reading

Hacking, Ian (ed.). *Scientific Revolutions.* Oxford: Oxford University Press, 1981.

Laudan, Larry. *Progress and Its Problems.* Berkeley: University of California Press, 1977.

Laudan, Larry. *Science and Values.* Berkeley: University of California Press, 1983.

Laudan, Larry. *Science and Relativism: Some Key Controversies in the Philosophy of Science.* Chicago: University of Chicago Press, 1990.

Laudan, Larry. *Beyond Positivism and Relativism: Theory, Method, and Evidence.* Boulder: Westview Press, 1996.

Pitt, Joseph C. *Pictures, Images, and Conceptual Schemes.* Dordrecht: D. Reidel, 1981.

Pitt, Joseph C. *Galileo, Human Knowledge and the Book of Nature: Method Replaces Metaphysics.* Dordrecht: Kluwer, 1991.

Pitt, Joseph C. *Thinking About Technology: Foundations of the Philosophy of Technology.* New York: Seven Bridges Press, 2000.

Price, Derek de Solla. *Big Science, Little Science.* New York: Columbia University Press, 1963.

CASE STUDY

Plate Tectonics

A major change in how geologists understand the world came about in the second half of the 20th century: plate tectonics. It has tremendous explanatory power and provides geologists with far greater predictive power than they had prior to their embracing of this view. In a nutshell, plate tectonics is the view that the earth's crust is constituted, in large part, by a collection of plates. These vast plates slowly move horizontally, caring the continents (or, at least parts of them). While the notion of continental drift was postulated and argued for, especially by Alfred Wegener, at the beginning of the 20th century, this view is not the same as plate tectonics. Wegener's views were regarded as highly controversial and were rejected by most geologists for decades. The related, but far fuller view of plate tectonics, emerged in the 1960s and within just a decade or two had dramatically transformed how geologists looked at the earth and its history. The two readings below provide synoptic detail of the history of plate tectonics and reflect on its scientific and philosophical significance. Consider how plate tectonics, which today nearly all geologists characterize as a revolution, not a mere refinement, in our geological understanding of the world, fits or does not fit with the models of scientific change discussed in Chapters Eight, Nine, and Ten (i.e., inductivism, Popper, Kuhn, Lakatos, Laudan, and Pitt). The readings below are by, first, Stephen Jay Gould and, second, Henry Frankel.

EVER SINCE DARWIN

Stephen Jay Gould

As the new Darwinian orthodoxy swept through Europe, its most brilliant opponent, the aging embryologist Karl Ernst von Baer, remarked with bitter irony that every triumphant theory passes through three stages: first it is dismissed as untrue; then it is rejected as contrary to religion; finally, it is accepted as dogma and each scientist claims that he had long appreciated its truth.

I first met the theory of continental drift when it labored under the inquisition of stage two. Kenneth Caster, the only major American paleontologist who dared to support it openly, came to lecture at my alma mater,

Antioch College. We were scarcely known as a bastion of entrenched conservatism, but most of us dismissed his thoughts as just this side of sane. (Since I am now in von Baer's third stage, I have the distinct memory that Caster sowed substantial seeds of doubt in my own mind.) A few years later, as a graduate student at Columbia University, I remember the a priori derision of my distinguished stratigraphy professor toward a visiting Australian drifter. He nearly orchestrated the chorus of Bronx cheers from a sycophantic crowd of loyal students. (Again, from my vantage point in the third stage, I recall this episode as amusing, but distasteful.) As a tribute to my professor, I must record that he experienced a rapid conversion just two years later and spent the remaining years joyously redoing his life's work.

Today, just ten years later, my own students would dismiss with even more derision anyone who denied the evident truth of continental drift—a prophetic madman is at least amusing; a superannuated fuddy-duddy is merely pitiful. Why has such a profound change occurred in the short space of a decade?

Most scientists maintain—or at least argue for public consumption—that their profession marches toward truth by accumulating more and more data, under the guidance of an infallible procedure called "the scientific method." If this were true, any question would have an easy answer. The facts, as known ten years ago, spoke against continental drift; since then, we have learned more and revised our opinions accordingly. I will argue, however, that this scenario is both inapplicable in general and utterly inaccurate in this case.

During the period of nearly universal rejection, direct evidence from continental drift—that is, the data gathered from rocks exposed on our continents—was every bit as good as it is today. It was dismissed because no one had devised a physical mechanism that would permit continents to plow through an apparently solid oceanic floor. In the absence of a plausible mechanism, the idea of continental drift was rejected as absurd. The data that seemed to support it could always be explained away. If these explanations sounded contrived or forced, they were not half so improbable as the alternative—accepting continental drift. During the past ten years, we have collected a new set of data, this time from the ocean basins. With these data, a heavy dose of creative imagination, and a better understanding of the earth's interior, we have fashioned a new theory of planetary dynamics. Under this theory of plate tectonics, continental drift is an inescapable consequence. The old data from continental rocks, once soundly rejected, have been exhumed and exalted as conclusive proof of drift. In short, we now accept continental drift because it is the expectation of a new orthodoxy.

I regard this tale as typical of scientific progress. New facts, collected in old ways under the guidance of old theories, rarely lead to any substantial revision of thought. Facts do not "speak for themselves"; they are read in the light of theory. Creative thought, in science as much as in the arts, is the motor of changing opinion. Science is a quintessentially human activity, not a mechanized robotlike accumulation of objective information, leading by laws of logic to inescapable interpretation. I will try to illustrate this thesis with two examples drawn from the "classical" data for continental drift. Both are old tales that had to be undermined while drift remained unpopular.

I. The late Paleozoic glaciation. About 240 million years ago, glaciers covered parts of what is now South America, Antarctica, India, Africa, and Australia. If continents are stable, this distribution presents some apparently insuperable difficulties:

A. The orientation of striae in eastern South America indicates that glaciers moved onto the continent from what is now the Atlantic Ocean (striae are scratches on bedrock made by rocks frozen into glacier bottoms as they pass over a surface). The world's oceans form a single system, and transport of heat from tropical areas guarantees that no major part of an open ocean can freeze.

B. African glaciers covered what are now tropical areas.

C. Indian glaciers must have grown in semitropical regions of the Northern hemisphere; moreover, their striae indicate a source in tropical waters of the Indian Ocean.

D. There were no glaciers on any of the northern continents. If the earth got cold enough to freeze tropical Africa, why were there no glaciers in northern Canada or Siberia?

All these difficulties evaporate if the southern continents (including India) were joined together during this glacial period, and located further south, covering the South Pole; the South American glaciers moved from Africa, not an open ocean; "tropical" Africa and "semitropical" India were near the South Pole; the North Pole lay in the middle of a major ocean, and glaciers could not develop in the Northern Hemisphere. Sounds good for drift; indeed, no one doubts it today.

II. The distribution of Cambrian trilobites (fossil arthropods living 500 to 600 million years ago). The Cambrian trilobites of Europe and North America divided themselves into two rather different faunas with the following peculiar distribution on modern maps. "Atlantic" province trilobites lived all over Europe and in a few very local areas on the far eastern border of North America—eastern (but not western) Newfoundland and southeastern Massachusetts, for example. "Pacific" province trilobites lived all over America and in a few local areas on the extreme western coast of Europe—northern Scotland and northwestern Norway, for example. It is devilishly difficult to make any sense of this distribution if the two continents always stood 3,000 miles apart.

But continental drift suggests a striking resolution. In Cambrian times, Europe and North America were separated: Atlantic trilobites lived in waters around Europe; Pacific trilobites lived in waters around America. The continents (now including sediments with entombed trilobites) then drifted toward each other and finally joined together. Later, they split again, but not precisely along the line of their previous junction. Scattered bits of ancient Europe, carrying Atlantic trilobites, remained at the easternmost border of North America, while a few pieces of old North America stuck to the westernmost edge of Europe.

Both examples are widely cited as "proofs" of drift today, but they were soundly rejected in previous years, not because their data were any less complete but only because no one had devised an adequate mechanism to move continents. All the original drifters imagined that continents plow their way through a static ocean floor. Alfred Wegener, the father of continental drift, argued early in [the 20th] century that gravity alone could put continents in motion. Continents drift slowly westward, for example, because attractive forces of the sun and moon hold them up as the earth rotates underneath them. Physicists responded with derision and showed mathematically that gravitational forces are far too weak to power such a monumental peregrination. So Alexis du Toit, Wegener's South African champion, tried a different tack. He argued for a local, radioactive melting of oceanic floor at continental borders, permitting the continents to glide through. This *ad hoc* hypothesis added no increment of plausibility to Wegener's speculation.

Since drift seemed absurd in the absence of a mechanism, orthodox geologists set out to render the impressive evidence for it as a series of unconnected coincidences.

In 1932, the famous American geologist Bailey Willis strove to make the evidence of glaciation compatible with static continents. He invoked the deus ex machina of "isthmian links"—narrow land bridges flung with daring abandon across 3,000 miles of ocean. He placed one between eastern Brazil and western Africa, another from Africa all the way to India via the Malagasy Republic, and a third from Vietnam through Borneo and New Guinea to Australia. His colleague, Yale professor Charles Schuchert, added one from Australia to Antarctica and another from Antarctica to South America, thus completing the isolation of a southern ocean from the rest of the world's waters. Such an isolated ocean might freeze along its southern margin, permitting glaciers to flow across into eastern South America. Its cold waters would also nourish the glaciers of southern Africa. The Indian glaciers, located above the equator 3,000 miles north of any southern ice, demanded a separate explanation. Willis wrote: "No direct connection between the occurrences can reasonably be assumed. The case must be considered on the basis of a general cause and the local geographic and topographic conditions." Willis's inventive mind was equal to the task: he simply postulated a topography so elevated that warm, wet southern waters precipitated their product as snow. For the absence of ice in temperate and arctic zones of the Northern Hemisphere, Willis reconstructed a system of ocean currents that permitted him to postulate "a warm, subsurface current flowing northward beneath cooler surface waters and rising in the Arctic as a warm-water heating system." Schuchert was delighted with the resolution provided by isthmian links:

Grant the biogeographer Holarctis, a land bridge from northern Africa to Brazil, another from South America to Antarctica (it almost exists today), still another from this polar land to Australia and from the latter across the Arafura Sea to Borneo and Sumatra and so on to Asia, plus the accepted means of dispersal along shelf seas and by wind and water currents and migratory birds, and he has all the possibilities needed to explain the life dispersion and the land and ocean realms throughout geological time on the basis of the present arrangement of the continents.

The only common property shared by all these land bridges was their utterly hypothetical status; not an iota of direct evidence supported any one of them. Yet, lest this saga of isthmian links be read as a warped fairy tale invented by dogmatists to support untenable orthodoxy, I point out that to Willis, Schuchert, and any right-thinking geologist of the 1930s, one thing legitimately seemed ten times as absurd as imaginary land bridges thousands of miles long—continental drift itself.

In the light of such highly fertile imagination, the Cambrian trilobites could present no insuperable problem. The Atlantic and Pacific provinces were interpreted as different environments, rather than different places—shallow water for the Pacific, deeper for the Atlantic. With a freedom to invent nearly any hypothetical geometry for Cambrian ocean basins, geologists drew their maps and hewed to their orthodoxy.

When continental drift came into fashion during the late 1960s, the classical data from continental rocks played no role at all: drift rode in on the coattails of a new theory, supported by new types of evidence. The physical absurdities of Wegener's theory rested on his conviction that continents cut their way through the ocean floor. But how else could drift occur? The ocean floor, the crust of the earth, must be stable. After all, where could it go, if it moved in pieces without leaving gaping holes in the earth? Nothing could be clearer. Or could it?

"Impossible" is usually defined by our theories, not given by nature. Revolutionary theories trade in the unexpected. If continents must plow through oceans, then drift will not occur; suppose, however, that continents are frozen into the oceanic crust and move passively as pieces of crust shift about. But we just stated that the crust cannot move without leaving holes. Here, we reach an impasse that must be bridged by creative imagination, not just by another field season in the folded Appalachians—we must model the earth in a fundamentally different way.

We can avoid the problem of holes with a daring postulate that seems to be valid. If two pieces of ocean floor move away from each other, they will leave no hole if material rises from the earth's interior to fill the gap. We can go further by reversing the causal implications of this statement: the rise of new material from the earth's interior may be the driving force that moves old sea floor away. But since the earth is not expanding, we must also have regions where old sea floor founders into the earth's interior, thus preserving a balance between creation and destruction.

Indeed, the earth's surface seems to be broken into fewer than ten major "plates," bounded on all sides by narrow zones of creation (oceanic ridges) and destruction (trenches). Continents are frozen into these plates, moving with them as the sea floor spreads away from the zones of creation at oceanic ridges. Continental drift is no longer a proud theory in its own right; it has become a passive consequence of our new orthodoxy—plate tectonics.

We now have a new mobilist orthodoxy, as definite and uncompromising as the staticism it replaced. In its light, the classical data for drift have been exhumed and proclaimed as proof positive. Yet these data played no role in validating the notion of wandering continents; drift triumphed only when it became the necessary consequence of a new theory.

The new orthodoxy colors our vision of all data; there are no "pure facts" in our complex world. About five years ago, paleontologists found on Antarctica a fossil reptile named *Lystrosaurus*. It also lived in South Africa, and probably in South America as well (rocks of the appropriate age have not been found in South America). If anyone had floated such an argument for drift in the presence of Willis and Schuchert, he would have been howled down—and quite correctly. For Antarctica and South America are almost joined by a string of islands, and they were certainly connected by a land bridge at various times in the past (a minor lowering of sea level would produce such a land bridge today). *Lystrosaurus* may well have walked in comfort, on a rather short journey at that. Yet the *New York Times* wrote an editorial proclaiming on this basis along, that continental drift had been proved.

Many readers may be disturbed by my argument for the primacy of theory. Does it not lead to dogmatism and disrespect for facts? It can, of course, but it need not. The lesson of history holds that theories are overthrown by rival theories, not that orthodoxies are unshakable. In the meantime, I am not distressed by the crusading zeal of plate tectonics, for two reasons. My intuition, culturally bound to be sure, tells me that it is basically true. My guts tell me that it's damned exciting—more than enough to show that conventional science can be twice as interesting as anything invented by all the von Dänikens and in all the Bermuda triangles of this and previous ages of human gullibility.

THE NON-KUHNIAN NATURE OF THE RECENT REVOLUTION IN THE EARTH SCIENCES

Henry Frankel

Prior to the acceptance of plate tectonics twentieth century geoscientists attacked and solved problems from competing and contrasting traditions. These traditions may be aptly labeled "fixism" and "mobilism." Fixists denied the possibility of any relative horizontal displacement of the continents, and utilized only vertical movements to account for various geological phenomena. Mobilists proposed large scale horizontal displacements of the continents and argued that belief in such displacements provided solutions to various problems falling within the general domain of the earth sciences. Plate tectonics constitutes the latest and most successful version of mobilism, while Alfred Wegener's continental drift theory, originally proposed in 1912, was the major version of mobilism during the first part of [the twentieth] century. This tradition underwent substantial change throughout its evolution into plate tectonics, and eventually became dominant in the later half of the [nineteen] sixties. Prior to acceptance of plate tectonics and its immediate predecessor, seafloor spreading, there were relatively few mobilists. Fixism held sway within the geological community. At present few major geologists are fixists. Mobilism, in the form of plate tectonics, is espoused in various degrees by most practicing earth scientists—there are presently as few fixists as there once were mobilists . . .

Although two Americans, Howard Baker and Frank Taylor, developed versions of mobilism, Alfred Wegener was the first person to propose an extensive version of mobilism, namely, his theory of continental drift. His first extensive presentation of his theory occurred in 1915 with the publication of his *Die Entstehung der Kontinente und Ozeane* [*The Origin of Continents and Oceans*]. The basic tenets of Wegener's theory are easily summarized. He regarded the continents as ships of light sialic material floating upon a heavier basaltic material which formed the ocean floor. He claimed that the continents underwent horizontal displacement by ploughing through the denser basaltic ocean floor. During the Carboniferous Period all the continents were united together forming a supercontinent which he labeled "Pangea." Pangea began to split apart during Late

Cretaceous or Early Tertiary. By the Eocene North and South America had broken away from Europe and Africa, opening up the Atlantic Ocean, and Asia had moved away from Antarctica and southern Africa by migrating northward and rotating counterclockwise. By the beginning of the Quaternary Australia finally split off from Antarctica, the Americas continued to migrate westward, and Asia kept drifting and rotating.

Wegener argued that his version of mobilism offered solutions to the following empirical problems:

1. Why the contours of the coastlines of eastern South America and western Africa fit together so well, and why there were many similarities between the respective coastlines of North American and Europe. Here his solution was simply to postulate that the continents had originally been one landmass.

2. Why there were numerous geological similarities between Africa and South America, and others between North America and Europe. Wegener had appealed to similarities in the Cape mountains of South Africa and the sierras of Buenos Aires, numerous similarities in the huge gneiss plateaux of Brazil and Africa and the pleistocene terminal moraines. He also spoke of the continuity of the three major systems of folds between North America and Europe, viz., the Armorican, Caledonian and Algonkian, so as to extend his thesis to North American and Europe. Finally, Wegener cited similarities in the geological structure of India, Antarctica, Australia, New Zealand and New Guinea, in an attempt to show that his version of mobilism accounted for many geological problems. Again Wegener simply argued that the previous joining of the continents solved the problems.

3. Why the paleontological record indicated that many plant and animal species had lived in both South America and Africa prior to the Paleozoic and why the record also indicated that the presence of similar species decreased enormously after the Paleozoic. Here Wegener argued that the problem could be solved by supposing that the continents had been joined prior to the Paleozoic and then had subsequently separated. Wegener also argued that the evidence in favor of his drift theory was enhanced by the fact that it solved problems (1) through (3) with respect to South America and Africa.

4. Why mountain ranges were usually located along the coast lines of continents, and why orogenic regions were long and narrow in shape. Wegener argued that mountain ranges form on the leading edge of a drifting continent as the sialic edge is compressed and folded due to the resistance of the simatic ocean floor. Moreover, he argued that the Himalayas, which are not located along a coastline, had formed when India had slid into and under Asia.

5. Why the earth's crust exhibited two basic elevations, one corresponding to the elevation of the continental tables, the other to the ocean floors. Wegener claimed that "there simply were at one time two undisturbed primal levels" which have remained relatively unchanged, since, according to his theory the major diastrophic disturbances were horizontal rather than vertical.

6. How to account for the Permo-Carboniferous moraine deposits found in South Africa, Argentina, southern Brazil, India and in western, central, and eastern Australia. Wegener's solution was simply to suppose that the respective continents had been united during the Permo-Carboniferous and that there had been an extensive icecap during that period.

Wegener also argued that many of the above-mentioned solutions were superior to those solutions proposed by various fixist theories. The major thrust of Wegener's argument centered around his claim that competing theories either had solutions saddled with conceptual problems or no solution at all. Those fixists who hypothesized the existence of former landbridges to account for the paleontological similarities had an enormous conceptual problem, namely, that there was no known mechanism for the subsequent sinking of the postulated landbridges once they had served as migratory routes which was consistent with the principle of isostasy. While those theorists who rejected the previous existence of landbridges as a solution to the paleontological problems, because of incompatibility with the isostasy principle, had no solution whatsoever.

Wegener admitted that his own theory was faced with a conceptual problem for which he offered tentative solutions and attempted to play down its importance. The problem in Wegener's terms was that there was no known force sufficient to propel the continents such vast distances through the ocean floor. Given the views concerning the rigidity of the earth, Wegener had to propose some mechanism for the drifting of the continents, or at least show it was possible, for the continents to move through the seafloor. He suggested two mechanisms which might be responsible for the horizontal displacement, namely, tidal and pole-flight force. *Pohlflucht* is a differential gravitational force due to the elliptical shape of the earth. The centrifugal force would cause the continents to move away from the center of the earth. Thus, the continents would supposedly flee from the poles, since the equatorial radius of the earth is larger than the polar radius. Tidal force, on the other hand, was taken by Wegener to provide the requisite westward drift of the continents. These tidal forces were actually stresses brought about by the gravitational action of the sun and the moon. Wegener claimed that these tidal stresses, which slowed the earth's diurnal eastward motion, would act most strongly on the surface of the earth. As a result, their action would lead to a slow sliding motion of the whole crust or of the individual continental block" in a westward direction. In addition, Wegener, in his 1929 edition of *The Origin of Continents and Oceans*, attempted to ameliorate the seriousness of the mechanism objection.

> The Newton of drift theory has not yet appeared. His absence need cause no anxiety; the theory is still young and still often treated with suspicion. In the long run, one cannot blame a theoretician for hesitating to spend time and trouble on explaining a law about whose validity no unanimity prevails. It is probable, at any rate, that the complete solution of the problem of the drifting forces will still be along time coming, for it means the unraveling of a whole tangle of interdependent phenomena where it is often hard to distinguish what is cause and what is effect. (Page 167)

The reception of Wegener's mobilism was extremely unfavorable. Only a few geologists, albeit some prestigious ones, endorsed the theory; most geologists were and remained fixists. Indeed, the unfavorable reception of Wegener's theory by most participants at the first international meeting on mobilism, The American Association of Petroleum Geologists' 1926 meeting organized by Van der Gracht, was typical. Most of the participants were fixists, and argued that the overall problem-solving effectiveness of mobilism was much less than that of fixism. In general, the substantive aspects of the criticisms were of three varieties. First, critics argued that some of the empirical problems Wegener had solved were merely pseudo-problems. Second, opponents argued that their own theories provided equally as good or better solutions to some of the empirical problems. Third, and most important, critics argued that the conceptual problem of finding a mechanism for the drifting of continents compatible with the estimated rigidity of the earth was insurmountable. In short, critics argued that Wegener had grossly overestimated the problem-solving effectiveness of his version of mobilism; that it created more difficulties than it solved. This third objection was the most serious. There were, I believe, several reasons why it carried so much weight. The mechanism problem was directed at part of the [very center] of Wegener's theory, namely, that the continents had displaced themselves horizontally by ploughing through the seafloor. This idea was at the heart of Wegener's theory; it served as a crucial premise in every one of his empirical solutions except the one concerning the two basic elevations of the earth's crust. A central aspect of the fixist tradition was the denial of any lengthy horizontal movement of the continents because of the conceptual difficulties such a supposition presented. The mechanism objection was actually more extensive than first suggested by Wegener. Wegener originally viewed the problem as simply finding forces of sufficient strength to propel the continents, but critics were quick to claim that the problem also concerned, among other things, whether the continents could survive such vast movements without crumbling, regardless of whether there were sufficient forces to propel them.

Other versions of mobilism made their appearance from the late teens throughout the twenties and thirties. Emile Argand was an early defender of Wegener's drift. In his initial defense of Wegener's position in 1916, he stressed the superiority of Wegener's theory to account for the similarity of fauna and flora in regions presently separated by vast oceans, and argued that it had the best solution to the problem of the Permo-Carboniferous Icecap. Then, he greatly expanded his defense of mobilism in his opening address of 1922 before the XIIth International Geological Congress in Brussels, and in 1924 published his own version of mobilism, *Tectonics of Asia*, in the proceedings of the Congress. Argand, a first-rate structural geologist, greatly improved upon Wegener's solutions to orogenic problems through offering a more detailed account of the formation of mountain ranges and island festoons. He stressed the mobilist requirement of an extremely plastic sima and drew out the orogenic consequences of such a requirement. He admitted that "almost nothing is known about the forces responsible for continental drift," remained judiciously silent about tidal and pole-flight forces, but spoke of "passive transport of the sial by currents of the sima" and made passing reference to various internal forces. In 1923 John Joly argued that tidal and pole-flight forces were, *ceteris paribus*, too weak to displace the continents through the ocean floor. But, he suggested that the seafloor might on occasion weaken from the release of heat caused by radioactivity at which time the combined action of tidal and precessional forces might propel the continents. In 1937, Alex Du Toit, a South African geologist, presented an alternative history for the breakup of the continents, and attempted to correct many of Wegener's mistakes in outlining the geological similarities between Africa and South America. Arthur Holmes in 1928 and later in 1931 presented a detailed alternative version of mobilism which was designed to circumvent the "mechanism" problem. During the late teens and early twenties Holmes had become disenchanted with the contractionist variant of fixism primarily because the abundance of radioactivity in the earth's crust and upper mantle provided too much heat for the earth to contract from cooling. Holmes, impressed with the ability of mobilism to solve the above-mentioned empirical problems—especially the one concerned with the Permo-Carboniferous Icecap—developed an alternative version of mobilism. In his view the continents were displaced by convection currents fueled by heat generated through radioactivity. Moreover, Holmes' version of mobilism did not require that the continent plough their way through the seafloor. Rather, his proposal, which we may call "seafloor stretching," had the continents separate from one another as a rising limb of a convection cell turned along the horizontal and stretched out the simatic layer of the crust and upper mantle, i.e., the seafloor. Consequently, the continents did not plough their way through the seafloor but were carried along with it. Holmes' proposal had little effect on the acceptability of mobilism for most earth scientists. For example, Harold Jeffreys, one of the most vehement opponents of mobilism as well as a major proponent of fixism, argued that although Holmes's mobilism was not an impossibility, the chances of the appropriate convection currents arising was extremely unlikely.

During the forties mobilism gained few advocates. Wegener and Argand respectively died in 1930 and 1940, and Holmes, Du Toit and a few others continued to support the tradition. In contrast, fixists had developed solutions to many of the problems solved by mobilism, and did not face any problems as serious as the mechanism problem that plagued the mobilist tradition. Bailey Willis, for example, had already provided fixists with alternative solutions to the problems of Permo-Carboniferous glaciation and the presence of similar flora and fauna in regions separated by vast oceans. Harold Jeffreys expanded his contractionist version of fixism, and provided fixists with sophisticated solutions to problems concerned with mountain formation and other geophysical phenomena. Other fixists like Vening Meinesz, Ph. Kuenen, J. Umbgrove and the young Harry Hess proposed and developed an alternative version of fixism. They postulated the existence of convection currents in the earth's mantle, and argued that such convection currents offered solutions to problems connected with island arc formation, mountain range formation, and the evolution of island arcs into mountain ranges. Both these fixist alternatives found more support than mobilism, and they continued to attract proponents well into the late fifties and throughout the sixties. In 1944 the status of mobilism was especially poor. Bailey Willis argued that mobilism should be leveled the deathblow since it was an obstruction to knowledge, and an apparent confirmation of the westward drift by the Danish Geodetic Institute was shown to be incorrect by Longwell. In short, proponents of mobilism weren't greatly improving its problem-solving effectiveness, and mobilism, if anything, lost ground as an acceptable theory among members of the geological community.

Mobilism, however, had a resurgence in the fifties through its ability to offer solutions to empirical problems arising from paleomagnetic and oceanographic studies. The initial work led to an international symposium held in 1956 arranged by S.W. Carey at the University of Tasmania. Carey, a strong advocate for continental drift, presented his own version of mobilism wherein he argued for an expanding earth, and used such an hypothesis as a solution to the recalcitrant mechanism problem. Then, in 1960, Harry Hess presented his own version of mobilism, labeled by Dietz as "seafloor spreading." Hess's seafloor spreading offered solutions to numerous problems which arose through empirical studies in oceanography and paleomagnetism, but the geological community did not accept seafloor spreading until the late sixties.

Hess proposed that the seafloor was created at midocean ridges, spread out toward the trenches, and then descended into the mantle. He then related his model for seafloor spreading to mobilism by suggesting that the continents were carried along by the spreading seafloor.

> . . . a continent's leading edges are strongly deformed when they impinge upon the downward moving limbs of convecting mantle . . . [that] Rising limbs coming up from under continental areas move the fragmented parts away from one another at a uniform rate so a truly median ridge forms as in the Atlantic Ocean . . . [and that] The cover of oceanic sediments and the volcanic seamounts also ride down into the jaw crusher of the descending limb, are metamorphosed, and eventually probably are welded onto continents.

And

> Paleomagnetic data presented by Runcorn (1959), Irving (1959) and others strongly suggest that the continents have moved by large amounts in geologically comparatively recent times. One may quibble over the details but the general picture on paleomagnetism is sufficiently compelling that it is much more reasonable to accept it than to disregard it . . . . This strongly indicates independent movement in direction and amount of large portions of the Earth's surface with respect to the rotational axis. This could be most easily accomplished by a convecting mantle system which involves actual movement of the Earth's surface passively riding on the upper part of the convecting cell.

In addition, Hess claimed that his version of mobilism avoided the recalcitrant mechanism problems.

> The mid-ocean ridges could represent the traces of the rising limbs of convection cells while the circum-Pacific belt of deformation and volcanism represents the descending limbs. The Mid-Atlantic Ridge is median because the continental areas on each side of it have moved away from it at the same rate . . . . This is not exactly the same as continental drift. The continents do not plow through oceanic crust impelled by unknown forces, rather they ride passively on mantle material as it comes to the surface at the crest of the ridge and then moves laterally away from it.

It is beyond question that Hess's proposal related together a vast variety of data, and thereby turned much puzzling data into solved problems. His model of seafloor spreading made sense of such items as the following: the median position of the ridges, the occurrence of shallow earthquakes along the ridges, the high temperature of the ridges, and their apparent ephemeral nature, the negative gravity anomalies along the trenches, their cold temperature, and the occurrence of intermediate and deep earthquakes at trench sites, apparent transcurrent faulting off the California coast, the uniform thickness of the bottom crustal layer, and the widening of fracture zones along the Mid-Atlantic Ridge as it crossed Iceland.

Despite the explanatory success of Hess's proposal, initially it gained few advocates. Part of the reason why the geological community—even the community of geophysicists and oceanographers working on the same set of problems solved by Hess—did not accept it at the time it was proposed was because there were fixist alternative solutions that explained much of the data. Maurice Ewing, head of the Lamont Institute (now Lamont-Doherty) at Columbia, that had supplied Hess with much of the oceanographic data, proposed a fixist alternative solution to the formation of the oceanic ridges. His hypothesis utilized convection currents but did not involve seafloor spreading or continental drift. Tuzo Wilson, who later became a major proponent of mobilism, proposed in the late fifties an improved version of contractionism that accounted for much of the new oceanographic data. In addition, many geophysicists argued that the paleomagnetic data which indicated horizontal displacement of the continents was either unreliable or subject to fixist interpretation, while several respected oceanographers argued that the newly discovered thinness of seafloor sediment deposits indicated highly compacted sediment as opposed to a lack of sediment.

Hess's seafloor spreading hypothesis spawned two auxiliary hypotheses: the Vine-Matthews-Morley hypothesis and the Wilson transform fault hypothesis. Both of these hypotheses were virtually corollaries of Hess's seafloor spreading hypothesis. Confirmation of the former was the central event which led to the dramatic shift of the overall geological community from endorsement of fixism to pursuit and outright acceptance of mobilism, while elaboration and confirmation of the latter led directly to the development of plate tectonics. In 1963 Vine, Matthews and Morley suggested that, *ceteris paribus*, if seafloor spreading were occurring then there would be strips of seafloor material having reversed polarity spreading out systematically and parallel to the ridges. They also linked their hypothesis with seafloor spreading. Vine and Matthews argued that it

> is consistent with, in fact virtually a corollary of, current ideas on ocean floor spreading and periodic reversals inn the Earth's magnetic field. If the main crustal layer (Seismic layer 3) of the oceanic crust is formed over a convection upcurrent in the mantle at the centre of an oceanic ridge, it will be magnetized in the current direction of the Earth's field. Assuming impermanence of the ocean floor, the whole of the oceanic crust is comparatively young, probably not older than 150 million years, and the thermo-remanent component of its magnetization is therefore either essentially normal, or reversed with respect to the present field of the Earth. Thus, if spreading of the ocean floor occurs, blocks of alternately normal and reversely magnetized material would drift away from the centre of the ridge and parallel to the crest of it.

When Vine, Matthews and Morley introduced their hypothesis, there was not enough analyzed data available to test it. The first profiles by Lamont personnel were taken off the Mid-Atlantic Ridge, and the interpretation of the profiles was taken to be inconsistent with Vine-Matthews-Morley. But, by the end of 1966, analyses of several profiles from the Pacific-Antarctic Ridge—especially Eltanin-19—and the Reykjanes Ridge supplied the confirmatory data. Walter Pitman, the person primarily responsible for the cleanest profile, Eltanin-19, has said the following:

> It hit me like a hammer . . . . In retrospect, we were lucky to strike a place where there are no hindrances to sea-floor spreading. We don't get profiles quite that perfect from any other place. There were no irregularities to distract or deceive us. That was good, because by then people had been shot down an awful lot over sea-floor spreading. I had thought Vine and Matthews was a fairly dubious hypothesis at the time, and Fred Vine had told me he was wholly convinced of his own theory until he saw Eltanin-19. It does grab you. It looks very just like the way a profile ought to look and never does. On the other hand, when another man here saw it his remark was "Next thing, you'll be proving Vine and Matthews."

This particular profile, Eltanin-19, convinced most personnel at Lamont that Hess's version of mobilism was worthy of concentrated pursuit, if not outright acceptance. The data from the Atlantic which had been taken to be inconsistent with Vine-Matthews-Morley was reinterpreted in light of Eltanin-19, and it was now seen to be consistent with the general idea of seafloor spreading. In addition, seismologists at Lamont, excited about Eltanin-19, turned to their data to determine if they could find support for Tuzo Wilson's work on transform faults, which like Vine-Matthews-Morley was a virtual corollary of Hess's mobilism.

In 1965 Tuzo Wilson, beginning with the notion of seafloor spreading, reasoned that the faulting which would occur if seafloor spreading takes place should be transform rather than transcurrent. He described transform faults in the following terms:

> Faults in which the displacement suddenly stops or changes form and direction are not true transcurrent faults. It is proposed that a separate class of horizontal shear faults exist which terminate abruptly at both ends, but which nevertheless may show great displacements . . . . The name transform fault is proposed for the class . . . The distinctions between (transform and transcurrent faults) might appear trivial until the variation in habit of growth of the different types is considered . . . . These distinctions are that ridges expand to produce new crust, thus leaving residual inactive traces in the topography of their former positions. On the other hand oceanic crust moves down under island arcs absorbing old crust so that they leave no traces of past positions.

Moreover, he explicitly linked his hypothesis with mobilism.

> Transform faults cannot exist unless there is crustal displacement and their existence would provide a powerful argument in favor of continental drift and a guide to the nature of the displacement involved.

Once Vine-Matthews-Morley was confirmed, seismologists at Lamont, who had seen the confirmatory profiles and were quite impressed with their quality, set out to test Wilson's hypothesis. They obtained their confirmatory results in 1967.

The central notions of plate tectonics, that the earth's surface is made of rigid crustal blocks, that the blocks are created at ridges, destroyed at trenches and move along transform faults, and that the continents ride passively atop these crustal blocks, came almost directly out of Wilson and Hess.

CHAPTER ELEVEN

Science and Technology

IN THIS CHAPTER, WE WILL

- Examine different views on the nature of the relationship between science and technology

- Identify some metaphysical, epistemological, and axiological issues related to technology

- Consider various claims about some important epistemological and axiological issues related to technology

We saw in Chapter Ten that Joseph Pitt argues that change and progress in science has been, and increasingly is, the result of advances in technology. Indeed, science today seems inconceivable without the use of computers and countless other sophisticated technological implements, devices, tools, and equipment. The connection between science and technology seems to most people so close that when asked about the basic and most important ways in which science affects their lives, most people mention things like computers, cell phones, automobiles, airplanes, perhaps nuclear weapons, and so on. That is, they mention technology! (They do not mention things like relativity theory, plate tectonics, cell theory, etc., i.e., major scientific theories that have altered our scientific view and understanding of the world.) Nevertheless, when many professional scientists are asked about what they do, they often emphasize that they are scientists, not engineers or technicians. The favor is returned by many engineers and technicians; they duly note that they are not scientists. Just what is the nature of the relationship between science and technology? That is the focus of this chapter and we will see, from a philosophy of

science perspective that the nature of this relationship has—
you guessed it!—metaphysical, epistemological, and axiological
aspects to it.

Technology

I will begin with a working definition of "technology." This definition is taken from the philosopher Frederick Ferré, who argues
that technology is *practical implementations of intelligence*. (He actually uses the term "technology" to be shorthand for "technologies," because there are many kinds of processes and products that
are technological.) There is quite a bit packed into this short
definition. First, Ferré identifies technology as a species of intelligence, which itself implies that technology is a form of knowledge.
As a form of knowledge, technology is not to be equated with
tools or machines or artifacts or any other material object (though
it often involves them). In addition, it is not simply a form of
knowledge, but it is an intelligence, meaning that technology is
related to thinking agents—and not necessarily human; other animals also engage in intelligent activity—and that it is related to
problem-solving and learning and responding to something outside itself.

Besides technology being a species of intelligence, it is the
practical implementation of that intelligence. As an "implementation," it is embodied in things like tools, machines, artifacts,
and so on (yes, it is those things, but not merely those things), as
well as in abstract things such as social organizations and relationships. As "practical," it is not an end in itself, but is focused
toward achieving some goal; it is a goal-directed activity as much
as a physical apparatus.

This working definition—again, *practical implementations of
intelligence*—carries with it a number of implications. For example, says Ferré, technologies do not necessarily have to be material or physical, though they usually are. Also, technologies are
not necessarily science-based. As we will see, one of the issues
that philosophers of science and of technology focus on is the
relation between science and technology. Ferré claims that
some technologies flow from the discoveries of science, but
some do not.

As noted above, although technology is a species of intelligence, it is not necessarily human intelligence. That is, other animals clearly engage in practical implementations in order to achieve some goal. At a minimal level, there is a large amount of evidence of animals making use of tools, even fashioning tools, in order to cope with their environments. An important corollary to this is, for Ferré, that technology is not at all necessarily unnatural. This is an important issue because many critics of technology claim that technology is the cause of waste and pollution and other ills (e.g., weapons of mass destruction). As such, technology is a human artifact, not a product of nature (that is, unnatural). For Ferré, technologies are natural in some respects and are indeed artifactual in some respects.

Before looking more closely at several philosophical concerns about technology, there are a few preliminary issues to discuss about science and technology. Throughout this book, we have looked at science and aspects of science in terms of content (what science involves), methods (how science proceeds and changes), and aims (why we investigate the things we do and why we use the methods we do in order to investigate those things). Now, many people claim that the content, methods, and aims of science are quite different than those of technology (or, minimally, the content, methods, and aims do not need to be the same). For example, scientists study the evolution of biological species and the life cycle of stars, technologists do not. In terms of methods, although there might be commonalities between science and technology at the "local" level—for instance, both might employ double blind studies—at a broader, more "global" level, science is driven by research programs or research traditions, and so on (the issues covered in the previous three chapters), but technology is not. Likewise, the aim of science, many claim, is a complete, coherent, true model of the world, where the aim of technology is to create ways to control the world (in the sense of building a better mousetrap or washing machine or oven or airplane, and so on). Others disagree that the content, methods, and aims of science and technology are significantly different. Especially given the sources of funding for scientific research, some say, the aims of science are never merely to understand and describe the world, but always in the background (and perhaps not very far in the background) the aim is to control the world for human purposes, particularly the purposes of those who "do" the science (either as researchers or as funders of the research). We will take up that issue of science and society more fully in Chapter Fourteen. The point here is that, when discussing the topic of the relation of science and technology, a major concern is the question of the what, how, and why of each.

There are metaphysical issues related to technology. For example, although you have certainly heard of *artificial intelligence* and questions about just how similar computers are (or can become) to humans, you might be less familiar with the fact that during the past couple of decades there has been an increasing interest in the notion of *artificial life* and asking what types of features or properties of things would be necessary and sufficient for something to be considered living. The expanding field of robotics also reflects a metaphysical aspect of technology.

Technology and knowledge

This chapter, however, will focus on two other topics associated with technology and its relation to science. The first topic is primarily epistemological, the second primarily axiological. The epistemological topic revolves around the notion of technology as knowledge (or, for Ferré, as an intelligence). We will look at two related, although different, views on the epistemological nature of technology. Before turning directly to them, I will mention a long-standing distinction, associated with Aristotle that has been made about types of knowledge. That distinction involves three Greek terms: *theoria, praxis,* and *techné.* Theoria, or theoretical knowledge, is concerned with knowing; praxis, or practical knowledge, is concerned with doing; techné, or technical knowledge, is concerned with making. Theoria, said Aristotle, is aimed at its own sake, that is, it has as its goal understanding. Praxis is aimed at performance, or doing well. Techné aims at production, or knowing how to do something. For Aristotle, these different kinds of knowledge were reflective of different aims and were manifested in different activities. So, theoretical knowledge was associated with activities such as philosophy, theology, mathematics, physics, and so on (the sciences). Practical knowledge was associated with activities such as politics and economics. Technical knowledge was associated with activities such as medicine and architecture (the arts). This triad of types of knowledge reflects a distinction that is still held today by some people, including the first philosopher discussed on the following page, James Feibleman. That distinction is between theoretical, or pure, science (theoria), applied science (praxis), and technology (techné). Not everyone agrees and, in fact, some critics of this view claim that such a view perpetuates the notion that, although technology is obviously value-laden, science is not, because its goal is pure understanding. In the next chapter we will take up more directly the issue of values and science. For now, just note that the epistemological topic of what kind of knowledge technology invokes and embodies is a topic that has value implications. But for the moment, we will turn to the readings.

The first reading is by James Feibleman, the second by I.C. Jarvie. Feibleman argues that although there is a close connection between science and technology (and that connection is closer today than in previous centuries), nevertheless, they are in fact different in terms of aims and results. In a nutshell, says Feibleman, the aim of science is to know and the aim of technology is to do. Where science strives to formulate universal laws, technology strives for empirical generalizations; where science can and does often deal with abstract, idealized objects (e.g., constructing models using frictionless planes or mass points), technology deals with concrete objects in more particularized contexts. Prior to enunciating these differences, Feibleman argues for a distinction between pure science and applied science and then between applied science and technology. Applied science, he says, truly is the application of pure, theoretical science, but technology is not. Both conceptually and historically, technology spawns from a difference source. For example, humans knew how to smelt metals long before they had an understanding of the basic structures revealed in physical chemistry. Applied science, then, is not just another name for technology, says Feibleman, nor even a "middle ground" between (pure) science and technology. It is a form of science and should not be confused with technology. Having drawn these distinctions, he goes on to argue that the two fields of science and technology have an impact of each other and the differences are sometimes (moreso now than before) blurry, but there are differences nonetheless. Here's Feibleman:

PURE SCIENCE, APPLIED SCIENCE, AND TECHNOLOGY: AN ATTEMPT AT DEFINITIONS
James Feibleman

It is not the business of scientists to investigate just what the business of science is. Yet the business of science is in need of investigation. If we are to consider the relations between science and engineering, the relation between pure and applied science will have first to be made very clear; and for this purpose we shall need working definitions. Once stated, these definitions may seem an elaboration of the obvious and an oversimplification. But the elaboration often seems obvious only *after* it has been stated, and the definitions may have to be simple in order to bring out the necessary distinctions.

By *pure science* or *basic research* is meant a method of investigating nature by the experimental method in an attempt to satisfy the need to know. Many activities in pure science are not experimental, as, for instance, biological taxonomy; but it can always be shown that in such cases the activities are ancillary to experiment. In the case of biological taxonomy the classifications are of experimental material. Taxonomy is practiced in other areas where it is not scientific, such as in the operation of libraries.

By *applied science* is meant the use of pure science for some practical human purpose.

Thus science serves two human purposes: to know and to do. The former is a matter of understanding, the latter a matter of action. Technology, which began as an attempt to satisfy a practical need without the use of science, will receive a fuller treatment in a later section.

Applied science, then, is simply pure science applied. But scientific method has more than one end; it leads to explanation and application. It achieves explanation in the discovery of laws, and the laws can be applied. Thus both pure science and applied science have both aims and results. Pure science has as its aim the understanding of nature; it seeks explanations. Applied science has as its aim the control of nature; it has the task of employing the findings of pure science to get practical tasks done. Pure science has as a result the furnishing of laws for application in applied science. And, as we shall learn later in this essay, applied science has as a result the stimulation of discovery in pure science.

Applied science puts to practical human uses the discoveries made in pure science. Whether there would be such a thing as pure science alone is hard to say; there are reasons for thinking that there would be, for pure science has a long history and as we have noted, another justification. There could be technology without science; for millennia, in fact, there was. But surely there could be no applied science without pure science: applied science means just what it says, namely, the application of science, and so without pure science there would be nothing to apply.

Logically, pure science pursued in disregard of applied science seems to be the *sine qua non* [necessary condition] of applied science, while historically the problems toward which applied science is directed came before pure science.

It has been asserted, for instance, that Greek geometry, which is certainly pure, arose out of the interest in land-surveying problems in Egypt, where the annual overflow of the Nile obliterated all conventional boundaries. Certainly it is true that the same concept of infinity is necessary for the understanding of Euclidean geometry and for the division of farms. Be that as it may, it remains true that the relations between pure and applied science are often varied and subtle, and will require exploration . . .

Technology

There has been some misunderstanding of the distinction between applied science and technology; and understandably so, for the terms have not been clearly distinguished. Primarily the difference is one of type of approach. The applied scientist as such is concerned with the task of discovering applications for pure theory. The technologist has a problem which lies a little nearer to practice. Both applied scientist and technologist employ experiment; but in the former case guided by hypotheses deduced from theory, while in the latter case employing trial and error or skilled approaches derived from concrete experience. The theoretical biochemist is a pure scientist, working for the most part with carbon compounds. The biochemist is an applied scientist when he explores the physiological effects of some new drug, perhaps trying it out to being with on laboratory animals, then perhaps on himself or on volunteers from his laboratory of from the charity ward of some hospital. The doctor or practicing physician is a technologist when he prescribes it for some of his patients.

Speaking historically, the achievements of technology are those which developed without benefit of science; they arose empirically either by accident or as a matter of common experience. The use of certain biochemicals in the practice of medicine antedates the development of science: notably, ephedrine, cocaine, curare, and quinine. This is true also of the prescientific forms of certain industrial processes, such as cheese-making, fermentation, and tanning.

The applied scientist fits a case under a class; the technologist takes it from there and works it out, so to speak, *in situ*. Applied science consists in a system of concrete interpretations of scientific propositions directed to some end useful for human life. Technology might now be described as a further step in applied science by means of the improvement of instruments. In this last sense, technology has always been with us; it was vastly accelerated in efficiency by having been brought under applied science as a branch.

Technology is more apt to develop empirical laws than theoretical laws, laws which are generalizations from practice rather than laws which are intuited and then applied to practice. Empirical procedures like empirical laws are often the product of technological practice without the benefit of theory. Since 1938, when Certelli and Bini began to use electrically induced convulsions in the treatment of schizophrenia, the technique of electroshock therapy has been widespread in psychiatric practice. Yet there is no agreement as to what precisely occurs or how the improvement is produced; a theory to explain the practice is entirely wanting . . .

The development of technology has a strong bearing on its situation today and may be traced briefly. It the Middle Ages, there was natural philosophy and craftsmanship. Such science as existed was in the hands of the natural philosophers, and such technology as existed was in the hands of the craftsmen. There was precious little of either, for the exploration of the natural world was conducted by speculative philosophers, while the practical tasks were carried out by handicrafts employing comparatively simple tools, although there were exceptions: the windmill, for instance. There was little commerce between them, however, for their aims were quite different, and the effort to understand the existence of God took precedence over lesser pursuits.

Gradually, however, natural philosophy was replaced by experimental science, and handicraft by the power tool. The separation continued to be maintained, and for the same reasons; and this situation did not change until the end of the eighteenth century. At that time the foundations of technology shifted from craft to science. Technology and applied science ran together into the same powerful channels at the same time that the applications of pure science became more abundant. A craft is learned by the apprentice method; a science must be learned from the study of principles as well as from the practices of the laboratory, and while the practice may come from applied science the principles are those of pure science.

There is now only the smallest distinction between applied science, the application of the principles of pure science, and technology. The methods peculiar to technology: trial and error, invention aided by intuition, have merged with those of applied science: adopting the findings of pure science to the purposes of obtaining desirable practical consequences. Special training is required, as well as some understanding of applied and even pure science. In general, industries are based on manufacturing processes which merely reproduce on a large scale effects first learned and practiced in a scientific laboratory. The manufacture of gasoline, penicillin, electricity, oxygen were never developed from technological procedures, but depended upon work first done by pure scientists. Science played a predominant role in such physical industries as steel, aluminum, and petroleum; in such chemical industries as pharmaceuticals and potash; in such biological industries as medicine and husbandry.

A concomitant development, in which the triumph of pure science over technology shows clear, is the design and manufacture of instruments. The goniometer, for the determination of the refractive index of fluids (used in the chemical industries); the sugar refractometer, for the reading of the percentages by weight of sugar (used in sugar manufacture); the pyrometer, for the measurement of high temperatures (used in the making of electric bulbs and gold and silver utensils); the polarimeter, for ascertaining the amount of sugar in urine (used by the medical profession); these and many others—such as for instance the focometer for studies in the length of objectives, the anomaloscope for color blindness, and the spectroscope for the measurement of wave lengths—are precision instruments embodying principles not available to the technologist working unaided by a knowledge of pure science.

From Practice to Theory

In the course of pursuing practical ends abstract principles of science hitherto unsuspected are often discovered. The mathematical theory of probability was developed because some professional gamblers wished to know the odds of games of chance. Electromagnetics stimulated the development of differential equations, and hydrodynamics function theory. Carnot founded the pure science of thermodynamics as a result of the effort to improve the efficiency of steam and other heat engines. Aerodynamics and atomic physics were certainly advanced more swiftly because of the requirements of war. Air pollution, which accompanies big city "smog," has led a number of physical chemists to investigate the properties of extreme dilution. Hence it is not surprising that many advances in pure science have been made in industrial laboratories: from the Bell Telephone laboratories alone have come the discoveries by Davisson and Germer of the diffraction of electrons, by Jansky of radio astronomy, and by Shannon of information theory . . .

Of course, applied science and technology cannot be independent of pure science, nor can pure science be independent of applied science and technology. The two developments work together and are interwoven. Gilbert discovered that the freely suspended magnetic needle (i.e., the compass) could be a practical aid to navigation at the same time he proposed that perhaps the earth was a gigantic magnet.

Problems which arise in the midst of practical tasks often suggest lines of theoretical inquiry. But there is more. Pragmatic evidence has always been held by logicians to have little standing. A scientific hypothesis needs more support than can be obtained from the practical fact that "it works." For who knows how long it will work or how well? What works best today may not work best tomorrow. A kind of practice which supports one theory may be supplanted by a more efficient kind of practice which supports quite a different theory. Relativity mechanics gives more accurate measurements than Newtonian mechanics. That use does not determine theory can be easily shown. Despite the theoretical success of the Copernican theory as refined and advanced by Kepler, Galileo, and Newton, we have never ceased to use the Ptolemaic conception in guiding our ships or in regulating clocks. However, if the practical success achieved by the application of certain theories in pure science cannot be construed as a proof of their truth, neither can it be evidence of the contradictory: workability is no evidence of falsity, either. Newton is still correct within limits. Practicality suggests truth and supports the evidence in its favor even if offering no final proof. The practical uses of atomic energy do not prove that matter is transformable into energy, but they offer powerful support. Hence, the use of a scientific law in the control of nature constitutes the check of prediction and control.

I.C. Jarvie offers a related, though distinct, view of the epistemological nature of technology. Reflecting the view we noted at the beginning of this chapter that science and technology have different (or, at least, not necessarily the same) aims, Jarvie claims that the aim of science is truth and, ultimately, universal descriptions and explanations of nature, while the aim of technology is effectiveness (building things that work), which are much more environment-specific. In terms of the epistemology of science and technology, Jarvie says that science is concerned with knowledge *that* and technology is concerned with knowledge *how*. (This is similar to, but not quite the same distinction as the theoria/praxis/techné distinction already mentioned.) In Chapter One, a distinction was made between *propositional knowledge,* or knowledge involving the content of some proposition, and *practical knowledge,* or knowledge of how to carry out some practice. This is another way of speaking of knowledge that (i.e., knowledge that some proposition is the case) and knowledge how (i.e., knowing how to do something). Again, Jarvie supports this distinction and claims it applies to science and technology. He follows a discussion of this distinction by addressing the question of whether or not science is just technology in the sense that science is a tool, a tool for predicting (and, hence, controlling) nature. Jarvie's answer to this question is that science is not a tool and, so, is not a form of technology. The reason for this, he says, is that the aim of science is truth, while the aim of technology is effectiveness and the two are not identical. For example, he argues, Newtonian mechanics is not true, but for most human concerns it is effective (since we almost never become involved in speeds approaching the speed of light or in distances approaching light years). Although Newtonian mechanics is just fine in terms of effectiveness for almost all of our concerns, says Jarvie, it would be disastrous for science to be satisfied with "mere" effectiveness. Finally, in a view that many see as controversial, Jarvie claims that in settling scientific questions, nature provides the answers, although in settling technological questions, both nature and society provide the answers. As he puts it: "Whereas science in a way puts the question to nature, technology puts the question both to society and to nature." This is controversial because, as we will discuss much more fully in Chapter Fourteen, many people claim that science also answers to society. Let's let Jarvie speak for himself:

TECHNOLOGY AND THE STRUCTURE OF KNOWLEDGE
Ian Jarvie

It would seem obvious enough that technology is a species of knowledge. Our so called "age of technology" seems to have more of this commodity we can call "technological knowledge" than any previous age or society. One would expect, then, that technology as a species of knowledge would be highly revered, widely studied, and generally well understood in our society. One would think, in fact, that a paper with my title would be no more required than one on "science and the structure of knowledge." This happens not to be so. Technology is *not* generally revered, especially by intellectuals, *not* well understood and studied, and even has its claims to be a species of knowledge disputed. I take it as my task to try to dispel such views. What I shall suggest in the course of what follows is that from one angle technology is only a part of the logical structure of our knowledge; and that from another angle the whole of our knowledge can be regarded as a substructure, as included under technology. Viewed logically, technology is a substructure of knowledge; it is knowledge of what physicists call the "initial conditions." Viewed anthropologically, knowledge is part of man's multiform attempts to adapt to his environment which we call his technology. Resistance to recognition of these facts is fed, I shall suggest, partly by ancient snobbery and partly by sheer mistaken identification of technology with machine technology.

. . . Technology does have somewhat different aims than science, it aims to be effective rather than true—and it can be the one without the other. Yet technology is knowledge of sorts; such know-how as we have tells us about what works in this world. Its position in the structure of knowledge is thus peculiar, because what happens to be effective in our part of the world may be a purely contingent matter and will also depend on what degree of effectiveness we happen to demand of technology. It may be enough for us to say of this drug that it cures this illness 90 percent of the time. We may then feel that we know *that* drug x has a 90 percent effectiveness in curing illness y. We also know *that* it has a failure rate of 10 percent with illness y. The causes of illness y and the reasons drug x cures it may be completely unknown. Some of our drug technology, then, is based on the contingent fact that drug x sometimes cures illness y. Now in much of our medical technology we regard 90 percent effectiveness as very good; if we raise our demand—as we tend to do, human beings never being satisfied— we also make more urgent the question of cause and cure in its pure form. For except in the few cases where we stumble across an 100 percent effective cure by accident, the obvious way to effect an 100 percent cure is to find out the cause of the disease and devise a true cure that deals with that cause in a well-understood and controllable way.

This argument aims to show the sharp differences created by making the aim of an activity effectiveness rather than truth. What is effective may be true, or it may be false—Newtonian celestial mechanics is a very effective navigating tool but has been superceded in science by Einstein's relativistic mechanics—or it may be unknown, as in the case of drug x. Now, because we also value truth, attempts will be made to find out why drug x works as it does, but meanwhile it will go on being good technology, effective 90 percent of the time.

So truth is not the same as effectiveness. And when we talk of knowledge we usually mean knowledge of truth. What I suggest is that knowledge of effectiveness is knowledge of truth, too, even if it is on a different logical level. It is, so to speak, true knowledge of *what* is effective. It is not true knowledge of *why* it is effective; it does not *explain* anything. But it is part and parcel of the whole truth, nevertheless.

. . . science aims at true laws which cover the entire physical world and explain the facts of the case about it. Know-how is knowing what works, how to do things in a small part of that world, with a precision as high as is demanded.

. . . Technology is our tools, invented by the inventor, shown to be possible by the pure scientist, and actually explained by the deductions and calculations of the applied scientist.

Technology, *qua* know-how, *qua* tools, however, cannot be knowledge. A tool is not knowledge. A chisel is not knowledge, nor is a lathe; they are things. Knowing *that* real chisels exist, knowing *how* a chisel can be used, knowing *how* to construct a chisel, *these* may be knowledge, but the chisel itself cannot be so considered. So perhaps those philosophers who have suggested that technology was a "knowing how" rather than a "knowing that" were right after all.

To sum up so far: If technology is tools, or what the inventor invents, or what applied scientists do to show how a theory explains, then it has no place in the structure of knowledge. Such a view may sound odd, but it has often been entertained by philosophers. Some have gone so far as to identify all of science with technology; to say that science itself is no more than a tool or an instrument for predicting and controlling nature. It follows from their view that this tool can make no claim to be knowledge.

. . . The view that technology = science = not making knowledge claims, strikes me as both dangerous and as having some truth in it. The view is dangerous because of the stress in technology on effectiveness. And as we have already seen, effectiveness is by no means coincident with truth. But when we compare the celestial mechanics of Newton and Einstein, the results differ so minutely in so few cases, and the equations of relativity are so much more involved, one wonders whether or not if they were judged by their effectiveness Newton would not still be accepted uncritically. Here lies the danger of pragmatism, that we can go on with a theory because it works, making adjustments here and there and blinding ourselves to the possibility that it is just false and needs to be replaced by a theory in better accord with the facts. Merging technology and science, I would suggest to you, could actually inhibit scientific progress since it would allow only doubts about effectiveness but not doubts about the overall truth of the theory. The grain of truth which I said could be found in the identification of science with technology I will come to at the end. For the moment I think we can separate science from technology by saying the following: the laws of science lay out the boundaries of what is possible, but within these boundaries there are many contingent variations closely connected with technology. What technology does is to explore and explain the fine detail of the facts of our world. This is to take technology as embracing applied science, invention, engineering, and so on . . .

Now while science sets the laws of the physical world, these are quite general laws. Technology, however, is quite specific. Even on the surface of the earth what is good technology in one place is not in another. Technology is what we might call "environment-specific." The technology of house-building in Greenland, Tokyo, and Arizona is quite different because of the different environments. If you consider some of the basic problems technology constantly grapples with, such as food, shelter, and transportation, you will see how the demands that are made on technology and the kinds of solutions it suggests are environment-specific. What is suitable food in Greenland may go bad in hours in Arizona. What will shelter a man in Arizona will not shelter him in a jet airplane, or on the moon. What technology knows is, within the general laws of nature, how to solve these problems of feeding, housing, and sheltering in different parts of the universe. Physics places no barrier to space travel; but our technology is only slowly getting to a point where it can solve all the environment-specific problems of the space environment. Our know-how is only slowly beginning to catch up to this task.

So when I say that technology fills in the fine detail within the framework set by the laws of nature I mean it this way. Technological knowledge is knowledge within the boundary of the circle I have described which coincides with the laws of science. What technology handles within that boundary are the practical problems set it by the society. Whereas science in a way puts the question to nature, technology puts the question both to society and to nature. When a physicist seeks the relationship between mass and energy he does not ask society what it wants the outcome to be. But in technology it is not as simple as that. Ask a traffic engineer to solve the problem of traffic congestion in a city and he will counterquestion: "How far are you prepared to go, how much can you spend?" The asker may be a politician who needs votes and who says, "Don't ask me to ban cars and don't ask me to raise taxes more than a percent or two." Within that limit the engineer goes to work. We all knew traffic is eased if you ban cars. Few of us know that one-way street systems, banning turns, synchronizing chains of stop lights, isolating pedestrians, building flyovers and bypasses could do this until the traffic engineers taught us it was so. They have increased our knowledge, but it is not knowledge of the deepest, in the metaphysical sense of deep, kind. Let me add that this metaphysical sense of "deep" carries, as far as I am concerned, no snobbish overtones. It is not necessarily more difficult, or more worthwhile knowledge: it is simply not knowledge about the structure of the world . . .

Before I come to my final point, I would like to expatiate briefly on the fact that technology is not widely studies and admired by intellectuals. That is, I think, because of the identification of science with knowledge and the identification of technology of grubbing around in the workshop. There is a snobbery about the workshop which is at least as old as the ancient Greeks, and which can be found earlier and even more nakedly expressed in China . . . That this obvious point has not been taken for granted is perhaps explained by the superficial identification of technology with machines . . .

And this brings me to a point I left aside previously. Earlier on, I remarked that the identification of science with technology had a grain of truth in it. That is what I know want to explain. To begin with, we must go back to the argument that a tool, like a chisel, cannot be knowledge. Is this really true? I would suggest that we may be being misled by a word. Certainly a tool like a chisel is not, in addition to being a thing, a piece of knowledge. What about a piece of knowledge, though, isn't it a thing, and can't it also be a tool? $E = mc^2$ is a piece of knowledge, a theory, or an equation, if you like. Is it not also a tool? Did we not use this piece of knowledge to plan and build and calculate the effect of the atomic bomb? Isn't a tool simply something man uses to increase his power over the environment? Isn't in this sense the whole of scientific and even intellectual endeavor an outgrowth of our attempts to cope with our environment by learning about it? Sir Karl Popper, in a beautiful lecture, has suggested this view. Placing us firmly in the struggle for survival in a hostile environment, he sees language and the quest for understanding as superb adapting mechanisms, no longer blind and chance-like like mutations, but controlled and intelligent.

Technology for me, then, is coterminous with our attempts to come to terms with our world; that is, our culture and our society; and, as such, it contains within it both pure tools and all knowledge.

Technology and values

Although Feibleman and Jarvie are primarily concerned with epistemological factors relating to technology (and science), they raise value questions, as well. Indeed, it is the impact of technology on our lives, and the good or bad impact, that concerns most people. There are values *within* technology that technologists especially are concerned with, such as sustainability, cost, reliability, and so on. For most us, though (and for the technologists, too), it is value *about* technology that really matters. In what ways has/does technology improve or worsen our lives? We can all list many good results of technology: warm, dry buildings; electric lights so we do not have to sit in the dark; modes of transportation to move us and products (like food) around quickly and safely; the internet; and so on. Of course, we can all list many bad results of technology, also: pollution, weapons of mass destruction, loss of privacy, and so on.

The following reading, by Emmanuel Mesthene, highlights the relationships among technology, society, and values. Mesthene believes that people have a spectrum of what he labels as "unhelpful" views about technology. These views range from (1) an uncritical sense that technology is an unalloyed blessing, seen as the motor or progress and solution to society's problems to (2) its opposite, that technology is an unmitigated curse, responsible for society's ills and destroying human dignity to (3) technology is "no big deal," it really does not have a deep or long-lasting impact on human history. That being said, Mesthene points out various ways, both positive and negative, in which technology and values intersect: how technology creates change, how society responds to technology and the changes it creates, how technology both challenges current values and causes changes in values.

THE ROLE OF TECHNOLOGY IN SOCIETY
Emmanuel Mesthene

. . . [W]hether modern technology and its effects constitute a subject matter deserving of special attention is largely a matter of how technology is defined. The research studies of the Harvard Program on Technology and Society reflect an operating assumption that the meaning of technology includes more than machines. As most serious investigators have found, understanding is not advanced by concentrating single-mindedly on such narrowly drawn yet imprecise questions as "What are the social implications of computers, or lasers, or space technology?" Society and the influences of technology upon it are much too complex for such artificially limited approaches to be meaningful. The opposite error, made by some, is to define technology too broadly by identifying it with rationality in the broadest sense. The term is then operationally meaningless and unable to support fruitful inquiry.

We have found it more useful to define technology as tools in a general sense, including machines, but also including linguistic and intellectual tools and contemporary analytic and mathematical techniques. That is, we define technology as the organization of knowledge for practical purposes. It is in this broader meaning that we can best see the extent and variety of the effects of technology on our institutions and values. Its pervasive influence on our very culture would be unintelligible if technology were understood as no more than hardware.

It is in the pervasive influence of technology that our contemporary situation seems qualitatively different from that of past societies, for three reasons. (1) Our tools are more powerful than any before. The rifle wiped out the buffalo, but nuclear weapons can wipe out man. Dust storms lay whole regions waste, but too much radioactivity in the atmosphere could make the planet uninhabitable. The domestication of animals and the invention of the wheel literally lifted the burden from man's back, but computers could free him from all need to labor. (2) This quality of finality of modern technology has brought our society, more than any before, to explicit awareness of technology as an important determinant of our lives and institutions. (3) As a result, our society is coming to a deliberate decision to understand and control technology to good social purpose and is therefore devoting significant effort to the search for ways to measure the full range of its effects rather than only those bearing principally on the economy. It is this prominence of technology in many dimensions of modern life that seems novel in our time and deserving of explicit attention.

How Technological Change Impinges on Society

. . . Technological change would appear to induce or "motor" social change in two principle ways. New technology creates new opportunities for men and societies, and it also generates new problems for them. It has both positive and negative effects, and it usually has the two *at the same time and in virtue of each other* . . .

The close relationship between technological and social change itself helps to explain why any given technological development is likely to have both positive and negative effects. The usual sequence is that (1) technological advance creates a new opportunity to achieve some desired goal; (2) this requires (except in trivial cases) alterations in social organization if advantage is to be taken of the new opportunity, (3) which means that the functions of existing social structures will be interfered with, (4) with the result that other goals which were served by the older structures are now only inadequately achieved . . .

How Society Reacts to Technological Change

The heightened prominence of technology in our society makes the interrelated tasks of profiting from its opportunities and containing its dangers a major intellectual and political challenge of our time.

Failure of society to respond to the opportunities created by new technology means that much actual or potential technology lies fallow, that is, not used at all or is not used to its full capacity. This can mean that potentially solvable problems are left unsolved and potentially achievable goals unachieved, because we waste our technological resources or use them inefficiently. A society has at least as much stake in the efficient utilization of technology as in that of its natural or human resources.

There are often good reasons, of course, for not developing or utilizing a particular technology. The mere fact that it can be developed is not sufficient reason for doing so. The costs of development may be too high in the light of the expected benefits, as in the case of the project to develop a nuclear-powered aircraft. Or, a new technological device may be so dangerous in itself or so inimical to other purposes that it is never developed . . .

Containing the Negative Effects of Technology

The kinds and magnitude of the negative effects of technology are no more independent of the institutional structures and cultural attitudes of society than is realization of the new opportunities that technology offers. In our society, there are individuals or individual firms always on the lookout for new technological opportunities, and large corporations hire scientists and engineers to invent such opportunities. In deciding whether to develop a new technology, individual entrepreneurs engage in calculations of expected benefits and expected costs to themselves, and proceed if the former are likely to exceed the latter. Their calculations do not take adequate account of the probable benefits and costs of the new developments to others than themselves or to society generally. These latter are what economists call external benefits and costs.

The external benefits potential in new technology will thus not be realized by the individual developer and will rather accrue to society as a result of deliberate social action, as has been argued above. Similarly with external costs. In minimizing only expected costs to himself, the individual decision maker helps to contain only some of the potentially negative effects of the new technology. The external costs and therefore the negative effects on society at large are not of principle concern to him and, in our society, are not expected to be.

Most of the consequences of technology that are causing concern at the present time—pollution of the environment, potential damage to the ecology of the planet, occupational and social dislocations, threats to the privacy and political significance of the individual, social and psychological malaise—are negative externalities of this kind. They are with us in large measure because it has not been anybody's explicit business to foresee and anticipate them. They have fallen between the stools of innumerable individual decisions to develop individual technologies for individual purposes without explicit attention to what all these decisions add up to for society as a whole and for people as human beings. This freedom of individual decision making is a value that we have cherished and that is built into the institutional fabric of our society. The negative effects of technology that we deplore are a measure of what this traditional freedom is beginning to cost us. They are traceable, less to some mystical autonomy presumed to lie in technology, and much more to the autonomy that our economic and political institutions grant to individual decision making . . .

Technology's Challenge to Values

Despite the practical importance of the techniques, institutions, and processes of knowledge in contemporary society, political decision making and the resolution of social problems are clearly not dependent on knowledge alone. Numerous commentators have noted that ours is a "knowledge" society, devoted to rational decision making and an "end of ideology," but none would deny the role that values play in shaping the course of society and the decisions of individuals. On the contrary, questions of values become more pointed and insistent in a society that organizes itself to control technology and that engages in deliberate social planning. Planning demands explicit recognition of value hierarchies and often brings into the open value conflicts which remain hidden in the more impersonal working of the market . . .

This is another way of pointing to the tension alluded to earlier, between the need for social action based on knowledge on the one hand, and the pull of our traditional values on the other. The increased questioning and reformulation of values . . . coupled with a growing awareness that our values are in fact changing under the impact of technological change, leads many people to believe that technology is by nature destructive of values. But this belief presupposes a conception of values as external and unchanging and therefore tends to confuse the valuable with the stable. The fact that values come into question as our knowledge increases and that some traditional values cease to function adequately when technology leads to changes in social conditions does not mean that values per se are being destroyed by knowledge and technology . . .

Technology as a Cause of Value Change

Technology has a direct impact on values by virtue of its capacity for creating new opportunities. By making possible what was not possible before, it offers individuals and society new options to choose from. For example, space technology makes it possible for the first time to go to the moon or to communicate by satellite and thereby adds those two new options to the spectrum of choices available to society. By adding new options in this way, technology can lead to changes in values in the same way that the appearance of new dishes on the heretofore standard menu of one's favorite restaurant can lead to changes in one's tastes and choices of food. Specifically, technology can lead to value change either (1) by bringing some previously unattainable goal within the realm of choice or (2) by making some values easier to implement than heretofore, that is, by changing the costs associated with realizing them . . .

One example related to the effect of technological change on values is implicit in our concept of democracy. The ideal we associate with the old New England town meeting is that each citizen should have a direct voice in political decisions. Since this has not been possible, we have elected representatives to serve our interests and vote our opinions. Sophisticated computer technology, however, now makes possible rapid and efficient collection and analysis of voter opinion and could eventually provide for "instant voting" by the whole electorate on any issue presented to it via television a few hours before. It thus raises the possibility of instituting a system of direct democracy and gives rise to tensions between those who would be violently opposed to such a prospect and those who are already advocating some system of participatory democracy.

This new technological possibility challenges us to clarify what we mean by democracy. Do we construe it as the will of an undifferentiated majority, as the resultant of transient coalitions of different interest groups representing different value commitments, as the considered judgment of the people's elected representatives, or as by and large the kind of government we actually have in the United States, minus the flaws in it that we would like to correct? By bringing us face to face with such questions, technology has the effect of calling society's bluff and thereby preparing the ground for changes in its values.

In the case where technological change alters the relative costs of implementing different values, it impinges on inherent contradictions in our value system. To pursue the same example, modern technology can enhance the values we associate with democracy. But it can also enhance another American value—that of "secular rationality," as sociologists call it—by facilitating the use of scientific and technical expertise in the process of political decision making. This can in turn further reduce citizen participation in the democratic process. Technology thus has the effect of facing us with contradictions in our value system and of calling for deliberate attention to their resolution . . .

Individual Man in a Technological Age

What do technological change and social and value changes that it brings with it mean for the life of the individual today? It is not clear that the effects are all one-way. For example, we are often told that today's individual is alienated by the vast proliferation of technical expertise and complex bureaucracies, by a feeling of impotence in the face of "the machine," and by a decline in personal privacy. It is probably true that the social pressures placed on individuals today are more complicated and demanding that they were in earlier times. Increased geographical and occupational mobility and the need to function in large organizations place difficult demands on the individual to conform or "adjust." It is also evident that the privacy of many individuals tends to be encroached upon by sophisticated eavesdropping and surveillance devices, by the accumulation of more and more information about individuals by governmental and many private agencies, and by improvements in information-handling technologies such as the proposed institution of centralized statistical data banks. There is little doubt, finally, that the power, authority, influence, and scope of government are greater today than at any time in the history of the United States . . .

It is not clear, finally, that technological and social complexity must inevitably lead to reducing the individual to "mass" or "organization" man. Economic productivity and modern means of communication allow the individual to aspire to more than he ever could before. Better and more easily available education not only provides him with skills and with the means to develop his individual potentialities, but also improves his self-image and his sense of value as a human being . . .

Recognition that the impact of modern technology on the individual has two faces, both negative and positive, is consistent with the double effect of technological change that was discussed above. It also suggests that appreciation of that impact in detail may not be achieved in terms of old formulas, such as more or less privacy, more or less government, more or less individuality.

Criticism of technology

Although Mesthene's essay frequently points to real or potential threats and problems associated with technology, his overall assessment is a positive one. Because of this, he has been criticized by a number of commentators. One critic in particular, John McDermott, charged Mesthene with offering a "sanitary" view of technology. (Many philosophers of technology see the Mesthene-McDermott exchange as the classic debate about technology and social values.) In an essay called, "Technology: The Opiate of the Intellectuals," McDermott claimed that Mesthene's view of technology (whether or not Mesthene intended it as such) reflects a "newly aggressive right-wing ideology." Mesthene, remember, defined technology as "the organization of knowledge for practical purposes." This, for McDermott, is part of the sanitizing of technology; he offers an alternative characterization of technology: "systems of rationalized control over large groups of men, events, and machines by small groups of technically skilled men operating through organizational hierarchy." Quite a different picture! McDermott's claim is that technology itself is not value-free; it is created and promulgated by individuals and groups who have social power and special interests. Agreeing with Mesthene that technology is not to be equated with machines, but instead needs to be seen as systems of organization, McDermott argues that technology is actually strongly antidemocratic. Especially in today's society, advanced technological systems are "management intensive," so much so, he claims, that technology "creates its own politics." Although the term, "military-industrial complex," which was coined by President Eisenhower at the end of the 1950s, has rather gone out of favor today, we all understand the claim that big corporations (i.e., big technology) has a strong influence on politics. This is precisely McDermott's point in saying that technology creates its own politics.

Besides Mesthene's sanitizing of this fundamental aspect of technology, McDermott argues that Mesthene's view is dangerous because it holds that the problems created (or increased) by technology should be addressed and solved by yet more technology. This view that technology is self-corrective—much like the economic view that the free market is self-corrective—is one that McDermott sees as mistaken and dangerous. Technology, he says, with its concentration in the hands of larger and larger corporations with greater and greater social and political power, is fostering sharper and sharper class differences within society.

Public policy

One final axiological aspect of the relation between science and technology that we will consider in this chapter is that of public policy. The previous reading by Mesthene and its criticism by McDermott both touch on this issue, but neither delve very far into it. Others have. On page 391, we will see one such consideration, by a team consisting of a philosopher of science and a political scientist.

That science and technology are important with respect to public policy is obvious. As just one example of this, the 2006

U.S. federal government budget for research and development was more than $134 billion. This included a 1.7% increase over the previous year's budget, though 97% of that increase went to weapons development and human space exploration technologies. In terms of federal funding for particular agencies connected to science and technology, the National Institutes for Health has a much larger budget ($27.7 billion) than the Department of Energy, the Environmental Protection Agency, the National Science Foundation, NASA, and other agencies. Indeed, the Department of Energy's budget declined from the previous year. The point here is that one very obvious and important connection between science and technology on the one hand and public policy on the other is governmental financial support for research and development.

The selection on the following page is by Anne L. Hiskes and Richard P. Hiskes. They look at how views about science and technology have historically affected public policy-making. Of particular concern to us, as philosophers of science, is that they argue that public policy concerning science and technology rests on assumptions about the nature of science and technology (i.e., rests on philosophy of science and technology views!). As they say: "Policy for science and technology is not spun out of thin air; it rests on prior assumptions about the nature of these enterprises. It is based on an image of how these activities best function and grow and of how science and technology interact." In addition, though they do not say this as explicitly, it rests on other related political agendas and values by those who wield the public purse strings. As we all know, depending upon who runs the White House and who runs Congress, different policy about things like stem cell research, global warming, etc. will emerge. But—and this is the important point stressed by the authors—that policy is also shaped in large part by their views about the nature of science and technology.

In their essay, the authors claim that over the years public views about science (and technology) have wavered from very favorable to mixed to unfavorable. This has been, in large part, because of results of science and technology, but also of underlying views of what the aims and nature of science and technology are. They argue that if science and technology are seen as quite different enterprises, because of different aims and methods and content/results, then policy issues (especially funding) for them will be seen quite differently than if science and technology are seen as much more closely aligned. So, one very important practical axiological issue about the relationship between science and technology is how that relationship is understood and how that then has an impact on public policy with respect to them. Here they are:

SCIENCE, TECHNOLOGY, AND POLICY DECISIONS
Anne L. Hiskes and Richard P. Hiskes

On Christmas 1932 at the meetings of the American Association for the Advancement of Science, newspaper journalists and over two thousand physical scientists packed the room reserved for a symposium on the nature of cosmic rays. The atmosphere was one of tense anticipation. Two Nobel Prize-winning physicists, Robert A. Millikan and Arthur H. Compton, were about to debate the merits of their opposing theories after two years of well-publicized rivalry. Millikan claimed that cosmic rays consist of photons produced by the fusion of hydrogen atoms. Compton claimed that cosmic rays consist of charged particles; in 1931 he launched a worldwide investigation to gather evidence for his theory, personally traveling fifty thousand miles over five continents.

The press was not disappointed with the debate. Millikan passionately defended his theory even though he had just received word privately that his anticipated confirmatory evidence was nonexistent. In a pique of temper after the debate, Millikan refused to shake Compton's hand. Headlines from New York City to Pasadena, California, carried the news to the eager public: The controversy remains unsolved—even Nobel Prize winners interpret data differently—even Nobel Prize winners are unable to live up to an ideal of dispassionate objectivity.

The level of interest shown by the press and by the public in the highly theoretical Millikan-Compton debate may seem puzzling. What was so important about the nature of cosmic rays? Why should the public care? The answer seems to be that public interest in the debate was motivated by growing doubts about the social value of science—doubts already serving as fuel for a public revolt against science and technology . . .

Widespread disillusionment with the direction of science and technology ultimately forced leaders in science, industry, and government to ask some hard questions about policy. Issues raised by these leaders in the 1930s concerned the appropriate relations between science, society, and government. Should government take a more active role in funding research? If so, how should this role be defined? How much control was justified and by whom? Answers to these questions are as crucial today as they were in the 1930s . . .

As a general conclusion, we may say that policy reevaluation is appropriate whenever public debate indicates that a discrepancy exists between what the public believes science and technology should be achieving and what science and technology actually seem to achieve. This discrepancy can stem from the public's unrealistic expectations for science and technology, but it might also result from policy that fails to develop the full potential of these enterprises. Both factors seemed to play a role in the critiques of science and technology in the 1930s. During that time the public apparently believed that science should provide absolute and definitive answers to all important questions and that scientific research would automatically improve the quality of life. These expectations were naïve in 1930, and they would be naïve today. But, as we will discuss in the next sections, the problem may have been rooted equally in a policy-making framework that was based on an inaccurate conception of the nature of science and technology.

Policy and a Philosophy of Science and Technology

An optimal policy-making framework for science and technology would seem to be one that produces the best possible fit between social values and the internal dynamics of science and technology. An optimal framework, it would seem, must therefore be based on an accurate conception of the nature of science and technology. Policy should be based on realistic conceptions of the possible achievements of science and technology and of their relations to each other and to their social context. Positions on these issues are components of a philosophy of science and technology.

In the following sections, we will sketch two opposing philosophies of science and trace their implications for technology and policy making. The first position is logical empiricism; the second position is sometimes called "the new pragmatism" or simply "the new philosophy of science."

We use the term *logical empiricism* to denote a philosophical framework that covers a class of philosophical positions that, although they differ on some points, agree on fundamental assumptions about science. The picture of science as painted by the logical empiricists is probably familiar. From about 1900 to 1965 some form of logical empiricism was accepted by most scientists, philosophers, and historians as the framework within which scientific endeavor should, and in fact usually did, take place. Textbooks and popularizations of science during this period transmitted the logical empiricist view of science to the public. We assume, therefore, that many policy makers also saw science from a logical empiricist perspective. The "new philosophy of science" emerged during the 1960s within the fields of the history, philosophy, and sociology of science, and that approach is still controversial.

Although the philosophies of logical empiricism and the new pragmatism differ on crucial points, they share noncontroversial assumptions held by students of twentieth-century science. All accounts of science identify the acquisition of knowledge as the ultimate aim of scientific research and hold that a claim should be accepted as knowledge only when there are good reasons to believe that it is probably true or approximately true. Furthermore, accounts of modern science agree that the primary test of truth within science is consistency with the data of experiment and observation. Scientists, however, are not only concerned with collecting data that describe particular, observed events. They also aim at discovering laws, like Newton's laws of inertia and of universal gravitation and Boyle's laws of gases, that describe general patterns in nature. Scientists similarly construct theories, like Einstein's theory of relativity, Newton's theory of mechanics, and Darwin's theory of evolution. In this context a theory is a unified system of abstract concepts and general principles that serves to explain and organize a wide range of observable phenomena. Newton's theory of mechanics, for example, served to explain the orbits of the planets, the tides of the oceans, and the fall of an apple through the related concepts of gravity, inertia, and mass.

Although logical empiricism and the new pragmatism agree on all these points, their proponents employ different concepts of scientific truth and have different views on the nature of objectivity within science. Because of this disagreement, the two positions diverge on their characterization of the differences between science and technology and also on their accounts of the relations between science, technology, and society. In our opinion these differences have important implications for the connection between science and social and political values and for the legitimacy of public participation in setting research goals. The emergence of the new pragmatic conception of science and technology, we believe, calls for a reevaluation of policy goals.

Let's pause for a moment to flesh out these two views of science that they have mentioned, logical empiricism and the new pragmatism. We have actually already encountered them in a way. Logical empiricism is often closely associated with inductivism, and for many also with falsificationism (look again at Chapter Eight). The new pragmatism, on the other hand, is Anne Hiskes' and Richard Hiskes' way of talking about Kuhn and to some extent those models of scientific change in Chapters Nine and Ten that followed him. For these authors (and many others), a logical empiricism view of science is that science aims at the discovery and understanding of natural laws, whereas technology aims at manipulating and controlling nature for some practical purpose; data is obtained through careful observation and experimentation and, if truly obtained carefully enough, is objective; data (at least objectively obtained) represent independent facts; good science is value-free, or value-neutral, as independent facts are tested via clear, objective tests and using clear standards of evaluation. Technology, on the other hand for logical empiricists, is value-laden, as its aims are value-laden. The new pragmatist view, they say, rejects this view of science and technology, including the objectivity said to be carefully obtained as well as the value-neutrality; for the new pragmatists, though science and technology are not identical with one another, there is not a sharp distinction between them, either in terms of content or methods or aims.

Given these two different conceptions of science and technology, there will follow different views on the nature and ways in which science and technology relate to society and, hence, on how policy-making is and should be done. So, assuming first the logical empiricist view of science, what policy implications flow from this view? Here is what they say:

SCIENCE, TECHNOLOGY, AND POLICY DECISIONS *(continued)*

Anne L. Hiskes and Richard P. Hiskes

Policy Options for Science

According to the logical empiricists' image of science as concerned with the production of objective knowledge, science must be protected from external social forces in order to function successfully. Scientists must be free to pursue interesting scientific questions as they arise, choosing them because of their potential contributions to the body of scientific knowledge. Furthermore, scientists must select answers to these questions on the basis of data and logic and not because the answers serve some political ideology or some economic or social value.

Government Funding

One aspect of science policy, therefore, could be to provide protection for science from external social forces. At most, government may supply funds for pure research. The scientific community should be in charge of disbursing these funds on the basis of scientific merit, presumably through a panel of experts chosen from all scientific disciplines. The government should not target specific research topics or approaches for preferential treatment, and lay participation in choosing research topics is entirely inappropriate . . .

Payoff of Scientific Research

We have seen that governmental funding of pure research is compatible with the philosophical ideal of scientific knowledge as long as government acts simply as a source of money. But now the policy maker faces an important issue: Public money should be spent on projects of clear social value and it should be budgeted in proportion to the social importance of the project. What justification can be given for funding pure scientific research, particularly if the money spent on science far exceeds that spent on the arts and humanities, or on social programs? The attainment of scientific knowledge is undoubtedly a worthwhile endeavor, which contributes to our general cultural enrichment. But is there any additional social payoff from pure research? If so, the social payoff must come from science-based technology.

Since 1945 policy makers have typically justified government support of pure research in terms of what historian George Wise called "the assembly line model" of science and technology. According to many policy makers, the assembly line model accurately represents the relation between twentieth-century science and technology. The model, as described by Wise, locates the origin of all modern technology in prior scientific knowledge, and it explains the development of technology in terms of an "assembly line" of stages beginning with the initial conception of a scientific idea and ending with some consumer product. The model identifies research for the sake of knowledge with science, and it identifies research for the sake of consumer products with technology. The assembly line model, therefore, is compatible with a logical empiricist philosophy of science and technology.

Wise depicts the assembly line model of technology as follows, where the arrows should be interpreted as representing a one-way process of development.

> Scientific Idea → Scientific Research → Knowledge → Applied
> Research → Invention → Development → Engineering → Marketing

If they assume the accuracy of the assembly line model and the social value of technology, policy makers can justify spending large amounts of money on pure research in the interests of promoting technology . . .

The New Synthesis [i.e., Pragmatism]: Policy Implications

A policy maker assuming the new, historically based image of science and technology has more flexibility in developing a legitimate policy. He or she may allow government to target specific basic research areas or approaches for special funding, perhaps even eliminating public support for an entire field. Funding decisions can be based on the projected practical applications of the research, and they may affect the future of science. Because contemporary scientific research is expensive, out of necessity scientists and science students would gravitate toward fields with money.

By adopting the historical approach our policy maker may also consider ways of effectively combining science and technology. The current highly complex state of technology requires the guidance of reliable scientific knowledge for innovations and improvements to continue. Improving the design of nuclear reactors and safely disposing of nuclear waste are problems . . . that can no longer be solved by the previously harmless technological method of trial and error tinkering: Action in such areas must be based on reliable principles governing the relevant processes. Many scientific problems of great social concern are also best addressed by a strategy that combines science and technology. Developing a cure for cancer, for example, requires the directed efforts of both basic and applied researchers.

Science has therefore become a valuable and necessary resource for technology, but as long as the "pure" scientific community operates in isolation from the "impure" technological community, this resource is not effectively used. Under the historically based image of science and technology, our policy maker is free to develop policy that would help merge the scientific and technological communities. He or she may legitimately explore new avenues for coordinating the efforts of the two communities, perhaps using the example of an industrial research laboratory directed by a research entrepreneur as a model for national laboratories.

A policy maker who adopts the historically based image of science and technology faces deeper and more difficult issues than a policy maker who regards science as isolated from social concerns and influences. Because the former policy maker believes that social forces always influence the direction and outcome of research, he or she bears the responsibility of selecting, and even of creating, the operative kinds of forces. But what values should be given priority? These questions are particularly pressing in light of the potentially great scope and power of a combined science and technology. But what kinds of concerns should be given priority?

Furthermore, scientific knowledge combined with technological expertise is a powerful tool for creating new ways of manipulating and controlling nature with greater and longer lasting effects. The consequences of manipulating the energy of the atom or of altering the genetic heritage of the human species, for example, are of a new order of magnitude: they affect life and health over the long term, as opposed to consequences that merely affect one's level of material comfort.

Chapter Summary

People often conflate science and technology, though most scientists and technologists claim they are related yet different. From a philosophical perspective, what are of interest about the nature of the relationship between science and technology are issues of content (and results), methods, and aims. Beginning with a working definition of technology as the practical implementations of intelligence, questions about technology and knowledge immediately arise. Is technological knowledge different than scientific knowledge and, if so, in what ways? This is the focus of the writings of James Feibleman and I. C. Jarvie. Besides epistemological concerns relating to technology, there are value concerns. One such concern is the issue of how technology has an impact on society's values. Emmanual Mesthene argues that technology is a double-edged sword, or tool, with both positive and negative impact, but overall technology is positive, creating new opportunities for society. James McDermott disagrees and sees technology as both reflecting and generating social power in the hands of specific social interest groups. A second axiological concern relating to technology and its relation to science is that of public policy. Anne L. Hiskes and Richard P. Hiskes argue that public policy relating to science and technology is shaped, at least in part, on underlying conceptions of the nature of them.

CASE STUDY

Genetically Modified Organisms

Genetic modification is a collection of technologies for modifying and changing the genetic makeup of living organisms. Scientists and technologists know how to combine genes from different organisms, including splicing genes from one organism and transplanting those genes into a different organism. The result is genetically modified organisms, often called GMOs (though sometimes the terms "genetically engineered" or "transgenic" are used). The products of genetic modification include medicines, waste management processes, and crops as well as foods for human consumption, food ingredients, and even animals (most of which are raised for human consumption). These technologies have become an important part of industrial economies. Nevertheless, there are many philosophical (especially moral) and social concerns that have been raised about the processes and products of genetic modification. Critics have used terms such as "Frankenfood" to refer to these products and have sought to at least monitor and restrict such technologies, if not eliminate them altogether. The readings below include an argument (by Lee Silver, molecular biologist from Princeton University) in favor of such technologies and an argument (by Normand Ellstrand, geneticist from the University of California, Riverside) against. Although the two readings seem at first to be talking about different kinds of genetic modification and different applications of such knowledge, together they highlight part of the range of concerns and issues connected to this topic.

WHY GM IS GOOD FOR US
Lee Silver

Farm-raised pigs are dirty, smelly animals that get no respect. They're also an environmental hazard. Their manure contains phosphorus, which, when it rains, runs off into lakes and estuaries, depleting oxygen, killing fish, stimulating algae overgrowth and emitting greenhouse gases. During the 1980s, phosphorus pollution killed all aquatic life in the 42km-long Mariager Fjord of Denmark—an ecological disaster that prompted European governments to impose strict regulations on pig farming. It didn't solve the problem.

Doing away with the pig is not an option. Pigs provide more dietary protein, more cheaply, to more people than any other animal. Northern Europe still maintains the highest pig-to-human ratio in the word (2-1 in Denmark), but East Asia is catching up. During the 1990s, pork production doubled in Vietnam and grew by 70 percent in China—along densely populated coastlines, pig density exceeds 100 animals per square kilometer. The resulting pollution is "threatening fragile coastal marine habitats including mangroves, coral reefs and sea grasses," according to a report released in February [2006] by the Food and Agriculture Organization of the United Nations.

As it turns out, there is a solution to the pig problem, but it requires a change of mind-set among environmentalists and the public. Two Canadian scientists have created a pig whose manure doesn't contain very much phosphorus at all. If this variety of pig were adopted widely, it could greatly reduce a major source of pollution. But the Enviropig, as they call it, is the product of genetic modification—which is anathema to many Westerners.

The Enviropig is one of many new technologies that are putting environmentalists and organic-food proponents in a quandary: should they remain categorically opposed to genetically modified (GM) foods even at the expense of the environment? Pigs can also be modified to digest grasses and hay (as cows and sheep do), reducing the energy-intensive use of corn as pig feed. Elsewhere, trees grown for paper could be made amenable to much more efficient processing, reducing both energy usage and toxic chemical bleach in effluents from paper mills. The most significant GM applications will be ones that help alleviate the problem of agriculture, which accounts for 38 percent of the world's landmass and is crowding out natural ecosystems and species habitats. GM crops that can be produced more efficiently would allow us to return land to nature.

Standing in opposition to these advances are advocates of an organic food philosophy that holds to the simplistic notion that "natural" is good and "synthetic" is bad. Genetic modification is unacceptable to organic farmers merely because it is performed in a laboratory. Says Charles Margulis, a spokesman for Greenpeace USA, "We think the Enviropig is a Frankenpig in disguise."

Technically, however, all domesticated plants and animals were created by human selection of random mutations that occur in nature. High-energy cosmic rays break chromosomes into pieces that reattach randomly; in this way, nature sometimes creates genes that didn't previously exist. Lab work, however, is more nuanced than nature: scientists can make subtle and precise changes to an organism's DNA. Canadian biologists Cecil Forsberg and John Phillips, for instance, have constructed a novel DNA molecule that, when planted in a pig embryo, imbues the Enviropig with the ability to secrete a phosphorus-extracting enzyme in its saliva. The results so far are dramatic—the new pigs can extract all the phosphorus they need from grain alone, without the phosphorus supplements that farmers now use. This reduces the phosphorus content of their manure by up to 75 percent.

Of course, stringent testing is needed to show that a genetic modification works and that the product is not harmful to humans. Scientists can do both of these things with techniques that allow them to examine and compare the structure and activity of every one of the animal's genes. An added advantage with the Enviropig, in particular, is that the single extra enzyme in its saliva is also present naturally in billions of bacteria inhabiting the digesting tract of every normal human being, which suggests that the Enviropig will be as safe for human consumption as non-GM pigs.

Organic farmers have always boasted that their approach to agriculture is, by its very nature, better for the environment than so-called conventional farming. The European Commission states that "organic farmers use a range of techniques that help sustain ecosystems and reduce pollution." But if you think that concern for the environment will ever persuade organic farmers to accept the Enviropig or any other animal modified to reduce pollution, you'd be wrong. According to self-imposed organic rules, precision genetic modification of any kind for any purpose is strictly forbidden. If conventional farmers begin to grow Enviropigs, organic pig farms will cause much more pollution per animal—unless environmental protection agencies step in and shut them down.

Even in the realm of health, organic food doesn't measure up to the hype. Consumers tend to assume that all organic crops are grown as advertised without chemical pesticides. This is false. Organic farmers can spray their crops with many chemicals including pyrethrin, a highly toxic pesticide, and rotenone, a potent neurotoxin recently linked to Parkinson's disease. Because these substances occur in nature—pyrethrin is produced by chrysanthemums and rotenone comes from a native Indian vine—they are deemed acceptable for use on organic farms.

In fact, although all commonly used pesticides dissipate so quickly that they pose a miniscule health risk to consumers, allergic food reactions to natural products kill hundreds of children each year. Genetically modified foods could greatly reduce this risk. U.S. Department of Agriculture scientist Eliot Herman has already created a less-allergenic soybean—an imported crop for baby foods. Through genetic surgery, Herman turned off the soy gene responsible for 65 percent of allergic reactions. Not only was the modified soy less allergenic in tests, but, as Herman explained, "the yield looks perfectly normal, plants develop and grow at a normal rate and they seem to have the same kinds of protein, oil and other good stuff in them." Other scientists have reported promising results in shutting off allergy-causing genes in peanuts and shrimp.

Should these advances be turned into products, organic soy or peanut products will be certifiably more dangerous to human health than comparable nonorganic products.

Unfortunately, this won't happen any time soon. Because no society has ever banned allergenic foods, conventional farmers have no incentive to plant reduced-allergy seeds. And many members of the public have been led to believe that all genetic modifications create health risks. In this climate, much of the needed research isn't being pursued. Chances are, farmers will continue to grow their polluting organic pork, their allergenic organic soy and their neurotoxin-sprayed organic apples. Worse still, they will make sure that no one else gets a choice in the matter of improving the conditions of life on earth—unless, that is, others rise up and demand an alternative.

WHEN TRANSGENES WANDER, SHOULD WE WORRY?
Norman C. Ellstrand

It is hard to ignore the ongoing, often emotional public discussion of the impacts of the products of crop biotechnology. At one extreme of the hype is self-righteous panic, and at the other is smug optimism. While the controversy plays out in the press, dozens of scientific workshops, symposia, and other meetings have been held to take a hard and thoughtful look at potential risks of transgenic crops. Overshadowed by the loud and contentious voices, a set of straightforward, scientifically based concerns have evolved, dictating a cautious approach for creating the best choices for agriculture's future.

Plant ecologists and population geneticists have looked to problems associated with traditionally improved crops to anticipate possible risks of transgenic crops. Those that have been most widely discussed are: (a) crop-to-wild hybridization resulting in the evolution of increased weediness in wild relatives, (b) evolution of pests that are resistant to new strategies for their control, and (c) the impacts on nontarget species in associated ecosystems (such as the unintentional poisoning of beneficial insects) . . . .

Exploring each of these in detail would take a book, and such books exist . . . . However, let us consider the questions that have dominated my research over the last decade to examine how concerns regarding engineered crops have evolved. Those questions are: How likely is it that transgenes will move into and establish in natural populations? And if transgenes do move into wild populations, is there any cause for concern? It turns out that experience and experiments with traditional crops provide a tremendous amount of information for answering these questions.

The possibility of transgene flow from engineered crops to their wild relatives with undesirable consequences was independently recognized by several scientists [e.g., R.E. Colwell, N. Ellstrand, P.J. Dale]. Among the first to publish the idea were two Calgene scientists [R.M. Goodman and N. Newell], writing: "The sexual transfer of genes to weedy species to create a more persistent weed is probably the greatest environmental risk of planting a new variety of crop species." The movement of unwanted crop genes into the environment may pose more of a management dilemma than unwanted chemicals. A single molecule of DDT . . . remains a single molecule or degrades, but a single crop allele has the opportunity to multiply itself repeatedly through reproduction which can frustrate attempts at containment . . .

When I gave seminars on the results of these experiments, I was met with a new question: "If gene flow from crops to their wild relatives was a problem, wouldn't it already have occurred in traditional systems?" A good question. I conducted a thorough literature review to find out what was known about the consequences of natural hybridization between the world's most important crops and their wild relatives.

Crop-to-weed gene flow has created hardship through the appearance of new or more difficult weeds . . . Crop-to-wild gene flow can create another problem. Hybridization between a common species and a rare one can, under the appropriate conditions, send the rare species to extinction in a few generations . . . It is clear that gene flow from crops to wild relatives has, on occasion, had undesirable consequences.

Are transgenic crops likely to be different from traditionally improved crops? No, and that is not necessarily good news. It is clear that the probability of problems due to gene flow from any individual cultivar is extremely low, but when those problems are realized, they can be doozies. Whether transgenic crops are more or less likely to create gene flow problems will depend in part on their phenotypes. The majority of the "first generation" transgenic crops have phenotypes that are apt to give a weed a fitness boost, such as herbicide resistance or pest resistance. Although a fitness boost in itself may not lead to increased weediness, scientists engineering crops with such phenotypes should be mindful that those phenotypes might have unwanted effects in natural populations. In fact, I am aware of at least three cases in which scientists decided not to engineer certain traits into certain crops because of such concerns . . .

It is interesting that little has been written regarding the possible downsides of within-crop gene flow involving transgenic plants. Yet a couple of recent incidents suggest that crop-to-crop gene flow may result in greater risk than crop-to-wild gene flow. The first is a report of triple herbicide resistance in canola in Alberta, Canada . . . Volunteer canola plants were found to be resistant to the herbicides Roundup (Monsanto, St. Louis), Liberty (Aventis, Crop Science, Research Triangle Park, NC), and Pursuit (BASF, Research Triangle Park, NC). It is clear that two different hybridization events were necessary to account for these genotypes. It is interesting that the alleles for resistance to Roundup and Liberty are transgenes, but the allele for Pursuit resistance is the result of mutation breeding. Although these volunteers can be managed with other herbicides, this report is significant because, if correct, it illustrates that gene flow into wild plants is not the only avenue for the evolution of plants that are increasingly difficult to manage.

The second incident is a report of the Starlink Cry9C allele (the one for creating the fuss in Taco Bell's taco shells [in which transgenic genes that were not approved for human consumption were found in the corn used for these taco shells]) appearing in a variety of supposedly nonengineered corn . . . Although unintentional mixing of seeds during the transport or storage may explain the contamination of the traditional variety, inter-varietal crossing between seed production fields could be just as likely. This news is significant because, if correct, it illustrates how easy it is to lose track of transgenes. Without careful checking, there are plenty of opportunities for them to move from variety to variety. The field release of "third generation" transgenic crops that are grown to produce pharmaceutical and other industrial biochemicals will pose special challenges for containment if we do not want those chemicals appearing in the human food supply.

The products of plant improvement are not absolutely safe, and we cannot expect transgenic crops to be absolutely safe either. Recognition of that fact suggest that creating something just because we are now able to do so is an inadequate reason for embracing a new technology. If we have advanced tools for creating novel agricultural products, we should use the advanced knowledge from ecology and population genetics as well as social sciences and humanities to make mindful choices about how to create the products that are best for humans and our environment.

Further Reading

Dusek, Val. *Philosophy of Technology: An Introduction*. New York: Blackwell, 2006.

Ferré, Frederick. *Philosophy of Technology*. Englewood Cliffs: Prentice Hall, 1988.

Hickman, Larry (ed.). *Philosophy, Technology and Human Affairs*. College Station: Ibis Press, 1985.

Hiskes, Anne L. and Richard P. Hiskes. *Science, Technology, and Policy Decisions*. Boulder: Westview Press, 1986.

Ihde, Don. *Philosophy of Technology: An Introduction*. New York: Paragon House, 1993.

Kaplan, David M. (ed.). *Readings in the Philosophy of Technology*. Lanham, NJ: Rowman & Littlefield, 2004.

MacKenzie, Donald and Judy Wajcman (eds.). *The Social Shaping of Technology, 2nd edition*. Philadelphia: Open University Press, 1999.

Mitcham, Carl and Robert Mackey (eds.). *Philosophy and Technology*. New York: Free Press, 1972.

Pitt, Joseph C. *Thinking About Technology*. New York: Seven Bridges Press, 2000.

Scharff, Robert C. and Val Dusek (eds.). *Philosophy of Technology*. New York: Blackwell, 2003.

Teich, Albert H. (ed.). *Technology and the Future, 7th edition*. New York: St. Martin's Press, 1997.

Volti, Rudi (ed.). *Society and Technological Change, 3rd edition*. New York: St. Martin's, 1995.

CHAPTER TWELVE

Science and Values

IN THIS CHAPTER, WE WILL

■ Consider values about science and values within science

■ Identify some metaphysical, epistemological, and axiological issues related to values and science

■ Examine claims regarding both moral values and epistemic values inherent in scientific research and practice

Every year since 1991 there has been an "Ignoble Prize" ceremony held at Harvard University to "honor" what many scientists see as funny, if not simply silly, scientific research identified during the previous year. For example, among the 2005 awardees were James Watson for his scholarly study, "The Significance of Mr. Richard Buckley's Exploding Trousers" (published in *Agricultural History* the year before), Claire Rind and Peter Simmons for their study, "Orthopteran DCMD Neuron: A Reevaluation of Responses to Moving Objects," in which they electronically monitored the activity of a brain cell in a locust while the locust was watching selected highlights from the movie "Star Wars" (published in *Journal of Neurophysiology* in 1992), and Victor Benno Meyer-Rochow and Jozsef Gal for their study, "Pressures Produced When Penguins Pooh—Calculations on Avian Defecation," which detailed basic principles of physics to calculate pressure that builds up inside a penguin (published in *Polar Biology* in 2003).

However, funny (or silly or bizarre) these studies might seem, they might well be considered *good* science if the research was carried out in rigorous ways, conforming to accepted standards of scientific practice. Nevertheless, they do point to the issue of what constitutes good science vs. bad science. One feature of what is taken as good science is that it is as value-free or value-neutral as possible. That is, values—whether personal values of the scientists or social, political values of society at large—should not shape the methods and processes used by the scientists nor the scientific standards by which the research is analyzed and evaluated. Putting this point another way, one sign of *bad* science is when values do enter into the methods and evaluative criteria of scientific practice.

One especially notorious example of this is the case of Trofim Lysenko, a Russian biologist during the era of the Soviet Union, who orchestrated agricultural science in the Soviet Union for several decades, beginning in the 1930s. The prevailing theory of genetics was based on Mendel's work and had been expanded in the early 20th century, particularly by the work of Thomas Morgan. Much of the emphasis of this view was that the heredity of an organism—its traits—were dependent (almost) exclusively on its genes and very little, if any at all, on its environment. Inherited characteristics, not acquired characteristics, are what matter. Lysenko rejected this view of genetics for a number of reasons. One of them was that he claimed that Marxist values, which were the official policy of the Soviet regime, focused on the importance of the environment in shaping organisms. Lysenko claimed that changes in heredity are the result of changes in the conditions of life upon the development of an organism, so that, indeed, acquired traits can be inherited by changing the environment (or "conditions of life"). The result of Lysenko's control of Soviet agricultural science was that (1) he orchestrated a devastating agricultural failure and (2) he led the purge (including arrest and death) of Soviet scientists who disagreed with him and challenged his scientific competence.

There are many other cases of what is often called bad, or junk, science, in which moral, social, and political values influence and even drive scientific research, but the Lysenko case is particularly well-documented and public. With respect to the lesson learned, many people claim that science is bad science to the extent that values enter into it. Others, as we will see, argue that values are not necessarily dangerous to or in conflict with good science. This chapter focuses on the nature and ways in which values play a role in science.

Values about science and within science

We all know that there are issues related to values *about* science. That is, there are concerns with the impact of scientific research on our lives. This could be in the sense of scientific and technological apparatuses that affect our lives, such as computers. It could also be in the sense of a scientific "picture" of who we are, such as how and in what ways we are influenced by our heredity and genetics. We might, as we in fact will do in the next two chapters, consider how and in what ways science challenges or shapes (or is challenged and shaped by) religion and social concerns. It is obvious, then, that there are values about science, about how we understand and assess the importance of science on our lives.

These values about science can be concerned primarily with what throughout this book has been called the metaphysics of science and epistemology of science and even axiology of science. For example, we might focus on the importance of what science investigates. Indeed, many people have asked about the significance of, say, spending millions of dollars on investigating black holes in outer space. Could or should that money be better spent on, say, heart disease research or perhaps on simply feeding and housing more people? In addition, there are questions about whether or not there is information about the world that scientists should not investigate, even though they can and could. For example, we could investigate pain thresholds in humans by torturing them and doing it in a rigorous, well-designed scientific procedure (well-designed in order to insure that the data is reliable). However, just because we could do this, it does not follow that we ought to do this.

With respect to epistemological issues, are the ways that science investigates the world the best ways to do so? For instance, with respect to social scientific research methods, some claim that a commitment to remain "detached" from the people being studied can lead and has led to failing to aid people who need help in the name of staying objective as a researcher. A famous example of this is the case of a young girl, code-named Genie, who was discovered in a Los Angeles suburb in 1970. She had been severely mistreated by her parents, who kept her isolated from the outside world and punished her for any vocalizations. The result was that when she was discovered by others at the age of 13, she had essentially no language skills whatever, certainly none beyond the skills of a normal infant. Over the next five or six years, many groups of scientists "investigated" Genie while she was being introduced into society. Among those scientists were linguists who saw Genie as a very fruitful case for studying hypotheses about language acquisition and development. While the scientists involved claimed that they cared very much for Genie's well-being, critics claimed that they focused too much on her as a test case for their research and not enough on her as a person. The point here is that there are values about how science is practiced, not just on what science investigates.

Finally, there are concerns related to science itself as a social institution. Of course, there are questions about funding levels for various scientific projects. But even broader, there are questions about how and in what ways science relates to—as noted above—matters of broad social influence. Is science, as a social institution, more or less important than other social institutions, for instance, the arts? How and in what ways and at what levels should science education be mandated?

Without question, then, there are obvious issues regarding values *about* science. But there are also philosophical and conceptual issues regarding values *within* science. That is, there is the question of how and in what ways values are part of science itself, in particular part of the very methods and practices of doing science. On the one hand, few people today, including scientists, would say that science is totally value-free. After all, if nothing else, science is done by scientists, who are themselves part of society and influenced by social and political and moral matters. On the other hand, good science tries to weed out the influence of these "outside" values. Good science tries to be as value-free or value-neutral as possible. Indeed, a major virtue of science is that it strives very hard, through a system of rigorous checks and balances, to eliminate or at least reduce values in the doing of science. For example, there is the expectation that experimental results, if valid, can be repeated by other experimenters. If they cannot, the scientific community is very hesitant to accept the results or to use them for further research. A fairly well-known case of this from the 1980s was the case of cold fusion. In this case, two experimenters claimed to have created, in a "tabletop" experiment, excess energy as a result of fusing sub-atomic particles. Most of the rest of the physics community said this simply could not be done under the experimental conditions that these researchers claimed. Immediately, many teams of physicists tried to replicate the claimed results of the original researchers and were unable to do so. The cold fusion claims of this original experiment were subsequently rejected by the physics community. The point, again, is that the scientific community largely claims that, although there might indeed be values that enter into scientific practice, those values are eliminated or diminished dramatically and it is a conscious part of scientific research that they are eliminated as much as possible. Good science, then, at least strives to be value-free.

Nevertheless, there is the issue of values within science, and within good science. In 1953 the journal *Philosophy of Science* published an article by Richard Rudner, entitled, "The Scientist Qua Scientist Makes Value Judgments." Rudner claimed that no hypothesis of science is ever completely verified. By accepting a hypothesis, then, scientists must make the decision that the evidence that supports the hypothesis is sufficiently good enough to justify accepting the hypothesis. This decision of what counts as being good enough evidence is a function of the importance—and, for Rudner, this importance is inescapably a matter of morality—of accepting or rejecting the hypothesis. If the hypothesis under consideration is about the effectiveness of some drug for treating a disease or ailment and could have potentially serious health consequences, then we would desire a very high degree of confidence in the level of support before accepting the hypothesis that the drug is safe for consumption. On the other hand, if the hypothesis is about whether or not one dye for fabrics is longer-lasting than an alternative dye, the level of desired degree of confidence in the hypothesis would be less. How sure we need to be before we accept a hypothesis, said Rudner, will depend on how serious a mistake would be. Scientists *must* make a value decision about the required level of confidence in the acceptability of evidence regarding any hypothesis. This is integral to the doing of scientific research. The main point of this argument is that values *within* science—and, yes, within good science—are inescapable. There simply cannot be value-free science, said Rudner.

Moral values

Although there is no question that moral, social, and political values influence the applications and uses of scientific knowledge, indeed, often the funding of science, Nicholas Rescher has argued that moral values are inherent in the very doing of science. That is, he has claimed that scientific research simply cannot take place absent many moral decisions being made. And, again, these are not moral decisions regarding the uses of scientific information once it has been attained; moral decisions permeate the very possibility of doing scientific research at all.

In the following selection Rescher identifies at least seven areas of scientific research in which values are an inherent part. Those seven areas are: (1) choice of research goals, (2) staffing of research activities, (3) research methods, (4) standards of proof, (5) dissemination of research findings, (6) control of misinformation, and (7) allocation of credit for research achievements. Far from values being in conflict with good science, Rescher argues that values are inescapable for scientific research.

THE ETHICAL DIMENSION OF SCIENTIFIC RESEARCH
Nicholas Rescher

It has been frequently asserted that the creative scientist is distinguished by his objectivity. The scientist—so it is said—goes about his work in a rigidly impersonal and unfeeling way, unmoved by any emotion other than the love of knowledge and the delights of discovering the secrets of nature.

This widely accepted image of scientific inquiry as a cold, detached, and unhumane affair is by no means confined to the scientifically uninformed and to scientific outsiders, but finds many of its most eloquent spokesmen within the scientific community itself. Social scientists in particular tend to be outspoken supporters of the view that the scientist does not engage in making value judgments, and that science, real science, deals only with what is, and has no concern with what ought to be. Any recitation of concrete instances in which the attitudes, values, and temperaments of scientists have influenced their work or affected their findings is dismissed with the scornful dichotomy that such matters may bear upon the psychology or sociology of scientific inquiry, but have no relevance whatever to the *logic* of science.

This point of view that science is "value free" has such wide acceptance as to have gained for itself the distinctive, if somewhat awesome, label as the thesis of the *value neutrality of science*.

Now the main thesis that I propose is simply that this supposed division between the evaluative disciplines on the one hand and the nonevaluative sciences on the other is based upon mistaken views regarding the nature of scientific research. In paying too much attention to the abstract logic of scientific inquiry, many students of scientific method have lost sight of the fact that science is a human enterprise, carried out by flesh and blood men, and that scientific research must therefore inevitably exhibit some normative complexion. It is my aim to examine the proposition that evaluative, and more specifically *ethical*, problems crop up at numerous points within the framework of scientific research. I shall attempt to argue that the scientist does not, and cannot, put aside his common humanity and his evaluative capabilities when he puts on his laboratory coat.

Ethical Issues and the Collectivization of Scientific Research

Before embarking on a consideration of the ethical dimension of scientific research, a number of preliminary points are in order.

In considering ethical issues within the sciences, I do not propose to take any notice at all of the various moral problems that arise in relation to what is *done with* scientific discoveries once they have been achieved. I want to concern myself with scientific work as such, and insofar as possible to ignore the various technological and economic applications of science. We shall not be concerned with the very obviously ethical issues that have to do with the use of scientific findings for the production of the instrumentalities of good or evil. The various questions about the morality of the *uses* to which scientific discoveries are put by men other than the scientists themselves—questions of the sort that greatly exercise such organizations as, for example, the Society for Social Responsibility in Science—are substantially beside the point. We all know that the findings of science can be used to manufacture wonder drugs to promote man's welfare, or bacteriological weapons to promote his extermination. Such questions of what is done with the fruits of the tree of science, both bitter and sweet, are not problems that arise *within* science, and are not ethical choices that confront the scientist himself. This fact puts them outside of my limited area of concern. They relate to the exploitation of scientific research not to its pursuit, and thus they do not arise *within* science in a way that concerns us here.

Before turning to a description of some of the ethical issues that affect the conduct of research in the sciences, I should like to say a word about their reason for being. Ethical questions—that is, issues regarding the rightness and wrongness of conduct—arise out of people's dealings with each other, and pertain necessarily to the duties, rights, and obligations that exist in every kind of interpersonal relationship. For a Robinson Crusoe, few, if any, ethical problems present themselves. One of the most remarkable features of the science of our time is its joint tendency toward collectivization of effort and dispersion of social involvement.

The solitary scientists laboring in isolation in his study or laboratory has given way to the institutionalized laboratory, just as the scientific paper has become a thing of almost inevitably multiple authorship, and the scientific calculation has shifted from the back of an envelope to the electronic computer. Francis Bacon's vision of scientific research as a group effort has come to realization. The scientist nowadays usually functions not as a detached individual unit, but as a part of a group, as a "member of a team."

This phenomenon of the collectivization of scientific research leads increasingly to more prominent emphasis upon ethical considerations within science itself. As the room gets more crowded, if I may use a simile, the more people involved in a given corner of scientific research, the more likely ethical issues are apt to arise. It seems that these phenomena of the collectivization and increasing social diffusion of modern science are the main forces that have resulted in making a good deal of room for ethical considerations within the operational framework of modern science.

Ethical Problems Regarding Research Goals

Perhaps the most basic and pervasive way in which ethical problems arise in connection with the prosecution of scientific research is in regard to the choice of research problems, the setting of research goals, and the allocation of resources (both material and human) to the prosecution of research efforts. This ethical problem of choices relating to research goals arises at all levels of aggregation—the national, the institutional, and the individual. I should like to touch upon each of these in turn.

The National Level

As regards to the national level, it is commonplace that the United States government is heavily involved in the sponsorship of research . . . In our country, the responsibility for such choices [of allocating federal support funds] is, of course, localized. The President's Science Advisory Committee and the Federal Council for Science and Technology give a mechanism for establishing an overall science budget and thereby for making the difficult decisions regarding resource allocation. These decisions, which require weighing space probes against biological experimentation and atomic energy against oceanography are among the most difficult choices that have to be made by, or on behalf of, the scientific community. The entrance of political considerations may complicate, but cannot remove, the ethical issues that are involved in such choices . . .

The Institutional Level

Let me now turn to the institutional level—that of the laboratory or department or research institute. Here again the ethical issue regarding research goals arises in various ways connected with the investment of effort, or, to put this same matter the other way around, with the selection of research projects.

One very pervasive problem at this institutional level is the classical issue of pure, or basic, versus applied, or practical, research. This problem is always with us and is always difficult, for the more "applied" the research contribution, the more it can yield immediate benefits to man; the more "fundamental," the deeper is its scientific significance and the more can it contribute to the development of science itself. No doubt it is often the case unfortunately that the issue is not dealt with on this somewhat elevated plane, but is resolved in favor of the applied end of the spectrum by the mundane, but inescapable, fact that this is the easier to finance.

I need scarcely add that this ethical issue can also arise at the institutional level in far more subtle forms. For instance, the directorship of a virology laboratory may have to choose whether to commit its limited resources to developing a vaccine which protects against a type of virus that is harmless as a rule but deadly to a few people, as contrasted with a variant type of virus that, while deadly to none, is very bothersome to many.

The Individual Level

The most painful and keenly felt problems are often not the greatest in themselves, but those that touch closest to home. At the level of the individual, too, the ethical question of research goals and the allocation of effort—namely, that of the individual himself—can arise and present difficulties of the most painful kind. To cite one example, a young scientist may well ponder the question of whether to devote himself to pure or to applied work. Either option may present its difficulties for him, and these can, although they need not necessarily, be on an ethical nature . . .

Ethical Problems Regarding the Staffing of Research Activities

The recruitment and assignment of research personnel to particular projects and activities poses a whole gamut of problems of an ethical nature. I will confine myself to two illustrations.

It is no doubt a truism that scientists become scientists because of their interest in science. Devotion to a scientific career means involvement with scientific work: *doing* science rather than *watching* science being done. The collectivization of science creates a new species—the science administrator whose very existence poses practical and ethical problems . . . And this is surely a problem with ethical implications derived from the fact that scientists have a certain obligation to the promotion of science itself as an ongoing human enterprise. On the other hand, there is the ethical problem of the scientist himself, for a scientist turned administrator is frequently a scientist lost to his first love.

My second example relates to the use of graduate students in university research. There seems to me to be a very real problem in the use of students in the staffing of research projects. We hear a great many pious platitudes about the value of such work for the training of students. The plain fact is that the kind of work needed to get the project done is simply not always the kind of work that is of optimum value for the basic training of a research scientist in a given field. Sometimes instead of doing the student a favor by awarding him a remunerative research fellowship, we may be doing him more harm than good. In some instances known to me, the project work that was supposedly the training ground of a graduate student in actuality derailed or stunted the development of a research scientist.

Ethical Problems Regarding Research Methods

Let me now take up a third set of ethical problems arising in scientific research—those having to do with the *methods* of the research itself. Problems of this kind arise perhaps most acutely in biological or medical or psychological experiments involving the use of experimental animals. They have to do with the measures of omission and commission for keeping experimental animals from needless pain and discomfort . . . It goes without saying that problems of this sort arise in their most acute form in experiments that risk human life, limb, well-being, or comfort.

Problems of a somewhat similar character come up in psychological or social science experiments in which the possibility of a compromise of human dignity or integrity is present, so that due measures are needed to assure treatment based on justice and fair play.

Ethical Problems Regarding Standards of Proof

I turn now to a further set of ethical problems relating to scientific research—those that are bound up with what we may call the standards of proof. These have to do with the amount of evidence that a scientist accumulates before he deems it appropriate to announce his findings and put forward the claim that such-and-so may be regarded as an established fact. At what juncture should scientific evidence be reasonably regarded as strong enough to give warrant for a conclusion, and how should the uncertainties of this conclusion be presented?

The problem of standards of proof is ethical, and not merely theoretical or methodological in nature, because it bridges the gap between scientific understanding and action, between thinking and doing. The scientist cannot conveniently sidestep the whole of the ethical impact of such questions by saying to the layman, "I'll tell you the scientific facts and then *you* decide on the proper mode of action." These issues are usually so closely interconnected that it is the scientific expert alone who can properly adjudge the bearing of the general scientific consideration upon the particular case in hand . . .

Ethical Problems Regarding the Dissemination of Research Findings

A surprising variety of ethical problems revolve around the general topic of the dissemination of research findings. It is so basic a truth as to be almost axiomatic that, with the possible exception of a handful of unusual cases in the area of national security classification, a scientist has not only the right, but even the duty, to communicate his findings to the community of fellow scientists, so that his results may stand or fall in the play of the open market place of ideas.

. . . It has become a widespread practice to make prepublication announcements of findings, or even pre-prepublication announcements. The ethical problem is posed by the extent and direction of such exchanges, for there is no doubt that in many cases favoritism comes into the picture, and that some workers and laboratories exchange findings in a preferential way that amounts to a conspiracy to maintain themselves ahead of the state of the art in the world at large. There is, of course, nothing reprehensible in the natural wish to overcome publication lags or in the normal desire for exchanges of ideas with fellow workers. But when such practices tend to become systematized in a prejudicial way, a plainly ethical problem comes into being.

Let us consider yet another ethical problem regarding the dissemination of research findings. The extensive dependence of science upon public opinion, in connection with its support both by the government and the foundations, has already been touched upon. This factor has a tendency to turn the reporting of scientific findings and the discussion of issues relating to scientific research into a kind of journalism. There is a strong incentive to create a favorable climate of public opinion for certain pet projects or concepts. Questions regarding scientific or technical merits thus tend to get treated not only in the proper forum of the scientific journals, but also in the public press and in Congressional or foundation committee rooms. Not only does this create the danger of scientific pressure groups devoted to preconceived ideas and endowed with the power of retarding other lines of thought, but it also makes for an unhealthy emphasis on the spectacular and the novel, unhealthy, that is, from the standpoint of the development of science itself. For such factors create a type of control over the direction of scientific research that is disastrously unrelated to the proper issue of strictly scientific merits . . .

Ethical Problems Regarding the Control of Scientific "Misinformation"

Closely bound up with the ethical problems regarding the dissemination of scientific information are what might be thought of as the other side of the coin—the control, censorship, and suppression of scientific misinformation. Scientists clearly have a duty to protect both their own colleagues in other specialties and the lay public against the dangers of supposed research findings that are strictly erroneous, particularly in regard to areas such as medicine and nutrition, where the public health and welfare are concerned. And quite generally, of course, a scientist has an obligation to maintain the professional literature of his field at a high level of content and quality. The editors and editorial reviewers in whose hands rest access to the media of scientific publication clearly have a duty to preserve their readership from errors of fact and trivia of thought. But these protective functions must always be balanced by respect for the free play of ideas and by a real sensitivity to the possible value of the unfamiliar . . .

It is worth emphasizing that this matter of "controlling" the dissemination of scientific ideas poses special difficulties due to an important, but much underrated, phenomenon: *the resistivity to novelty and innovation by the scientific community itself.* No feature of the historical course of development of the sciences is more damaging to the theoreticians' idealized conception of science as perfectly objective—the work of almost disembodied intellects governed by purely rational considerations and actuated solely by an abstract love of truth. The mere assertion that scientists can resist, and indeed frequently have resisted, acceptance of scientific discoveries clashes sharply with the stereotyped concept of the scientist as the purely objective, wholly rational, and entirely open-minded man . . .

But let us return to the ethical issues involved [in controlling pseudo-science]. These have to do not with the uncontroversial thesis that pseudo-science must be controlled, but with procedural questions of the *means* to be used for the achievement of this worthy purpose. It is with this problem of the means for its control that pseudo-science poses real ethical difficulties for the scientific community.

The handiest instrumentalities to this end and the most temptingly simple to use are the old standbys of thought control—censorship and suppression. But these are surely dire and desperate remedies. It is no doubt highly unpleasant for a scientist to see views that he regards as "preposterous" and "crackpot" to be disseminated and even to gain a considerable public following. But surely we should never lose sensitivity to the moral worth of the methods for achieving our ends or forget that good ends do not justify questionable means. It is undeniably true that scientists have the duty to prevent the propagation of error and misinformation. But this duty has to be acted on with thoughtful caution. It cannot be construed to fit the conveniences of the moment. And it surely cannot be stretched to give warrant to the suppression of views that might prove damaging to the public "image" of science or to justify the protection of one school of thought against its critics . . .

Ethical Problems Regarding the Allocation of Credit for Scientific Research Achievements

The final set of ethical problems arising in relation to scientific research that I propose to mention relate to the allocation of credit for the achievements of research work. Moral philosophers as well as students of jurisprudence have long been aware of the difficulties in assigning to individuals the responsibility for corporate acts, and thus to allocate to individual wrongdoers the blame for group misdeeds. This problem now faces the scientific community in its inverse form—the allocation to individuals of credit for the research accomplishments resulting from conjoint, corporate, or combined effort. Particularly in this day of collectivized research, this problem is apt to arise often and in serious forms.

Let no one be put off by stories about scientific detachment and disinterestedness. The issue of credit for their findings has for many centuries been of the greatest importance to scientists. Doubts on this head are readily dispelled by the prominence of priority disputes in the history of science . . . [T]he problem of credit allocation can come up nowadays in forms so complex and intricate as to be almost inconceivable to any mind not trained in the law. For instance, following out the implications of an idea put forward as an idle guess by X, Y, working under W's direction in Z's laboratory, comes up with an important result. How is the total credit to be divided? It requires no great imagination to think up some of the kinds of problems and difficulties that can come about in saying who is to be credited with what in this day of corporate and collective research.

Epistemic values

As we just saw, Rescher claims that moral values are an inherent part of scientific research. Not only should they not be eliminated from science, but they cannot be eliminated. Moral values are just as much an inescapable part of science, including good science, as are experiments and observations. There are other types of values, however, that Rescher does not discuss and these are values about the nature of science as providing us with reliable knowledge about the world. The philosopher Ernan McMullin, in the selection beginning on the next page, calls such values *epistemic* values. He calls them epistemic, he says, "because they are presumed to promote the truth-like character of science, its character as the most secure knowledge available to us of the world we seek to understand. An epistemic value is one we have reason to believe will, if pursued, help toward the attainment of such knowledge." As we have noted already, we want reliable scientific data to be replicable, to be precise and accurate. It is usual in science to expect that the results of experiments to be clearly quantifiable. Yet these features of being replicable, precise, accurate, quantifiable (and others) are not "in the data themselves." They are values that we hold regarding the validity and reliability of the data. Such values, says McMullin, are inherent and inescapable for science.

In the following reading, McMullin first analyzes various notions of value, distinguishing, for example, between value-judgment and value-clarification, as well as what he calls characteristic value (such as a particular organism having a certain colored plumage, with its respective survival value for that organism). The primary focus of his argument, however, is on epistemic values and their role in science, especially in assessing rival theories. Finally, he says, although we need to guard against the undue role of moral, social, and political values in theory-assessment (i.e., guard against cases like Lysenko), this can still be done within the context of acknowledging and understanding the role of epistemic values in science. Like Rescher, then, though for different reasons, McMullin claims that values in science are not incompatible with good science.

VALUES IN SCIENCE
Ernan McMullin

[In 1953] Richard Rudner argued in a brief essay in [the journal] *Philosophy of Science* that the making of value-judgments is an essential part of the work of science. He fully realized how repugnant such a claim would be to the positivist orthodoxy of the day, so repugnant indeed that its acceptance (he prophesied) would bring about a "first-order crisis in science and methodology." [Rudolf] Carnap, in particular, has been emphatic in excluding values from any role in science proper. His theory of meaning had led him to conclude that "the objective validity of a value . . . cannot be asserted in a meaningful statement at all." The contrast between science, the paradigm of meaning, and all forms of value-judgment could scarcely have been more sharply drawn: "it is altogether impossible to make a statement that expresses a value-judgment." No wonder, then, that Rudner's thesis seemed so shocking.

[Now] the claim that science is value-laden might no longer even seem controversial, among philosophers of science, at least, who have been accustomed to see the pillars of positivism fall one by one. One might even characterize the recent deep shifts in theory of science as consequences (many of them, at least) of the growing realization of the part played by value-judgments in scientific work . . . I shall try to show that the watershed between "classic" philosophy of science (by this meaning, not just logical positivism but the logicist tradition in theory of science stretching back through Immanuel Kant and René Descartes to Aristotle) and the "new" philosophy of science can best be understood by analyzing the change in our perception of the role played by values in science . . . .

The Anatomy of Value

"Value" is one of those weasel words that slip in and out of the nets of the philosopher. We shall have to try to catch it first, or else what we have to say about the role of values in science may be of small use. It is not much over a hundred years since the German philosopher, Hermann Lotze, tried to construct a single theory of value which would unite the varied value-aspects of human experience under a single discipline. The venture was, of course, not really new since Plato had attempted a similar project long before, using the cognate term "good" instead of "value." Aristotle's response to Plato's positing of the Good as a common element answering to one idea was to point to the great diversity of ways in which the term "good" might be used. In effect, our response to Lotze's project of a general axiology would likewise be to question the usefulness of trying to find a single notion of value that would apply to all contexts equally well.

Let us begin with the sense of "value" that the founders of value-theory seem to have preferred. They took it to correspond to such features of human experience as attraction, emotion, and feeling. They wanted to secure an experiential basis for value in order to give the realm of value an empirical status just as valid as that of the (scientific) realm of fact. The reality of *emotive* value (as it may be called) lies in the feelings of the subject, not primarily in a characteristic of the object. Value-differences amount, then, to differences of attitude or of emotional response in specific subjects.

If one takes "value" in this sense, the value decision becomes a matter of clarifying emotional responses. To speak of *value-judgment* here (as indeed is often done) is on the whole misleading since "judgment" could suggest a cognitive act, a weighing-up. When the value of something is determined by one's attitude to it, the declaration of this value is a matter of value-*clarification* rather than of judgment, strictly speaking . . .

It seems plausible to hold that emotive values are alien to the work of natural science. There is no reason to think that human emotionality is a trustworthy guide to the structures of the natural world. Indeed, there is every reason, historically speaking, to view emotive values, as Francis Bacon did, as potentially distortive "Idols," projecting in anthropomorphic fashion the pattern of human wants, desires, and emotions on a world where they have no place. When "ideology" is understood as a systematization of such values, it automatically becomes a threat to the integrity of science. The notion of value which is implicit in much recent social history of science, as well as in many analyses of the science-ideology relationship, is clearly that of emotive value.

A second kind of "value" is more important for your quest. A property or set of properties may count as a value in an entity of a particular kind because it is desirable for an entity of that kind. (The same property in a different entity might *not* count as a value.) The property can be a desirable one for various sorts of reasons. Speed is a desirable trait in wild antelope because it aids survival. Sound heart action is desirable in an organism with a circulatory system because of the functional needs of that organism. A retentive memory is desirable for a lawyer because of the nature of the lawyer's task. Sharpness is desirable in a knife because of the way in which it functions as a utensil. Efficiency is desirable in a business firm if the firm is to accomplish the ordinary ends of business . . . .

Let us focus on what these examples have in common. (In another context, we might be more concerned about their differences.) In each case, the desirable property is an objective characteristic of the entity. We can thus call it a *characteristic* value. In some cases, it is relative to a pattern of human ends; in others, it is not. In some cases, a characteristic value is a means to an end served by the entity possessing it; in others, it is not. In all cases, it serves to make its possessor function better as an entity of that kind.

Assessment of characteristic values can take on two quite different forms. One can judge the extent to which a particular entity realizes the value. We may be said to *evaluate* when we judge the speediness of a particular antelope or the heart-beat of a particular patient. On the other hand, we may be asked to judge whether or not (or to what extent) this characteristic really *is* a value for this kind of entity. How much do we *value* the characteristic? Here we are dealing, not with particulars, but with the more abstract relation of characteristic and entity under a particular description. Why *ought* one value speed in an antelope, rather than strength, say? How important *is* a retentive memory to a lawyer? . . .

Value-judgment, in the sense of evaluation could thus fall on the side of the factual, and the old dichotomy between fact and value could still be maintained. Value-judgment in the sense either of valuing or of evaluating, where the characteristic value is *not* sharply defined, was still to be rigorously excluded from science. Such value-judgment (so the argument went) is necessarily subjective; it involves a decision which is not rule-guided, and therefore has an element of the arbitrary. It intrudes individual human norms into what should ideally (if it were to be properly scientific) be an impersonal mapping of propositions onto the world . . .

What I want to argue here is that value-judgment [in the fuller sense] *does* play a central role in science. Both evaluation *and* value are involved. The attempt to construe all forms of scientific reasoning as forms of deductive or inductive inference fails. The sense of my claim that science is value-laden is that there are certain characteristic *epistemic* values which are integral to the entire process of assessment in science . . .

My argument for the effective presence of "values in science" does not, then, refer to the constitutive role in science of the value of truth; nor does it refer to the ethical values required for the success of science as a communal activity, or to the values implicit in decision-making in applied science. Rather, it is directed to showing that the appraisal of theory is in important respects closer in structure to value-judgment than it is to the rule-governed inference that the classic traditional in philosophy of science took for granted . . .

Theory-Choice as Value-Judgment

. . . The watershed between classic theory of science and our as yet unnamed post-logicist age has been variously defined since [1950]. But for our purposes here, it can best be laid out in four propositions, three of them familiar, the other (P3) less so.

P1: The goal of science is theoretical knowledge.

P2: The theories of science are underdetermined by the empirical evidence.

P3: The assessment of theories involves value-judgment in an essential way.

P4: Observations in science are theory-dependent.

P1 tells us that the basic explanatory form of science is theory, not law, and thus that retroduction, not induction, is the main form of scientific validation. Theories by their very nature are hypothetical and tentative; they remain open to revision or even to rejection. P2 reminds us that there is no direct logical link, of the sort that classical theories of science expected, between evidence and theory. Since one is not compelled, as one would be in a logical or mathematical demonstration, one has to rely on oblique modes of assessment. And P3 tells us that these take the form of value-judgments.

P4 serves to emphasize that a thesis in regard to theory-appraisal has broader scope. To the extent that scientific observation is theory-dependent, it is also indirectly value-impregnated. This last point is not stressed any further in what follows, but it is well that it should be kept in mind lest it be thought that only *one* element of science, theory-choice, is affected by the shift sustained at all other points . . .

The fact that theory-appraisal is a sophisticated form of value-judgment explains one of the most obvious features of science, a feature that could only appear as a mystery in the positivist scheme of things. Controversy, far from being rare and wrong-headed, is a persistent and pervasive presence in science at all levels. Yet if the classical logicist view of science had been right, controversy would be easily resolvable. One would simply employ an algorithm, a "method," to decide which of the contending theories is best confirmed by the evidence available. At any given moment, there would then be a "best" theory, to which scientists properly versed in the craft ought to adhere.

But, of course, not only is this *not* the case, but it would be a disaster if it *were* to be the case . . . The clash of theories, Popper has convinced us, is needed in order that weak spots may be probed and potentialities fully developed. Popper's own theory of science made it difficult to see how such a pluralism of theories could be maintained. But once theory-appraisal is recognized to be a complex form of value-judgment, the persistence of competing theories immediately follows as a consequence . . .

Epistemic Values

Even though we cannot *definitively* establish the values appropriate to the assessment of theory, we saw just a moment ago that we can provide a tentative list of criteria that have gradually been shaped over the experience of many centuries, the values that are implicit in contemporary scientific practice. Such characteristic values I will call *epistemic*, because they are presumed to promote the truth-like character of science, its character as the most secure knowledge available to us of the world we seek to understand. An epistemic value is one we have reason to believe will, if pursued, help toward the attainment of such knowledge. I have concentrated here on the values that one expects a good *theory* to embody. But there are, of course, many other epistemic values, like that of reproducibility in an experiment or accuracy in measurement.

When I say that science is value-laden, I would not want it to be thought that these values derive from theory-appraisal only. Value-judgment permeates the work of science as a whole, from the decision to allow a particular experimental result to count as "basic" or "accepted" (the decisional element that Popper stressed), to the decision not to seek an alternative to a theory which so far has proved satisfactory. Such values as these may be pragmatic rather than epistemic; they may derive from the finiteness of the time or resources available to the experimenter, for example. And sometimes the borderline between the epistemic and the pragmatic may be hard to draw, since (as Pierre Duhem and Karl Popper among others have made clear) it is essential to the process of science that pragmatic decisions be made, on the temporary suspension of further testing, for example.

Of course, it is not pragmatic values that pose the main challenge to the epistemic integrity of the appraisal process. If values are needed in order to close the gap between underdetermined theory and the evidence brought in its support, presumably all sorts of values can slip in: political, moral, social, and religious. The list is as long as the list of possible human goals. I shall lump these values together under the single blanket term, "non-epistemic." The decision as to whether a value is epistemic or non-epistemic in a particular context can sometimes be a difficult one. But the grounds on which it should be made are easy to specify in the abstract. When no sufficient case can be made for saying that the imposition of a particular value on the process of theory choice is likely to improve the *epistemic* status of the theory, that is, the conformity between theory and the world, this value is held to be non-epistemic in the context in question. The decision is itself, of course, a value-judgment and there is an obvious danger of a vicious regress at this point . . .

The Place of Act in a World of Values

. . . [L]et me return to the question that must by now be uppermost in the reader's mind. What is left of the vaulted objectivity of science, the element of the factual, in all this welter of value-judgment? Once the camel's nose is inside, the tent rapidly becomes uncomfortable. Is there any reasoned way to stop short of a relativism that would see in science no more than the product of a contingent social consensus, bearing testimony to the historical particularity of culture and personality much more than to an objective truth about the world? I think there is, but I can at this stage only provide an outline of the argument needed. It requires two separate steps.

Step one is to examine the epistemic values employed in theory-appraisal, the values that lie at the heart of the claim that theory assessment in science is essentially value-laden, and to ask how they in turn are to be validated, and how in particular, circularity is to be avoided in doing this. First, let me recall how the skills of epistemic value-judgment are *learnt*. Apprentice scientists learn them not from a method book but from watching others exercise them. They learn what to expect in a "good" theory. They note what kinds of considerations carry weight, and why they do so. They get a feel for the relative weight given the different kinds of considerations, and may quickly come to realize that there are divergences here in practice. Their own value-judgments will gradually become more assured, and will be tested against the practice of their colleagues as well as against historical precedent . . .

We can endeavor to *account for* [particular values'] desirability in terms of a higher-order epistemological account of scientific knowing. This is to carry retroductions to the next level upwards. It is asking the philosopher to provide a theory in terms of which such values as fertility would be shown to be appropriate demands to lay on scientific theory. The philosopher's ability to provide just such a theory (and it is not difficult to do this) in turn then testifies to the reliability of taking these criteria to be proper values for theory-appraisal in the first place. This is only the outline of an argument, and much more remains to be filled in. But perhaps I have said enough to indicate how one could go about showing that the characteristic values scientists have come to expect a theory to embody are a testimony to the *objectivity* of the theory, as well as of the involvement of the subjectivity of the scientist in the effort to attain that objectivity . . .

And so, to conclude step one, there is reason to trust in the values used commonly in current science for theory-appraisal as something much more than the contingent consensus of a peculiar social sub-group.

But a further step is needed, because these values do not of themselves *determine* theory-choice, a point I have stressed from the beginning. And so other values *can* and *do* enter in, the sorts of values that sociologists of science have so successfully been drawing our attention to of late, as they scrutinize particular episodes in the history of science. I am thinking of such values as the personal ambition of the scientist, the welfare of the social class to which he or she belongs, and so on. Has the camel not, then, poked its wet nose in beside us once again?

It has, of course, but perhaps we can find a way to push it out—or almost out—one final time. The process of science is one long series of test and tentative imaginative extensions. When a particular theory seems to have triumphed, . . . it is not as though the view that has prevailed is allowed to reign in peace. Other scientists attempt to duplicate experimental claims; theoreticians try to extend the theories involved in new and untried ways; various tests are devised for the more vulnerable theoretical moves involved, and so on. This is not just part of the mythology of science. It really *does* happen, and it is easy to document.

To the extent that non-epistemic values and other non-epistemic factors have been instrumental in the original theory-decision (and sociologists of science have rendered a great service by revealing how much more pervasive these factors are than one might have expected), they are gradually sifted by the continued application of the sort of value-judgment we have been describing here. The non-epistemic, by very definition, will not in the long run survive this process. The process is designed to limit the effects not only of fraud and carelessness, but also of ideology, understood in its perjorative sense as distortive intrusion into the slow process of shaping our thought to the world.

Chapter Summary

There are value issues relating to values about science. The distinction between good science and bad science is sometimes said to be in part a function of science being as value-free as possible. The history of science, as well as contemporary scientific practice, is filled with examples of values degrading the worth of scientific research and results, whether those values were broad social and political values or the values of the participating researchers. There are well-known cases, such as that of Trofim Lysenko, in which social and political values permeated scientific theory and research, resulting in bad science. There are also cases of funding organizations, both private and public, squelching the results of scientific research when those results were not desired by the funding organizations. There are also value issues relating to values within science. In particular, Nicholas Rescher argues that moral values are inherent in multiple aspects of scientific research, such as the choice of research goals, standards of proof, dissemination of research findings, and allocation of credit for research achievements. Ernan McMullin argues that epistemic values are inherent in theory-assessment. They are values such as quantifiability, predictability, replicability, and so on. Epistemic values, says McMullin, are presumed to promote the truth-like character of science, its character as the most secure knowledge available to us of the world we seek to understand. Both Rescher and McMulllin claim that values are inescapable as a part of science and that they are not inconsistent with the practice and assessment of good science.

CASE STUDY
Does Race Exist?

The notion that humanity is composed of various different races—for example, Caucasian, Negroid, Asiatic, Semitic—is long-standing. The proposed criteria for just what constitute a race, or the very concept of race, has changed over time. That is, what were identified in 1800 (by some people, at least) as the different races of humans are not the same as what are identified today (by some people, at least) as the different races of humans. Indeed, the very notion of humanity as being divisible into races—in other words, the very concept of race—has been challenged recently. Much of this challenge stems from the claim that there is minimal, if any, scientific (primarily genetic) basis for the concept. Following are two readings related to the question: does race exist? The first reading, by Loring Brace, rejects the notion of race, although the second reading, by George Gill, accepts it. As you read them, look for both explicit and implicit values both about the topic and the science related to it as well as values within the science itself.

DOES RACE EXIST? AN ANTAGONIST'S PERSPECTIVE
Loring Brace

I am going to start this essay with what may seem to many as an outrageous assertion. There is no such thing as a biological entity that warrants the term "race."

The immediate reaction of most literate people is that this is obviously nonsense. The physician will retort, "What do you mean, 'there is no such thing as race'? I see it in my practice everyday!" Jane Doe and John Roe will be equally incredulous. Note carefully, however, that my opening declaration did not claim that "there is no such thing as race." What I said is that there is no "biological entity that warrants the term 'race'." "You're splitting hairs," the reader may retort. "Stop playing verbal games and tell us what you really mean!"

And so I shall, but there is another charge that has been thrown my way, which I need to dispel before explaining the basis for my statement. Given the tenor of our times at the dawn of the new millennium, some have suggested that my position is based mainly on the perception of the social inequities that have accompanied the classification of people into "races." My stance, then, has been interpreted as a manifestation of what is being called "political correctness." My answer is that it is really the defenders of the concept of "race" who are unwittingly shaped by the political reality of American history.

But all of this needs explaining. First, it is perfectly true that the long-term residents of the various parts of the world have patterns of features that we can easily identify as characteristic of the areas from which they come. It should be added that they have to have resided in those places for a couple of hundred thousand years before their regional patterns became established. Well, you may ask, why can't we call those regional patterns "races"? In fact, we can and do, but it does not make them coherent biological entities. "Races" defined in such a way are products of our perceptions. "Seeing is believing" will be the retort, and, after all, aren't we seeing reality in those regional differences?

I should point out that this is the same argument that was made against Copernicus and Galileo almost half a millennium ago. To this day, few have actually made the observations and done the calculations that led those Renaissance scholars to challenge the universal perception that the sun sets in the evening to rise again at the dawn. It was just a matter of common sense to believe that the sun revolves around the Earth, just as it was common sense to "know" that the Earth was flat. Our beliefs concerning "race" are based on the same sort of common sense, and they are just as basically wrong.

The Nature of Human Variation

I would suggest that there are very few who, of their own experience, have actually perceived at first hand the nature of human variation. What we know of the characteristics of the various regions of the world we have largely gained vicariously and in misleadingly spotty fashion. Pictures and the television camera tell us that the people of Oslo in Norway, Cairo in Egypt, and Nairobi in Kenya look very different. And when we actually meet natives of those separate places, which can indeed happen, we can see representations of those differences at first hand. But if one were to walk up beside the Nile from Cairo, across the Tropic of Cancer to Khartoum in the Sudan and on to Nairobi, there would be no visible boundary between one people and the other. The same thing would be true if one were to walk north from Cairo, through the Caucasus, and on up into Russia, eventually swinging west across the northern end of the Baltic Sea to Scandinavia. The people at any adjacent stops along the way look like one another more than they look like anyone else since, after all, they are related to one another. As a rule, the boy marries the girl next door throughout the whole world, but next door goes on without stop from one region to another.

We realize that in the extremes of our transit—Moscow to Nairobi, perhaps—there is a major but gradual change in skin color from what we euphemistically call white to black, and that this is related to the latitudinal difference in the intensity of the ultraviolet component of sunlight. What we do not see, however, is the myriad other traits that are distributed in a fashion quite unrelated to the intensity of ultraviolet radiation. Where skin color is concerned, all the northern populations of the Old World are lighter than the long-term inhabitants near the equator. Although European and Chinese are obviously different, in skin color they are closer to each other than either is to equatorial Africans. But if we test the distribution of the widely known ABO blood-group system, then Europeans and Africans are closer to each other than either is to Chinese.

Then if we take that scourge sickle-cell anemia, so often thought of as an African disease, we discover that, while it does reach high frequencies in some parts of sub-Saharan Africa, it did not originate there. Its distribution includes southern Italy, the eastern Mediterranean, parts of the Middle East, and over into India. In fact, it represents a kind of adaptation that aids survival in the face of a particular kind of malaria, and wherever that malaria is a prominent threat, sickle-cell anemia tends to occur in higher frequencies. It would appear that the gene that controls that trait was introduced to sub-Saharan Africa by traders from those parts of the Middle East where it had arisen in conjunction with the conditions created by the early development of agriculture.

Every time we plot the distribution of a trait possessing a survival value that is greater under some circumstances than under others, it will have a different pattern of geographical variation, and no two such patterns will coincide. Nose form, tooth size, relative arm and leg length, and a whole series of other traits are distributed each in accordance with its particular controlling selective force. The gradient of the distribution of each is called a "cline" and those clines are completely independent of one another. This is what lies behind the aphorism, "There are no races, there are only clines." Yes, we can recognize people from a given area. What we are seeing, however, is a pattern of features derived from common ancestry in the area in question, and these are largely without survival value. To the extent that the people in a given region look more like one another than they look like people from other regions, this can be regarded as "family resemblance writ large." And as we have seen, each region grades without break into the one next door.

There is nothing wrong with using geographic labels to designate people. Major continental terms are just fine, and sub-regional refinements such as Western European, Eastern African, Southeast Asian, and so forth carry no unintentional baggage. In contrast, terms such as "Negroid," "Caucasoid," and "Mongoloid" create more problems than they can solve. Those very terms reflect a mix of narrow regional, specific ethnic, and descriptive physical components with an assumption that such separate dimensions have some kind of common tie. Biologically, such terms are worse than useless. Their continued use, then, is in social situations where people think they have some meaning.

America and the Race Concept

The role played by America is particularly important in generating and perpetuating the concept of "race." The human inhabitants of the Western Hemisphere largely derive from three very separate regions of the world—Northeast Asia, Northwest Europe, and Western Africa—and none of them has been in the New World long enough to have been shaped by their experiences in the manner of those long-term residents in the various separate regions of the Old World.

It was the American experience of those three separate population components facing one another on a daily basis under conditions of manifest and enforced inequality that created the concept in the first place and endowed it with the assumption that those perceived "races" had very different sets of capabilities. Those thoughts are very influential and have been enshrined in laws and regulations. This is why I can conclude that, while the word "race" has no coherent biological meaning, its continued grip on the public mind is in fact a manifestation of the power of the historical continuity of the American social structure, which is assumed by all to be essentially "correct."

Finally, because of America's enormous influence on the international scene, ideas generated by the idiosyncrasies of American history have gained currency in ways that transcend American intent or control. One of those ideas is the concept of "race," which we have exported to the rest of the world without any realization that this is what we were doing. The adoption of the biologically indefensible American concept of "race" by an admiring world has to be the ultimate manifestation of political correctness.

DOES RACE EXIST: A PROPONENT'S PERSPECTIVE
George Gill

Slightly over half of all biological/physical anthropologists today believe in the traditional view that human races are biologically valid and real. Furthermore, they tend to see nothing wrong in defining and naming the different populations of *Homo sapiens*. The other half of the biological anthropology community believes either that the traditional racial categories for humankind are arbitrary and meaningless, or that at a minimum there are better ways to look at human variation than through the "racial lens."

Are there differences in the research concentrations of these two groups of experts? Yes, most decidedly there are. As pointed out in a recent 2000 edition of a popular physical anthropology textbook, forensic anthropologists (those who do skeletal identification for law-enforcement agencies) are overwhelmingly in support of the idea of the basic biological reality of human races, and yet those who work with blood-group data, for instance, tend to reject the biological reality of racial categories.

I happen to be one of those very few forensic physical anthropologists who actually does research on the particular traits used today in forensic racial identification (i.e., "assessing ancestry," as it is generally termed today). Partly this is because for more than a decade now U.S. national and regional forensic anthropology organizations have deemed it necessary to quantitatively test both traditional and new methods for accuracy in legal cases. I volunteered for this task of testing methods and developing new methods in the late 1980s. What have I found? Where do I now stand in the "great race debate?" Can I see truth on one side or the other—or on both sides—in this argument?

Findings

First, I have found that forensic anthropologists attain a high degree of accuracy in determining geographical racial affinities (white, black, American Indian, etc.) by utilizing both new and traditional methods of bone analysis. Many well-conducted studies were reported in the late 1980s and 1990s that test methods objectively for percentage of correct placement. Numerous individual methods involving midfacial measurements, femur traits, and so on are over 80 percent accurate alone, and in combination produce very high levels of accuracy. No forensic anthropologist would make a racial assessment based upon just *one* of these methods, but in combination they can make very reliable assessments, just as in determining sex or age. In other words, multiple criteria are the key to success in all of these determinations.

I have a respected colleague, the skeletal biologist C. Loring Brace [see above], who is as skilled as any of the leading forensic anthropologists at assessing ancestry from bones, yet he does not subscribe to the concept of race. Neither does Norman Sauer, a board-certified forensic anthropologist. My students ask, "How can this be? They can identify skeletons as to racial origins but do not believe in race?" My answer is that we can often *function* within systems that we do not believe in.

As a middle-aged male, for example, I am not so sure that I believe any longer in the chronological "age" categories that many of my colleagues in skeletal biology use. Certainly parts of the skeletons of some 45-year-old people look older than the corresponding portions of the skeletons of some 55-year-olds. If, however, law enforcement calls upon me to provide "age" on a skeleton, I can provide an answer that will be proven sufficiently accurate should the decedent eventually be identified. I may not believe in society's "age" categories, but I can be very effective at "aging" skeletons. The next question, of course, is how "real" is age biologically? My answer is that if one can use biological criteria to assess age with reasonable accuracy, then age has some basis in biological reality even if the particular "social construct" that defines its limits might be imperfect. I find this true not only for age and stature estimations but for sex and race identification.

The reality of "race" therefore depends more on the definition of reality than on the definition of race. If we choose to accept the system of racial taxonomy that physical anthropologists have traditionally established—major races: black, white, etc.—then one can classify human skeletons within it just as well as one can classify living humans. The bony traits of the nose, mouth, femur, and cranium are just as revealing to a good osteologist as skin color, hair form, nose form, and lips to the perceptive observer of living humanity. I have been able to prove to myself over the years, in actual legal cases, that I am *more* accurate at assessing race from skeletal remains than from looking at living people standing before me. So those of us in forensic anthropology know that the skeleton reflects race, whether "real" or not, just as well if not better than superficial soft tissue does. The idea that race is "only skin deep" is simply not true, as any experienced forensic anthropologist will affirm.

Position on Race

Where I stand today in the "great race debate" after a decade and a half of pertinent skeletal research is clearly more on the side of the reality of race than on the "race denial" side. Yet I do see why many other physical anthropologists are able to ignore or deny the race concept. Blood-factor analysis, for instance, shows many traits that cut across racial boundaries in a purely *clinal* fashion with very few if any "breaks" along racial boundaries. (A cline is a gradient of change, such as from people with a high frequency of blue eyes, as in Scandinavia, to people with a high frequency of brown eyes, as in Africa.)

Morphological characteristics, however, like skin color, hair form, bone traits, eyes, and lips tend to follow geographical boundaries coinciding often with climatic zones. This is not surprising since the selective forces of climate are probably the primary forces of nature that have shaped human races with regard not only to skin color and hair form but also the underlying bony structures of the nose, cheekbones, etc. (For example, more prominent noses humidify air better.) As far as we know, blood-factor frequencies are *not* shaped by these same climatic factors.

So, serologists who work largely with blood factors will tend to see human variation as clinal and races as not a valid construct, while skeletal biologists, particularly forensic anthropologists, will see races as biologically real. The common person on the street who sees only a person's skin color, hair form, and face shape will also tend to see races as biologically real. They are not incorrect. Their perspective is just different from that of the serologist.

So, yes, I see truth on both sides of the race argument.

Those who believe that the concept of race is valid do not discredit the notion of clines, however. Yet those with the clinal perspective who believe that races are not real do try to discredit the evidence of skeletal biology. Why this bias from the "race denial" faction? This bias seems to stem largely from socio-political motivation and not science at all. For the time being at least, the people in "race denial" are in "reality denial" as well. Their motivation (a positive one) is that they have come to believe that the race concept is socially dangerous. In other words, they have convinced themselves that race promotes racism. Therefore, they have pushed the politically correct agenda that human races are not biologically real, no matter what the evidence.

Consequently, at the beginning of the 21st century, even as a majority of biological anthropologists favor the reality of the race perspective, not one introductory textbook of physical anthropology even presents that perspective as a possibility. In a case as flagrant as this, we are not dealing with science but rather with blatant, politically motivated censorship. But, you may ask, are the politically correct actually correct? Is there a relationship between thinking about race and racism?

Race and Racism

Does discussing human variation in a framework of racial biology promote or reduce racism? This is an important question, but one that does not have a simple answer. Most social scientists over the past decade have convinced themselves that it runs the risk of promoting racism in certain quarters. Anthropologists of the 1950s, 1960s, and early 1970s, on the other hand, believed that they were combating racism by openly discussing race and by teaching courses on human races and racism. Which approach has worked best? What do the intellectuals among racial minorities believe? How do students react and respond?

Three years ago, I served on a NOVA-sponsored panel in New York, in which panelists debated the topic "Is There Such a Thing as Race?" Six of us sat on the panel, three proponents of the race concept and three antagonists. All had authored books or papers on race. Loring Brace and I were the two anthropologists "facing off" in the debate. The ethnic composition of the panel was three white and three black scholars. As our conversations developed, I was struck by how similar many of my concerns regarding racism were to those of my two black teammates. Although recognizing that embracing the race concept can have risks attached, we were (and are) more fearful of the form of racism likely to emerge if race is denied and dialogue about it lessened. We fear that the social taboo about the subject of race has served to suppress open discussion about a very important subject in need of dispassionate debate. One of my teammates, an affirmative-action lawyer, is afraid that a denial that races exist also serves to encourage a denial that racism exists. He asks, "How can we combat racism if no one is willing to talk about race?"

Who will Benefit?

In my experience, minority students almost invariably have been the strongest supporters of a "racial perspective" on human variation in the classroom. The first-ever black student in my human variation class several years ago came to me at the end of the course and said, "Dr. Gill, I really want to thank you for changing my life with this course." He went on to explain that, "My whole life I have wondered about why I am black, and if that is good or bad. Now I know the reasons why I am the way I am and that these traits are useful and good."

A human-variation course with another perspective would probably have accomplished the same for this student if he had ever noticed it. The truth is, innocuous contemporary human-variation classes with their politically correct titles and course descriptions do not attract the attention of minorities or those other students who could most benefit. Furthermore, the politically correct "race denial" perspective in society as a whole suppresses dialogue, allowing ignorance to replace knowledge and suspicion to replace familiarity. This encourages ethnocentrism and racism more than it discourages it.

Further Reading

Bronowski, J. *Science and Human Values.* New York: Harper Torchbooks, 1956.

Graham, Loren. *Between Science and Values.* New York: Columbia University Press, 1981.

Grünfeld, Joseph. *Science and Values.* Amsterdam: B.R. Grüner, 1973.

Holton, Gerald and Robert S. Morrison (eds.). *Limits of Scientific Inquiry.* New York: W.W. Norton, 1979.

Joravsky, David. *The Lysenko Affair.* Chicago: University of Chicago Press, 1970.

Lacey, Hugh. *Is Science Value Free?* New York: Routledge, 2004.

Laudan, Larry. *Science and Values.* Berkeley: University of California Press, 1983.

Lewontin, R. C. *Biology As Ideology.* New York: HarperPerenniel, 1992.

Mayo, Deborah G. and Rachelle D. Hollander (eds.). *Acceptable Evidence.* Oxford: Oxford University Press, 1991.

Resnik, David B. *The Ethics of Science.* New York: Routledge, 1998.

Sigma Xi. *Ethics, Values, and the Promise of Science: Forum Proceedings.* Research Triangle Park: Sigma Xi, 1993.

Stevenson, Leslie, et al. *The Many Faces of Science.* Boulder: Westview, 2000.

CHAPTER THIRTEEN

Science and Religion

IN THIS CHAPTER, WE WILL

- Identify some metaphysical, epistemological, and axiological aspects of religion as it relates to science

- Identify several ways that science and religion are said to be related, whether in conflict or dialogue or independent of one another

- Examine the question of scientific and religious methods

- Examine the issue of evolutionary theory and design

- Consider the axiological issue of human dignity

We have all heard of the Big Bang, the theory that the universe began sometime between 13 to 14 billion years ago with a sudden and dramatic expansion of everything that makes up the physical cosmos. Many of us have also heard of Bishop James Usser, who in 1620 calculated the beginning of the universe to have been in the year 4004 B.C. We know of the controversy about teaching creationism in schools. In 1996, *Time Magazine* ran an article on the power of prayer to improve a person's physical health.

Whether or not individuals would consider themselves religious, in the sense that they have personal beliefs or convictions connected to God or spirituality, the examples above show how religion is related to all of us. In the introductory chapter of this book, we looked at issues of metaphysics, epistemology, and axiology. As was noted, there are metaphysical issues related to religion, such as the very nature of a divine being. Just what does the name "God" refer to? We know what the name "Babe Ruth" refers to; it's that guy who played baseball for the New York Yankees. We can say things about him that we know are true or false (he hit many home runs; he weighed 800 pounds). But can we do the same with God? Besides metaphysical issues, such as the nature of God, and epistemological issues, such as how we can know the nature of God, there are many axiological questions related to religion, such as the appropriate role of religion in public education or why bad things happen to good people. This chapter will examine some metaphysical, epistemological, and axiological issues connected to the relations between science and religion.

What is religion?

In addressing these relations, we will first need to look at features of religion. To begin with, what is religion? Consider the various definitions, or at least characterizations, of religion given below:

- Religion is the belief in an everlasting God, that is, in a Divine Mind and Will ruling the Universe and holding moral relations with mankind. (James Marineau)
- Religion is the recognition that all things are manifestations of a Power which transcends our knowledge. (Herbert Spencer)
- By religion, then, I understand a propitiation or conciliation of powers superior to man which are believed to direct and control the course of Nature and of human life. (J. G. Frazer)
- Religion is rather the attempt to express the complete reality of goodness through every aspect of our being. (F. H. Bradley)
- Religion is ethics heightened, enkindled, lit up by feeling. (Matthew Arnold)
- Religion is, in truth, that pure and reverential disposition or frame of mind which we call piety. (C. P. Tiele)
- The essence of religion consists in the feeling of absolute dependence. (Friedrich Schleiermacher)

There are, of course, countless other characterizations of religion. These attempts to state the nature of religion differ in a variety of ways. For instance, some but not all include belief in God (or perhaps gods) as basic to what religion is. Some but not all focus on religion as purpose or meaning connected to human self-understanding. Notice that none of these statements about the fundamental nature of religion speak to specific religions, such as Christianity or Islam or Hinduism. Instead, the sorts of features are ones that emphasize a family of aspects. One such aspect is the existence of divine, or supernatural, beings. Another aspect is the distinction between what is taken to be sacred and holy on the one hand, and what is taken to be profane, or irreverent. This distinction between the sacred and profane points to conduct that is required or permitted or forbidden to believers. Some of this conduct might involve rituals that connect believers to sacred objects or beings (such as prayer) or connect believers to a community of other believers (such as taking communion in church). Especially important elements of human life are often highlighted and even legitimated through such rituals (such as baptism or marriage).

Although these aspects of religion are basic to what religion is, how most people encounter religion in their daily lives is in terms of their personal faith and connection with what is sacred, as well as in terms of their connections with other people, for example, belonging to a church or religious community. It is their understanding of their own identity that is significant, their identity as an individual person and their identity as a part of some larger group (whether that group is one's immediate local church congregation or, say, as a larger religious denomination or even simply as part of God's creation). For religious believers, religion speaks to who we are, where we come from, and in terms of our personal and collective destiny, where we are going.

One important point to note when considering the nature of the relationship between science and religion is that historically, the relationship has actually been quite varied and complex. Most people think the historical connection has been a hostile one. They support this view by pointing to some rather notorious cases from the history of science. For example, people often bring up Galileo's struggles with the Catholic Church and the fact that he was forced to back away from his open support of a Copernican view of the solar system. Shortly prior to Galileo's famous struggles, Nicholas Bruno was burned at the stake for advocating a view that there were many worlds in the universe possibly with life. Of course, the whopper of them all is the case of Darwin and evolution. We'll get to that shortly.

In spite of these examples, much of the history of science displays a much more mutually supporting relationship between science and religion. Isaac Newton, for instance, wrote to Reverend Dr. Richard Bentley: "When I wrote my treatise about our system, I had an eye upon such principles as might work with considering men for the belief in a Deity; and nothing can rejoice me more than to find it useful for that purpose." Indeed, much of the achievements throughout the history of science were the result of the research by clergy and churchmen, such as Gregor Mendel.

Relation between science and religion

I began this chapter with the claim that we have all heard of the Big Bang theory of the beginning of the Universe. And, of course, we all know of the controversies around evolutionary theory versus creationism (or the more recent intelligent design view), as well as religious concerns over human cloning and stem cell research. Religion and science, as two broadly fundamental ways that we understand the world seem all-too-often at odds with each other. But why is that, and do they have to be?

(CALVIN AND HOBBES ©1988 Watterson. Dist. By UNIVERSAL PRESS SYNDICATE.
Reprinted with permission. All rights reserved.)

A few years back there was a Calvin & Hobbes cartoon strip that showed the two of them leaning up against a tree. This cartoon illustrates what many take to be a basic difference between religion and science; religion, they say, asks about the meaning of events (*why* things happen), whereas science asks about the nature and cause of the events (*how* things happen). This might be over-simplistic, but you get the point. For religious purposes, we want to know the significance of events for understanding who we are and where we have come from and where we are going (our identity, origin, and destiny). For scientific purposes, we want to know how things work and know how to use them. Of course, as scientists we might also care about our origins and destiny (that's what a lot of cosmology is about), but in a different sense than for religious concerns.

Does this mean that religion and science are necessarily at odds? Not at all. That is, the content, methods, and goals of science and of religion are not *necessarily* at odds. And, in fact, there is and has been quite a varied relationship between religious concerns and scientific concerns. Before looking directly at some of the kinds of relationships between religion and science, I will say something about the very terms "religion" and "science." As we saw at the start of this chapter, there are many different conceptions of what religion is. There are many different religions and many different religious doctrines and practices. The same holds for science. There are many different sciences and they vary with respect to what they study and what methods they use and what aims they have. Anthropologists study quite different things than radio astronomers do and they use quite different methods and they have quite different goals (at least some different goals). So, the first thing to note is that when we ask about the relation between religion and science, we are using two very broad and imprecise terms. Although many people get quite agitated about what evolutionary theory says about human nature, not many people think that the periodic chart of the elements that chemists use is religiously objectionable. Also, not many people get upset on religious grounds that some scientific experiments involve double-blind studies, where neither the experimenter nor the subject know who is in the control group and who is not. So, to talk about the relationship between religion and science really needs a lot of unpacking and more careful treatment.

Nonetheless, we can see various ways that religious concerns and scientific concerns might and do relate. One basic mode of relation between them is that they *conflict*. That is, both religion and science make claims about the world or things in it and those claims clash with each other. If a cosmologist says that the world is 13 billion years old and Bishop Usser says it is 6,000 years old, and if they are both making factual claims about the real age of the world, then obviously they cannot both be true. They are making contrary claims and they are rival views. Very often this is how religion and science are portrayed.

A second view of the relationship between religion and science is that they are really quite *independent* of each other. Each has its appropriate, relevant sphere of concern. They do not contradict each other because they are talking about different things, even when they sometimes seem to be talking about the same thing. So, when a theist says that God parted the waters or separated the land and the sea, this is not necessarily meant to contradict a scientific account of how this could or did happen. The point is that religious claims are not necessarily meant as physical descriptions of the world. Instead, they are metaphorical or allegorical and are meant to speak about the meaning or significance of events in the world.

A third view is that there is and can be important *dialogue* and *integration* across the spheres of religion and science. There might well be "boundary questions" that both speak to, so they are not completely isolated from each other. For example, both religion and science wrestle with the question of the origin of humanity and the nature of who we are as persons (the notion of a soul). Much of the history of science is a testimony to religious believers trying to understand the physical world. This area of study is often called "natural theology," in which one studies God's creation in order to better understand God the creator. So, there might well be areas of mutual concern between religion and science (they are not totally independent of each other) and yet they have separate concerns as well (they are not total rivals of each other). The question then becomes when, if ever, religious claims are meant to be empirical, and hence rival claims to science. Just as well, it would be appropriate to ask when, if ever, what is said in the name of science is meant to function like religion, that is, tell us about the meaning and significance of events. Certainly, in terms of claims about the world, many—probably most—scientific claims are consistent with religious claims and beliefs. There is nothing about electrons having a negative charge and protons having a positive charge that runs against religious concerns. Even claims that might seem more controversial are not necessarily so. For example, a theist could easily agree that the moon's orbit is the result of a balance of gravitational and inertial forces, yet still hold to the belief that there is a creator of the universe or intelligent design to the universe.

Method

An important topic about the relation of religion and science is how we can best characterize the nature of science, particularly in terms of method, and ask if it really is that different than religion. Throughout this book so far, we have looked at a number of complex and complicated issues connected to how science works (e.g., chapters on explanation, evidence, theories and models). Are scientific methods for gathering, analyzing, and evaluating information different than (and perhaps in conflict with) religious methods? This question was raised in 1981 (and on many occasions before and since), when the Arkansas General Assembly voted to enact a state law requiring that creationism be taught in public schools. In the following two selections, we see different views about the nature of science and how it relates to religion. In the first selection, Larry Laudan argues that the criteria we usually apply to science, but not to religion, are mistaken. In the second selection, Michael Ruse responds to Laudan.

SCIENCE AT THE BAR—CAUSES FOR CONCERN
Larry Laudan

In the wake of the decision in the Arkansas Creationism trial (*McLean v. Arkansas*), the friends of science are apt to be relishing the outcome. The creationists quite clearly made a botch of their case and there can be little doubt that the Arkansas decision may, at least for a time, blunt legislative pressure to enact similar laws in other states. Once the dust has settled, however, the trial in general and Judge William R. Overton's ruling in particular may come back to haunt us; for, although the verdict itself is probably to be commended, it was reached for all the wrong reasons and by a chain of argument which is hopelessly suspect. Indeed, the ruling rests on a host of misinterpretations of what science is and how it works.

The heart of Judge Overton's Opinion is a formulation of "the essential characteristics of science." These characteristics serve as touchstones for contrasting evolutionary theory with Creationism; they led Judge Overton ultimately to the claim, specious in its own right, that since Creationism is not "science," it must be religion. The Opinion offers five essential properties that demarcate scientific knowledge from other things: "(1) It is guided by natural law; (2) it has to be explanatory by reference to natural law; (3) it is testable against the empirical world; (4) its conclusions are tentative, i.e., are not necessarily the final word; and (5) it is falsifiable."

These fall naturally into families: properties (1) and (2) have to do with lawlikeness and explanatory ability; the other three properties have to do with the fallibility and testability of scientific claims. I shall deal with the second set of issues first, because it is there that the most egregious errors of fact and judgment are to be found.

At various key points in the Opinion, Creationism is charged with being untestable, dogmatic (and thus non-tentative), and unfalsifiable. All three charges are of dubious merit. For instance, to make the inter-linked claims that Creationism is neither falsifiable nor testable is to assert that Creationism makes no empirical assertions whatever. That is surely false. Creationism makes a wide range of testable assertions about empirical matters of fact. Thus, as Judge Overton himself grants (apparently without seeing its implications), the creationists say that the earth is of very recent origin (say 6,000 to 20,000 years old); they argue that most of the geological features of the earth's surface are diluvial in character (i.e., products of the postulated Noachian deluge); they are committed to a large number of factual historical claims with which the Old Testament is replete; they assert the limited variability of species. They are committed to the view that, since animals and man were created at the same time, the human fossil record must be paleontologically co-extensive with the record of lower animals. It is fair to say that no one has shown how to reconcile such claims with the available evidence—evidence that speaks persuasively to a long earth history, among other things.

In brief, these claims are testable, they have been tested, and they have failed those tests. Unfortunately, the logic of the Opinion's analysis precludes saying any of the above. By arguing that the tenets of Creationism are neither testable nor falsifiable, Judge Overton (like those scientists who similarly charge Creationism with being untestable) deprives science of its strongest argument against Creationism . . . The correct way to combat Creationism is to confute the empirical claims it does make, not to pretend that it makes no such claims at all.

It is true, of course, that some tenets of Creationism are not testable in isolation (e.g., the claim that man emerged by a direct supernatural act of creation). But that scarcely makes Creationism 'unscientific.' It is now widely acknowledged that many scientific claims are not testable in isolation, but only when embedded in a larger system of statements, some of whose consequences can be submitted to test . . .

Perhaps what Judge Overton had in mind was the fact that some of Creationism's core assumptions (e.g., there was a Noachian flood, that man did not evolve from lower animals, or that God created the world) seem closed off from any serious modification. But historical and sociological researches on science strongly suggest that the scientists of any epoch likewise regard some of their beliefs as so fundamental as not to be open to repudiation or negotiation. Would Newton, for instance, have been tentative about the claim that there were forces in the world? Are quantum mechanicians willing to contemplate giving up the uncertainty relation? Are physicists willing to specify circumstances under which they would give up energy conservation?

. . . What about the other pair of essential characteristics which the *McLean* Opinion cites, namely; that science is a matter of natural law and explainable by natural law? I find the formulation in the Opinion to be rather fuzzy; but the general idea appears to be that it is inappropriate and unscientific to postulate the existence of any process or fact which cannot be explained in terms of some known scientific laws—for instance, the creationists' assertion that there are outer limits to the change of species "cannot be explained by natural law." . . . For centuries scientists have recognized a difference between establishing the existence of a phenomenon and explaining that phenomenon in a lawlike way. Our ultimate goal, no doubt, is to do both. But to suggest, as the *McLean* Opinion does repeatedly, that an existence claim (e.g., there was a worldwide flood) is unscientific until we found the laws on which the alleged phenomenon depends is simply outrageous. Galileo and Newton took themselves to have established the existence of gravitational phenomena, long before anyone was able to give a causal or explanatory account of gravitation. Darwin took himself to have established the existence of natural selection almost a half-century before geneticists were able to lay out the laws of heredity on which natural selection depended. If we took the *McLean* Opinion seriously, we should have to say that Newton and Darwin were unscientific. . . .

Rather than taking on the creationists obliquely in wholesale fashion by suggesting that what they are doing is "unscientific" *tout court* (which is doubly silly because few authors can even agree on what makes an activity scientific), we should confront their claims directly and in piecemeal fashion by asking what evidence and arguments can be marshaled for and against each of them. The core issue is not whether Creationism satisfies some undemanding and highly controversial definitions of what is scientific; the real question is whether the existing evidence provides stronger arguments for evolutionary theory than for Creationism. Once that question is settled, we will know what belongs in the classroom and what does not.

PRO JUDICE
Michael Ruse

As always, my friend Larry Laudan writes in an entertaining and provocative manner, but in his complaint against Judge William Overton's ruling in *McLean v. Arkansas*, Laudan is hopelessly wide of the mark. Laudan's outrage centers on the criteria for the demarcation of science which Judge Overton adopted, and the judge's conclusion that, evaluated by these criteria, creation-science fails as science. I shall respond directly to this concern—after making three preliminary remarks.

First, although Judge Overton does not need defense from me or anyone else, as one who participated in the Arkansas trial, I must go on record as saying that I was enormously impressed by his handling of the case . . . Second, Judge Overton, like everyone else, was fully aware that proof that something is not science is not the same proof that it is religion . . . Third, whatever the merits of the plaintiffs' case, the kinds of conclusions and strategies apparently favored by Laudan are simply not strong enough for legal purposes. His strategy would require arguing that creation-science is weak science and therefore ought not to be taught . . . Unfortunately, the U.S. Constitution does not bar the teaching of weak science. What it bars (through the Establishment Clause of the First Amendment) is the teaching of religion. The plaintiffs' tactic was to show that creation-science is less than weak science or bad science. It is not science at all.

Turning now to the main issue, I see three questions that must be addressed. Using the five criteria listed by Judge Overton, can one distinguish science from non-science? Assuming a positive answer to the first question, does creation-science fail as genuine science when it is judged by these criteria? And, assuming a positive answer to the second, does the Opinion in *McLean* make this case?

The first question has certainly tied philosophers of science in knots in recent years. Simple criteria that supposedly give a clear answer to every case . . . will not do. Nevertheless, although there may be many grey areas, white does seem to be white and black does seem to be black. Less metaphorically, something like psychoanalytic theory may or may not be science, but there do appear to be clear-cut cases of real science and real non-science. For instance, an explanation of the fact that my son has blue eyes, given that both parents have blue eyes, done in terms of dominant and recessive genes and with an appeal to Mendel's first law, is scientific. The Catholic doctrine of transubstantiation (i.e., that in the Mass the bread and wine turn into the body and blood of Christ) is not scientific.

Furthermore, the five cited criteria of demarcation do a good job of distinguishing the Mendelian example from the Catholic example. Law and explanation through law come into the first example. They do not enter the second. We can test the first example, rejecting it if necessary. In this sense, it is tentative, in that something empirical might change our minds. The case of transubstantiation is different. God may have His own laws, but neither scientist nor priest can tell us about those which turn bread and wine into flesh and blood. There is no explanation through law. No empirical evidence is pertinent to the miracle. Nor would the believer be swayed by any empirical facts. Microscopic examination of the Host is considered irrelevant. In this sense, the doctrine is certainly not tentative . . .

What about the criterion of tentativeness, which involves a willingness to test and reject if necessary? Laudan objects that real science is hardly all that tentative: "[H]istorical and sociological researches on science strongly suggest that the scientists of any epoch likewise regard some of their beliefs as so fundamental as not to be open to repudiation or negotiation."

It cannot be denied that scientists do sometimes—frequently—hang on to their views, even if not everything meshes precisely with the real world. Nevertheless, such tenacity can be exaggerated. Scientists, even Newtonians, have been known to change their minds. Although I would not want to say that the empirical evidence is all-decisive, it plays a major role in such mind changes. As an example, consider a major revolution of our own time, namely that which occurred in geology. When I was an undergraduate in 1960, students were taught that continents do not move. Ten years later, they were told that they do move. Where is the dogmatism here? Furthermore, it was the new empirical evidence—e.g., about the nature of the sea-bed—which persuaded geologists . . .

Let us move on to the second and third questions, the status of creation-science and Judge Overton's treatment of the problem. The slightest acquaintance with the creation-science literature and Creationism movement shows that creation-science fails abysmally as science. Consider the following passage, written by one of the leading creationists, Duane T. Gish, in *Evolution: The Fossils Say No!*: "CREATION. By creation we mean the bringing into being by a supernatural Creator of the basic kinds of plants and animals by the process of sudden, or fiat, creation. We do not know how the Creator created, what process He used, *for He used processes which are not now operating anywhere in the natural universe.* That is why we refer to creation as Special Creation. We cannot discover by scientific investigations anything about the creative processes used by the Creator."

. . . By their own words, therefore, creation-scientists admit that they appeal to phenomena not covered or explicable by any laws that humans can grasp as laws. It is not simply that the pertinent laws are not yet known . . . Furthermore, there is nothing tentative or empirically checkable about the central claims of creation-science . . .

Finally, what about Laudan's claim that some parts of creation-science (e.g., claims about the Flood) are falsifiable, and that other parts (e.g., about the originally created "kinds") are revisable? Such parts are not falsifiable or revisable in a way indicative of genuine science. Creation-science is not like physics, which exists as part of humanity's common cultural heritage and domain. It exists solely in the imagination and writing of a relatively small group of people. Their publications (and stated intentions) show that, for example, there is no way they will relinquish belief in the Flood, whatever the evidence. In this sense, their doctrines are truly unfalsifiable.

There is, of course, much more to say about comparing scientific methods and religious methods. Prayer is a method used in the context of religion for understanding events that occur or trying to change the world in some way. Clearly, this is not a method used in the sciences to understand or change things. Double-blind studies, with the expectation that their results could be (nearly) replicated, are basic to many of the experimental sciences, yet they simply are not part of religious practice. A useful exercise, both in and out of a philosophy of science class, is to consider what sorts of particular methods sciences and religions use for particular goals. An entire book could be devoted to this topic, but we need to move on to other issues.

Evolutionary theory

As we all know, one of the most notorious points of contact between science and religion is with respect to evolutionary theory. Conceptions of the transformation of organisms and whole species were around long before Charles Darwin published *The Origin of Species* in 1859. Charles' own grandfather, Erasmus Darwin, advocated an evolutionary view at the turn of the 19th century, as did Jean Baptiste Lamarck. Although these two advocates (along with many others) saw evolutionary theory as consistent with their religious views, Charles Darwin was explicit in questioning and challenging any supposed consistency.

Darwin was aware of conflict, at least potential conflict, between his evolutionary *explanation* of the traits of organisms and the origin of species and an intelligent design explanation. Shortly, we will touch on the notion of design, but first it would be helpful to have a better sense of just what Darwinian evolutionary theory says. Many people, and I mean *many* people, have mistaken notions of it, such as "we all come from monkeys!" Even people who claim to accept evolutionary theory often have mistaken notions of it, such as "giraffes have long necks because over generations they have stretched to reach leaves to eat." (A fancier way of putting that bit about giraffes is to say that acquired traits are heritable.) Well, Darwinian evolutionary theory does not say we come from monkeys or that acquired traits are heritable. What it does say is fairly simple and straightforward, yet, at the same time, it is a constellation of various theses. In his book, *Toward a New Philosophy of Biology,* evolutionary biologist Ernst Mayr argued that what goes by the name of "Darwinian evolution" are really five theories. (I would prefer to call them five dimensions or components of a single theory, but that is not crucial.) Here is what Mayr said:

TOWARD A NEW PHILOSOPHY OF BIOLOGY
Ernest Mayr

Under the circumstances I consider it urgently necessary to dissect Darwin's conceptual framework of evolution into a number of major theories that formed the basis of his evolutionary thinking. For the sake of convenience I have portioned Darwin's evolutionary paradigm into five theories, but of course others might prefer a different division . . . For Darwin himself these five theories were apparently much more a unity than they appear to a person who analyzes them with modern hindsight. The five theories were: (1) evolution as such, (2) common descent, (3) gradualism, (4) multiplication of species, and (5) natural selection . . .

Evolution as Such

This is the theory that the world is neither constant nor perpetually cycling but rather is steadily and perhaps directionally changing, and that organisms are being transformed in time . . . . Evolution as such is no longer a theory for a modern author. It is as much as fact as that the earth revolves around the sun rather than the reverse. The changes documented by the fossil record in precisely dated geological strata are a fact that we designate as evolution. It is the factual basis on which the other four evolutionary theories rest. For instance, all the phenomena explained by common descent would make no sense if evolution were not a fact.

Common Descent

The case of the species of Galapagos mockingbirds provided Darwin with an important new insight. The three species had clearly descended from a single ancestral species on the South American continent. From here it was only a small step to postulate that all mockingbirds were derived from a common ancestor—indeed, that every group of organisms descended from an ancestral species. This is Darwin's theory of common descent . . . None of Darwin's theories was accepted as enthusiastically as common descent; it is probably correct to say that no other of Darwin's theories had such enormous immediate explanatory powers. Everything that had seemed to be arbitrary or chaotic in natural history up to that point now began to make sense . . . Nothing helped the rapid adoption of evolution more than the explanatory power of the theory of common descent. Soon it was demonstrated that even animals and plants, seemingly so different from each other, could be derived from a common, one-celled ancestor. This Darwin had already predicted, when he suggested that "all our plants and animals (have descended) from some one form, into which life was first breathed." The studies of cytology (meiosis, chromosomal inheritance) and biochemistry fully confirmed the evidence from morphology and systematics for a common origin. It was one of the triumphs of molecular biology to be able to establish that eukaryotes and prokaryotes have the identical genetic code, thus leaving little doubt about the common origin even of these groups . . . There was only one area in which the application of the theory of common descent encountered vigorous resistance: the inclusion of man into the total line of descent. To judge from contemporary cartoons, none of the Darwinian theories was less acceptable to the Victorians than the derivation of man from the other primates. Yet at the present time this derivation is not only remarkably well substantiated by the fossil record, but the biochemical and chromosomal similarity of man and the African ape is so great that it is quite puzzling why they are so relatively different in morphology and brain development.

Gradualism

Darwin's third theory was that evolutionary transformation always proceeds gradually, never in jumps. One will never understand Darwin's insistence on the gradualism of evolution, nor the strong opposition to this theory, unless one realizes that virtually everyone at the time was an essentialist. The occurrence of new species, documented by the fossil record, could take place only by new origins, that is, by saltations. Since the new species were perfectly adapted, however, and since there was no evidence for the frequent production of maladapted species, Darwin saw only two alternatives. Either the perfect new species had been specially created by an all-powerful and all-wise Creator, or else—if such a supernatural process were unacceptable—the new species had evolved gradually from pre-existing species by a slow process, at each stage of which they maintained their adaptation. It was this second alternative that Darwin adopted.

The source of Darwin's strong belief in gradualism is not quite clear . . . Most likely gradualism is the extension of Lyell's uniformitarianism from geology to the organic world. Lyell's failure to do so had rightly been criticized by Bronn. Darwin, of course, also had strictly empirical reasons for his insistence on gradualism. His work with domestic races, particularly his work with pigeons and his conversations with animal breeders, convince him how strikingly different the end products of slow, gradual selection could be. This fitted well with his observations on the Galapagos mockingbirds and tortoises, which were best explained as the result of gradual transformation.

Finally, Darwin had didactic reasons for insisting on the slow accumulation of rather small steps. He answered the argument of his opponents that one should be able to "observe" evolutionary change owing to natural selection by saying: "As natural selection acts solely by accumulating slight successive favorable variations, it can produce no great or sudden modifications; it can act only by very short and slow steps." There is little doubt that the general emergence of population thinking in Darwin strengthened his adherence to gradualism. As soon as one adopts the concept that evolution occurs in populations and slowly transforms them—and this is what Darwin increasingly believed—one is automatically forced also to adopt gradualism. Gradualism and population thinking probably were originally independent strands in Darwin's conceptual framework, but eventually they reinforced each other powerfully . . .

The Multiplication of Species

This theory of Darwin's dealt with the explanation of the origin of the enormous organic diversity. It is estimated that there are 5 to 10 million species of animals and 1 to 2 million species of plants on earth. Even though in Darwin's day only a fraction of this number was known, the problem of why there are so many species and how they originated was already present. Lamarck had ignored the possibility of a multiplication of species in his *Philosophie Zoologique* (1809). For him diversity was produced by differential adaptation. New evolutionary lines originated by spontaneous generation, he thought. In Lyell's steady-state world, species number was constant and new species were introduced to replace those that had become extinct. Any thoughts of the splitting of a species into several daughter species was absent among these earlier authors . . .

Although Darwin deserves credit, together with Wallace, for having posed concretely for the first time the problem of the multiplication of species, the pluralism of his proposed solution lead to a history of continuous controversy that is not ended to this very day. At first, from the 1870s to the 1940s, sympatric speciation was perhaps the more popular theory of speciation, although some authors, particularly ornithologists and specialists of other groups displaying strong geographic variation, insisted on exclusive geographic speciation. The majority of entomologists, however, and likewise most botanists, even though admitting the occurrence of geographic speciation, considered sympatric speciation to be the more common and thus more important form of speciation. After 1942 allopatric speciation was more or less victorious for some twenty-five years, while now the controversy is again in full swing . . .

There are three reasons why speciation is still an open problem 125 years after the publication of *Origin*. The first is that, as in so much of evolutionary research, the evolutionist analyzes the results of past evolutionary processes and is thus obliged to reach conclusions by inference. Consequently, one encounters all the well-known difficulties meet in the reconstruction of historical sequences. The second difficulty is that in spite of all the advances of genetics, we are still almost entirely ignorant as to what happens genetically during speciation. And finally, there are reasons to believe that rather different genetic mechanisms may be involved in the speciation of different kinds of organisms and under different circumstances. Yet Darwin's model of speciation, as first developed on the basis of the Galapagos mockingbirds, is still very much alive, and presumably essentially correct.

Natural Selection

Darwin's theory of natural selection was his most daring, most novel theory. It dealt with the mechanism of evolutionary change and, more particularly, how this mechanism could account for the seeming harmony and adaptation of the organic world. It attempted to provide a natural explanation in place of the supernatural one of natural theology. His theory for the natural mechanism that would be able to direct evolutionary change was unique . . . It replaced teleology in nature with an essentially mechanical explanation . . . To judge from his writings, Darwin had a much simpler concept of natural selection than the modern evolutionist. For him there was a steady production of individuals, generation after generation, with those that were "superior" having a reproductive advantage. It seemed essentially to be a single-step process, the conveying of reproductive success. The modern evolutionist agrees with Darwin that the individual is the target of selection; but we now also know that the production of a new individual is an exceedingly complex process. Indeed, we realize that natural selection is actually a two-step process, the first one consisting of the production of genetically differing individuals, while in the second step the survival and reproductive success of these individuals is determined . . .

Although I call the theory of natural selection Darwin's *fifth* theory, it is actually, in turn, a small package of theories. This includes the theory of the perpetual existence of a reproductive surplus (superfecundity), the theory of the heritability of individual differences, the discreteness of the determinants of heredity, and several others. Many of these were not explicitly stated by Darwin but are implicit in his model as a whole.

The theory of natural selection was the most bitterly resisted of all of Darwin's theories . . . . The most determined resistance came from those who had been raised under the ideology of natural theology. They were quite unable to abandon the idea of a world designed by God and to accept a mechanical process instead. More importantly, a consistent application of the theory of natural selection meant a rejection of any and all cosmic teleology. Sedgwick and K.E. von Baer were particularly articulate in resisting the elimination of teleology.

Natural selection represents not only the rejection of any finalistic causes that may have a supernatural origin, but it rejects any and all determinism in the organic world. Natural selection is utterly "opportunistic," as G.G. Simpson has called it; it is a "tinkerer." It starts, so to speak, from scratch in every generation . . . Curiously, in the controversies over natural selection, the process has been described sometimes as "pure chance" (Herschel and many other opponents of natural selection) or as a strictly deterministic optimization process. Both classes of claimants overlook the two-step nature of natural selection and the fact that in the first step chance phenomena prevail, while the second step is decidedly of an anti-chance nature.

Given Mayr's characterization of Darwinian evolutionary theory as consisting of these five theories or theses, we can now, in a more informed way, turn to the question of how they relate to religious claims. (Remember, the five theories were: (1) evolution as such, (2) common descent, (3) gradualism, (4) multiplication of species, and (5) natural selection.)

Is the claim of "evolution as such" in conflict with religious claims? Let's not forget that there are many religions, so, just limiting ourselves to Christian religious claims, is there a conflict between "evolution as such" and particular Christian claims? What Christian claim conflicts with the view that the world is neither constant nor perpetually cycling but rather is steadily and perhaps directionally changing, and that organisms are being transformed in time? How is this view related to the claim that there exists a creator of the universe? How is it related to the claim that humans have a non-physical soul that survives the body's death? How is it related to the claim that Jesus is the personal savior of persons? I confess, for me, it is not obvious how they relate at all. (This might be a worthwhile topic for class discussion. Perhaps I just don't get it.)

Or, take Mayr's third Darwinian theory, gradualism: evolutionary transformation always proceeds gradually, never in jumps. Is this in conflict with the claim that there is a creator of the universe or a non-physical human soul, and so on? As Mayr points out, this theory is one concerning the pace of transformation and the time needed, but it is also a theory about essences and the nature of change of traits that species undergo. There seems to be no necessary connection between those and whether or not God exists. Of course, there have been (and still are) people who deny the "deep time" that evolutionary theory accepts. There, then, is a point of conflict: two claims about the age of the world, where both parties hold that their views are descriptive of the facts. If one person says that the universe is 13 billion years old and another person says that it is 6,000 years old, and assuming both people mean their claims to be literally true, then, surely, there is a conflict. This is obviously because it cannot be the case that both claims are true, where it is not obvious that two other claims (the universe is 13 billion years old and humans have a non-physical soul) cannot both be true.

Now, I will not go through each of the five Darwinian theories, as Mayr lays them out, but I will point to two issues that very often are raised in the context of evolutionary theory and religion: (1) *design* (or the relation between God and nature), and (2) *human nature* (or the relation between humans and nature, particularly human origins) and *human dignity* (or the relation between humans and progress or human destiny).

Design

As we have seen, one major point of contention connected to evolutionary theory is that things in nature, and the universe as a whole, displays such order that many people insist the most reasonable inference is that this orderliness, or design, is the result of a designer, not of random chance events. What are the sorts of features that we associate with something having been designed? They are orderly, or at least organized; they are often quite complex; they seem purposive, that is, intended to fulfill some purpose or other; they are frequently quite precise or fine-tuned. When we look at nature, this is just what we find, an orderliness and harmony and complexity of things such that it makes the most sense to infer that these things were designed. And, of course, many people claim, if there is design, then there is a designer. That designer of nature is God.

A famous version of this proof comes from the 18th-century clergyman William Paley. His most famous argument is an analogy, often known as the "watch analogy". Watches are such complicated and orderly devices that, if we were to stumble upon one out in the middle of nature, it would be much more reasonable (he says) to assume that it was the product of design rather than of natural forces and interactions. Perhaps it is not impossible that a watch could "naturally arise," but, surely, it is far more likely that it was produced by people and dropped there. Things that exhibit such order and complexity are more likely designed by some designer than not. In addition, says Paley, nature itself is far more complex and organized than any human contrivance. The human eye, for example, is far more complex and organized than any camera, and no computer (however powerful) is as complex and organized as the human brain. Beyond the complexity and organization of human organs and even of microscopic organisms, whole ecosystems are vastly more complicated. Surely, it is more reasonable to believe that such organization and complexity is the result of intelligent design and not mere random physical interactions. Perhaps it is the case that a million monkeys typing on a million keyboards for a million years would produce Shakespeare's works, but isn't it much more reasonable to assume that those works are the result of an intelligent author?

This sounds like a pretty convincing argument. However, as you can imagine, plenty of people have not found it compelling. For one thing, we can find many examples in nature of orderliness and complexity, yet it does not follow that there was necessarily an intelligent designer. The orderliness and complexity might well be the effect of non-intelligent causes. For example, we see orderliness and complexity in the structure of our solar system, with its eight planets (assuming that Pluto is not a planet) and many moons and other celestial objects. Each of these things has gravitational influence on all the others, yet somehow the solar system runs on and on in harmony, without planets and moons crashing into each other and in orbits that are highly structured. Intelligent design of this system is, of course, one explanation for the order that we see. However, the order might well be the result of non-intelligent forces. We can easily explain, say, the moon's orbit around the earth, as a balance of two forces, gravity and inertia. Gravity, which pulls the moon toward the Earth, is exactly balanced by the moon's inertia to move off in a straight line away from the Earth. It is the balance of these forces that produce the moon's orderly orbit. At least this is how an astronomer would explain the order. If the forces had not been balanced, the moon would not have its orbit. If gravity had been stronger, the moon would have crashed into the Earth, or if the moon's inertia had been stronger, it would have flown off away from the Earth. So, the fact that things are orderly or complex does not by itself demonstrate intelligent design.

Or, take another example. A common example used to talk about organisms adapting to their environments is the peppered moth in England. There are two varieties, the darker-winged variety and the lighter-winged variety. Prior to industrialization, there was a certain survival rate of these two varieties. With the oncoming of industrial pollution from coal-burning factories and the resulting soot-darkened trees and buildings, the darker-winged variety could more easily blend into its environment and escape predators than the lighter-winged variety. As a result, the survival rates of darker-winged moths increased relative to lighter-winged moths. This was not evidence of any intelligent design; it was simply the result of environmental changes. The point, of course, is again that orderliness and complexity by itself does not demonstrate intelligent design.

This issue of design has been at the center of recent social and political controversy, particularly with respect to teaching evolutionary theory in public schools and in the content of textbooks for primary and secondary schools. Underlying much of this controversy is the championing of intelligent design theory by scientists who oppose evolutionary theory, at least parts of evolutionary theory. This is the subject of this chapter's Case Study.

Human nature and dignity

A second issue I noted earlier that flows out of the relation between evolutionary theory and religious belief is that of human origin and dignity. We know that each religion makes claims about where humans, as a species, came from. (There usually is not a lot of controversy about where individual humans come from, at least not the biological, physical individual.) We also know that evolutionary theorists point to earlier humanoids (such as Cro-Magnons) and detail the descent of homo sapiens. The focus here will not be so much on the empirical question of what do the discoveries of anthropologists say about human origins. Rather, the focus will be on why this has seemed to be an issue with respect to religions and the acceptance of evolutionary theory. That is, how is the issue of human origin a matter of concern with respect to religious belief? Ian Barbour, who has written for decades on this topic, addresses this point directly:

ISSUES IN SCIENCE AND RELIGION
Ian Barbour

In the Western tradition, *man was set apart* from all other creatures. Man alone was a rational being; human reason was considered totally different in kind from whatever intelligence animals have. Man alone possessed an immortal soul, which defined his true being and his relationship to God. Man's distinctiveness put him in many respects "outside" nature, despite his sharing with other creatures a common dependence on God and a common finitude and temporality. This uniqueness of status now appeared to be denied by the theory of evolution. Distinctions between human and animal characteristics were indeed minimized by Darwin and his followers. Surviving primitive tribes, as Darwin portrayed them, almost closed the gap between man and animal. Huxley claimed that there is less difference between man and the highest apes than between higher and lower apes. Man himself, absorbed into nature, seemed to be the product of accidental variations and the struggle for survival, a child of blind chance and law.

Man's moral sense had always been considered one of his most distinctive capacities, but Darwin claimed that it too had originated by selection. In the early history of mankind a tribe whose members had strong social instincts, such as fidelity and self-sacrifice for the common good, would have had an advantage over other tribes. If morality conferred survival value, standards of conscience would have tended to rise. In the extinction of savage races in conflict with more civilized ones Darwin saw further evidence of built-in ethical advance. In a similar fashion he traced each of man's emotional and intellectual characteristics back to origins in the earlier stages of human and subhuman development . . .

It is perhaps understandable that Darwin overemphasized *the continuity of man and animal*. The earlier tradition had portrayed such an absolute discontinuity that to establish man's rootedness in nature Darwin looked for all the similarities he could find, overlooking the differences. The tremendous scope of the theory of evolution had been amply demonstrated, and it was easy to assume that all human phenomena could be exhaustively interpreted in essentially biological terms. It is also understandable that there were both scientists and theologians who, in reaction to such claims, insisted that natural selection could not account for man. Today we can see that in the long history of the world, man's emergence marks a genuinely new chapter—one not disconnected from previous chapters, and yet involving factors not previously present. Something radically different takes place when culture rather than genes becomes the principle means by which the past is transmitted to the future, and when conscious choice alters man's development.

Moreover, both opponents and proponents of evolution often seem to have made the implicit assumption that *man's descent determines his nature.* Much of the emotion accompanying the rejection of the idea that "we have apes in our family tree" can be traced to this notion that source fixes meaning. Belief in evolution was equated with belief that man is "nothing but an animal." Man's origins were too readily taken by both sides to be the chief clue to his significance; a subhuman past somehow came to imply a less than fully human present. This is a genetic or temporal form of "reductionism," which finds the significance of an entity not in its smallest parts, as with eighteenth-century materialism, but in its most primitive beginning; it is a philosophical assumption equally destructive to the dignity of man, and equally unwarranted as a conclusion from the data.

Not everyone agrees with Barbour's statement that there is a radical difference between culture and biology, or at least between culturally induced change and genetically induced change. However, his last point is especially important for this chapter, namely, that human's descent determines human's nature and that source fixes meaning. We certainly do not think this is the case for individual persons. We do not assert that since you came from a particular pair of parents that, therefore, who you are, what values you have, what you will accomplish, what impact you will have, are all set in stone. Hardly! Where we come from is not a final determiner of where we will go or of what importance we are. Barbour here is not explicitly taking a stand on whether evolutionary theory is "right" about human nature (or even if there is a human nature). Rather, he is asking the pragmatic question: what difference does it make? If evolutionary theory is correct, does that imply that there is no human dignity or that humans are not unique among species? If evolutionary theory is not correct, does that imply that humans are disconnected from their biology? Again, Barbour does not answer these questions, but he suggests that these are the questions that really lay at the interface between science and religion, at least with respect to evolutionary theory.

Chapter Summary

When examining the relation between science and religion, it is important to note that there are many religions, just as there are many sciences. There are metaphysical aspects of religion (such as the existence of deities or souls or miracles). There are epistemological aspects of religion (such as means of knowing and understanding, e.g., faith, revelation, natural signs). There are axiological aspects of religion (such as notions of sacredness and purpose, of obligatory and permitted and prohibited behavior, of rituals). There are various modes of relation between science and religion: conflict, independence, or dialogue and integration. With respect to philosophical concerns about the relation of science and religion, one area of concern is that of method; how are scientific methods like and unlike religious methods for investigating, evaluating, and understanding phenomena. Two philosophers of science, Larry Laudan and Michael Ruse, offer alternative views about science as method and religion as method, with Laudan claiming that they are not significantly different, but Ruse claiming they are. Evolutionary theory is a major focus on attention for the examination of the relation between science and religion. Biologist Ernst Mayr claims that evolutionary theory is actually a conglomeration of several different theses: evolution as such, common descent, gradualism, multiplication of species, and natural selection. Evolutionary theory is often at the focal point of interest in the relation between science and religion, particularly, for Ian Barbour, with respect to the issues of design and human nature, which have both metaphysical and axiological aspects.

CASE STUDY
Intelligent Design

The debates over the origin of life, origin of species, and the reasonableness of design have gone on for centuries. During much of the 20th century these debates were characterized as evolution versus creationism. Those on the "evolution" side of the debates sought and demanded natural (as opposed to supernatural) accounts for the origin of life and of species, arguing that whatever design there might be in nature was an effect, not a cause. Those on the "creationism" side of the debates sought and demanded, in the final analysis, supernatural accounts for the origin of life and of species, arguing that whatever design there might be in nature was the result of a purposeful designer (God). Following public discussion and court cases (such as the Arkansas case in the 1980s, noted above), supporters of purposeful design began arguing for their position under the label of "intelligent design theory" (ID theory). Though ID theory does not outright deny that species in fact change over time or openly advocate views such as the world being only 6,000 years old (hence distancing itself from at least some claims of creationism), ID theory focuses on rejecting evolutionary theory as being able to provide an adequate account of both the array of species we find in nature and of the complexity of life and of the basic features of life. ID theory claims that evolutionary theory is simply inadequate science (at best) and that intelligent design is a better scientific theory. Evolutionary theorists disagree on both counts. The readings on the following pages are from a 2002 special report on intelligent design that appeared in Natural History *magazine. Two of the selections, those by Michael Behe and Jonathan Wells, are by supporters of ID theory, whereas the other two selections, those by Kenneth Miller and Eugenie Scott, reject ID theory. As you read them, consider what metaphysical, epistemological, and axiological claims, assumptions and implications are being made. Consider, also, in what ways exactly the ID proponents and opponents see the relation between science and religion (that is, between scientific their scientific claims and assumptions and their non-scientific claims, assumptions, and implications). Are their views, whether explicitly or implicitly, that science and religion are in conflict, are independent of each other, or overlap in meaningful ways?*

THE CHALLENGE OF IRREDUCIBLE COMPLEXITY
Michael J. Behe

Scientists use the term "black box" for a system whose inner workings are unknown. To Charles Darwin and his contemporaries, the living cell was a black box because its fundamental mechanisms were completely obscure. We know that, far from being formed from a kind of simple, uniform protoplasm (as many nineteenth-century scientists believed), every living cell contains many ultrasophisticated molecular machines.

How can we decide whether Darwinian natural selection can account for the amazing complexity that exists at the molecular level? Darwin himself set the standard when he acknowledged, "If it could be demonstrated that any complex organ existed which could not possibly have been formed by numerous, successive, slight modifications, my theory would absolutely break down."

Some systems seem very difficult to form by such successive modifications—I call them irreducibly complex. An everyday example of an irreducibly complex system is the humble mousetrap. It consists of (1) a flat wooden platform or base; (2) a metal hammer, which crushes the mouse; (3) a spring with extended ends to power the hammer; (4) a catch that releases the spring; and (5) a metal bar that connects to the catch and holds the hammer back. You can't catch a mouse with just a platform, then add a spring and catch a few more mice, then add a holding bar and catch a few more. All the pieces have to be in place before you catch any mice.

Irreducibly complex systems appear very unlikely to be produced by numerous, successive, slight modifications of prior systems, because any precursor that was missing a crucial part could not function. Natural selection can only choose among systems that are already working, so the existence in nature of irreducibly complex biological systems poses a powerful challenge to Darwinian theory. We frequently observe such systems in cell organelles, in which the removal of one element would cause the whole system to cease functioning. The flagella of bacteria are a good example. They are outboard motors that bacterial cells can use for self-propulsion. They have a long, whiplike propeller that is rotated by a molecular motor. The propeller is attached to the motor by a universal joint. The motor is held in place by proteins that act as a stator. Other proteins act as brushing material to allow the driveshaft to penetrate the bacterial membrane. Dozens of different kinds of proteins are necessary for a working flagellum. In the absence of almost any of them, the flagellum does not work or cannot even be built by the cell.

Another example of irreducible complexity is the system that allows proteins to reach the appropriate subcellular compartments. In the eukaryotic cell there are a number of places where specialized tasks, such as digestion of nutrients and excretion of wastes, take place. Proteins are synthesized outside these compartments and can reach their proper destinations only with the help of "signal" chemicals that turn other reactions on and off at the appropriate times. This constant, regulated traffic flow in the cell comprises another remarkably complex, irreducible system. All parts must function in the synchrony or the system breaks down. Still another example is the exquisitely coordinated mechanism that causes blood to clot.

Biochemistry textbooks and journal articles describe the workings of some of the many living molecular machines within our cells, but they offer very little information about how these systems supposedly evolved by natural selection. Many scientists frankly admit their bewilderment about how they may have originated, but refuse to entertain the obvious hypothesis: that perhaps molecular machines appear to look designed because they really *are* designed.

I am hopeful that the scientific community will eventually admit the possibility of intelligent design, even if that acceptance is discreet and muted. My reason for optimism is the advance of science itself, which almost every day uncovers new intricacies in nature, fresh reasons for recognizing the design inherent in life and the universe.

THE FLAW IN THE MOUSETRAP
Kenneth R. Miller

To understand why the scientific community has been unimpressed by attempted to resurrect the so-called argument from design, one need look no further than Michael J. Behe's own essay. He argues that complex biochemical systems could not possibly have been produced by evolution because they possess a quality he calls irreducible complexity. Just like mousetraps, these systems cannot function unless each of their parts is in place. Since "natural selection can only choose among systems that are already working," there is no way that Darwinian mechanisms could have fashioned the complex systems found in living cells. And if such systems could not have evolved, they must have been designed. That is the totality of the biochemical "evidence" for intelligent design.

Ironically, Behe's own example, the mousetrap, shows what's wrong with this idea. Take away two parts (the catch and the metal bar), and you may not have a mousetrap but you do have a three-part machine that makes a fully functional tie clip or paper clip. Take away the spring, and you have a two-part key chain. The catch of some mousetraps could be used as a fishhook, and the wooden base as a paperweight; useful applications of other parts include everything from toothpicks to nutcrackers and clipboard holders. The point, which science has long understood, is that bits and pieces of supposedly irreducibly complex machines may have different—but still useful—functions. Behe's contention that each and every piece of a machine, mechanical or biochemical, must be assembled in its final form before *anything* useful can emerge is just plain wrong. Evolution produces complex biochemical machines by copying, modifying, and combining proteins previously used for other functions. Looking for examples? The systems in Behe's essay will do just fine. He writes that in the absence of "almost any" of its parts, the bacterial flagellum "does not work." But guess what? A small group of proteins from the flagellum *does* work without the rest of the machine—it's used by many bacteria as a device for injecting poisons into other cells. Although the function performed by this small part when working alone is different, it nonetheless can be favored by natural selection.

The key proteins that clot blood fit this pattern, too. They're actually modified versions of proteins used in the digestive system. The elegant work of Russell Doolittle has shown how evolution duplicated, retargeted, and modified these proteins to produce the vertebrate blood-clotting system.

And Behe may throw up his hands and say that *he* cannot imagine how the components that move proteins between subcellular compartments could have evolved, but scientists actually working on such systems completely disagree. In a 1998 article in the journal *Cell*, a group led by James Rothman, of the Sloan-Kettering Institute, described the remarkable simplicity and uniformity of these mechanisms. They also noted that these mechanisms "suggest in a natural way how the many and diverse compartments in eukaryotic cells could have evolved in the first place." Working researchers, it seems, see something very different from what Behe sees in these systems—they see evolution.

If Behe wishes to suggest that the intricacies of nature, life, and the universe reveal a world of meaning and purpose consistent with a divine intelligence, his point is philosophical, not scientific. It is a philosophical point of view, incidentally, that I share. However, to support that view, one should not find it necessary to pretend that we know less than we really do about the evolution of living systems. In the final analysis, the biochemical hypothesis of intelligent design fails not because the scientific community is closed to it but rather for the most basic of reasons—because it is overwhelmingly contradicted by the scientific evidence.

ELUSIVE ICONS OF EVOLUTION
Jonathan Wells

Charles Darwin wrote in 1860 that "there seems to be no more design in the variability of organic beings and in the action of natural selection, than in the course which way the wind blows." Although many features of living things appear to be designed, Darwin's theory was that they are actually the result of undirected processes such as natural selection and random variation.

Scientific theories, however, must fit the evidence. Two examples of the evidence for Darwin's theory of evolution—so widely used that I have called them "icons of evolution"—are Darwin's finches and the four-winged fruit fly. Yet both of these, it seems to me, show that Darwin's theory cannot account for all features of living things.

Darwin's finches consist of several species on the Galápagos Islands that differ mainly in the size and shape of their beaks. Beak differences are correlated with what the birds eat, suggesting that the various species might have descended from a common ancestor by adapting to different foods through natural selection. In the 1970s, biologists Peter and Rosemary Grant went to the Galápagos to observe this process in the wild.

In 1977 the Grants watched as a severe drought wiped out 85 percent of a particular species on one island. The survivors had, on average, slightly larger beaks that enabled them to crack the tough seeds that had endured the drought. This was natural selection in action. The Grants estimated that twenty such episodes could increase average beak size enough to produce a new species.

When the rains returned, however, the average beak size returned to normal. Ever since, beak size has oscillated around a mean as the food supply has fluctuated with the climate. There has been no net change, and no new species have emerged. In fact, the opposite may be happening, as several species of Galápagos finches now appear to be merging through hybridization.

Darwin's finches and many other organisms provide evidence that natural selection can modify existing features—but only within established species. Breeders of domestic plants and animals have been doing the same thing with artificial selection for centuries. But where is the evidence that selection produces new features in new species?

New features require new variations. In the modern version of Darwin's theory, these come from DNA mutations. Most DNA mutations are harmful and are thus eliminated by natural selection. A few, however, are advantageous—such as mutations that increase antibiotic resistance in bacteria and pesticide resistance in plants and animals. Antibiotic and pesticide resistance are often cited as evidence that DNA mutations provide the raw materials for evolution, but they affect only chemical processes. Major evolutionary changes would require mutations that produce advantageous *anatomical* changes as well.

Normal fruit flies have two wings and two "balancers"—tiny structures behind the wings that help stabilize the insect in flight. In the 1970s, geneticists discovered that a combination of three mutations in a single gene produces flies in which the balancers develop into normal-looking wings. The resulting four-winged fruit fly is sometimes used to illustrate how mutations can produce the sorts of anatomical changes that Darwin's theory needs.

But the extra wings are not new structures, only duplications of existing ones. Furthermore, the extra wings lack muscles and are therefore worse than useless. The four-winged fruit fly is severely handicapped—like a small plane with extra wings dangling from its tail. As is the case with all other anatomical mutations studies so far, those in the four-winged fruit fly cannot provide raw materials for evolution.

In the absence of evidence that natural selection and random variations can account for the apparently designed features of living things, the entire question of design must be reopened. Alongside Darwin's argument against design, students should also be taught that design remains a possibility.

THE NATURE OF CHANGE

Eugenie C. Scott

Without defining "design," Wells asserts that "many features of living things appear to be designed." Then he contrasts natural selection (undirected) with design (directed), apparently attempting to return to the pre-Darwinian notion that a Designer is directly responsible for the fit of organisms to their environments. Darwin proposed a scientific rather than a religious explanation: the fit between organisms and their environments is the result of natural selection. Like all scientific explanations, his relies on natural causation.

Wells contends that "Darwin's theory cannot account for all features of living things," but then, it doesn't have to. Today scientists explain features of living things by invoking not only natural selection but also additional biological processes that Darwin didn't know about, including gene transfer, symbiosis, chromosomal rearrangement, and the action of regulator genes. Contrary to what Wells maintains, evolutionary theory is not inadequate. It fits the evidence just fine.

Reading Wells, one might not realize the importance of the Grants' careful studies, which demonstrated natural selection in real time. That the drought conditions abated before biologists witnessed the emergence of new species is hardly relevant; beak size does oscillate in the short term, but given a long-term trend in climate change, a major change in average size can be expected. Wells also overstates the importance of finch hybridization: it is extremely rare, and it might even be contributing to new speciation. The Galápagos finches remain a marvelous example of the principle of adaptive radiation. The various species, which differ morphologically, occupy different adaptive niches. Darwin's explanation was that they all evolved from a common ancestral species, and modern genetic analysis provides confirming evidence.

Wells admits that natural selection can operate on a population and correctly looks to genetics to account for the kind of variation that can lead to "*new* features in *new* species." But he contends that mutations such as those that yield four-winged fruit flies do not produce the sorts of anatomical changes needed for major evolutionary change. Can't he see past the example to the principle? That the first demonstration of a powerful genetic mechanism happened to be a nonflying fly is irrelevant.

Edward Lewis shared a Nobel Prize for the discovery of the role of these genes, known as the *Ubx* complex. They are of extraordinary importance because genes of this type help explain body plans—the basic structural differences between a mollusk and a mosquito, a sponge and a spider.

Ubx genes are among the *HOX* genes, found in animals as different as sponges, fruit flies, and mammals. They turn on or off the genes involved in—among other things—body segmentation and the production of appendages such as antennae, legs, and wings. What specifically gets built depends on other, downstream genes. The diverse body plans of arthropods (insects, crustaceans, arachnids) are variations on segmentation and appendage themes, variations that appear to be the result of changes in the *HOX* genes. Recent research shows that fly *Ubx* genes suppress leg formation in abdominal segments but that crustacean *Ubx* genes don't; a very small *Ubx* change results in a big difference in body plan.

Mutations in these primary on/off switches are involved in such phenomena as the loss of legs in snakes, the change from lobe fins to hands, and the origin of jaws in vertebrates. *HOX*-initiated segment duplication allows for anatomical experimentation, and natural selection winnows the result. "Evo-Devo"—the study of evolution and development—is a hot new biological research area, but Wells implies that all it has produced is crippled fruit flies.

Wells argues that natural explanations are inadequate and, thus, that "students should also be taught that design remains a possibility." Because in his logic, design implies a Designer, he is in effect recommending that science allow for nonnatural causation. We actually *do* have solid natural explanations to work with, but even if we didn't, science only has tools for explaining things in terms of natural causation. That's what Darwin did, and that's what we're trying to do today.

Further Reading

Barbour, Ian. *Issues in Science and Religion.* Englewood Cliffs, NJ: Prentice Hall, 1966.

Barbour, Ian. *Religion and Science*, rev ed. New York: Harper, 1997.

Barbour, Ian. *When Science Meets Religion.* New York: Harper, 2000.

Bender, David L. and Bruno Leone (eds.). *Science and Religion: Opposing Viewpoints.* St. Paul, MN: Greenhaven Press, 1988.

Brooke, John Hedley. *Science and Religion: Some Historical Perspectives.* New York: Cambridge University Press, 1991.

Cantor, Geoffrey and John Hedley Brooke. *Reconstructing Nature: The Engagement of Science and Religion.* New York: Oxford, 2000.

Clements, Tad S. *Science Versus Religion.* Amherst, NY: Prometheus, 1990.

Ferngren, Gary B. (ed.). *Science and Religion: A Historical Introduction.* Baltimore: Johns Hopkins University Press, 2002.

Gould, Stephen Jay. *Rocks of Ages: Science and Religion in the Fullness of Life.* New York: Ballantine Books, 1999.

Grant, Edward. *Science and Religion, 400 B.C. to A.D. 1550: From Aristotle to Copernicus.* Westport, CT: Greenwood Press, 2004.

Huchingson, James E. *Religion and the Natural Sciences: The Range of Engagement.* New York: Harcourt, Brace, Jovanovich, 1993.

Kurtz, Paul (ed.). *Science and Religion: Are They Compatible?* Amherst, NY: Prometheus, 2003.

Lindberg, David and Ronald Numbers (eds.). *God and Nature.* Berkeley, CA: University of California Press, 1986.

McGrath, Alister E. *Science and Religion: An Introduction.* Oxford: Blackwell, 1998.

Olson, Richard G. *Science and Religion, 1450-1900: From Copernicus to Darwin.* Westport, CT: Greenwood Press, 2004.

Peters, Ted (ed.). *Bridging Science and Religion.* Minneapolis, MN: Augsburg Fortress Publishers, 2003).

Polkinghorne, John. *Quarks, Chaos, and Christianity: Questions to Science and Religion.* New York: Crossroad Classic, 1995.

Polkinghorne, John. *Serious Talk: Science and Religion in Dialogue.* Philadelphia, PA: Trinity Press International, 1995.

Richardson, W. Mark (ed.). *Religion and Science: History, Method, Dialogue.* New York: Routledge, 1996.

Ruse, Michael. *Can a Darwinian be a Christian?: The Relationship between Science and Religion.* Cambridge: Cambridge University Press, 2000.

CHAPTER FOURTEEN

Science and Society

IN THIS CHAPTER, WE WILL

- Consider various conceptions and criticisms of "traditional" science
- Identify some metaphysical, epistemological, and axiological issues related to science and society
- Examine feminist and sociology of science claims about science and society

In the mid-1990s sociologist Raymond Eve collected a series of anecdotes concerning beliefs that Americans had about science and the natural world. These included cases of a person who tied knots in the electric cords of kitchen appliances in order to reduce the monthly utility bill and a person living in Texas who concluded that NASA faked pictures of the moon landings during the 1960s and 1970s because of the fact that she could not receive TV signals transmitted from New York, so then pictures supposedly being transmitted all the way from the moon could not possibly be received in her home. In various polls conducted in 2005 and 2006, the results showed that more Americans believed in creationism than in Darwinian evolution as an explanation for the origin of humans. At the same time, exit tests of college graduates showed that only a minority of those graduates could give the answers that scientists accept for basic natural phenomena such as why the Earth's northern hemisphere is colder in winter than in summer.

One well-known acknowledgement and analysis of the reality and significance of this general social unawareness of science comes from C.P. Snow. Back in the 1950s, Snow, both a physicist and a novelist, coined the term "two cultures" to refer to what he saw as a present and widening gap between the sciences and the humanities, or, to expand that, between scientific knowledge and the general public's knowledge of science. This gap was exemplified, he said, by asking his literary colleagues how many of them could describe the Second Law of Thermodynamics. None could and Snow remarked that this was a scientific equivalent of asking, "Have you read a work of Shakespeare?" Not only is the gap one of factual knowledge, but also of attitude and ethos. Both scientists and—for lack of a better term—humanists view the other with indifference, suspicion, and even distrust. Snow not only bemoaned this state of affairs, but also claimed it was harmful to understanding and fruitfully dealing with the role of science in society. Sadly, said Snow, this was the case in the 1950s and the two cultures were growing further apart. An especially notorious reminder of this notion of two cultures made a splash in the mid-1990s, what came to be known as the *Sokal Hoax* (or, the Sokal Affair). Physicist Alan Sokal purposefully submitted an article (entitled, "Transgressing the Boundaries: Toward a Transformative Hermeneutics of Quantum Gravity") to a prominent cultural studies journal, *Social Text,* in which he wrote a sociological and philosophical analysis and scathing critique of aspects of contemporary physics. The article was accepted and published. The problem was that the article was a complete hoax. Sokal intentionally wrote material that he knew was false and often simply nonsensical and he did this to find out if it would get published, but more so (he said later) in order to debunk what he saw as the extreme relativist and ignorant views of many social critics of science, especially among academicians.

For all of the talk that we live in a scientific age and for all of the reliance that we have every day on technology and the applications of science, the role of science and its relation to society, as Snow noted, often seems perplexing and even strained. The previous several chapters on technology, values, and religion all speak to particular aspects of the relation between science and society. This chapter will focus on the general issue of science as knowledge and how that relates to some conceptions of the social role of science, broadly speaking. In particular, we will look at several criticisms—or, at least, different notions—of what science is and how it relates to society. Those views will include the claim that science is (at least as it is mostly practiced) sexist; that science is a dangerous ideology; that the goals of science should be emancipation, not truth (or, at least, truth only as a means toward emancipation); that science is just one way of explaining the world and phenomena in the world, a way that is no more privileged in being true than other ways (or narratives) that are offered to explain the world and its phenomena. After considering these various views, we will then look at a rejection of them.

Science as sexist

In Chapter Eleven, we looked at the relation between science and values. Some of those values were moral values and we saw that Nicholas Rescher claimed that such values were inescapable in the context of scientific research. In addition, we saw Ernan McMullin argue that there are inherent epistemic values in science; that we cannot evaluate or appraise theories without invoking values such as replicability, precision, fecundity, quantifiability, and so on. As we will see, many people claim that those very epistemic values flow from and perpetuate sexism in science, even if that sexism is unintentional. Those very epistemic values, these thinkers argue, reflect experiences and goals that are primarily male-oriented experiences and goals.

When feminists (whether they are men or women) claim that science is sexist, they do not necessarily mean that the individual scientists intend to be sexist. Rather, the sexism is often structural and implicit. (Of course, sometimes it is open and intentional!) Science, they argue, can be, and generally is, sexist in terms of what gets investigated, how it gets investigated, and why it gets investigated (yes, you guessed it, in terms of metaphysical, epistemological, and axiological aspects). With respect to what gets investigated, feminists argue that the choice of research topics, especially what gets high levels of funding, are not topics that are of particular importance to women's lives; weapons research receives more funding, for instance, than reproduction technologies. How science investigates the world, feminists claim, reflects particular interests and values. For example, as Ruth Hubbard argues in the following selection, experimental designs that require a separation of experimenter and experimental subjects reflects (and perpetuates) what she sees as a masculinist approach to gaining knowledge. The aims and goals of scientific research (why some phenomena are investigated) also reflect masculinist biases, say feminists, because these aims and goals often promote or support—even if unintentionally—status quo and ongoing social structures and institutions that are part of the suppression of women. For feminists, not only are moral values inescapable within the various areas of scientific research that Rescher covered, but also those values are typically masculinist. This holds not simply for the choice of research topics, but in terms of the staffing of research activities (in which women are rarely the lead investigator), the dissemination of findings and control of misinformation (in which control and authority are the primary concerns, values that feminists claim are masculinist), and the other areas that Rescher discussed. In addition, the epistemic values that McMullin highlighted, such as replicability, quantifiability, precision, fecundity, and so on, are ones that feminists claim are much more reflective of men's lives than of women's in large part, again, because they are centered around control and authority. If these sorts of epistemic values define what counts as good science, then there is a masculinist bias built into the very conception of good science. One example of this, says Hubbard below, is that some areas of knowledge discovery—what Hubbard calls the "household"—are devalued as not yielding legitimate scientific knowledge.

In the reading below, Hubbard makes these various points about the what, how, and why of science being masculinist in the context of what she calls *fact-making*. Facts, she says, including scientific facts, are not simply bits of information that we discover about the world. Rather, facts are aspects of the world that we deem to be significant to our interests, such that they get recognized and legitimized. What is important about this is the issues of whose interests generate the making of facts and whose interests are served by the recognition of these constructed facts. Here is what she says:

SCIENCE, FACTS, AND FEMINISM
Ruth Hubbard

The Facts of Science

The Brazilian educator, Paulo Freire, has pointed out that people who want to understand the role of politics in shaping education must "see the reasons behind the facts." I want to begin by exploring some of the reasons behind a particular kind of facts, the facts of natural science. After all, facts aren't just out there. Every fact has a factor, a maker. The interesting question is: as people move through the world, how do we sort those aspects of it that we permit to become facts from those that we relegate to being fiction—untrue, imagined, imaginary, or figments of the imagination—and from those that, worse yet, we do not even notice and that therefore do not become fact, fiction, or figment? In other words, what criteria and mechanisms of selection do scientists use in the making of facts?

One thing is clear: making facts is a social enterprise. Individuals cannot just go off by themselves and dream up facts. When people do that, and the rest of us do not agree to accept or share the facts they offer us, we consider them schizophrenic, crazy. If we do agree, either because their facts sufficiently resemble ours or because they have the power to force us to accept their facts as real and true—to make us see the emperor's new clothes—then the new facts become part of our shared reality and their making, part of the fact-making enterprise.

Making science is such an enterprise. As scientists, our job is to generate facts that help people understand nature. But in doing this, we must follow rules of membership in the scientific community, and go about our task of fact-making in professionally sanctioned ways. We must submit new facts to review by our colleagues and be willing to share them with qualified strangers by writing and speaking about them (unless we work for private companies with proprietary interests, in which case we still must share our facts, but only with particular people). If we follow proper procedure, we become accredited fact-makers. In that case our facts come to be accepted on faith and large numbers of people believe them even though they are in no position to say why what we put out are facts rather than fiction. After all, a lot of scientific facts are counterintuitive, such as that the earth moves around the sun or that if you drop a pound of feathers and a pound of rocks, they will fall at the same rate.

What are the social or group characteristics of those of us who are allowed to make scientific facts? Above all, we must have a particular kind of education that includes graduate, and post-graduate training. That means that in addition to whatever subject matter we learn, we have been socialized to think in particular ways and have familiarized ourselves with that narrow slice of human history and culture that deals primarily with the experiences of western European and North American upper class men during the past century or two. It also means that we must not deviate too far from accepted rules of individual and social behavior and must talk and think in ways that let us earn the academic degrees required of a scientist.

Until the last decade or two, mainly upper-middle and upper class youngsters, most of them male and white, have had access to that kind of education. Lately, more white women and people of color (women and men) have been able to get it, but the class origins of scientists have not changed appreciably. The scientific professions still draw their members overwhelmingly from the upper-middle and upper classes . . .

Thus science is made, by and large, by a self-perpetuating, self-reflexive group: by the chosen for the chosen. The assumption is that if the science is "good," in a professional sense, it will also be good for society. But no one and no group are responsible for looking at whether it is. Public accountability is not built into the system.

. . . Natural science requires a conjunction of head and hand because it is an understanding of nature *for use*. To understand nature is not enough. Natural science and technology are inextricable, because we can judge that our understanding of nature is true only to the extent that it works. Significant facts and laws are relevant only to the extent that they can be applied and used as technology. The science/technology distinction, which was introduced one or two centuries ago, does not hold up in the real world of economic, political and social practices.

Woman's Nature: Realities versus Scientific Myths

. . . Sociobiologists have tried to prove that women's disproportionate contributions to child- and homecare are biologically programmed because women have a greater biological "investment" in our children than most men have. They offer the following rationale: an organism's biological fitness, in the Darwinian sense, depends on producing the greatest possible number of offspring, who themselves survive long enough to reproduce, because this is what determines the frequency with which an individual's genes will be represented in successive generations. Following this logic a step further, sociobiologists argue that women and men must adopt basically different strategies to maximize opportunities to spread our genes into future generations. The calculus goes as follows: Eggs are larger than sperm and women can produce many fewer of them than men can produce sperm. Therefore each egg that develops into a child represent a much larger fraction of the total number of children a woman can produce, hence of her "reproductive fitness," than a sperm that becomes a child does of a man's "fitness." In addition, women "invest" the nine months of pregnancy in each child. Women must therefore be more careful than men to acquire well-endowed sex partners who will be good providers to make sure that their few investments (read, children) mature. Thus, from seemingly innocent biological asymmetries between sperm and eggs flow such major social consequences as female fidelity, male promiscuity, women's disproportional contribution to caring for home and children, and the unequal distribution of labor by sex. As sociobiologist, David Barash, says, "mother nature is sexist," so don't blame her human sons.

In devising these explanations, sociobiologists ignore the fact that human societies do not operate with a few superstuds; nor do stronger or more powerful men as a rule have more children than weaker ones. Men, in theory, could have many more children than women can, but in most societies equal numbers of men and women engage in producing children, though not in caring for them. These kinds of absurdities are useful to people who have a stake in maintaining present inequalities. They mystify procreation, yet have a superficial ring of plausibility and thus offer naturalistic justifications for discriminatory practices . . .

Subjectivity and Objectivity

I want to come back to Paulo Friere, who says: "Reality is never just simply the objective datum, the concrete fact, but is also people's (and I would say certain people's) perception of it." And he speaks of "the indispensable unity between subjectivity and objectivity in the act of knowing."

The recognition of this "indispensable unity" is what feminist methodology is about. It is especially necessary for a feminist methodology in science because the scientific method rests on a particular definition of objectivity that we feminists must call into question. Feminists and others who draw attention to the devices that the dominant group has used to deny other people access to power—be it political power or the power to make facts—have come to understand how that definition of objectivity functions in the processes of exclusion I discussed at the beginning.

Natural scientists attain their objectivity by looking upon nature (including other people) in small chunks and as isolated objects. They usually deny, or at least do not acknowledge, their relationship to the "objects" they study. In other words, natural scientists describe their activities as though they existed in a vacuum. The way language is used in scientific writing reinforces this illusion because it implicitly denies the relevance of time, place, social context, authorship, and personal responsibility. When I report a discovery, I do not write, "One sunny Monday after a restful weekend, I came into the laboratory, set up my experiment and shortly noticed that . . ." No; proper style dictates, "It has been observed that . . ." This removes relevance of time and place, and implies that the observation did not originate in the head of a human observer, specifically my head, but out there in the world. By deleting the scientist-agent as well as her or his participation as observer, people are left with the concept of science as a thing in itself, that truly reflects nature and that can be treated as though it were as real as, and indeed equivalent to, nature.

A blatant example of this kind of context-stripping that is commonly called objectivity is the way E.O. Wilson opens the final chapter of his *Sociobiology: The New Synthesis*. He writes: "Let us now consider man in the free spirit of natural history, as though we were zoologists from another planet completing a catalog of social species on earth." That statement epitomizes the fallacy we need to get rid of. There is no "free spirit of natural history," only a set of descriptions put forward by the mostly white, educated Euro-American men who have been practicing a particular kind of science during the past two hundred years. Nor do we have any idea what "zoologists from another planet" would have to say about "man" (which, I guess is supposed to mean "people") or about other "social species on earth," since that would depend on how these "zoologists" were used to living on their own planet and by what experiences they would therefore judge us. Feminists must insist that subjectivity and context cannot be stripped away, that they must be acknowledged if we want to use science as a way to understand nature and society and to use the knowledge we gain constructively . . .

The problem is that the context-stripping that worked reasonably well for the classical physics problem of falling bodies has become the model for how to do every kind of science. And this even though physicists since the beginning of [the 20th] century have recognized that the experimenter is part of the experiment and influences its outcome. That insight produced Heisenberg's uncertainty principle in physics: the recognition that the operations the experimenter performs disturb the system so that it is impossible to specify simultaneously the position and momentum of atoms and elementary particles. So, how about standing the situation on its head and using the social sciences, where context stripping is clearly impossible, as a model and do all science in a way that acknowledges the experimenter as a self-conscious subject who lives, and does science, within the context in which the phenomena she or he observes occur? Anthropologists often try to take extensive field notes about a new culture as quickly as possible after they enter it, before they incorporate the perspective and expectations of that culture, because they realize that once they know the foreign culture well and feel at home in it, they will begin to take some of its most significant aspects for granted and stop seeing them. Yet they realize at the same time that they must also acknowledge the limitations their own personal and social backgrounds impose on the way they perceive the foreign society. Awareness of our subjectivity and context must be part of doing science because there is no way we can eliminate them. We come to the objects we study with our particular personal and social backgrounds and with inevitable interests. Once we acknowledge those, we can try to understand the world, so to speak, from inside instead of pretending to be objective outsiders looking in.

. . . If feminists are to make a difference in the ways science is done and understood, we must not just try to become scientists who occupy the traditional structures, follow established patterns of behavior, and accept prevailing systems of explanation; we must understand and describe accurately the roles women have played all along in the process of making science. But we must also ask why certain ways of systematically interacting with nature and of using the knowledge so gained are acknowledged as science whereas others are not.

I am talking of the distinction between the laboratory and that other, quite differently structured, place of discovery and fact-making, the household, where women use a different brand of botany, chemistry, and hygiene to work in our gardens, kitchens, nurseries, and sick rooms. Much of the knowledge women have acquired in those places is systematic and effective and has been handed on by word of mouth and in writing. But just as our society downgrades manual labor, it also downgrades knowledge that is produced in other than professional settings, however systematic it may be. It downgrades the orally transmitted knowledge and the unpaid observations, experimentation and teaching that happen in the household. Yet here is a wide range of systematic, empirical knowledge that has gone unnoticed and unvalidated (in fact, devalued and invalidated) by the institutions that catalog and describe, and thus define, what is to be called knowledge. Men's explorations of nature also began at home, but later were institutionalized and professionalized. Women's explorations have stayed close to home and their value has not been acknowledged.

What I am proposing is the opposite of the project the domestic science movement put forward at the turn of the [20th] century. That movement tried to make women's domestic work more "scientific" in the traditional sense of the word. I am suggesting that we acknowledge the scientific value of many of the facts and knowledge that women have accumulated and passed on in our homes and in volunteer organizations.

I doubt that women as gendered beings have something new or different to contribute to science, but women as political beings do. One of the most important things we must do is to insist on the political content of science and on its political role. The pretense that science is objective, apolitical and value-neutral is profoundly political because it obscures the political role that science and technology play in underwriting the existing distribution of power in society. Science and technology always operate in somebody's interest and serve someone or some group of people. To the extent that scientists are "neutral" that merely means that they support the existing distribution of interests and power.

Science as (just one) narrative

Just as feminists have claimed that "traditional" science is laden with values that reflect and perpetuate men's experiences and lives at the expense of women's, other writers, including many social scientists, have argued that science is one means of accounting for phenomena in the world, but only one of a number of means of doing so. Science is a narrative, they say, no more or less "privileged" than other narratives. By not being "privileged" they mean that it has no more necessary connection to giving a single, correct account of the world than do other narratives. Science is no more objectively true than other narratives, if by "objective" we mean independent of interests and values and goals. Science is a social institution, conducted by individuals and groups who are shaped and influenced by many social forces. One particularly well-known version of this perspective is called the sociology of knowledge (and also the Strong Programme), a school of thought associated with the works of Bruno Latour, Steve Woolgar, Barry Barnes, David Bloor, Harry Collins, and others. The sociology of knowledge, especially scientific knowledge, focuses on the distribution of belief and the factors that influence it. For example, by observing the actual day-to-day practices of scientists over the course of months in their laboratories and noting such things as patterns and chains of communication, these investigators concluded that, with respect to actual scientific practice, there is not a sharp distinction between facts and artifacts (or "discovered" facts and "created" artifacts); rather facts are fabricated or constructed depending upon what the scientists did with the initial proposed "fact." Reality, as the sociologists of knowledge say, is a consequence of the settlement of a dispute, not its cause. Scientific investigation, they say, is largely "agonistic," meaning that scientists' activities are directed not so much toward natural phenomena but rather toward providing a coherent account of them, relative to background beliefs, interests, and goals. As Latour and Woolgar remark, "Nature is a usable concept only as a by-product of agonistic activity." Contrary to the standard notion that science is constrained by nature, by events in the natural world that are independent of our investigations of them, the sociologists of knowledge argue that "nature" is a concept and that "facts" do not speak for themselves; they are given voices via decisions by scientists. Likewise, notions such as "truth" and "correspondence" are not simply terms that describe independent features about the world, but are normative terms that direct us or exhort us to act in certain ways. Those ways might be fruitful and indeed lead to information or technological devices that we deem to be useful and important, but those ways are nonetheless based on our beliefs and interests and goals, not, say the sociologists of knowledge, on objective facts. Again Latour and Woolgar state:

LABORATORY LIFE
Bruno Latour and Steve Woolgar

. . . [T]he set of statements considered too costly to modify constitute what is referred to as reality. Scientific activity is not "about nature," it is a fierce fight to *construct* reality . . .

The result of the *construction* of a fact is that it appears unconstructed by anyone; the result of rhetorical *persuasion* in the agonistic field is that participants are convinced that they have not been convinced [by humans rather than by objective facts]; the result of *materialization* is that people can swear that material considerations are only minor components of the "thought process"; the result of the investments of *credibility*, is that participants can claim that economics and beliefs are in no way related to the solidity of science; as to the *circumstances*, they simply vanish from accounts, being better left to political analysis than to an appreciation of the hard and solid world of facts!

Science as a dangerous ideology and as inherently political

If facts of nature are not what constrain scientific knowledge and if scientific knowledge is not a matter of a correspondence between independent phenomena in the world and our beliefs about them, and if science is based on particular beliefs and interests and goals, then science is just one narrative about the world, since there are other beliefs and interests and goals that might (and do) drive other narratives. The following two readings present the claim that science today is not simply one more narrative about the world, but in fact is a dangerous one. According to Paul Feyerabend, in the first selection, science is an ideology, a worldview that its advocates take as being true and inconsistent with alternative worldviews. Consequently, science has become restrictive of other views of the world; it is domineering and stifles other perspectives. In addition, it is built upon a somewhat idealized picture of its own successes and nature. In particular, Feyerabend argues, science falsely claims that its method and results show its superiority to alternative world-views. Imagine, for instance, if someone seriously suggested that the National Science Foundation should provide lots of money to set up a clinic to train people to practice voodoo medicine or to promote intelligent design theory. (The second reading related to the claim that science is a dangerous narrative will emphasize the political nature and aspects of science.) First, though, here is what Feyerabend has to say:

HOW TO DEFEND SOCIETY AGAINST SCIENCE
Paul Feyerabend

I want to defend society and its inhabitants from all ideologies, science included. All ideologies must be seen in perspective. One must not take them too seriously. One must read them like fairytales which have lots of interesting things to say but which also contain wicked lies, or like ethical prescriptions which may be useful rules of thumb but which are deadly when followed to the letter.

Now—is this not a strange and ridiculous attitude? Science, surely, was always in the forefront of the fight against authoritarianism and superstition. It is to science that we owe our increased intellectual freedom vis-à-vis religious beliefs; it is to science that we owe the liberation of mankind from ancient and rigid forms of thought. Today these forms of thought are nothing but bad dreams—and this we learned from science. Science and enlightenment are one and the same thing—even the most radical critics of society believe this. Kropotkin wants to overthrow all traditional institutions and forms of belief, with the exception of science. Ibsen criticizes the most intimate ramifications of 19th century bourgeois ideology, but he leaves science untouched. Levi-Strauss has made us realize that Western Thought is not the lonely peak of human achievement it was once believed to be, but he excludes science from his relativization of ideologies. Marx and Engels were convinced that science would aid the workers in their quest for mental and social liberation. Are all these people deceived? Are they all mistaken about the role of science? Are they all the victims of a chimera?

To these questions my answer is a firm *Yes and No*.

Now, let me explain my answer.

My explanation consists of two parts, one more general, one more specific.

The general explanation is simple. Any ideology that breaks the hold a comprehensive system of thought has on the minds of men contributes to the liberation of man. Any ideology that makes man question inherited beliefs is an aid to enlightenment. A truth that reigns without checks and balances is a tyrant who must be overthrown and any falsehood that can aid us in the overthrow of this tyrant is to be welcomed. It follows that 17th and 18th century science indeed *was* an instrument of liberation and enlightenment. It does not follow that science is to *remain* such an instrument. There is nothing inherent in science or in any other ideology that makes it *essentially* liberating. Ideologies can deteriorate and become stupid religions. Look at Marxism. And that the science of today is very different from the science of 1650 is evident at the most superficial glance.

For example, consider the role science now plays in education. Scientific "facts" are taught at a very early age and in the very same manner in which religious "facts" were taught only a century ago. There is no attempt to waken the critical abilities of the pupil so that he may be able to see things in perspective. At the universities the situation is even worse, for indoctrination is here carried out in a much more systematic manner. Criticism is not entirely absent. Society, for example, and its institutions, are criticized most severely and often most unfairly and this is already at the elementary school level. But science is excepted from the criticism. In society at large the judgment of the scientist is received with the same reverence as the judgments of bishops and cardinals was accepted not too long ago . . .

. . . Human life is guided by many ideas. Truth is one of them. Freedom and mental independence are others. If Truth, as conceived by some ideologists, conflicts with freedom then we have a *choice*. We may abandon freedom. But we may also abandon Truth. (Alternatively, we may adopt a more sophisticated idea of truth that no longer contradicts freedom; that was Hegel's solution.) My criticism of modern science is that it inhibits freedom of thought. If the reason is that it has found the truth and now follows it then I would say that there are much better things than first finding, and then following such a monster.

This finishes the general part of my explanation.

There exists a more specific argument to defend the exceptional position science has in society today. Put in a nutshell the argument says (1) that science has finally found the correct *method* for achieving results and (2) that there are many *results* to prove the excellence of the method. This argument is mistaken—but most attempts to show this lead into a dead end. Methodology has by now become so crowded with empty sophistication that it is extremely difficult to perceive the simple errors at the basis. It is like fighting the hydra—cut off one ugly head, and eight formalizations take its place. In this situation the only answer is superficiality: when sophistication loses content then the only way of keeping in touch with reality is to be crude and superficial. That is what I intend to be.

With respect to (1) above (scientific method), Feyerabend claims that the various views concerning scientific change and progress (what we covered in Chapters Eight through Ten)—what he means by "scientific method"—have all proven to be faulty, minimally in being incomplete as adequate accounts of science having a method of providing us with knowledge about the world. One lesson to be learned by these attempts to account for scientific change is that there is no clear and obvious method that produces scientific knowledge that can objectively be shown to be "truer" or "better" for us. Not only, says Feyerabend, is there no scientific method that guarantees objective truth, but also there is no legitimate argument that the methods that sciences use produce knowledge that is truer or better; some other methods might work just as well.

His argument against the claims for the results of science (argument (2) above) is two-fold. First, he claims, a careful look at the history of science shows that much of the "progress" of science—including what we take as the factual results—came about from contributions that indeed run counter to what scientific method propounds. For example, when Copernicus introduced his sun-centered view of the solar system, he relied on astrologers as much as astronomers and on philosophical assumptions that he never questioned or tested. Likewise, Johannes Kepler, who formulated a precise mathematical model of the orbits of the planets in our solar system, relied heavily on mystical and religious commitments that he took for granted and never questioned. Second, Feyerabend says, for the "results of science" argument to be valid, it would need to be demonstrated that other methods do not produce results that provide true or good knowledge of the world. But, he claims, this has not been done, certainly not in any way that does not already presuppose the truth of scientific claims already. Science, he says, is just one ideology among many. Being an ideology is not necessarily bad, claims Feyerabend, but being a domineering ideology is, and this is just what he thinks religion was in the past and what science is today. The implications? Feyerabend states: "The most important consequence is that there must be a *formal separation between state and science* just as there is now a formal separation between state and church. Science may influence society but only to the extent to which any political or other pressure group is permitted to influence society."

Feyerabend said he would be crude and superficial! Nevertheless, he raises points and offers a view that many others share, namely, the view that science is one sort of "narrative" or meaningful account among others. In addition, as he said, truth is one value among others. Freedom is another value. Focusing on this notion of freedom, some contemporary thinkers have argued for what they call the *emancipation* view of science, as opposed to the *explanation* view of science. What they mean is this: the "traditional" view of science is that its goal is to explain phenomena about the world and leave to politics or society at large the decisions about what to do with these scientific explanations. The emancipation view of science, however, sees the ultimate goal of science to be that of making people more free, free not only of political and social restraints and oppression, but in the sense of free to be able to accomplish more and, hence, flourish and enhance their well-being. Not only, say advocates of this view, is it not possible for science not to be intimately connected to politics, but it should not strive not to be. It should embrace its status as one narrative among others and see as its goal the emancipation of people. Providing scientific explanations of phenomena should be a means to a larger end, namely, enhancing freedom.

One example of such a view comes from a group called Science for the People. The reading below argues that science is deeply intertwined with politics and economics. Because of this, scientists should be openly involved in particular kinds of activities that are good (i.e., emancipatory) rather than bad (i.e., oppressive).

PEOPLE'S SCIENCE
Bill Zimmerman, et al

In the fifteenth century, Leonardo da Vinci refused to publish plans for a submarine because he anticipated that it would be used as a weapon. In the seventeenth century, for similar reasons, Boyle kept secret a poison he had developed. In 1946, Leo Szilard, who had been one of the key developers of the atom bomb, quit physics in disillusionment over the ways in which the government had used his work. By and large, this kind of resistance on the part of scientists to the misuse of their research has been very sporadic, from isolated individuals, and generally in opposition only to particular, usually repugnant projects. As such, it has been ineffective. If scientists want to help prevent socially destructive applications of science, they must forego acting in an ad hoc or purely moralistic fashion and begin to respond collectively from the vantage point of a political and economic analysis of their work. This analysis must be firmly anchored in an understanding of the U.S. corporate state.

We will argue below that science is inevitably political, and in the context of contemporary U.S. corporate capitalism, that it contributes greatly to the exploitation and oppression of most of the people both in this country and abroad. We call for a reorientation of scientific work and will suggest ways in which scientific workers can redirect their research to further meaningful social change.

Science in Capitalist America
There are basically two reasons why [science's] advancements and new developments cannot be left to the "natural" progress of scientific-technological knowledge, why they must be foreseen and included in the social-economic planning of the ruling class. First is the mammoth investment in present-day plant, equipment and organizational apparatus of the major monopolies.

The sudden obsolescence of a significant part of their apparatus would be an economic disaster which could very well endanger their market position . . . Secondly, the transformation of the process of production entails a major reorganization of education, transportation, and communication. This has far-reaching social and political consequences which cause profound strains in traditional class, race, and sex relationships, which have already generated and will continue to generate political and social crises. For the ruling class to deal with these crises it is necessary to be able to plan ahead, to anticipate new developments so that they do not get out of hand.

In our view, because planning and programmed advances in technology are absolutely central to ruling class strategy, an entirely new relationship is required between the ruling and the technical-scientific sectors of society, a relationship which has been emerging since the Second World War, and which, deeply rooted in social-economic developments, cannot be reversed. If one looks at the new sciences which have been developed in this period—cybernetics, systems analysis, management science, linear programming, game theory—as well as the direction of developments in the social sciences, one sees an enormous development in the techniques of gathering, processing, organizing, and utilizing information, exactly the type of technological advance most needed by the rulers . . .

Theoretical and experimental physicists, working on problems of esoteric intellectual interest, provided the knowledge that eventually was pulled together to make the H-bomb, while mathematicians, geophysicists, and metallurgists, wittingly or unwittingly, made the discoveries necessary to construct intercontinental ballistic missiles. Physicists doing basic work in optics and infrared spectroscopy may have been shocked to find that their research would help government and corporate engineers build detection and surveillance devices for use in Indochina. The basic research of molecular biologists, biochemists, cellular biologists, neuropsychologists, and physicians was necessary for CBW (chemical-biological warfare) agents, defoliants, herbicides, and gaseous crowd-control devices . . .

Unfortunately, the problem of evaluating basic research does not end with such obscure misapplications as these. One must also examine the economic consequences of basic research, consequences which flow from the structure of corporate capitalism under which we live. Scientific knowledge and products, like any other products and services in our society, are marketed for profit—that is, they are not equally distributed to, equally available to, or equally usable by all of the people. While they often contribute to the material standard of living of many people, they are channeled through an organization and distribution of scarcity in such a way as to rationalize the overall system of economic exploitation and social control. Furthermore, they frequently become the prerogative of the middle and upper classes and often result in increasing the disadvantages of those sectors of the population that are already most oppressed.

For example, research in comparative and developmental psychology has shown that enriching the experience of infants and young children by increasing the variety and complexity of shapes, colors, and patterns in their environment might increase their intelligence as it is conventionally defined. As these techniques become more standardized, manufacturers are beginning to market their versions of these aids in the form of toys aimed at and priced for the upper and middle classes, and inaccessible to the poor . . .

Science is Political

An analysis of scientific research merely begins with a description of how it is misapplied and maldistributed. The next step must be an unequivocal statement that scientific activity in a technological society is not, and cannot be, politically neutral or value free. Some people, particularly after Hiroshima and Nuremberg, have accepted this statement. Others still argue that science should be an unbridled search for truth, not subject to a political or a moral critique. J. Robert Oppenheimer, the man in charge of the Los Alamos project which built and tested the first atomic bombs, said in 1967 that "our work has changed the conditions in which men live, but the use made of these changes is the problem of governments, not of scientists."

The attitude of Oppenheimer and others, justified by the slogan of "truth for truth's sake," is fostered in our society and has prevailed. It is tolerated by those who control power in this country because it furthers their aims and does not challenge their uses of science. This attitude was advanced centuries ago by people who assumed that an increase in available knowledge would automatically lead to a better world. But this was at a time when the results of scientific knowledge could not easily be anticipated. Today, in a modern technological society, this analysis becomes a rationalization for the maintenance of repressive or destructive institutions, put forth by people who at best are motivated by a desire for the intellectual pleasure of research, and often are merely after money, status, and soft jobs. We believe it would be lame indeed to continue to argue that the possible unforeseen benefits which may arise from scientific research in our society will inevitably outweigh the clearly foreseeable harm. The slogan "truth for truth's sake" is defunct, simply because science is no longer, and can never again be, the private affair of scientists . . .

Political Organizing in the Health Fields

There is a wide range of activities that might constitute a Science for the People. This work can be described as falling into six broad areas:

Technical Assistance to Movement Organizations and Oppressed People
The free people's health centers have already been described as an example of this approach. Another example would be designing environmental poisoning detection kits for groups trying to protect themselves from pollution and trying to organize opposition to the capitalist system which hampers effective solutions to pollution problems . . .

Foreign Technical Help to Revolutionary Movements
American scientific workers can provide material aid to assist struggles in other countries against U.S. or other forms of imperialism, or against domestic fascism . . .

People's Research
. . . [T]here are areas in which scientists should take the initiative and begin developing projects that will aid struggles that are just beginning to develop. For example, workers in the medical and social sciences and in education could help design a program for client-controlled day care centers which would both free women from the necessity of continual child care and provide a thoroughly socialist educational experience for the children . . .

Exposés and Power Struggle Research
. . . [T]here is a growing need for research in the biological and physical sciences to expose how the quest for corporate profits is poisoning and

destroying irreplaceable and critical aspects of our environment. This information, in a form anyone can understand, should be made available to action-oriented community ecology groups.

Ideological Struggle

Ruling-class ideology is effectively disseminated by educational institutions and the mass media, resulting in misinformation that clouds people's understanding of their own oppression and limits their ability to resist it . . . The elitist bias of most American social sciences oppress students from working-class and poor backgrounds, as well as women and minorities, by failing to adequately portray their history and culture . . . To combat this, the social scientist should work to make available to the people their true history and cultural achievements . . . For example, courses in any of the biological sciences should deal with the political reasons why our society is committing ecological murder/suicide. Courses in psychopathology should spend at least as much time on our government officials and our insanely competitive economic system as they do on the tortured victims incarcerated in our mental "hospitals," many of whom would not be there in the first place if they lived in a society where normality and sanity were synonymous.

Demystification of Science and Technology

No one would deny that science and technology have become major influences in the shaping of people's lives . . . In the interests of democracy and people's control, the false mystery surrounding science and technology must be removed and the hold of experts on decision making must be destroyed. Understandable information can be made available to all those for whom it is pertinent. For example, the women's liberation movement has taken the lead in teaching the facts about human reproduction biology to the people who need it the most for control over their own bodies.

. . . Attempts to demystify science must take place at many levels. The doctrine that problems of technology can be met with technological rather than political solutions is increasingly being incorporated into the ruling ideology. The counterargument should be made that only political reorganization will be effective in the long run, and this argument will need to be bolstered by more research. On the level of daily practice, elitist tendencies can be undermined in laboratories and classrooms by insisting that *all* workers or students participate in decision making that affects what they do and by creating conditions that ensure them the information necessary to make those decisions. The elitism and hierarchical structuring of most scientific meetings and conventions can be opposed by members forcefully insisting that they be given some control over the selection of speakers and that all scheduled speakers address themselves to the political implications of their work . . . Scientists must succeed in redirecting their professional activities away from services to the forces and institutions they oppose and toward a movement they wish to build. Short of this, no matter how much they desire to contribute to the solution, they remain part of the problem.

Rejection of "New Age" criticisms of science

Throughout this chapter so far, we have encountered a number of focused and vehement criticisms of science. A common feature of them is that they assert that science is not simply value-laden, but the values with which it is laden are negative. Science, these critics have stated, is no more a vehicle for getting a true picture of the world than are other world views. Indeed, the very notion of some independent truth that science—or any other narrative—*could* get is mistaken. We also noted at the beginning of this chapter what has come to be called the Sokal Affair, one attempt by a practicing scientist to challenge these criticisms by demonstrating that many of them are based, first, on a misunderstanding of science, or perhaps even outright ignorance, and, second, on intentional unwarranted attacks on science, attacks coming from intellectual, philosophical, and political agendas that come from relativist assumptions and carry ultimately repressive consequences. This attitude is reflected in the reading on the next page, by the philosopher of science, Noretta Koertge. Koertge lumps together the various kinds of criticisms of science that have come from feminists, sociologists of science, and others under the label of "New Age" Science. She criticizes these attacks on "traditional" science and claims that they are infiltrating science education. Although there are reasonable bases for some of their criticisms, she argues, those bases are all-too-often taken to unacceptable extreme conclusions.

One result, to the extent that these "New Age" views of science become part of the educational curriculum, is that society will become even more ignorant of good science. Here is Koertge:

POSTMODERNISMS AND THE PROBLEM OF SCIENTIFIC LITERACY

Noretta Koertge

I begin by surveying some of the general recommendations for a new kind of science literacy that are coming out of the sociological and cultural studies approach to science studies. There is no doubt that much of the work is intended to be directly applied to science education. Harry Collins and Trevor Pinch [in their book, *The Golem*] subtitle their controversial book, which compares science to a golem, "What Everyone Should Know about Science." Part of Cambridge University Press's Canto series, their book is intended for a general audience, including preuniversity students. Research in women's studies is also directed toward revolutionizing science pedagogy . . . [Such writers] proclaim that students as citizens need to know more about science, although as we shall see, their picture of science is a very controversial one, indeed. Even more controversial is their denial of the proposition that laypeople need to have a better understanding of the basic content of modern science. Collins and Pinch, in a section entitled "Science and the Citizen," are quite emphatic on this point: The idea that knowing more science would help the public make more sensible decisions "ranks among the greatest fallacies of our age." Through their case studies, they claim to "have shown that scientists at the research front cannot settle their disagreements through better experimentation, more knowledge, more advanced theories, or clearer thinking. It is ridiculous to expect the general public to do better."

These commentators also widely agree that students should be explicitly disabused of any ideas they might have picked up about the epistemic desirability of reproducible experiments, controlling variables, statistical analysis, and all the other methodological staples of modern science. Again, Collins and Pinch are quite clear. After describing the bungling efforts of schoolchildren to determine the boiling point of water, they claim that the "negotiation" of their results in the classroom does not differ significantly from the behavior of great scientists working at the frontier: "Eddington, Michelson, Morley . . . are Zonkers, Brians, and Smudgers with clean white coats and 'PhD' after their names."

In tandem with this trivialization of scientific methodology are proposals that would negate central features of the scientific approach. For example, [Sue V.] Rosser's recipes for making science more "female friendly" prescribe the inclusion and validation of personal experiences as part of the laboratory exercise and a deemphasis on objectivity [in "Female Friendly Science: Including Women in Curricular Content and Pedagogy in Science," *Journal of General Education* 42 (1993): 191-220]. Noting that "well-controlled experiments in a laboratory environment may provide results that have little application . . . outside the classroom," she recommends that students investigate problems of a more "holistic, global scope," using "interactive methods" instead of trying to set up isolated systems or controlling variables. Rosser is convinced that female students would find this new kind of methodology more "friendly." Be that as it may, such recommendations cannot be viewed as friendly amendments to standard conceptions of fruitful scientific methodology . . .

Postmodern mathematics

. . . [Take] Luce Irigaray's speculations about the history of fluid mechanics. Irigaray's prose—in either French or English translation—is difficult to understand; her influence on educators has come primarily through an essay by Katherine Hayles, an English professor and contributor to the *Social Text* issue on the "science wars." Here is Hayles's summary:

> The privileging of solid over fluid mechanics, and indeed the inability of science to deal with turbulent flow at all, she [Irigaray] attributes to the association of fluidity with femininity. Whereas men have sex organs that protrude and become rigid, women have openings that leak menstrual blood and vaginal fluids. Although men, too, flow on occasion—when semen is emitted, for example—this aspect of their sexuality is not emphasized. It is the rigidity of the male organ that counts, not its complicity in fluid flow.

> These idealizations are reinscribed in mathematics, which conceives of fluids as laminated planes and other solid forms. In the same way that women are erased within masculinist theories and language, existing

only as not-men, so fluids have been erased from science, existing only as not-solids.

From this perspective it is no wonder that science has not been able to arrive at a successful model for turbulence. The problem of turbulent flow cannot be solved because the conceptions of fluids (and of women) have been formulated so as necessarily to leave unarticulated remainders. [From "Gender encoding in fluid mechanics: masculine channels and feminine flows" *Differences* 4 (1992): 16–44.]

The speculative nature of Irigaray's musings should be obvious to anyone, although they might seem plausible to those inclined toward psychoanalytic historiography. The more one knows about the history of science, however, the more preposterous these assertions seem. For starters, fluids have hardly been "erased" from science. Thales, the first pre-Socratic discussed by Aristotle, thought that the whole world was formed from one element, water. Aristotle made water one of his four elements and designated "the moist" and "the yielding" as primary qualities. In early modern science, Descartes's cosmology was based on the vortex motions of a continuous fluid, and to refute his account, Newton had to develop an alternative treatment of vortices. Eighteenth-century explanations of electrical phenomena posited either one or two electrical fluids. Imponderable fluids such as "caloric" or the "ether" were prominent in the ontology of nineteenth-century physics, and many of the most important theoretical advances in chemistry dealt with the properties of solutions. Furthermore, Irigaray's description of the mathematical models used in hydrodynamics is completely distorted . . .

Female-Friendly Science

Feminist suggestions for science pedagogy are another mixed bag. Let us look briefly at one of the seemingly more moderate and sympathetic approaches, the "Model for Transforming the Natural Sciences," proposed by Sue V. Rosser, a former senior program officer at the National Science Foundation. Although Rosser presents her proposal as a modest one, it is immediately evident that it is science itself that is to be transformed, not just science education.

The initial recommendations are sensible—one should include the names of women scientists who have made important discoveries and provide whenever possible hands-on experiences for the students instead of making them rely on textbook descriptions. Rosser then moves on to the familiar feminist injunction to "use less competitive models and more interdisciplinary methods to teach science." (It is anybody's guess what that might entail, but it sounds innocent enough.)

The last phases of Rosser's planned transformation, however, are explicitly based on cultural studies's critiques of science. For example, when Rosser recommends not having laboratory exercises in introductory courses in which students must kill animals, what is surprising is not the recommendation itself—there has already been a dramatic decrease in the use of animal subjects—but the reason Rosser gives: "[Carolyn] Merchant and [Susan] Griffin . . . document the extent to which modern mechanistic science becomes a tool men use to dominate both women and animals. Thus many women may particularly empathize with animals."

Rosser goes on to criticize all of modern biology for being reductionistic because of its emphasis on cell and molecular biology. From the beginning, she says, students should be encouraged to develop hypotheses that are "relational, interdependent, and multi-causal rather than hierarchical, reductionistic, and dualistic," and curricula should include "fewer experiments likely to have applications of direct benefit to the military." The goal is to arrive at a new kind of science, one that is "redefined and reconstructed to include us all."

. . . Rosser describes her approach as an application of women's studies, whose central message is that the overall impact of science on the lives of women (and minorities) has been oppressive. Claims that science and technology have eliminated drudgery and many of the dangers of childbirth and provided improved contraceptive devices are said to be outweighed by science's contributions to warfare, the decline in midwifery, and the devaluation of more intuitive, holistic approaches to problem-solving.

The methods and values of science are claimed to be intrinsically sexist. Instead of viewing science as an important component of the Enlightenment (a term with positive connotations), many feminists see the rise of modern science as responsible for "the death of nature" (as the historian of science Carolyn Merchant argues in a book with that title). For a variety of reasons (some would posit "womb envy"; others cite the "object relations" successor to Freudian theory), men are seen as more inclined to treat living things as "objects" and to value them only to the extent that they can dissect and control them. Science—with its emphasis on analysis, abstraction, quantification, and prediction—is then viewed, to repeat Mary Daly's terminology, as a paradigm case of patriarchal, phallocratic necrophilia . . .

Sophistication versus Cynicism in the Classroom

What unifies the various commentators on science education that I have called postmodern are the convictions that science has too much authority in our society and that there is too much respect for scientific reasoning within the general population. To combat these alleged tendencies toward science worship or sciences boosterism, these commentators believe that science education must be transformed so as to present students with a less heroic and less idealistic picture of scientific inquiry. Once students learn that scientific knowledge is constructed just like every other segment of our cultural beliefs and once they realize that the results of scientific experiments are the product of social negotiations, just as are the appraised values of the damage caused by a tornado, then, the social constructivists believe, students will grow up to be less admiring of scientific findings and better able to cope as citizens in a complex technological world.

Since allegedly there can be no compelling evidential basis for scientific claims, the discerning citizen needs to ask not whether the claim is well supported but, rather, whose political interests are served by such a claim. Since science supposedly has a long history of oppressing women and minorities, young people in these groups are thought to have a special need for inoculation against a naïve belief in the products and procedures of traditional science.

What are we to make of such a program? Even if we reject extreme versions of social constructivism, are there at least some beneficial practical reforms coming out of these critiques? First, we all can agree with the postmodernists—and C.P. Snow—that citizens need to know more about science, but only if what they are told is reasonably accurate and only if it is not presented as a substitute for learning more of the content of science. Of course, students need to learn about scientific controversies like the interesting cases Collins and Pinch discuss in their book. But the study of scientific debates is hardly a novel pedagogical innovation. Old textbooks, such as Holton and Roller and the Harvard Case Histories, gave rich accounts of historical controversies that clearly illustrated the strengths and weaknesses of both positions and the difficulties in settling the matter. The most conventional of the current science books offer alternative accounts of why the dinosaurs became extinct, how the moon was formed, how life began, and how best to model the bonds in benzene. Let us concede to Collins and Pinch, however, that students also need to learn more about professional rivalries in science and the politics of science journalism . . . but the picture must not be reduced to a cynical cartoon of real science. Students must also learn about the role of evidence and rational debate in scientific conflict resolution and also successful theory construction and refinement and how they were achieved.

Second, let us agree with the cultural critics of science—and Sir Karl Popper—that students need to learn more about the fallibility of scientific theories. We also freely grant that the hypotheses that spring most readily to the scientist's mind often reflect the commonsense beliefs, metaphysical systems, and ideological predilections of the times. But what we must add to the cultural studies picture and give prominence to is the old Popperian point about the refutability of false scientific theories and the possibility of learning from our mistakes. However obnoxious various outdated scientific theories of reproduction, intelligence, and human differences may be, it still was possible to discredit them through the routine application of the ordinary self-corrective devices of scientific inquiry. These methodological procedures do not always operate as efficiently as we would like, and they also can be subverted by political pressure. But there is no historical warrant for building into the curriculum a cynical, worst-case-scenario view of science.

Third, let us welcome all those who support the proposition that science education at all levels should become more accessible to and welcoming of women and minorities. Professional scientific organizations have long been concerned about the gender gap and racial gaps in scientific literacy. On average, members of these groups are more prone to math anxiety and score lower on standardized math tests, are less likely to take nonrequired sciences courses in high school, are less inclined to major in science or engineering, and are more liable to drop out if they do choose a science-based career. Sociological studies of attitudes toward science also report interesting gender differences in the patterns of attraction to pseudoscience and belief in paranormal phenomena. In accord with their explicit political commitments, postmodernist commentators on science emphasize the problem of the alienation of such groups from science. But too often their solution is to give each political identity its own special ethnoscience, tailor-made in ontology, methodology, and content to match the ideology and interests of that community. They believe that by denying the transcultural validity of scientific results, they will somehow undermine the power of transnational corporations and military alliances. Somehow feminist science will empower women, and ethnomathematics will improve the lot of the Navajo people.

But here their misunderstanding of the nature of science can have tragic consequences for the very people they want to liberate. It is not easy to generate truth claims about the world, and the scientific process does not always succeed in doing so, but when it does, what wonderful stones they provide for David's sling! To give just one example: I submit that DNA testing—a product of the reductionistic, nonholistic science that cultural critics of science deplore—promotes more justice to rape victims than do the special pleadings of feminist psychologists about the veracity of female plaintiffs. At the same time, DNA testing can promote justice for those African American men who have been falsely accused of rape. The science underlying DNA testing is universal science, not ethnoscience or genderized science, and that is why it can be used to arbitrate disputes between groups in such a manner that the politically less powerful can prevail. What a tragedy to educate members of disadvantaged groups in ersatz science and mathematics, all in the name of multiculturalism. And how dangerous it is to suggest to the powerful in our society that science is part of their rightful patriarchy because after all, as Sandra Harding put it, "science is politics by other means" [in her book, *Whose Science? Whose Knowledge? Thinking From Women's Lives*]. A denigration or subversion of the ideals of science can never be politically progressive in the long run.

Chapter Summary

Science, especially scientific knowledge, is important to society in terms of its impact on people's lives. Yet, there appears to be a significant ignorance of science among the general population. That ignorance applies to the content of science (i.e., scientific information), the processes of science (i.e., methods for acquiring and assessing scientific information), and the aims of science (i.e., goals both within science and about science). Although many scientists (and nonscientists) see the problem as one of better educating the public about science, many others are critical of what they see as "traditional" science. These critics include many feminists and sociologists of science, among others. They argue that science is one narrative about the world, and like any other narrative, it is based on beliefs, interests, and goals. For Ruth Hubbard, the values that underlie traditional science are fundamentally sexist. Paul Feyerabend and others, although not directly addressing sexist values, claim that science is a political ideology. The basic relation of science and society then is to recognize science as ideology and address its role in oppressing or emancipating people. Noretta Koertge challenges many of these claims and criticisms, arguing that many of them are based on misconceptions, ignorance, or political agendas of their own.

CASE STUDY
Science Education

One issue noted in several readings above is the importance of science education as it relates to the broad topic of science and society. C.P. Snow bemoaned what he saw as the ignorance of many people, even humanist intellectuals, about science. Saying we have become, in effect, two cultures, he argued in public forums that more focused science education was needed to bridge these two cultures. As this issue became more publicly addressed, the language of the discussion shifted to what became called science literacy. *The following are two readings, written nearly 50 years apart, concerning what kinds of scientific knowledge, or knowledge about science, is important for citizens to have.*

ON UNDERSTANDING SCIENCE
James Conant

. . . [W]e need a widespread understanding of science in this country, for only thus can science be assimilated into our secular cultural pattern. When that has been achieved, we shall be one step nearer to the goal which we now desire so earnestly, a unified, coherent culture suitable for our American democracy in this new age of machines and experts . . .

Understanding Science

In my experience, a man who has been a successful investigator in any field of experimental science approaches a problem in pure and applied science, even in an area in which he is quite ignorant, with a special point of view. I designate this point of view "understanding science." Note carefully that it is independent of a knowledge of the scientific facts or techniques in the new area to which he comes. Even a highly educated and intelligent citizen without research experience will almost always fail to grasp the essentials in a discussion which takes place among scientists concerned with a projected inquiry. This will be so not because of the layman's lack of scientific knowledge or his failure to comprehend the technical jargon of the scientist; it will be to a large degree because of his fundamental ignorance of what science can or cannot accomplish, and his consequent bewilderment in the course of a discussion outlining a plan for a future investigation. He has no "feel" for the Tactics and Strategy of Science.

In the last five years I have seen repeated examples of such bewilderment of laymen. If I am right in this diagnosis (and it is a fundamental premise of this book), the remedy does not lie in a greater dissemination of scientific information among nonscientists. Being well informed about science is not the same thing as understanding science, though the two propositions are not antithetical. What is needed are methods for imparting some knowledge of the Tactics and Strategy of Science to those who are not scientists. Not that one can hope by any short-cut methods to produce in a layman's mind the same instinctive reaction toward scientific problems that is the hallmark of an investigator, but enough can be accomplished, I dare hope, to bridge the gap to some degree between those who understand science because science is their profession and those who have only studied the results of scientific inquiry—in short, the layman.

But even if we agree that it is not more knowledge about science (more facts and principles) but some understanding of science that is required by the general public our pedagogic problem is not solved. For there are two ways of probing into complex human activities and their products: one is to retrace the steps by which certain end results have been produced, the other is to dissect the result with the hope of revealing its structural pattern and exposing the logical relations of the component parts, and, incidentally, exposing also the inconsistencies and flaws. Philosophic and mathematical minds prefer the logical approach, but it is my belief that for nine people out of ten the historical method will yield more real understanding of a complex matter.

For example, consider our form of government here in the United States with its complicated interplay of state and federal relations so baffling to even a highly educated visitor from another democratic nation. In one sense, only a few lawyers, statesmen, and political scientists understand the American Commonwealth. The rest of us can find time only to try to obtain some understanding by the study of a few books. Shall we follow Lord Bryce, for example, in looking for insight into the American constitution, or read Beard balanced by Charles Warren? For me, the answer is easy: if I have to choose, the historian's story will provide more understanding than the statesman's analysis. Whether this is true for a large majority of students, only the teachers of political science and history could say. But I venture the analogy to illustrate two ways in which an understanding of science may be to some degree attained by a relatively small amount of study. You may turn to the philosopher's interpretation or you may study examples of science in the making.

As far as the scientific education of the layman is concerned, I believe there is no real choice. It may be a toss-up as to whether the political scientist or the historian can give the better understanding of our government in a limited amount of time, but the odds are all against the philosopher, I believe, who has a parallel assignment in regard to science. To be sure, he has had a clear field for the most part, for the histories illustrating the Tactics and Strategy of Science are as yet unwritten. But in spite of this lack of competition I doubt if the philosophical treatments of science and scientific method have been very successful when viewed as an educational enterprise. No one questions, of course, the importance of this type of penetrating analysis. There must be constant critical appraisal of the progress of science and in particular of scientific concepts and operation. This is one of the prime tasks of philosophers concerned with the unity of science and the problems of cosmology. But when the learned discussions of these difficult matters are the sole source of popular knowledge about the ways of science, education in science may be more handicapped than helped by their wide circulation. I am inclined to think that, on the whole, the popularization of the philosophical analysis of science and its methods has led not to a greater understanding but to a great deal of misunderstanding about science . . .

The Tactics and Strategy of Science

Let me now be specific as to my proposal for the reform of the scientific education of the layman. What I propose is the establishment of one or more courses at the college level on the Tactics and Strategy of Science. The objective would be to give a greater degree of understanding of science by the close study of a relatively few historical examples of the development of science . . .

The case histories would almost all be chosen from the early days in the evolution of the modern discipline. Certain aspects of physics in the seventeenth and eighteenth centuries; chemistry in the eighteenth and nineteenth; geology in the early nineteenth; certain phases of biology in the eighteenth; others in the nineteenth. The advantages of this method of approach are twofold: first, relatively little factual knowledge is required either as regards the science in question or other sciences, and relatively little mathematics; second, in the early days one sees in clearest light the necessary fumblings of even intellectual giants when they are also pioneers; one comes to understand what science is by seeing how difficult it is in fact to carry out glib scientific precepts.

A few words may be in order as to the principles which would guide me in selecting case histories for my course in the Tactics and Strategy of Science. I should wish to show the difficulties which attend each new push forward in the advance of science, and the importance of new techniques; how they arise, are improved, and often revolutionize a field of inquiry. I should hope to illustrate the intricate interplay between experiment, or observation, and the development of new concepts and new generalizations; in short, how new concepts evolve from experiments, how one conceptual scheme for a time is adequate and then is modified or displaced by another. I should want also to illustrate the interconnection between science and society about which so much has been said in recent years by our Marxist friends. I should have very little to say about the classification of facts, unless it were to use this phrase as a straw man. But I should hope that almost all examples chosen would show the hazards which nature puts in the way of those who would examine the facts impartially and classify them accurately. The "controlled experiment" and the planned or controlled observation would be in the forefront of every discussion. The difference in methods between the observational sciences of astronomy, geology, systematic biology on the one hand, and the experimental sciences of physics, chemistry, and experimental biology on the other should be emphasized.

. . . A discussion of the evolution of new conceptual schemes as a result of experimentation would occupy a central position in the exposition. This being so, there would be no escape from a consideration of the difficulties which historically have attended the development of new concepts. Is a vacuum really empty, if so, how can we see through it? Is action at a distance imaginable? These questions at one time in the forefront of scientific discussion are well worthy of careful review. The Newtonian theory of gravitation once disturbed "almost all investigators of nature because it was founded on an uncommon intelligibility." It no longer disturbs us because "it has become a common unintelligibility." To what extent can the same statement be made about other concepts which have played a major part in the development of modern science? When we say that the chemists have "established" that chlorophyll is essential for photosynthesis and that they also have "established" the spatial arrangements for the carbon, hydrogen, and oxygen atoms in cane sugar, are we using the word "establish" in two different senses? These and similar questions should be explored in sufficient degree to make the student aware of some of the complexities which lie hidden behind our usual simplified exposition of the basic ideas of modern science in an elementary course.

However, I cannot emphasize too often that the course in question must *not* be concerned with the fruits of scientific inquiries, either as embodied in scientific laws or theories or cosmologies, or in the application of science to industry or agriculture or medicine. Rather, the instructor would center his attention on the ways in which these fruits have been attained. One might call it a course in "scientific method" as illustrated by examples from history, except that I am reluctant to use this ambiguous phrase. I should prefer to speak of the methods by which science has been advanced, or perhaps we should say knowledge has been advanced, harking back to Francis Bacon's famous phrase, the advancement of learning.

THE MYTH OF SCIENTIFIC LITERACY

Morris H. Shamos

The current state of science education, as well as most of its problems, is clearly influenced by a single overriding premise: the *primary* function of formal science education, whether precollege or college, is to ensure a steady supply of scientists and science-related professionals, including, of course, science educators. Everything else that is done in science education, regardless of its educational worth or numbers of students involved, turns out to be secondary to this goal. Not that this is its avowed purpose, of course. Science educators persistently try to persuade themselves, and the community at large, to believe that there is a loftier purpose to science education, namely, to educate the general public—to achieve widespread scientific literacy—and indeed many educators have visions of such an ideal. But the reality behind such grand objectives is that the practical goal of producing future scientists must (and does) come first. Urging students into science as a profession is clearly part of the responsibility of science educators, but one must bear in mind that here we are dealing with only about 5 to 10 percent of the high school student population. To face the issue squarely, it is obvious that science departments, whether in our schools or colleges, are no different from most other disciplines in seeking to increase the enrollment of nonmajors in their courses; their underlying motive is more to attract critical masses of faculty and adequate equipment budgets for research than to satisfy some *compelling* educational need of the general (nonscience) student.

The competition is keen in most faculties to be included in the distribution requirements for all students, and equally acute in most science departments to design courses that will attract these students, regardless of whether such courses will have a lasting effect on them . . . So, unseemly as it may be, a major factor in the pursuit of scientific literacy is self-justification and perpetuation of the science and science education professions. Many university science departments survive only by virtue of the "point credits" they earn through their introductory courses. How else to account for such promotional titles as Physics for Poets, Kitchen Chemistry, Biology for Living, etc. Not that this is altogether improper, for it is essential that university science departments be able to support "critical masses" of faculty to carry on research and prepare future scientists. Whether this is equally true for all students a the high school level is open to question.

A second premise concerns general education in science. If the purpose of such education is to create a scientifically literate public, the principle target audience, namely the student population, may be ill-chosen. However one chooses to define scientific literacy, its main objective seems clear enough: society (and the individual) will somehow benefit if its members are sufficiently literate to participate intelligently in science-based societal issues. Assuming this is true, and on the surface it seems perfectly sensible, is the proper target audience the student or the adult population? Obviously, if the purpose of such literacy is to benefit society, it is really only the adult population that is in a position to contribute to the public good. So while student may attain some level of scientific literacy relating to the individual science courses they take in school, what good is it if they fail to retain this knowledge into adulthood?

The mistake we make is in assuming that because some, perhaps even many, of our students perform well in school science, they have achieved a measure of scientific literacy that will serve them as adults. Most science teachers leave their classes feeling that they have communicated successfully with some number of nonscience students, and most likely they have. But the end effect of this is a delusion. Good school performance, even a reasonable level of scientific literacy while one is a student, provides no assurance that the individual will retain enough science when he or she becomes a responsible adult, presumably contributing to the overall good of society. It would be different if science education for the general student were justified solely on the grounds of a cultural or intellectual imperative, but while many may believe that it should be, science educators in general fear that doing so would spell its doom by relegating it to purely elective status in the schools.

Here lies the crux of the matter. Whatever we may do to turn students on to science, to make them acutely aware of the world around them, and get them to at least appreciate what the scientific enterprise is about, if not so much science itself, we are guided in the schools by immediate feedback rather than long-term retention. After all, to be pragmatic about it, having literate students who turn out to be scientific illiterates as adults does not do much for society. We know that the staying power of science courses is very poor, but what is particularly depressing is the fact that although most students lapse back into scientific illiteracy soon after they graduate, they nevertheless think they are reasonably literate in science . . .

The Dimensions of Scientific Literacy

For the present, let us assume, as do most science educators, that scientific literacy requires some level of *understanding* of science. If so, attempts to fashion a simple definition of the phrase in absolute terms must fail because a meaningful definition can be expressed only in behavioral terms or measurable outcomes, that is, what should be expected of a science literate or one who "understands" something about science? . . . Few educated individuals are totally illiterate in science; everyone knows some facts of nature and has some idea of what science is about, however naïve or misconceived these notions may be. Hence, it is an oversimplification to assume that an individual is either literate or illiterate in science. Instead, one might distinguish several levels of literacy, levels that are normally attained sequentially by science-bound students, for example, during their formal exposure to science. Following are descriptions (definitions, if you will) of three such levels of literacy, which build upon one another in degree of sophistication as well as in the chronological development of the science-oriented mind, and which, because of their vertical structure, may be useful as criteria for judging scientific literacy, if a knowledge of science is indeed to be included in such literacy.

1. *Cultural Scientific Literacy.* Clearly the simplest form of literacy is . . . [a recognition of] many of the science-based terms (the jargon) used by the media, which is generally [most people's] only exposure to science, and such recognition probably provides some measure of comfort that they are not totally illiterate in science. But for the most part, this is where their knowledge of science ends.

2. *Functional Scientific Literacy.* Here we add some substance to the bare skeleton of cultural literacy by requiring that the individual not only have command of a science lexicon, but also be able to converse, read, and write coherently, using such science terms in perhaps a nontechnical but nevertheless meaningful context. This means using the terms correctly, for example, knowing what might be called "some of the simple, everyday facts of nature," such as

having some knowledge of our solar system, of how the Earth revolves around the Sun and the Moon revolves around the Earth, and how eclipses occur . . . Or to get a bit more sophisticated, expecting the individual to identify the ultimate source of our energy, or the "greenhouse effect," or knowing what "clean air" means or how we get the oxygen we breathe. And getting still more sophisticated, hoping that the individual knows the difference between electrons and atoms, or what DNA is and the role it plays in living things . . .

3. *"True" Scientific Literacy.* At this level the individual actually knows something about the overall scientific enterprise. He or she is aware of some of the major conceptual schemes (the theories) that form the foundations of science, how they were arrived at, and why they are widely accepted, how science achieves order out of a random universe, and the role of experiment in science. This individual also appreciates the elements of scientific investigation, the importance of proper questioning, of analytical and deductive reasoning, of logical thought processes, and of reliance upon objective evidence. These are the same mental qualities that John Dewey called "scientific habits of the mind" nearly a century ago and which he proposed as the main rationale for compulsory science education, a rationale that today is often called "critical thinking." Whatever term one chooses, however, it remains a mental state that has never come to pass in the general population. This is obviously a demanding definition of scientific literacy and some may argue that it is designed to make such literacy unattainable by the public at large. But it means only that the term itself, "scientific literacy," has been used too loosely in the past and that, when viewed realistically, true scientific literacy, as defined here, is unlikely to be achieved in the foreseeable future . . .

Science Appreciation

Turning to the basic question of what the educated person should know about science, we should first discard our current notion of "scientific literacy" as being a meaningless goal and seek other criteria that may be more practical. [One such criterion was given by Edward Teller in 1957, when we argued]: "The mass of our children should be given something which may not be terribly strenuous but should be interesting, stimulating and amusing. They should be given science appreciation courses just as they are sometimes given music appreciation courses."

Teller's message of science *appreciation*, coming at a time when the American public, and particularly the Congress, was highly sensitive to the issue of Soviet competition in space, and just when massive NSF support for precollege science education was in its formative stage, fell on deaf ears as the nation girded itself for a far more ambitious role in science education, namely, to achieve in the educated public what had never before been achieved—the intellectual state that came to be known as "scientific literacy." While not clearly defined at the time (nor even now), this objective carried such a comforting pedagogical feel that one could hardly challenge its premise, and for the next quarter of a century the science education community sought to justify virtually everything it did as bringing us closer to the goal of scientific literacy. It tried valiantly, but . . . it failed badly.

In our zeal to achieve the ideal we failed to question the goal itself rather than the means to attain it. The science education community was reluctant to concede the possibility that the answer might lie in a goal other than scientific literacy, one that would be more acceptable to the general student and yet achieve a useful end result. The science and engineering communities, and our nation generally, would be better served by a society that, while perhaps illiterate in science in the formal academic sense, at least is aware of what science is, how it works, and its horizons and limitations . . .

Almost fifty years ago, the approach taken by James B. Conant in his well-known Harvard Case Histories in Experimental Science marked a significant effort in [the direction of scientific appreciation]. Its premise, however, that appreciation of science might grow out of the historical development of some of the great ideas in science, evidently did not fully satisfy the need, as seen more in the eyes of the Harvard faculty than by its students. [Nor] would it fully satisfy the needs of science awareness, although a strong case can be made for it as part of any science curriculum. The main advantage of a historical approach is that the science it deals with, when viewed from a modern perspective, is generally much simpler and the reasoning involved is likely to be more transparent than in a contemporary example. However, it would be inconceivable today, largely because of its societal import, to omit contemporary science from a student's formal education. Thus any modern science curriculum, even one taking the case history approach to demonstrate the process of science, must also lean heavily on contemporary science, particularly on some of the scientific advances that gave rise to modern technology and its consequent social issues . . . .

Science Awareness: A New Scientific Literacy

Having delineated the many problems confronting the scientific literacy movement, we now address the question of how to reformulate the goal itself. After all these years of trying to achieve scientific literacy in the student population we have made no discernible progress. Everyone seems to have a vague, ill-defined notion of what *should* be, but we've had no clear specifics, least of all on how to achieve our goals. All is not lost, however. The fact that there is no general acceptance of what the elusive scientific literacy actually means, or should mean, is itself significant, for it forces us to reflect on why we think scientific literacy is important, whatever one takes it to mean. Since the curriculum, in effect, sets the tone of a science program, on what should curriculum developers (and textbook writers) concentrate in any new approach to science education?

Putting aside science as a cultural imperative, there are two valid reasons for seeking widespread public understanding of science—three, if one includes the practical but unspoken objective of getting critical masses of students into our science courses. The first is the desire of the science and science education communities to have the public (and particularly public officials) appreciate and support these enterprises to ensure their continued vitality. This purpose might better be classed under the science or technology *appreciation* alluded to earlier. The second is the desire, mainly of the social science community, to have the public participate directly in the decision-making process on societal issues having a scientific base, issues that are actually based for the most part on technology . . . .

This is what most people take scientific literacy to mean, and is where the bottleneck actually occurs. Prodded mainly by the social science community, we have been laboring to find ways of educating all Americans in science to the point where they can reach *independent* judgments on such issues. Such *social* or *civic literacy* is really the underlying goal of the scientific literacy movement, and particularly its STS (science/technology/society) component, and it is time we all recognize this as an impossible task and get on with the normal business of science education. Not even professional scientists can always be relied upon to vote with their heads instead of their feet, and no *reasonable* amount of science education can ever get the average person to the point where he or she is able to judge such issues independently and dispassionately.

The answer is simple and straightforward, if one takes as a given that the only practical way of resolving the primarily technical aspects of a given issue is to seek the advice of experts in the field. With this assumption, the three guiding principles for presenting science to the general (nonscience) student should be:

Teach science mainly to develop appreciation and awareness of the enterprise, that is, as a *cultural* imperative, and not primarily for content. Designing curricula aimed at this objective is not difficult, provided one does not attempt to cover everything.

To provide a central them, focus on technology as a *practical* imperative for the individual's personal health and safety, and on an awareness of both the natural and man-made environments. Several very good materials along these lines already exist.

For developing social (civic) literacy, emphasize the *proper* use of scientific experts, an emerging field that has not yet penetrated the science curriculum.

Further Reading

Alic, Margaret. *Hypatia's Heritage.* Boston: Beacon Press, 1986.

Barnes, Barry, David Bloor, and John Henry. *Scientific Knowledge: A Sociological Analysis.* Chicago: University of Chicago Press, 1996.

Chalmers, Alan. *Science and Its Fabrication.* Minneapolis: University of Minnesota Press, 1990.

Feyerabend, Paul. *Science in a Free Society.* London: Verso, 1982.

Grinnell, Richard W. (ed.). *Science and Society.* New York: Longman, 2007.

Gross, Paul and Norman Levitt. *Higher Superstition: The Academic Left and Its Quarrels with Science.* Baltimore: The Johns Hopkins University Press, 1994.

Hess, David J. *Science Studies.* New York: New York University Press, 1997.

Kitcher, Philip. *Science, Truth, and Democracy.* Oxford: Oxford University Press, 2001.

Kourany, Janet A. (ed.). *The Gender of Science.* Upper Saddle River: Prentice Hall, 2002.

Latour, Bruno and Catherine Porter. *Politics of Nature.* Cambridge: Harvard University Press, 2004.

McComas, William F. (ed.). *The Nature of Science in Science Education.* Dordrecht: Kluwer, 1998.

Polanyi, Michael. *Science, Faith and Society.* London: Oxford University Press, 1946.

Rouse, Joseph. *Engaging Science.* Ithaca: Cornell University Press, 1996.

Snow, C.P. *The Two Cultures and a Second Look.* New York: New American Library, 1963.

Sokal, Alan and Jean Bricmont. *Fashionable Nonsense.* New York: Picador USA, 1998.

Tuana, Nancy (ed.). *Feminism and Science.* Bloomington: Indiana University Press, 1989.

Zammito, John H. *A Nice Derangement of Epistemes.* Chicago: University of Chicago Press, 2004.

CHAPTER FIFTEEN

Mass Extinctions

IN THIS CHAPTER, WE WILL

- Consider the facts of the ongoing mass extinctions debates
- Identify and examine various philosophical issues related to the mass extinctions debates

I suspect that you have heard that what caused the dinosaurs to go extinct was a meteor (or asteroid or comet) smashing into the earth. You might not have heard that this view was only relatively recently proposed among scientists. It is now the received view among both professional academics and lay persons that the demise of the dinosaurs was part of a mass extinction event that occurred 65 million years ago (mya) and was caused by bolide impact (i.e., by an extraterrestrial object striking the earth). This was not the received view before 1980 and, for professional paleontologists, was not broadly accepted until the early- and even mid-1990s, once the Chicxulub crater site (in Mexico) was identified as the impact site datable to the Cretaceous-Tertiary (K-T) boundary. Nevertheless, controversy and debate have remained regarding mass extinctions, even the K-T extinction, as is evidenced in the following quotations:

> Sixty-five million years ago, a comet or asteroid larger than
> Mt. Everest slammed into the Earth, causing an explosion
> equivalent to the detonation of a hundred million hydrogen
> bombs. Vaporized impactor and debris from the impact were
> blasted out through the atmosphere, falling back to Earth all
> around the globe . . . Controversial and widely attacked during the
> 1980s, the impact theory received confirmation from the discovery

of the giant impact crater it predicted, buried deep beneath younger strata at the north coast of the Yucatan Peninsula.

This quote is from the book *T-Rex and the Crater of Doom*, written by Walter Alvarez, professor of geology and geophysics at UC, Berkeley and one of the originators of the impact account of K-T extinction. The book was published in 1997 by Princeton University Press. This contrasts with another quotation from the same time:

> The demise of the dinosaurs (along with a host of other more or less contemporaneous life-forms) clearly occurred for other and more complicated reasons than impacts from space . . . The Alvarez hypothesis has collapsed under the weight of accumulated geologic and other evidence to the contrary, as well as from an increasingly obvious absence of scientific evidence proffered in its support.

This quote is from the book *The Great Dinosaur Extinction Controversy*, written by Charles Officer and Jake Page, Officer being a well-known geologist at Dartmouth. The book was published in 1996 by Weidenfeld and Nicolson. Its jacket states the book "chronicles the fantastic story of how (the impact) hypothesis became so widespread" and the "ample scientific research that proves the theory wrong."

There is little that warms the heart of a philosopher or historian of science more than categorically claimed contradictory comments, especially coming from renowned and respected scientific practitioners! The sight of a good scientific fight is a call to action for fruitful analysis of debate and controversy within science as well as meta-scientific views about science. This chapter is an investigation of the presentation, both inside and outside of academia, of the ongoing debates concerning mass extinctions of life on the earth. Since the early 1980s, shortly following the landmark Alvarez article announcing the impact theory, these debates have been addressed to the lay public at the same time as among professionals. In this chapter we will look at these ongoing debates about mass extinctions and see how this case relates to the various topics we have covered in this book. This is a very exciting and complex case of scientific practice and debate and it is still ongoing! There are far more features about this case to discuss than can be covered in a single chapter, so I hope that you will wrestle with these issues beyond what I will do here. But let's begin. First, we will look at a brief summary of what scientists have said, focusing on the time period since 1980, about mass extinctions.

Summary of the mass extinctions debates

Extinctions of species happen all the time and the history of life on the earth reveals evidence of varied rates of extinctions. Sometimes paleontologists speak of extinction events, relatively short periods of time (geologically speaking), in which extinction rates rise above the "normal" rates of extinctions. Just about all paleontologists speak of the "Big Five" extinction events (see Figure 1): End-Ordovician (440 mya), Late Devonian (360 mya), End-Permian (250 mya), End-Triassic (220 mya), and End-Cretaceous (65 mya). During these "Big Five" events,

Era	Period	Epoch	Age in 10^6 years	Major extinction events
Cenozoic	Quaternary (Sub-period)	Holocene	0.01	
		Pleistocene	2	
		Pliocene	5	
		Miocene	25	
		Oligocene	38	
		Eocene	55	
		Palaeocene	65	*
Mesozoic	Cretaceous		144	
	Jurassic		200	*
	Triassic		250	*
Palaeozoic	Permian		286	
	Carboniferous		360	*
	Devonian		408	
	Silurian		438	*
	Ordovician		505	
	Cambrian		545	

Figure 1   (From *Catastrophes and Lesser Calamities*, Tony Hallam. Oxford: Oxford University Press, 2004. Page 26.)

extinction rates rose to as much as (and even more than) half of all known species going extinct; in addition, the extinctions were global. From the early 1980s until the late 1990s, it was the End-Cretaceous extinction event that received most of the attention, certainly for the nonspecialist public. Since the late 1990s, however, the End-Permian extinction event has generated more attention, again both inside and outside academia. As early as 1983 a book on the End-Cretaceous extinction, Michael Allaby and James Lovelock's *The Great Extinction,* was published for a nonprofessional audience. By the end of 1983 there appeared in *The New York Times* a story on the possible periodicity (that is, a repeated temporal pattern) of extinctions, what came to be dubbed "The Nemesis Hypothesis."

Briefly stated, the Nemesis hypothesis is this: A star with an orbit elliptical to the plane of our solar system has come close enough to our solar system every 26 million years so as to disrupt the Oort Cloud, a hypothetical bubble of material enveloping our solar system; the result of this disruption has been that some of this material was deflected toward the inner planets and subsequently, in the forms of asteroids or meteorites, has bombarded the Earth with the resulting impacts causing mass extinctions of life. The most famous victims of one such bombardment were the dinosaurs at the end of the Cretaceous period.

This characterization of the Nemesis hypothesis, as simple as it is, is actually rather complex because it carries with it several other hypotheses. These other hypotheses include the following: (1) there have been mass extinction events (i.e., relatively sudden and widespread extinctions of a large percentage of species) of terrestrial life, (2) there has been a periodicity to these mass extinctions, (3) the periodicity is one of approximately 26 million years, (4) the periodicity has an extraterrestrial cause, (5) that extraterrestrial cause is Nemesis, and (6) the mass extinction of life at the Cretaceous-Tertiary, or K-T, boundary (65 million years ago), including the extinction of dinosaurs, was caused by the impact of an extraterrestrial body (and indirectly caused by Nemesis).

Each hypothesis in this web of hypotheses has been championed and challenged independently of the others. For example, not everyone in the scientific community accepts the impact view with respect to the extinction at the K-T boundary (e.g., Orth, 1981; Hallam, 1987). Indeed, not everyone accepts that there was an extinction *event* at the K-T boundary (Briggs, in Glen, 1994), meaning that the extinction occurred over a relatively quick time period. Even accepting impact for that particular extinction event does not entail accepting periodicity of extinction events (e.g., Stigler and Wagner, 1988). Similarly, accepting periodicity does not entail accepting a periodicity of 26 million years (e.g., Rampino and Strothers, 1984), nor does it entail acceptance of Nemesis as the cause of periodicity (e.g., Rampino and Strothers, 1984; Schwartz and James, 1984).

A (very!) brief and selective chronology of work among professionals with respect to these hypotheses is as follows: In 1977, Fischer and Arthur published a paper postulating a periodicity of mass extinctions of 32 million years. This paper was met with some criticism, but mostly with silence. (Seven years earlier, Digby McLaren, in his presidential address to the Paleontological Society, had suggested impact as the cause of a mass extinction 365 million years ago.) In June 1980, the research team led by Louis Alvarez published its famous paper (Alvarez, 1980) suggesting an extraterrestrial impact as the cause of the extinctions at the K-T boundary. The predominant evidence was the pronounced levels of iridium at the boundary. By the end of 1983, the Alvarez team reported at least 22 sites, scattered around the world, exhibiting the iridium anomaly at the K-T boundary. The initial Alvarez paper was immediately criticized in terms of its evidence and its conclusions. Challenges included whether the iridium anomaly was a true anomaly, whether it entails an extraterrestrial cause, where the impact crater is, and whether a single catastrophic event could account for late Cretaceous extinctions (which apparently span numbers of centuries).

In early 1984, Raup and Sepkoski (1984) announced a periodicity of mass extinctions of 26 million years, based on computer simulations producing a "best fit" analysis of family extinctions. This analysis was immediately criticized and continues to be. In April 1984, two causes were proposed to account for a 26-million-year periodicity. First, Rampino and Strothers (1984) as well as Schwartz and James (1984) suggested that periodicity is caused by our solar system's oscillation with respect to the galactic plane. Second, both Whitmore and Jackson (1984) and Davis, Hut, and Muller (1984) suggested an unseen companion to our sun. This yet-to-be-found star was baptized "Nemesis." In January 1985, Whitmore and Matese (1985) offered a third proposal, that the cause of the periodicity is an unseen tenth planet in our solar system, which they dubbed "Planet X." Meanwhile, by the beginning of 1985, corroborating evidence for the Alvarez claim of impact included Luck and Turekian's (1983) evidence of anomalous levels of osmium isotope ratios at the K-T boundary, Bohor's (1987) findings of shocked quartz at the K-T boundary sites, as well as reports of worldwide distribution of iridium anomalies at the K-T boundary. The three proposals—galactic oscillation, a tenth planet, and a companion star—all met with criticisms. The galactic oscillation view, although requiring no new or mysterious ontological objects, suffered the fate of not being in sync with the purported mass extinctions. As the solar system bobs up and down relative to the galactic plane, the mass extinctions should have occurred when the solar system was approaching the galactic plane, but that has not happened. The Planet X view received little attention, but suffered the fate of the planet not having been found. This is true as well for Nemesis (i.e., not having been found), but its defenders claim it is less likely that we would have missed a planet in our solar system than a (very likely dim) star that is not within our solar system, but only approaches it enough to have its gravitational field affect the Oort Cloud.

The summer of 1986 brought renewed objection to an extraterrestrial cause of extinction at the K-T boundary and increased skepticism of an extraterrestrial cause for any other extinction event. These objections included claims for largespread volcanic activity as the causal agent (e.g., Loper, 1988), questions concerning whether there was truly a sudden extinction event at K-T (e.g., Hallam), and a lack of evidence for the K-T impact site (i.e., a crater). At the same time, bits of further evidence—if not corroborating the impact hypothesis and the periodicity hypothesis, then at least being consistent with them—included the discovery of an impact crater off the coast of Nova Scotia, dated at 200 million years ago.

By the end of 1988, the impact hypothesis had gained more adherents, especially with respect to impact at the K-T boundary. Nevertheless, proponents of terrestrial mechanisms for extinction pointed to data that did not fit the impact (or periodicity) view. An apparent extinction event 92 million years ago contained evidence (such as enhanced levels of scandium and titanium, more characteristic of material from the Earth's upper mantle than from meteorites or asteroids) that was deemed more easily explainable by volcanic activity. In addition paleoclimatic studies seemed to indicate that there was significant cooling of the Earth just prior to the K-T extinction. By early 1989 two additional pieces of evidence bolstered the impact view: McHone and Nieman's (1989) isolation of stishovite (having been found only at crater sites and very rare in the Earth's crust) at the K-T boundary, along with Zhao and Bada's (1989) discovery of two rare amino acids (alpha-amino-isobutyric acid and racemic isovaline), normally associated with meteorites.

By the early 1990s, no impact site had been conclusively identified as the point of K-T impact, though several had been suggested (and rejected), including sites in Iowa, Cuba and Haiti. By the end of 1992, however, an impact site on the Yucatan peninsula, Chicxulub, had been identified as the K-T impact site and by the end of 1994 was accepted by most investigators as "the real thing." On the other hand, the volcanists (i.e., advocates of high-level volcanic activity) continued to point not only to the Deccan Traps of India as evidence of volcanic activity as the most likely mechanism of extinctions, but claimed the discovery of vast deposits of volcanic basalts, known as the Siberian Traps, to be further corroboration of their position. In addition, several pieces of evidence claimed by proponents of impact as supporting the impact hypothesis came under challenge, including the claim that a variety of foraminifera suddenly became extinct at the K-T boundary. Keller (1989) and others argued that they did not suddenly become extinct, but gradually died out. Rampino and Haggerty (1995) continued to argue for a 26 to 30 million year periodicity while others claimed that evidence of "hypercanes" (extremely massive hurricanes) contributed to the End-Cretaceous extinction.

The upshot of this is that at the end of 1995, 15 years after the initial Alvarez article, none of the various hypotheses associated with the Nemesis hypothesis was established to the complete satisfaction of the scientific community. The hypotheses that there have been mass extinctions and that there was an extinction event at the K-T boundary enjoyed the greatest acceptance by the relevant investigators. Even the hypothesis that the K-T extinction was caused by impact was accepted by a majority of scientists. The hypotheses of periodicity of extinction events and specifically of the specific timing and cause of such periodicity received far less support and were treated much more as (more or less promising) speculation.

In 1996, attention shifted to conflicting claims regarding the End-Permian extinction event, with both terrestrial causes cited (e.g., massive quantities of carbon dioxide released from the oceans) to impact as evidenced by shocked quartz. By the beginning of 1998 another extraterrestrial, but non-impact, cause of End-Cretaceous extinction was resurrected, namely high-energy radiation from gamma-ray bursts outside the solar system. At the same time, additional geochemical data, the isotopic composition of chromium, was said to "confirm" impact (e.g., Shukolyukov and Lugmair, 1998). In 2001, Becker et al. (2001) claimed that extraterrestrial noble gases in fullerenes at the Permian-Triassic boundary strongly indicate an impact event as the cause of the End-Permian extinction. Soon after evidence of elevated iridium levels amidst fern spikes, as well as shocked quartz, was found in Pennsylvania at the Triassic-Jurassic boundary, suggesting impact at the End-Triassic extinction. In 2003, Ellwood et al. (2003) claimed evidence for bolide impact at the Late Devonian extinction. Meanwhile, evidence of increased levels of carbon dioxide and methane gases along with lack of an associated impact crater, led others to question impact as the cause of End-Permian extinction. In early 2004, however, Becker suggested that such a crater, the Bedout Crater off the northwest coast of Australia, might indeed be the associated impact site, though this has not yet been established. In 2006, evidence was uncovered of an impact site, the Wilkes Land 300-mile-wide crater, in Antarctica dated to around 250 mya. In Figure 2, Tony Hallam, a critic of the impact view, offers a summary of proposed

	Bolide Impact	Volcanism	Cooling	Warming	Regression	Anoxia/ transgression
Late Precambrian						●
Late Early Cambrian					●	●
Late Cambrian biomeres			○			●
End-Ordovician			●	●	●	●
Frasnian-Famennian			○		○	●
Devonian-Carboniferous			○			●
Late Guadaloupian					●	
End-Permian		●		●	○	●
End-Triassic		●		○	●	○
Early Toarcian		●		○		
Cenomanian-Turonian			○			●
End-Cretaceous	●	●	●		●	○
End-Palaeocene		●		●		●
Late Eocene			●			

Figure 2 (From *Catastrophes and Lesser Calamities*. Tony Hallam. Oxford: Oxford University Press, 2004. Page 197.)

causes for various mass extinctions, in an attempt to visually summarize the predominant view of most paleontologists at the beginning of this century. I say "most paleontologists" because there is not anything near universal agreement (even among the paleontologists) about this. For example, there are quite a few paleontologists, indeed a growing number, who support the notion of an End-Permian impact hypothesis.

Philosophical concerns: Basic components of science

Given this sketchy survey of the mass extinction debates over the past quarter century, we will take the rest of this chapter to consider how these debates connect up with the philosophy of science issues that we have looked at throughout this book.

As you now know, there are a variety of facets of science that philosophers attend to in the process of analyzing the norms and practices of science. These facets range from the gathering of information (e.g., observation, measurement, experimentation) to organizing such information (e.g., models, theories, paradigms) to accounting for such information (e.g., explanation, prediction, hypothesis testing, reduction). There are numerous ways in which the conduct of the scientific community involved in the extinction debates exhibited these facets and it would be beneficial for philosophers of science to look carefully at these numerous ways.

For example, with respect to information gathering and hypothesis formation, a variety of experimental techniques were used, including thought experiments, computer simulation experiments, as well as "traditional" one-shot case studies. Or, the multiple interpretations, reinterpretations, and apparent invulnerability to falsification of much of the proposed evidence both for and against impact can provide fecund material for both philosophers and sociologists of science. In this first section, we will examine issues of the mass extinctions debates as they relate to the topics of observation/measurement, experimentation, theories/models, explanation, evidence, and unity of science.

First, then, what are some features of observation and measurement that were noted in Chapter Two that relate to this case? There are many, but I will focus on only a few. I will begin with one small incident, what came to be called "the 3-meter gap." In Montana, at one excavation site of dinosaur fossils, there was a gap of 3 meters between the K-T boundary and where scientists found the latest dinosaur bones (by "latest" meaning closest to the present time). In addition, mammalian fossils that were identified as belonging to the Tertiary Period (so, after the K-T extinction event) were found between the dinosaur bones and the K-T boundary layer. Now, what might appear to be a straightforward case of going out into the field and observing this data, and upon finding none above the K-T boundary—and, so, concluding that the impact hypothesis is correct—or finding some above the K-T boundary—and, so, concluding that the impact hypothesis is incorrect—turns out not to be so straightforward. A 3 meter gap suggested to some scientists that the impact hypothesis was false, as 3 meters of sediment could represent millions of years. But there are deeper conceptual issues here just about observation. For instance, the observation that there were no dinosaur fossils found above the K-T boundary hinges on a prior conception of what constitutes a fossil, as well as what constitutes a dinosaur fossil. That is, odd fragments and isolated bones by themselves do not constitute either, because these things could easily have simply been buried or exhumed by erosion. Their presence at a particular location does not in itself mean they were deposited where they died, when they died, and just remained there.

Much of what is observed with respect to these debates are incomplete and ambiguous records of what actually happened millions of years ago. As Charles Officer, critic of the impact hypothesis, claims, hiatuses do not appear in the geologic record and such hiatuses might make a gradual extinction appear abrupt, since layers of sediment can take varying amounts of time to form. Beyond that, some scientists have argued that microbes living in the sediment can and have changed iridium deposits, including in some cases of the K-T boundary itself. In one experiment, for example, scientists compared pieces of nickel-iron meteorite immersed in a bacteria-containing solution with other pieces in a sterile solution. They found that the bacteria caused iridium to leave the meteorite and enter the solution, suggesting that microbes might have erased part of the original iridium layer or spread it into deeper sediments. In another trial, they found that fungi and bacteria actually concentrated iridium that was dissolved in water, indicating that they could have enhanced the iridium layer. Given this information, there would be no need to hypothesize (or accept a hypothesis that) bolide impact explains, and indeed is needed to explain, the iridium anomaly at the K-T boundary.

We saw in Chapter Two that Norman Hanson claimed that observation is theory-laden. How this would relate to the present case would be to see if background theory influenced what different scientists observed. An example Hanson might point to it this: In 1988 Gerta Keller argued that the extinctions at K-T were more gradual than abrupt and she pointed to the fossil record to support this claim. She claimed that the fossil record, particularly with foraminifera, showed a slow, gradual decline leading up to the K-T boundary. Jan Smit, however, looking at the same record, disagreed. Smit found that virtually all of his 30 species of Cretaceous foraminifera at a particular site continues up to within two centimeters of the K-T boundary. They both acknowledged that they were looking at the same phenomena, but seeing different things. Likewise, one phenomenon that has been seen as supporting the impact hypothesis is shocked quartz (because the force of the impact caused the structure of the quartz to be altered). Charles Officer, however, claimed to have found shocked quartz spread across Gubbio, not just at the K-T boundary, suggesting that shocked quartz is not a clear-cut indication of impact.

Besides examples such as these about what is observed and how to interpret those observations, there are issues of what is not observed and has not been observed. First and foremost, what has not been observed is Nemesis. No "death star" has been found, even after more than 25 years of searching for one. On the other hand, brown dwarf stars have been found relatively close to the solar system. There is obviously the question of what is not observed when assessing the hypothesis of periodicity. That is, what can actually be observed is not a periodicity, but particular phenomena in some sort of pattern, which in this case is a temporal pattern. But, then, what is actually observed that constitutes a temporal pattern? Hanson claims this is theory-laden. Scheffler claims it is a categorization, allowing us to "file" the actual observations into a coherent package. So, just to be able to summarily talk about various issues of observation, there are questions of what is actually observed. Is it a pattern, a relative frequency, a comparative level, and so on.

This case is not simply about seeing bones or iridium or whatever, but observing information that is gleaned from phenomena such as comparative levels of iridium and placement of fossils and levels of radioactive isotopes, and so on. Once stated that way, it is clear that observation is a very complex matter, especially observation involving historical events from the distant past.

There are similar concerns with respect to measurement. We saw from Jones' argument in Chapter Two that measurement involves various conceptual steps: identifying the "object" being measured, identifying the measuring "device" (and scales), comparing the salient features of the object with those of the measuring device. In the case of the mass extinctions debates, the objects being measured are, again, sometimes patterns or rates or relative frequencies. Sometimes time is what is being measured: how old is some fossil or some crater, for example. What length of time does the K-T boundary represent? If it is millions of years, that is not a very meaningful boundary, at least to signify an event. If it is a few years, it is profoundly meaningful. If it is tens of thousands of years, is it then meaningful? Ten thousand years could represent millions of generations of some organisms, hence not be very informative about an extinction event (after all, it is not unlikely that over the course of millions of generations a species could gradually die off or evolve). The measuring devices in these debates might be extremely sophisticated matters, both in terms of equipment and conceptualization. For example, argon dating of craters involves both highly precise equipment and highly complex and abstract physical theory.

Another basic component of science that we identified earlier in this book (Chapter Three) was experimentation. Many of the experiments involved in the debates have been computer simulation experiments. For example, David Raup ran a simulated bombarding of Australia by bolides. He created a computer program with which he could simulate bombarding the globe and see what extinctions ensued, if any. At first, he structured the program so that comets struck randomly, but when they failed to produce desired local mass extinctions, he changed the program so he could aim the comets (aiming them at Australia in particular), thinking to wipe out marsupials. Other experiments were primarily fact-finding ones, such as seeing if comparatively high levels of iridium were to be found at crater sites. So, some experiments were designed to simply collect data, other to test some particular hypothesis.

Now, in Chapter Three, we read of Pierre Duhem's view that there is no "crucial" experiment, in the sense that any particular experiment by itself confirms or refutes a given hypothesis. That is because, he claimed, that whenever we test any give hypothesis, we are also, at least implicitly, testing many background (or auxiliary) hypotheses. This view seems to be borne out in the extinctions debate. For instance, Charles Officer remarks that about the K-T boundary, "In itself, this clay layer tells us very little about how the extinctions took place. In other words, from the standpoint of foraminifera species, what *exactly* happened during that revolutionary period is unknown from this section. Paleontologists could get a better idea if they could find a layer of limestone somewhere else . . ." (*The Great Dinosaur Extinction Controversy*, pages 57–58). In other words, the data do not speak for themselves, either for or against impact. The iridium anomaly at the K-T boundary requires an interpretation. Not only does it require an interpretation, but also without the background beliefs that meteorites occasionally strike the earth, that iridium is common in them but rare on the earth's surface, and so on, the impact hypothesis would not have been formulated at all. Perhaps it is one or more of these background hypotheses that are (seemingly) falsified.

A conceptual point related to experimentation is that of scientific realism. As we saw in Chapter Three, some philosophers of science claim that scientific practice, especially scientific progress, makes sense only to the extent that what they do matches up with real phenomena in the world (independent of any of our theories or models). Others claim that realism provides no fruitful explanation for the phenomena that we encounter. Now, we certainly assume that many of the features of this case are "real": there really are particular levels of iridium at various locations, that there really are crater impact sites, that species really went extinct, that something caused those extinctions, and so on. On the other hand, many of these scientists speak of geologic eras, periodicity of events, comparative levels of iridium, an absence of Nemesis, and so on. Do they take, say, geologic eras to be real, on a par with fossil bones? Eras are much more abstract than bones and seem to be much more a function of theories and models. By this, I do not mean the epistemological issue of just how we know when some era occurred (for example, when the Cretaceous Period occurred vs. the Tertiary Period), but in what sense an era is a phenomenon "out there in the world" independent of our theories or models. Even with what we would take to be more of an independent phenomenon, say, the Nemesis star, it is not clear how various scientists take it with respect to its "reality" status. It has never been observed, which for many scientists is sufficient to say it does not exist. However, some scientists have argued that we cannot infer that it does not exist simply on the basis of it not having been found over the past quarter century. It might well be out there! Another possibility is that it is real and in the past affected our planet's history, but since then has been deflected in its own orbit, so no longer is near our solar system. (Yes, we can come up with all kinds of scenarios to account for why it has not been found.) But: is Nemesis real? Again, there is a metaphysical take on this question as well as an epistemological one. Both are relevant to assessing how philosophical concerns about realism versus various competitors to realism to explain and account for scientific practice.

What is the role and nature of theories and models with respect to the mass extinctions debates? It is not obvious that there are any full-fledged theories involved, at least on a par with evolutionary theory or plate tectonics or quantum theory. That is, there is not really an Impact Theory that is universal or even general enough to explain not only the extinction events that have occurred in the earth's past but could provide meaningful predictions about future (possible) extinction events. There are certainly theories that are connected to the mass extinction debates, such as evolutionary theory and plate tectonics. For example, volcanists might well argue that plate tectonics can account for slow, gradual, but significant changes in the earth's ecosystems, resulting in the extinctions that we know have happened. But there seems to be no overall theory of extinctions. This raises an issue about the role and significance of theory for scientific change and progress. Certainly the scientists involved in these debates claim that we have a much better understanding of the earth's history as well as of more specific issues (such as crater dating) than we had prior to 1980 and the rise of the impact hypothesis, along with the ensuing surge in interest in mass extinctions. Yet the change and progress appears not to be the direct result of any significant theory, whether the emergence of some new theory or the novel application of existing theory. This is not to dismiss the importance of theory, say in terms of theory-ladenness of observation, but it does raise the question of the role and nature of theory as a (the?) major force in scientific change and progress. One wrinkle on this issue is that some scientists have argued that underlying the basic receptiveness or hostility to the impact view is a deeper—and theory-based—view about an earlier debate among geologists, namely a debate between catastrophism and uniformitarianism, where the former claims that dramatic events in the earth's past were the result of sudden catastrophic episodes and the latter claims that events in the earth's past, including what we see as dramatic events, were the result of slow, gradual, uniform changes. The scientists who speak about this underlying debate claim that the impact hypothesis has revived this debate by resurrecting a catastrophist view, so that underlying the scientists' attitudes and practices in this debate are deeply held theoretical commitments. We will actually speak more about this when we look at how Kuhn's view of scientific change relates to the extinctions debates.

There are, as we have seen, various models and hypotheses about more specific aspects within these extinction debates. When we looked at models in Chapter Four, we noted that sometimes models have primarily an exploratory function and other times an explanatory function. This is true of various models here. The impact model not only was intended to account in an explanatory way for the iridium anomaly, but in an exploratory way to investigate matters of iridium levels and presence of shocked quartz at numerous impact crater sites, as well as refining crater dating. Likewise, the volcanist hypothesis had both explanatory and exploratory functions.

When considering the features of models, we saw that models have a normative nature; they are focused, purposive, and often "idealized." In addition, they are structural representations of some phenomena. We saw that Morrison and Morgan argued that there are four basic elements related to models: how they are constructed, how they function, what (and how) they represent, and how we learn from them. How do these elements relate to the extinction debates? Although the impact model seems to have been constructed as a result of the discovery of the Gubbio iridium anomaly, many geologists and paleontologists claim that this model was constructed on the basis of that anomaly only by and because the Alvarez team was not trained in geology and paleontology. They were primarily physicists, so naturally (say the critics) they would construct (concoct, say the critics) a model based on extraterrestrial causes. Because this impact model then served as an exploratory function, it was just as much background theory and assumptions that led to the model as any data from the K-T boundary.

The question of what and how models represent is tied up with various conceptual issues we have already noted. For instance, much of the focus of concern in these extinction debates is on timings, patterns, rates, relative frequencies, and so on. So, what is being represented? Sometimes species, sometimes genera, families, and broader groupings of organisms. This relates to, for instance, the issue of realism, in the sense that most biologists speak of species as real (that is, independent of our theories and models), but broader groupings such as genera as being constructed on the basis of our theories and models. There is also the issue of how phenomena are represented in the various models in these debates. As we already saw, sometimes they are represented as elements of computer simulations.

Another basic component of science, as we covered in Chapter Five, is explanation. The focus of science is not merely to describe phenomena, but to explain them. We noted various models of scientific explanation: Covering Law, Causal, Pragmatic, Unification, and Information. How these different models of explanation relate to the mass extinctions debates is quite complex, because there are so many hypotheses and claims (and counter-claims) that are made in the debates. So, we will focus on just one topic and see how these models relate to it: the relatively high levels of iridium found (often, but not always) at the K-T boundary. How can we best explain the presence of these relatively high levels? As we know, the impact advocates say that, because there is such a dramatic spike in the levels, this indicates that there was a high level of iridium that occurred in a very short period of time. That, coupled with previous knowledge that iridium is relatively rare on the earth's surface and relatively common in meteorites, points to the high iridium levels as having an extraterrestrial source. We also know that the impact critics claim that high levels of iridium are found in areas of significant volcanic activity (so, no extraterrestrial source is needed) and that the claims of an iridium spike at K-T are exaggerated (so, no need for a short period of time to produce the high levels). Both agree that there is a phenomenon to be explained, but they do not necessarily agree on just what that phenomenon is. This makes it somewhat difficult to relate the models of explanation to this topic, since it is not settled just what needs to be explained! Nevertheless, let's see what we can say.

In the Covering Law model, the high iridium levels are the explanandum (the thing to be explained). The explanans (what does the explaining) would include some law(s) that cover this phenomenon and some particular conditions that relate this phenomenon to those laws. What are the relevant laws in this case and what are the relevant particular conditions? It is not obvious! As we just saw, the claim is that the iridium levels at K-T are significantly higher than in the surrounding sediments. The iridium levels at these other sediment points might be considered relevant particular conditions as would be the background information that iridium is rarely found on the earth's surface. But nothing here points to any covering laws.

The Causal model seems to fare better in explaining this situation. That is, both advocates and critics can agree that, if there really are significantly high levels of iridium at K-T, identifying the cause would constitute an (the?) explanation. That is, if they both agreed that there are high iridium levels to be explained, they agree that there must be a cause for those levels and identifying that cause (or those causes) would provide an explanation. They just disagree on what the cause is (impact vs. volcanic activity).

The Pragmatist model would not necessarily disagree that scientists are content with identifying the cause of the high levels, but would note that this makes sense only in the larger picture of three elements of any explanation: theory, fact, and context. Recall that this model of explanation claims that any phenomenon to be explained is never simply an isolated instance, but is always part of some contrast class. So, we would want to really ask: Why are the iridium levels high *at this point in the geologic column?*, which is a different question than: Why are the *iridium* levels high at this point in the geologic column? Of course, the scientists involved in these debates have been fairly clear that it is the second question (with the emphasis on iridium) that they are asking. Given that contrast class (iridium vs. other elements), they now seem to be content with looking for an acceptable cause or mechanism to produce those levels.

Another model of explanation was the Unification model, which stated that we explain some phenomenon only when we can make it coherent with other accepted knowledge; that is, when we can unify it with other knowledge. This, too, seems to be much of the focus of the practicing scientists. For example, the volcanists claim that, yes, a bolide impact *could* be the cause and, hence, explanation of high iridium levels, but that is something akin to pulling a rabbit out of the hat. There is a lot of evidence to support a cause that this not a sudden, dramatic, unpredictable one-time (or, at least, extremely rare) event such as a bolide impact. The phenomenon can be squared with events and forces of strictly terrestrial origin and that would be more scientific, because less "miraculous." What is important here is the drive for seeking coherence among background assumptions (theories, knowledge, practices) and the particular phenomenon to be explained. Of course, this drive for unification is also prevalent among the impact advocates. They claim that the worldwide presence of high iridium levels at K-T are more consistent with impact than with volcanic activity. Likewise, they argue that other kinds of evidence, such as shocked quartz, is more consistent with impact than with volcanic activity and, so, supports the claim for bolide impact as the cause of high iridium levels.

Finally, the Information model suggests that what constitutes an explanation is the relative surprise or informativeness of some phenomenon given background knowledge. This model, too, could be content with identifying some cause and showing that this cause is part of a coherent, consistent, unifying account. But, what makes this explanatory, according to this model, is that we actually learned something; it was informative, or surprising given background knowledge. Certainly, the claim of a bolide impact as the causal agent would be surprising and this was part of the criticisms of the volcanists—it is too surprising; it results in making reasonable predictions too unwieldy.

This last model of explanation, the Information model, actually points to the issue of evidence, as well, especially the Bayesian view of evidence. This is because even critics of the information model could agree that the informativeness of an explanation is really a measure of the evidentiary value of it. That is, high iridium levels lend support for the claim of a bolide impact, and indeed are evidence of one, to the extent that those levels raise the probability of the impact hypothesis being true. This can be seen as another way of saying that it is informative!

Of course, as we saw in Chapter Six, Bayesianism is one view about evidence and there are objections to that view as being what scientists want and need in terms of an understanding of the nature of evidence. In the case of the mass extinctions debates, what is important is to see what kinds of phenomena the scientists who were involved saw as being relevant to providing grounds for exploration and explanation. The kinds of data that were appealed to included sea level changes, oxygen depletion (as well as over-abundance), geophysical and geochemical analysis of terrestrial craters, fossils of both flora and fauna, indications of long-term climate change, normal evolutionary forces and pressures, and so on. Different scientists weighed different evidence differently! As we have seen, many supporters of the impact hypothesis called the Chicxulub crater as the "smoking gun," that is, final and sufficient evidence of a bolide impact at K-T, whereas others (though fewer) did not. Impact advocates saw the K-T iridium levels as significant in support of their view, whereas critics downplayed it as significant evidence, and certainly did not see it as sufficient. Volcanists have argued that there is an abundance of evidence to show that extinctions were gradual or perhaps stepwise, but certainly not instantaneous (geologically speaking).

With respect to Achinstein's claims about evidence, and that scientists use four different concepts of evidence (subjective, epistemic-situation, potential, and veridical), it is not clear exactly how they shed light on the practices of the involved scientists. For instance, Achinstein claims that potential evidence is the most important concept of evidence and further that what scientists really want is veridical evidence (though they cannot be sure if/when they ever have it). This seems plausible. But there are questions to raise here. First, can the same phenomenon be supporting evidence for different, and even conflicting, hypotheses? Both the advocates and the critics of the impact hypothesis cite the iridium spike as supporting evidence for their respective hypotheses. Achinstein, I take it, would disagree, at least with respect to what he calls "veridical evidence." Because the hypotheses conflict, they cannot both be true, so, at least in terms of veridical evidence, the iridium spike cannot be evidence for both, any more than, say, a particular solar eclipse could count as veridical evidence for both Ptolemaic and Copernican planetary models. Yet both advocates and critics of impact *do* cite the iridium spike as supporting evidence and this is not simply to be shunted aside by saying that it counts as "epistemic-situation evidence" as opposed to "veridical evidence," because both parties are in the same epistemic situation. They agree on what phenomenon has occurred, that is, that there is a specific aberrant iridium level at the K-T boundary, but they disagree on what explains this phenomenon and on what it signifies. If they are not in the same epistemic-situation, then it becomes less and less clear what an epistemic-situation is.

There is one last basic component of science that we looked at earlier in this book, reductionism and the unity of science. Charles Officer recounts in his book, *The Great Dinosaur Extinction Controversy* (pp. 76–78), attitudes that were expressed between some physicists (who supported the impact hypothesis) and geologists/paleontologists (who rejected the impact hypothesis). At a conference in the 1980s, he recalled William Clemens (a critic of impact) saying that the impact view was "codswollop" and Robert Bakker, a noted dinosaur specialist as remarking about the physicists: "The arrogance of these people is simply unbelievable. They know next to nothing about how real animals evolve, live and become extinct. But despite their ignorance, the geochemists feel that all you have to do is crank up some fancy machine and you've revolutionized science. The real reasons for the dinosaur extinctions have to do with temperature and sea-level changes, the spread of diseases by migration and other complex events. In effect, they're saying this: 'we high-tech people have all the answers, and you paleontologists are just primitive rockhounds.'" Luiz Alvarez (Nobel Prize winning physicist and leader of the team that published the ground-breaking 1980 impact article) was quoted as saying, "I don't like to say bad things about paleontologists, but they're really not very good scientists. They're more like stamp collectors."

The mass extinctions debates have obviously involved scientists from many different fields and specialties. As a result, their working assumptions and practices and histories have varied. Likewise, they appeal to varied theories and models. Just how related are they, then, and what does this say about any unity of science? As we saw in Chapter Seven, we can think of unity of science, and also of reduction, in terms of ontology, epistemology, and axiology.

That is, we can ask about unity (or reduction) of what science investigates, how it investigates, and why (what goals it has). One view of unity, as we saw, was that there is a single world out there, so in the final analysis, there is a single, correct description of the world. Another sense of unity is that there is (or should be) unity of method, of how to investigate the world. We noted that this focus on epistemology is sometimes played out in terms of theoretical reduction, that is, that the theories (and models) of higher-level sciences are reducible to theories (and models) of the more basic sciences. To the physicists in these debates, any geological or biological or paleontological claim that contradicts basic physical theories would simply have to be rejected. Along with this view is the notion that physics can and does "trump" paleontology, in the sense that if they conflict, the claims of physics will not be abandoned. Of course, not all scientists or philosophers of science agree with this view (as we saw in Chapter Seven, Jerry Fodor did not). It is just this view that many scientists involved in these debates, especially the non-physicists and non-chemists, raise as being crucial to the ongoing nature of the debates. That is, they argue that the typical models and practices of physics do not reflect the complexities of geological and biological phenomena. Here is Charles Officer again: "Physics is a different world altogether from geology. In physics, typically, one can build a machine and devise an experiment to test a given hypothesis (both of which Alvarez was exceptionally good at), and then the experiment can be repeated by others to verify the results. Subsequent experiments can be conducted to test logical corollaries to the original hypothesis, and in due course—*quod erat demonstrandum.* In geology, matters are not so clean, test procedures not so precise. All one has is data—and precious little of that—left from an "experiment" conducted tens to hundreds of millions of years ago. Not only can the experiment not be repeated, but a basic question is often, *What was the experiment?* What data is available can almost always be interpreted in a variety of ways, and only by surrounding the problem with more and different kinds of data can consensus be reached. Furthermore, that consensus can evaporate in the face of new data, either quickly or slowly as in the case of continental drift. Also, a geological consensus bears little or no relation to a proof in physics" (pp. 14–15).

Now, it seems fairly clear that in one sense there is no unity of science here, certainly not in the sense of any commitment or agreement that the different sciences involved can all be reduced to physics. Does this mean that there is no unity of science or that reductionism (whether ontological or epistemological) is wrong? No, that does not follow. But, if we look at actual scientific practice in the context of these debates, we do not see a unity of science cashed out in terms of theoretical reduction, not even a desire for it!

So, how do these issues of basic components of science relate to the mass extinctions debates? Well, I hope it is obvious, even after all these pages, to see that they relate in many ways and in detailed and complex ways. We have been able to touch only briefly on each of these topics and I hope that you consider them in much further detail. Nonetheless, even at just this level of treatment, I hope you see how the philosophical and conceptual issues both illuminate and inform the events and activities of the practicing scientists in this case as well as those philosophical and conceptual issues being themselves illuminated and informed by those events and activities. But there are more philosophical issues to consider, so let's move on.

Philosophical concerns: Models of scientific change

In this section, we will focus on the issues of theory evaluation and change/progress in science. How, especially since the 1980 Alvarez article, has the scientific community dealt with the Nemesis hypothesis (and its attendant hypotheses of impact, periodicity, etc.)? Has the scientific community acted in ways that have been captured adequately by models proposed by philosophers of science (e.g., Kuhn)? If not, and if these proposed models are meant prescriptively, has the scientific community acted "irrationally" or in ways that could be aided by such models? We will address these questions by concentrating on models covered in Chapters Eight, Nine, and Ten.

In Chapter Eight we looked at two models of scientific change (or progress), inductivism and falsificationism (Popper). Inductivism, we saw, argued that science begins with particular observations (unbiased, one hopes), formulates hypotheses to account for those observations, tests those hypotheses, leading (again, one hopes) to empirical generalizations, which, in turn, case be tested further. Eventually, laws and theories emerge (i.e., are inductively inferred) to provide explanations for these generalizations. Under Popper's falsificationist view, bold conjectures and rigorous attempts to falsify hypotheses are the signs of genuine science, which will perhaps provide greater and greater verisimilitude, but never proof of the truth of any hypothesis. How do these two models fare with respect to the actual practice of the scientists involved in the mass extinctions debates?

Even the scientists themselves, in their explicit remarks about science, reject these two models. For example, David Raup (an impact advocate) says, "Science is not the pure, isolated endeavor that is usually depicted. It is rarely a simple process of posing hypotheses, devising experimental tests, and waiting for Yes or No answers. Although the answers are occasionally simple, getting them published and accepted by the scientific community is not. And scientists are victims of the same emotions and belief systems as other people" (*The Nemesis Affair*, p. 18). Likewise, Charles Officer (a volcanist advocate) states, "Scientists, contrary to the popular archetype, are often unobjective in their pursuit of truth" (*The Great Dinosaur Extinction Controversy*, p. 184). Beyond these types of explicit comments, however, we saw above that the inductivist notion of science beginning with (unbiased) observation is questionable at best. Even the stumbling onto the iridium anomaly at Gubbio was not an inductivist matter of formulating a hypothesis and then going out to test it. Where impact advocates saw an iridium anomaly, volcanists did not; where some scientists saw evidence for stepwise extinction, others did not; where some "saw" a spreading out of shocked quartz, others did not. In a word (well, a few words), the data did not speak for itself nor did inferences move smoothly from (unbiased) observations to tested hypotheses to empirical generalizations to theories.

How about Popper's falsificationist model? There certainly has been a lot of testing of hypotheses in these debates! Have they followed the Popperian line? Well, not so obviously. For example, most of the scientists involved have dropped the Nemesis hypothesis, but they did so for various reasons and at various times throughout the past two decades. Some rejected it outright, whereas others eventually dismissed it because no compelling evidence supported it (not because there was a clean proof that it was false). Or, to repeat the case of the 3-meter gap noted above, some scientists accepted certain observations as definitive and others did not. In addition, other hypotheses such as the reality of periodicity and the timing of a periodicity have been challenged and championed by different scientists. Also, as more and more data emerged, hypotheses and models were sometimes modified rather than abandoned wholesale. The larger point of these examples is that, in terms of actual scientific practice—and what is acknowledged by most scientists as good scientific practice—shows that how and when a hypothesis is falsified is not at all obvious or uniform.

Kuhnian language and characterizations often are used by scientific commentators, including those who have dealt with the extinction debates (e.g., Glen, 1994; Muller, 1988). That is, they often characterize the activities of the scientific community in Kuhnian terms. Very briefly, remember that Kuhn's view is that change and progress in science involves the replacement of paradigms, not the simple accumulation of "objective facts." Those paradigms are what the scientific community shares, in the form of disciplinary matrices and exemplars. Much of what constitutes a given discipline or endeavor as scientific is that it is engaged in within the context of a guiding, dominant paradigm. Normal science, science done within a paradigm, is puzzle-solving activity, in which the paradigm is assumed, not tested. Anomalies can—indeed, almost undoubtedly will—arise and if they are pronounced and irresolvable, can lead to a crisis. A crisis can lead to "profound professional insecurity," resulting in the emergence of extraordinary science and perhaps even a revolution (i.e., the abandonment of one paradigm for another). Shifts in paradigms can be of a "gestalt switch" nature, in which phenomena are seen in very new and different lights and there is incommensurability between the old and new paradigms.

Recognizing that this is a very elementary statement of Kuhn's view, can we properly characterize the history of the extinction debates as Kuhnian? I think not. Although certain features of this history fit Kuhn's model, there are other telling features that do not. First, despite the claims by various scientists (e.g., Gould, in Glen, 1994; Hsü, in Glen, 1994) that the controversy over Nemesis and impact arose because it represented a neo-catastrophist challenge to the reigning uniformitarian paradigm, it is difficult if not impossible to show that the pre-Alvarez work was substantially different than the post-Alvarez work. "Normal science" did not change, nor has there been a "gestalt switch" in which data and phenomena are now incommensurable with pre-Alvarez claims and assumptions. Indeed, advocates on both sides of the various hypotheses point to the same evidence, the same analytic techniques, and so on to make their case. Much of the "standard paradigm," if there is one, of practicing paleontologists has remained untouched, for example, a commitment to plate tectonics. It certainly is the case that, with a strong advocacy for volcanism alongside with the strong advocacy for impact, there is no dominant paradigm at present. Nor could one make a strong case that the paleontological community is in a period of crisis; there still is widespread consensus on what questions are important to pursue and what techniques are to be followed. Few proponents of impact have been deterred from their view by the presence of apparently inconsistent or even falsifying data (e.g., evidence for the gradual decline and extinction of species prior to the K-T boundary). Nor have many proponents of volcanism been deterred from their view by the presence of apparently inconsistent or falsifying data (e.g., stichovite and shocked quartz at crater sites). Changes that are occurring in the scientific community are not the result of dramatic, sudden gestalt switches even though a gradual acceptance of catastrophism seems to be taking place and is a significant conceptual change.

Does Lakatos's view of research programs better account for the nascence or the reception of these debates? Yes and no. That is, there are aspects of the history of the extinction debates that fit well with Lakatos's view and other aspects that fit less well. For Lakatos, research programs, not Kuhnian paradigms, are the real vehicles for scientific change and progress. Research programs consist of methodological rules, some—the positive heuristic—specifying paths of research to follow and others—the negative heuristic—specifying paths of research to avoid. The negative heuristic includes a hard core of hypotheses that do not get tested and a protective belt of auxiliary hypotheses that do. The positive heuristic gives suggestions on how to develop the protective belt.

A research program is successful if the revisions of the auxiliary hypotheses result in a progressive problem-shift and unsuccessful if it leads to a degenerating problem-shift, where a problem-shift means the focus on and resolution of certain empirical and theoretical problems leads to the formulation and subsequent resolution of new problems. Research programs are appraised for their heuristic power always with respect to rival programs, so overall change and progress is not the linear replacement of one paradigm by another, but the explanatory advantages of one research program with respect to a rival research program; falsification and rejection of a research program can only occur if there is a rival research program that is progressive (and so shows the first program to be degenerating).

Does the history of this case reflect a Lakatosian view? There clearly are many Lakatosian elements here. There seem to be rival programs, the impact program and the volcanist program, at least with respect to what mechanism is identified as the cause of the K-T extinction. But these supposed programs do not directly speak to periodicity of extinctions or even the actuality of extinction events, as opposed to gradual, stepwise extinctions. Proffered evidence does seem to be assessed not simply for one program or another, but in relation to both programs. That is, some evidence, such as the worldwide K-T iridium levels or the correlation between crater dating and extinction events, suggest that the impact program is progressive with respect to the volcanist program because those pieces of information cohere much better with the impact program than with the volcanist program. On the other hand, other evidence, such as the Deccan and Siberian Traps along with evidence of dinosaur survival in arctic climates (e.g., Clemens and Nelms, 1993), suggest that the volcanist program is progressive with respect to the impact program. In addition, it is unclear what exactly would constitute the impact program's hard core and what would constitute its protective belt (and likewise for the volcanist program). Proponents for both programs acknowledge the iridium anomaly and do not seem to take that as a part of the protective belt of either program. Also, both accept the vast lava flows found in the volcanic traps, and so would not consider such evidence as being in need of testing; rather they disagree on their accounts of how those flows came to be. It is difficult, then, to enunciate the content of the hard core or protective belt of either program and so, it is difficult to enunciate whether or not either program is progressive. To the extent that Lakatos' construal of scientific research programs is meant as normative (i.e., as a rational reconstruction with a prescriptive sense of what is *good* science), no light is shed because the very elements of the programs (the hard core and protective belt) cannot be clearly explicated.

Laudan has proposed an account of scientific change and progress that shares some features with the Kuhnian view and with the Lakatosian view, but is sufficiently different than both of them to stand as a distinct alternative model. Rather than speaking of "paradigms" or "research program," Laudan speaks of "research traditions" as the vehicle for scientific change and progress. Science, he claims, is concerned with cognitive problems, which involve both empirical problems and conceptual problems. In terms of theory choice and appraisal, Laudan states that the most important test is whether a theory provides satisfactory solutions to important problems and that doing so is more significant than whether or not the theory is true, corroborated, well-confirmed, or otherwise justifiable within the framework of contemporary epistemology. That is, science is first and foremost concerned with solving specific problems and the crucial goal for science is to solve as many problems as possible; the proper measure for theory choice and appraisal is problem-solving effectiveness. Scientific rationality is quite simply the process of making the most progressive decisions, so that, contra Lakatos, scientific rationality for Laudan is defined in terms of progress, which in turn is defined in terms of problem-solving effectiveness (again, where problems can be both empirical and conceptual).

Have the activities of the scientific community with respect to this case been essentially ones focused on problem-solving effectiveness? To a large degree, yes. The Alvarez team, seeing the need to give a coherent interpretation of the iridium anomaly, was not concerned with whether or not the interpretation fit into a larger theoretical structure such as uniformitarianism; they were concerned to give an interpretation of the data that would maximize problem-solving, both in the sense of making sense of the empirical information and in the sense of not creating future empirical or conceptual problems. That is, by suggesting impact as the cause of the iridium anomaly, they tried to give an account that cohered with other empirical information (indeed, they sought empirical coherence by looking at sites around the world where the K-T boundary was exposed) and they tried to minimize conceptual problems (by looking, say, for the simplest explanation for world-wide iridium anomalies). Much of the criticism of impact (and of periodicity and of Nemesis) has been in the form of proposing specific empirical and conceptual problems. For example, the suggestion that dinosaurs lived in cold climates was offered in part to show that even if impact occurred at the K-T boundary, this would not (did not) cause the extinction of the dinosaurs; there is no necessary conceptual link between impact and extinction. Or, the presence of the Deccan and Siberian Traps are empirical phenomena that do not necessarily have any connection to impact, hence an empirical problem for the impact proponents. Likewise, the best account for the presence of not only iridium anomalies, but shocked quartz, stishovite, osmium anomalies, etc., say the impact proponents, is that impact did occur; volcanists face empirical and conceptual problems in making sense of these phenomena. So, to a large degree, the extinctions controversy does fit with Laudan's view. On the other hand, Laudan's conclusion that problem-solving effectiveness defines scientific rationality does not follow. Both sides of the controversy share commitments to standards of testing to techniques of analysis to appropriate forms of data collection, and so on. Different standards or levels of rationality is not what separates the sides of this controversy and both sides demand verifiable, quantifiable, replicable experimental and field data and both sides demand interpretations of phenomena that are internally coherent and externally consistent with established knowledge.

Finally, in Chapter Ten, we considered Pitt's technologism model of scientific change. How does it fare when relating it to the mass extinctions debates? Recall that Pitt emphasizes that scientific change and progress are mainly the result of what he calls the technological infrastructure of science. By that he means "the historically defined set of mutually supporting sets of artifacts and structures without which the development and refinement of scientific knowledge is not possible." He is not speaking just of instruments and equipment (though he is speaking of those), but the political, social, communicative structures that underlie scientific ideas. The development of new information in a mature science is, by and large, a function of its technological infrastructure. In short, he says, scientific discovery today depends almost completely on the technological context without which modern science would be impossible. So, how does this make sense of the activities of the scientists involved in the extinction debates? With respect to much of the data collection and analysis, obviously sophisticated instruments and equipment were paramount. For example, being able to identify and measure the varying levels of iridium against norms of background layers required highly precise instruments. Likewise, being able to (approximately) date crater impact sites depends upon extremely sophisticated equipment as well as background physical and chemical theory.

Of course, by the technological infrastructure, Pitt means much more than the instruments used to gather and analyze data. This is the more important aspect of his model of scientific change, since any such model would acknowledge the importance of good equipment. But, it is just this further aspect of his view that fails to shed much light on why the involved scientists have acted the way they have (or should). That is, if these other aspects of the technological infrastructure are things like the political, social, and communicative structures underlying scientific practice, it is just not at all obvious or clear how these have shaped or influenced what these scientists have done. Certainly, they do not seem to shape how the scientists have assessed the reliability of biochemical information. As an example, one issue is whether or not marine species died off because of a lack of or an overabundance of oxygen in the world's oceans at the time of an extinction event. There just is no evidence that political or social or communicative structures influenced the collection or analysis of the data that they scientists used in evaluating anoxia (lack of oxygen) versus hypoxia (overabundance of oxygen). Of course, the scientists involved had, for instance, certain communicative structures that they favored—some folks talked more to others or attended the same conferences or read the same journals—but it is not as if they ignored the findings or criticisms of their opponents. Quite the opposite; one of the reasons that the debates continue is because they are aware of their opponents and of the data that is inconclusive with respect to generating fairly complete consensus among the scientists. It might very well be the case that the technological infrastructure that Pitt speaks of is necessary even for the debates to be taking place, not to mention for them to be ongoing, but such technological infrastructure does not seem to provide much of a illuminating explanation for why certain data is treated as confirming by some scientists but not by others or why some scientists formulate particular hypotheses to account for certain data while others formulate quite different hypotheses. This is not to say that Pitt's model is wrong, but that it is certainly not sufficient.

What are we to say, then, about the mass extinction debates as they relate to philosophical issues of models of scientific change and theory evaluation? It seems that as a case study, the conduct of the scientific community involved in this controversy has not fully been captured by any one of these models. Are the models failures then? By no means. No more than the impact view is a failure because it has not (yet) accounted for cold climate dinosaurs and no more than the volcanist view is a failure because it has not (yet) accounted for shocked quartz. Of course, the scientific community as a whole seems to be edging toward the impact view for some extinction events though not all because on the whole that view seems more promising, just as on the whole the philosophical community has edged away from much of the specifics of Kuhn's view because it seems less promising.

But what can then be said for philosophical models of scientific change and theory evaluation? In addressing this larger issue, we might ask what desiderata do we have for philosophical models? In Chapter Four, we noted that for scientific models (or theories), several desiderata can be stated. They should be extensive (meaning they correlate large amounts and varied sorts of phenomena), fecund (meaning they stimulate new research), predictable and explanatory (meaning they are testable against observations), plastic (meaning they are easily modifiable to accommodate new information), simple (meaning having few assumptions and laws, in part so as to be extensive), internally consistent and externally coherent, and (probably) quantitative. Are these the desiderata for *philosophical* models? What I have tried to do here is to show that an ongoing scientific controversy can be a fruitful subject for future philosophical reflection and that this controversy can also serve as a testing ground for the value of philosophical models of scientific change and theory evaluation. The various philosophical models of scientific change (and progress), I believe, have been found promising but inadequate.

Philosophical concerns: Values and society

As we mentioned at the beginning of this chapter, since 1980 it has become commonplace for people to say that the dinosaurs died because a meteorite (or asteroid or comet) collided with the earth. This view has become so commonplace that there are even cartoons, such as this one, that are based on the assumption that people are familiar with this notion.

If Ellen thought falling stars were romantic, Lou figured she'd melt for an impact-crater demonstration.

(From *American Scientist,* Nov.-Dec., 2000, page 507.)

In addition, there have been movies made of the basis of a bolide impact, not to mention books and magazine articles. *Time* magazine did a cover story on it in 1985. There was even a rock group, Shriekback, who composed a song called "Nemesis," about this topic. In Chapters Eleven through Fourteen of this book, we looked at various issues relating science to values and society. Some of those issues are not directly pertinent to the mass extinctions debates. For example, issues about the relations between science and religion are only indirectly connected to these debates. Also, issues about the relation between science and technology are only indirectly related. However, many of the topics that we covered in the chapters on science and values and on science and society are directly connected to these debates.

Perhaps the most direct and obvious connection is with the issue of epistemic values. Remember, McMullin claimed that epistemic values are those that are presumed to promote the truth-like character of science, its character as the most secure knowledge available to us of the world we seek to understand. An epistemic value is one we have reason to believe will, if pursued, help toward the attainment of such knowledge. Examples of epistemic values are replicability, quantifiability, simplicity, fecundity, predictability, coherence, and so on. Clearly, scientists, including those involved in these debates, are concerned with these values. For example, regarding internal coherence, Charles Officer questions how impact advocates could explain what he took as the missing crater for the K-T extinction by their suggestion that the meteorite (or asteroid or comet) fell into the ocean, yet at the same time claim shocked quartz on land as evidence for the impact. Regarding external consistency, the impact advocates claim that comparatively high levels of iridium at different K-T boundary sites around the world provide support for impact. In addition, critics of impact question how an abrupt impact can be consistent with evidence that the extinctions are gradual.

One epistemic value that McMullin speaks of is unifying power, that is, the ability of a theory or model to bring together disparate areas of inquiry or explain how various phenomena are linked. The impact view is, of course, claimed to do just that: it provides an account for how the iridium anomaly, shocked quartz, tektites, microdiamonds, soot, and so on are all found at the K-T boundary. Another epistemic value is fecundity, the fruitfulness of a theory or model to stimulate new research and new questions. Clearly, the impact hypothesis did that. Very quickly, scientists around the world began to look for new evidence that would shed light on this hypothesis and began to reexamine phenomena and data that had previously been collected. Even critics of the impact view, such as Anthony Hallam, have noted that "judged by its heuristic value the impact hypothesis of mass extinctions . . . has been a brilliant success" because it focused attention on the issue of mass extinctions and generated unprecedented research in the field.

Simplicity is also an epistemic value (although not simplicity at the expense of reliability). This feature of simplicity is at the forefront of different assessments of the impact hypothesis. It is seen as a virtue by impact advocates, namely there is a fairly simple causal explanation of how an extinction event occurred at K-T (and possibly at other extinction points). Critics, though, see this simplicity as a vice; it is too simple of an account and fails to acknowledge the many and varied phenomena that make up the full causal picture of the different extinction events. (See again Figure 2 on page 523.)

Besides epistemic values being related to science in general and to this case, ethical values enter into scientific research at multiple points, according to Nicholas Rescher. Recall, he identifies at least seven dimensions in which ethical decisions are part of scientific research: (1) choice of research goals, (2) staffing of research activities, (3) research methods, (4) standards of proof, (5) dissemination of research findings, (6) control of misinformation, and (7) allocation of credit for research achievements. Each of these points, it turns out, is indeed reflected in the actual events and activities of the scientists involved in the extinctions debates, though I will touch on only a couple of them here.

The "behind the scenes" events and activities are especially spelled out in various publications including David Raup's *The Nemesis Affair*, Charles Officer's *The Great Dinosaur Extinction Controversy*, and Walter Alvarez' *T-Rex and the Crater of Doom*. For example, Raup discusses the gentle controversy concerning the publication of his (and colleague Jack Sepkoski) 1984 paper in the *Proceedings of the National Academy of Sciences*, in which they proposed a 26-million-year periodicity of extinctions. One reason this was gently controversial is because there was/is no peer review required for this journal. This is because, according to Raup, the journal is "ostensibly an outlet for its members." The Academy was established by the U.S. Congress for the purpose of advising the federal government on science issues and its membership is not open to any and everyone, but is determined by selection by the current membership. Raup claimed that he and Sepkoski chose to publish their paper in the *PNAS* because of its relatively quick publication timeline and in order to get their paper in front of these "top" scientists. Critics suggested that they were bypassing peer review.

Besides where Raup chose to publish his research, he speaks also of choosing not to publish some of it, at least at a particular point in time. He writes about having run his computer simulation experiments in which he "bombed" Australia: "When the research I have just described was complete, I naturally thought of publication. Even though the results were not quite what I had expected, it was a useful evaluation of the Öpik scenario for extinction in that I was able to put some mathematical limits on the effects of the scenario. [This is a reference to E.J. Öpik, who had earlier written about impact as a possible cause of extinctions.] *But I made no attempt to publish this research because I knew it would be laughed at, or worse.* So, I filed away all the data and computer programs and went on to other research projects" (*The Nemesis Affair*, page 45.)

Also, with respect to the dissemination of findings, Rescher, in his analysis of ethical dimensions of scientific research, remarked that there is a strong incentive to create a favorable climate of public opinion for certain projects. Charles Officer, in his criticisms of the impact view, noted that after the flurry of popular press attention to the issue, most of it accepting the impact view, it became more and more difficult to get "equal time" in presenting objections and criticisms (except among particular groups of scientists). Not only that, but also there was "pressure" to support the impact view (which we will see on the following pages).

I will mention two final points in connection with issues of science, values, and society. One of them is Ruth Hubbard's claim that facts are made, not discovered; the other is the claim by the group Science for the People that all science is political. With respect to Hubbard's claim that facts are made, we saw in the previous chapter that what she means by that is not that phenomena in the world are made, but what we focus on and identify, and hence determine to be facts, are decisions on our part. Is it a fact that there is periodicity of extinction events in the earth's past? What we see is that different scientists argue that the evidence either is there or is not there in sufficient form to say. Yes, we want to say that what actually happened in the past actually happened! But is that a fact, when what we mean by "fact" is a claim that has been substantiated by sufficient evidence and that serves as a reliable basis and guide for future research? It is just these criteria of being sufficiently substantiated and being a reliable basis and guide that Hubbard means by fact-making, as opposed to fact-discovering. Remember, by saying that we make facts, Hubbard does not mean that we make them up (i.e., just claim them on no basis). Did the Alvarez team discover or make the fact of the K-T iridium spike? Walter Alvarez explains how the team came to detect the spike, by analyzing sediment samples in a neutron activator: "The rock sample is put in a nuclear reactor and irradiated with neutrons which are absorbed by atoms in the rock, making some of the atoms unstable so that they decay radioactively. This is the 'neutron activation' in neutron activation analysis. When an unstable, activated atom decays, it gives off a gamma ray—a single photon of intense light. The photons coming from each element have a specific, characteristic energy, which is a marker for the presence of that particular element. [There is] a detector that registers a count each time a gamma ray with the energy characteristic of activated iridium, for example, passes through it. This is the 'analysis' in neutron activation analysis" (*T-Rex and the Crater of Doom*, p. 67). So, phenomena are detected (discovered), but the "fact" of iridium levels is a matter of sophisticated activity based on complex background theory, and, in this sense, made.

Now, there is the further point of Hubbard's view, that prevailing science is not just a matter of fact-making, but is sexist. Although many scientists would agree with the fact-making aspect of Hubbard's view, many would not (and do not) agree with the further claim of inherent sexism. In this particular case of the extinctions debates, gender seems quite removed, certainly in terms of the content of the debates. Is it removed in terms of the goals of the debates or the methods used by scientists? There certainly does not appear to be any overt issue about gender with respect to the goals, namely, wanting to know what caused extinctions or whether or not there is a periodicity to them, and so on. Is it sexist because resources are going into these questions rather than others? Well, how can one answer this? Was it sexist that Charles Babbage, in the 1800s, devoted his time to developing an early computer rather than putting his efforts into, say, working on women's nutritional needs? Given that now computers can and do empower women just as they empower men, has it turned out that Babbage's efforts were not sexist? I do not mean these questions rhetorically; rather, it is difficult to assess any and all scientific activity on its "oppressive" or "emancipatory" value without seeing what results from it in the future. There is no obvious emancipatory value in determining what happened 65 mya (much less 250 mya), but there is no obvious oppressive value there, either. Nor is it obvious that addressing phenomena in the world with questions that have no apparent emancipatory value means that those questions, or that addressing, are thereby oppressive.

Finally, one clear point connected to the extinctions debates that relates to the view of Science for the People is what many of the scientists referred to as the global winter scenario. The connection to society, noted by impact supporters and critics, is to what often is called the nuclear winter scenario, that is, the climatic impact of a nuclear war. As David Raup remarked in *The Nemesis Affair*, about supposed environmental effects of a meteorite impact: "The interesting point here is that the experiment and computer modeling that went into the dinosaur-extinction problem were soon picked up by Carl Sagan and others and applied to the environmental effects of a major thermonuclear war." Once that connection was made, according to Charles Officer, some saw it as the scientists' duty to not dispute the claims regarding the environmental effects of either, on the grounds that believing in the nuclear winter scenario could help to prevent such a war from ever happening: ". . . people in the Alvarez camp took to suggesting that early opponents of their hypothesis were willy-nilly undermining the nuclear winter hypothesis and thus lending comfort to war-mongers!" (*The Great Dinosaur Extinction Controversy*, p. 88). It would not be beyond reason to claim that Science for the People would not disagree with this attitude. Whether or not they would, it is certainly true that social and political "lessons" were claimed by some people to be learned from the extinction debates. The activities by the scientists themselves involved in the debates certainly do not appear political. That is, they gathered data, formulated hypotheses, tested them, considered alternative explanations, etc., all in the context of trying to explain phenomena in the world. Of course, Science for the People would not see these activities as politically value-neutral. The simple fact that resources went into these topics of research rather than others is itself political, they claim. One can, and many do, respond that every time a chose is made, it is a value-based decision, but calling that, then, political, is playing on an ambiguity. There are no political motives or pressures in investigating and deciding whether or not sea-level changes caused the End-Permian extinction 250 mya, at least no political motives or pressures that have any significance. If the data is there, say scientists across the political spectrum, consensus will emerge and will emerge for scientists who have very different political views and values. Still, as Officer's remarks show, even something as seemingly removed from politics as debates about what happened millions of years in the earth's past is not without political implications. Minimally, the events and activities by the scientists engaged in the mass extinctions debates reveal the prevalence and inescapable presence of values in the day-to-day doings of science.

Chapter Summary

The mass extinctions debates, which emerged in full force in the 1980s and are still ongoing, involve scientists from many and varied disciplines. These debates focus on questions about the existence, causes, timings, pace, and extent of major extinctions of life on the earth. They emerged as a significant area of research in large part because of the publication in 1980 of findings that suggested the mass extinction at the end of the Cretaceous

Era (approximately 65 million years ago) was caused by a bolide impact, that is, an extra-terrestrial object—for example, meteorite, asteroid, comet—struck the earth. Over the course of the next quarter century, scientists investigated many aspects and hypotheses connected to questions of the history of terrestrial mass extinctions, and those investigations are still going on. Some hypotheses, originally seen as highly suspect are now accepted by most of the scientific community, for example, that there was a bolide impact at the K-T boundary (65 million years ago). Other hypotheses, associated with these same debates, have received less support, for example, that there is a periodicity, or regular recurring timing, of terrestrial mass extinctions. These debates provide a very fertile case study for the many topics in the philosophy of science, including the metaphysical topics (the *what* of science), epistemological topics (the *how* of science), and axiological topics (the *why* of science). This case study provides fruitful material for considering the nature of observation and measurement, scientific explanation, models of scientific change, the nature and kinds of values within science, and many other philosophical and conceptual issues.

Further Reading

Allaby, Michael and James Lovelock. *The Great Extinction*. London: Martin Secker and Warburg, Ltd., 1983.

Alvarez, L., et al. Extraterrestrial cause for the Cretaceous-Tertiary extinction. *Science* 1980; 208:1095–1108.

Alvarez, Walter. *T. Rex And The Crater Of Doom*. Princeton: Princeton University Press, 1997.

Archibald, J. David. *Dinosaur Extinction And The End Of An Era*. New York: Columbia University Press, 1996.

Becker, L., et al. Impact event at the Permian-Triassic boundary: evidence from extraterrestrial noble gases in fullerenes. *Science* 2001; 291:1530–1533.

Benton, Michael. *When Life Nearly Died*. London: Thames and Hudson, 2003.

Berggren, W. A. et al. (eds.). *Catastrophes And Earth History*. Princeton: Princeton University Press, 1984.

Bohor, B. F., et al. Shocked quartz in the Cretaceous-Tertiary boundary clays: evidence for a global distribution. *Science* 1987; 236:705–708.

Carlisle, David Brez. *Dinosaurs, Diamonds, And Things From Outer Space*. Stanford: Stanford University Press, 1995.

Clemens, W. A. and L. G. Nelms. Paleoecological implications of Alaskan terrestrial vertebrate fauna in latest Cretacean time at high paleolatitudes. *Geology* 1993; 21:503–506.

Courtillot, Vincent. *Evolutionary Catastrophes: The Science of Mass Extinction.* Cambridge: Cambridge University Press, 1999.

Davies, John K. *Cosmic Impact.* New York: St. Martin's Press, 1986.

Davis, M., P. Hut, and R. A. Muller. Extinction of species by periodic comet showers. *Nature* 1984; 308:715–717.

Donovan, Stephen K. (ed.). *Mass Extinctions: Processes And Evidence.* New York: Columbia University Press, 1989.

Ellwood, B., et al. Impact ejecta layer from the Mid-Devonian: possible connection to global mass extinctions. *Science* 2003; 300:1734–1737.

Erickson, Jon. *Target Earth!* Blue Ridge Summit, PA: TAB Books, 1991.

Erwin, Douglas H. *The Great Paleozoic Crisis.* New York: Columbia University Press, 1993.

Erwin, Douglas H. *Extinction.* Princeton: Princeton University Press, 2006.

Fischer, A. G. and M. A. Arthur. Secular variations in the pelagic realm. In H. E. Cook and P. Enos (Eds.) *Deep-water carbonate environments. Soc. of Econ. Paleontol. and Mineral. Spec. Publ.* 1977; 25:19–50.

Frankel, Charles. *The End Of The Dinosaurs.* Cambridge: Cambridge University Press, 1999.

Glen, William (ed.). *The Mass-Extinction Debates: How Science Works In A Crisis.* Stanford: Stanford University Press, 1994.

Goldsmith, Donald. *Nemesis: The Death Star And Other Theories Of Mass Extinction.* New York: Walker and Company, 1985.

Gribbin, John and Mary. *Fire On Earth.* New York: St. Martin's Griffin, 1996.

Hallam, A. *Great Geological Controversies.* Oxford: Oxford University Press, 1989.

Hallam, A. *Catastrophes and Lesser Calamities: The Causes of Mass Extinctions.* Oxford: Oxford University Press, 2004.

Hallam, A. and P. B. Wignall. *Mass Extinctions And Their Aftermath.* Oxford: Oxford University Press, 1997.

Hallam, A. End-Cretaceous mass extinction event: argument for terrestrial causation. *Science* 1987; 238:1237–1242.

Hecht, Jeff. *Vanishing Life: The Mystery Of Mass Extinctions.* New York: Charles Scribner's Sons, 1993.

Hsü, Kenneth J. *The Great Dying.* New York: Harcourt Brace Jovanovich, 1986.

Keller, G. Extended Cretaceous/Tertiary boundary extinctions and delayed population changes in planktonic foraminifera from Brazos River, Texas. *Paleooceanography* 1989; 4:287–332.

Loper, D. E. Shocked quartz found at the K/T boundary. *Eos* 1988; 69:961, 971–972.

Luck, J. M. and K. K. Turekian. Osmium-187/Osmium-186 in manganese nodules and the Cretaceous-Tertiary boundary. *Science* 1983; 222:613–615.

Macleod, Norman and Greta Keller (eds.). *Cretaceous-Tertiary Mass Extinctions*. New York: W. W. Norton, 1996.

McGhee, Jr., George R. *The Late Devonian Mass Extinction*. New York: Columbia University Press, 1996.

McHone, J. F. and R. L. Nieman. K/T boundary stishovite: detection by solid-state nuclear magnetic resonance and power x-ray diffraction. *Geological Society of American Abstracts*, 1989; A120.

McMenamin, Mark and Diana. *The Emergence of Animals*. New York: Columbia University Press, 1990.

Martin, Ronald E. *One Long Experiment*. New York: Columbia University Press, 1997.

Muller, Dr. Richard. *Nemesis: The Death Star*. New York: Weidenfeld and Nicolson, 1988.

Officer, Charles and Jake Page. *The Great Dinosaur Extinction Controversy*. New York: Addison-Wesley, 1996.

Orth, C. J., et al. An iridium abundance anomaly at the paleontological Cretaceous-Tertiary boundary in northern New Mexico. *Science* 1981; 214:1341–43.

Osterbrock, Donald E. and Peter H. Raven (eds.). *Origins And Extinctions*. New Haven: Yale University Press, 1988.

Powell, James Lawrence. *Night Comes To The Cretaceous*. New York: W. H. Freeman, 1998.

Prothero, Donald R. *The Eocene-Oligocene Transition*. New York: Columbia University Press, 1994.

Rampino, M. R. and R. B. Strothers. Terrestrial mass extinctions, cometary impacts and the Sun's motion perpendicular to the galactic plane. *Nature* 1984; 308:709–712.

Rampino, M. and B. Haggerty. Mass extinctions and periodicity. *Science* 1995; 269:617–618.

Raup, D. M. and J. J. Sepkoski. Periodicity of extinctions in the geologic past. *Proceedings of the National Academy of the Sciences* 1984; 81:801–805.

Raup, David. *Extinction*. New York: W. W. Norton, 1991.

Raup, David. *The Nemesis Affair*. New York: W. W. Norton, 1986. (Revised edition, 1999.)

Schwartz, R. D. and P. B. James. Periodic mass extinctions and the Sun's oscillation about the galactic plane. *Nature* 1984; 308:712–713.

Shukolyukov, A. and G. W. Lugmair. Isotopic evidence for the Cretaceous-Tertiary impactor and its type. *Science* 1998; 282:927–929.

Stanley, Steven M. *Extinction*. New York: Scientific American Library, 1987.

Stigler, S. M. and M. J. Wagner. Response to D. M. Raup and J. J. Sepkoski, Jr.: testing for periodicity of extinction. *Science* 1988; 241:96–98.

Verschuur, Gerrit L. *Impact!* Oxford: Oxford University Press, 1996.

Ward, Peter. *The End Of Evolution*. New York: Bantam, 1994.

Ward, Peter. *Gorgon*. New York: Viking Penguin, 2004.

Whitmire, D. P. and A. A. Jackson. Are periodic mass extinctions driven by a distant solar companion? *Nature* 1984; 308:713–715.

Whitmire, D. P. and J. J. Matese. Periodic comet showers and Comet X. *Nature* 1985; 313:36–38.

Zhao, M. and J. L. Bada. Extraterrestrial amino acids in Cretaceous-Tertiary boundary sediments at Stevns Klint, Denmark. *Nature* 1989; 339:463–465.

GLOSSARY

analytic approach the philosophical method of analyzing concepts, usually by identifying necessary and/or sufficient conditions for that concept (ch. 1)

anomaly a phenomenon that is contrary to expectation and cannot be explained within a prevailing theory or paradigm (ch. 9)

anti-realism an umbrella term for a variety of views that reject the notion that (1) the goal of scientific investigation is to arrive at a single, true description of the world or (2) that "being true" provides any explanatory force to a claim (cf., *constructive empiricism, constructivism, idealism, instrumentalism, phenomenalism*) (ch. 3)

axiology the study of value(s), including the conditions, sources, and justification of value claims (ch. 1)

Bayes' Theorem $P(h|e) = P(e|h)P(h)/P(e)$, where h is some hypothesis, e is some (purported) evidence, $P(e/h)$ is the probability of the evidence e being true given hypothesis h, and $P(h/e)$ is the probability of hypothesis h being true given evidence e (ch. 6)

Bayesianism the view that is committed to *Bayes' Theorem* as correctly capturing the concept of scientific evidence, i.e., that what makes some phenomenon evidence for a given hypothesis is that the hypothesis is more probably true on the basis of that phenomenon (ch. 6)

bolide impact the impact on the Earth's surface of an extraterrestrial object such as a meteorite or comet; suggested as a cause of *mass extinctions* on Earth (ch. 15)

bridge law a generalized statement that displays or asserts a connection between the items in the higher-level science and items in the lower-level science; these laws serve as a bridge between the two sciences by showing how the items from the one can be defined (and, hence, reduced) to the items of the other (ch. 7)

categorization the grouping, partitioning, or classification of phenomena (ch. 2)

causal model a model of scientific explanation that identifies the cause(s) of a phenomenon as the explanatory factor of that phenomenon (ch. 5)

ceteris paribus a Latin phrase that literally means, "other things being equal;" usually used in contexts to suggest the absence of unusual, irrelevant, or even interfering conditions (ch. 4)

Chicxulub the site at Mexico's Yucatan peninsula of an impact crater dated at approximately 65 million years ago and identified as the very likely site of *bolide impact,* responsible for the mass extinction at the *K-T* boundary (ch. 15)

confirmation the relation between phenomena and a hypothesis (or *model* or *theory*) in which the phenomena support the hypothesis to a significant, though vague, level (ch. 6)

conflict/independence/dialogue, integration types of relationships between scientific claims and religious claims (ch. 13)

construction/evaluation relationships involving (usually) *models* or *theories* in terms of their production and their testing (ch. 4)

constructive empiricism the view that the goal of science is to provide empirically adequate accounts of the phenomena that we encounter; it is successful prediction and explanation of phenomena that matters, not truth (ch. 3)

constructivism the view that we construct conceptions of the world, that there are multiple correct ways of describing the world; that we do not just discover what kinds of things there are in the world, but (at least in part) we construct them; that we do not "cut nature at its joints," but we determine what joints there are to be cut (ch. 3)

corroboration the relationship between evidence and hypotheses such that there is an attempt to falsify a hypothesis and the evidence in fact supports the hypothesis; usually associated with Popper's falsificationist model of scientific change (ch. 8)

covering-law model a model of scientific explanation in which explanation is seen as an argument form, with general laws (that cover a range of phenomena) as an essential part of the *explanans* (ch. 5)

degrees of belief a (subjective) level of credibility that something is the case; associated with *Bayes' Theorem* and *Bayesianism* (ch. 6)

demarcation problem the concern to establish criteria to distinguish science(s) from non-science(s) (ch. 8)

disciplinary matrix a term to capture aspects of a paradigm that refers to various elements of scientific practice, such as ways of expressing generalizations or metaphysical commitments, that are shared by common practitioners of a scientific field; associated mostly with Kuhn's model of scientific change (ch. 9)

emancipatory science science engaged in with the (intended) purpose of improving the lives of persons (ch. 14)

empirical/conceptual problem broad distinction of types of problems that concern scientists; highlighted by Laudan in his research traditions model of scientific change (ch. 10)

entity realism the view (distinguishable from *theory realism*) that there is a commitment to the reality of entities that scientists use to manipulate phenomena in the world, e.g., "if you can spray them, they exist" (ch. 3)

epistemic reduction (theory/explanatory/methodological) the notion that various sorts of concepts, models, theories, etc. that scientists use to explore and explain phenomena can themselves be reduced to the concepts, models, theories, etc. of the more basic sciences; associated, but also contrasted, with *ontological reduction* (ch. 7)

epistemic values values that are presumed to promote the truth-like character of science, its character as secure knowledge of the world; e.g., values such as replicability of experiments, quantifiability of experimental findings, fruitfulness of generating future hypotheses (ch. 12)

epistemology the study of knowledge, including the conditions, sources, and justification of knowledge claims (ch. 1)

evidence some phenomenon, or phenomena, said to support some hypothesis or to support the fact that something is the case (ch. 6)

exemplar shared, sometimes idealized, examples that are common to a scientific discipline and often held to be particularly notable instances of a paradigm; mostly associated with Kuhn's model of scientific change (ch. 9)

explanandum a Latin phrase that literally means, "that which is to be explained;" the phenomenon to be explained in a scientific explanation (ch. 5)

explanans a Latin phrase that literally means, "that which explains" (ch. 5)

exploratory/explanatory a distinction relating to types and purposes of experiments, hypotheses, models, and theories; e.g., some (exploratory) experiments primarily seek new information while other (explanatory) experiments primarily test and provide evidence for a given phenomenon (ch. 4)

extinction event against the background of constant and "normal" extinctions, the extinction of large numbers of species or families within a geological relatively short period of time (ch. 15)

falsificationism the model of scientific change that holds that the appropriate form and standard of assessing (purported) scientific claims is the effort to falsify hypotheses; associated primarily with Popper's answer to the *demarcation problem* (ch. 8)

hard core aspects of a scientific research program that are accepted and not directly subject to testing or attempts at falsification; said to be protected by the *protective belt* of aspects that are tested; usually associated with Lakatos' model of scientific change (ch. 9)

idealism the view that what is really real, or most real, are ideas in some mind, not physical substances in themselves; to the extent that things "out there" in the world are real, it is because they are experienced or conceived (ch. 3)

incommensurability a relationship between two sets of phenomena such that they are not directly translatable into the other or capable of being put into a one-to-one relationship with each other; usually associated with Kuhn's model of scientific change (ch. 9)

inductivism the model of scientific change based primarily on inductive principles of inference, often associated with a cumulative amassing of empirical knowledge and a bottom-up, observationally based view of scientific method (ch. 8)

information model a model of scientific explanation that focuses on explanation as a measure of information or surprise relative to background knowledge (ch. 5)

instrumentalism the view that scientific models and theories are instruments, tools, for allowing us to make sense of phenomena that we encounter; as tools, the concern is how well they work, not on whether or not they are true (ch. 3)

K-T (Cretaceous/Tertiary) the geological boundary, identified at approximately 65 million years ago, separating the Cretaceous and Tertiary periods (ch. 15)

logical empiricism (positivism) philosophical model of science, often associated with *inductivism,* emphasizing the criterion of empirical observation as the basis for meaningfulness and embracing a dichotomy between facts and values (ch. 11)

mass extinctions again a background of constant and "normal" extinctions, the extinction of large numbers of species or families (ch. 15)

metaphysics the study of reality, including what kinds of things are real and the most general features of the world (ch. 1)

Mill's Methods a set of principles of inductive inference, especially for identifying causes, associated primarily with the writings of John Stuart Mill (ch. 8)

model a representation, style, or design of something; a standard of excellence; a structural isomorphism to theories or objects (ch. 4)

modus tollens a form of argument structure, usually represented as: given that a hypothesis entails some observation, and given that the observation does not occur, then the hypothesis is false (or, symbolically: $H \rightarrow O$, $\sim O$, $\therefore \sim H$) (ch. 8)

natural ontological attitude (NOA) the view, attributed to Arthur Fine and usually associated with a rejection of *realism,* that scientific claims and truths are not importantly different from "homely truths," that is, everyday, common sense notions of what things there are, how we come to know them and call claims about them true or false, and what we want science to do for us (ch. 3)

necessary condition a condition or state of affairs that is required for another condition or state of affairs to be; e.g., being unmarried is a necessary condition for being a bachelor (ch. 1)

negative/positive heuristic the aspects of scientific research programs that implicitly or explicitly identify what types of questions and issues to test (the positive heuristic) and not to test (the negative heuristic); associated with Lakatos' model of scientific change (ch. 9)

Nemesis a purported (brown dwarf) star, suggested as a cause of the mass extinction of life on the Earth approximately 65 million years ago and perhaps of other extinction events (ch. 15)

normal science science practiced within the domain of a reigning paradigm, in which fundamental aspects of the paradigm are assumed, not tested; associated with Kuhn's model of scientific change (ch. 9)

ontological reduction the notion that one kind of phenomenon is, or in principle can be, shown to be really an instance of another, more basic, kind of phenomenon; e.g., water just is H_2O; associated, but also contrasted, with *epistemic reduction* (ch. 7)

paradigm a framework, including ontological, epistemological, and axiological assumptions, of a scientific discipline within which scientific practice and activities (e.g., those relating to theories, models, experiments, etc.) are carried out; usually associated with Kuhn's model of scientific change (ch. 9)

paradigm shift a change in commitments to a particular *paradigm* for a given scientific discipline (ch. 9)

periodicity the state of having or being a regular or recurrent pattern; some researchers have suggested that there has been a periodicity of mass extinction events on Earth (ch. 15)

phenomenalism the view that we perceive only the appearances of things (i.e., phenomena) as they arise in our experiences, so the only meaningful reality to talk about is the reality of phenomena (ch. 3)

philosophy literally, the love of wisdom, often associated with seeking both clarity of concepts (cf., *analytic approach*) and interconnectedness of concepts (cf., *synthetic approach*) (ch. 1)

philosophy of science the analysis and evaluation of basic concepts and practices within science and about science (ch. 1)

practical implementations of intelligence characterization of technology, highlighting its concrete, abstract, and purposive nature (ch. 11)

pragmatist model a model of scientific explanation that stresses the view that relevance is central to explanation but that it is also a matter of context, of what pragmatic concerns are in play for a given explanation (ch. 5)

problem of induction the problem of justifying an inference about the future on the basis of past and present phenomena; often associated with the inductivist model of scientific change as well as concerns about evidence and confirmation (ch. 8)

problem shift a series of scientific theories which replace each other over time, noting a shift in the problems to be solved by scientists; associated with Lakatos' model of scientific change and the notion of *research programs* (ch. 9)

properties features or characteristics of things (where "things" can include physical objects, events, processes, etc.); e.g., having fur is a property of cats but not of fish (ch. 1)

protective belt the implicit or explicit set of problems that scientists test within a *research program;* said to protect the *hard core* of the research program; usually associated with Lakatos' model of scientific change (ch. 9)

pure/applied science a distinction, made by some though challenged by others, primarily on the basis of different goals, with the goal of pure science said to be understanding and explanation and the goal of applied science to be the practical application of the results of pure science; both are said to be related to but not identical with technology (ch. 11)

raven paradox a paradox regarding *confirmation* in which any phenomenon that serves as evidence for a given hypothesis also serves as evidence for any logically equivalent hypothesis, with counter-intuitive results; e.g., the existence of blue books counting as evidence that all ravens are black (ch. 6)

realism the view that (1) the goal of scientific investigation is to arrive at a single, true description of the world and/or (2) that "being true" provides any explanatory force to a claim; models and theories are successful because they reflect the way the world really is (ch. 3)

reductionism the notion that higher-level entities can be explained (i.e., reduced) in terms of lower-level entities; some forms of reductionism are epistemic, others are ontological (ch. 7)

relations features or ways in which things can be with respect to each other (where "things" can include physical objects, events, processes, etc.); e.g., a father is older than his daughter (where "older than" is a relation between them) (ch. 1)

research program the broad unit or structure of theories and practices that constitute scientific activity, including *negative/positive heuristics;* associated with Lakatos' model of scientific change (ch. 9)

research tradition the broad unit or structure of theories and practices that constitute scientific activity, characterized primarily on the notion of historically sensitive problem solving; associated with Laudan's model of scientific change (ch. 10)

revolution a significant change in scientific accounts of the world, usually involving metaphysical (a change in theories, models, postulated and acknowledged kinds of entitles), epistemological (a change in methods, procedures, and practices), and axiological (a change in goals and values) aspects; especially associated with Kuhn's model of scientific change (ch. 9)

simulacrum something having merely the form or appearance of a certain thing, without possessing its substance or proper qualities; associated with scientific models (ch. 4)

sufficient condition a condition or state of affairs that satisfies or brings about another condition or state of affairs; e.g., having 100 pennies is sufficient for having a dollar (ch. 1)

synthetic approach   the philosophical method of demonstrating consequences and interconnections among concepts (ch. 1)

technological infrastructure   the political, economic, and other social networks that underlie and make possible the material conditions for scientists to do their work (ch. 10)

teleological explanation   an account for phenomena that are, or seem to be, goal-directed (ch. 5)

theoria/praxis/techné   three conceptions of knowledge; theoria is theoretical knowledge with the goal of theoretical understanding; praxis is practical knowledge, concerned with doing; techné, or technical knowledge, is concerned with making and producing (ch. 11)

theory   an element of scientific accounts of the world that is broad in scope and unifying in function, with predictive and explanatory power (ch. 4)

theory-laden   the view that basic epistemic activity, such as observation and measurement, are influenced by background assumptions, categories, and theories (ch. 2)

theory realism   the view (distinguishable from *entity realism*) that theories are true to the extent that they describe the way the world really is; theories explain phenomena because, and to the extent that, they are true of the real world that is independent of them (ch. 3)

Two Cultures   term coined by C.P. Snow to indicate the growing separation between the sciences and non-sciences (ch. 14)

unification model   a model of scientific explanation that emphasizes the goal of explanation as understanding, along with the sense that understanding the world is enhanced to the extent that we recognize and establish interconnections among phenomena and placing them in a broader context of knowledge, i.e., by unifying them (ch. 5)

unity of science (language/laws/method)   the notion that the goal, genuine possibility, and underlying assumption of scientific investigation is to formulate an account of the world, which is itself unified (ch. 7)

verisimilitude   the truthlikeness of a hypothesis (or model or theory); associated with Popper's model of scientific change (ch. 8)

vulcanism   the view that mass extinctions are the result of, and explainable by, terrestrial volcanic activity (ch. 15)

CREDITS

Achinstein, Peter. From *The Book of Evidence*, (2001). Reprinted by permission of Oxford University Press, Inc.

Barbour, Ian G. *Issues in Science & Religion*, 1st Edition, © 1966, pgs. 90–92. Reprinted by permission of Pearson Education, Inc., Upper Saddle River, NJ.

Behe, Michael J. "The Challenge of Irreducible Complexity" from Special Report on Intelligent Design reprinted from *Natural History*, April 2002, copyright © Natural History Magazine, Inc., 2002.

Bernard, Claude. From "Introduction to the Study of Experimental Medicine" translated by A. S. Weber, in *Nineteenth Century Science: An Anthology*, (ed.) A. S. Weber. Copyright © 2000, by A. S. Weber. Reprinted by permission of Broadview Press.

Campbell, Norman. From *What Is Science?* (1953), Dover Publications, Inc.

Cartwright, Nancy. From *How the Laws of Physics Lie*, (1983). Reprinted by permission of Oxford University Press.

Conant, James. From *On Understanding Science*, Copyright © 1951 Yale University Press. Reprinted by permission of Yale University Press.

Descartes, René. From *Principles of Philosophy*, translated by Valentine Roger Miller and Reese P. Miller. Copyright © 1983 D. Reidel. With kind permission from Springer Science and Business Media.

Einstein, A. From "On the Method of Theoretical Physics" (1933). Used by permission of Oxford University Press, Inc.

Ellstrand, Norman. From "When Transgenes Wander, Should We Worry?" in *Plant Physiology*, 125, April 2001: 1543–1545. Copyright © 2001 by Sage Publications, Inc. Journals. Reproduced with permission of American Society of Plant Biologists in the format Textbook via Copyright Clearance Center.

Feibleman, James K. "Pure Science, Applied Science, and Technology: An attempt at Definitions" from *The Two-Story World* edited by Huntington Cairns. Copyright © 1966 by James K. Feibleman. Reprinted by permission of Henry Holt and Company, LLC.

Feyerabend, Paul. From "How to Defend Society Against Science" from *Radical Philosophy* 11 (1975). Reprinted by permission of Radical Philosophy.

Fine, Arthur. From "The Natural Ontological Attitude" in *Scientific Realism*, edited by Jarrett Leplin, 1984, University of California Press. Reprinted by permission of University of California Press.

Fodor, Jerry. From "Special Sciences" from Synthese, Vol. 28, No. 2 (October 1974), pp. 97–115. Copyright © 1974 Synthese. With kind permission from Springer Science and Business Media and the author.

Fraassen, Bas van. From *The Scientific Image* (1980). Reprinted by permission of Oxford University Press.

Frankel, Henry. From "The Non-Kuknian Nature of the Recent Revolution in the Earth Sciences" in *PSA 1978: Volume Two*, (eds.) Peter Asquith and Ian Hacking, 1981, Philosophy of Science Association, pp. 197–207. Used by permission of The University of Chicago Press.

Friedman, Michael. From "Explanation and Scientific Understanding" in *Journal of Philosophy* 71, 1974. Reprinted by permission of the *Journal of Philosophy* and the author.

Godfrey-Smith, Peter. From *Theory and Reality*. Copyright © 2003 University of Chicago Press. Reprinted by permission of University of Chicago Press and the author.

Gould, Stephen Jay. From *Every Since Darwin: Reflections in Natural History*. Copyright © 1977 Stephen Jay Gould. Copyright © 1973, 1974, 1975, 1976, 1977 by The American Museum of Natural History. Used by permission of W. W. Norton & Company, Inc.

Hacking, Ian. From *Representing and Intervening*, Copyright © 1983 by Cambridge University Press. Reprinted by permission.

Hallam, Tony. "Summary of the proposed causes of the main Phanerozoic mass-extinction events" from *Catastrophes and Lesser Calamities* (2004). Reprinted by permission of Oxford University Press.

Hallam, Tony. "Timescale for the Phanerozoic eon" in *Catastrophes and Lesser Calamities* (2004). Reprinted by permission of Oxford University Press.

Hanna, Joseph F. From "Explanation, Prediction, Description, and Information" in *Synthese*, Vol.20, No. 3, 1969, pp. 308–309, 316–317, 320, with kind permission from Springer Science and Business Media.

Hanson, Norman R. From *Patterns of Discovery*, 1958, Cambridge University Press. Reprinted by permission.

Hempel, Carl and Paul Oppenheim. From "Studies in the Logic of Explanation" in *Philosophy of Science* 15 (1948): 567–579. Used by permission of The University of Chicago Press.

Hiskes, Anne and Richard Hiskes. From *Science, Technology, and Policy Decisions*. Copyright © 1986 by Anne L. Hiskes and Richard P. Hiskes. Reprinted by permission of the authors.

Hubbard, Ruth. From "Science, Facts, and Feminism" in *Feminism and Science*, (ed.) Nancy Tuana, 1989, Indiana University Press. Reprinted by permission of the author.

Jarvie, Ian. From "Technology and the Structure of Knowledge" in *Philosophy and Technology*, (eds.) Carl Mitcham and Robert Mackey, 1972, Free Press. Reprinted by permission of the author.

Jones, Roger. From *Physics as Metaphor*, 1982, New American Library. Reprinted by permission of the author.

Kline, Morris. From *Mathematics and the Physical World*, 1959, Dover Publications, Inc.

Koertge, Noretta. From "Postmodernisms and the Problem of Scientific Literary" in *A House Built on Sand*, edited by Noretta Koertge (1998). Reprinted by permission of Oxford University Press, Inc.